The History Of The Kirk Of Scotland, Volume 2

CALDERWOOD'S HISTORY

OF

THE KIRK OF SCOTLAND.

VOLUME SECOND.

THE WODROW SOCIETY,

INSTITUTED MAY, 1841,

FOR THE PUBLICATION OF THE WORKS OF THE FATHERS AND EARLY
WRITERS OF THE REFORMED CHURCH OF SCOTLAND.

vol. 8

THE

HISTORY

OF THE

KIRK OF SCOTLAND.

BY

MR DAVID CALDERWOOD,

SOME TIME MINISTER OF CRAILING.

EDITED FROM THE ORIGINAL MANUSCRIPT PRESERVED IN
THE BRITISH MUSEUM,

BY THE

REV. THOMAS THOMSON.

VOLUME SECOND.

EDINBURGH:
PRINTED FOR THE WODROW SOCIETY.
M.DCCC.XLIII.

EDINBURGH PRINTING COMPANY, SOUTH ST DAVID STREET.

CONTENTS

OF

THE SECOND VOLUME.

VOL. II.   b

1

CALDERWOOD'S HISTORIE

OF

THE KIRK OF SCOTLAND.

QUEENE MARIE, SOVERANE.

AMBASSADERS FROM FRANCE TO ENGLAND TO TREAT OF PEACE.

BEFORE the death of the queene regent, the Frenche king not being able to send an armie in time, for succour of his companeis lying at Leith, sent two ambassaders, Monsieur Randon and Monsieur Monlucke, Bishop of Valence. Their commission was, to treat with the Queen of England upon peace; for the Frenche king thought it an indignitie to send to the Scotish nobilitie, his subjects. The Queene of England sent her principall secretarie, Sir William Cecill, Knight, and Doctor Wotton, Deane of Yorke. The English and Scots fearing deceate, sought, by all meanes, to have the contract sure. The Frenche, to gratifie those who sent them, protracted the time till these within Leith were skarse of victuall; and the Frenche within Inchekeith had almost perished, if by some stratageme they had not gottin a shippe with victualls, and some munitioun, upon Midsommer Eve, wherof they triumphed not a little. Yitt in end, peace was concluded upon the * * of Julie 1560, as followeth :—

"THE ARTICLES TRANSACTED AND AGREED UPON BY JOHNE
BISHOP OF VALENCE, AND MONSIEUR RANDAN, DEPUTEIS FOR
THE KING AND QUEEN OF SCOTLAND, SIR WILLIAM CECILL
AND NICOL WOTTON, AMBASSADERS FOR THE QUEENE OF ENG-
LAND, UPON THE MATER PRESENTED TO THEM BY WAY OF
PETITION, FOR THE PART OF THE NOBILITIE AND PEOPLE OF
SCOTLAND.

" In the first, upon the complaint and petition of the said nobilitie and the people of this countrie, anent the number of men of
warre susteaned by their majesteis in these parts in time of peace :
It is humblie requested to the said deputeis, that they would provide opportune remedie therupon, to the solace and releefe of the
countrie. The saids deputeis considering the said desire to be just,
and conforme to reasoun, consented, concorded, and affirmed, that
the king and queene sall procure no Frenche men of warre, nor no
other natioun, to come to thir parts in time comming. But if
strangers would pretend to enter into this realme with an armie or
navie, to occupie the same, in the which case provisioun sall be
made by their majesteis, the judgement and counsell of the estats
of the realme being had therunto ; and that the Frenche men of
warre being now in the toun of Leith, sall be sent to France, the
same time that the armie and navie of Englishmen and Scotishmen
sall be skailled both by sea and land ; the which sall be done in the
best maner may be, as at more lenth consideratioun sall be had
therupon. And as to the bands of Scotish men of warre being in
the said place, they sall be brokin, and the men of warre licentiat
to depart. Moreover, as to the forts of Dumbar and Inchekeith,
there sall remaine in them a hundreth and twentie Frenche men
allenarlie, which sall be parted and distributed in thir two places.
And there sall remaine no moe in Dumbar but sixtie men of warre,
so it be not affirmed by the captans chosin to that effect by both the
parteis, that for the keeping of the same anie greater number is
not needfull : also to depart when the estats of the realme can find

anie good and sure remedie, upon the expenses made in the same places, to keepe the same from perell of invasion, or deprivatioun therof frome them that would pretend to occupie the same: they sall immediatlie shew the same unto their majesteis als hastilie as may be done; and in the meane time, the number of the said men of warre sall not be augmented. And, in like maner, it sall not be lawfull to anie of the said men of warre to doe anie injureis to anie persoun, nor yitt to mainteane and defend anie Scotish man of what qualitie so ever he be of, against the will and authoritie of the magistrats of the realme; nor to receave them in the said place, that the minister of justice may not putt hands in them; nor yitt sall intromett with them anie maner of way with the querrells and discords of the lords, and other particular men of this realme; but they themselves sall be bound, in cases of anie querrell, to be punished after the lawes and constitutions of this realme, and to answere for themselves before the judges ordinarie of the same. Last of all, that frome hencefurth they be not compelled to tak on credite, they sall be everie moneth satisfeid of their wages, so that two Scotish lords, chosin by the counsell, may present it at weapon-showing and musters of the said men of warre; and also to visite the said forts, to see if the number of them be eeked. And it sall not be lawfull for the saids men of warre to tak anie victualls for their sustentatioun, for munitioun of the said places, but by payment of readie money munerat, and with the pleasure of them that deliver the same to them. And, therefore, the said lords oblishe them to give them so muche as is needfull unto them, they having to pay therefore.

" *Item*, Upon the petition presented unto the saids lords deputeis, anent the demolitioun of the fortifications, the said deputeis consent, concord, and affirme, that the fortificatioun of Leith sall be demolished, and that two, three, or foure captans sall be chosin by both the parteis, to visite the castell of Dumbar. And if it be found by them that the reparatioun, amplificatioun, and fortifeing made therof now after the peace, greater number of men to the keeping therof is required, the reparatioun and fortificatioun therof sall be demolished so soone as may be done; and sall remain onlie untuiched that thing which may make the castell more sure, and in least danger from invasioun, providing notthelesse, that no greater number of men therin be required for keeping of the same. Moreover, in times comming, the king and queene sall mak no moe new forts within the realme; and sall not augment them that are elles made; and sall not repair them that are demolished, without counsell and consent of the estats; nor yitt sall transport to their parts anie artillerie, munitioun of warre, powder, or victuals, but so muche as may serve for keeping of the said places by the space of six moneths, or a yeere.

" *Item,* Anent the petitioun made anent the debts contracted by the Frenche men of warre in this countrie, the saids lords concorded, that the king and queene sall caus restore all that which happeneth to be found, given, and granted to the king's lieutenants, and his captans, and others officers, for the nourishment, sustentatioun, and maintenance of the said Frenche men, or that which is found ought to be the lieutenant's, for service of his majestie, that may appeare by writting and confessioun of parteis.

" *Item,* Upon the petitioun made anent the conventioun of estats in this realme, the saids deputeis consent, concord, &c., that the estats of this realme may conveene, and hold parliament the 20th day of the moneth of Julie nixt to come; upon the which day the parliament sall be continued, as use is, unto the first day of the moneth of August following. Providing alwise, that before they beginne to treate of anie thing in the said parliament, all tumult of warre be discharged and ceasse, that they that are present may be free, without feare of men of warre or others; and that in this meane time a messinger be sent by the said deputeis to the king and queene, to certifie them of the things agreed, treated, and concorded, requesting their majesteis humblie to be content with the same. And the said conventioun sall be als lawfull in all respects as the same had beene ordeaned and done by expresse commandement of their majesteis, providing that no mater be treated therin before the said first day of August.

" *Item*, Upon the article presented anent warre and peace, the saids deputeis consented, concorded, &c., that the king and queene neither make peace nor warre in thir parts, but by the counsell, judgement, and consent of the estats, according to the ordinance of the countrie, and as was observed by their predecessors.

" *Item*, Upon the petitioun presented to the said deputeis, concerning the governement and regiment of the policie, they have consented, &c., that twentie-foure worthie men of this realme be chosin by the three estats, of the which the king and queene sall choose seven, and the estats five, which, in their majesteis absence, sall tak order, and mak an ordinarie counsell, for the administratioun foresaid ; so that no man, of whatsoever qualitie he be, sall have the power to order anie thing to be done tuiching the said bussinesse, without the mediatioun, authoritie, and consent of them ; so that the said counsellers sall conveene together als oft as they may. But they sall conveene no lesse than six together ; and when anie mater of importance occurreth, they sall be called to consult, or tak order, by them, or the most part of them, if need be. And if it happin anie of the said seven, chosin by the king and queene, to deceasse, their majesteis sall choose another furth of the said number of twentie-foure, in place of him that deceased. And if anie of the said five chosin by the estats dieth, the remnant foure chosin by them sall name another, of the number of twentie-foure. Moreover, if it be thought expedient to the said estats, that other two be augmented to the said number of twelve, then, and in that case, the king and queene sall choose one, and the estats another." (And so was this article agreed under conditioun ; that is to say, that the same be no prejudice in times comming to the king and queene, and the rightes of the crowne. And the said deputeis offered their labours to make mediatioun to the king and queene, for maintcaning pensiouns and expenses of the said counsellers, and ordinarie officers of the said counsell, to be provided of the rents and revenues of the crowne.)

" *Item*, Upon the petitioun made to the saids deputeis, anent the officers of this realme, they consented and concorded, &c., that in

time to come, the king and queene sall not depute anie stranger in the
administratioun of the civill and commoun justice, and likewise in the
office of chancerie, keeper of the seale, treasurer, comptroler, and
other like offices; and sall not use them, but sall be content with their
owne subjects, borne in the realme. Moreover, it sall not be lawfull to putt the office of treasurie, comptroller, in the hands of anie
churcheman, or other which are not able to exercise the said offices;
the which treasurer and comptroller sall be provided of sufficient
commissioun to use the said offices. But it sall not be lawfull to
them to dispone or sell wards of mariages, or other casualteis, or
anie other things whatsoever they be perteaning to their offices,
without counsell or consent of the said counsell to that effect, that
the counsell may know that all things be done to the profite of the
king and queene. And yitt they will not bind nor astrict the king
or queene to this article, that they may not give when they think
expedient.

" *Item*, They concorded, that in the first conventioun and parliament of the estats of this realme, there sall be constituted, ordeaned, and established, a law of oblivioun, which afterward sall
be confirmed by the king and queen's majesteis, by the which all
remembrance of bearing of armour, and other things which have
beene done, sall be bureid and forgottin, frome the sixt day of the
moneth of Marche, in the yeere of our Lord 1558 yeeres. And
by the same law, they which have gainsaid the lawes of the realme,
sall be excused and free of all paines conteaned therin, suche like
as if it never had beene gainsaid, providing that the priviledges of
the said law be not extended to them which the estats of the realme
sall judge unworthie therof.

" *Item*, It is agreed and concluded, that in the said conventioun
or parliament, the estats of the realme, as the use is, and of the
maner is required, sall be called, in the which all they that have
used to conveene and be present may come without all feare, or
force done, or to be done to them, by any persoun; so that the
said estats sall oblishe them, that where, in time comming, anie seditioun or conventioun of men of warre sall happin to be, without

command of the counsell, being of the number of twelve, the realme and countrie sall repute the causers therof, and they that conveene, as rebells; and sall persue them as suche like, that they may be punished by the lawes of the realme; so that the king and queene sall not be compelled, in time comming, to send anie men of warre, strangers, in thir parts, for obteaning the due obedience of their subjects.

" *Item*, They offered, concorded, and agreed, that there sall be a generall peace and reconciliatioun amongst all lords and subjects of this realme, so that they that are called of the Congregatioun, and they which are not of the same, sall putt no reproche to others for the things which are done frome the said sixt day of Marche, 1558.

" *Item*, They offered, concorded, and affirmed, that the king and queene sall not persue, revenge, nor mak anie persecutioun for the things that have beene done; nor yitt sall they suffer the same to be done by their subjects, Frenchemen; but sall have all things in oblivioun, as the same had never beene done. And suche like the lords of this realme of Scotland sall doe, of all bussinesse betwixt them and the Frenchemen, on their parts. And if by sinister informatioun, or anie other occasioun, their majesteis have conceaved evill opinioun against their subjects, they sall utterlie forgett and change the same; nor they sall not deprive anie of them, nor denude anie of them, or of their subjects, of the offices, benefices, or estats which they have bruiked in the said realme before, by reasoun of anie things they have medled with, frome the said 6th day of Marche, 1558. And further, sall make no occasioun of deprivatioun nor depouning of them by anie other colour, without caus; but rather they sall esteeme and treat them, in time comming, as good and obedient subjects, providing that the saids lords and other subjects, on their part, make to their majesteis all obedience, suche like as other faithfull and naturall subjects owe to their soverans.

" *Item*, It is concorded and agreed, that it sall be lawfull to none of the lords of the nobilitie of Scotland, or anie other, to make convocatioun of men of warre, but in the ordinarie caus approved by the law and custome of the realme; and yitt, none of them sall caus anie men of warre, strangers, to come to thir parts, and muche lesse sall attempt to doe anie thing against the king and queene, or against the authoritie of the counsell or other magistrats of the realme; and they who have presented the petitioun sall be bound therunto. And in cace anie of them, or others, find occasioun to invade, or tak armour against anie man, as he pretendeth, after that he hath communicated the mater with the counsell of the realme, he sall present his complaint to their majesteis. And, generallie, they sall oblishe them, under the said pains, to doe the things which perteane to good and faithfull subjects, for the quietnesse and tranquillitie of the realme, and rights of their soverans.

" *Item*, It is agreed, that if anie bishops, abbots, or other churchmen, sall find or alledge them to have receaved anie injureis, either in their persons or in their goods, the plaint sall be seene and considered by the estats of the said conventioun and parliament; and there sall be made redresse, as they sall find, according to reasoun: and, in the meane time, no man sall stoppe them, but they sall brooke their goods; nor sall doe anie hurt, injurie, or violence to them. And if anie doth controveen this article, he sall be persued by the lords, as a perturber of a good commoun weale.

" *Item*, It is concorded, &c., that the saids lords sall bind them to observe, and caus to be observed, all and sundrie points and articles agreed in this treatie. And if it happen that anie of them, or anie other, would gainsay the same, the remanent lords and residue of the whole people sall be enemeis to him, and sall persue him, till he be chastised and punished according to his demerits.

" *Item*, It is concluded, &c., that all the whole realme may know, that the king and queene are not willing to keepe anie remembrance of the troubles and differences past; and so farre as concerneth the nobilitie and other subjects of this realme, that their majesteis desire to treate them humanelie, and to be favourable unto them, the said deputeis have promised and concorded, that the Duke of Chattelerault, and all other noblemen of Scotland, sall be remitted, and

putt again in all their goods and beneficee which they had and injoyed in France, that they may brooke and injoy the same, in the
same maner as they did before these debates, the said sixt day of
Marche, and yeere aforesaid, even as the said controverseis had
never chanced. And also, that all capitulatiouns and articles agreed
upon in times past, and speciallie these that were appointed in the
king and queen's contract, sall be observed and keeped, als weill
for the part of their majesteis, as for the part of the nobilitie and
people of Scotland. And as concerning David, sonne to the said
Duke of Chattelerault, now being in Brys de Vincent, libertie sall
be granted to him to returne to Scotland, and doe as he pleaseth.

"Moreover, when the said deputeis exponed, that some time it
might chance, that the king might misse of his great gunnes and
artillerie in France, the said lords having consideration therof,
concorded, that no other artillerie be translated out of this realme,
but these which were sent and brought in, frome the day of the
deceasse of Francis, King of France, of good memorie, to these
parts; and that all other artillerie and munitioun be reponed into
the places where they were taken furth of, and in speciall, that
have the armes of Scotland, sall be putt in the place where they
were takin furth of, &c., and there sall be noblemen of Scotland
appointed therefore; and two, for the part of the king's majestie, are
to be deputed to cognosce the samine, before the shipping therof.

"And, moreover, that where for the part of the nobilitie and
people of Scotland, certan articles concerning religioun and other
points were presented, which the said deputeis would not tuiche,
but considering the weight and importance of them, remitted the
same to be acknowledged and decided by their majesteis; the saids
lords and nobilitie doe promise, that a certan number of noblemen
sould be chosin in the nixt conventioun and parliament, to be sent
to their majesteis, which sall expone to their Highnesse these things
that sall be thought needfull for the estate of their bussinesse; and
for the fore-mentioned, and other articles and points undecided by the
said deputeis, to the effect that they may know their majesteis' intentioun and benevolence upon these things, which sall be exponed

for the part of the countrie. The which also sall have with them
a confirmatioun and ratificatioun by the estats of the realme, of
these articles which are concorded and agreed by the said deputeis; to whom also the same time, or before, sall be givin and delivered like confirmatioun and ratificatioun made by their majesteis, so being, that the said estats send their ratificatioun aforesaid."

THE PROCLAMATION OF THE THINGS ABOVE WRITTIN.

" To the loving of the most puissant, and comfort of all Christians:
The most puissant prince and princesse, and most Christian King
and Queene of France, Francis and Marie, by the grace of God
King and Queene of France and Scotland, and by the most puissant princesse Elizabeth, by the same grace, Queene of England
and Ireland, &c., it is concorded, and reconciliatioun of peace and
amitie made, which is to be observed inviolablie amongst them,
their subjects, realms, and countreis. Forasmuche as in name
of the said prince and princesse it is commanded, and straitlie
charged to all maner of persons under their obedience, or being in
their service, frome hencefurth to desist from all hostilitie both by
sea and land, and to keepe good peace one with the other; and
with charge to the breakers under their great perell."

THE DEPARTURE OF THE FRENCHE AND ENGLISH.

Peace being proclaimed, as said is, the most part of the Frenche
were transported to France, in English vessells. They careid with
them the whole spoile of Leith. That was the secund benefite
Leith receaved of their promised libertie. The English armie departed by land the 16th of Julie. The most part of the noblemen,
professors of the true religioun, convoyed them honorablie.

PREPARATION FOR THE PARLIAMENT.

After the return of the lords from the convoy of the English, the counsell beganne to consult upon the affaires of the commoun wealth, speciallie the establishement of religioun, and to prepare and order things needfull for the parliament. The preachers exhorted them to be thankfull to God for their deliverance; nixt, to see ministers placed in the countrie, as necessitie required.

PUBLIC THANKSGIVING AND PLANTING OF SUPERINTENDANTS AND MINISTERS.

A day was appointed, wherin the whole nobilitie, and the greatest part of the Congregatioun, assembled in the Great Kirk of Edinburgh, where, after sermoun made for the purpose, thanks were givin to God for his mercifull deliverance frome the tyrannie of the Frenche, the substance wherof is extant in some prayers, and formes of thanksgiving prefixed before the Psalmes. Commissioners of burghes, with some of the nobilitie and barons, were appointed to see ministers placed, who for the time were in Edinburgh, for the most part. Mr Knox was appointed minister in Edinburgh; Christopher Gudman, who for the most part remained in Air, in the time of the troubles, was placed in Sanct Andrewes; Adam Heriot in Aberdeen; Mr Johne Row in Sanct Johnstoun; Paul Methven in Jedburgh; William Christesone in Dundie; David Fergusone in Dumfermline; Mr David Lindsay in Leith. Mr Johne Spotswood was nominated to be superintendent of Lothiane, Mr Johne Wynrame of Fife, Mr Johne Willocke for Glasgow and the west, the Laird of Dun for Angus and Mernes, Mr Johne Carswell for Argile and the Isles; unlesse the countreis whereto they were appointed could, in the meane time, find out men more able and sufficient, or elles shew suche causes as might make them unable for that dignitie.

THE SPIRITUALL LORDS PRESENT AT THIS PARLIAMENT.

The parliament approaching, all that by law or ancient custome had, or might clame place therin, were advertised by the counsell. The assemblie was great, notwithstanding some, as weill of these that be called spirituall, as of these that be called temporall lords, absented themselves contemptuouslie. Yitt the Bishop of Sanct Andrewes, Dumblane, and Dunkeld, with some other of inferior sort of the Popish factioun, presented themselves. The Bishop of Galloway, the Abbots of Lindores, Culrosse, Sanct Colme's Inch, Newbottle, Halyrudhous, the Pryour of Sanct Andrewes, Colding-hame, Sanct Marie Ile, the Sub-pryour of Sanct Andrewes, and diverse others who had renounced Poperie, were present also.

In time of parliament, Mr Knox taught publicklie upon the pro-phecie of Haggee. He was fervent in applicatioun. William Mat-lane of Lethington said in mockage, " We must now forgett our-selves, and beare the barrow, to build the hous of God." Howbeit some mocked, yitt others were moved, and assembled together, to consult what things were to be proponned to the present par-liament. After deliberation, this subsequent supplicatioun was pre-sented :—

> " The Barons, Gentlemen, Burgesses, and others, true subjects
> of this realme, professing the Lord Jesus within the same,
> to the Nobilitie and States of Parliament presentlie assem-
> bled within the said realme, desire grace, mercie, and
> peace, from God, the Father of our Lord Jesus Christ,
> with the encreasse of his Holie Spirit.

" Please your honours to reduce to your remembrance, how di-verse and sundrie times we, with some of your selves, most hum-blie desired, at the feete of the late queene regent, freedome and libertie of conscience, with a godlie reformatioun of abuses, which,

by the malice of Satan and negligence of men, are creeped in into
the religioun of God, and are mainteaned by suche as tak upon
them the name of clergie.   And albeit that our godlie and most
reasonable sute was then disdainfullie rejected, wherof no small
trubles have ensued, as your honours weill know, yitt seing
that the same necessitie yitt remaineth that then moved us; and,
moreover, that God of his mercie hath now putt into your hands
suche order as God thereby may be glorifeid, this commoun wealth
quietted, and the policie therof established, we cannot ceasse to
crave of your honours the redresse of suche enormiteis as manifestlie are, and of long time have beene committed by the place-
holders of the ministrie, and others of the clergie within this realme.
And first, seing that God of his great mercie hath, by the light of
his Word, manifested to no small number of this realme, that the
doctrine of the Roman church receaved by the said clergie, and
mainteaned through their tyrannie by fire and sword, conteaneth
in itself manie pestiferous errours, which cannot but bring damnatioun to the soules of suche as therewith sall be infected; suche as
are the doctrine of transubstantiation; of the adoratioun of Christ's
bodie under the forme of bread, as they terme it; of the merits of
works, and justificatioun that they alledge cometh thereby; together with the doctrine of the Papisticall indulgences, purgatorie,
pilgrimage, and praying to sancts departed, which all either repugne to the plaine Scriptures, or elles have no ground of the doctrine of our Master, Jesus Christ, his prophets, nor apostles: We
humblie therefore crave of your honours, that suche doctrine and
idolatrie, as by God's Word are both condemned, so may they be
abolished by act of this present parliament, and punishement appointed for the transgressers.   Secundarilie, seing that the Sacraments of Jesus Christ are most shamfullie abused and profaned by
that Roman harlott, and her sworne vassalls, and also, becaus that
the true discipline of the ancient church is utterlie now among that
sect extinguished; for who within the realme are more corrupt in
life and maners than are they that are called the clergie, living in
whoordom, adulterie, deflouring virgins, corrupting matrons, and

doing all abominatioun without feare of punishement?—we humblie, therefore, desire your honours to find remedie against the one and the other. Thridlie, becaus that Man of Sinne most falslie clameth unto himself the titles of the Vicar of Christ, the Successour of Peter, the Head of the Church; that he cannot erre, that all power is graunted unto him, &c., by the which usurped authoritie, he taketh upon him the distributioun and possessioun of the whole patrimonie of the church, wherby the true ministrie of the Word of God long time hath altogether beene neglected, godlie learning despised, the schooles not provided, and the poore not onlie defrauded of their portioun, but also most tyrannouslie oppressed, we likewise heerof desire remedie. And least that your honours sould doubt in anie of these premisses, we offer ourselves evidentlie to prove, that in all the rable of the clergie there is not one lawfull minister, if God's Word, the practises of the apostles, the sinceritie of the primitive church, and their owne ancient lawes, sall judge of lawfull electioun. We further offer ourselves to prove them all theeves and murtherers, yea, rebells and tratours to the lawfull authoritie of emperours, kings, and princes; and, therefore, unworthie to be suffered in anie commoun wealth. How maliciouslie they have murthered our brethrein, for no other caus, but for that they have offered to us the light of God's Word, your honours cannot be ignorant; and into what hazard their tyrannie hath brought this whole realme, the ages after will consider. If yee looke for anie other fruict of them in times to come, than yee have seene in them whom we accuse, we are assured yee sall be deceaved. Now hath God, beyond all expectatioun of man, made yourselves, who sometime were suppliants with us for reformatioun, judges, as it were, in the caus of God: at least, he hath subdued your enemeis unto you, that by violence they are not able to suppresse the Veritie, as heeretofore they have done. We, therefore, in the bowells of Jesus Christ, crave of your honours, that either they may be compelled to answere to our former accusatiouns, and unto suche others as justlie we have to lay to their charges, or elles, that all affectioun layed aside, yee pronounce them suche by censure of this parliament, and caus them to be so reputed, as by us most justlie they are accused : especiallie, that they may be decerned unworthie of honour, authoritie, charge, or cure within the Church of God, and so frome hencefurth never to injoy vote in parliament. Which, if yee doe not then in the feare of God, and by the assurance of his Word, we forewarne you, as yee leave a greevous yoke and burthein intolerable upon the Kirk of God within this realme, so sall they be thornes in your eyes, and prickes in your sides, whom after, when yee would, yee sall have no power to remove. God, the Father of our Lord Jesus Christ, give you upright hearts, seeking his glorie; and true understanding what this day He who hath delivered you frome boundage, both spirituall and temporall, craveth of you by his servants.   And your honours' answere most humblie we require."

This supplicatioun being read in audience of the whole assemblie, as some favoured uprightlie the caus of God, so were there manie that for worldlie respects abhorred a perfyte reformatioun.   Yitt were the barons and ministers called, and commandement givin to them, to draw, in plaine and severall heads, the summe of that doctrine which they would mainteane, and desire the parliament to establishe.   This was gladelie undertaken, and within foure dayes after, this Confessioun following was presented :—

" THE CONFESSION OF FAITH

" PROFESSED AND BELEEVED BY THE PROTESTANTS WITHIN THE REALME OF SCOTLAND ; RATIFEID BY THE ESTATS OF PARLIAMENT, AS WHOLESOME AND SOUND DOCTRINE, GROUNDED UPON THE INFALLIBLE TRUTHE OF GOD'S WORD.

" *And this glade tidings of the kingdome sall be preached throughout the whole world, for a witnesse unto all nations. And then sall the end come.*"—Matt. xxiv.

" THE PREFACE.

" The Estats of Scotland, with the Inhabitants of the same,
professing Christ Jesus his holie Gospell, to their naturall
countrie men, and unto all other realmes and nations professing the same Lord Jesus with them, wishe grace, mercie, and peace from God, the Father of our Lord Jesus
Christ, with the spirit of righteous judgment, for saluta-
tion.

" Long have we thristed, deere brethrein, to have notifeid unto
the world the summe of that doctrine which we professe, and for
which we susteaned infamie and danger. But suche hath beene
the rage of Satan against us, and against Christ Jesus his eternall
Veritie, latelie borne amongst us, that to this day no time huth
beene granted unto us to cleare our consciences, as most gladelie
we would have done. For how we have beene tossed a whole yeere
past, the most part of Europ (as we doe suppose) doth understand.
But seing that of the infinite goodnesse of our God, (who never
suffereth his afflicted utterlie to be confounded,) above expectatioun have we obteaned some rest and libertie, we would not but
sett furth this breefe and plaine confessioun of suche doctrine as is
propouned unto us, and as we beleeve and professe, partlie for satisfactioun of our brethrein, whose hearts (we doubt not) have beene,
and yitt are wounded by the dispitefull railing of suche as yitt
have not learned to speeke weill, and partlie for stopping of the
mouths of impudent blasphemers, who boldlie condemne that which
they neither heard nor understood. Not that we judge, that the
cankered malice of suche is able to be cured by this simple confessioun: no, we know that the sweete savour of the Gospell is and
sall be death unto the sonnes of perditioun. But we have cheefe
respect to our weake and infirme brethrein, to whome we would
communicat the bottom of our hearts, least that they be troubled,
or careid away with diversitie of rumors which Satan sparseth

against us, to the defacing of this our godlie enterprise ; protesting, that if anie man will note in this our confessioun, anie articles or sentence repugning to God's holie Word, that it would please him of his gentlenesse, and for Christian charitie's sake, to admonishe us of the same in writting, and we of our honours and fidelitie doe promise unto him satisfactioun frome the mouth of God, that is, frome the Holie Scripture, or elles reformatioun of that which he sall prove to be amisse. For God we take to record in our consciences, that from our hearts we abhorre all sects of heresie, and all teachers of erroneous doctrine ; and that with all humilitie we embrace the puritie of Christ's Gospell, which is the onlie food of our soules, and, therefore, so precious unto us, that we are determined to suffer the extremitie of worldlie danger, rather than that we sall suffer ourselves to be defrauded of the same. For heerof we are most certanlie perswaded, that whosoever denyeth Christ Jesus, or is ashamed of him in presence of men, sall be denyed before the Father, and before his holie angels. And, therefore, by the assistance of the mightie Spirit of the same our Lord Jesus, we firmelie purpose to abide to the end in the confessioun of this our faith.

" 1. Of God.

" We confesse and acknowledge one onlie God, to whome we must cleave, whom onlie we must worship, and in whom onlie we put our trust ; who is eternall, infinite, immeasurable, incomprehensible, omnipotent, invisible, one in substance, and yitt distinct in three persons, the Father, the Sonne, and the Holie Ghost ; by whom we confesse and beleeve all things in heaven and earth, as weill visible as invisible, to have beene created, to be reteaned in their being, and to be ruled and guided by his inscrutable providence, to suche end as his eternall wisdome, goodnesse, and justice, hath appointed them, to the manifestatioun of his owne glorie.

" 2. Of the Creation of Man.

" We confesse and acknowledge this our God to have created man, (to witt, our first father Adam,) of whom also God formed

VOL. II.　　　　　　　　　　　　　　　　　B

the woman, to his owne image and similitude; to whom he gave
wisdome, lordship, justice, free-will, and cleere knowledge of himself, so that in the whole nature of man there could be noted no
imperfectioun : from which honour and perfectioun man and woman did both fall, the woman being deceaved by the serpent, and
man obeying the voice of the woman; both conspiring against
the soverane majestie of God, who, in expresse words, had before threatned death, if they presumed to eate of the forbiddin
tree.

" 3. *Of Originall Sinne.*

" By which transgressioun, commounlie called Originall Sinne,
was the image of God utterlie defaced in man, and he and his posteritie, of nature, become enemeis to God, slaves to Satan, and servants to sinne, in so muche, that death everlasting hath had, and
sall have, power and dominioun over all that have not beene, are
not, or sall not be regenerated from above; which regeneration is
wrought by the power of the Holie Ghost working in the hearts of
the elect of God an assured faith in the promises of God reveeled
to us in his Word, by which faith they apprehend Christ Jesus,
with the graces and benefits promised in him.

" 4. *Of the Revelation of the Promises.*

" For this we constantlie beleeve, that God, after the fearefull
and horrible defection of man from his obedience, did seeke Adam
again, call upon him, rebooke his sinne, convict him of the same, and
in the end made unto him a most joyful promise, to witt, that the seed
of the woman sould breake doun the serpent's head; that is, he
sould destroy the works of the devill. Which promise, as it was
repeated and made more cleere frome time to time, so was it embraced with joy, and most constantlie reteaned of all the faithfull
frome Adam to Noah, frome Noah to Abraham, and from Abraham
to David, and so furth to the incarnation of Jesus Christ, who all
(we meane the faithfull fathers under the law) did see the joyfull
dayes of Christ Jesus, and did rejoice.

" 5. *The Continuance, Increasse, and Preservation of the Church.*

" We most constantlie beleeve, that God preserved, instructed, multiplied, honoured, decored, and from death called to life his church in all ages, from Adam till the comming of Christ Jesus in the flesh. For Abraham he called from his father's countrie ; him he instructed, his seed he multipleid, the same he mervellouslie preserved, and more mervellouslie delivered frome the boundage and tyrannie of Pharaoh ; to them he gave his lawes, constitutions, and ceremoneis ; them he possessed in the land of Canaan ; to them, after judges, and after Saul, he gave David to be king, to whom he made promise, that of the fruict of his loynes sould one sitt for ever upon his royall seate. To this same people frome time to time he sent prophets, to reduce them to the right way of their God, frome which often times they declynned by idolatrie. And, albeit that for their stubborne contempt of justice, he was compelled to give them in the hands of their enemeis, as before was threatned by the mouth of Moses, in so muche that the holie citie was destroyed, the temple burnt with fire, and the whole land left desolate the space of seventie yeeres, yitt of mercie did he reduce them againe to Je-rusalem, when the citie and temple were re-edifeid, and they, against all tentations and assaults of Satan, did abide, till the Messias came, according to the promise.

" 6. *Of the Incarnation of Christ Jesus.*

" When the fulnesse of time came, God sent his Sonne, his Eter-nall Wisdome, the substance of his owne glorie, into this world, who tooke the nature of manhead, of the substance of a woman, to witt, of a virgin, and that by operatioun of the Holie Ghost ; and so was borne the just seed of David, the Angell of the great coun-sell of God, the verie Messias promised ; whome we confesse and acknowledge Immanuel, verie God and verie man, two perfyte na-tures united and joyned in one persoun. By which our confessioun, we condemne the damnable and pestilent hereseis of Arrius, Mar-cion, Eutyches, Nestorius, aud suche others as either did denie the eternitie of his Godhead, or the veritie of his humane nature; or confounded them, or yitt divided them.

" 7. Why it behoved the Mediator to be verie God and verie Man.

" Wee acknowledge and confesse, that this most wonderous conjunctioun betwixt the Godhead and the manhead in Christ Jesus, did proceed frome the eternall and immutable decree of God, frome which all our salvatioun springeth and dependeth.

" 8. *Election.*

" For that same eternall God and Father, who of meere grace elected us in Christ Jesus his Sonne, before the foundatioun of the world was layed, appointed him to be our Head, our Brother, our Pastor, and great Bishop of our soules. But becaus that the inimitie betwixt the justice of God and our sinnes was suche, that no fleshe by itself could, or might have atteaned unto God, it behoved that the Sonne of God sould descend doun unto us, and take himself a bodie of our bodie, fleshe of our fleshe, and bone of our bones, and so become the Mediator betwixt God and man; giving power to so manie as beleeve in him to be the sonnes of God, as himself doth witnesse : " I passe up to my Father and unto your Father, to my God and unto your God." By which most holie fraternitie, whatsoever we have lost in Adam is restored to us again. And for this caus are we not affrayed to call God our Father, not so muche becaus he hath created us, (which we have commoun with the reprobat,) as for that he hath givin unto us his onlie Sonne to be our brother, and givin unto us grace to acknowledge and embrace him for our onlie Mediator, as before is said. It behoved, further, the Messias and Redeemer to be verie God and verie man, becaus he was to underly the punishement due for our transgressiouns ; and to present himself in the presence of his Father's judgement, as in our persoun, to suffer for our transgressioun and inobedience, by death to overcome him that was the author of death. But becaus the onlie Godhead could not suffer death, neither yitt could the onlie manhead overcome the samine, He joyned both together in one persoun, that the imbecillitie of the one sould suffer and be subject to death, which we had deserved, and the infinite and invincible power of the other, to witt, of the Godhead, sould triumphe, and purchase to us life, libertie, and perpetuall victorie.   And so we confesse, and most undoubtedlie beleeve.

" 9. *Christ's Death, Passion, and Buriall.*

" That our Lord Jesus offered himself a voluntarie sacrifice unto his Father for us; that he suffered contradictioun of sinners; that he was wounded and plagued for our transgressions; that he, being the cleane innocent Lambe of God, was damned in the presence of an earthlie judge, that we sould be absolved before the tribunal seate of our God; that he suffered not onlie the cruell death of the crosse, (which was accursed by the sentence of God,) but also that he suffered for a seasoun the wrathe of his Father, which sinners had deserved.   But· yitt we avow, that he remained the onlie welbeloved and blessed Sonne of his Father, even in the middest of his anguishe and torment which he suffered in bodie and soule, to mak full satisfactioun for the sinnes of the people; after the which, we confesse and avow, that there remaineth no other sacrifice for sinne. Which, if anie affirme, we nothing doubt to avow, that they are blasphemers against Christ's death, and the everlasting purgatioun and satisfactioun purchased to us by the same.

" 10. *Resurrection.*

" Wee undoubtedlie beleeve, that in so muche as it was impossible that the dolours of death sould reteane in boundage the Author of life, that our Lord Jesus, crucifeid, dead, and bureid, who descended into hell, did arise againe for our justificatioun, and destroying of him who was the author of death; brought life againe to us who were subject to death, and to the boundage of the same. We know that his resurrectioun was confirmed by the testimonie of his verie enemeis; by the resurrectioun of the dead, whose sepulchres did open, and they did rise, and appeared to manie within the citie of Jerusalem. It was also confirmed by the testimonie of his angels, and by the senses and judgements of his apostles, and of others who had conversatioun, and did eate and drinke with him after his resurrectioun.

"11. *Ascension*.

" We nothing doubt, but the self-same bodie which was borne of the Virgin was crucifeid, dead, and bureid; and which did rise again, did ascend unto the heavens, for the accomplishment of all things; where, in our names, and for our comfort, He hath receaved all power in heaven and earth; where He sitteth at the right hand of his Father, inaugurat in his kingdome, Advocat, and onlie Mediator for us. Which glorie, honour, and prerogative, He alone amongst the brethrein sall possesse, till that all his enemeis be made his footstoole, as that we undoubedlie beleeve they sall be, in the finall judgement; to the executioun wherof we certanlie beleeve, that the same our Lord Jesus sall visiblie return, as that he was seene to ascend. And then we firmelie beleeve, that the time of refreshing and restitutioun of all things sall come, in so muche that these, who frome the beginning have suffered violence, injurie, and wrong, for righteousnesse' sake, sall inherite that blessed immortalitie promised frome the beginning. But contrariwise, the stubborne, inobedient, cruell oppressours, filthie persons, idolaters, and all suche sorts of unfaithfull, sall be cast in the dungeon of utter darknesse, where the worme sall not dee, neither yitt the fire sall be extinguished. The remembrance of which day, and of the judgement to be executed in the same, is not onlie to us a bridle whereby our carnall lusts are refrained, but also suche inestimable comfort, that neither may the threatning of worldlie princes, neither yitt the feare of temporall death and present danger, move us to renounce and forsake that blessed societie which we, the members, have with our Head and onlie Mediator, Christ Jesus; whome we confesse and avow to be the Messias promised, the onlie Head of his Kirk, our just Lawgiver, our onlie High Preest, Advocat, and

Mediator. In which honours and offices, if man or angell presume to intruse themselves, we utterlie detest them as blasphemous to our Soverane and supreme Governour, Christ Jesus.

"12. *Faith in the Holie Ghost.*

"This our faith, and the assurance of the same, proceedeth not from flesh and blood, that is to say, frome naturall powers within us, but is the inspiratioun of the Holie Ghost; whome we confesse God equall with the Father and with his Sonne; who sanctifeith us, and bringeth us into all veritie by his owne operatioun; without whome we sould remaine for evermore enemeis to God, and ignorant of his Sonne Christ Jesus. For of nature we are so dead, so blind, and so perverse, that neither can we feele when we are pricked, see the light when it shineth, nor assent unto the will of God when it is reveeled, unlesse the Spirit of the Lord Jesus quicken that which is dead, remove the darkenesse frome our mindes, and bow our stubborne hearts to the obedience of his blessed will. And so, as we confesse that God the Father created us when we were not, as his Sonne, our Lord Jesus, redeemed us when we were enemeis to him, so also do we confesse, that the Holie Ghost doth sanctifie and regenerat us, without all respect of anie merite proceeding of us, be it before, or be it after our regeneratioun. To speeke this one thing yitt in more plaine words: as we willinglie spoile our selves of all honour and glorie of our owne creatioun and redemptioun, so doe we also of our regeneratioun and sanctificatioun. For of ourselves we are not sufficient to thinke a good thought; but He who hath begunne the work in us, is onlie He who continueth us in the same, to the praise and glorie of his undeserved grace.

"13. *The cause of Good Works.*

"So that the caus of good works we confesse to be, not our free-will, but the Spirit of the Lord Jesus, who, dwelling in our hearts by true faith, bringeth furth suche works as God hath prepared us for to walk in. For this we must boldlie affirme, that blasphemie

it is to say, that Christ abideth in the hearts of suche as in whome
there is no spirit of sanctificatioun. And, therefore, we feare not
to affirme, that murtherers, oppressors, cruell persecutors, adulterers, whoormongers, filthie persons, idolaters, drunkards, theeves,
and all workers of iniquitie, have neither true faith, neither anie
portioun of the Spirit of the Lord Jesus, so long as obstinatlie they
continue in their wickednesse. For how soone the Spirit of the
Lord Jesus (which God's elect childrein receave by true faith)
taketh possessioun in the heart of anie man, so soone doth He regenerat and renue the same man; so that he beginneth to hate
that which before he loved, and beginneth to love that which before he hated. And from thence commeth that continuall battell
which is betwixt the flesh and the Spirit in God's childrein, whill
the flesh and naturall man, according to the owne corruptioun,
lusteth for things pleasant and delectable to the self; and grudgeth
in adversitie, is lifted up in prosperitie, and at everie moment is
prone and readie to offend the Majestie of God. But the Spirit of
God, which giveth witnessing to our spirit that we are the sonnes
of God, maketh us to resist filthie pleasures, and to grone in God's
presence for deliverance frome this boundage of corruptioun; and
finallie to triumphe over sinne, that it raigne not in our mortall
bodeis. This battell hath not the carnall man, being destitute of
God's Spirit; but doth follow and obey sinne with greedinesse,
and without repentance, even as the devill and their corrupt lusts
doe pricke them. But the sonnes of God, as before was said, doe ·
fight against sinne; doe sob and mourne, when they perceave themselves tempted to iniquitie; and if they fall, they rise againe with
earnest and unfained repentance. And thir things they doe, not
by their owne power, but by the power of the Lord Jesus, without whom they were able to doe nothing.

> " 14. *What Works are reputed good before God.*

" We confesse and acknowledge, that God hath givin to man
his holie law, in which not onlie are forbiddin all suche works as
displease and offend his godlic Majestie, but also are commanded

all suche as please him, and as he hath promised to reward. And thir works be of two sorts. The one are done to the honour of God, the other to the profite of our nighbours; and both have the reveeled will of God for their assurance. To have one God, to worship and honour him, to call upon him in all our troubles, reverence his holie name, to heare his Word, beleeve the same, communicat with his holie Sacraments, are the works of the First Table. To honour father and mother, obey their charges, (not repugning to the commandement of God,) to save the lives of innocents, to represse tyrannie, to defend the oppressed, to keepe our bodeis cleane and holie, to live in sobernesse and temperance, to deale justlie with all men both in word and deed, and, finallie, to represse all appetite of our nighbour's hurt, are the good works of the Secund Table, which are most pleasing and acceptable to God, as these works that are commanded by himself. The contrarie wherof is sinne most odious, which alwise displeaseth him, and provoketh him to anger: as not to call upon him alone when we have need, not to heare his Word with reverence, to contemne and despise it, to have or worship idols, to mainteane and defend idolatrie, lightlie to esteeme the reverend name of God, to profane, abuse, or contemne, the Sacraments of Christ Jesus, to disobey or resist anie that God hath placed in authoritie, (whill they passe not over the bounds of their office,) to murther or to consent thereto, to beare hatred, or to lett innocent blood be shed if we may withstand it. And, finallie, the transgressioun of anie other commandement in the First or the Secund Table, we confesse and affirme to be sinne, by which God's anger and displeasure is kindled against the proud, unthankfull world. So that good works we affirme to be these onlie that are done in faith, and at God's commandement, who in his law hath expressed what the things be that please him. And evill works we affirme not onlie these that expreslie are done against God's commandement, but these also that in maters of religioun and worshipping of God have no other assurance but the invention and opinion of man, which God from the beginning hath ever rejected; as by the prophet Isay, and by our Master, Christ

Jesus, we are taught in thir words, 'In vaine doe they worship me, teaching for doctrins the precepts of men.'

"15. *The Perfection of the Law, and Imperfection of Man.*

" The law of God we confesse and acknowledge most just, most equall, most holie, and most perfyte, commanding these things which being wrought in perfectioun were able to give life, and able to bring man to eternall felicitie. But our nature is so corrupt, so weake, and so imperfyte, that we are never able to fulfill the works of the law in perfectioun; yea, if we say we have no sinne even after we are regenerated, we deceave ourselves, and the veritie of God is not in us. And, therefore, it behoveth us to apprehend Christ Jesus, with his justice and satisfactioun, who is the end and accomplishment of the law; by whom we are sett at this libertie, that the curse and maledictioun of God fall not upon us, albeit we fulfill not the same in all points. For God the Father, beholding us in the bodie of his Sonne Christ Jesus, accepteth our imperfyte obedience as it were perfyte, and covereth our works, which are defiled with manie spots, with the justice of his Sonne. We doe not meane that we are so sett at libertie, that we owe no obedience to the law; (for that before we have plainlie confessed;) but this we affirme, that no man in earth (Christ Jesus onlie excepted) hath givin, giveth, or sall give in worke, that obedience to the law which the law requireth. But when we have done all things, we must fall doun, and unfainedlie confesse that we are unprofitable servants. And, therefore, whosoever boast themselves of the merits of their owne works, or putt their trust in the works of supererogatioun, boast themselves in that which is nought, and putt their trust in damnable idolatrie.

"16. *Of the Kirk.*

" As we beleeve in one God, Father, Sonne, and Holie Ghost, so doe we most constantlie beleeve, that frome the beginning there hath beene, and now is, and to the end of the world sall be, a Kirk; that is to say, a companie and multitude of men chosin of God, who rightlie worship and embrace him by true faith in Christ Jesus, who is the onlie Head of the same Kirk, which also is the bodie and spous of Christ Jesus: which Kirk is Catholick, that is, universall, becaus it conteaneth the elect of all ages, of all realmes, natiouns, and tongues, be they of the Jewes, or be they of the Gentiles, who have communioun and societie with God the Father, and with his Sonne Christ Jesus, through the sanctificatioun of his Holie Spirit. And therefore is it called the communioun, not of profane persons, but of sancts, who, as citicens of the heavenlie Jerusalem, have the fruitioun of the most inestimable benefites; to witt, of one God, of one Lord Jesus, one faith, and one baptisme; out of which Kirk there is neither life nor eternall felicitie. And, therefore, we utterlie abhorre the blasphemie of them that affirme, that men who live according to equitie and justice sall be saved, what religioun that ever they have professed. For as without Christ Jesus there is neither life nor salvatioun, so sall there none be participant thereof, but suche as the Father hath givin unto his Sonne Christ Jesus, and they that in time come unto him, avow his doctrine, and beleeve into him: (we comprehend the childrein with the faithfull parents.) This Kirk is invisible, knowne onlie to God, who alone knoweth whom he hath chosin; and comprehendeth as weill, as said is, the elect that be departed, commounlie called the kirk triumphant, as those that yitt live and fight against sinne and Satan, or sall live heerafter.

" 17. *The Immortalitie of the Soule.*

" The elect departed are in peace, and rest from their labours. Not that they sleepe, and come to a certan oblivioun, as some phantasticks doe affirme; but that they are delivered from all feare and torment, and all tentatioun to which we, and all God his elect are subject in this life, and therefore doe beare the name of the kirk militant: as contrariwise, the reprobat and unfaithfull departed have anguish, torment, and paine that cannot be expressed. So that neither are the one nor the other in suche sleepe, that they feele not joy or torment, as the parable of Christ Jesus, in the 16th

of Luke, his words to the theefe, and thir words of the soules crying under the altar, 'O Lord, thou art righteous and just: how
long sall thou not revenge our blood upon these that dwell in the
earth,' doe declare.

" 18. *Of the Notes by which the True Kirk is discerned from the False, and who sall be Judge of the Doctrine.*

" Becaus that Satan from the beginning hath laboured to decke
his pestilent synagogue with the title of the Kirk of God, and hath
inflammed the hearts of cruell murtherers to persecute, trouble, and
molest the true Kirk and members therof; as Cain did Abel, Is-
mael Isaack, Esau Jacob, and the whole priesthood of the Jewes
Christ Jesus himself, and his apostles after him, it is a thing most
requisite, that the true Kirk be discerned frome the filthie syna-
gogues, by cleere and perfyt notes, least we, being deceaved, receave and embrace, to our owne condemnatioun, the one for the
other. The notes, signes, and sure tokens wherby the immaculat
spous of Christ Jesus is knowne frome the horrible harlot, the kirk
malignant, we affirme, are neither antiquitie, title usurped, lineall
descent, place appointed, nor multitude of men approving an errour.
For Cain, in age and title, was prefered to Abel and Seth. Jerusalem had prerogative above all places of the earth, where also
were the preests lineallie descended from Aaron. And greater
number followed the scribes, Pharisees, and preests, than unfainedlie beleeved and approved Christ Jesus and his doctrine. And yitt,
as we suppose, no man of sound judgement will graunt, that anie
of the forenamed were the Kirk of God. The notes, therefore, of
the true Kirk of God, we beleeve, confesse, and avow to be, First,
The true preaching of the Word of God, into the which God hath
reveeled himself unto us, as the writtings of the prophets and apostles doe declare: Secundlie, The right administratioun of the sacraments of Christ Jesus, which must be annexed unto the Word and
promises of God, to seale and confirme the same in our hearts:
Last, Ecclesiasticall discipline uprightlie ministered as God his
Word prescribeth, whereby vice is repressed and vertue nourished.

Wheresoever, then, these former notes are seene, and of anie time continue, (be the number never so few; about two or three;) there, without all doubt, is the true Kirk of Christ, who, according to his promise, is in the middest of them. Not that universall, of which we have before spokin; but particular, suche as was in Corinthus, Galatia, Ephesus, and other places in which the ministrie was planted by Paul, and were of himself named the Kirks of God. And suche kirks we, the inhabitants of the realme of Scotland, professors of Christ Jesus, professe our selves to have in our citeis, touns, and places reformed. For the doctrine taught in our kirks is conteaned in the writtin Word of God, to witt, in the bookes of the Old and New Testament: in these bookes, we meane, which of the ancients have beene reputed canonicall, in the which we affirme, that all things necessarie to be beleeved for the salvatioun of man are expressed, the interpretation wherof we confesse, neither apperteaneth to privat nor publick persoun, neither yitt to anie kirk, for anie pre-eminence or prerogative, personallie or locallie, which one hath above another; but apperteaneth to the Spirit of God, by the which also the Scripture was writtin. When controversie then happeneth, for the right understanding of anie place or sentence of Scripture, or for reformatioun of anie abuse within the Kirk of God, we ought not so muche to looke what men before us have said or done, as unto that which the Holie Ghost uniformclie speeketh within the bodie of the Scriptures, and unto that which Christ Jesus himself did, and commanded to be done. For this is a thing universallie graunted, that the Spirit of God, which is a spirit of unitie, is in nothing contrarious to himself. If, then, the interpretation, determination, or sentence of anie doctor, kirk, or counsell, repugne to the plaine Word of God writtin in anie other place of Scripture, it is a thing most certane, that there is not the true understanding and meaning of the Holie Ghost, although that councels, realmes, and natiouns have approved, and receaved the same. For we darre not receave nor admitt anie interpretatioun which repugneth to anie principall point of our faith, or to anie other plaine text of Scripture, or yitt to the rule of charitie.

" 19. *The Authoritie of the Scriptures.*

" As we beleeve and confesse the Scriptures of God sufficient to instruct and make the man of God perfyte, so doe we affirme and avow the authoritie of the same to be of God, and neither to depend of men nor angells. We affirme, therefore, that suche as alledge the same to have no other authoritie than that which it hath receaved from the kirk, to be blasphemous against God, and injurious to the true church, which alwayes heareth and obeyeth the voice of her owne spous and pastor, and taketh not upon her to be mastresse over the same.

" 20. *Of General Councels; of their Power, Authoritie, and Cause of their Convocation.*

" As we doe not rashlie damne that which godlie men assembled together in generall councell, lawfullie gathered, have propouned unto us, so, without just examination, darre we not receave whatsoever is obtruded unto men under the name of generall councels. For plaine it is, as they were men, so have some of them manifestlie erred, and that in maters of great weight and importance. So farre, then, as the councel proveth the determinatioun and commandement that it giveth be the plaine Word of God, so soone doe we reverence and embrace the same. But if man, under the name of a councell, pretend to forge unto us new articles of our faith, to make constitutions repugning to the Word of God, then utterlie we must refuse the same, as the doctrine of devills, which draweth our soules frome the voice of our onlie God, to follow the doctrins and constitutions of men. The caus, then, why that generall councels were conveened was, neither to make anie perpetuall law which God before had not made; neither yitt to forge new articles of our beleefe, nor to give the Word of God authoritie; muche lesse to make that to be His word, or yitt the true interpretatioun of the same, which was not before by his holie will expressed in his Word. But the caus of councels (we meane of suche as merite the name of councels) was partlie for confutatioun of hereseis, and for giving

publick confessioun of their faith to the posteritie following; which
both they did by the authoritie of God's writtin Word, and not by
anie opinioun or prerogative, that they could not erre, by reasoun
of their generall assemblie. And this we judge to have beene the
cheefe caus of generall councels. The other was, for good policie
and order, to be constituted and observed in the kirk, which, as in
the hous of God, it becometh all things to be done decentlie and in
order. Not that we thinke anie policie, and one order in ceremoneis,
can be appointed for all ages, times, and places : for as ceremoneis,
suche as men have devised, are but temporall, so may and ought
they to be changed, when they rather foster superstitioun, than
that they edifie the kirk using the same.

" 21. *Of the Sacraments.*

" As the fathers under the law, besides the veritie of the sacri-
fices, had two cheefe sacraments, to witt, Circumcision and the Pass-
over, the despisers and contemners wherof were not reputed of
God's people, so doe we acknowledge and confesse, that we now,
in the time of the Evangell, have two cheefe sacraments onlie,
instituted by the Lord Jesus, and commanded to be used of all
these that will be reputed members of his bodie ; to witt, Baptisme
and the Supper, or Table of the Lord Jesus, called the Communion
of his bodie and blood. And thir sacraments, as weill of Old as of
New Testament, now instituted of God, not onlie to make a visible difference betwixt his people and these who were without his
league, but also to exercise the faith of his childrein, and by participation of the same sacraments, to seale in their hearts the assurance of his promise, and of that most blessed conjunctioun, unioun,
and societie, which the elect have with their head, Christ Jesus.
And thus, we utterlie damne the vanitie of them that affirme the
sacraments to be nothing elles but naked and bare signes. No ;
we assuredlie beleeve, that by baptisme we are ingrafted in Christ
Jesus, to be made partakers of his justice, by which our sinnes are
covered and remitted ; and also that in the Supper, rightlie used,
Christ Jesus is so joyned with us, that he becometh the verie

nourishement and foode of our soules. Not that we imagine anie transubstantiatioun of bread into Christ's bodie, and of wine into his naturall blood, as the Papists have perniciouslie taught, and damnablie beleeved; but this union and conjunctioun which we have with the bodie and blood of Christ Jesus, in the right use o the sacraments, wrought by the operatioun of the Holie Ghost, who, by true faith, carieth us above all things that are visible, carnall, and earthlie, and maketh us to feede upon the bodie and blood of Christ Jesus, which was once brokin and shed for us, which now is in heaven, and appeareth in the presence of his Father for us. And yitt, notwithstanding the farre distance of place, which is betwixt his bodie now glorifeid in heaven, and us now mortall in this earth, yitt we must assuredlie beleeve, that the bread which we breake is the communioun of Christ's bodie, and the cuppe which we blesse is the communioun of his blood. So that we confesse and undoubtedlie beleeve, that the faithfull, in the right use of the Lord's Table, doe so eate the bodie and drinke the blood of the Lord Jesus, that he remaineth in them, and they in him : yea, they are so made flesh of his flesh, and bone of his bones, that as the eternall Godhead hath givin to the flesh of Christ Jesus (which of the owne conditioun and nature was mortall and corruptible) life and immortalitie, so doth Christ Jesus his flesh and blood, eatin and drunkin by us, give unto us the same prerogatives. Which, albeit we confesse are neither givin unto us at that time onlie, neither yitt by the proper power and virtue of the •sacrament onlie, yitt we affirme, that the faithfull, in the right use of the Lord's Table, have conjunctioun with Christ Jesus, as the naturall man cannot apprehend. Yea, and farther, we affirme, that albeit the faithfull, oppressed with negligence and namelie[1] infirmitie, doe not profite so muche as they would in the verie instant actioun of the Supper, yitt sall it after bring furth fruict, as livelie seede sowin in good ground : for the Holie Spirit, which can never be divided from the right institutioun of the Lord Jesus, will not frustrate the faithfull of the fruict of that mysticall actioun.

---

[1] Conspicuous, noted.

1

But all thir, we say, come of-true faith, which apprehendeth Christ Jesus, who onlie maketh this sacrament effectuall unto us. And, therefore, whosoever slaunders us that we affirme or beleeve sacraments to be naked and bare signes, doe injurie unto us, and speeke against the manifest truthe. But this liberallie and frankelie we confesse, that we mak a distinctioun betwixt Christ Jesus in his eternall substance, and betwixt the elements of the sacramentall signes. So that we neither worship the signes in place of that which is signifeid by them, neither yitt doe we despise them as unprofitable and vaine, but doe use them with all reverence ; examining ourselves diligentlie before that so we doe, becaus we are assured by the mouth of the apostle, that suche as eate of that bread, and drinke of that cuppe, unworthilie, are guiltie of the bodie and blood of Jesus Christ.

" 22. Of the right Administration of the Sacraments.

" That sacraments be rightlie ministred, we judge two things requisite. The one, that they be ministred by lawfull ministers, whome we affirme to be onlie these that are appointed to the preaching of the Word, into whose mouths God hath putt some sermoun᾿ of exhortatioun, they being men lawfullie chosin therto by some kirk. The other, that they be ministred in suche elements, and suche sort, as God hath appointed, elles we affirme that they ceasse to be the right sacraments of Christ Jesus. And therefore it is that we flee the doctrine of the Papisticall kirk, in participatioun of their sacraments ; First, Becaus their ministers are no ministers of Christ Jesus, yea, (which is more horrible,) they suffer weomen, whom the Holie Ghost will not suffer to teache in the congregatioun, to baptize ; and, Secundlie, Becaus they have so adulterated the one sacrament and the other with their owne inventiouns, that no part of Christ's actioun abideth in the originall puritie. For oyle, salt, spittal, and suche like, in baptisme, are but men's inventiouns. Adoratioun, veneratioun, bearing through streetes and touns, and keeping of bread in boxes or boostes,[1] are profanatioun of Christ's

---

[1] Chests.

sacraments, and no use of the same. For Christ Jesus said, ' Tak,
eat, etc. Doe yee this in remembrance of me.' By which word and
charge, he sanctifeid bread and wine to the sacrament of his holie
bodie and blood, to the end that the one sould be eaten, and that
all sould drinke of the other; and not that they sould be keeped
to be worshipped and honoured as God, as the Papists have done
heeretoforè, who also committed sacriledge, stealing frome the people the one part of the sacrament, to witt, the blessed cuppe.
Moreover, that the sacraments be rightlie used, it is required, that
the end and caus why the sacraments were instituted be understand
and observed, as weill of the ministers as of the receivers. For if
the opinioun be changed in the receaver, the right use ceasseth;
which is most evident by the rejectioun of the sacrifice, (as also if
the teacher plainlie teache false doctrine,) which were odious and
abominable before God, (albeit they were his owne ordinance,) becaus that wicked men use them to another end than God hath ordeaned. The same affirme we of the sacraments in the Papisticall
kirk, in which we affirme the whole actioun of the Lord Jesus to
be adulterated, as weill in the externall forme, as in the end and
·opinioun. What Christ did, and commanded to be done, is evident by the evangelists, and by Sanct Paul : what the preest doeth
at his altar we need not to rehearse. The end and caus of Christ's
institutioun, and why the self-same sould be used, is expressed in
thir words : ' Doe yee this in remembrance of me. Als oft as yee
sall eate of this bread, and drinke of this cuppe, yee sall shew furth
(that is, extoll, preache, magnifie, and praise) the Lord's death till
he come.' But to what end, and in what opinioun, the preests say
their masse, lett the word of the same, their owne doctrines, and
writtings witnesse : to witt, that they, as mediators betwixt Christ
and his kirk, doe offer unto God the Father a sacrifice propitiatorie
for the sinnes of the quick and the dead. Which doctrine, as blasphemous to Christ Jesus, and making derogatioun to the sufficiencie of his onlie sacrifice once offered for purgation of all these that
sall be sanctifeid, we utterlie abhorre, detest, and renounce.

" 23. *To whom Sacraments apperteane.*

" We confesse and acknowledge, that baptisme apperteans as
weill to the infants of the faithfull, as unto them that be of age and
discretioun. And so we damne the errour of the Anabaptists, who
denie baptisme to apperteane to childrein before they have faith
and understanding. But the Supper of the Lord we confesse onlie
to apperteane to suche as be of the houshold of faith, and can trie
and examine themselves, as weill in their faith, as in their duetie toward their nighbour. Suche as eate or drinke at that holie table
without faith, or being at dissensioun and divisioun with their brethrein, doe eate unworthilie. And therefore it is that in our kirk
our ministers tak publick and particular examinatioun of the knowledge and conversatioun of suche as are to be admitted to the table
of the Lord Jesus.

" 24. *Of the Civill Magistrat.*

" We confesse and acknowledge impyres, kingdoms, dominions,
and citeis, to be distructed and ordeaned by God : the powers
and authoritie in the same, be it of emperours in their impyres, of
kings in their realmes, dukes and princes in their dominions, and
of other magistrats in citeis, to be God's holie ordinance, ordeaned
for manifestatioun of his owne glorie, and for the singular profyte
and commoditie of mankinde. So that whosoever goeth about to
tak away, or to confound the whole state of civill policeis now long
established, we affirme the same men not onlie to be enemeis to
mankinde, but also wickedlie to fight against God his expressed
will. We further confesse and acknowledge, that suche persons as
are placed in authoritie are to be loved, honoured, feared, and
holdin in most reverend estimation, becaus that they are the lieutenants of God, in whose sessiouns God himself doth sitt and judge,
yea, even the judges and princes themselves, to whom, by God, is
givin the sword, to the praise and defense of good men, and to
punishe all open malefactors. Moreover, to kings, princes, rulers,
and magistrats, we affirme that cheeflie, and most principallie, the

conservatioun and purgatioun of religioun apperteaneth; so that
not onlie they are appointed for civill policie, but also for maintenance of true religioun, and for suppressing of idolatrie and superstitioun whatsoever, as in David, Josephat, Ezekias, Josias, and
others highlie commended for their zeale in this case may be espied.

" 25. *The Gifts freelie given to the Kirk.*

" Albeit that the Word truelie preached, and the sacraments
rightlie ministred, and discipline executed according to the Word of
God, be the certan and infallible signes of the true kirk, we meane
not, that everie particular persoun joyned with suche companie is
an elect member of Christ Jesus: for we acknowledge and confesse,
that dornell, cockle, and chaffe may be sowin, grow, and in great
abundance ly in the middest of the wheat. That is, the reprobat
may be joyned in the societie of the elect, and may externallie use
with them the benefytes of the Word and Sacraments. But suche
being but temporall professors in mouth, but not in heart, doe fall
backe, and continue not unto the end; and therefore have they no
fruict of Christ's death, resurrectioun, nor ascensioun. But suche
as with heart unfainedlie beleeve, and with mouth boldlie confesse
the Lord Jesus, as before we have said, sall most assuredlie receave
thir gifts: First, In this life, remissioun of sinnes, and that by
onlie faith in Christ's blood, in so muche, that albeit sinne remaine,
and continuallie abide in thir our mortall bodeis, yitt it is not
imputed unto us, but remitted, and covered with Christ's justice.
Secundlie, In the generall judgement, there sall be givin to everie
man and woman resurrectioun of the flesh. For the sea sall give
her dead, the earth these that be therin inclosed; yea, the Eternall, our God, sall stretche out his hand on the dust, and the dead
sall arise incorruptible, and that in the substance of the self-same
flesh that everie man now beareth, to receave, according to their
works, glorie or punishement. For suche as now delite in vanitie,
crueltie, filthinesse, superstitioun, or idolatrie, sall be adjudged to
the fire unquenchable, in which they sall be tormented for ever, as

weill in their owne bodeis, as in their soules, which now they give
to serve the devill in all abominatioun.   But suche as continue in
weill doing to the end, boldlie professing the Lord Jesus, we constantlie beleeve that they sall receave glorie, honour, and immortalitie, to raigne for ever in life everlasting with Christ Jesus, to
whose glorifeid bodie all his elect sall be made like, when he sall
appeare again in judgement, and sall rander up the kingdome to
God his Father, who then sall be, and ever sall remaine, in all
things, God, blessed for ever; to whom, with the Sonne, and with
the Holie Ghost, be all honour and glorie, now and ever.   So
be it.

" Arise, O Lord, lett thy enemeis be confounded; lett them flee
from thy presence that hate thy godlie name.   Give thy servants
strenth to speeke thy words in boldnesse, and lett all nations cleave
to thy true knowledge.   Amen."

THE CONFESSIOUN OF FAITH RATIFEID BY THE ESTATS.

These articles were read in face of parliament, and ratifeid by
the three estats at Edinburgh, the 17th day of Julie, 1560.   The
Confessioun was read publicklie, first, in audience of the Lords
of the Articles.   The forenamed bishops, and some other of the
temporall estate, were charged in the name of God to object, if they
could, anie thing against that doctrine.   Some of the ministers were
present, standing upon their feete, readie to have answered.   Whill
no objectioun was made, a day was appointed for conference.   The
Confessioun of Faith was read, everie article by it self, and everie
man's voice required accordinglie.   None of the temporall estat
voted in the contrare, except the Erle of Atholl, Lord Somervell,
and Lord Borthwicke.   " We will beleeve," said they, " as our
fathers beleeved."   The Popish bishops spake nothing.   The rest
of the three estats approved the doctrine by their votes; manie the
rather becaus the bishops would not, nor durst say nothing in the
contrare.   The Erle of Marshall said, " It is long since I had some

favour to the truthe; but praised be God, I am this day fullie resolved: for seing my lord bishops, who, for their learning, can, and
for their zeale they owe to the truthe, would, as I suppose, gainsay anie thing repugning to the same, yitt speeke nothing against
the doctrine propouned, I cannot but hold it the verie truthe of
God, and the contrarie to be deceavable doctrine. Therefore, so
farre as in me lyeth, I approve the one, and damne the other; and
doe farther aske of God, that not onlie I, but also my posteritie,
may injoy the comfort of the doctrine that this day our eares have
heard. Farther, I protest, if anie persons ecclesiasticall sall heerafter
oppone themselves to this our Confessioun, that they have no place
nor credite, considering that time of advisement being granted to
them, and they having full knowledge of this our Confessioun, none
is now found in lawfull, free, and quiett parliament, to oppone
themselves to that which we professe. And, therefore, if anie
of this generatioun pretend to doe it after this, I protest he be
reputed rather one that loveth his owne commoditie, and the
glorie of the world, than the truthe of God, and salvatioun of men's
soules."

TWO ACTS AGAINST THE MASSE AND THE POPE'S JURISDICTION.

After the ratificatioun of the Confessioun of Faith, two acts were
made. One, that no maner of person, in time coming, administrat
anie of the sacraments secreetlie, or anie other way, but onlie these
that are admitted, and have power to that effect; nor say masse,
nor heare masse, nor be present thereat, under the paine of confis-
cation of all their goods, and punishing of their bodeis, at the discretioun of the magistrats within whose jurisdiction suche persons
happin to be apprehended, for the first fact; banishment out of the
realme for the secund fact; and death for the thrid fact. Another,
that none of the subjects sute or desire in time comming, title or
right by the Bishop of Rome, or his sect, to anie thing within this
realme, under the pain of baratrie; that is to say, proscriptioun,
banishment, and never to brooke honour, office, nor dignitie within

this realme : that the controveeners be called before the justice or
his deputs, or before the Lords of the Sessioun, and be punished
conforme to the lawes; their furnishers with fynings of money :
that the purchasers of their title or right, or mainteaners and defenders of them, sall incurre the same paines ; and that no bishop,
or other prelat within this realme, use anie jurisdictioun in time to
come by the said Bishop of Rome's authoritie, under the paine forsaid.   These two acts and the Confessioun of Faith are extant in
print, in the Acts of Parliament ratifeid and confirmed in the yeere
1567, James Erle of Murrey being regent.

THE DEATH OF THE KING OF FRANCE.

The estats directed to France, to the king and queene, Sir James
Sandelands, Lord of Sanct Johne, with the Acts of Parliament, to
be ratifeid by them, according to the promises made by their commissioners in the contract above mentioned. He came to France
in a verie unfitt time ; for the Gwisians ruled the court, and sought
the ruine of those that mislyked their governement. Whom they
could not oppresse under colour of religioun, they intended against
them accusatioun of treasoun and lesemajestie. The King of Navarre was committed to waird, the Prince of Condie adjudged to
death, Montmorancy and his sister's sonnes were appointed for the
slaughter. They had the names of ten thowsand in scroll, whome
they purposed to vexe and oppresse one way or other. The toun
of Orleance was in the meane time possessed by souldiours. Some
few courteours satt in judgement upon the lives, goods, and credite
of honest men. The prison houses were filled : steeples, turrets,
blocke-houses, and other places upon the walls, were, for a time, converted into prisons. It was determined at court, that als soone as
the yce thowed, and the river of Loyr were navigable, the king
sould take journey to Chinon, and the Gwisians, with some few,
sould remaine, to putt in executioun the sentences of the judges.
In the meane time came Sir James Sandelands to court, not so
muche to seeke pardoun for anie bypast offences, as to purge his

countriemen, and to lay the blame of the late tumults upon the Frenche. The Gwisians rebooked him sharplie, that he, being a Knight of the Holie Order,[1] sould have takin upon him anie message or instructions frome rebells, for that execrable religioun, which had beene latelie condemned in the Councell of Trent by the consent of all other Christian natiouns. Manie woundered that the Scots, not sufficientlie provided of munitioun or armour, and divided among themselves, durst provoke so mightie a king. Whill they were thus freating and threatning, the king was stricken suddenlie with an aposthume in that deafe eare that never would heare the truthe of God, when he was sitting at masse, readie to have departed out of Orleance immediatlie therafter: for his hous in Orleance was brokin up, his beds, coffers, tapestrie, sent away, and his bootes putt on. There was none professing the truthe within the toun that looked not for extremitie; for the walls and gates were, night and day, keeped by garrisouns of the Gwisians. Innocent men were daylie brought in, to suffer punishement. None were suffered to depart furth but at the pleasure of the Duke of Gwise, the Cardinall of Loran, and their factioun. When all things were in readinesse for shedding of the blood of the innocent, the Lord beganne to work as yee see. The king was careid to a voide hous, and layed upon a palliesse, till a cannabie was sett up above him.

THE LAST PARLIAMENT A LAWFULL PARLIAMENT.

Sir James Sandelands was dismissed frome the court of France soone after the king was stricken in his deafe eare, without anie ratificatioun of the Acts and Confessioun of Faith. The professours sent him not to beg anie strenth to their religioun, which

---

[1] Sir James Sandilands of Calder, after having resided some years at Malta, and become a Knight of the Order of Saint John, was, on account of his high reputation and talents, promoted to the Mastership of the Preceptory of Torphichen in 1543, with the title of Lord Saint John of Jerusalem. In consequence, therefore, of the ecclesiastical as well as military character of which his office partook, his secession to the Reformers was regarded by the Papists as a double apostacy.

needed not the suffrages of men, so muche as to show their obedience. Where as some alledge this parliament above mentioned was but a privat conventioun, becaus neither king nor queene was present, sword, scepter, or crowne borne, and some principall lords absent, they may be easilie answered. First, Through whose default was the queene absent; or who procured her to be sent to France, but the Papists themselves? Nixt, The estats of the realme were assembled in her name. They had her and her husband's full power and commissioun to hold a parliament, and to doe all which may be done in a lawfull parliament, even as if they had beene there in their proper persouns. Wheresoever the king's counsellers, with his power and commissioun, are assembled to doe anie thing at his commandement, there is the king's presence and authoritie. If the power of princes were to be limited to their bodilie presence, kings sould be compelled to be content not onlie with one realme, but also with one citie. There was no greater freedome in anie parliament holdin for an hundreth yeere before; for in it men's voices were free, and givin of conscience: in others they were bought, or givin at the devotioun of the prince. The careing of the sword, scepter, and crowne, is rather a glorious ceremonie than a substantiall and necessar point. The absence of some prejudgeth not these that were present, for all were warned.

THE CHURCH POLICIE DRAWIN AT THE DESIRE OF THE NOBILITIE.

The parliament being dissolved, consultatioun was had how a good and godlie policie might be established in the church, which, by the Papists, was altogether defaced. Commissioun and charge were givin to Mr Knox, Mr Johne Wynrame, Subpryour of Sanct Andrewes, Mr Johne Spotswod, Mr Willockes, Mr Johne Dowglas, Rector of the Universitie of Sanct Andrewes, and Mr Johne Row, to draw a plat forme of the church policie, as they had done of the doctrine. They obeyed, and presented it to the nobilitie, who perused it manie dayes. Some approved it, and wished it to be ratifeid by law : others perceaving their carnall libertie to be restrained, and worldlie commoditie to be somwhat impaired thereby, grudged, in so muche that the name of the Booke of Discipline became odious unto them. What crossed their corrupt appetites was termed by them in mockage a " devote imaginatioun." Some were licentious, some had gripped greedilie to the kirk rents, others thought they would not laike their part. The Lord Areskine was the cheefe man among the professours who refused to subscribe the Booke of Discipline. No wonder; for beside that he had an evill wife, if the poore, the schooles, and the ministrie had gottin their owne competent part, his kitchen would have laiked two parts and more of that which he possessed. None were more unmercifull to the poore ministers than they that had the greatest share of the kirk rents. Yitt a great part of the nobilitie subscribed the Booke of Discipline in Januarie following, as we sall shew.

THE ERLE OF ARRAN PROPONED IN MARIAGE TO THE QUEENE OF ENGLAND.

The Erles Morton and Glencarne, and William Matlane of Lethington, younger, were sent from the counsell, soone after the parliament, to England, to crave the constant assistance of the Queene of England against all forraine invasioun; and to propone in mariage to the queene the Erle of Arran, who then was in no small estimatioun among the godlie. But the Queene of England and her counsell willed them not to depend upon suche hopes, for it was not her minde to marie hastilie. But before their returne, the King of France, Francis the Secund, departed this life about the beginning of December. Therefore the Erle of Arran did beare the repulse the more patientlie, for he was not altogether out of hope that the Queene of Scotland careid some favour to him. He wrote to her, and sent for credite a ring, which she knew verie weill. She receaved both the letter and the ring. After answere returned, he pursued no farther, howbeit he bare it heavilie in heart.

THE CASTELL OF SEMPILL BESIEGED AND TAKIN.

The castell of Sempell was besieged and takin soon after the parliament, becaus the lord therof disobeyed the lawes and ordinances of the counsell; speciallie becaus he would mainteane the masse, and had besett the Erle of Arran with a great number of his freinds, whill as he was ryding out the way with his accustomed companie.

THE HOPES OF THE FRENCHE FACTIOUN.

The Papists looke for a new armie frome France at the nixt spring. There was no small appearance; for France utterlie refused to confirme the peace contracted at Leith, or to ratifie the Acts of Parliament, dismissed the Lord of Sanct Johne without a resolute answere, beganne to gather new bands of throtcutters, and to make great preparatioun for ships. The Gwisians vowed to revenge upon England and Scotland the displeasure of their sister. Beton, Bishop of Glasgow, Durie, Abbot of Dumfermline, Lord Seton, Mr Johne Sinclar, Deane of Restalrig, and others of the Frenche factioun, fostered them in their malice. They openlie renounced anie portioun of Scotland, unlesse it were under the governement of the Frenche men. The Lord Seton, who went with the Frenche out of Leith, and some other practisers, were sent before to raise new troubles. Manie were affrayed. Sundrie feared that England would not sustcane so great charges as they had done in former times for their defence. The preachers assured them, that God would perfyte his owne worke, for it was not theirs, but his owne; exhorted the professors to proceed in reformatioun of abuses, and planting the ministrie, and then committ the successe to God, who is able to dispose of kingdoms. The godlie had skarse begunne to call for helpe at God, and to shew some signes of obedience to his Word, when he sent a wonderfull deliverance. For by the death of the King of France, the faithfull in France were delivered, as it were, frome present death; and the professours in

Scotland, who by their foolishnesse had made themselves slaves to strangers, were restored again to the freedome and libertie of a free realme. Mr Knox had received letters out of France (for he had intelligence both with the churches and the court there) that the king was deadlie sicke, and would not recover. Whill he was conferring with the duke and Lord James, in the duke's loodging, in the Church of Feild, upon these newes, and was comforting them, and they him for the death of his wife, Marjorie Bowes, there came a messinger frome Berwick, sent by my Lord Gray, to certifie them of the death of the King of France. The death of this king made great alteratioun in France, England, and Scotland. A conventioun of the nobilitie was appointed to be holdin at Edinburgh, the 15th day of Januarie following.

THE FIRST GENERALL ASSEMBLIE.

The first Generall Assemblie of the reformed Kirk of Scotland was holdin at Edinburgh, the 20th day of December. That the reader may perceave what raritie of pastors there was in the infancie of our kirk, and what were the small beginnings of our Assembleis, we will sett doun the names of the commissioners and members of this first Assemblie.

THE NAMES OF THE MINISTERS AND COMMISSIONERS OF PARTICULAR KIRKS.

Johne Knox, minister; James Baron and Edward Hope, commissioners for Edinburgh.

Christopher Gudman, minister; David Spence and Mr Robert Kynpont, for St Andrewes.

Mr Johne Row, minister, for the kirk of Perth.

William Daroch and William Norwell, for Stirline.

Charles Drummond, provcist, James Witherspoone and Andrew Mill, for Linlithquho.

Hugh Wallace of Carnall, Johne Foullarton of Dreghorne, and Charles Campbell of Skeldum, for the kirk of Kyle.

George Hume of Spott, for the kirks of East Lothiane.

David Lindsay, minister; Andrew Lambe and Patrik Boyman, for Leith.

William Harlaw, minister; and Robert Fairlie of Braid, for the West Kirk, beside Edinburgh.

William Christesone, minister; George Lowell and William Carmichaell, for Dundie.

Alexander Guthrie of Hackerton, and William Durhame of Grange, for Forfar.

Johne Areskine of Dun, and Andrew Mill, for Montrose.

The Lairds of Tulyvarde and Fethercarne, for the kirks of the Mernes.

The Laird of Garleis, younger, for the kirks of Nithisdaill.

Mr David Wemes, for the kirk of Carnbie.

Mr Walter Balfour, for the kirk of Linton.

Johne Browne, Thomas Boyd, and James Polwart, for Torphichin.

William Lambe, William Bonkle, for Dumbar.

James Dowglas, James Moir, for Calder comitis.

Mr Robert Wynrame, for Ratho.

Johne Kincaid, for Kirkliston.

THE NAMES OF SUCHE AS WERE THOUGHT BEST QUALIFEID FOR PREACHING OF THE WORD, AND MINISTRING OF THE SACRAMENTS, AND READING OF THE COMMOUN PRAYERS PUBLICKLIE IN ALL KIRKS AND CONGREGATIONS, GIVIN UP BY THE MINISTERS AND COMMISSIONERS WITHIN THEIR OWNE BOUNDS.

In Kyle, for reading; Rankene Davidsone, Richard Bannatyne, Robert Campbell, Hugh Wallace, Andrew Lokhart, Andrew Chalmer, James Dalrumpell, Adam Landels, all readers, and Johne Chalmer, apt to teache.

In Sanct Andrewes, for ministering and teaching; Mr Johne Rutherford, Mr William Ramsay, Mr James Wilkie, Mr Robert

Hammiltoun, Mr Patrik Consteane, Mr William Rynde, **Mr William** Skeene, Mr Archibald Hammiltoun, Mr Alexander Arbuthnet, Mr James Kirkaldie, Mr David Collesse, Mr William Scot, Mr David Wemes, Mr Thomas Buchanan, Mr David Spence, Mr Robert Kynpont, Johne Wynrame of Kirknesse, Mr Alexander Spence, Mr Johne Wood, Mr David Guild, Mr Robert Patersone.

Others thought apt and able by the ministers and commissioners foresaid to minister :—Johne Arcskine of Dun, Johne Foulertone of Kynnaber, David Forresse, Patrik Kinninmonth, Mr James Melvill, Richard Melvill, Mr Johne Kello, Mr Robert Montgomrie, Mr Johne Hepburne, Mr Thomas Hepburne, Mr George Hepburne, William Lambe. Mr Johne Ramsay was presented by Sir Johne Borthwicke to serve at the kirks of Aberdour and Fyvie.

RESTALRIG UNITED TO LEITH.

It was found reasonable and expedient that the parochiners of Restalrig sould repaire to the kirk of Leith, and that the kirk of Restalrig be razed, and utterlie destroyed, as a monument of idolatrie.

ACTS.

Mariage within the secund, thrid, and fourth degrees of affinitie and consanguinitie, and suche others as are not prohibited expreslie by the Word, were approved as lawfull. The admissioun of ministers, elders, and deacons, is ordeaned to be made publicklie in the kirk, and pre-mentioun to be made upon the Lord's day preceding. It was ordeaned, that parteis for carnall copulatioun committed betwixt the promise and solemnizatioun of mariage, sall make publick confessioun of their fault. It was ordeaned, that suche as have borne office in the Popish church sould be supported with the almesse of the kirk, as other poore, if their conversatioun were honest.

PETITIONS.

It was thought expedient, that earnest supplicatioun sould be made to the estats in parliament, Lords of Secreit Counsell, that none be suffered to be Lords of the Sessioun, shireffs, stewarts, bailiffes, or other suche judges ordinar, but suche as were professors of the reformed religioun.

Item, To desire the estats in parliament to tak order, with confirmatioun of testaments, that pupills and orphans be not defrauded, and that lawes might be made therupon in their favours.

Item, To requeist the estats in parliament, and Lords of Secreit Counsell, to inflict sharpe punishement upon the persons whose names were to be presented to them, and other idolaters and mainteaners of idolatrie, in contempt of God, his true religioun, and acts of parliament, who say masse, or caus masse to be said, or are present at the same within the places which were to be named and presented to them.

This assemblie was continued to the 15th day of Januarie. It was appointed, that one commissioner sould be sent, at least, from everie kirk, for requiring suche things of the parliament as sall be thought profitable for the weale of the church.

Item, That everie one bring with him a roll of the whole tithes, lands, annuells, profites, and emoluments of the paroche kirks nixt adjacent to them, and of the names of the tacksmen, and what duetie they payed for their tacks. Everie commissioner present promised to come, or caus others to be sent from the kirks.

M.D.LXI.

LORD JAMES SENT TO THE QUEENE BY THE CONVENTION.

At the conventioun holdin at Edinburgh, the 15th day of Januar, 1561, Lord James was appointed to goe to France, to the queene, and a parliament was appointed to beginne the 20th day of May, at which time they looked for his returne. He was for-

warned of dangers which might befall him, and admonished not to
consent that the queene sould have masse publicklie or privatlie
within the realme of Scotland; for if he so did, he sould betray
the caus of God, and expone religioun to the uttermost danger.
He answered, he would never consent that she sould have masse
publicklie, but he could not stoppe her to have masse in her chamber privatlie. He departed from Edinburgh the 18th of Marche,
and was at the queene in Aprile. Howbeit he susteaned the
charges of his convoy upon his owne expenses, yitt went there no
man out of this countrie so weill accompaneid before.

A DEPUTATION BEFORE THE CONVENTION.

At this conventioun, Mr Alexander Andersone, sub-principall of
Aberdeen, a man more subtile and craftie than either learned or
godlie, being called to dispute for his faith, refused, using a place
of Tertullian to cloke his ignorance. It was answered, that Tertullian must not prejudge the authoritie of the Holie Ghost, who,
by the mouth of Peter, commandeth us to give a reasoun of our
faith to everie one who requireth the same of us : and farther, that
they neither required him, nor anie other man, to disput in anie
point concerning their faith which is fullie expressed in the Scriptures ; for all that they beleeve without controversie. But they
required of him, as of all other Papists, that they would suffer their
doctrine, constitutions, and ceremoneis to come to triell ; and speciallie the masse to be layed to the square rule of God's Word, and
to the right institutioun of Jesus Christ. Mr Alexander denied
that the preest tooke upon him Christ's office to offer for sinne, as
was alledged. A masse booke was produced, and in the beginning
of the canon were these words read, " *Suscipe, Sancta Trinitas,
hanc oblationem, quam ego, indignus peccator, offero tibi vivo Deo, vero,
pro peccatis meis, pro peccatis totius ecclesiæ vivorum et mortuorum,*"
&c. "Now," said the reasouner, "if to offer for the sinnes of the
whole church was not the office of Christ Jesus, yea, that office
which to him onlie might and may apperteane, lett the Scripture

judge : and if a vile knave, whom yee call preest, proudlie taketh
the same upon him, lett your owne bookes witnesse." Mr Alexander answered, that none could offer the propitiatorie sacrifice but
onlie Christ; " but we," said he, " offer the remembrance." It
was answered, that they praised God he denied a sacrifice propitiatorie in the masse; and offered to prove, that in moe than an
hundreth places, it is affirmed by their Popish doctors, that the
masse is a propitiatorie sacrifice. Where he alledged that they
offered Christ in remembrance, it was asked, to whome did they
offer in remembrance, and by what authoritie; for in God there
did fall no oblivioun. And if they would say, they offer not as if
God were forgetfull, but as willing to applie Christ's merits to his
church, it was asked, what warrant and commandement had they
so to doe? for there is a commandement to tak, eate, drinke; but
to offer Christ's bodie either for remembrance or applicatioun, there
is none, and therefore they tooke upon them an office which was
not givin. Mr Alexander being more than astonished, would have
shifted; but the lords willed him to answere directlie. He said,
he was better seene in philosophie then in theologie. Then Mr
Johne Leslie, then Parson of Une, after Abbot of Lindores, at
lenth Bishop of Rosse, was commanded to answere to the former
argument. He beganne to answere with great gravitie, " If our
Master have nothing to say to it, I have nothing; for I know nothing but the cannon law. The greatest reasoun that ever I found
there is, *Nolumus* and *Volumus*." Yitt this man afterward was
the onlie patrone for the masse! No wounder, for he was a preest's
gette. Therefore the old proverb holdeth true, " *Patrem sequitur
sua proles.*" The nobilitie perceaving that neither the one nor the
other would answere directlie, said, " We have beene miserablie
deceaved heretofore; for, if the masse may not obteane remissioun
of sinnes to the quick and the dead, wherefore were all the abba-
cies doted so richelie with temporall lands ?"

THE BOOKE OF DISCIPLINE SUBSCRIBED.

At the same conventioun, the Booke of Discipline was subscribed by a great part of the nobilitie, to witt, the duke's Grace, the Erles of Arran, Argile, Glencarne, Marshall, Menteith, Morton, Rothesse; Lord James, Lord Yester, Lord Lindsay, Lord Boyd, Lord Uchiltrie, the Master of Maxwell, and the Master of Lindsay; Barons Dumlanrig, Lochinvar, Garleis, Barganie, and Mr Alexander Gordoun, Bishop of Galloway, Alexander Campbell, Deane of Murrey, with a great number moe, in the Tolbuith of Edinburgh, the 27th day of Januarie, in the yeere of our Lord 1561, according to the new accompt frome Januarie. Their approbatioun is signifeid in these words following :—

" We, which have subscrived these presents, having advised with the articles heerin specifeid, and as is above mentiouned frome the beginning of this booke, thinke the same good, and conforme to God's Word in all points, conforme to the notes and additiouns thereto eeked, and promitt to sett the same fordward to the uttermost of our powers, providing that the bishops, abbots, pryors, and other prelats and beneficed men, which elles have joyned themselves to us, brooke the revenues of their benefices during their lyftyme, they susteaning and upholding the ministrie and ministers, as is heerin specifeid, for preaching of the Word, and ministring of the Sacraments."

The preachers afterward exhorted the professors to establishe the Booke of Discipline by act and publick law, affirming, that if they suffered things to hang in suspense when God had givin to them sufficient power, they sould after sob for it, but sould not gett it. We have thought expedient to insert the booke in this part of our Historie, that the posteriteis to come may judge what worldlings refused, and what was the godlie policie the ministers required; with this advertisement, that the penners wished the posteritie, if God granted them occasion and libertie, to establishe a more perfyte discipline, which was done twentie yeeres after, when some speciall points of this booke, speciallie about superintendents

and readers, were altered and amended, as we sall see in the Secund Booke of Discipline. The maner of electioun and admissioun
of ministers, elders, and deacons, and of superintendents for the
time, the order of discipline, and censuring of offenders, the maner
of ministratioun of the sacraments, visitation of the sicke, order of
buriall, and how free they were of corruptioun and superstitioun,
may be gathered not onlie of the First Booke of Discipline, but
also out of the Liturgie, or maner of ministratioun of the sacraments, and forme of divine service, which is sett doun before the
Psalmes.

THE PREFACE TO THE FIRST BOOKE OF DISCIPLINE.

TO THE GREAT COUNCELL OF SCOTLAND, ETC.

THE FIRST HEAD: OF DOCTRINE.

" *Seing that Christ Jesus is he whome God the Father,*" &c.

OF THE MINISTERS.

*Their Electioun and Admissioun.   What things are cheefelie
required in the Ministers.*

Lett the church first diligentlie consider, that the minister which
is to be chosin be not found culpable of anie suche faults which
Sanct Paul reprehendeth in a man of that vocatioun; but, contrariwise, indewed with suche vertues, that he may be able to
undertake his charge, and diligentlie execute the same. Secundlie,
that he distribute faithfullie the Word of God, and minister the
Sacraments; ever carefull, not onlie to teache his flocke publicklie,
but also privatlie to admonishe them, remembring alwayes, that
if anie thing perishe through his default, the Lord will require it
at his hands.[1]

[1] Acts i. 13, 14; 1 Tim. iii. 2; 2 Tim. ii. 4; Ezech. xxxiii·; Jerem. iii. ;

Of their Office and Duetie.

Becaus the charge of the Word of God is of greater importance than that anie man is able to dispense therewith, and Sanct Paul exhorteth to esteeme them as ministers of Christ and disposers of God's mystereis, not lords or rulers, as Sanct Peter sayeth, over the flocke; therefore, the pastor or minister's cheefe office standeth in preaching the Word of God, and ministring the Sacraments; so that in consolatiouns, judgements, electiouns, and other politicall affaires, his counsell, rather than authoritie, taketh place. And if so be the congregatioun upon just caus agree to excommunicate, then it belongeth to the minister, according to their generall determinatioun, to pronounce the sentence, to the end that all things may be done orderlie, and without confusioun.[1]

The maner of electing the Pastors or Ministers.

The ministers and elders, at suche times as there wanteth a minister, assemble the whole congregatioun, exhorting them to advise and consider who may best serve in that roome and office; and if there be choise, the church appoint two or three upoun some certane day, to be examined by the ministers and elders :[2]

First, as tuiching their doctrine, whether he that sould be minister have good and sound knowledge in the Holie Scriptures, and fitt and apt gifts to communicate the same to the edificatioun of the people : for the tryell wherof, they propose him a theame or text, to be treated privatlie, whereby his abilitie may the more manifestlie appeare unto them.[3]

Secundlie, they inquire of his life and conversatioun; if he have in times past lived without slaunder, and governed himself in suche sort, as the Word of God hath not heard evill, or beene slaundered through his occasioun; which being severallie done, they signifie

Johne xxi.; Esai lxii.; 2 Cor. ix.; 2 Tim. ii.; 1 Cor. iv.; Matt. xxv.; 2 Cor. i.; Acts xx.; Tim. iv.; Ezech. iii.

[1] 2 Cor. ix.; 1 Cor. ix.; Acts vi.; Luc. xii.; 1 Cor. iv.; 2 Cor. iv.; 1 Peter v. 2; Col. i.; Matt. xx.; Matt. xxvi.; Mal. ii.; 1 Pet. iv.; Acts iii. 16; 1 Cor. i. 15; Acts xx.; 2 Cor. iv.; 1 Cor. v.; 1 Cor. xiv.

[2] Acts xi. 1; Tit. i.   [3] Tit. i. 9; Tit. ii.

unto the congregatioun, whose gifts they found most meete and
profitable for that ministrie: appointing also by a generall consent
eight dayes at the least, that everie man may diligentlie inquire of
his life and maners.[1]

At the which time the minister exhorteth them to humble themselves to God by fasting and prayer, that both their electioun may
be agreeable to his will, and also profitable to the church.[2]

And if in the meane seasoun anie thing be brought against
him, wherby he may be found unworthie by lawfull probatiouns,
then is he dismissed, and some other presented. If nothing be alledged, upoun some certane day one of the ministers at the morning sermoun presenteth him againe to the church, framing his sermoun, or some part thereof, to the setting furth of his duetie.

Then, at after noone, the sermoun ended, the minister exhorteth them to the electioun, with the invocatioun of God's name,
directing his prayer as God sall move his heart. In like maner,
after the electioun, the minister giveth thanks to God, with requeist of suche things as sall be necessarie for his office. After
that he is appointed minister, the people sing a psalme, and depart.[3]

Of the Elders, and as tuiching their Office and Election.

The elders must be men of good life and godlie conversatioun;
without blame and all suspicioun; carefull for the flocke, wise, and
above all things fearing God. Whose office standeth in governing
with the rest of the ministers; in consulting, admonishing, correcting, and ordering all things appertaining to the state of the congregatioun. And they differ frome the minister, in that they
preache not the Word, nor minister the Sacraments. In assem-
bling the people, neither they without the ministers, nor the ministers without them, may attempt anie thing. And if anie of the
just number want, the minister, by the consent of the rest, warneth
the people therof, and finallie admonisheth them to observe the

[1] Rom. ii. ; James i. ; 1 Sam. ii. ; 1 Tim. v. [2] Acts xiii. 14 ; Luc. iii.
[3] 2 Cor. x. ; Col. iii. ; Mat. ix. ; 1 Thes. v. ; Col. iv. ; Ephes. v. ; Phil. 1.

same order which was used in choosing the ministers, as farre furth
as their vocatioun requireth.[1]

Of the Deacons, and their Office and Election.

The deacons must be men of good estimatioun and report,
descreit, of good conscience, charitable, wise; and, finallie, endued
with suche vertues as Sanct Paul requireth in them. Their office
is to gather the almes diligentlie, and faithfullie to distribute it,
with the consent of the ministers and elders: also to provide for
the sicke and impotent persouns; having ever a diligent care, that
the charitie of godlie men be not wasted upoun loiterers and idle
vagabounds. Their electioun is, as hath beene afore rehearsed, in
the ministers and elders.

We are not ignorant, that the Scriptures make mentioun of a
fourth kinde of ministers left to the Church of Christ, which also
are verie profitable, where time and place doe permitt.

These ministers are called teachers, or doctors, whose office is
to instruct and teache the faithfull in sound doctrine; providing
with all diligence, that the puritie of the Gospell be not corrupt,
either through ignorance or evill opiniouns. Notwithstanding,
considering the present estate of things, we comprehended under
this title suche meanes as God hath in his church that it sould not
be left desolate, nor yitt his doctrine decay for default of ministers
therof.

Therefore, to terme it by a word more usuall in these our dayes,
we may call it the order of schooles, wherin the highest degree,
and most annexed to the ministrie and governement of the church,
is the expositioun of God's Word contained in the Old and New
Testament.

But becaus men cannot so weill profite in that knowledge except they be first instructed in the tongues, and humane sciences,
(for now God worketh not commounlie by miracles,) it is necessarie that seede be sowen for the time to come, to the intent the

---

[1] Num. xi.; Acts xiv.

church be not left barren and waste to our posteritie ; and that schooles also be erected, and colledges maintained with just and sufficient stipends, wherin the youth may be trained up in the knowledge and feare of God, that in their ripe age they may prove worthie members of our Lord Jesus Christ, whether it be to rule in civill policie, or serve in the spirituall ministrie, or elles to live in godlie reverence and subjectioun.

The Weeklie Assemblie of the Ministers, Elders, and Deacons.

To the intent that the ministrie of God's Word may be had in reverence, and not brought to contempt through the evill conver- satioun of such as are called therunto ; and also, that faults and vices may not by long sufferance grow at lenth to extreame incon- veniences, it is ordained, that everie Thursday the ministers and elders, in their assemblie or consistorie, diligentlie examine all suche faults and suspiciouns as may be espied, not onlie among others, but cheeflie among themselves ; least they seeme to be culpable of that which our Saviour Christ reproved in the Pharisees, who could espie a mote in another man's eye, and could not see a beame in their owne.

And becaus the eye ought to be more cleare than the rest of the bodie, the minister may not be spotted with anie vice bot to the great slaunder of God's Word, whose message he beareth. Therefore it is to be understand, that there be certane faults, which, if they be deprehended in a minister, he ought to be deposed ; as heresie, papistrie, schisme, blasphemie, perjurie, fornicatioun, thift, drunkennesse, usurie, fighting, unlawfull games, with suche like. Others are more tolerable, if so be that after brotherlie admoni- tiouns he amend his fault ; as strange and unprofitable fashioun in preaching the Scriptures, curiositie in seeking vaine questiouns, negligence as weill in his sermons and studeing the Scriptures, as in all other things concerning his vocatioun, scurrilitie, flattering, lieing, backbiting, wantoun words, deceate, covetousnes, taunting, dissolutioun in apparrell, gesture, and other his doings ; which vices, as they be odious in all men, so in him that ought to be as an exemple to others of perfectioun, in no wise are to be suffered, especiallie if so be, that according to God's rule, being brotherlie advertised, he acknowledge not his fault and amende.

Interpretation of the Scriptures.

Everie weeke once, the congregatioun assemble, to heare some place of the Scriptures orderlie expounded. At the which time, it is lawfull for everie man to speeke or inquire, as God sall move his heart, and the text minister occasioun, so that it be without pertinacie or disdaine, as one that rather seeketh to profite than contend. And if so be, anie contentioun arise, then suche as are appointed moderators, either satisfie the partie, or elles, if he seeme to cavill, exhort him to keepe silence, referring the judgement therof to the ministers and elders, to be determined in their assemblie before-mentioned.

THE FORME AND ORDER OF THE ELECTION OF THE SUPERINTENDENT, WHICH MAY SERVE IN ELECTION OF ALL OTHER MINISTERS. AT EDINBURGH, THE 9TH OF MARCHE, ANNO 1560. JOHNE KNOX BEING MINISTER.

First was made a sermoun, in the which these heads were intreated: First, the necessitie of ministers and superintendents: Secund, the crimes and vices that might unable them of the ministrie: Thrid, the vertues required in them: Fourth and Last, whether suche as, by publick consent of the church, were called to suche office, might refuse the same.

The sermoun finished, it was declared by the same minister, maker therof, that the Lords of Secreit Counsell had given charge and power to the churches of Lothiane to choose Mr Johne Spottiswod superintendent; and that sufficient warning was made by publick edict to the churches of Edinburgh, Linlithquo, Stirline, Tranent, Hadintoun, and Dumbar, as also to erles, lords, barouns, gentlemen, and others, that have, or might claim to have, voice in electioun, to be present that day, at the same houre. And therefore inquisitioun was made who were present, and who were absent.   After was called the said Mr Johne, who answering, the minister demaunded if anie man knew anie crime or offense to the said Mr Johne, that might unable him to be called to that office ; and that he demanded thrise.   Secundarilie, questioun was moved to the whole multitude, if there was anie other whome they wold putt in electioun with the said Mr Johne.   The people were asked if they wold have the said Mr Johne superintendent ?   If they wold honour and obey him as Christ's minister, and comfort and assist him in every thing pertaining to his charge ?   They answered, " We will; and we doe promise unto him suche obedience as becometh the sheepe to give to their pastor, so long as he remaineth faithfull in his office."

The answeres of the people, and their consent receaved, these questions were proponed to him that was to be elected.

Question. " Seing that yee hear the trust and desire of this people, doe yee not thinke your self bound in conscience before God to support them that so earnestlie call for your comfort, and the fruict of your labours ?"

Answere. "If anie thing were in me able to satisfie their desire, I acknowledge myself bound to obey God, calling by them."

Question. " Doe yee seeke to be promoted to this office and charge for anie respect of worldlie commoditie, richesse, or glorie ?"

Answere. " God knoweth the contrarie."

Question. " Beleeve yee not, that the doctrine of the prophets and apostles, contained in the bookes of the New and Old Testament, is the onlie true and most absolute foundatioun of the universall church of Christ Jesus, in so muche, that in the same Scripture are contained all things necessarie to be beleeved for the salvatioun of mankinde ?"

Answere. " I verilie beleeve the same; and doe abhorre and utterlie refuse all doctrine alledged necessarie to salvatioun, that is not expressedlie contained in the same."

Question. " Is not Christ Jesus, man of man according to the fleshe, to witt, the sonne of David, the seede of Abraham, conceaved of the Holie Ghost, borne of the Virgine Marie his mother, the onlie Head and Mediator of his church ?"

Answere. " He is, and without him there is neither salvation to man, nor life to angell."

Question. " Is not the same Lord Jesus the onlie true God, the eternall Sonne of the eternall Father, in whome all that sall be saved were elected before the foundatioun of the world was layed ?"

Answere. " I acknowledge and confesse Him in the unitie of his Godhead to be God above all things, blessed for ever."

Question. " Sall not they whome God, in his eternall counsell, hath elected, be called to the knowledge of his Sonne, our Lord Jesus ; and sall not they who of purpose are called, in this life, be justifeid ; and where justificatioun and free remissioun of sinnes is obtained in this life by free grace, sall not the glorie of the Sonne of God follow in the generall resurrectioun, when the Sonne of God sall appeare in his glorious majestie ?"

Answere. " This I acknowledge to be the doctrine of the apostles, and the most singular comfort of God's childrein."

Question. " Will yee not then containe your self in all doctrine within the bounds of this foundatioun ? Will yee not studie to promove the same, as weill by your life as by your doctrine ? Will yee not, according to the graces and utterance that God sall graunt unto you, professe, instruct, and maintaine the puritie of the doctrine contained in the sacred Word of God ; and to the uttermost of your power will yee not gainstand, and convince the gainsayers, and the teachers of men's inventiouns ?"

Answere. " That doe I promise in the presence of God, and of his congregation, heir assembled."

Question. " Know yee not that the excellencie of this office unto the which God hath called you, requireth that your conversatioun and behaviour be suche, as that yee may be irreprehensible, yea, even in the eyes of the ungodlie ?"

Answere. " I unfainedlie acknowledge, and humblie desire the church of God to pray with me, that my life be not slaunderous to the glorious Evangell of Christ Jesus."

Question. " Becaus yee are a man compassed with infirmiteis, will yee not charitablie, and with lownesse of spirit, receive admonitioun of your brethrein ? And if yee sall happen to slide, or offend in anie point, will yee not be subject to the discipline of the church, as the rest of your brethrein ?"

Answere. " I acknowledge my self a man subject to infirmitie, and one that hath need of correctioun and admonitioun, and, therefore, I most willinglie subject my self to the wholsome discipline of the church, yea, to the discipline of the same church by the which I am now called to this office and charge; and heere, in God's presence and yours, do promise obedience to all admonitiouns secreetlie or publicklie given : unto the which if I be found inobedient, I confesse myself most worthie to be ejected, not onlie frome this honour, but also from the societie of the faithfull, in case of my stubburnesse. For the vocatioun of God to beare charge within his church maketh not men tyrants nor lords, but appointeth them servants, watchemen, and pastors to the flocke."

This ended, question must be asked againe of the multitude :

Question. " Require ye anie farther of this your superintendent ?"

Answere. " If no man answere, lett the minister proceid :

" Will yee not acknowledge this your brother for the minister of Christ Jesus ? Will yee not reverence the Word of God that proceedeth frome his mouth ? Will yee not receave of him the sermoun of exhortatioun with patience, not refusing the wholsome medicine of your soules, although it be bitter and unpleasaunt to the fleshe ? Will yee not finallie mainteane and comfort him in his ministrie against all suche as wickedlie wold rebell against God, and his holie ordinances ?"

Answere. " We will, as we will answere to the Lord Jesus, who hath commaunded his ministers to be had in reverence, as his ambassaders, and as men that carefullie watche for the salvatioun of our soules."

Lett the Nobilitie be urged with this.

" Yee have heard the duetie and professioun of this our brother, by your consents appointed to this charge; as also, the duetie and obedience which God requireth of us towards him heir in this ministrie. But becaus that neither of both are able to performe anie thing without the speciall grace of our God in Christ Jesus, who hath promised to be present with us even to the consummatioun of the world, with unfained hearts lett us crave of him his benedictioun and assistance in this worke begunne to his glorie, and for the comfort of his church."

" O Lord, to whome all power is given in heaven and earth; thou that art the eternall Sonne of the eternall Father; who hath not onlie so loved thy church, that for the redemptioun and purgatioun of the same, thou hath humbled thyselfe to the death of the crosse, and therupoun hath shedde thy most innocent blood to prepare to thy self a spouse without spott; bot also to retaine this thy most excellent benefite in recent memorie, hath appointed in thy church teachers, pastors, and apostles, to instruct, comfort, and admonishe the same: looke upon us mercifullie, O Lord, thou that art onlie King, Teacher, and Hie Preest to thy owne flocke; and send unto this our brother, whome, in thy name, we have charged with the cheefe care of thy church, within the bounds of L., suche portioun of thy Holie Spirit, as thereby he may rightlie divide thy Word, to the instructioun of thy flocke, and to the confutatioun of pernicious errors, and damnable superstitions. Give unto him, good Lord, a mouth and wisdome, whereby the enemeis of thy truthe may be confounded, the woolves expelled and driven frome thy fold, thy sheepe may be fed in the wholesome pastures of thy most holie Word, the blind and ignoraunt may be illuminated with true knowledge: finallie, that the dregges of superstitioun and idolatrie which now resteth within this realme being purged and removed, we may all not onlie have occasioun to glorifie thee our Lord and Saviour, bot also daylie to grow in godlinesse and obedience of thy most holie will, to the destructioun of the bodie of sinne, and to the restitutioun of that image to the which we were once created, and to the which, after our fall and defectioun, we are renewed by participatioun of thy Holie Spirit, which by true faith in the * * * *[1] of whome the perpetuall increasse of thy graces we crave, as by thee our Lord, King, and onlie Bishop, we are taught to pray, Our Father," &c.

The prayer ended, the rest of the ministers, if anie be, and elders of that church present, in signe of their consent, sall take the elected by the hand. The cheefe minister sall give the benedictioun as followeth :—

"God, the Father of our Lord Jesus Christ, who hath commaunded his Gospell to be preached to the comfort of his elect, and hath called thee to the office of a watcheman over his people, multiplie his graces with thee; illuminate thee with his Holie Spirit; comfort and strenthen thee in all vertue; governe and guide thy ministrie to the praise of his holie name, to the propagatioun of Christ's kingdome, to the comfort of his church; and, finallie, to the plaine discharge and assurance of thy owne conscience in the day of the Lord Jesus; to whome, with the Father, and with the Holie Ghost, be all honour, praise, and glorie, now and ever. So be it."

The last Exhortation to the Elected.

"Take heede to thyself, and unto the flocke committed to thy charge: feede the same carefullie, not as it were by compulsioun, but of verie love which thou beareth to the Lord Jesus: walke in simplicitie and purenesse of life, as it becometh the true servaunt, and the ambassader of the Lord Jesus. Usurpe not dominioun, nor tyrannicall authoritie over thy brethrein. Be not discuraged in adversitie, but lay before thy self the exemples of the prophets, apostles, and of the Lord Jesus, who in their ministrie sustained contradictioun, contempt, persecutioun, and death. Feare not to

[1] A blank in the MS.

rebooke the world of sinne, justice, and judgement. If anie thing
succeede prosperouslie in thy vocatioun, be not puft up with pride,
neither yitt flatter thy self as that the good successe proceeded
frome thy vertue, industrie, or care. But lett ever that sentence
of the apostle remaine in thy heart, ' What hath thou which thou
hath not receaved ? If thou have receaved, why glorieth thou ?'
Comfort the afflicted, support the poore, and exhort others to support them. Be not solicite for things of this life, but be fervent
in prayer to God for the increasse of his Holie Spirit. And, finallie, behave thyself in this holie vocatioun with suche sobrietie, as
God may be glorifeid in thy ministrie, and so sall thou shortlie obtaine the victorie, and sall receave the crowne promised, when the
Lord Jesus sall appear in his glorie ; whose omnipotent Spirit assist thee and us, to the end."

Sing the twentie-thrid Psalme.

THE ORDER OF THE ECCLESIASTICALL DISCIPLINE.

The Necessitie of Discipline.

As no citie, toun, house, or familie, can maintaine their estate,
and prosper, without policie and governance, even so the church of
God, which requireth more purelie to be governed than anie citie
or familie, cannot, without spirituall policie and ecclesiasticall discipline, continue, increase, and floorishe.

What Discipline is.

And as the Word of God is the life and soule of this church, so
this godlie order and discipline is, as it were, sinews in the bodie,
which knitt and joyne the members together with decent order and
comelinesse, Ephes. v. It is a bridle to stay the wicked frome
their mischeefes ; it is a spurre to pricke fordward such as be slow
and negligent ; yea, and for all men it is the Father's rodde ever
in readinesse to chastise gentlie the faults committed, and to caus
them afterward to live in more godlie feare and reverence. Final-

lie, it is an order left by God unto his church, whereby men learne to frame their wills and doings according to the law of God, by instructing and admonishing one another, yea, and by correcting and punishing all obstinate rebells, and contemners of the same.

For what Cause it ought to be used.

There are three causes cheeflie which move the church of God to the executing of discipline. First, That men of evill conversatioun be not numbred among God's childrein, to their Father's reproache, as if the church of God were a sanctuarie for naughtie and vile persouns. The secund respect is, That the good be not infected with accompaneing the evill; which thing Sanct Paul foresaw, when he commanded the Corinthians to banishe frome among them the incestuous adulterer, saying, " A little leaven maketh sowre the whole lumpe of dowe," 1 Cor. v.; Galat. v. The thrid caus is, That a man thus corrected or excommunicate might be ashamed of his fault, and so through repentance come to amendement : the which thing the apostle calleth delivering to Satan, that his soule may be saved in the day of the Lord, (1 Thes. ix.; 1 Cor. v.;) meaning that he might be punished with excommunicatioun, to the intent his soule sould not perishe for ever.

The Order of Proceiding in Privat Discipline.

First, therefore, it is to be noted, that this censure, correctioun, or discipline, is either private or publick : private, as if a man committ either in maners or doctrine anie fault against thee, to admonishe him brotherlie, betweene him and thee. If so be he stubbornlie resist thy charitable advertisements, or elles, by continuance in his fault, declareth that he amendeth not, then, after he hath beene the secund time warned in presence of two or three witnesses, and continueth obstinatlie in his errour, he ought, as our Saviour Christ commandeth, to be disclosed and uttered to the church, so that, according to publick discipline, he either may be receaved through repentance, or elles be punished as his fault requireth, Matt. xviii.; Luc. xvii.; James v.; Levit. ix.; 2 Thes. viii.

What things are to be observed in Private Discipline.

And heere, as tuiching private discipline, three things are to be noted: First, That our admonitiouns proceede of a godlie zeale and conscience; rather seeking to winne our brother than to slaunder him. Nixt, That we be assured that his fault be reproveable by God's Word. And, finallie, That we use suche modestie and wisdome, that if we somewhat doubt of the mater whereof we admonishe him, yitt, with godlie exhortatiouns, he may be brought to the knowledge of his fault; or if the fault appertaine to manie, or be knowne of diverse, that our admonitioun be done in presence of some of them. Breeflie, If it concerne the whole church, in suche sort, that the concealing therof might procure some daunger to the same, that then it be uttered to the ministers and seniors, to whome the policie of the church doth appertaine.

Of Publick Discipline, and of the end thereof.

Also, in publick discipline, it is to be observed, that the minister pretermitt nothing at anie time unchastised with one kinde of punishement or other, if they perceave anie thing in the congregatioun either evill in example, slaunderous in maners, or not beseeming their professioun: as if there be anie covetous persoun; anie adulterer, fornicator, forsworne, theefe, briber, false witnesse-bearer, blasphemer, drunkard, slaunderer, usurer; anie persoun disobedient, seditious, or dissolute; anie heresie or sect, as Papisticall, Anabaptisticall, and suche like: breeflie, whatsoever it be that might spott the Christian congregatioun; yea, rather, whatsoever is not to edificatioun, ought not to escape their admonitioun or punishment, Ephes. vii.

Excommunication is the last Remedie.

And becaus it cometh to passe, sometime in the church, that

4

when other remedeis assayed profite nothing, they must procede
to the apostolicall rod and correctioun, as unto excommunicatioun,
(which is the greatest and last punishment belonging to the spirituall ministrie,) it is ordained, that nothing be attempted in that
behalfe without the determinatioun of the whole church.

Rigour in Punishment ought to be avoided.

Wherin also they must beware, and take good heed, that they
seeme not more readie to expell frome the congregatioun, than to
receave againe those in whome they perceave worthie fruicts of
repentance to appeare ; neither yit to forbid him the hearing of sermouns, which is excluded frome the sacraments and other dueteis
of the church, that he may have libertie and occasioun to repent.

God's Word is the onlie Rule of Discipline.

Finallie, That all punishments, correctiouns, censures, and admonitiouns, stretche no further than God's Word, with mercie, may
lawfullie beare.

Matt. xviii.—" *If anie refuse to heare the congregation, lett him
be to thee as a heathen, and as a publican.*"

THE ORDER OF EXCOMMUNICATIOUN AND PUBLICK REPENTANCE
USED IN THE CHURCH OF SCOTLAND, AND COMMANDED TO BE
PRINTED BY THE GENERALL ASSEMBLIE OF THE SAME, IN THE
MONETH OF JUNE, 1571.

To the Reader.

Albeit that in the Booke of Discipline, the causes, as weill of
publick repentance as of excommunication, are sufficientlie expressed, yit, becaus the forme and order are not sett furth, that
everie church and minister may have assurance that they agree
with others in proceeding, it is thought expedient to drawe that
order which, universallie within this realme, sall be observed.

The Crimes of Excommunication.

And, first, We must understand what crimes be worthie of excommunication, and what of publick repentance.

In the first, it is to be noted, That all crimes that by the law of God deserve death, deserve also excommunicatioun frome the societie of Christ his Church, whether the offender be Papist or Protestant: for it is no reasoun that, under pretence of diversitie of religioun, open impietie sould be suffered in the visible bodie of Christ Jesus. And, therefore, wilfull murtherers, adulterers, (lawfullie convict,) sorcerers, witches, conjurers, charmers, and givers of drinkes to destroy childrein, and open blasphemers, (as if anie renunce God, denie the truthe and the authoritie of his holie Word, railing against his blessed sacraments;) suche, we say, ought to be excommunicate frome the societie of Christ's Church, that their impietie may be the more deepelie wounded, perceaving themselves abhorred of the godlie. Against suche open malefactors the processe may be summouned. For the crime being knowne, advertisement ought to be given to the superintendent of the diocesse, either by the minister, or by suche as can best give informatioun of that fact; except in reformed touns and other places, where the ministrie is planted with ministers and elders, according to the act of the Generall Assemblie, made the 26th of December, 1568. And if there be no superintendent where the crime is committed, then ought the informatioun to passe frome suche as are offended to the nixt superintendent, who, with expeditioun, ought to direct his letters of summouns to the parish church where the offender hath his residence, if the ministrie be there planted. And if it be not, or if the offender have no certane dwelling place, then ought the summouns to be direct to the cheefe toun, and best reformed church in that diocesse where the crime was committed, appointing to the offender a certane day, time, and place, where and when he sall appeare before the superintendent and his assessors, to heare that crime tryed, as tuiching the truthe of it, and to answere himself why the sentence of excommunicatioun sould not be pronounced publicklie against him. If the offender, lawfullie warned, appeare not, inquisitioun being taken of the crime, charge may be given by the superintendent to the ministers, so manie as sall be thought needful for publicatioun of that sentence, to pronunce the same the nixt Sunday, the forme wherof sall after be declared. But and if the offender appeare, and alledge for himself anie reasonable defense, to witt, that he will not be fugitive frome the law, bot will abide the censure for that offense, then may the sentence of excommunicatioun be suspended, till that the magistrat be required to trie that cause; wherin, if the magistrats be negligent, then ought the church frome secreit inquisitioun proceed to publick admonitioun, that the magistrats may be vigilant in that cause of blood, which crieth vengeance upoun the whole land where it is shed without punishment. If no remedie by them can be found, then justlie may the church pronunce the offender excommunicate, as one suspect, besides his crime, to have corrupt the judges, revengers of the blood. And so ought the church to proceed to excommunicatioun, whether the offender be fugitive frome the law, or whether he procure pardoun, or illude the severitie of justice by meanes whatsoever, besides the triell of his innocencie.

If the offender abide an assise, and by the same be absolved, then may not the church pronunce excommunicatioun; but justlie may exhort the man by whose hand the blood was shed to enter in consideratioun with himself, how pretious is the life of man before God, and how severelie God commaunded blood (howsoever it be shed, except it be by the sword of the magistrate) to be punished: and so may enjoyne unto him suche satisfactiouns to be made publicklie to the church, as may beare testificatioun of his obedience and unfained repentance. If the offender be convict, and executioun follow according to the crime, then, upoun the humble sute of him that is to suffer, may the elders and ministers of the church not onlie give unto him consolatioun, but also pronunce the sentence of absolutioun, and his sinne to be remitted, according to his repentance and faith. And this muche for excommunicatioun of publick offenders. And yit further, we must consider, that if the offender be fugitive frome the law, so that punishement cannot be executed against him, in that case the church ought to delay no time; bot upoun the notice of his crime, and that he is fled frome the presence of the judge, it ought to pronunce him excommunicated publicklie, and so continuallie to repute him, untill suche time as the magistrate be satisfeid. And so, whether the offender be convict in judgement, or be fugitive frome the law, the church ought to proceede to the sentence of excommunicatioun, the forme wherof followeth :—

THE FORME.

The Minister, in publick audience of the People, sall say :—

" It is cleerelie knowne to us that N., sometime baptized in the name of the Father, of the Sonne, and of the Holie Ghost, and so reputed and counted for a Christian, hath fearefullie fallen frome the societie of Christ's bodie, by committing cruell and wilfull murther, (or by committing filthie adulterie, &c.) which crime, by the law of God, deserveth death. And becaus the civill sword is in the hand of God's magistrats, who, notwithstanding, oft winke at suche crimes, we, having place in the ministrie, with greefe and dolour of our hearts, are compelled to draw the sword graunted by God to his church; that is, to excommunicate frome the societie of Christ Jesus, frome his bodie, the church, frome participatioun of sacraments and prayers with the same, the said N.

" And, therefore, in the name and authoritie of the eternall God, and of his Sonne Jesus Christ, we pronunce the said N. excommunicate and accursed in that his wicked fact; and charge all that favour the Lord Jesus so to repute and hold him, (or her,) until suche time as that either the magistrat have punished the offender as God's law commaunds, or that the same offender be reconciled to the church againe, by publick repentance. And, in the mean time, we earnestlie desire all faithfull to call upoun God to move the hearts of the upper powers so to punishe suche horrible crimes, that malefactors may feare to offend, even for feare of punishment; and also so to tuiche the heart of the offender, that he may deepelie consider how fearefull it is to fall in the hands of the eternall God, that by unfained repentance he may apprehend mercie in Jesus Christ, and so avoide eternall condemnatioun."

The sentence of excommunicatioun once pionunced, the church may not suddanlie admit the murtherer, or convict adulterer, to repentance and societie of the faithfull, albeit that pardoun be purchased of the magistrat. But first ought inquisitioun be taken, if the murtherer have satisfeid the partie offended, that is, the kinne and freinds of the man slaine : which, if he have not done, neither is understand willing so to doe, the church in no wise may heare him. But and if he be willing to satisfie, and the freinds exceede measure, and the possibilitie of him that hath committed the crime, then ought the church to putt moderatioun to the unreasonable, in case the civill magistrate hath not so done before, and so proceid with him that offereth repentance, that the wilfulnesse of the indiscreete be not hinderance to the reconciliatioun of him that earnestlie craved the benefite and societie of the church.

And yit may not the church receave anie excommunicate at his first requeist ; bot in suche greevous crimes as before are expressed, (of others sall be after spoken,) fourtie dayes at the least after his first offer may be appointed, to trie whether the signes of repentance appeare in the offender or not. And yit, in the meane time, the church may comfort him by wholsome admonitiouns, assuring him of God's mercie, if he be verilie penitent : he may also be admitted to the hearing of the Word, but in no wise to participatioun of prayers, neither before nor after sermoun. The first fourtie dayes expired, upoun his new sute, the superintendent or sessioun may enjoyne suche paines as may trie whether he be penitent or not : the least are, the murtherer must stand three severall Sundayes in a publick place before the church doore, barefooted and bare-headed, clothed in base and abject apparell, having the same weapoun which he used in the murther, or the like, bloodie, in his hands, and in conceaved words sall say to suche as sall enter into the church :—

The Confession of the Penitent.

" So farre hath Satan gotten victorie over me, that cruellie I have shed innocent blood, for the which I have deserved death corporall and eternall; and so I graunt my self unworthie of the commoun light, or yit of the companie of men. And yit, becaus in God there is mercie that passeth all measure, and becaus the magistrat hath not taken frome me this wretched life, I most earnestlie desire to be reconciled againe with the church of Christ Jesus, frome the societie whereof mine iniquitie hath caused me to be excommunicated. And, therefore, in the bowells of Christ Jesus, I crave of you to pray with me unto God, that my greevous crime may be of him remitted; and also that ye will be suppliants with me to the church, that I abide not thus excommunicate unto the end."

At the last of the three Sundayes, certane of the elders sall receave him into the church, and present him before the preaching place, and sall declare unto that minister, that all that was enjoyned to that offender was obedientlie fulfilled by him. Then sall the minister recite unto him, as weill the greevousnesse of his sinne as the merceis of God, if he be penitent; and therafter sall require of the church, if that they desire anie further satisfactioun. And if no answere be given, then sall the minister pronunce his sinne to be remitted according to his repentance; and sall exhort the church to embrace him as a brother, after that prayer and thanksgiving be givin to God, as after sall be described. And thus far to be observed for the order in receaving of them who have committed capitall crimes, be it murther, adulterie, incest, witchcraft, or others before expressed.

Resteth yitt another kinde of offenders who deserve excommunicatioun, albeit not so summarilie; to witt, suche as have beene partakers with us in doctrine and sacraments, and have returned backe againe to Papistrie, or have given their presence to anie part of their abominatioun; or yitt, that of anie long continuance with-draw themselves frome the societie of Christ's bodie, and frome the participatioun of the sacraments, when they are publicklie mini-stred.　Suche, no doubt, declare themselves worthie of excommu-nicatioun.　But first, they must be called, either before the superin-tendent with some joyned with him, or elles before the elders and sessioun of the best and nixt reformed church where the offenders have their residence, who must accuse their defectioun, exhort them to repentance, and declare them the danger wherin they stand. Whome, if the offender heareth, the sessioun or superintendent may appoint him a day to satisfie the church publicklie, whome by his defectioun he had offended.　But if he continue stubburne, then may the sessioun or superintendent commaund the minister or mi-nisters to declare, the nixt Sunday, the defectioun of suche a per-soun, and his obstinate contempt.　And this advertisement given two Sundayes, the thrid may the sentence of excommunication be pronounced.

Offenses that deserve Publick Repentance, and order to proceede therein.

Such offenses as fall not under the civill sword, and yit are slaunderous and offensive in the church, deserve publick repent-ance; and of these, some are more haynous than others.　Forni-catioun, drunkennesse used, swearing, cursed speaking, chiding, fighting, browling, and commoun contempt of the order of the church, breaking of the Sabboth, and suche like, ought to be in no persoun suffered.　But the slaunder being knowne, the offender sould be called before the ministrie; his crime proved, accused, re-booked, and he commaunded publicklie to satisfie the church: which if the offender refuse, they may proceede to excommunica-tioun, as after sall be declared.　If the offender appeare not, sum-mouns ought to passe to the thrid time; and then, in case he ap-peare not, the church may decerne the sentence to be pronunced.

Other, if it be lesse haynous, and yit deserve admonitioun, as wantoun and vaine words, uncomelie gestures, negligence in hearing the preaching, or abstaining frome the Lord's Table when it is ministred, suspicioun of avarice or of pride, superfluitie or ryotousnes in cheare or rayment; these, we say, and suche others that of the world are not regarded, deserve admonitioun among the members of Christ's bodie, first, secreitlie, by one or two of these that first espie the offense. Which, if the persoun suspected heare, and give declaratioun of amendiment, then there needeth no farther processe. But if he contemne the admonitioun, then sould the former admonishers take to themselves two or three faithfull and honest witnesses, in whose presence the suspected offender sould be admonished, and the causes of their suspicioun declared. To whome, if then he give significatioun of repentance, and promise of amendiment, they may cutt off all farther accusation. But and if he obstinatlie contemne both the said admonitiouns, then ought the first and secund brethrein signifie the mater to the minister and elders in their sessioun, who ought to call the offender, and before the complainers accuse him, as weill of the crime, as of the contempt of the admonitioun. If then he acknowledge his offense, and be willing to satisfie the brethrein before offended, and the sessioun then present, there needeth no farther publicatioun of that offense. But if he declare himself inobedient to the sessioun, then, without delay, the nixt Sunday ought the crime, and the order of admonitiouns passed before, be publicklie declared to the church, and the persoun (without specificatioun of his name) be admonished to satisfie in publick that which he refused to doe in secreit; and that for the first. If he offer himself to the church before the nixt Sunday, the discretioun of the ministrie may take suche order as may satisfie, as weill the private persouns that were first offended, as the church, declaring the repentance and submissioun of that brother that before appeared stubburne and incorrigible. But and if he abide the secund admonitioun publick, when that his name sall be expressed, and his offenses and stubburnnesse declared, then can no satisfactioun be receaved but in publick: yea, it may not be receaved before he have humblie required the same of the ministrie and sessioun of the church, in their appointed assemblie.

If he continue stubburne, then the thrid Sunday ought he be charged publicklie to satisfie the church for his offense and contempt, under the paine of excommunicatioun, the order wherof sall after be declared.

And thus a small offense or slaunder may justlie deserve excommunicatioun, by reasoun of the contempt and disobedience of the offender. If the offender shew himself penitent betweene the first admonitioun and the secund, and satisfie the ministrie of the church, and the brethrein that before were offended in their assemblie, then it may suffice, that the minister, at commandement of the sessioun, declare the nixt Sunday (without comparing or expressing of the persoun) his repentance or submissioun, in these, or other words:

" It was signifeid unto you before, (dearelie beloved,) that ane certane brother (or brethrein) was noted, or, at least, suspected of some offense, whereof he being admonished by one or two, appeared lightlie to regarde the same; and therefore was he and his offense notifeid unto the ministrie, in their assemblie, who, according to their duetie and charge, accused him of the same. And not finding in him suche obedience as the professioun of a Christiane requireth, fearing that suche offenses and stubburnnesse sould engender contempt, and infect others, they were compelled to notifie unto you the crime, and proceiding of the sessioun, minding to have sought the uttermost remedie, in case the offender had continued obstinate. Bot seing that it hath pleased God to mollifie the heart of our brother, whose name we neede not to expresse, so that he hath not onlie acknowledged the offense, bot also hath fullie satisfeid the brethrein that first were offended, and us the ministrie, and hath promised to abstaine frome all appearance of suche evill as wherof he was suspected and admonished, we have no just cause to proceede to anie farther extremitie; but rather to glorifie God for the submissioun of our brother, and unfainedlie pray unto him, that in the like case we, and everie one of us, may give the like obedience."

The Forme and Order of Publick Repentance.

It is first to be observed, that none may be admitted to publick repentance, except that first they be admitted thereto by the sessioun and assemblie of the ministers and elders ; in the which they ought sharplie to be examined, what feare and terrour they have of God's judgements, what hatred of sinne, and dolour for the same, and what sense and feeling they have of God's mercies ; in the which if they be ignoraunt, they ought diligentlie to be instructed. For it is but a mockage to present suche to publick repentance, as neither understand what sinne is, what repentance is, what is grace, nor by whome is God's favour and mercie purchased. After, then, that the offender sall be in the assemblie instructed, so that he hath some taste of God's judgements, bot cheefelie of God's mercies in Christ Jesus, he may be presented before the publick church, upoun a Sunday after the sermoun, and before the prayers and psalme ; and then the minister sall say :—

" Beloved and deerest brethrein, we, by reasoun of our charge and ministrie, present before you this brother, that by infirmitie of flesh and craft of Satan hath fearefullie fallen frome the obedience of his God, by committing N. of a crime, &c., (lett the sinne be expressed,) by the which he hath not onlie offended against the Majestie of God, bot also by the same hath given great slaunder and offense to his holie congregatioun ; and, therefore, doth to his owne confusioun (bot to the glorie of God, and our great comfort) present himself heere before you, to witnesse and declare his unfained repentance, the thirst and the care he hath to be reconciled with God through Jesus Christ, and with you, his brethrein, whome he hath offended. And, therefore, it is requisite that yee and he understand what assurance we have to require suche publick satisfactioun of him, what profite we ought to learne in the same, and what profite and utilitie redoundeth to both, of this his humiliatioun.

" That publick repentance is the institutioun of God, and not man's inventioun, may be plainlie gathered of the words of our Master, commanding, that if anie have offended his brother, in

what sort soever it be, that he sall goe to him, and be reconciled
unto his brother. If the offense committed against one brother requireth reconciliatioun, the offense committed against manie brethrein requireth the same. And if a man be charged by Christ
Jesus to goe to a man whome he hath offended, and there, by confessing of his offense, require reconciliatioun, muche more is he
bound to seeke a whole multitude whome he hath offended, and
before them with all humilitie require the same. For that woe
which our Master, Christ Jesus, pronounceth against everie man
that hath offended the least one within his church, remaineth
upoun everie publick offender, untill suche time as he declare himself willing to remove the same; which he can never doe, untill
suche time as he lett the multitude whome he hath offended understand his unfained repentance. But becaus that all men of upright judgement agree in this, that publick offenses require publick
repentance, we passe to the secund head, which is, What it is that
we have to consider, in the fall and sinne of this our brother. If
we consider his fall, and sinne in him onlie, without consideratioun
of ourselves, and of our owne corruptioun, we sall profite nothing :
for so sall we but despise our brother; and flatter ourselves. But
if we sall earnestlie consider what nature we beare, what corruptioun lurketh in it, how prone and readie everie one of us is to
suche, and greater impietie, then sall we, in the sinne of this our
brother, accuse and condemne our owne sinnes ; in his fall, sall we
consider and lament our sinfull nature; also sall we joyne our repentance, teares, and prayers, with him and his, knowing that no
fleshe can be justifeid before God's presence, if judgement proceid
without mercie. The profite which this our brother and we have
of this his humiliatioun is, that we and he may be assured, that
more readie is our Lord God to receave us to mercie through
Jesus Christ, his onlie Sonne, than we are to crave it. It is not
sinne, be it never so greevous, that sall separate us frome his favour, if we seeke to his mercie : for as all have sinned, and are by
themselves destitute of God's grace, so is He readie to shew mercie
unto all that unfainedlie call for the same. Yea, He doth not onlie

receave such as come, bot He, by the mouth of his deare Sonne, calleth upon suche as be burdenned and loadened with sinne, and solemnelie promiseth that He will refreshe them. We have, besides, an other commoditie, to witt, that if we sall heerafter fall in the like, or greater, (for we stand not by our owne power, but by grace onlie,) that we be not ashamed in this same sort to humble our selves, and confesse our offense. Now, therefore, brother, as we all praise God in this your humiliatioun, beseeching him, that it be without hypocrisie, so it becometh you earnestlie to consider of what minde, and with what heart, yee present your self heere before this assemblie. It is not your sinne that sall separate you frome your God, nor frome his mercie in Jesus Christ, if you repent the same ; but hypocrisie and impenitencie (which God remove frome you and us) is no wise tolerable before his presence."

The offender ought to protest before God that he is sorie for his sinne, and unfainedlie desireth God to be mercifull unto him, and that for the obedience of his deare Sonne, our Lord Jesus Christ.

The Minister.

" We can onlie see that which is without, and according to your confessioun judge, leaving the secreits of the heart to God, who onlie can trie and searche the same. But becaus unfained repentance for sinne, and simple confessioun of the same, are the meere gifts of God, we will joyne our prayers with yours, that the one and the other may be graunted to you and us.

" Eternall and everliving God, Father of our Lord Jesus Christ, thou that by the mouth of thy holy prophets and apostles hath plainly pronunced, that thou desireth not the death of a sinner, bot rather that he may convert and live ; who also hath sent thy onlie Sonne, to suffer the cruell death of the crosse, not for the just, bot suche as find themselves oppressed with the burthein of sinnes, that by Him and his advocatioun they may have accesse to the throne of thy grace, being assured, that before thee they sall find favour and mercie : We are assembled, O Lord, in thy presence, and that in the name of this same our Lord Jesus, thy deare Sonne, to accuse before thee our sinnes, and before the feete of thy Majestie to crave mercie for the same. We most humblie beseeche thee, O Father of mercies, first that thou will touche and move our hearts by the power of thy Holie Spirit, in suche sort, that we may come to a true knowledge of our sinnes. But cheefelie, O Lord, that it will please thee to move the heart of this our brother, N., &c., who, as he hath offended thy Majestie, and a great number of this thy holie congregatioun, by his greevous and public sinne, so doth he not refuse publicklie to acknowledge and confesse the same, as that this his humiliatioun, given to the glorie of thy name, presentlie doth witnesse. But becaus, O Lord, the externall confessioun, without the dolour of the heart, availeth nothing in thy presence, we most humblie beseeche thee, that thou will so effectuallie move his heart, and ours also, that he and we, without hypocrisie damning that which thy law pronounceth unjust, may attaine to some sense and feeling of thy mercie, which thou hath abundantlie shewed unto mankinde in Jesus Christ our Lord. Graunt, O Lord, unto this our brother, the repentance of the heart, and sincere confessioun of his mouth, to the praise of thy name, to the comfort of thy church, and to the confusioun of Satan. And to us graunt, O Lord, that albeit we cannot be altogether cleane of sinne, yit that we fall not in horrible crimes, to the dishonour of thy most holie name, to the slaunder of our brethrein, and infamie of thy holie Evangell which we professe. Lett thy godlie power, O Lord, so strenthen our weaknesse, that neither the craft of Satan, nor the tyrannie of sinne, draw us utterlie frome thy obedience. Give us grace, O Lord, that, by holinesse and innocencie of life, we may declare to this wicked generatioun, what difference there is betwixt the sonnes of light and the sonnes of darknes, that men, seing our good works, may glorifie thee, and thy Sonne Jesus Christ, our onlie Saviour and Redeemer; to whome, with thee and the Holie Spirit, be all honour, praise, and glorie, now and ever. Amen."

The prayer finished, the minister sall turne him to the penitent brother, and in full audience sall say:

" Ye have heard, brother, what is your duetie toward the church which yee have offended; to witt, that willinglie yee confesse that crime that you have committed, asking God mercie for the same, and so that yee may reconcile your self to the church which yee have offended. Yee have heard also the affection and care of the church toward you, their penitent brother, notwithstanding your greevous fall; to wit, that we all heere present joyne our sinnes with your sinne; we all repute and esteeme your fall to be our owne; we accuse our selves no lesse than we accuse you: now, finallie, we joyne our prayers with yours, that we and you may obtaine mercie, and that by the meanes of our Lord Jesus Christ. Let us, therefore, brother, have this comfort of you, that yee will openlie and simplie confesse your crime, and give to us attestation of your unfained repentance."

The penitent sall then openlie confesse the crime, whatsoever it be, and sall desire God's mercie, and pray the church to call to God for mercie with him; and unfainedlie desire that he may be joyned again to their societie and number.

If the penitent be confounded with shame, or such a one as cannot distinctlie speeke to the comfort and instruction of the church, the minister sall make repetition, that everie head may be understood by it self; and therefore sall aske the penitent if that be his confession, and if so he beleeveth. His answere affirmative being receaved, the minister sall aske the congregation if they judge anie further to be required for their satisfaction and reconciliation of that brother. No contradiction being made, the minister sall say to the penitent, "We have heard, deare brother, your confession, for the which, from our hearts we praise God. For in it the Spirit of Jesus Christ hath confounded the devill, and broken doun his head and power, in that, that yee to the glorie of God have openlie damned yourself and your impietie, imploring grace and mercie, for Christ Jesus, his Sonne's sake. This strenth, submission, and obedience, cannot proceed frome flesh and blood, bot is the singular gift of the Holie Ghost. Acknowledge, therefore, it to be given unto you by Jesus Christ our Lord. And now, take heed, least at any time yee be unmindfull of this great benefite, which, no doubt, Satan doth envie, and will assaile by all meanes possible, that you may abuse it. He will not cease to tempt you to fall againe in suche, or crimes more horrible. But resist the devill, and he sall flee frome you. Live in sobrictie; be instant in prayer; commend yourself unfainedlie unto God, who, as he is faithfull, so sall he give to us victorie over sinne, death, and Satan, and that by the meanes of our Head, and soverane Campioun, Jesus Christ, to whom be all praise, glorie, and honour, now and ever. Amen."

An Admonition to the Church.

" It is your duetie, brethrein, to tak exemple of this our penitent brother, First, that yee be unfainedlie displeased in your owne hearts for your sinnes: Secundarilie, that with this our brother yee accuse them in the sight of God, imploring grace and mercie for your offenses committed; and last, if anie of you sall after this publicklie offend, that yee refuse not, with the like reverence, to satisfie the Church of God, offended by you. Now onlie resteth, that yee remitt and forget all offenses which yee have conceaved heeretofore, by the sinne and fall of this our brother; accept and embrace him as a member of Christ's bodie. Let none take upon him to reproache and accuse him for any offenses that before this houre he hath committed. And that he may have the better assurance of your good will and reconciliation, prostrate yourselves before God, and render him thanks for the conversion and repentance of this our brother."

The Thanksgiving.

" Heavenlie Father, fountane of all mercie and consolation, we confesse ourselves unworthie to be counted among thy childrein, if thou have respect to the corruption of our nature. But, seing it hath pleased thy Fatherlie goodnes, not only freelie to choose us in thy deare Sonne, our Lord Jesus Christ, by his death to redeeme us, by his Evangell to call us, and by his Holie Spirit (which both are thine) to illuminate us; but also, that thou hath commanded the Word and holie Evangell to be preached, to the end that the penitent sall have an assurance of the remission of their sinnes, not onlie for a time, bot even so oft as men frome sorrowful heart sall call for thy grace and mercie: In consideration of this thy Fatherlie adoption, and ineffable clemencie showen upon us, we can not but praise and magnifie thy Fatherlie mercie, a testimonie whereof we not onlie feele in ourselves, bot also see the same evident in the conversion of this our brother, whom Satan for a time held in boundage, but now is set at freedome by the power of our Lord Jesus Christ, and is returned againe to the societie of thy bodie. Graunt unto us, Heavenlie Father, that he and we may more and more be displeased for our sinnes, and proceed in all maner of good works, to the praise of thy holie name, and edification of thy church, by Jesus Christ, our Lord, and onlie Saviour. So be it."

The thanks finished, the minister sall require of the penitent, if he will be subject to the discipline of the church, in case that he after offend. Who, answering that he will, the minister sall say in maner of absolution:

" If thou unfainedlie repent thy former iniquitie, and beleeve in the Lord Jesus, then I, in his name, pronounce and affirme that thy sinnes are forgiven, not onlie in earth, but also in heaven, according to the promises annexed with the preaching of his Word, and to the power putt in the ministrie of his church."

Then sall the elders and deacons, with the ministers, (if anie be,) in name of the whole church, take the reconciled brother by the hand, and embrace him, in signe of full reconciliation. Then, after, sall the church sing the 103d Psalme, so muche as they think expedient; and so sall the assemblie with the benediction be dismissed.

The Forme of Excommunication.

After that all admonition, both privat and public, be past, as before is said, then must the church proceed to excommunicatioun, if the offender remaine obstinate. The Sunday, therefore, after the thrid publick admonition, the minister being before charged by the session or elders, sall thus signifie unto the church after sermoun:

3

"It is not unknowen to you, with what lenitie and carefulnesse the ministrie and the whole church, by publick and privat admonitions, hath sought N., &c., to satisfie the church, and to declare himself penitent for his greevous crimes and rebellion, by the which he hath offended God's majestie, blasphemed his holie name, and offended his church, in whome to this day we finde nothing bot stubburnnesse. We cannot, therefore, of conscience, winke any longer at the disobedience of the said N., least that his exemple infect and hurt others. We are compelled, therefore, in the feare of God, to give the said N. into the hands and power of the devill, to the destruction of the flesh, if that by that meane he may be broght to the consideration of himself, and so repent, and avoide that fearefull condemnation that sall fall on all inobedient, in the day of the Lord Jesus. And, least that anie sall thinke that we doe this of manlie presumption, without the assurance of the Scripture, yee sall shortlie heare what commandement and authoritie we have so to doe.

" First, we have the commandement of our Master and Saviour, Jesus Christ, to hold suche for ethnicks and publicans as will not heare the voice of the church. But plaine it is, that this obstinate N. hath contemptuouslie refused all wholsome admonitions, and therefore we, not one or two, but the whole church, must hold him as a publicane; that is, as one cutt off frome the bodie of Christ, and unworthie of anie societie with him, or with the benefites of his church, till his new conversion, and his receaving againe.

" Secundarilie, we have the command of the apostle Sanct Paul, and that fearefull sentence which he, being absent, did notwithstanding pronounce against the incest; with his sharpe rebooke to the Corinthians, that with greater zeale and expedition they expelled not from among them that wicked man. And, if anie thinke that the offense of this forenamed obstinat is not so hainous as that of the incest, lett such understand, that mercie and favour may be rather granted to anie other sinne, than to the contempt of wholsome admonitions, and of the just and lawfull ordinances of the church. For other sinnes, how hainous so ever they be, (so be it

that they deserve not death,) as by unfained repentance they are remitted before God, so, upon the same humblie offered unto the
church, order may be taken, that the offender may be comforted,
and at lenth restored to the societie of the church again. But such
as proudlie contemne the admonition of the church, privat or publick, declare themselves stubburne, rebellious, and altogether impenitent, and, therefore, most justlie ought they to be excommunicate.

"The precept of God given under the law, to expel frome the
middest of God's people suche as were leprous, (without exception
of person,) is to us an assurance, that we ought to expell frome the
societie of Christ's bodie suche as be stricken with spirituall leprosie; for the one is no lesse infective and dangerous than is the
other. Now, seing that we know excommunication is God's ordinance, lett us, in few words, understand the utilitie and use of the
same.

"By it, first, the church is purged of open wicked doers, which
is no small commoditie, considering that we fight in the middest
and eyes of this wicked generation, which seeketh in us nothing
more than occasioun of slaunder. Secundarlie, by it is the church,
and everie member of the same, retained in obedience and feare,
wherof all have need, if the frailtie of our flesh sall be rightlie considered. Thridlie, by it we exercise a singular work of charitie,
whill that we declare ourselves carefull to keepe the flocke of Christ
in puritie of maners, and without danger to be infected. For, as it
were a worke both uncharitable and cruell, to joyne together in
one bed persons infected with pestilent and other contagious and
infective sores with tender childrein, or with suche as are whole, so
it is no lesse crueltie to suffer among the flocke of Christ suche obstinat rebells: for, true is that sentence of the apostle's, 'A little
leaven corrupteth the whole masse." But, least that we sould
seeme to usurpe power over the church, or to doe anie thing without
the knowledge and consent of the whole bodie, for this present we
delay the sentence, willing such as have anie thing to object in the
contrarie to propone the same the nixt sessioun day, or elles to sig-

nifie the same to some of the ministers or elders, that answere may be given thereto; and, in the meane time, we will call to God for the conversion of the impenitent.

The Prayer for the Obstinat.

" Eternall and ever-living God, Father of our Lord Jesus Christ, whose verie propertie is to shew mercie, and to restore life, when to man's judgement death hath gotten dominion over thy creatures: for thou hath first sought, called, accused, and convicted our father Adam, after his transgression, and being so deid in sinne, and thrall to Satan, that he could neither confesse his offense, nor yit aske mercie for the same: thou, by thy free promises of mercie and grace, gave unto him a new life, and strenth to repent. The same order must thou keepe, O Lord, with all thy chosen childrein of his posteritie; for in man's corrupt nature there can be no obedience, untill that thou, by operation of thy Holie Spirit, work the same. And, therefore, we most humblie beseeke thee, for Jesus Christ thy Sonne's sake, pitifullie to looke upon this thy creature, who was once baptized in thy name, and hath professed himself subject to thy religion, and to the discipline of thy church, whom Satan (alas!) now so blindeth, that obstinatlie he contemneth the one and the other. We have followed, O Lord, the rule prescribed unto us by thy deare Sonne, our Lord Jesus Christ, in admonishing and threatning him; but hitherto have profited nothing concerning him and his humiliation.

" But, O Lord, as thou alone knoweth, so may thou alone change and mollifie the hearts of the proud and impenitent. Thou, by the voice of thy prophet Nathan, wakened David frome his deadlie securitie. Thou, without anie prophet, did beate doun the pride of Manasseh in the prisoun, after he had shed the blood of thy servants, and had replenished Jerusalem with all kinde of impietie. Thou turned the heart of Peter, at the looke of thy deare Sonne, our Lord Jesus Christ, after that fearefullie, with horrible imprecations, he had thrise openlie denied him.

" O Lord, thy mercies without measure endure for ever, to the which we, after long travell, doe remitt this obstinat and impenitent; earnestlie desiring thee, O Father of mercies, first so to peirce his heart with the feare of thy severe judgements, that he may beginne to understand, that thus contemning all wholsome admonitions, he provoketh thy wrath and indignation against himself. Open his eyes, that he may see how fearefull and terrible a thing it is to fall into thy hands. And, therefore, mollifie and anoint his heart with the unction of thy Holie Spirit, that he may unfainedlie convert unto thee, and give unto thee that honour and obedience that thou requireth in thy holie Word; and so to our comfort, that now mourne for his rebellion, that he may subject himself to the just ordinance of thy church, and avoide that fearefull vengeance that most assuredlie sall fall upon all the inobedient. These thy graces, Heavenlie Father, and farther, as thou knoweth to be expedient for us, and for thy church universall, we call, according as we be taught to pray by our soverane Master, Christ Jesus, saying, 'Our Father,' &c."

The second Sunday, after sermon and publick prayers, the minister sall, in audience of the whole church, aske the elders and deacons, who must sitt in an eminent and proper place, that their answere may be heard:

The Minister.

"Hath he, whome the last day we admonished, under the paine of excommunication, to satisfie the church for his publick slander and contempt of the ministrie, by himself or by anie other, offered his obedience unto you?"

They sall answere, as the truthe is, Yea, or Nay.

If he hath sought the favour of anie within the ministrie, with promise of obedience, then sall farther processe be delayed, and he commanded to appeare before the session in their nixt assemblie, where order may be taken for his publick repentance, as in the former head is expressed. If he have not laboured to satisfie the church, then sall the minister proceed, and say:

"It cannot be but dolorous to the bodie, that anie one member therof sould be cut off and perish: and yit, it ought to be more fearefull to the member than to the bodie, for the member cut off can doe no thing but putrifie and perish, and yit the bodie may retaine life and strenth. But the rebellion of this obstinat may proceed, in one part, from ignorance; for it may be, that he understandeth not what excommunication is, and what is the danger of the same. I sall, therefore, in few words, open the one and the other.

"Lawfull excommunication (for the thundrings of that Roman Antichrist are but vanitie and winde) is the cutting off frome the bodie of Jesus Christ, frome participation of his holie sacraments, and frome publick prayers with his church, by publick and solemned sentence, all obstinat and impenitent persons, after due admonitions; which sentence, lawfullie pronounced in earth, is ratified in heaven, by binding of the same sinnes that they bind in earth. The danger heerof is greater than man can suddanlie espie: for seing, that without the bodie of Jesus Christ there abideth nothing but death and damnation to mankinde, in what estate sall we judge them to stand that justlie are cut off frome the same?

" Yea, what horrible vengeance hangeth upon them and their posteritie, notable and severe punishments may instruct us. Cain, the murtherer, was not accused within his owne person onlie, bot that same malediction ranne on his posteritie, and all that joyned therewith, till that all mankind was destroyed by water, (eight persons reserved.) Cham likewise was accursed in his sonne Canaan, the severitie wherof proceeded even to the rooting out of that whole race and nation. The simple word of our Master, Jesus Christ, caused the figge tree suddanlie to wither. At the voice of Peter, Ananias and Saphira were striken with death. The same God and Lord Jesus, with the power of his Holie Spirit, that then was potent and just, worketh even now in the ministrie of his church, the contempt wherof he will in no wise suffer unpunished. And, therefore, ye that have acquaintance or familiaritie with the forenamed obstinate, declare unto him these dangers, and will him not to tempt the uttermost. And thus, yett againe lett us pray to God for his conversion."

Lett the former Prayer be publicklie said.

The thrid Sunday, lett the first question be proponed by the minister to the elders and deacons, concerning the submissioun of the obstinate so oft admonished, as was proponed the secund. If repentance be offered, lett order be taken, as is aforesaid, with one charge to the church, to praise God for the conversion of that brother. If repentance be not offered, then sall the minister expone wherein the persoun that is to be excommunicate hath offended; how oft, and by whome he hath beene admonished, as weill privatlie as publicklie; and sall demand of the elders and deacons, if it be not so: whose answere receaved, the minister sall aske the whole church, if they thinke that suche contempt sould be suffered among them; and if then no man mak intercession for the obstinat, the minister sall proceed, and say:

" Of verie conscience we are compelled to doe that which to our hearts is most dolorous; to witt, to give over to the hands of the divell this forenamed obstinate contemner, N., whom once we esteemed a member of our bodie; and that not onlie for the crime which he hath committed, bot muche rather for his proud contempt and intolerable rebellion, least that our sufferance of him in this his impietie sould not onlie be imputed to us, bot also that he sould infect others with the same pestilence. And, therefore, we must use the last remedie, how greevous so ever it be unto us. And yit, I desire you, for more ample declaration of your Christian charitie toward him, ye pray with me unto God now, for the last, for his conversion.

The Last Prayer before the Excommunication.

" Omnipotent, eternall, and most mercifull Father, who, for that good will that thou beareth unto us in Jesus Christ, thy deare Sonne, will not the death and destructioun of a sinner, but rather that he by inspiration, and moving of thy Holie Spirit, convert and live: who also doth witnesse the vertue and strenth of thy Word to be suche, that it causeth the mountans to shake, the rocks tremble, and the floods to drie up : Behold, wee thy childrein and people heere prostrate before thee, most humblie beseeche thee, in the name of thy deare Sonne, our Lord Jesus Christ, that thou will move and pierce the heart of our impenitent brother, whom Satan so long hath endured and hardened. Lett it please thy Majestie, by the vertue of thy Holie Spirit, that thou will mollifie the same, expell his darknes, and, by the light of thy grace, that thou will so illuminat him, that now at lenth he may feele, First, how greevouslie he hath offended against thy Majestie ; and, Secundarilie, against thy holie church and assemblie. Give him thy grace to acknowledge, accuse, and damne, as weill before us whome he hath offended, as before thy presence, this his proud contempt ; least that we, by the same provoked, be compelled with all our greefes to cutt him off thy mysticall bodie, whom we, O Lord, unfainedlie desire to retaine within thy church, as a livelie member of thy deare Sonne, our Lord Jesus. Heare us, mercifull Father. Call backe againe this our impenitent brother that now tendeth to eternall destruction, that we all who before thy presence even for his rebellioun doe morne, may receave him again with gladnesse and joy, and so rander praise and honour to thee before thy holy congregation.

" We grant ourselves, O Lord, unworthie whom thou sould heare, becaus we ceasse not to offend thee, by our continuall transgressing thy holy precepts. Looke not upon us, mercifull Father, in this our corrupt nature ; bot looke thou to thy deare Sonne, whom thou of thy meere mercie hath appointed our Head, great Bishop, Advocat, Mediator, and onlie Propitiator. In him, and in the merits of his death, we humblie beseeche thee mercifullie to behold us, and suffer not the most innocent blood of thy deare Sonne shed for us, and for this our impenitent brother, to be profained by the tyrannie and slight of Satan. But, by the vertue of the same, lett this our impenitent brother be brought to unfained repentance, that so he may escape that fearefull condemnation in the which he appeareth to fall. This we aske of thee, O Heavenlie

Father, in the boldnes of our Head and Mediator, Jesus Christ, praying, as he hath taught, Our Father," &c.

If, after this prayer, the obstinat appeare not to offer his repentance, then sall the minister proceed, and say :

"Brethrein, seing that, as yee have heard, this obstinat and impenitent person hath so greevouslie offended against God, and against this his holie congregation, who by no meanes (as yee may perceave) can be broght to repentance ; wherof it is evident by the Word of God, that he is fallen from the kingdome of heaven, and the blessed societie of the Lord Jesus : and we (albeit with dolour of our hearts) may now execute that which the commandement of Jesus Christ, and the practise of his apostles, sheweth that of our office we ought to doe ; to witt, that we sall publicklie declare and pronounce suche to have no societie with us, as declare themselves obstinate and rebellious against all wholsome admonitions, and the blessed ordinances of his church.   And that we may doe the same, not of our owne authoritie, but in the name and power of our Lord Jesus Christ, before whom all knees are compelled to bow, lett us humblie fall doun before him, and on this maner pray, and pronounce this sentence :

The Invocation of the name of Jesus Christ to excommunicate the
Impenitent, together with the Sentence of Excommunication.

" O Lord Jesus Christ, the onlie and eternall King of all the chosin childrein of thy Heavenlie Father, the Head and Lawgiver of thy Church ; who by thy owne mouth hath commanded, that suche offenders as proudlie contemne the admonitions of thy church sall be cast out of the societie of the same, and sall be reputed of thy professors as profane ethnicks ; wee, willing to obey this thy precept, which also we have receaved by institution of thy apostles, are heere presentlie convented, to excommunicate, and cast furth frome the societie of thy holie bodie, and from all participation with thy church in sacraments or prayers, N.   Which thing we doe at thy commandement, and in thy power and authoritie, to the glorie of thy holie name, to the conservation and edification of this thy church, in the which it hath pleased thee to place us ministers, and to the extreme remedie of the stubburne obstinacie of the fore-named impenitent. And becaus thou hath promised thy self ever to be with us, bot speciallie with such as uprightlie travell in the ministrie of thy church, whom also thou hath promised to instruct and guide by the dictament of thy Holie Spirit, we most humblie beseeche thee so to governe and assist us in the execution of this our charge, that whatsoever we in thy name doe heere pronunce in earth, that thou will ratifie the same in the heaven. Our assurance, O Lord, is thy expressed Word. And, therefore, in boldnes of the same, here I, in thy name, and at the commandement of this thy present congregation, cutt off, seclude, and excommunicate frome thy bodie, and frome our societie, N., as ane persoun slanderous, proude, contemner, and a member for this present altogether corrupted, and pernicious to the bodie. And this his sinne (albeit with sorrow of heart) by vertue of our ministrie we bind, and pronunce the same to be bound in heaven and earth. We farther give over in the hands and power of the devill the said N., to the destruction of his flesh; straitlie charging all that professe the Lord Jesus, to whose knowledge this our sentence sall come, to repute and to hold the said N. accursed, and unworthie of the familiar societie of Christians; declaring unto all men, that suche as heerafter, before his repentance, sall haunt or familiarlie accompanie him, are partakers of his impietie, and subject to the like condemnatioun. This our sentence, O Lord Jesus, pronunced in thy name, we humblie desire thee to ratifie, according to thy promise. And yit, Lord, thou that came to save that which was lost, looke upon him with the eyes of thy mercie, if thy good pleasure be; and so pierce thou his heart, that he may feele in his breast the terrors of thy judgements, that by thy grace he fruitfullie may be converted to thee; and so damning his owne impietie, he may be with the like solemnitie receaved within the bosome of thy church, frome the which this day (with greefe and dolour of our hearts) he is ejected. Lord, in thy presence we protest, that our

owne affections move us not to this severitie, bot onlie the hatred
of sinne, and obedience that we give to thy owne commandement.
And, therefore, O Heavenlie Father, we crave the perpetuall assistance of thy Holie Spirit, not onlie to bridle our corrupt affections,
bot also so to conduct us in all the course of our whole life, that
we never fall to the like impietie and contempt; but that continuallie we may be subject to the voice of thy church, and unto
the ministers of the same, who truelie offer unto us the Word of
Life, the blessed Evangell of thy onlie beloved Sonne, Jesus
Christ; to whome with thee, and the Holie Spirit, be all praise,
glorie, and honour, now and ever.   So be it."

The sentence pronunced, and the prayer ended, the minister sall
admonishe the church, that all the faithfull doe hold the excommunicat as an ethnick, as before is said; that no man use his familiar companie; and yit, that no man accuse him of anie other
crime than of suche as he is convicted of, and for the which he is
excommunicate; bot that everie man sall secreitlie call to God for
grace to be granted to the excommunicate.   Such as have office in
the ministrie may, upon licence required of the church, speeke with
the excommunicate, so long as hope resteth of his conversion.   Bot
if he continue obstinat, then ought all the faithfull utterlie to abhorre his presence and communication.   And yit ought they more
earnestlie to call to God, that Satan in the end may be confounded,
and the creature of God free frome his snares, by the power of the
Lord Jesus.   And with the accustomed benediction, the assemblie
sall be dismissed, after they have sung the 101st Psalme, or one
portion therof, as it sall please the congregation.

The Order to receave the Excommunicate againe to the Societie of the Church.

First, we must observe, that suche as deserve death for that
crime committed, never be admitted to the societie of the church,
untill suche time as either the magistrat punish according to the
law, or elles pardoun the crime, as before we have said.   But such
as for other offenses, and for their contempt, are excommunicat,

may be receaved, when they sall earnestlie seeke the favours of
the church.   They must beginne at the ministrie, the elders, and
the deacons, who must expone their repentance to the minister or
ministers in their assemblie; a day may be appointed to the excommunicate to present himself before them.   The signes of his repentance ought to be diligentlie enquired; as, what hath beene his
behaviour since the time of his excommunication, what he will offer for satisfaction to the church, and unto whome he hath exponed
the greefe and dolor of his heart?   If the excommunicate be found
penitent, and obedient in all things, the minister, the nixt Sunday,
may give advertisement to the whole church of his humiliation,
and command them to call to God for increasse of the same.   The
nixt session day, the minister may appoint to the excommunicate
suche satisfaction as they thinke most expedient; to the which if
the excommunicate fullie agree, then may the said ministrie appoint
unto him a certane day, when he sall fulfill the same.   For this is
principallie to be observed, that no excommunicate person may be
receaved to the societie of the church againe, untill suche time that
he have stand at the church doore, at the least moe Sondayes than
one.   Which dayes being expired, and the whole satisfaction com-
pleat, some of the elders sall passe to the excommunicate, after that
the former prayer of the minister in the pulpit be ended, and sall
present him to a certane place appointed for the penitent; where
he sall stand in the same habite in the which he made satisfaction,
untill the sermon be ended.   And then sall the same elders that
broght him in the church present him to the minister, with these,
or the like words :—

    " This creature of God, N., that for his wickednes and obstinat re-
bellioun hath beene excommunicate frome the bodie of Jesus Christ,
bot now, by the power of the Spirit of God, is called backe againe by
repentance, so farre as the judgement of man can perceave.   For he
hath not onlie craved the favours of the ministrie, that he might
be receaved unto the bodie of the church againe, but also most
obedientlie hath subjected himself to all that we have commanded,
for tryell of his humiliation.   And, therefore, we present him before

you to be examined; and if his repentance be sufficient, to be receaved again to the bodie of the church."

Then sall the minister render thanks first to God, for that part
of his humiliation, and also desire the church of God to doe the
same with him. Therafter, he sall addresse him to the person excommunicate; and, first, sall lay before him his sinne; then, after,
the admonitions that were givin to him, to satisfie the church for
the same; and, last, his proud contempt, and long obstinacie, for
the which he was excommunicate; and of everie one he sall require his particular confession, with accusation of himself, and de-
testation of his impietie. Which being receaved, he sall rander
thanks to God as followeth :—

" We thanke the mercie and goodnes of God, through Jesus
Christ our Lord, for this thy conversion, N., into the which thou
hath not so muche shamed thy self, as that thou hath confounded
and overcome Satan, by whose venemous and deceavable entise-
ments thou hitherto hath beene rebellious to the wholsome admonitions of the church. And yit, becaus we can onlie see that which
is externall, we will joyne our prayers with thine, that thy humiliation may proceed frome the heart."

Lett the prayer appointed to be said in the receaving the penitent be said also heere; which ended, lett the church and the penitent be admonished, as is expressed, except that the crime of his
excommunication must ever be alledged and mentioned.

The Prayer conteaning his receaving to the Church.

" Lord Jesus Christ, King, Teacher, and our eternall Preest, who,
with the preaching of thy blessed Evangell, hath joyned the power
to bind and loose the sinnes of men; who hath also pronunced, that
whosoever by thy ministers is bound in earth sall be bound in
the heaven, and also, that whosoever is loosed by the same sall
be loosed and absolved with thee in the heaven: looke, O Lord,
mercifullie upon this thy creature, N., &c., whome Satan of long
time hath holden in boundage, so that not onlie he drew him to iniquitie, bot also that he so hardened his heart, that he despised all

admonitions, for the which his sinne and contempt we were compelled to excommunicate him frome our bodie. But now, O Lord,
seing that the Spirit of our Lord Jesus Christ hath so far prevailed
in him, that he is returned to our societie, it will please thee, for the
obedience of our Lord Jesus, to accept him, that his former inobedience be never layed to his charge; but that he may increasse in
all godlines, till that Satan finallie be trodden under his feete and
ours, by the power of our Lord Jesus Christ; to whom with thee,
and with the Holie Spirit, be all honour and glorie, now and ever.
So be it."

The Forme of Absolution.

" In the name and authoritie of Jesus Christ, I, the minister
of his blessed Evangell, with consent of this whole ministrie and
church, absolve thee, N., from the sentence of excommunication,
frome the sinne by thee committed, and from all censures ledde
against thee for the same before, according to thy repentance; and
pronunce thy sinne to be loosed in heaven, and thee to be receaved
again to the societie of Jesus Christ, to his bodie the church, to
the participation of his sacraments, and, finallie, to the fruition of
all his benefites, in the name of the Father, the Sonne, and the
Holie Spirit. So be it."

The absolution pronunced, the minister sall then call him, Brother, and give him admonition to watche and pray that he fall not
in the like tentation; that he be thankfull for the mercie showen
unto him, and that he shew the fruicts of his conversion in life and
conversation.

Therafter, the whole ministrie sall embrace him, and such others
of the church as be nixt unto him, and then sall ane psalme of
thanksgiving be sung.

This order may be enlarged or contracted, as the wisdome of the
discreit minister sall thinke expedient; for we rather shew the way
to the ignorant, than prescribe order to the learned, that cannot be
amended.

A Prayer.

" Preserve the publick face of thy church within this realme, O Lord: dilate the kingdome of thy Sonne, Jesus Christ, universallie; and so farther disclose, and breake doun the tyrannie of that Roman Antichrist, by the power of thy Sonne, our Lord Jesus Christ. So be it." Anno 1567.

Rom. xvi.

Soli sapienti Deo per Iesum Christum gloria in perpetuum. Amen.

This booke is thoght necessarie and profitable for the Church, and commaunded to be printed by the Generall Assemblie. Sett furth by John Knox, minister, and sighted by us whose names follow, as we war appointed by the said Generall Assemblie.

Johne Willocke.	David Lindsay.
Mr Johne Craig.	William Christeson.
Robert Pont.	James Creg, &c.
John Row.	

THE VISITATION OF THE SICK.

Becaus the visitation of the sicke is a thing verie necessarie, and yitt, notwithstanding, it is hard to prescribe all rules appertaining therunto, we referre it to the discretion of the godlie and prudent minister, who, according as he seeth the patient afflicted, either may lift him up with the sweete promises of God's mercie through Christ, if he perceave him much afrayed of God's threatnings; or contrariwise, if he be not tuiched with the feeling of his sinnes, may beate him doun with God's judgements; evermore, like a skilfull physician, framing his medicine according as the disease requireth. And if he perceave him to want anie necessaries, he not onlie releeveth him according to his abilitie, but also provideth by others, that he may be furnished sufficientlie. Moreover, the partie that is visited may at all times for his comfort send for the minister, who doth not onlie make prayers for him there presentlie, but also, if it so require, commendeth him in the publick prayers to the congregation.

A Prayer to be said in visiting of the Sicke.

" O, our good God, Lord, and Father, the Creator and conserver of all things, the fountaine of all goodnes and benignitie; like as (among other thine infinite benefites, which thou of thy great goodnes and grace doth distribute ordinarilie unto all men) thou giveth them health of bodie, to the end that they sould the better know thy great liberalitie, so that they might be the more readie to serve and glorifie thee with the same : so, contrariwise, when we have evill-behaved ourselves, in offending thy Majestie, thou hath accustomed to admonishe us, and call us unto thee, by diverse and sindrie chastisements, through the which it hath pleased thy goodnes to subdue and tame our fraile fleshe : but speciallie, by the greevous plagues of sicknesses and diseases; using the same as a meane, to awake and stirre up the great dullnesse and negligence that is in us all, and advertising us of our evill life by such infirmiteis and dangers; especiallie when, as they threaten the verie death, which (as assured messingers of the same) are all to the flesh full of extreme anguish and torments, although they be, notwithstanding, to the spirit of the elect as medicines both good and wholsome : for by them thou doth move us to turne unto thee for our salvation, and to call upon thee in our afflictions, to have thine helpe which art our deare and loving Father.

" In consideration wherof, we most earnestlie pray unto thee, our good God, that it wold please thine infinite goodness to have pitie upon this thy poore creature whome thou hath, as it were, bound and tyed to the bed by most greevous sicknesse, and broght to great extremitie by the heavinesse of thine hand. O Lord, enter not into accompt with him, to render the reward due unto his works : bot through thine infinite mercie remitt all his faults, for

the which thou hath chastised him so gentlie; and behold rather
the obedience which thy deare Sonne, Christ Jesus our Lord, hath
rendered unto thee, to witt, the sacrifice which it pleased thee to
accept as a full recompense for all the iniquities of them that receave him for their justice and satisfaction, yea, for their onlie Saviour. Lett it please thee, O God, to give him a true zeal and affection to receave and acknowledge Him for his onlie Redeemer.
To the end also that thou mayest receave this sicke person to thy
mercie, qualifieng all the troubles which his sinnes, the horrour of
death, and dreadfull feare of the same, may bring to his weake conscience; neither suffer thou, O Lord, the assaults of the mightie
adversarie to prevaile, or to take frome him the comfortable hope
of salvation which thou giveth to thy dearlie beloved childrein.

" And, forasmuche as we are all subject to the like state and condition, and to be visited with like battell, when it sall please thee
to call us unto the same, we beseeche thee humblie, O Lord, with
this thy poore creature, whome thou presentlie chastiseth, that
thou will not extend thy rigorous judgement against him; but that
thou wold vouchsafe to show him thy mercie, for the love of thy deare
Sonne, Jesus Christ our Lord, who having suffered the most shame-
full and extreme death of the crosse, beare willinglie the fault of
this poore patient, to the end that thou might acknowledge him as
one redeemed with his precious blood, and receaved into the communion of his bodie, to be participant of eternall felicitie, in the
companie of thy blessed angells. Wherefore, O Lord, dispose and
move his heart to receave, by thy grace, with all meeknesse, this
gentle and Fatherlie correctioun, which thou hath layed upon him;
that he may endure it patientlie, and with willing obedience; sub-
mitting himself with heart and minde to thy blessed will, and favourable mercie, wherin thou now visiteth him after this sort, for
his profite and salvation. It may please thy goodnes, O Lord, to
assist him in all his anguishes and trubles. And although the
tongue and voice be not able to execute their office, in this behalfe,
to sett furth thy glorie, that yitt, at the least thou will stirre up his
heart to aspire unto thee onlie, which are the onlie fountaine of all

goodnes ; and that thou fast roote and sattle in his heart the sweete promises which thou hath made unto us in Christ Jesus, thy Sonne, our Saviour, to the intent he may remain constant against all the assaults and tumults which the enemie of our salvation may raise up to trouble his conscience.

" And seing it hath pleased thee that, by the death of thy deare Sonne, life eternall sould be communicated unto us; and by the shedding of his blood, the washing of our sinnes sould be declared; and that by his resurrection also, both justice and immortalitie sould be given us, it may please thee to apply this holie and wholsome medicine to this thy poore creature, in suche extremitie ; taking frome him all trembling and dreadfull feare, and to give him a stout courage in the middest of all his present adversities.

" And for as muche as all things, O Heavenlie Father, be knowen unto thee, and thou can, according to thy good pleasure, minister unto him all suche things as sall be necessarie and expedient, lett it please thee, O Lord, so to satisfie him by thy grace, as may seeme meete for thy divine majestie. Receave him, Lord, into thy protectioun, for he hath his recourse and accesse unto thee alone ; and make him constant and firme in thy commandements and promises: and also pardoun all his sinnes, both secreit and these which are manifest, by the which he hath most greevouslie provoked thy wrathe and severe judgements against him ; so as, in place of death, (the which both he and all we have justlie merited,) thou will grant unto him that blessed life which we also attend and looke for, by thy grace and mercie. Neverthelesse, O Heavenlie Father, if thy good pleasure be, that he sall yit live longer in this world, it may then please thee to augment in him thy graces, so as the same may serve unto thy glorie; yea, Lord, to the intent he may conforme himself the more diligentlie, and with more carefulnesse, to the exemple of thy Sonne, Christ Jesus; and that in renuncing himself, he may cleave fullie to Him who, to give consolation and hope to all sinners to obtaine remission of all their sinnes and offenses, hath caried with him into the heavens the theefe which was crucified with him upon the crosse.

" But if the time by thee appointed be come, that he sall depart frome us unto thee, make him to feele in his conscience, O Lord, the fruict and strenth of thy grace; that thereby he may have a new taste of thy Fatherlie care over him frome the beginning of his life unto the verie end of the same, for the love of thy deare Sonne, Jesus Christ, our Lord.

" Give him thy grace, that with a good heart, and full assurance of faith, he may receave to his consolation so great and excellent a treasure, to witt, the remission of his sinnes in Christ Jesus thy Sonne, who now presenteth him to this poore persoun in distresse, by the vertue of thy promises reveeled unto him by thy Word, which he hath exercised with us, in thy church and congregation, and also in using the sacraments which thou therin hath established, for confirmatioun of all their faith that trust in thee unfainedlie. Lett true faith be unto him, O Lord, as a most sure buckler, thereby to avoide the assaults of death, and more boldlie walke for the advancement of eternall life to the end; that he, having a most lyvelie apprehensioun therof, may rejoyce with thee in the heavens eternallie.

" Lett him be under thy protection and governance, O Heavenlie Father. Althogh he be sick, yitt can thou heale him: he is cast doun, bot thou can lift him up : he is sore trubled, bot thou can send redresse : he is weake, thou can send strenth : he acknowledgeth his uncleannesse, his spots, his filthinesse, and iniquities, but thou can washe him, and make him cleane : he is wounded, bot thou can minister most soverane salves : he is fearefull and trembling, bot thou can give good curage and boldnesse. To be short, he is, as it were, utterlie lost, and a strayed sheepe, bot thou can call him home to thee againe. Wherefore, O Lord, seing that this poore creature (thine owne workmanship) resigneth him whollie into thy hands, receave him into thy mercifull protection. Also, we poore miserable creatures which are, as it were, in the feild, readie to fight till thou withdraw us frome the same, vouchsafe to strenthen us by thine Holie Spirit, that we may obtaine the victorie, in thy name, against our deidlie and mortall enemie ; and, furthermore, that the afflic-

tion and the combate of this thy poore creature, in most greevous torments, may move us to humble ourselves with all reverent feare and
trembling under thy mightie hand, knowing that we must appeare
before thy judgement-seate, when it sall please thee so to appoint.
But, O Lord, the corruption of our fraile nature is suche, that we
are utterlie destitute of anie meane to appeare before thee, except
it please thee to make us suche as thou thy self requireth us to be ;
and, further, that thou give us the spirit of meeknes and humilitie,
to rest and stay whollie on these things which thou onlie commandeth.

" But forasmuche as we be altogether unworthie to enjoy suche
benefites, we beseeche thee to receave us in the name of thy deare
Sonne, our Lord and Master, in whose death and satisfaction standeth whollie the hope of our salvation.

" It may also please thee, O Father of comfort and consolatioun,
to strenthen with thy grace these which employ their travell and
diligence to the aiding of this sicke person, that they faint not by
overmuche and continuall labour, bot rather to goe heartilie and
cheerefullie fordward in doing their endeavoures toward him : and
if thou take him frome them, then of thy goodnesse to comfort them,
so as they may patientlie beare suche departing, and praise thy
name in all things. Also, O Heavenlie Father, vouchsafe to have
pitie on all other sicke persons, and suche as be anie otherwise
or meanes afflicted ; and also on those who as yit are ignorant of
thy truthe, and appertaine neverthelesse unto thy kingdome : in
like maner on those that suffer persecution, tormented in prisons,
or otherwise trubled by the enemies of the Veritie, for bearing testimonie to the same : finallie, on all the necessities of thy people, and
upon all the ruines or decayes which Satan hath brought upon thy
church. O Father of mercie, spread forth thy goodnesse upon all
those that be thine, that we, forsaking ourselves, may be the more
inflammed and confirmed to rest onlie upon thee alone. Grant
these our requests, O our deare Father, for the love of thy deare
Sonne, our Saviour, Jesus Christ, who liveth and raigneth with

thee in unitie of the Holie Ghost, true God for evermore. So
be it."

THE BURIALL.

The corps is reverentlie broght to the grave, accompaneid with
the congregatioun, without anie farther ceremoneis. Which being
bureid, the minister, if he be present, and required, goeth to the
church, if it be not farre off, and maketh some comfortable exhortation to the people tuiching death and resurrection.

THE ORDER OF BAPTISME.

First, note, that forasmuche as it is not permitted by God's
Word that weomen sould preache, or minister the sacraments ; and
it is evident that the sacraments are not ordained of God to be
used in private corners, as charmes or sorcereis ; but left to the
congregation, and necessarilie annexed to God's Word, as seales of
the same ; therefore, the infant which is to be baptized sall be
broght to the church, on the day appointed to commoun prayer and
preaching, accompaneid with the father and god-father : so that,
after the sermon, the childe being presented to the minister, he de-
mandeth this questioun :

" Doe you heere present this childe to be baptized, earnestlie
desiring that he may be engrafted in the mysticall bodie of Jesus
Christ ?"

The answere.—" Yea, we require the same."

The minister proceedeth :

" Then lett us consider, dearelie beloved, how Almightie God
hath not onlie made us his childrein by adoption, (Rom. viii. ; Galat. iv. ; Eph. i.,) and receaved us into the fellowship of his church,
but also hath promised, that he will be our God, and the God of
our childrein, unto the thowsand generation, Gen. xvii. ; Isa. lvi.
Which things, as he confirmed to his people of the Old Testament

by the sacrament of Circumcision, so hath he also renewed the same to us in his New Testament by the sacrament of Baptisme, doing us thereby to witt, that our infants appertaine to him by covenant, and, therefore, ought not to be defrauded of those holie signes and badges, whereby his childrein are knowen from infidels and pagans, Gen. xvii.; Col. ii.; Acts x.

" Neither is it requisite, that all these that receave this sacrament have the use of understanding and faith ; bot cheeflie that they be contained under the name of God's people, so that, remission of sinnes in the blood of Christ Jesus doth appertaine unto them by God's promise ; which thing is most evident by Sanct Paul, who pronounceth the childrein begotten and borne (either of the parents being faithfull) to be cleane and holie, 1 Cor. vii. Also our Saviour Christ admitteth childrein to his presence, embracing and blessing them, Mark x.; Matt. x.; Luke xviii.; Psal. xxii. Which testimonies of the Holie Ghost assure us, that infants be of the number of God's people, and that remission of sinnes doth also appertaine to them in Christ. Therefore, without injurie they cannot be debarred frome the commoun signe of God's childrein. And yit is not this outward action of suche necessitie, that the lacke therof sould be hurtfull to their salvation, if that, prevented by death, they may not convenientlie be presented to the church. But we (having respect to that obedience which Christians owe to the voice and ordinance of Christ Jesus, who commanded to preach and baptize all, without exceptioun) doe judge them onlie unworthie of anie fellowship with him, who contemptuouslie refuse suche ordinarie meanes as his wisdome hath appointed to the instruction of our dull senses, Mar. xvi.; Matt. xxi.

" Furthermore, it is evident, that baptisme was ordained to be ministred in the element of water, to teache us, that like as water outwardlie doth wash away the filth of the bodie, so, inwardlie, doth the vertue of Christ's blood purge our soules frome that corruptioun, and deadlie poysoun, wherewith by nature we were infected ; whose venemous dregges, althogh they continue in this our flesh, yit, by the merits of his death, are not imputed unto us, becaus

the justice of Jesus Christ is made ours by baptisme, Matt. v.;
1 Pet. v.; 1 Johne v.; 1 Cor. x.; Eph. ii. Not that we thinke anie
suche vertue or power to be included in the visible water, or outward action ; for manie have beene baptized, and yit never inwardlie purged ; but that our Saviour, Christ, who commanded baptisme
to be ministred, will, by the power of his Holie Spirit, effectuallie
worke in the hearts of his elect, in time convenient, all that is meant
and signified by the same. And this the Scripture calleth our regeneration, which standeth cheefelie in these two points : in mortifica-
tion, that is to say, a resisting of the rebellious lusts of the flesh ;
and in newnes of life, whereby we continuallie strive to walke in
that purenesse and perfection wherewith we are cled in baptisme.

  " And althogh we, in the journey of this life, be encumbered
with manie enemies, which, in the way, assaile us, yit fight we not
without fruict. For this continuall battell which we fight against
sinne, death, and hell, is a most infallible argument, that God the
Father, mindefull of his promise made unto us in Christ Jesus,
doth not onlie give us motions and curage to resist them, bot also
assurance to overcome, and obtaine victorie. Wherefore, dearelie
beloved, it is not of necessitie onlie that we be once baptized :
but also, it muche profiteth oft to be present at the ministration
thereof, that we (being putt in minde of the league and covenant
made betweene God and us, that he will be our God, and we his
people ; he our Father, and we his childrein) may have occasioun as
weill to trie our lives past, as our present conversation ; and to
prove ourselves, whether we stand fast in the faith of God's elect,
or contrariwise have strayed frome him, through incredulitie and ungodlie living, Jer. xxxi. ; Heb. viii., vi. Wherof if our consciences
doe accuse us, yit, by hearing the loving promises of our heavenlie
Father, (who calleth all men to mercie by repentance,) we may,
frome henceforth, walke more warilie in our vocatioun. Moreover,
yee that be fathers and mothers, may take heereby most singular
comfort, to see your childrein thus receaved into the bosome of
Christ's congregation ; whereby you are daylie admonished, that yee
nurishe and bring up the childrein of God's favour and mercie, over

whome his Fatherlie providence watcheth continuallie.   Which thing, as it ought greatlie to rejoyce you, knowing that nothing can come unto them without his good pleasure, so ought it to make you diligent and carefull to nurture and instruct them in the true knowledge and feare of God; wherin, if yee be negligent, yee doe not onlie injurie unto your childrein, hiding frome them the good will and pleasure of Almightie God, their Father, but also heape damnation upon yourselves, in suffering his childrein, bought with the blood of his deare Sonne, so traterouslie for lacke of knowledge to turne backe frome him.   Therefore, it is your duetie, with all diligence to provide that your childrein, in time convenient, be instructed in all doctrine necessarie for a true Christian : cheefe-lie, that they be taught to rest upon the justice of Christ Jesus alone, and to abhorre and flee all superstitioun, Papistrie, and idolatrie.   Finallie, To the intent that we may be assured, that you, the father and the suretie, consent to the performance heerof, declare heere, before the face of his congregation, the summe of that faith wherin you beleeve, and will instruct this childe."

Then the father, or, in his absence, the god-father, sall rehearse the articles of his faith; which done, the minister exponeth the same, as after followeth :—

" The Christiane faith, wherof yee have now breeflie heard the summe, is commounlie divided in twelve articles; but that we may the better understand what is conteaned in the same, we sall divide it into foure principal parts.   The first sall concerne God the Fa-ther; the secund, Jesus Christ our Lord; the thrid sall expresse unto us our faith in the Holie Ghost; and the fourth and last sall declare what is our faith concerning the church, and of the graces of God freelie given unto the same.

I beleeve in God, the Father Almightie, Maker of heaven and earth.

" First, of God we confesse three things, to witt, that he is our Father, Almightie, Maker of heaven and earth.   Our Father we call him, and so by faith beleeve him to be, not so muche becaus he hath created us, (for that we have commoun with the rest of

creatures, who yit are not called to that honour, to have God to
them a favourable Father;) but we call him Father, by reason of
his free adoption, by the which he hath chosen us to life everlasting in Jesus Christ.   And this his most singular mercie we preferre to all things earthlie and transitorie.   For without this, there
is to mankinde no felicitie, no comfort, nor finall joy; and having
this we are assured, that by the same love by the which He once
hath freelie chosen us, he sall conduct the whole course of our life;
that in the end, we sall possesse that immortall kingdome that he
hath prepared for his chosin childrein.   For frome this fountaine
of God's free mercie, or adoption, springeth our vocatioun, our
continuall sanctificatioun, and, finallie, our glorificatioun, as witnesseth the apostle, Rom. viii.

" The same God, our Father, we confesse Almightie, not onlie
in respect of that he may doe, but in consideration, that by his
power and godlie wisdome are all creatures in heaven and earth,
and under the earth, ruled, guided, and keeped in that order that
his eternall knowledge and will hath appointed them.   And that is
it which in the thrid part we doe confesse, that he is Creator of
heaven and earth; that is to say, that the heaven, and the earth,
and the contents thereof, are so in his hands, that there is nothing
done without his knowledge, neither yitt against his will, but that
he ruleth them so, that in end his godlie name sall be glorified in
them.   And so, we confesse and beleeve, that neither the devills,
nor yit the wicked of the world, have anie power to molest or
trouble the chosin childrein of God, but in so farre as it pleaseth
him to use them as instruments, either to prove and trie our faith
and patience, or elles to stirre us to more fervent invocatioun of
his name, and to continuall meditatioun of that heavenlie rest and
joy that abideth us after these transitorie trubles.   And yit sall not
this excuse the wicked, becaus they neither looke in their iniquitie
to please God, nor yit to obey his will.

And in Jesus Christ, his onlie Sonne, our Lord.

" In Jesus Christ we confesse two distinct and perfect natures,

to witt, the eternall Godhead and the perfect manhead joyned together; so that we confesse and beleeve, that that eternall Word,
which was frome the beginning, and by the which all things were
created, and yit are conserved and keeped in their being, did, in
the time appointed in the counsell of his heavenlie Father, receave
our nature of a Virgin, by operation of the Holie Ghost.

Conceaved by the Holie Ghost.

" So that in his conceptioun we acknowledge and beleeve, that
there is nothing but puritie and sanctification, yea, even in so
muche as he is become our brother. For it behoved him that sould
purge others frome their sinnes to be pure, and cleane frome all
spott of sinne, even frome his conception. And as we confesse
and beleeve him conceaved by the Holie Ghost, so doe we confesse
and beleeve him to be borne of a Virgine, named Marie, of the
tribe of Juda, and of the familie of David, that the promise of God
and the prophecie might be fulfilled, to witt, ' That the seed of the
woman sall breake doun the serpent's head ;' and that ' A Virgine
sould conceave, and beare a childe, whose name sould be Immanuel,
that is to say, God with us,' Isa. vii. The name of Jesus, signifieng
a Saviour, was given to him by the angell, to assure us, that it is
he alone that ' saveth his people frome their sinnes,' Matt. i. He is
called Christ, that is, anointed, by reasoun of the offices given him by
God his Father; to witt, that he alone is appointed King, Preest,
and Prophet. King, in that, that all power is given to him in heaven
and earth, so that there is none other but He in heaven or earth
that hath just authoritie and power to make lawes to binde the
consciences of men ; neither yitt is there anie other that may defend our soules frome the boundage of sinne, nor yitt our bodies
frome the tyrannie of man. And this He doeth by the power of
his Word, by the which he draweth us out of the boundage and
slaverie of Satan, and maketh us to raigne over sinne, whiles that
we live, and serve our God in righteousnes and holines of our life.
A Preest, and that perpetuall and everlasting, we confesse him,
becaus that, by the sacrifice of his owne bodie, which he once of-

fered up upon the crosse, he hath fullie satisfied the justice of his
Father in our behalfe; so that whosoever seeketh anie meanes besides his death and passioun, in heaven or in earth, to reconcile
unto them God's favour, they doe not onlie blaspheme, bot also, so
farre as in them is, renunce the fruict and efficacie of that his onlie
one sacrifice. We confesse him to be the onlie Prophet, who had
reveeled unto us the whole will of his Father in all things pertaining to our salvatioun. This our Lord Jesus we confesse to be the
onlie Sonne of God, becaus there is none suche by nature bot he
alone. We confesse him also our Lord, not onlie by reason we are
his creatures, but cheefelie becaus he hath redeemed us by his precious blood, and so hath gotten just dominioun over us, as over the
people whome he hath delivered frome the bondage of sinne, death,
hell, and the divell, and hath made us kings and preests to God
his Father.

Suffered under Pontius Pilate, was crucified.

" We farther confesse and beleeve, that the same our Lord Jesus
was accused before an earthlie judge, Pontius Pilate, under whom,
albeit oft and diverse times he was pronounced to be innocent, he
suffered the death of the crosse, hanged upon a tree betwixt two
theeves. Which death, as it was most cruell and vile before the
eyes of men, so was it accursed by the mouth of God himself, saying, ' Cursed is everie one that hangeth on a tree.'

Died, and buried, and descended into hell.

" And this kinde of death sustained he in our persoun, becaus
he was appointed of God his Father to be our pledge, and he that
sould beare the punishment of our transgressiouns. And so we acknowledge and beleeve, that he hath taken away that curse and
malediction that hanged on us by reasoun of sinne. He verilie
died, rendering up his spirit into the hands of his Father, after that
he had said, ' Father, into thy hands I commend my spirit.' After
his death, we confesse his bodie was buried, and that he descended
to the hell.

The thrid day he rose again from the dead.

" But becaus he was the Author of Life, yea, the verie life it self, it was impossible that he sould be retained under the dolours of death. And, therefore, the thrid day he rose agane, victor and conqueror of death and hell; by the which his resurrectioun he hath brought life againe to the world, which he by the power of his Holie Spirit communicateth unto his livelie members, so that now unto them corporall death is no death, but an entrance into that blessed life wherin our Head, Jesus Christ, is now entered.

He ascended into heaven, and sitteth on the right hand of God, the Father Almightie.

" For after that he had sufficientlie proved his resurrectioun to his disciples, and unto suche as constantlie did abide with him to the death, he visiblie ascended into the heaven, and was taken frome the eyes of men, and placed at the right hand of God, the Father Almightie, where presentlie he remaineth in his glorie, onlie Head, onlie Mediator, and onlie Advocat, for all the members of his bodie. Of which we have most especiall comfort, First, for that by his ascension, the heavens are opened to us, and entrance made unto us, that boldlie we may appeare before the throne of our Father's mercie; and, Secundarilie, that we know that his honour and authoritie is given to Jesus Christ, our Head, in our name, and for our profite and utilitie. For albeit that in bodie he now be in heaven, yitt, by the power of his Spirit, he is present heere with us, as weill to instruct us, as to maintaine and comfort us in all our trubles and adversities; frome the which he sall finallie deliver his whole church, and everie true member of the same, in that day when he sall visiblie appeare againe, Judge of the quicke and the dead.

From thence he sall come to judge the quicke and the dead.

" For this finallie we confesse of our Lord Jesus Christ, that as he was seene visiblie to ascend, and so left the world as tuiching that bodie that suffered and rose againe, so do we constantlie beleeve that he sall come frome the right hand of his Father, when all eyes sall see him, yea, even those that have pierced him. And then sall be gathered, as weill those that then sall be found alive, as those that before have sleeped. Separatioun sall be made betwixt the lambes and the goates, that is to say, betwixt the elect and the reprobate. The one sall heare this joyfull voice, ' Come, yee blessed of my Father, possesse the kingdome that is prepared for you before the beginning of the world;' the other sall heare that fearefull and irrevocable sentence, ' Depart frome me, ye workers of iniquitie, to the fire that never sall be quenched.' And for this cause, this day in the Scripture is called the day of refreshing, and of the revelation of all secreits, becaus that then the just sall be delivered from all miseries, and sall be possessed in the fulnes of their glorie : contrariwise, the reprobate sall receave judgement and recompense of all their impietie, be it openlie or secreitlie wrought.

I beleeve in the Holie Ghost.

" As we constantlie beleeve in God the Father, and in Jesus Christ, as before is said, so we doe assuredlie beleeve in the Holie Ghost, whom we confesse God, equal with the Father and the Sonne; by whose working and mightie operation our darknes is removed, our spirituall eyes are illuminated, our soules and consciences sprinkled with the blood of Jesus Christ, and we retained in the truthe of God, even to our lives' end. And for these causes we understand, that this eternall Spirit, proceiding frome the Father and the Sonne, hath in the Scriptures diverse names. Sometimes called Water, by reason of his purgation, and giving strenth to this our corrupt nature to bring furth good fruicte, without whom this our nature sould utterlie be barren, yea, it sould utterlie abound in all wickednes. Sometimes the same Spirit is called Fire, by reason of the illumination, and burning heate of fire that he kindleth in our hearts. The same Spirit is called also Oyle, or

Unction, by reason that his working mollifieth the hardnes of our heart, and maketh us receave the print of that image of Jesus by whom onlie we are sanctified.

The Holie Catholick Church, the Communion of Sancts.

"We constantlie beleeve that there is, was, and sall be, even till the comming of the Lord Jesus, a church which is holie and universall, to witt, the Communion of Sancts. This church is holie, becaus it receaveth free remission of sinnes, and that by faith onlie in the blood of Jesus Christ. Secundlie, becaus it being regenerate, it receaveth the Spirit of sanctification, and power to walke in newnesse of life, and in good workes, which God hath prepared for his chosen to walke in. Not that we thinke the justice of this church, or anie member of the same, ever was, is, or yitt sall be, so full or perfect, that it needeth not to stoupe under mercie; but that, becaus the imperfections are pardoned, and the justice of Jesus Christ imputed to suche as by true faith cleave unto him: which church we call universall, becaus it consisteth and standeth of all tongues and nations, yea, of all estats and conditions of men and weomen whom, of his mercie, God calleth frome darknes to light, and frome the boundage and thraldome of sinne, to his spirituall service and puritie of life; unto whome he also communicateth his Holie Spirit, giving unto them one faith, one Head and soveraigne Lord, the Lord Jesus, one baptisme, and right use of sacraments; whose heart also he knitteth together in love and Christiane concord.

The Forgivenesse of Sinnes, the Resurrection of the Bodie, and Life Everlasting.

"To this church, holie and universall, we acknowledge and beleeve three notable gifts to be granted; to witt, remission of sinnes, which by true faith must be obtained in this life. Resurrection of the flesh, which all sall have, albeit not in equall condition; for the reprobat, as before is said, sall rise bot to fearefull judgement and condemnation, and the just sall rise to be possessed in glorie. And this resurrection sall not be an imagination, or that one bodie sall rise for another, but everie man sall receave in his owne bodie as he hath deserved, be it good or evill. The just sall receave the life everlasting, which is the free gift of God, given and purchased to his chosen by Jesus Christ, our onlie Head and Mediator; to whome, with the Father, and the Holie Ghost, be all honour and glorie, now and ever. Amen."

Then followeth this prayer:

"Almightie and everlasting God, which of thine infinite mercie and goodnes hath promised unto us, that thou will not onlie be our God, but also the God and Father of our children; we beseeche thee, that as thou hath vouchsafed to call us to be partakers of this thy great mercie in the fellowship of faith, so it may please thee to sanctifie with thy Spirit, and to receave into the number of thy childrein this infant, whome we sall baptize according to thy Word; to the end that he, comming to perfyte age, may confesse thee onlie the true God, and whome thou hath sent, Jesus Christ: and so serve him, and be profitable unto his church, in the whole course of his life, that, after his life ended, he may be broght, as a livelie member of his bodie, unto the full fruition of thy joyes in the heavens, where thy Sonne, our Saviour, Christ reigneth, world without end: in whose name we pray, as he hath taught us, Our Father," &c.

When they have prayed in this sort, the minister requireth the child's name; which knowen, he sayeth, "N., I baptize thee in the name of the Father, of the Sonne, and of the Holie Ghost."— Matt. xviii.; Mark xvi.; Acts ii.

And as he speeketh these words, he taketh water in his hand, and layeth it upon the childe's forehead: which done, he giveth thanks, as followeth:—

"Forasmuch, most holie and mercifull Father, as thou doth not onlie beautifie and blesse us with commoun benefites, like unto the rest of mankinde, bot also heapeth upon us most abundantlie rare and wonderfull gifts; of duetie we lift up our eyes and mindes unto thee, and give thee most humble thanks for thy infinite goodnes, which hath not onlie numbred us among thy sancts, bot also of thy

free mercie doth call our childrein unto thee, marking them with
this sacrament, as a singular token and badge of thy love. Wherefore, most loving Father, thogh we be not able to deserve this so
great a benefite; yea, if thou would handle us according to our
merites, we sould suffer the punishment of eternall death and damnation, yit, for Christ's sake, we beseeche thee, that thou will confirme this thy favour more and more toward us, and take this
infant in thy tuition and defense, whome we offer and present unto
thee, with commoun supplications. And never suffer him to fall in
suche unkindnes, whereby he sould lose the force of baptisme ; but
that he may perceave thee continuallie to be his mercifull Father,
throgh thine Holie Spirit working in his heart, by whose divine
power he may so prevaile against Satan, that in the end, obtaining
the victorie, he may be exalted into the libertie of thy kingdome.
So be it."

The maner of the Lord's Supper.

The day when the Lord's Supper is ministred, which commounlie
is used once a moneth, or so oft as the congregation sall think expedient, the minister useth to say as followeth :—

" Lett us marke, deare brethrein, and consider, how Jesus Christ
did ordaine unto us his holie Supper, according as Sanct Paul maketh rehearsall, in the eleventh chapter of the First Epistle to the
Corinthians, saying, ' I have receaved of the Lord that which I
have delivered unto you, to witt, that the Lord Jesus, the same
night that he was betrayed, tooke bread ; and when he had given
thanks, he brake it, saying, Take yee, eate yee ; this is my bodie
which is broken for you : doe yee this in remembrance of me. Likewise after supper he tooke the cuppe, saying, This cuppe is the
new testament, or covenant, in my blood ; doe yee this, so oft as yee
sall drinke thereof, in remembrance of me. For so oft as yee sall
eate this bread, and drinke of this cuppe, yee sall declare the Lord's
death untill his comming. Therefore, whosoever sall eate this
bread, and drinke of the cuppe of the Lord, unworthilie, he sall be
guiltie of the bodie and blood of the Lord. Then see that everie

man prove and trie himself, and so lett him eate of this bread, and drinke of this cuppe: for whosoever eateth and drinketh unworthilie, he eateth and drinketh his owne damnation, for not having due regard and consideration of the Lord's bodie.'"

This done, the minister proceedeth to the exhortation :—

"Dearelie beloved in the Lord, forasmuche as we be now assembled, to celebrate the holie communion of the bodie and blood of our Saviour Christ, lett us consider these words of Sanct Paul, how he exhorteth all persons diligentlie to trie and examine themselves, before they presume to eate of that bread, and drinke of that cuppe. For as the benefite is great, if with a true penitent heart, and livelie faith, we receave that holie sacrament, (for then we spirituallie eate the flesh of Christ, and drinke his blood : then we dwell in Christ, and Christ in us ;) so is the danger great if we receave the same unworthilie : for then we be guiltie of the bodie and blood of Christ our Saviour, and eate and drinke our owne damnation, not considering the Lord's bodie ; we kindle God's wrath against us, and provoke him to plague us with diverse diseases, and sindrie kindes of death.

"And, therefore, in the name and authoritie of the eternall God, and of his Sonne, Jesus Christ, I excommunicate frome this table all blasphemers of God, all idolaters and murtherers, all adulterers, all that be in malice or envie, all disobedient persons to father or mother, princes or magistrats, pastors or preachers, all theeves and deceavers of their nighbours, and, finallie, all suche as (leade) a life · directlie fighting against the will of God; charging them, as they will answere in the presence of Him who is the righteous Judge, that they presume not to profane this most holie table. And yit, this we pronunce, not to seclude anie penitent person, how greevous so ever his sinnes before have beene, so that he feele in his heart unfained repentance for the same; bot onlie suche as continue in sinne without repentance. Neither yit is this pronunced against such as aspire to a greater perfection than they can in this life attaine unto.

"For albeit we feele in ourselves muche frailtie and wretched-

3

nes; as that we have not our faith so perfyte and constant as we ought, being manie times readie to distrust God's goodnes, through our corrupt nature; and also, that we are not so throughlie given to serve God, neither have so fervent a zeale to sett furth his glorie as our duetie requireth; feeling still suche rebellioun in ourselves, that we have need daylie to fight against the lusts of our flesh, yet, neverthelesse, seing that our Lord hath dealt thus mercifullie with us; that he hath printed his Gospell in our hearts, so that we are preserved frome falling into desperation and misbeleefe; and seing, also, that he hath endued us with a will and desire to renunce and withstand our owne affections, with a longing for his righteousnes, and the keeping of his commandements, we may be now right weill assured, that these defaults and manifold imperfections in us sall be no hinderance at all against us, to cause him not to accept, and to impute us as worthie to come to his spirituall table. For the end of our comming thither is, not to make protestation that we are upright or just in our lives; bot contrariwise, we come to seeke our life and perfection in Jesus Christ, acknowledging, in the meane time, that we of our selves be the childrein of wrathe and damnation.

" Lett us consider then, that this sacrament is a soverane medicine for all poore, sicke creatures, a comfortable helpe to weake soules, and that our Lord requireth no other worthinesse on our part, bot that we unfainedlie acknowledge our naughtinesse and imperfection. Then, to the end that we may be worthie partakers of his merits, and most comfortable benefites, (which is the true eating of his flesh, and drinking of his blood,) lett us not suffer our mindes to wander about the consideration of these earthlie and corruptible things, (which we see present to our eyes, and feele with our hands,) to seeke Christ bodilie present in them, as if he were enclosed in the bread or wine, or as if these elements were turned and changed into the substance of his flesh and blood.[1] For

---

[1] " Transubstantiation, Transelementation, Transmutation, and Transformation, as the Papists use them, are the doctrine of devills."—*Note in the MS.*

the onlie way to dispose ourselves to receave nurishment, releefe, and quickening of his substance, is to lift up our mindes, by faith, above all things worldlie and sensible, and thereby to enter into heaven, that we may find Christ where he dwelleth undoubtedlie, verie God and verie man, in the incomprehensible glorie of his Father, to whome be all praise, honour, and glorie, now and ever. Amen."

The exhortation ended, the minister cometh doun frome the pulpit, and sitteth at the table, everie man and woman, in like wise, taking their place as occasioun best serveth. Then he taketh bread, and giveth thanks, either in these words following, or like in effect :—

"O Father of mercie, and God of all consolation ; seing all creatures doe acknowledge and confesse thee as Governour and Lord, it becometh us, the workmanship of thine owne hands, at all times to reverence and magnifie thy godlie Majestie, first, for that thou hath created us to thine owne image and similitude, but, cheefelie, becaus thou hath delivered us frome that everlasting death and damnation into the which Satan drew mankinde by the meane of sinne, frome the boundage wherof, neither man nor angell was able to make us free. But thou, O Lord, riche in mercie, and infinite in goodnes, hath provided our redemptioun to stand in thine onlie and welbeloved Sonne, whom, of verie love, thou did give to be made man, like unto us in all things, sinne except, that in his bodie he might receave the punishment of our transgression, by his death to make satisfaction to thy justice, and by his resurrection to destroy him that was author of death ; and so to bring againe life to the world, frome which the whole ofspring of Adam most justlie was exiled.

"O Lord, we acknowledge that no creature is able to comprehend the lenth and breadth, the deepnesse and hight of that thy most excellent love, which moved thee to shew mercie where none was deserved ; to promise and give life where death had gottin victorie ; to receave us in thy grace, when we could do nothing but rebell against thy justice. O Lord, the blind dulnesse of our corrupt nature will not suffer us sufficientlie to weigh thy most ample benefites.   Yit, neverthelesse, at the commandement of Jesus Christ our Lord, we present ourselves to this table, (which he hath left, to be used in remembrance of his death, untill his comming againe,) to declare and witnesse before the world, that by him alone we have receaved libertie and life; that by him alone thou doth acknowledge us thy childrein and heyres; that by him alone we have entrance to the throne of thy grace; that by him alone we are possessed in our spirituall kingdome, to eat and drinke at his table, with whom we have our conversation presentlie in heaven, and by whom our bodies sall be raised up againe frome the dust, and sall be placed with him in that endlesse joy, which thou, O Father of mercie, hath prepared for thine elect, before the foundation of the world was layed.   And these most inestimable benefites, we acknowledge and confesse to have receaved of thy free mercie and grace, by thine onlie beloved Sonne, Jesus Christ, for the which, therefore, we, thy congregatioun, moved by thy Holie Spirit, render all thanks, praise, and glorie, for ever and ever."

This done, the minister breaketh the bread, and delivereth it to the people, who distribute and divide the same among themselves, according to our Saviour Christ's commandement: and likewise giveth the cuppe, during the which time, some place of Scripture is read, which doth livelie sett furth the death of Christ, to the intent, that our eyes and senses may not onlie be occupied in these outward signes of bread and wine, which are called the visible Word, but that our hearts and mindes also may fullie be fixed in the contemplation of the Lord's death, which is, by this holie sacrament, represented.   And after this action is done, he giveth thanks, saying:—

" Most mercifull Father, we render unto thee all thanks, praise, and glorie, for that it hath pleased thee, of thy great mercie, to grant unto us, miserable sinners, so excellent a gift and treasure, as to receave us into the fellowship and companie of thy deare Sonne, Jesus Christ our Lord, whome thou hath delivered to death for us; and hath given him to us, as a necessarie foode and nurish-

ment unto everlasting life. And now, we beseeche thee also, Heavenlie Father, to grant us this request, that thou never suffer us to
become so unkinde as to forgett so worthie benefites.   But rather
imprint and fasten them sure in our hearts, that we may grow and
increase daylie more and more in true faith, which continuallie is
exercised in all maner of good works.   And so muche the rather,
O Lord, confirme us in these perellous dayes, and rages of Satan,
that we may constantlie stand and continue in the confessioun of
the same, to the advancement of thy glorie, who art God over all
things, blessed for ever. So be it."

The action thus ended, the people sing the 103 Psalme: " My
soule, give laud," &c., or some other of thanksgiving; which ended,
one of the blessings before mentioned is recited, and so they rise
frome the table and depart.

TO THE READER.

Why this Order is observed rather than anie other.

If there be anie that wold mervell, why we follow rather this
order than anie other, in the administration of this sacrament, lett
him diligentlie consider, that, first of all, we utterlie renunce the
errour of the Papists: Secundlie, We restore unto the sacrament
his owne substance, and to Christ his proper place.   And as for
the words of the Lord's Supper, we rehearse them, not becaus they
sould change the substance of bread or wine, or that the repetition
thereof, with the intent of the sacrificer, sould make the sacrament,
(as the Papists falslie beleeve,) but they are read and pronounced,
to teache us how to behave ourselves in that action; and that
Christ might witnesse unto our faith, as it were, with his owne
mouth, that he hath ordained these signes to our spirituall use and
comfort.   We doe first, therefore, examine ourselves, according to
Sanct Paul's rule, and prepare our mindes, that we may be worthie
partakers of so high mysteries.   Then, taking bread, we give
thanks, breake, and distribute it, as Christ our Saviour hath taught
us.   Finallie, the ministration ended, we give thanks again, accord-

ing to his exemple ; so that without his Word and warrant, there is nothing in this holie action attempted.

THE FORME OF MARIAGE.

After the bannes or contract hath beene published three severall dayes, in the congregation, (to the intent, that if anie person have interest or title to either of the parties, they may have sufficient time to make their challenge,) the parties assemble at the beginning of the sermon, and the minister, at time convenient, sayeth as followeth :—

Of Mariage.

" Dearlie beloved brethrein, we are heere gathered together in the sight of God, and in the face of his congregation, to knitt and joyne these parties together, in the honourable estate of matrimonie, which was instituted and authorized by God himself in Paradise, man being then in the estate of innocencie. For what time God had made heaven, and earth, and all that is in them, and had created and facioned man after his owne similitude and likenesse, unto whom he gave rule and lordship over all the beasts of the earth, fishes of the sea, and foules of the aire, he said, ' It is not good that man live alone : lett us make ane helper like unto himself.' And God broght a fast sleepe upon him, and tooke one of his ribbes, and shaped Evah therof, giving us therby to understand, that man and wife are one bodie, one flesh, and one blood ;[1] signifeing also unto us, the mysticall union that is betweene Christ and his Church ; for the which cause, man leaveth his father and mother, and taketh him to his wife, to keepe companie with her ; the which also we ought to love, even as our Saviour loveth his church, that is to say, his elect and faithfull congregatioun, for which he gave his life.

[1] " In Hebrew, man is called *isch*, and the woman *ischa*, whereby is weill expressed the naturall affinitie betwixt man and his wife."—*Note in the MS.*

" And semblablie also, it is the wive's duetie to studie to please and obey her husband, serving him in all things that be godlie and honest; for she is in subjectioun, and under the governance of her husband, so long as they continue both alive.   And this holie mariage being a thing most honourable, is of suche vertue and force, that thereby the husband hath no more right and power over his owne bodie bot the wife, and, likewise, the wife hath no more power over her owne bodie bot the husband, forasmuche as God hath so knitt them together in his mutuall societie, to the procreation of childrein, that they sould bring them up in the feare of the Lord, and to the increase of Christ's kingdome.

" Wherefore, they that be thus coupled together by God cannot be severed or putt apart, unlesse it be for a seasoun with the consent of both parties, to the end, to give themselves the more ferventlie to fasting and prayer ; giving diligent heede in the meane time, that their long being apart be not a snare, to bring them into the danger of Sathan, through incontinencie. And, therefore, to avoide fornication, everie man ought to have his owne wife, and everie woman her owne husband; so that so manie as cannot live chast are bound, by the commandement of God, to marie, that therby the holie temple of God, which is our bodies, may be keeped pure and undefiled : for since our bodies are now become the verie members of Jesus Christ, how horrible and detestable a thing is it, to make them the members of ane harlott! Everie one ought, therefore, to keepe his vessell in all purenesse and holinesse; for whosoever polluteth and defileth the temple of God, him will God destroy."

Here the minister speeketh to the parties that sall be maried, on this wise :—

" I require and charge you, as ye will answere at the day of judgement, when the secreets of all hearts sall be disclosed, that if either of you know anie impediment why yee may not be lawfullie joyned together in matrimonie, that yee confesse it. For be yee weill assured, that so manie as be coupled otherwise than

God's Word doth allow, are not joyned together by God, neither is their matrimonie lawfull."

If no impediment be by them declared, then the minister sayeth to the whole congregatioun :—

" I take you to witnesse, that be heere present, beseeching you all to have good remembrance heerof. And, moreover, if there be anie of you that know, that either of these parties be contracted to anie other, or knoweth anie other lawfull impediment, lett them now make declaration thereof."

If no cause be alledged, the minister proceedeth, saying :—

" Forasmuche as no man speeketh against this thing, you, N., sall protest heere, before God, and his holie congregatioun, that you have taken, and are now contented to have, M., heere present, for your lawfull wife ; promising to keepe her, to love and entreate her in all things, according to the duetie of a faithfull husband, forsaking all other during her life, and breefelie to live in an holie conversation with her, keeping faith and truthe in all points, according as the Word of God and his holie Gospell doth command."

The Answere.

" Even so I tak her, before God, and in the presence of this his congregation."

The minister to the spouse also sayeth :—

" You, M., sall protest heere, before the face of God, and in the presence of this holie congregatioun, that yee have taken, and are now contented to have, N., heere present, for your lawfull husband ; promising to him subjection and obedience, forsaking all other during his life, and, finallie, to live in a holie conversatioun with him, keeping faith and truthe in all points, as God's Word doth prescribe."

The Answere.

" Even so I take him, before God, and in the presence of this his congregation."

The minister then sayeth :—

" Give diligent care, then, to the Gospell, that yee may understand how our Lord wold have this holie contract keeped and observed; and how sure and fast a knott it is, which may, in no wise, be loosed, according as we be taught in the 19th chapter of Sanct Matthew's Gospell :—' The Pharisees came unto Christ, to tempt him, and to grope his minde, saying, Is it lawfull for a man to putt away his wife for everie light cause?' He answered, saying, ' Have yee not read, that he which created man in the beginning made them male and female; saying, For this thing sall man leave father and mother, and cleave unto his wife, and they twaine sall be one flesh? So that they are no more two, but one flesh. Lett no man, therefore, putt asunder that which God hath coupled together.'

" If yee beleeve assuredlie these words which our Lord and Saviour did speeke, (according as yee have heard them now rehearsed out of the holie Gospell,) then may yee be certaine, that God hath even so knitt you together in this holie state of wedlocke. Wherefore, applie yourselves to live together, in godlie love, in Christian peace, and good exemple, ever holding fast the band of charitie without anie breache; keeping faith and truthe the one to the other, even as God's Word doth appoint."

Then the minister commendeth them to God, in this or suche like sort :—

" The Lord sanctifie and blesse you : the Lord powre the richesse of his grace upon you, that yee may please him, and live together in holie love to your lives' end. So be it."

Then is sung the 128 Psalme, " Blessed are they that feare the Lord," &c., or some other appertaining to the same purpose.

AN ADULTERER IN EDINBURGH RESCUED OUT OF THE HANDS OF THE MAGISTRATS.

As the servants of God travelled to have vice punished, the devill beganne to bestirre himself more furiouslie. There was an Act made in Edinburgh, that fornicators and adulterers sould be carted through the town, and banished, till their repentance were offered and receaved. It was found, that a fleshiour, named Sandersone, had putt away his lawfull wife, under colour, that they were lawfullie divorced after the Popish maner, and had takin another into his hous. Triell being takin that he was not mareid with the secund woman, nor able to prove that he was divorced lawfullie frome his first wife, was committed to the hands of the magistrats, who commanded him to be carted, according to their Act. The rascall multitude, inflammed by some ungodlie craftsmen, brake the cart, and tooke away the malefactor. This was the beginning of farther evills.

THE QUEENE RETIRETH TO LORAINE.

After the death of King Francis, the queene withdrew herself frome the court of France, and went to Lorane, with her uncles, either becaus not willing to remaine longer at court, when, through the strenth of the King of Navarre, her mother-in-law did draw to herself, by little and little, the governement of the whole realme, or elles to seeke a retired place for mourning. Lord James came to her in Loraine. Mr Johne Leslie, Officiall of Aberdeene, after Bishop of Rosse, came to her the day before, sent to her frome the Erle of Huntlie, and other lords spirituall and temporall, in the north. He suggested falselie to the queene, that he came to perswade her to committ the governement of the kingdome to him, to which he aspired more than the overthrow of religioun; and ad-

vised her, to caus deteane him till she were arrived in Scotland,
and had pacifeid tumults at home; to land in the north parts,
where there sould be twentie thowsand men readie to guarde her,
and convoy her to Edinburgh. But she would not seeme to follow
his advice.

A DELIBERATION ABOUT THE QUEEN'S RETURN.

It was reasouned among the queene her freinds whether she
sould returne or not. Some pretended the difficultie of the journey, the malcontentment of the English queene, the seditious
spirits of her subjects at home, who could hardlie be conteaned in
awe by the governement of men; who had shortened the dayes of
her father and mother with displeasure. It was answered, that
kings not preassing to infringe the liberteis of the countrie, raigned
among them in securitie and great honour. The cheefe way now
to preserve peace was, to make no alteratioun in religioun. Her
uncles inclynned this way for their owne respects, for they thought
she would be farther at their devotioun if she were out of France,
where the state of the countrie was so troubled; and with the hope
of her mariage might gaine friends, and in the meane time appoint
one of their owne factioun to be gouvernour in Scotland. She
herself inclynned to returne, that she might commande as a soverane. Her brother, Lord James, promised she sould find the countrie in quiett.

NOAL SENT IN AMBASSADGE FROM FRANCE.

Whill Lord James was in France, there came an ambassader,
Noalius, a senator of Burdeaux. He craved, that the league betwixt Scotland and England might be brokin, the ancient league
betweene Scotland and France might be renued, the bishops and
churchmen restored to their places, and suffered to intromett with

their rents. The counsell delayed answere till the parliament appointed to be holdin in May following.

PRACTISES IN ABSENCE OF THE QUEENE.

In the meane time, the Papists practised with the ambassader.
The Erles of Huntlie, Atholl, Bothwell, and others, intended to
have takin Edinburgh before the time indicted for the parliament.
The bishops held counsell in Stirline. Some whispered, that the
duke and the Bishop of Sanct Andrewes were too familiar: some
feared that the duke, as secund persoun, sould have usurped the
authoritie of the queene in her absence; for so had some of his
freinds urged him, immediatlie after the death of the King of
France. The professours prevented them, and came to Edinburgh.
The Erle of Arran stoode constant with his brethrein. Mr James
Mackgill, and some others, travelled earnestlie and stoutlie, that
nothing sould be done prejudiciall to the queene's authoritie in absence of Lord James, but were evill recompensed after.

AN INSURRECTION IN EDINBURGH.

The Papists hunt for occasiouns of broyle. The play of Robin-
hoode[1] was left off for manie yeeres, and forbiddin by act of parliament;[2] yitt would the rascall multitude of Edinburgh trouble

---

[1] Many of the popular games, sports, and festivals, which Strutt and other writers
have recorded as belonging exclusively to England, were equally common to Scotland, in consequence of the Saxon origin of both nations; but the May-day play, or
pageant of Robin Hood, was at first confined to England, from whence it was introduced into Scotland, probably about the beginning of the sixteenth century. As
these popular festivals were, in many cases, grossly profane, as well as opportunities
for dissipation and licentiousness, the Scottish Reformers, at the commencement of
their labours, endeavoured to suppress them.

[2] The following Act of the Scottish Parliament, A.D. 1557, is the one referred to.
" It is statut and ordanit, that in all tymes cumming, na maner of persoun be chosin

the toun, even in the verie night. The bailiffe tooke frome them some swords and an ensigne. Heerupon they possessed the gates of the toun, and intended to have pursued some honest men in their owne houses. The mutinie stayed upon restitutioun of their swords and ensigne; yitt ceassed they not to molest the inhabitants of the toun, and countrie men resorting to the toun, taking their money frome them, or threatning farther violence. The magistrats apprehended a cheefe actor, one named Killon, a cordiner, who had spoiled one named Johne Mowbray of ten crownes. He was putt to an assise, and a gibbet sett up beneath the croce. Whether by pactioun of the proveist and some other, or by instigatioun of the craftsmen, it is uncertane; but certane it is, that the jayle was brokin up, and not onlie the said Killon, but also all other malefactors, sett at freedome, the gibbet pulled down, and despitefullie brokin in peeces. The proveist and some of the counsell assembled in the clerk's chamber. The rascall multitude, together with some cheefe craftsmen, ringleaders, intended to invade the chamber. The proveist, and suche as were with him in companie, went to the tolbuith, not suspecting they would make new pursute, after they had obteaned their intent. But they came rushing doun frome the Castellhill, and with stones, gunnes, and

Robert Hude nor Littill John, Abbot of Unressoun, Quenis of Maij, nor vtherwyse, nouther in burgh nor to landwart, in ony tyme to cum : And gif ony prouest, baillies, counsal, and communitie, chesis sic ane personage as Robert Hude, Lyttill Johne, Abbottis of Unressoun, or Quenis of Maij, within burgh, the chesaris of sic sall tyne thair fredome for the space of fyue zeiris, and vtherwise salbe punist at the quenis grace will, and the acceptar of siclyke office salbe banist furth of the realme : And gif ony sic persounis sic as Robert Hude, Lyttill Johne, Abbottis of Unressoun, Quenis of Maij, beis chosin outwith burgh, and uthers landwart townis, the chesaris sall pay to our souerane lady x. pundis, and thair persounis put in waird, thair to remaine during the quenis grace plesoure : And gif ony wemen or uthers, about simmer treis singand, makis perturbatioun to the quenis liegis in the passage throw burrowis and vther landwart townis, the women perturbatouris for skafrie of money or vtherwyse salbe takin, handellit, and put vpon the cukstulis of euerie burgh or towne."—Acts of the Parliaments of Scotland, folio edit., vol. ii. p. 500. In spite of this prohibition, the proscribed festival was such a favourite, that, by the end of the century, the General Assembly continued to complain of the excesses that were occasioned by " the making of Robin Hude."

other weapons, came to the tolbuith, and rushed at the doore, till
they were forced to retire, partlie by stones cast doun, partlie by a
pistoll shott by Robert Norwell, wherewith one Twedie was hurt.
Yitt ceased they not to cast stones, and shoot at the windowes,
threatning death to all that were within.   And, indeed, the craftsmen, suspected authors of that tumult, careid no good will to some
that were with the proveist.   Archibald Dewar, Patrik Changie,
had before willed Mr Knox to solist the proveist.   He had answered, that he had often solicited in their favours; but his conscience accused him, that they used his travells for no other end
but to be a patrone to their impietie.   He had interceeded before
for William Harlaw, James Frissell, and others that were convicted of a tumult.   They threatned, that both he and the bailiffes
sould have caus to repent, if the execution were not stayed.   He
answered, he would not hurt his conscience for fear of man.   So
they departed, and the tumult rose immediatlie, which continued
frome two after noone till eight at night.   When the craftsmen
were required to assemble, and to free the proveist frome the furie
of the multitude, they went to their foure houres pennie,[1] and without regard of their oath or duetie, jesting, they said, " They would
be magistrats alone, lett them rule the multitude alone."   To pacifie the multitude, the proveist and bailiffes were forced to subscrive, that they sould never pursue anie of these who were guiltie
of that tumult, for anie crime committed in that behalfe.   This
assurance was proclamed at the Croce after nyne of the clocke at
night.   The nobilitie, notwithstanding, vowed punishement, wherupon a number of that factioun absented themselves till the arrivall
of the queene.   The cheefe authors were reputed as excommunicat,
till they satisfeid the magistrats, and made humble supplicatioun
to the church.

---

[1] The name of the afternoon refreshment of ale, wine, or usquebaugh, which was
taken at four o'clock, and most commonly in some tavern or alehouse. Hard drinking was at this period a particular characteristic of the Scots, and the " four hours
pennie" was one of the many practices by which the general evil had been confirmed.
The phrase is equivalent to our modern " tea-time."

The Papists, a little before the parliament, resorted in diverse
companeis to the toun, and beganne to brag. The professours
heereupon assembled, and went up and doun the streets in companeis, but in peaceable manner, so that the bishops and their
bands forbare the High Street. The brethrein, understanding
what they intended, conveened upon the twentie-seventh of May,
and, after consultatioun, concluded that an humble supplicatioun
sould be presented, together with some articles, to the Lords of
Secreit Counsell, and the whole Assemblie then conveened. The
Master of Lindsay, the Laird of Lochinvar, the Laird of Phairnihirst, elder, the Laird of Quhittinghame, Thomas Menzeis,
Proveist of Aberdeene, and George Lowell, Burges of Dundie,
were directed as commissioners to present the Articles and Supplicatioun.

THE ARTICLES.

1. First, That idolatrie, and all monuments therof, sould be suppressed throughout the whole realme : that the sayers, hearers,
mainteaners, and frequenters to the masse, sould be punished according to the Act of Parliament.

2. That speciall and certane provisioun be appointed for the sustentatioun of superintendents, ministers, exhorters, and readers :
that superintendents and ministers be planted where none were
alreadie planted, in places convenient : that suche as disobeyed
or contemned the superintendents in their functiouns sould be
punished.

3. That some punishement be appointed for the abusers of the
sacraments, and contemners of the same.

4. That no letters be givin furth by the Lords of Sessioun, to
answere or pay anie persoun their tithes, without speciall proviso,
that the parochiners reteane so muche in their hands as is allowed

to the ministrie : that suche as are alreadie givin be called in and discharged ; and likewise, that no shireffes give precepts to that effect.

5. That neither the Lords of Sessioun, nor anie other judges, proceed upon suche precepts or warning past, at the instance of these who of late have obteaned fewes of vicars' and parsons' manses and church-yards.   That six aikers, if there be so muche of the gleeb, be alwayes reserved to the minister, according to the appointment of the Booke of Discipline, and that everie minister may have letters therupon.   (This last claus is omitted in the Register.)

6. That no letters of the Lords of Sessioun, nor others, take place, whill the stipends conteaned in the Booke of Discipline for sustentatioun of the ministers be first consigned in the hands, at the least, of the principalls of the parish.

7. That some punishement be appointed for suche as purchasse, bring home, or execute within this realme, the Pope's bulls.

THE SUPPLICATION.

" Please your honours, and the wisdoms of suche as are pre-sentlie conveened with you in counsell, to understand, that by manie arguments we may perceave what the pestilent generatioun of the Roman Antichrist within this realme intendeth ; to witt, that they would of new erect their idolatrie, tak upon them impyre above our conscience, and so to command us, the true subjects of this realme, and suche as God of his mercie hath under our sove-rane subjected unto us, in all things to obey their appetites. Honestie craveth, and conscience moveth us, to make the veric secreets of our hearts patent to your honours in that behalfe, which is this : that before that ever these tyranns and dumbe dogges im-pyre above us, and above suche as God hath subjected unto us, that we, the barons and gentlemen professing Christ Jesus within this realme, are fullie determined to hazard life, and whatsoever we have receaved of God in temporall things.   Most humblie, therefore, beseeche your honours, that suche order may be takin, that we have not occasioun to take again the sword of just defense into our hands, which we have willinglie (after that God had givin victorie both to your honours and us) resigned over into your hands, to the end that God's Gospell may be publictlie preached within this realme, the true ministers therof reasonablie susteaned, idolatrie suppressed, and the committers therof punished according to the lawes of God and man. In doing wherof, your honours sall find us not onlie obedient unto you in all things lawfull, but also readie at all times to bring under order and obedience suche as would rebell against your just authoritie, which, in absence of our soverane, we acknowledge to be in your hands; beseeching your honours, with upright judgement and indifferencie, to looke upon these our few articles, and by these our brethrein to signifie unto us suche answere again as may declare your honours worthie of that place, wherunto God, after some danger susteaned, in his mercie hath called you. And lett these enemeis of God assure themselves, that if your honours putt not order unto them, that we sall shortlie take suche order, that they sall neither be able to doe what they list, neither yitt to live upon the sweate of the browes of suche as are no debters unto them. Lett your honours conceave nothing of us but all humble obedience in God. But lett the Papists be yitt once again assured, that their pride and idolatrie we will not suffer."

Upon this supplicatioun, and articles presented by the Commissioners of the Assemblie of the Kirk, an act and ordinance was made by the Lords of Secreit Counsell, answering to everie head of the forsaid articles, and that letters be answered therupon which were raised by sindrie ministers.

LORD JAMES IN DANGER AT PARISE.

After the queene resolved to come home, Lord James returned with speed. Beside great charges, and the losse of a boxe wherin

3

he putt his money, he escaped a great danger when he was to enter in his journey. The Papists intended, that when he came frome Rhems in Loraine, where the queene remained with the cardinall, to besett his loodging by night in Parise, or to assault him and his companie in the streets. Lord James was forewarned of that danger by the Ringrave, with whom he had contracted familiaritie before in Scotland. He resolveth to depart out of Parise the nixt day after he came, and in good order. Yitt they gett knowledge. They prepared a processioun upon the Change-bridge, where he was to passe. As one part of his companie passed by without uncovering their head, some were suborned to crie " Huguenots!" and to cast stones. But the Ringrave, and some other gentlemen accompaneing Lord James, rebooked the foolish multitude, road over some of the foremost; and so the rest were scattered.

LETTERS TO THE LORDS FROM THE QUEENE.

Lord James brought letters frome the queene to the lords, wherin she required, that they interteane quietnesse, and suffer nothing to be attempted against the contract of peace made at Leith till her owne returne; and to suffer religioun presentlie established to have free course.

THE ANSWERE GIVIN TO THE FRENCHE AMBASSADER.

The lords, after the reading of these letters, gave answere to the Frenche ambassader as followeth : First, That France had not deserved at their hands, that either they or their posteritie sould enter with them againe in anie league or confederacie, offensive or defensive, seing they had so cruellie persecuted them and their realme, and violated their liberteis, under pretence of mariage and amitie, and would have brought the people into miserable servitude.

Secund, That beside conscience, they could not tak upon them suche a shame, as without offense committed to breake the league

which in God's name they had made with them, whome He had
made instruments to sett Scotland at freedome frome the tyrannie
of the Frenche, at least of the Guisians and their factioun.

Last, for the thrid demand, That suche as they called bishops
and churchemen, they knew neither for pastors of the church, nor
yitt for anie just possessers of the patrimonie of the same; but
knew them perfytelie to be woolves, theives, murtherers, and idle
belleis. And, therefore, as Scotland hath forsakin the Pope and
Poperie, so could they not be debtors to his foresworne vassalls.
With these answeres departed the said ambassader.

THE REMANENT MONUMENTS OF IDOLATRIE DESTROYED.

The lords made an act, that all monuments of idolatrie sould be
destroyed. The Erle of Arran was directed to the west; the Erles
of Argile and Glencarne, together with the Protestants of the
west, were appointed to joyne with him. They demolished Failefurde, Kilwinning, a part of Cosraguell, and burnt Pasley. The
bastard bishop escaped narrowlie. Lord James was directed to
the north, where he made suche reformatioun as nothing contented
the Erle of Huntlie; yitt seemed he to approve all that was done.

THE QUEENE HER INTENTION.

The queene addressing herself to her voyage, her most inward
freinds advised her to dissemble in maters of religioun. Yitt Durie, Abbot of Dumfermline, and Johne Sinclar, designed Bishop of
Brechin, animated her to crueltie, wherto she inclyned, partlie by
her owne dispositioun, partlie by the perswasioun of her owne kinsmen. Sometimes speeches would escape out of her mouth, which
did bewray her inclinatioun. She would boast among her familiars,
that she would imitat Queene Marie. Her intention was, to depresse
by little and little the other factioun, till her owne was sufficientlie strenthened. Her uncles encuraged her with the apparent shew
of the strenth of the Popish factioun, wherof their eldest brother,

Francis, Duke of Guise, was appointed to be chiftane, according to a secreit and bloodie decree of the Councell of Trent. In the meane time, Charles, Cardinal of Lorane, counselled her to leave beside him her apparell and houshold stuffe, till it was seene what was the successe of her voyage. She being acquainted with his nature, answered, she could not see wherefore she sould be more carefull of her stuffe and apparell nor of her owne persoun.

SAFE PASSAGE INDIRECTLIE DENIED TO OUR QUEENE BY QUEENE ELIZABETH.

Monsieur d'Osell was sent frome our Queene to Queene Elizabeth, to trie her good will before she enter in her voyage. He was honourablie receaved, and sent backe with answere, that if she would come through England, she would take it as a great benefite; but if she would eschew to come by her, she would take it as a contumelie. There was jealousie betwixt the two queenes; for after the death of King Francis, the Queene of England had beene earnest with the Queene of Scots,.by Francis Erle of Bedford, and Nicolas Throgmorton, to ratifie the treatie of Edinburgh. She answered, she could not resolve without consent of the Scottish nobilitie; wherupon Queene Elizabeth did not absolutelie grant a safe conduct, neither for Monsieur d'Osell to returne through England, nor herself to passe by sea. Our queene sent for Throgmorton, and demanded what could be the reasoun of this indirect repulse. The other answered, he had no commissioun but to receave her answere anent the confirmatioun of the treatie at Edinburgh. What passed betwixt them may be collected by the letter sent by Throgmorton to Queene Elizabeth, dated at Parise, the 23d of June. The marginall observatiouns are Mr Knox's.

THROGMORTON'S LETTER TO THE QUEENE OF ENGLAND.

" The 18th of this present June, I sent Sommer to the Queene of Scots, for audience, who appointed me to come to her the same

day after dinner, which I did.   To her I did your Majestie's heartie
commendations, and declared unto her your Majestie's gladsomnesse
of her recoverie of her late sickenesse, whose want of health, as it
was greevous unto your Majestie, so did yee congratulate and
greatlie rejoice of the good tydings of health she was presentlie in.
After these offices, I putt her in remembrance again what had
passed frome the beginning in the mater of your Majestie's demand
of ratification, according to the proport of the said treatie, as weill
by me at the first, as afterward by my Lord Bedford at his being
heere; and also followed sithence again by me in audience, and by
my letter to her, being in Lorane; adding heereto your Majestie's
further commandement and recharge to me againe, presentlie to
renue the same demand, as before had beene done.

"The said queene made answere:

"'Monsieur L'Ambassader,—I thanke the queene, my good
sister, for this gentle visitatioun and congratulation of this my recoverie; and though I be not yitt in perfyte health, yitt, I thanke
God, I feele myself in verie good health in the comming to.   And
for answere to your demand of my ratificatioun, I doe remember
all these things that yee have recited unto me; and I would that
the queene my good sister sould thinke, that I doe respite the resolute answere in this mater, and performing therof, untill suche
time as I might have the advice of the nobles[1] and estats of myne
owne realme, which I trust sall not be long a doing; for I intend
to make my voyage thither shortlie.   And though this mater,'
quoth she, 'doth tuich me principallie, yitt doth it also tuich the
nobles and estats of my realme too.   And, therefore, it sall be
meete that I use their advices therin.   Heeretofore they have
seemed to be greeved that I sould doe anie thing without them;
and now, they would be more offended if I sould proceed in this
mater of myself without their advices.   I doe intend,' quoth she,

---

[1] "The nobles were no farther respected than they might serve to her corrupt affections."   This and the following quotations, which are here introduced in the form
of foot-notes, are in the original MS. placed in the margin, being a running com-
mentary on Throgmorton's Letter, by John Knox.

' to send Monsieur d'Osell to the queene, your mistresse, my good sister, who sall declare that unto her frome me that, I trust, sall suffice her, by whom I will give her to understand of my journey into Scotland. I meane to embark at Calice. The king hath lent me certane galeyes and ships, to convoy me home ; and I intend to require of my good sister these favours that princes use to do in these cases. And though the termes wherin we have stood heertofore have beene somewhat hard, yitt, I trust that frome hencefurth[1] we sall accord together as cousins and good nighbours. I meane,' quoth she, ' to retire all the Frenchemen from Scotland who have givin jealousie to the queene, my sister, and miscontentment to my subjects,[2] so as I will leave nothing undone to satisfie all parteis ; trusting the queene, my good sister, will doe the like, and that frome hencefurth none of my disobedient subjects sall find aide or support at her hands.'

" I answered, that I was not desirous to fall into discourse how these hard termes first beganne, nor by what meanes they were nourished, becaus therin I must charge some partie with injurie and perill offered to the queene, my mistresse, which was the verie ground of these maters.[3] But I was weill assured, that there could be no better occasion offered to putt the former unkindenesse in forgetfulnesse, than by ratifeing the treatie of peace, for that sould repay all injureis past. ' And, Madame,' quoth I, ' where it pleaseth you to suspend the ratificatioun, till yee have the advices of the nobles and estats of your realme, the queene, my mistresse, doth nothing doubt of their conformitie in this mater, becaus the treatie was made by their consents.'

" The queene answered, ' Yea, by some of them, but not by all.[4] It will appeare, when I come amongst them, whether they be of the same minde that you say they were then of. But of this I assure you, Monsieur l'Ambassader,' quoth she, ' I for my part am

---

[1] " Even till she might shew her evil will."
[2] " If France wold have susteaned them, they had not yitt departed."
[3] " The armes of England were usurped."
[4] " Your Papists and ours have practised, and still practise division."

verie desirous to have the perfyte and assured amitie of the queene, my good sister, and will use all the meanes I can to give her occasioun to thinke that I meane it indeed.'[1]

" I answered, 'Madame, the queene, my mistresse, you may be assured, will use the like towards you, to move you to be of the same opinioun towards her.' 'Then,' said she, 'I trust the queene, your mistresse, will not support nor encourage none of my subjects to continue in their disobedience,[2] nor to tak upon them things that apperteane not to subjects.[3] You know,' quoth she, ' there is muche adoe in my realme about maters of religioun. And though there be a greater number of the contrare religioun to me than I would there were, yitt there is no reasoun that subjects sould give[4] a law to their soverane, and speciallie in maters of religioun, which I feare,' quoth she, ' my subjects sall take in hand.'[5] I answered, 'Madame, your realme is in no other case this day than all other realmes through Christendome are, the proofe wherof yee see verifeid in this realme; and you see what great difficultie it is to give order in this mater, though the king and all his counsell be verie desirous therunto. Religioun is of the greatest force that may be. You have been long out of your owne realme, so that the contrarie religioun to yours had wonne the upper hand, and the greatest part of your realme. Your mother was a woman of great experience, of deepe dissimulatioun, and keeped that realme in quietnesse till she beganne to constraine men's consciences; and as you think it unmeete to be constrained by your subjects, so it may like you to consider, the mater is als

[1] " So that she might have had England to the Pope's religion, I think she leed not."

[2] " The feare of God in the heart of Elias was disobedience to cursed Jezebel."

[3] " This we may answere here; it apperteaneth to subjects to worship God as he hath commanded, and to suppresse idolatrie, by whosoever it be erected or mainteaned."

[4] " God giveth his law as weill to the prince as to the subjects."

[5] " Answere for the part of Scotland : and if so they had done, they escaped God's indignation, which had been felt, and still hanged over this realme, for the idolatrie and other abominations committed in the same, which shall not ceasse till that it be suppressed."

intolerable to them, to be constrained by you in maters of conscience. For the duetie due to God cannot be given to anie other without offense of his Majestie.'

" ' Why,' said she, ' God doth command subjects to be obedient to their princes; and commandeth princes to reade his law, and governe thereby themselves and the people committed to their charges.' ' Yea, Madame,' quoth I, ' in these things that be not against his commandements.' ' Weill,' quoth she, ' I will be plaine with you : the religioun which I professe, I tak to be the most acceptable to God, and, indeid, neither doe I know, nor desire to know, anie other.[1] Constancie becometh all folkes weill, but none better than princes, and suche as have rule over realmes, and speciallie in maters of religioun.[2] I have been brought up,' quoth she, ' in this religioun ; and who might credite me in anie thing if I sould shew myself light in this case ? And though I be young, and not weill learned, yitt have I heard this mater oft disputed by my uncle, my lord cardinall, with some that thought they could say somewhat in the mater ; and I found therin no great reasoun to change my opinioun.' [3]

" ' Madame,' quoth I, ' if you will judge weill in that mater, you may be conversant in the Scriptures, which are the tuichstone to trie the right frome the wrong. Peradventure you are so partiallie affected to your uncle's argument, that you could not indifferentlie consider the other parteis. Yitt this I assure you, Madame, your uncle, my lord cardinall, in conference with me about these maters, hath confessed, that there be great errours and abuses come into the church, and great disorders in the ministers and cleargie, insomuche that he desired and wished that there might be a reformatioun of the one and the other.' [4] ' I have oftentimes heard him

---

[1] " The consecration of the Cardinall will not suffer you."

[2] " The Turk is als constant in his Alcoron, as the Pope and his sect are in his constitutions."

[3] " Neither yet did Caiphas, when Christ Jesus did reasoun in his presence. But what was the Cardinall compelled to confesse at Poissie ?"

[4] " But the devill would putt order to himself."

say the like,' quoth she. Then I said, ' Weill, I trust God will inspire all you that be princes, that there may be some good order takin in this mater, so as there may be an unitie in religioun through all Christendome.' 'God grant!' quoth she; ' but for my part, you may perceave that I am none of these that will change my religioun everie yeere.[1] And, as I told you in the beginning, I meane to constraine none of my subjects, but would wish they were all as I am; and I trust they sould have no support to constraine me. I will send Monsieur d'Osell to you,' quoth she, ' before he goe, to know whether yee will anie thing into England. I pray you so order yourself in his mater betwixt the queene, my good sister, and me, that there may be perfyte and assured amitie betwixt us; for I know,' quoth she, ' ministers may doe muche good and harme.' I told her, I would faithfullie and truelie make declaratioun of all that she had said to me unto your Majestie, and trusted that she sould so satisfie your Majestie by Monsieur d'Osell in all things, as I sould heerafter have no more occasiouns to treate with her of anie things, but of the increasse of amitie. There sould be no want therin on her behalfe. This is the effect of the Queene of Scotland's answere to your Majestie's demand of the said ratificatioun, and of my negociatioun with her at this time."

THE QUEENE OF ENGLAND OFFENDED AT OUR QUEENE'S ANSWERES.

These advertisements somewhat exasperated, and not without caus, the Queene of England. For the armes of England were before usurped by the queene and her husband, and Queene Elizabeth reputed by the Gwisians little better than a bastard. Our queene tooke no little pleasure, speciallie after her husband was dead, of this title; for, thought she, "the shew of England sall allure manie wowers to me." The Gwisians and the Papists of

---

[1] " Change it not before you have it, for dancing and her sister is the ground of that which yitt yee have.'

both the realmes did not a little animate her in that persute. The
Queene of England, according to her promise, ratifeid the treatie
of peace contracted at Leith, by her seale and subscriptioun ;
but our queene frustrated her expectatioun with shifts and dela-
tours ; wherupon this Letter following was sent to the nobilitie and
states of Scotland :

THE QUEENE OF ENGLAND'S LETTER TO THE STATES OF SCOTLAND.

" Right trustie and right inteerlie beloved cousins, we greete
you. We doubt not but as our meaning is, and hath beene alwayes
sithence our raigne, in the sight of Almightie God, straight and
direct towards the advancement of his honour and truth in religioun, and, consequentlie, to procure peace and mainteane concord
betwixt both these realmes of England and Scotland, so also our
outward acts have weill declared the same to the world, and speciallie to you, being our nighbours, who have tasted and proved in
these, our freindship and earnest goodwill, more than we thinke
anie of your antecessers have ever receaved frome hence ; yea,
more than a great number of yourselves could weill hope of us,
all former exemples being weill weighed and considered. And this
we have to rejoice of. And so may yee be glade that where, in the
beginning of the troubles in that countrie, and of our succours
meant for you, the jealousie, or rather the malice of diverse, both
in that realme and others, was suche, both to deprive us in the yeelding, and you in requiring, our aide, that we were noted to have
meaned the surprise of that realme, by depriving your soverane, the
queene, of her crowne ; and you, or the greatest part of you, to have
intended by our succours the like ; and either to preferre some
others to the crowne, or ellis to make of that monarchie a commoun
weale ; maters verie slanderous and false. But the end and determinatioun, yea, the whole course and processe of the actioun on
both our parts have manifested, both to the slanderers and to all
others, that nothing was more meant and prosecuted than to establishe your soverane, the queene, our cousin and sister, in her estate

and crowne, the possessioun wherof was in the hands of strangers.
And although no words could weill satisfie their malice, yitt our
deeds doe declare, that no thing was sought, but the restitutioun
of that realme to the ancient libertie, and as it were, to redeeme
it from captivitie.

" Of these our purposes and deeds there remaineth, among other
arguments, good testimonie, by a solemne treatie and accord made
the last yeere at Edinburgh, by commissioners sent from us and
your queene with full authoritie in writting under both our hands,
and the Great Seales of both our realmes, in suche maner as other
princes, our progenitors, have alwise used. By which treatie and
accord, either of us have fullie accorded with other, to keepe good
peace and amitie betwixt ourselves, our countreis, and subjects.
And, in the same also, a good accord is made, not onlie of certan
querrells happened betwixt us, but also of some differences betwixt
the ministers of the late Frenche king, your soverane's husband,
and you, the estats of that realme, for the alteratioun of lawes and
customes of that countrie attempted by them. Upon which accord,
there made and concluded, hath hitherto followed, as you know,
suretie to your soverane's estate, quietnesse to yourselves, and a
better peace betwixt both the realmes than ever was heard of in
anie time past.

" Neverthelesse, how it happeneth we know not, that your soverane, either not knowing in this part her owne felicitie, or elles
dangerouslie seduced by perverse counsell, wherof we would be
most sorie, being of late at sundrie times required by us, according
to her band remaining with us, signed with her owne hand, and
sealed with the Great Seale of that realme, and allowed by you,
being the estats of the same, to ratifie her said treatie in like maner
as we by writting have done, and are readie to deliver it to her,
maketh suche dilatorie answeres therunto, as what we sall judge
therof, we perceave by her answere, that it is meete to require of
you. For, although she had alwayes answered since the death of
her husband, that in this mater she would first understand the
mindes of certan of you before she would make answere ; and so
having now, of long time, suspended our expectatioun, in the end,

notwithstanding that she had conference both by messingers, and by some of yourselves being with her, yitt she still delayed it; al ledging to our ambassader in France, (who said that this treatie was made by your consents,) it was not by consent of you all, and so would have us to forbeare, untill she sall returne in that her countrie.

"And, now, seing this her answere depended, as it sould seeme by her words, upon your opinions, we cannot but plainlie lett you all understand, that this maner of answere, without some more fruict, cannot long content us. We have meant weill to our sister, your queene, in time of offence given to us by her. We did plainlie, without dissimulatioun, charge her in her owne doubtfull state; whill strangers possessed her realme, we stayed it frome danger; and now having promised to keep good peace with her and you, her subjects, we have hitherto observed it, and sall be sorie if either yee or she sall give us contrarie caus. In a mater so profitable to both the realmes, we think it strange, that your queene hath no better advice; and, therefore, we doe require you all, being the estates of that realme, upon whome the burthein resteth, to consider this mater deepelie, and to make us answere whereunto we may trust. And if yee sall thinke meete she sall thus leave the peace imperfyte, by breaking her solemne promise, contrarie to the order of all princes, we sall be weill content to accept your answere, and sall be als carelesse to see the peace keeped, as yee sall give us caus. And doubt not, by the grace of God, but whosoever of you sall first inclyne thereto, sall soonest repent. You must be content with our plaine writting. And, on the other side, if you continue all in one minde to have the peace inviolablie keeped, and sall so by your advice procure the queene to ratifie it, we also promise you, that we will also continue our good dispositioun to keepe the same in suche good termes as now it is: and in so doing, the honour of Almightie God sall be duelie sought and promoted in both realmes, the queene, your soverane, sall injoy her estate with suretie, and yourselves possesse that which you have with tranquilitie, to the increasse of your f@mileis and posteriteis, which, by the frequent

warres heeretofore, your antecessors never had long in one estate.
To conclude, we require you to advertise us of what minde yee be;
speciallie, if you all continue in that minde, that you meane to have
the peace betwixt both the realmes perpetuallie keeped. And if
yee sall forbeare anie long time to advertise us, yee sall give to us
some occasioun of doubt, wherof more hurt may grow than good.
From," etc.

These letters receaved and perused, albeit the estats could not be
conveened, yitt did the counsell, and some others also in particular, returne answeres with reasonable diligence. The tenor of the
counsell's letter was this :—

"Please your Majestie, that with judgement we have advised
your Majestie's letters. And, albeit the whole estats could not
suddanlie be assembled, yitt we thought expedient to signifie somewhat of our mindes unto your Majestie. Farre be it frome us, that
either we take upon us that infamie before the world, or grudge of
conscience before our God, that we sould lightlie esteeme the observatioun of that peace latelie contracted betwixt these two realmes.
By what motives our soverane delayed the ratification therof, we
cannot tell. But of us (of us, we say, Madame, that have in God's
presence protested fidelitie in our promise) her Grace had none.
Your Majestie cannot be ignorant, that in this realme there are
manie enemeis; and, farther, that our soverane hath counsellers,
whose judgement she in all causes preferred to ours. Our obedience bindeth us, not onlie reverentlie to speeke and write of our soverane, but also to judge and thinke. And yitt your Majestie may
be weill assured, that in us sall be noted no blame, if that peace be
not ratifeid to your Majestie's contentment: for God is our witnesse,
that our cheefe care in this earth, nixt the glorie of our God, is that
constant peace may remaine betwixt these two realmes, wherof your
Majestie and realme may have sure experience so long as our coun-

sell or votes may stay the contrarie. The benefite that we have receaved is so recent, that we cannot suddanlie burie it in forgetfulnesse. We would desire your Majestie rather to be perswaded of us, that we, to our power, will studie to leave it in remembrance to our posteritie. And thus, with lawfull and humble commendatioun of our service, we committ your Majestie to the protectioun of the Omnipotent. At Edinburgh, the 16th day of Julie, 1561."

SHARPER ANSWERES TO THE MESSINGERS.

Some dealt more sharplie with the messingers, and willed them not to accuse nor threaten so sharpelie, till they were able to convict suche as had promised fidelitie of some evident faile ; which, although they were able to lay to the charge of some, yitt respect would be had to suche as long had declared themselves constant procurers of peace and quietnesse. In the meane time, Mr Stephen Wilson, Mr Johne Leslie, called *Nolumus* and *Volumus*, Mr James Thornton, and others that lived by traffick with the Roman Antichrist, directed letters, some to the Pope, some to the Cardinall of Lorane, some to our queene.

QUEENE MARIE HER VOYAGE HOMEWARD.

The English queene not being satisfeid with the answeres of our queene, neither for the wrong that was done in usurping her armes, nor by anie securitie of absteaning in time to come, was not a little discontented. Monsieur d'Osell, who was sent to receave the forts of Dumbar and Inchkeith from Monsieur Charle Boys, and to keepe them till her comming, was stayed in his passage through England, and came no farther than Londoun. Our queene was convoyed from Parise to Calice, with her six uncles, the Dukes of Gwise and d'Awmall, the Cardinall of Lorane and Gwise, the Grand Pryour, and the Marquesse d'Albeuf, the Duke of Nemeurs, and other her freinds and kinsmen. Two galeyes and certane other shippes were prepared for her convoy to Scotland. Her uncles, d'Awmall, the Grand Pryour, d'Albeuf, Monsieur d'Anveill, the Constable's sonne, and others of inferiour rank, accompaneid her. She arrived at Leith, the 20th day of August. The English queene had a navie in readinesse, under colour to pursue pyrats. Others doe interprete, that there was an intentioun to intercept the queene by the way, in case she intended to passe by without her consent. That Lord James was privie to this plott, as some maliciouslie alledge, there is no likelihood; for our queene was so farre from suspecting him, that she created him Erle of Murrey, she was so weill pleased with his service. Whatsoever was the Queene of England her intent, the mist was so thicke, that our queene past by; and onlie one shippe, wherin the Erle of Eglinton was a passinger, was takin, and brought to London, but soone after sett free againe.

THE QUEENE HER ARRIVALL.

Queene Marie arrived betwixt seven and eight houres in the morning, the 20th of August. She brought with her als faire jewells, pretious stones, and pearles, as were to be found in Europ. Her tapistrie and other stuffe was brought to Leith in October following. In the memorie of man was never seene, that day of the yeere, a more darke and unpleasant face of the heaven, than was at her arrivall, which continued two dayes after; for beside muche raine, the mist was so thicke, and the day so darke, that skarse could anie man espie another the lenth of two paire of butts. The sunne was not seene to shyne two dayes before, nor two dayes after. The multitude understanding of her arrivall by the sound of the galey cannons, repaired in great numbers to Leith. She was honorablie receaved by the Erle of Argile, the Lord Areskine, Lord James, and other noblemen, and the citicens of Edinburgh.

THE QUEENE COMETH TO HALYRUDHOUS.

Becaus the palace of Halyrudhous was not sufficientlie prepared, by reasoun of her suddan comming, she stayed in Leith till towards

the evening. The seditious craftsmen, who had latelie violated the
authoritie of the magistrats, mett her betwixt Leith and Edinburgh,
and craved her pardoun ; which was easilie granted, becaus what
was done was done in contempt of religioun. Fires of joy were
sett furth that night. Some honest citicens went, accompaneid
with some musicians, and saluted her at her chamber window with
musicke. She was so weill pleased with the melodie, as she alledged, that she willed the same to be continued some nights
after.

GREAT OFFENCE TAKEN AT THE QUEENE'S MESSE.

The lords repaired to her from all quarters. Nothing was knowne
but mirth till the Lord's day following, which was the 24th of August, when preparatioun beganne to be made for the idol, the
masse. The hearts of the godlie beganne to swell. Some said
plainlie, " Sall that idol be suffered to take place againe within this
realme ? It sall not." The Master of Lindsay, the gentlemen of
Fife, and others, cried out plainlie, in the Abbey closes, " The idolatrous preest sall dee the death, according to God's law !" Whill
one was careing the wax candels through the hall to the chappell,
the candels were brokin, and if some of the queene's houshold had
not come in time to helpe, the rest of the furniture had beene
throwne doun. This fact was interpreted diverslie. Some blamed
it as too great boldnesse ; others thought that men's patience was
tryed. Some said, the preest was worthie to be punished according to God's law. No Papist, nor anie that came from France,
durst whisper. But Lord James, the man whome all the godlie did reverence, tooke upon him the keeping of the chappell
doore. He pretended he would stoppe all Scots to enter ; but the
truthe was, he did it, that none sould trouble the preest. After
masse said, the preest was committed to the protectioun of Lord
Johne, Pryour of Coldinghame, and Lord Robert, Pryour of Halyrudhous, who then were both professours. So the godlie departed
with greefe of heart. After noone they repaired to the Abbey in

great companeis, and signifeid plainlie, that they could not suffer the land which God, by his mightie power, had delivered from idolatrie, to be polluted againe before their eyes.   Then followed complaint upon complaint.   Her owne servants, who had no remissioun of sinnes but by vertue of the masse, cried out, that they would returne to France without delay : they would not live without the masse.   The counsell considered upon the nixt remedie. Politick men were sent to the gentlemen with these and the like perswasiouns : "Fy, alas! will we chase our soveranc frome us? She will returne incontinent to her galeyes, and then, what will all the realme say of us?   May we not suffer her a little while?   We doubt not but she will desist.   If we were not assured she might be wonne, we sould be as great enemeis to her masse as yee sould be.   Her uncles will not stay; and after their departure, we sall rule all at our pleasure.   Would we not be als loath to endanger religioun as anie of you?"   With these and the like speeches the fervencie of the brethrein was quenched, and an act framed, the tenor wherof followeth :—

"Apud Edinburgh, 25 Augusti, 1561.

"Forsamekle as the queene's Majestie hath understand the great inconveniences that may come through the divisioun presentlie standing in this realme for the difference in maters of religioun, that her Majestie is most desirous to see it pacifeid by a good order, to the honour of God, and tranquilitie of her realme, and meanes to make the same by the advice of her estats, so soone as convenientlie may be ; and that her Majestie's godlie resolutioun may be hindered greatlie, in case anie tumult or sedition be raised among the leiges, if anie alteration or novation be preassed at, or attempted, before that the order be established ; therefore, for eshewing these inconveniences, her Majestie ordeans letters to be directed, to charge all and sundrie her leiges, by open proclamation at the Mercat Croce of Edinburgh, and other places needfull, that they and everie one of them content themselves in quietnesse, keep silence and civill societie among themselves, and in the meane time, whill the estats of the realme may be assembled, and that her Majestie have takin a finall order by their advice, and publick consent, which her Majestie hopeth sall be to the contentment of the whole: That none of them tak upon hand, privatlie or publicklie, to make anie alteratioun or innovatioun of the estate of religioun, or attempt anie thing against the same, which her Majestie found publicklie and universallie standing at her Majestie's arrivall in this her realme, under the paine of death. With certification, if anie subject in the realme sall come in the contrarie heerof, he sall be esteemed and holdin a seditious person, and raiser of tumult; and the said paine sall be executed against him with all rigour, to the exemple of others. Attour, her Majestie, with advice of her Lords of Secreit Counsell, commands and charges all her leiges, that none of them take upon hand to molest or trouble anie of her domesticall servants, or persons whatsomever, come furth of France in her Grace's companie at this time, in word, deed, or countenance, for anie caus whatsomever, either within the palace or without, or mak anie derisioun or invasioun upon anie of them, under whatsomever colour or pretence, under the said paine of death; albeit her Majestie be sufficientlie perswaded, that her good and loving subjects would doe the same, for the reverence and feare they beare to her persoun and authoritie, notwithstanding no suche commandement were published."

THE ERLE OF ARRAN'S PROTESTATION AGAINST THE PROCLAMATION.

This act, made by suche as professed true religioun, (for Papists had neither power nor vote at that time in counsell,) was proclamed at the Mercat Croce of Edinburgh, upon Monday the 25th of August. None made oppositioun, but onlie the Erle of Arran, who protested, that the lawes of God and the countrie made against idolaters, hearers and sayers of masse, be not violated. The tenor of the protestation followeth:—

" In so farre as by this proclamatioun it is understand by the

Kirk of God, and members therof, that the queene's Grace is mynded, that the true religioun and worship elles established proceed fordward that it may daylie increasse untill the parliament, that order may then be taken for extirpation of all idolatrie within this realme; we render most heartie thankes unto the Lord our God for her Grace's good minde; earnestlie praying that it might be encreassed in her Highness, to the honour and glorie of his name, and weill of his Kirk within this realme. And as tuiching the molestatioun of her Highness' servants, we suppose that none darre be so bold as once to move their finger at them, in doing of their lawfull bussinesse. And as for us, we have learned at our Master Christ's schoole to keepe peace with all men. And, therefore, for our part, we will promise that obedience unto her Majestie, (as is our duetie,) that none of her servants sall be molested, troubled, or once tuiched by the Kirk, or anie member therof, in doing their lawfull effaires. But since that God hath said, that the idolater sall dee the death, we protest solemnlie in the presence of God, and in the eares of the whole people that heare this proclamation, and speciallie in presence of you, Lyon Herald, and the rest of your colleagues, etc., makers of this proclamatioun, that if anie of her servants sall committ idolatrie, speciallie say masse, participat therewith, or take the defense therof, (which we were loath sould be in her Grace's companie,) in that case, that this proclamation be not extended to them in that behalfe, no more nor if they committ slaughter or murther, seing the one is muche more abominable and odious in the sight of God than the other; but that it may be lawfull to inflict upon them the paines conteaned in God's Word against idolaters, where ever they may be apprehended, without favour. And this our protestatioun we desire you to notifie unto her Grace, and give her the copie therof, least her Highness sould suspect an uproare, if we sould all come and present the same.

" At Edinburgh, the day and yeere forsaid."

THE FERVENCIE OF PROFESSORS COOLED.

This boldnesse did somwhat exasperat the queene, and suche as favoured her in that point. As the Lords, then called of the Congregatioun, repaired to the toun, at the first they seemed wonderfullie offended that the masse was permitted. Everie man, as he came, accused them that were before him. But after they had remained a space, they were as calme themselves. Heerupon, a zealous man, Robert Campbell of Kingzeancleughe, said to the Lord Uchiltrie, " Now, my lord, yee are come, and almost the last of all. I perceave that the fierie edge is not yitt off you. But I feare yee become als calme as the rest, when the holie water of the court sall be sprinkled upon you. For I have beene heere now five dayes. At the first, I heard everie man, when he came, say, ' Lett us hang the preest !' But after they had beene twice or thrice in the Abbey, all their fervencie was cooled. I thinke there be some enchantment in the court, wherby men are bewitched." And, indeid, the queene's flattering words, on the one side, ever crying, " Conscience! conscience! it is a sore mater to constraine the conscience ;" and the subtile perswasiouns of her supposts, men judged to be otherwise fervent for religion, upon the other part, putting men in hope she would be content to heare the preachings, and might be wonne, made all to suffer and winke at her masse for a time.

MR KNOX FINDETH FAULT WITH TOLERATION OF THE QUEENE'S MASSE.

The nixt Lord's day Mr Knox inveyed against idolatrie, and declared what plagues God had inflicted upon nations for the same. He added, that one masse was more fearfull to him than if ten thowsand armed enemeis were landed in anie part of the realme, to suppresse religioun. " For," said he, " in our God there is strenth to confound multitudes, if we unfainedlie depend upon him ; wherof we have had experience.   But when we joyne hand with idolatrie, there is no doubt but God's amiable presence and comfortable defense sall depart frome us.   And, then, I feare, alas ! that experience sall teache, to the greefe of manie, what sall then become of us."   The guiders of the court jested, and said plainlie, that suche feare was no point of their faith ; that his admonitioun was untymelie, and beside his text.   But he repeated the same words and manie moe, in December, 1565, when suche as now onlie mainteaned her masse were exiled, summouned upon treasoun, a decreit of forfalture intended against them.   He asked God mercie, in the audience of manie, that he was not more vehement and upright for suppressing of that idol in the beginning : " For," said he, " albeit I spake that which offended some, which this day they feele to be true, yitt did I not all that I might have done.   For God not onlie hath givin to me knowledge, and a tongue, to make the impietie of that idol knowne, but also credite with manie, who would have putt in executioun God's judgements, if I would have consented thereto.   But so carefull was I of the commoun tranquillitie, and loath to offend these of whome I conceaved a good opinioun, that in secreit I travelled to mitigat and coole the fervencie which God kindled in others, rather than to encurage them to putt to their hands to the Lord's warke.   Wherin, unfainedlie, I acknowledge myselfe to have done most wickedlie ; and frome the bottome of my heart crave God pardoun, for that I did not what in me lay to suppresse that idol in the beginning."

A CONFERENCE BETWIXT THE QUEENE AND MR KNOX.

The queene, whether by the counsell of others, or moved by herself, it is uncertan, had long conference with Mr Knox, none being present except Lord James.   Two gentlemen stood in the other end of the hous.   The queene layed to his charge, that he had raised a number of her subjects against her mother and herself : that he had

writtin a booke against her just authoritie, (she meant the treatise
against the regiment of weomen,) which she had, and against
which she would caus the most learned in Europe to write : that
he was the author of a great seditioun and slaughter in England :
that all that he did, he did it by necromancie, as she was informed.
He answered, " Madame, will please your Majestie patientlie to
heare my simple answeres ? First, if to teache the truthe in sinceritie, to rebooke idolatrie, to exhort people to worship God according to his Word, be to raise subjects against their princes,
then cannot I be excused. But, Madame, if the true knowledge of
God, and his right worship, be the cheefe causes which must move
men to obey frome their heart their lawfull princes, as it is certane
they are, wherin can I be blamed ? I am perswaded, your Grace
both had, and presentlie hath, als unfained obedience of suche
as professe the truthe in this realme, as ever your father or other
progenitors had, of these who were called Bishops. Tuiching that
booke which seemeth so highlie to offend your Majestie, it is true I
wrote it, and am content that all the learned in the world judge of
it. I heare that an English man hath written against it, but I have
not read him. If he have sufficientlie improved my reasouns, and
established his owne assertions, with als evident testimoneis as I
have done myne, I sall confesse my errour. But I have ever thought,
and doe still thinke, that, by myself alone, I am more able to susteane my assertions in that worke, than anie tenne in Europe sall
be able to confute." " Yee thinke," quoth she, " that I have no
just authoritie." " Please your Majestie," said he, " learned men,
in all ages, have had their judgements free, and often disagreeing
from the commoun judgements of the world ; and have published
the same, both by penne and tongue. They have borne, notwithstanding, with the errours which they could not amend. Plato, in
his booke of the Commoun wealth, damned manie things mainteaned
in the world ; yitt lived under suche formes of policie as were receaved, without troubling the estate. So have I, Madame, communicat my judgement to the world. If the estate find no inconvenience in the regiment of a woman, that which they sall allow,

I sall not dissallow, farther than within my owne breast, but sall be
als weill content to live under your Grace as Paul was to live under
Nero. I trust, so long as yee defile not your hands with the blood
of the sancts, that neither I, nor that booke, sall harme you of your
authoritie; for that booke was writtin speciallie against that wicked
Jesabell of England." " But," said she, " yee speeke of weomen
in general." " True it is," said he; " but wisdome sould teache
your Grace, not to call in question that which, to this day, hath
not troubled your Majestie, either in person or in authoritie; for
manie things have beene impugned of late, which before were
holdin for certane veriteis. No man is able to prove, that anie suche
questioun hath been moved in publick or in secreit. If I would have
troubled your estate becaus yee are a woman, I might have chosin
a time more convenient than this, when your Majestie is at home.
But, Madame, to answere to the other two imputations; I praise
God, that the wicked have no other crimes to lay to my charge,
than suche as the world knoweth to be false : for I was resident in
England onlie five yeeres ; two at Berwick, two at Newcastell, one
at Londoun. Now, if, during these times, anie can prove there
was either seditioun or mutinie in these places, I sall confesse my
self to have beene the shedder of the blood, or mover of the seditioun. I am not ashamed to averre farther, that God so blessed my
weake labours, that in Berwick, where there used commounlie to
fall furth slaughter by reasoun of querells rysing among souldiours,
there was als great quietnesse all the time I was there as there is
this day in Edinburgh. As for the slaunder of magick, necromancie, or anie other art forbidden by God, I have witnesses, beside my
owne conscience, all the congregatiouns that ever heard me, what I
spake against suche arts, and the practisers of suche impietie. It
behoveth me to beare patientlie the slaunders of suche as never delyted in the veritie, seing my Master was slaundered, as one possessed with Belzebub." " Yit," said she, " yee have taught the
people to receave another religioun than their princes can allow.
How can that doctrine be of God, seing God commandeth subjects
to obey their princes ?" " Madame," said he, " as right religioun

tooke neither originall nor authoritie from worldlie princes, but
frome the eternall God above, so are not subjects bound to frame
their religioun according to the appetite of princes; for often it fall-
eth furth, that princes are the most ignorant of all others of true
religioun. If the people of Israel had beene of the religioun of
Pharaoh, to whome they were a long time subjects, what religioun
would they have beene of? If, in the dayes of the Apostles, men
had reteaned the religioun of the Roman Emperours, what religioun sould have beene upon the face of the earth? The three
childrein said expresslie to Nebuchadnezar, 'We will make it
knowne to thee, O king, that we will not worship thy gods.' Da-
niel prayed publicklie to his God, against the expresse commandement of Darius." "Yitt," said she, "none of these lifted the
sword against their princes." "They who obey not the commandement givin doe," said he, "in some sort resist." "Yitt," said she,
"they resisted not by the sword." "God," said he, "Madame,
had not givin to them the power and the meanes." "Thinke you,
then," quoth she, "that subjects, having power, may resist their
princes?" "If their princes exceede bounds," quoth he, "Madame,
they may be resisted even by power: for there is not greater honour or obedience to be givin to kings and princes, than God hath
commanded to be givin to father and mother. If childrein joyne
together against their father, stricken with a phrenesie, and seeking to slay his owne childrein; apprehend him, take his sword
or other weapons frome him, bind his hands, and keepe him in prison till his phrenesie overpasse; doe they anie wrong? or will God
be offended with them for hindering their father frome committing
horrible murther? Even so, Madame, if princes would murther the
childrein of God, their subjects, their blind zeale is but a mad
phrenesie. To tak the sword from them, to bind their hands, and
cast them in prison, till they be brought to a sober minde, is not
disobedience, but just obedience, becaus it agreeth with the Word
of God."[1]

[1] "No appearance at this time of the imprisonment of Queene Marie."—*Note in the MS.*

The queene stood still, as one amazed, more than a quarter of an hour, and her countenance was changed. Lord James beganne to interteane her with faire speeches, and demanded, " What hath offended you, Madame ?" At lenth she said, " Weill, then, I perceave my subjects must obey you, and not me ; and sall doe what they please, and not what I command." "God forbid," said he, "that I tak upon me to command anie to obey me, or to sett subjects at libertie to doe what pleaseth them. It is my care, that both princes and subjects obey God. Think not, Madame, that wrong is done to you, when yee are willed to be subject to God ; for it is he that subjecteth people under princes. Yea, God craveth that kings be foster fathers, and queenes nurses to his people. This subjectioun to God, and service to his church, is the greatest dignitie fleshe and blood can gett upon earth." " But yee are not the kirk," said she, " which I will nourish. I will defend the kirk of Rome, which I thinke to be the true kirk." " Your will," said he, " is no reasoun, nor will your judgement make that Roman harlot, polluted with all kinde of spirituall fornicatioun, as weill in doctrine as in maners, to be the true spous of Christ. I offer to prove that the kirk of the Jewes, which crucifeid Christ, and denyed the Sonne of God, degenerated not so farre frome the ordinances and statuts of God, as the kirk of Rome hath declynned, more than five hundreth yeeres since, frome that puritie of religioun which was in the dayes of the apostles." " My conscience," said she, " perswadeth me not so." " Conscience," said he, " requireth knowledge, which I feare yee want." " I have both heard and read," said she. " So," said he, " did the Jewes who crucifeid Christ. But have yee heard anie teache, but suche as were allowed by the Pope and his cardinalls ?" " Yee interprete Scripture," said she, " after one maner, and they after another : whom sall I beleeve, or who sall be judge ?" " Further than the Word teacheth you," said he, " yee sall neither beleeve the one nor the other. The Word of God is plaine in itself. If there appeare anie obscuritie in one place, the Holie Ghost, who is never contrarious to himself, explaneth the same in other places. Papists alledge, that the masse is the institutioun of Christ Jesus, and a sacrifice for the quicke and the dead; we say, it is but the inventioun of man, and therefore an abomination before God, and no sacrifice commanded by God. So long as they are able to prove nothing, howbeit all the world beleeve them, they doe receave but the lees of men for the truthe of God. The Word of God doth plainlie assure us, that Christ neither said, nor commanded to be said, masse at the last Supper." "Yee are too hard for me," said she; "but if they were heere, whom I have heard, they would answere you." "Would to God," said he, "Madame, the most learned Papist in Europe, or whome yee would most beleeve, were heere present, and that yee would heare patientlie the mater reasouned to the end!" "Weill," said she, "yee will, perhaps, gett that sooner than yee beleeve.' "Assuredlie," said he, "if ever I gett it in my life, it is sooner than I beleeve: for the ignorant Papist cannot reasoun patientlie; the learned will never come in your audience, to have the ground of their religioun searched. They know they are not able to susteane reasouning, except fire and sword and their owne lawes be judges." "So say yee," quoth the queene. "So we have seene," said he, "to this day. For how oft have they beene required to come to conference; but it could not be obteaned, unlesse themselves were admitted judges. Therefore, Madame, it behoveth me to say againe, that they darre never dispute, but where themselves are both judge and partie."

The queene was called upon to dinner. At parting Mr Knox said to her, "I pray God, Madame, that yee may be als blessed within the commoun wealth of Scotland, as ever Deborah was in the commoun wealth of Israel." The Papists grudged and feared that which they needed not. The godlie rejoiced, and thought, that at least she would heare sermons: but they were deceaved. Mr Knox being asked by some of his familiars, what opinion he had himself of the queene? "If there be not in her," said he, "a proud minde, a craftie witt, and an indured heart against God and his truthe, my judgement faileth me."

THE COUNSELL CHOSIN.

When the nobilitie were conveened, the Lords of Privie Counsell were chosin : the duke, the Erles of Huntlie, Argile, Atholl,
Morton, Glencarne, Marshall, Bothwell; Lord Areskine, Lord
James, etc. Some were appointed to waite upon the court by
course, but that order endured not long.

D'AWMALL AND D'ANVEILL RETURNE TO FRANCE.

Duke d'Awmall returned with the galeyes to France, after he
had stayed for a certane time. The Grand Pryour and d'Anveill
stayed somewhat longer, and went through England. D'Albeuf
stayed till the nixt spring.

THE QUEENE'S PROGRESSE.

The queene entered in her Progresse in September. She travelled frome Edinburgh to Linlithquo; from thence to Stirline;
frome Stirline to Sanct Johnstoun, Dundie, and Sanct Andrewes,
all which parts she polluted with the masse. Fire followed her in
the most places. The Frenche were enriched with the propynes,
which were givin by the touns verie liberallie.

HER ENTRIE TO EDINBURGH.

In the beginning of October, the queene returned to Edinburgh.
Great preparations were made for her entrie to the toun. Faine
would fooles have counterfooted France. The keys were delivered
to her by a prettie boy, descending, as it were, frome a cloud. She
heard the verses made in her owne commendatioun with delyte,
and smyled. But when the Bible was presented, and the praise

therof sett furth, she beganne to frowne.[1] She could not refuse it
for shame; but she did little better, for she gave it to Arthure
Areskine, one of the most pestilent Papists within the realme.
The liquor of their prodigalitie was so sweete to her taste, that she
licked twice of that boxe after. This was Balfour's rule. The
queene cannot laike if the subjects have.

THE PROVEST AND BAILIFFES CHANGED AT THE QUEENE'S COMMAND.

Archibald Dowglas, Proveist of Edinburgh, Edward Hope, Adame
Foullerton, etc., Bailiffes, caused proclame, according to the custome, the statuts of the toun; and among the rest, that no adulterer, fornicator, notorious drunkard, masse-moonger, or obstinat
Papist, that corrupted the people, suche as preests, friers, and
others of that sort, sould be found within the toun, within fourtie-
eight houres, under the paines conteaned in the statuts.[2] Without
cognitioun of the caus, the queene caused the proveist and bailiffes to
be charged to waird in the castell, and commanded a new electioun

---

[1] Of this part of the pageant with which Mary was welcomed in her public entry
into Edinburgh, the following account is given in the " Diurnal of Occurents in Scotland," p. 68.—" Quhen hir grace come fordward to the butter trone of the said
burgh, the nobilitie and convoy foirsaid precedand, at the quhilk butter trone thair
was ane port made of tymber, in maist honourable maner, cullorit with fyne collouris,
hungin with syndrie armes; upon the quhilk port was singand certane barneis in the
maist hevinlie wyis; under the quhilk port thair wes ane cloud opynnand with four
levis, in the quhilk was put ane bony barne. And quhen the quenes hienes was
cumand throw the said port, the said cloud opynnit, and the barne discendit doun as
it had beene ane angell, and deliueret to her hienes the keyis of the toun, togidder
with ane Bybill and ane Psalme Buik, couerit with fyne purpourit veluot; and efter
the said barne had spoken some small speitches, he deliuerit alsua to her hienes
three writtings, the tennour thairof is vncertane. That being done, the barne as-
cendit in the cloud, and the said cloud stekit; and thairafter the quenis grace come
doun to the tolbuith." In the solemn pageantries with which the first visit of Queen
Elizabeth into the city of London was welcomed, only two years previous, a similar
exhibition was made, where a child, personating Truth, presented her with an English Bible. The more devout or more politic English queen kissed the gift, and
pressed it to her bosom.

[2] The penalties were, being branded on the cheek, and carted through the town.

to be made of proveist and bailliffes. Some oppouned to the new
electioun for a while. But when charge was doubled upon charge,
no man was found to oppone himself. Mr Thomas Mackalzean
was chosin proveist. The man was sufficientlie qualifeid for the
charge, but the depositioun of the other was against order. Some
of the burgesses themselves were blamed, that her will was so farre
obeyed. A contrarie proclamatioun was made, that the toun sould
be patent to all the queene's leiges : so murtherers, adulterers,
theeves, whoores, drunkards, idolaters, and all sort of offenders, gott
protectioun under her wings.

A PART OF MR KNOX'S LETTER TO MASTRESSE ANNA LOCKE.

Mr Knox, in a letter writtin to Mastresse Anna Locke, the secund of October, hath these words :—" The permissioun of that
odious idol, the masse, by suche as have professed themselves enemeis to the same, doth hourlie threaten a suddane plague. I thrist
to change this earthlie tabernacle, before that my wretched heart
sould be assaulted with anie suche new dolours. I feare this my
long rest sall not continue. If yee, or anie other thinke that I, or
anie other preacher within this realme, may amend suche enormiteis, yee are deceaved ; for we have discharged our consciences,
but remedie appeareth none, unlesse we would arme the hands of
the people in whome abideth yitt some sparke of God's feare. Our
nobilitie (I write with dolour of heart) beginne to find ease, good
service of God. If they be not troubled in their professioun, they
can weill eneugh abide the queene to have her masse, yea, in her
owne chappell, if she like. She hath beene in her progresse, and
hath considered the mindes of the people for the most part repugnant to her devilish opinioun ; and yitt, in her appeareth no
amendiment, but an obstinat proceeding frome evill to worse. I
have finished in open preaching the Gospell of Sanct Johne, saving
onlie one chapter. Oft have I craved the misereis of my dayes to
end with the same."

A REASONING ABOUT THE QUEENE'S MASSE.

The queene tooke upon her greater boldnesse than she and her bleeting preests had attempted before ; for upon Alhallow-day they bended up their masse with all mischeevous solemnitie. The ministers declared in publick the inconveniences. The nobilitie were sufficientlie admonished of their duetie. But as men, ledde with affectioun, called in doubt that wherin they seemed not long before to have beene most resolute, to witt, whether subjects might putt to their hands to suppresse the idolatrie of the prince, there was reasonning upon this questioun in Mr James Makgill, Clerk of Register his house, betwixt the Lord James, the Erles Morton and Marishall, Secretarie Lethington, the Justice-Clerk, Mr James Makgill, on the one side, Mr Knox, Mr Johne Row, Mr George Hay, Mr Robert Hammilton, ministers, on the other side. The noblemen and their assisters affirmed, that the subjects might not lawfullie take the masse frome her ; the ministers susteaned the contrarie. It was concluded, that the questioun sould be formed and directed, with some letters, to Geneva for resolutioun. Mr Knox offered his travells. Secretare Lethington alledged, that there stood muche in right informatioun ; promised to write. The event declared, that his promise was onlie a shift, to drive time. These that favoured the queene urged, that the queene might have free use of her owne religioun in her owne chappell, for her and her houshold. The ministers mainteaned the contrarie, adding, that her libertie would turne to their thraldome ere it was long. But nothing could move suche as were creeping in credite ; so the votes of the lords prevailed.

LORD JAMES HOLDETH A JUSTICE COURT IN JEDBURGH.

Whill the court was mindefull of nothing but pleasures and pro-digalitie, the borderers brake louse. Lord James, made Lieutenant since the queene's arrivall, as David was made captan by Saul against the Philistins, as was suspected, was sent to the borders to represse them. Yitt God assisted him, and bowed the hearts of men to feare and obedience. Bothwell himself assisted him, but he had a remissioun for Liddesdaill. There were hanged at the court in Jedburgh twentie-eight of one clan. He mett with the Lord Gray at Kelso. They agreed upon good order to be keeped in the borders.

A FAINED FRAY IN HALYRUDHOUS.

Whill Lord James was in the borders, the queene tooke greater libertie. Speeches escaped some time, which bewrayed her inclinatioun to tyrannie. She consulteth with her base brother, Johne, how to gett a guard of hyred souldiours. The ambitious man was resolved to obey her in all things, and was therefore the deerer to her. A fray was fained, as though the Erle of Arran had enclosed the palace of Halyrudhous about, and by force would carie the queene to his castell, fourteene myle frome thence. The inventioun had some appearance, becaus it was not unknowne to the people that the erle bare immoderat love to her, and that her affectioun was estranged frome him. The toun of Edinburgh was called to watche. Robert Lord Halyrudhous, and Johne Lord Coldinghame, keeped watche by course. Scouts were sent furth, and centinells commanded, under the paine of death, to keepe their stations. These who skowred the feilds all the night shew themselves before the palace gates. Some were offended, others jested at this sport. The authors or devisers knowing no man durst controll them, regarded not men's secreit judgements.

SIR PETER MEWTAS HIS COMMISSION TO THE QUEENE.

Soone after the returning of Lord James frome the borders, Sir Peter Mewtas came with commissioun frome the Queene of England, to require ratificatioun of the peace contracted at Leith. She answered as before, she behoved to advise, and then sould send answere. In presence of the counsell she was grave; but when she, her fidlers, and other dauncing companiouns, gott the hous alone, there might be seene unseemelie scripping, notwithstanding that she was wearing the doole weid. Her commoun speeche in secreit was, she saw nothing in Scotland but gravitie, which she could not agree weill with, for she was brought up in joyousitic. So termed she dancing, and other things thereto belonging.

THRID GENERALL ASSEMBLY.—DIVISION BETWIXT THE LORDS AND THE MINISTERS ABOUT HOLDING ASSEMBLEIS.

The Generall Assemblie was holdin at Edinburgh in December. The rulers of the court beganne to draw themselves apart from the brethrein, and to rage, that anie thing sould be consulted upon without their advice. They draw to themselves some of the lords, and remained in the Abbey. The cheefe commissioners of the kirks, the superintendants, and some ministers, went to them, where they were conveened in the abbot's loodging, within Halyrudhous. The lords compleaned that the ministers held their secreit coun- sels with gentlemen without their knowledge. The ministers deny- ed that they had done anie thing otherwise than commoun order required; and reproved them for not conveening with their bre- threin, seing they knew the order, and that the same was appoint- ed by themselves, as the Booke of Discipline, subscrived by the most part with their owne hands, would beare witnesse. Some beganne to denie that ever they knew such a thing as the Booke of Discipline; and called also in doubt whether it was ex- pedient that suche conventions sould be holdin : for gladelie would the queene and her flatterers have had all the assembleis of the godlie discharged. Her favourers alledged, that it was a mater of jealousie, that subjects sould hold Assembleis without knowledge of their prince. It was answered, That the prince understood there was a reformed kirk within this realme, and that they had their orders, and appointed times for conveening. " The queene knoweth weill eneugh," said Lethington : " But the questioun is, whether the queene alloweth suche conventiouns ?"   It was replyed, " If the libertie of the kirk sould stand upon the queene's allowance or dissallowance, we are assured we sall be deprived, not onlie of Assembleis, but also of the publick preaching of the Gospell." This reply was contemned, and the contrarie affirmed. " Time will try," said the replyer; " and I adde, take frome us the freedome of Assembleis, and take frome us the Evangell; for without Assembleis, how sall good order and unitie in doctrine be keeped ? It is not to be supposed that all ministers sall discharge their office so duelie, or behave themselves so weill in their conversatioun, as that they sall not need admonitioun. It may be, also, some refractorie persons will not admitt the admonitioun of simple ministers; for remeed wherof, it is necessar that there be Generall Assembleis holdin, in which the judgement and gravitie of manie may correct and represse the folleis and errours of a few." The most part of the nobilitie and barons approved this reason, and willed the reasoners for the queene to counsell her Grace, if she were jealous of anie thing to be treated, to send suche as she would appoint to heare.

THE RATIFICATION OF THE BOOKE OF DISCIPLINE REFUSED.

Thereafter it was propouned, that the Booke of Discipline might be ratifeid by the queene's Majestie. Lethington scripped[1] at this motioun, and asked, how manie of these that had subscrived it would be subject to it ? It was answered, " All the godlie." " Will the duke ?" said Lethington. " If he will not, I wishe he were scrapped out," said Uchiltrie, "not onlie out of that booke, but also out of our number and companie ; for to what purpose sall travell be takin to sett the kirk in order, if it be not keeped ; or to what end sall men subscrive, if they never meane to performe ?" Lethington answered, " Manie subscrived them, *in fide parentum*, as the barnes are baptized." " Ye thinke that stuffe proper," answered Mr Knox, " but it is als untrue as unproper. That booke was read in publick audience, and the heads therof reasouned upon diverse dayes, as all that sitt heere knowe verie weill, and yourself

---

[1] Sneered.

cannot denie. No man, therefore, was desired to subscrive that which he understood not." " Stand content," quoth one; " the ratificatioun of the booke will not be obteaned." " Lett God," said the other, " require the detriment which this kirk and commounwealth sall find by the want of things therin prescribed, from the hands of suche as stoppe the same."

THE BARONS CRAVE PROVISION FOR MINISTERS.

The barons perceaving that the ratification of the Booke of Discipline was refused, presented certan articles to the counsell, craving idolatrie to be suppressed, kirks to be planted with qualifeid ministers, sufficient stipends to be provided for them according to equitie and conscience; for till that time the ministers lived upon men's benevolence. Manie deteaned in their owne hands the fruicts which the bishops and others of that sect had before abused, and so some part was bestowed upon the ministers; but then the bishops beganne to grippe againe to that which most unjustlie they called their owne. The Erle of Arran was discharged to intromett with the rents of Sanct Andrewes and Dumfermline, wherwith he had intrometted before in name of factorie; and so were manie others. The barons required, therefore, that their ministers might be provided, or ellis they would not suffer anie longer anie thing to be lifted to the bishop's use, more than they did before the queene's arrivall; for their religioun, which the queene promised not to alter, could not continue without ministers, and ministers could not live without provisioun. The court flatterers were somewhat moved, for the rod of impietie was not then strenthened in her and their hands. To please the queene, and to satisfie the godlie on the other side, they devised that the kirk-men sall intromett with the two parts of their benefices, and that the thrid part be lifted up to the ministers' and the queene's use.

A RYOT IN EDINBURGH.

This winter, the Erle Bothwell, the Marquesse d'Albeuf, Johne Lord Coldinghame, brake up Cuthbert Ramsaye's gates and doores, searched his hous for his daughter-in-law, Alesone Craik, in despite of the Erle of Arran, whose harlot she was suspected to have beene. The Assemblie, and also the nobilitie for the most part, were in the toun. They were so commoved, that they concluded to crave justice, as they did, by this subsequent supplicatioun :

"To the Queen's Majestie and her Secreit and Great Counsell, Her Grace's faithfull and obedient Subjects, the Professors of Christ Jesus his holie Evangell, wish the spirit of righteous judgement.

" The feare of God, conceaved of his holie Word, the naturall and unfained love we beare to your Grace, the duetie which we owe to the quietnesse of our countrie, and the terrible threatenings which our God pronounceth against everie realme and citie where horrible crimes are committed openlie, and then by the committers obstinatlie defended, compell us, a great part of your subjects, humblie to crave at your Grace upright and true judgement against suche persons as have done what in them ly to kindle God's wrathe against this whole realme. The impietie by them committed is so haynous and so horrible, that as it is a fact most vile and rare to be heard within this realme, and principallie within the Bowes of this citie, so sould we thinke ourselves guiltie of the same, if negligentlie, or yitt for worldlie feare, we passed over with silence. Therefore, your Grace may not thinke that when we crave open malefactors condignelie to be punished, that we crave anie thing but that which God hath commanded us to crave, and also hath commanded your Grace to give to everie one of your subjects. For by this hooke hath God knitt together the prince and the people; that as he commandeth honour, feare, and obedience to be givin to the powers established by him, so doth he in expresse words command and declare what the prince owes to the subjects, to witt, that as he is the minister of God, bearing the sword, for vengeance to be takin upon evill doers, and for defence of peaceable and quiett men, so ought he to draw the sword without partialitie, so oft as in God's name he is required thereto. Seing so it is, Madame, that this crime so recentlie committed, and that in the eyes of the whole realme now presentlie assembled, is so haynous, (for who heertofore hath heard within the Bowes of Edinburgh, gates and doores under silence of night burst up, houses riped, and that with hostilitie, seeking a woman, as appeareth, to oppresse her?) seing, we say, this cryme is so heynous, that all godlie men feare not onlie God's sore displeasure to fall upon you and your whole realme, but also that suche libertie breede contempt, and in end seditioun, if remedic in time be not provided; which, in our judgement, is impossible, if severe punishement be not executed for the crime committed. Therefore, we most humblie beseeke your Grace, that, all affectioun sett aside, yee declare yourself so upright in this case, that yee may give evident demonstration to all your subjects, that the feare of God, joyned with the love of commoun tranquilitie, hath principallie seate in your Grace's heart. This farther, Madame, of conscience we speeke, that as your Grace, in God's name, doth crave of us obedience, (which to rander in all things lawfull we are most willing,) so, in the same name, doe we, the whole professors of Christ's Evangell, within this your Grace's realme, crave of you and your counsell sharpe punishement for this crime; and for performance therof, that, without delay, the principall actors of this most haynous crime, and the persuers of this intended villainie, may be called before the cheefe justice of this realme, to suffer an assise, and to be punished according to the lawes of the same. Your Grace's answere most humblie we beseeke."

BOTHWELL ATTEMPTETH A NEW RYOT.

This supplication was presented by diverse gentlemen. Court
flatterers at the first disclaimed, and asked, "Who durst avow
this?" The Master of Lindsay answered, "A thowsand gentlemen
within Edinburgh." Others ashamed to oppone in publick, suborned the queene to give a gentle answere, till the conventioun
was dissolved. She wanted not craft to cloke impietie. Her uncle
was a stranger, had young companie about him; "but," said she,
"I sall putt suche order to him, and all others, that heerafter there
sall be no occasioun to compleane." How sould she punishe in
others that vice, which, in France, was free of punishement, and
practised by the king and cardinalls; as the masking and dance of
Orleance can witnesse, when virgins and men's wives were made
als commoun to King Henrie and Charles the Cardinall their court
and pages, as harlots in brothells, to their companiouns? The transgressors frequented nightlie, masked. At lenth, the duke's freinds
assembled upon a night, in the High Street. The Abbot of Kilwinning, then joyned to the kirk, was the principall man at the beginning. Manie of the godlie repaired to him. Andrew Stewart,
Lord Uchiltrie, being informed of the whole proceedings, said,
"Nay, suche impietie sall not be suffered, so long as God sall assist us. The victorie that God, in his mercie, hath givin us, we
will, by his grace, mainteane;" and so commanded his sonne, the
Master, and his servants, to bring furth their speares and long weapons. Vowes were made by Bothwell, that the Hammiltons sould
be driven not onlie out of the toun, but also out of the countrie.
Johne Lord Coldinghame had mareid Bothwell's sister. This affinitie drew Lord Robert also to his assistance. The Master of Maxwell, after Lord Hereis, warned the Erle Bothwell, that if he stirred furth of his loodging, he, and suche as would assist him, sould
resist him in the face. These speeches bridled his furie. D'Albeuf,

being in his chamber, in the Abbey, start to an halbert. Ten men
were skarse able to hold him. But the danger was betweene the
Croce and the Tron. The Erle of Huntlie and Lord James came
from the queene to stay the tumult. Bothwell and his assisters
were commanded to keepe their loodgings under paine of treasoun.
But, in verie deed, either the duke had verie false servants, or elles
Lord James his death was contrived not onlie at that time, but
at other times. Upon a certane day, when Lord James was upon
horsebacke, readie to come to sermon, he was warned by one of
the duke's servants to returne, and stay with the queene. What
ground he had we cannot tell; but soone after, the duke and some
of the lords conveened at Glasgow. Their conclusions were keeped
secreit.

Upon the tenth of December, this act following was made, of the
two parts and thrids of the benefices.

" *Apud Edinburgh, decimo Decembris*, 1561.

" The which day, forsameikle as the queene's Majestie, by the
advice of the Lords of her Secreit Counsell, forseing the imminent
troubles which apparentlie were to rise among the leiges of this
realme, for maters of religioun; to stay the same, and to evite all
incommodities that might therupon ensue, intercommuned with a
part of the clergie and state ecclesiasticall, with whom then reasonning being had, it was thought good and expedient by her Highnesse, that a General Assemblie sould be appointed the 15th of
December instant, wherto the rest of the states might have repaired, and by advice of the whole, a reasonable overture made for
staying of appearing trouble, and quietting of the whole realme.
Which conventioun being by her Majestie appointed, and sundrie
dayes of counsell keeped, and the said ecclesiasticall estate oft times
required that the said order might be taken, and overture made for
staying of the trouble, and quietting of the countrie. Last of all, in
presence of the queene's Majestie, and Lords of Counsell forsaid,
and others of the nobilitie of this realme, compeared Johne Archbishop of Sanct Andrewes, Patrick Bishop of Murrey, Henric Bishop

of Rosse, and Robert Bishop of Dunkelden ; and for themselves respective offered unto the queene's Majestie, to be content of two parts
of the rents of their benefices, and the fourth part to be imployed as
her Majestie thought expedient. And, becaus the certantie therof
was not knowne, nor yitt what summes of money would susteane the
ministrie and ministers of God's Word within this realme, neither
yitt how muche was necessarie to support the queene's Majestie
above her owne rents for the commoun effaires of the countrie ;
therefore, it is decerned, concluded, and determined, by the queene's
Majestie, and Lords of her Counsell foresaid, and others of the nobilitie present, that if the fourth part of the fruicts of the whole
benefices within this realme may not be sufficient to susteane the
ministrie within this whole realme, and support the queene's Majestie, to interteane and sett fordward the commoun effaires of the
countrie ; failing whereof, the thrid part of the saids fruicts, or
more, whill it sall be sufficient to the effect forsaid, to be taken up
yeerelie, in time comming, till a generall order be taken therin, so
muche therof to be imployed to the queene's Majestie for the enter-
teaning and setting fordward of the commoun effaires of the countrie, and so muche therof to the ministers, and sustentatioun of the
ministrie, as may reasonablie susteane the same, at the sight and
discretioun of the queene's Majestie and counsell forsaid ; and the
excrescence and superplus to be assigned to the old possessors.
And, to the effect that the rents and yeerelie availe of the whole
benefices of this realme may be cleerelie knowne to the queene's
Majestie and counsell forsaid, it is statute and ordeaned, that the
whole rentall of the benefices of this realme be produced before her
Grace and lords forsaid, at the times underwrittin, that is to say,
of the benefices on this side of the Mounth, the 24th of Januarie
nixt to come, and beyond the Mounth, the 10th of Februarie nixt
therafter. And ordinar letters to be directed to the shireffs in that
part to passe, charge, and require, all and sundrie archbishops, bishops, commendatars, abbots, pryours, on this side of the Mounth,
personallie, if they can be apprehended ; and failing therof, at the
said archbishops', bishops', commendators', abbots', pryours' dwelling-

places, cathedrall, kirks, or abbeyes, and all archdeacons, deanes, chanters, subchanters, proveists, parsons, vicars, and other bene- ficed men whatsoever, their chamberlans or factors, personallie, or at their dwelling-places, or at the parish kirk where they sould remaine, to exhibite and produce before the queene's Majestie and lords forsaid, the said 24th day of Januarie nixt to come, a just and true rentall of the availes and rents of their benefices, to the effect forsaid ; and to charge the prelats, and other beneficed men on the yond side of the Mounth, in maner respective forsaid, to exhibite and produce the just and true rentalls of their benefices before the queene's Majestie and the lords forsaid, the said 10th day of Feb- ruarie, to the effect forsaid ; with certificatioun to them that faile, the queene's Grace and counsell will proceed heerin as accordeth. And siclyke, to charge the whole superintendants, ministers, elders, and deacons of the principall touns and shires of this realme, to give in before the queene's Grace, and Lords of Counsell forsaid, the 24th day of Januarie nixt to come, a formall and sufficient roll and memoriall, what may be sufficient and reasonable to susteane the ministrie, and whole ministers of the realme, that her Majestie, and Lords of Counsell forsaid, may take order therin as accordeth : and, farther, that the queene's Majestie, and Lords of Counsell forsaid, may rypelie and digestlie weygh and consider what necessarie sup- port is required to be takin yeerelie of the fruicts of the saids be- nefices, beside her Grace's owne yeerelie rent, to interteane and sett fordward the commoun effaires of this realme, against the said 24th day of Januarie nixt to come ; that then it may be proceeded in the said mater, all parteis satisfeid, and the whole countrie and leiges therof sett at quietnesse."

LETHINGTON'S AMBASSADGE TO ENGLAND.

William Matlane of Leithington, younger, being sent soone after the arrivall of our queene to Queene Elizabeth, returned before December. The effect of his negociation was to salute the queene in his mistresse's name ; to make knowne her good-will toward her,

and minde to interteane peace and unitie. He delivered also letters directed from our nobilitie, wherin they remembred courteouslie her former favour, requeisted her to provoke our queene to constant amitie by some tokins of her good affectioun; speciallie by
declaring her successour and heyre-apparent, in the nixt parliament : for that would be the most forcible meane to burie all former
rancour in oblivioun, and to exhaust the fountaine of discorde in
times to come. Queene Elizabeth answered, she expected another
ambassadge ; that his mistresse according to her promise made, to
ratifie the treatie at Leith, als soone as she returned home, and
might have the advice of her nobles. She had done so. The
other answered, that he was sent soone after her arrivall, before
she had medled with anie publick effaires : that she was busseid in
receaving courteous salutatiouns of her nobles, but most of all in
settling the estate of religioun : that manie of the nobilitie, namelie, suche as dwelt in the remote parts, were not then come to
court, without whose advices she could not resolve in suche a
mater. The queene replyed, " What needeth new consultatioun
for that to which she had alreadie bound herself by seale and subscriptioun ?" The other rejoyned, he had no commissioun for that
bussinesse. In end, the queene said, " In regarde his mistresse
hath not ratifeid the treatie, according to her promise, nor deserved
anie benefite at her hands, but rather had provoked her to anger by
usurping her armes, yitt she sould procure that nothing be done
in prejudice of her right, but leave it free to the estats to decide
betwixt her and her competitors. Successour she would declare
none. For unconstant people looke commounlie to the sunne
rysing, or designed successours, and forsake the sunne setting ;
and designed and confirmed successours cannot conteane themselves
within bounds, but animated with their owne hopes, or stirred
up by malcontents, affected present governement. I will not,"
quoth she, " be so foolish as to hang a wynding-sheet before myne
owne eyes ; or to make myself a funerall feast whill I am alive."
In end, the queene was drawin this farre, as to consent that some
commissioners sould meete for both sides, and reforme the treatie

after this maner: That the Queene of Scots absteane frome the
armes of England, and the titles of England and Ireland, during
her lyfe-time, and her childrein, if she had anie; and that neither
she, nor anie of her posteritie, seeke to waiken or diminishe anie
right our queene had to the crowne of England.

M.D.LXII.

COMMISSION GIVIN TO RECEAVE THE RENTALS OF BENEFICES.

It being ordeaned in December last past, that archbishops, bishops, abbots, and other beneficed men, their farmers and tacksmen, produce the rentall of the benefices before the queene and the
lords of her counsell, commissioun was given, becaus the queene
herself might not attend upon the recept of the rentals, the 24th
of Januarie, to Mr James Makgill of Rankeilour Neather, Clerk of
Register, Sir Johne Bellendine of Auchinnoul, knight, Justice-
Clerk, the Secretar, Treasurer, Advocat, and the Laird of Pittarow,
to call before them, within the burgh of Edinburgh, all and sundrie
prelats and beneficed men, which were charged now personnallie,
being in Edinburgh, or sall happin to repaire thither heerafter, and
require of them the rentals of their benefices. *Item*, To warne all
superintendants, ministers, elders, deacons, to give in to them the
names of the whole ministers, that her Highnesse may tak order
with the benefices, according to the tenor of the first ordinance
made therupon.

FACTORS AND CHAMBERLANS APPOINTED TO INTROMET WITH THE FRUICTS OF THE BENEFICES.

Notwithstanding of the former ordinance and commissioun, and
the waiting on of the commissioners since the 24th of Januar, yitt
few produced their rentals. It was ordeaned, therefore, by the
queene and lords of secreit counsell, the 12th of Februarie, that
factors and chamberlans be appointed to intromett, gather, uplift,

and receave, to the queene's use, all and sundrie mailes, formes, tiends, rents, provents, emoluments, gaines, profites, dueteis, of whatsomever benefices, wherof the rentals were not produced conforme to the said ordinance. And if anie rentals produced beare not the just availl, for their fraudulent dealing, to intromett with so muche of the profites and fruicts of the said benefice as were omitted : and that the producers of the rentals, and possessors of the benefices, sall never have actioun, to clame frome the tenents and occupyers more than was conteaned within the saids rentals alreadie produced by them. *Item*, That the Lords of Sessioun direct furth letters at the said factors' and chamberlans' instances, causing them to be answered of the fruicts of the saids benefices.

AN ORDINANCE FOR THE THRIDS.

Upon the 15th of Februarie it being considered, that the fourth part was not sufficient for the uses above mentioned, it was declared, that the whole thrid part of all benefices of which the rentals are produced, sall be takin up by the person or persons which sall be nominated by her Majestie ; that the samine be employed to the use forsaid, together with the whole fruicts of the benefices wherof the rentals were not produced; and that they beginne at the last crop, the yeere 1561, and that the thrid be takin up by the persons which sall be appointed for the uplifting therof : that this order sall continue till farther order be takin by the queene's Majestie, with advice of her estats. Moreover, it was ordeaned, that annuells, mailles, dueteis, within free burrows, and other touns perteaning to chapelreis, prebendareis, or friereis, together with the rents of friers' lands, where ever they be, setting and disponing therupon, be intrometted with by suche as her Grace sall appoint, and be imployed upon hospitals, schooles, and other godlie uses, as sall seeme most expedient to her Highnesse, with advice of her counsell. The Proveist and Bailiffes of Aberdeen, Elgine in Murrey, Innernesse, Glasgow, and other burrows where friereis were not demolished, were ordeaned to intertaine and uphold the saids

friers' places upon the commoun good therof, and to use the same
to the commoun weale and service of the said touns, till finall order
was takin therin, notwithstanding anie other gift, title, or interesse,
givin by the queene before to anie person, of the said places, their
yards, orchards, and other pertinents. No meane was found more
commodious for maintenance of the poore, of the schooles, and of
colledges.

THE MAKERS OF THE ACTS.

The Lords of Secreit Counsell, who were present at making of
the forsaid acts, were these following :—James Duke of Chattelerault, George Erle of Huntlie, Archibald Erle of Argile, William
Erle Marshall, Johne Erle of Atholl, William Erle of Montrose,
James Erle of Morton, Alexander Erle of Glencarne, James Commendatar of Sanct Andrewes, Johne Lord Areskine, the Treasurer,
the Secretare, the Clerk-Register, the Justice-Clerk, and the
Comptroller. The Erle of Huntlie said jesting, after making the
first act to the beneficed men : " Good day, my lords of the two
part !"

THE MINISTERS NOT CONTENT WITH THE DIVISION OF THE BENEFICES.

The ministers understood cleerelie wherat the queene and her
flatterers did shoot, and therefore spaired not to utter their minde
in publick. Mr Knox said openlie, " Weill, if the end of this order, pretended to be takin for the sustentatioun of ministers, be
happie, my judgement faileth me. I am assured, the Spirit of God
is not the author of it. I see two parts freelie givin to the devill,
and the thrid part must be divided betwixt God and the devill.
Weill," said he, " ere it be long, the devill sall have three parts of
the thrids : judge, then, what God's portioun sall be." These
speeches were unpleasant in the eares of manie. Secretare Lethington was not ashamed to affirme that the ministers being sus-

teaned, the queene would not gett at the yeere's end so muche as to buy a paire of new shoes.

MEANE STIPENDS MODIFEID TO MINISTERS.

The Erle of Argile, the Erle of Murrey, Morton, Lethington, the Justice-Clerk, and the Clerk-Register, were appointed to modifie ministers' stipends. The Laird of Pittarrow was appointed to pay them. Who would have thought, when Joseph ruled Egypt, his brethren would have returned to their famileis with emptie seckes? Least ministers sould be wanton, the modificators judged an hundreth merks sufficient to a single man, being a commoun minister. Three hundreth merks was the highest summe that was ordeaned for anie except superintendents, and some few others. The poore ministers, exhorters, and readers, compleaned at church assembleis, that neither were they able to live upon the stipends allowed, nor gett payment of that small portioun which was allowed. So faine would the comptroller have played a good varlett, and satisfeid the queene, or elles have made up his owne profite. Hence arose a commoun speeche: "The good Laird of Pittarrow was an honest, earnest professour of the true religioun; but the devill may runne away with the comptroller, for he and his collectors are become greedie factors." When ministers compleaned, some answered disdainfullie, "Manie lairds have not so muche to spend." It was replyed, that the functioun of ministers craved bookes, quietnesse, studie, and travell, to edifie the kirk, when manie lairds were waiting upon their worldlie bussinesse: the stipends of ministers, who had no trade, sould not be modifeid according to the rents of other commoun men, who might, and daylie did augment their rents by diverse meanes. They gott no other answere, but that the queene could not spaire greater summes. Oft was it cried in their eares, "O happie servants of the devill, and miserable servants of Jesus Christ, if after this life there was not a hell or a heaven! For to the servants of the devill, to your dumbe dogges, and horned bishops, to one of these idle belleis ten thowsand were little encugh. But to the servants of God, who painfullie teach Christ's Evangell, a thowsand pund is thought to passe measure." One day, in reasonning upon this mater, the secretar in choler said, " The ministers have this muche payed to them by yeere, but who among them gave ever the queene ' Gramercie ?' " One smiled, and answered, " Assuredlie I thinke, that suche as have receaved anie thing gratis of the queene are unthankfull if they acknowledge it not. I am assured ministers have receaved nothing gratis : yea, it may be called in question, whether they receave anie thing at all of the queene. The queene hath no better title to that which she usurpeth, whether in giving to others, or taking to herself, than these that crucifeid Christ had to divide his garments ; yea, not so good : for suche spoile ought to be the rewarde of suche men ; yitt the souldiours were more humane, for they parted not the garments of our Maister till he was crucifeid. But the queene and her flatterers part the spoile, whill poore Christ is preaching among us. Lett the Papists, who have the two parts, and some the thrids free, and others who have gottin abbaceis and kirk lands in few, thanke the queene, and sing, ' Placebo Domine :' the poore preachers will not yitt flatter for feeding of their belleis." These speeches bred no small displeasure against the speaker ; but the flatterers escaped not free of punishment.

THE ERLEDOM OF MURREY BESTOWED UPON LORD JAMES.

The queene made Lord James Erle of Marr. But becaus the Lord Areskine claimed right to the erledome, soone after the queene bestowed upon Lord James the Erledome of Murrey. The Erle of Huntlie, who had injoyed the Erledome of Murrey ever since the death of James Stuart, brother to King James the Fyft, hunted for all occasions to trouble the estat of the countrie, misconstrued all the actiouns of the new made erle, and presented to the queene a libell, wherin he charged him with affectatioun of tyrannie, but upon so slight grounds as that the accusatioun was not regarded. The excesse of the briddell made at the solemnization of the Erle of Murrey's mariage, upon the 8th of Februarie, offended manie of the godlie, so much the rather becaus he had hithertills behaved himself temperatlie.   Then beganne the mask-ing, which continued sum yeeres after.   He mareid **Agnes** Keith, daughter to the Erle Marshall.

ARRAN RECONCILED WITH BOTHWELL : ACCUSETH HIM SOONE
AFTER OF TREASOUN.

The Erle of Bothwell, by the mediatioun of James Baron, burges of Edinburgh, obteaned conference with Mr Knox.   They conferred first in James Baron's lodging, and after in Mr Knox his studie. The erle confessed the lewdnesse of his former life, and the wrongs he had done by the entysement of the queene regent.   He con-fessed he had misbehaved himself to the Erle of Arran, and that he was willing to redeeme his favour, if it were possible : "For," said he, " if I might have my Lord Arran's favour, I would await upon the court with a paidge, and some few servants, to spaire charges; where as now, I am constrained for my owne safetie to susteane a number of wicked men, to the utter consumptioun of that part of my patrimonie which yitt remaineth."   Mr Knox, after some pro-fessioun of Scotish kindnesse, becaus his grandfather, goodsir, and father, had served his predecessors, and some of them lost their lives under their service, counselled him to beginne at God, whose majestie he had offended ; with whom, if he were reconciled, he would bow the hearts of men to forgett all offences.   If he con-tinued in godlinesse, he promised he sould have him at command. The erle desired him to trie if the Erle of Arran would be content to accept him in his favours, which he promised to doe.   In the time of his travells, the Erle Bothwell persued the Laird of Ormis-ton, and tooke his sonne, Alexander Cockburne, careid him to Borthwicke, but sent him backe againe.   Mr Knox was offended ; yitt upon his excuse, and declaration of his minde, he re-entered in new travells, and brought the mater so to passe, that the Laird of Ormeston, upon whose satisfactioun stood the greatest stay of the

agreement, referred his satisfactioun in all things to the judgements
of the Erles of Arran and Murrey, to whome the said erle submitted himself in that heed, and therupon delivered his hand-writt.

So, being convoyed by certan of his freinds to the Kirk of Feild,
where the Erle of Arran loodged, and Mr Knox with him, to beare
witnesse to the agreement, as he entered in at the chamber doore,
and would have givin these honours which freinds had appointed,
the Erle of Arran went to him, embraced him, and said, " If the
heart be upright, few ceremoneis may serve." Mr Gawin Hammiltoun, Abbot of Kilwinning, and the Laird of Rickerton, were the
cheefe communers. Mr Knox said, " Now, my lords, God hath
brought you together by the labours of simple men. I know my
travells are alreadie takin in evill part : but seing I have the testimonie of a good conscience, that what I have done I have done
for the weill of you both, and for the hurt of none, I beare the more
patientlie the misreports and judgements of men. Now I leave you
in peace, and desire you who are freinds to be carefull that amitie
encrease." The erles embraced other, went to a window, and conferred together a certane space. The nixt day, the Erle Bothwell
convoyed the Erle of Arran to the kirk, to heare the sermoun,
wherat manie rejoiced. The Thursday nixt they dynned together.
Therafter, Bothwell and Mr Gawin Hammiltoun road to Kinneil to
the duke.

What communicatioun was amongst them was not knowne, but
so farre as the Erle of Arran made knowne to the queene's Grace
and the Erle of Murrey ; for, upon the fourth day after the reconciliation, the sermon being ended, the Erle of Arran came to Mr
Knox his hous. Mr Knox was occupeid, as commounlie he was
wont to be after sermoun, in directing of letters. In the meane
time, the Erle openeth the greefe of his minde to Mr Richard
Strang and Alexander Guthrie. When Mr Knox had ended, he
called these three together, and said, " I am treasonablie betrayed." With these words he beganne to weepe. " My lord,
who hath betrayed you ?" said Mr Knox. " One Judas or other,"
said he : " I know it is but my life that is sought ; but I regarde it

not." Then said Mr Knox, "I understand not suche darke maner
of speeking." "Weill," said he, "I take you three to witnesse,
that I reveele this to you, and I will write to the queene. An
act of treasoun is layed upon me. The Erle of Bothwell hath
shewed to me that he sall take the queene, and putt her in my
hands, in the castell of Dumbartane; and that he sall slay the Erle
of Murrey, Lethington, and others that now misguide her, and so
sall I and he rule all. I know this is devised to bring me within
compasse of treasoun, for he will informe the queene of it. But I
take you to witnesse, that here I reveele it to you; and I will goe
write incontinent to the queene's Majestie, and to my brother, the
Erle of Murrey." "Did you consent to anie part?" said Mr Knox.
He answered, "Nay." Then said he, "In my judgement his words
cannot harme you. The performance of the fact depended upon
your will. Ye say yee have disassented; so the purpose sall vanishe and dee of itself, unlesse yee waken it. It is not to be supposed that he will harme you in that which himself devised, and
wherto yee would not consent." "O," said he, "wounder not what
craft is used against me. It is treasoun to conceale treasoun."
"My lord," said he, "treasoun must import consent and determinatioun. In my judgement, it sall be more sure and honorable to
relie upon your owne innocencie, and abide the unjust accusatioun
of another, if anie follow therupon, as I thinke there sall not, than
to accuse, speciallie after so late reconciliatioun." "I know," said
the erle, "he will offer the combat to me. That will not be suffered
in France; but I will doe that which I have said." So he went to
his loodging, and tooke with him Mr Richard Strang and Alexander Guthrie. He wrote a letter, and directed it with diligence to
the queene, then resident in Falkland, and road after to Kinneill to
the duke his father. From thence he directed a letter to the Erle
of Murrey, writtin with his owne hand in ciphers, wherin he compleaned of the rigorous handling by his father and freinds. He assureth him that he feared his life, in case remedie were not provided in time. But he stayed not upon anie remedie, but brake
the chamber doore where he was enclosed, and with great paine

1

went to Stirline. Frome thence he was convoyed to Halyards.
He stayed till the Erle of Murrey came to him, and convoyed
him to Falkland, to the queene, who was then informed sufficientlie; and, upon suspicioun conceaved, caused apprehend Mr
Gawin Hammiltoun and the Erle Bothwell, who knowing nothing of the former advertisements, were come to Falkland, which
augmented the former suspicioun. But Mr Knox, by his letters, procured all things to be used more circumspectlie. He willed the
Erle of Murrey not to give great credite to the Erle of Arran his
words and inventions, for he perceaved him to be stricken with
phrenesie. As he advertised, so it came to passe; for, within few
dayes, he imagined he had seene wonderfull signes in the heavens.
He alledged he was bewitched. He would have beene in the
queene's bed, and affirmed that he was her husband. He behaved
himself so foolishlie, that his phrenesie could not be hid; yitt Bothwell and the Abbot of Kilwinning were keeped in the castell of
Sanct Andrewes. When they were called before the counsell, Arran constantlie affirmed that Bothwell proponed suche things
wherof he advertised the queene's Grace; but he stiffelie denyed
that his father, the abbot, or his freinds, understood anie thing of
that mater, or that they intended anie violence against him, and alledged he was inchanted so to thinke and write. The queene,
highlie offended therat, committed him to prisoun, with the other
two, in the castell of Sanct Andrewes. They were after convoyed
to the castell of Edinburgh. James Stuart of Cardonald, called
Captan James, appointed to be the erle's keeper, was evill bruited
for the evill interteanement of him in this estate. It was concluded
in counsell, the 18th of Aprile, that in consideratioun of the former
suspicioun and accusatioun, the duke sall rander to the queene the
castell of Dumbartan. The custodie of it had beene granted to him
by appointment, till the queene had lawfull issue of her owne bodie;
but will prevailed against promise, so the castell was randered to
Captan Anstruther, as having power frome the queene.

Thus have I related this part of the historie, as Mr Knox hath
sett it doun in the Fourth Booke of his Historie. Mr Buchanan his

relatioun is somewhat different. He writeth that James Hepburne, Erle Bothwell, resolved to raise trouble in the countrie, that so he might fish in drumlie waters, or to attempt some flagitious crime whereby he might recover his estate. First, he preasseth to perswade the Erle of Murrey to seeke the overthrow of the Hammiltons. But, finding him to abhorre his counsell, he offered to the Hammiltons to assist to the murther of the Erle of Murrey : " For then," said he, " the queene, will she, nill she, must be enthralled as you please. The most convenient time for the murther, and conveying away of the queene, will be," said he, " when the Erle of Murray cometh furth with her to the hunting, in the parke of Falkland." A time was appointed for executioun. The Erle of Arran, abhorring the fact, advertised the Erle of Murrey by a missive. Answere was returned by the same messinger; but the Erle of Arran being absent, the letters were delivered to his father. His father, after consultatioun with his freinds, committeth him to strait custodie. The erle escaped by night, came to Falkland on the morne, and discovered the whole mater and maner. Soone after, the Erle of Bothwell and the Abbot of Kilwinning, who sould have putt the device in executioun, were apprehended at Falkland, at the queene's command, and a guarde sett to keepe them. Spyes sent furth to try the feilds, reported they had seene horsemen appeare in sundrie places. Arran was more particularlie inquired what sould have beene the maner ? The immoderat love he careid to the queene, and sure freindship with the Erle of Murrey, on the one side, the care he had, out of naturall love, to exeme his father out of the number of the conspirators, distracted his minde. He gott no rest the night following; and the day after, was perceaved to be distracted in his witts. There proceeded other occasiouns as preparatives; for where as he wont to be weill accompaneid, his father being somewhat needie and counselled by his freinds, allowed him but one servant to waite upon him. Bothwell was sent to the castell of Edinburgh, Arran to the castell of Sanct Andrewes. When his witts were sattled by intervalls, he sent letters to the queene, writtin so judiciouslie and accuratlie, that he was suspected to have fained madnesse, to free his father frome guiltinesse. The rest he accused so constantlie, and with suche vehemencie, that when he could not prove before the counsell, by witnesses, so secreit a plott, he offered to fight the single combat with Bothwell. The duke first wrote to the queene, and after went to her to Sanct Andrewes, whither she was then come, and requeisted that Bothwell and Kilwinning might be delivered unto him upon sufficient pledges, which was refused. The queene demanded the castell of Dumbartane, which the duke ever held since he was governour, and it was at her command delivered. Thus you have the two different reports of our writters. Mr George Buchanan writeth farther, that George Erle of Huntlie, conceaving now a greater hatred against the Erle of Murrey, becaus the duke, father-in-law to his sonne, was brought in danger, procured a tumult to be raised in Edinburgh, wherof we have made mentioun before; hoping that the Erle of Murrey would runne up frome the Abbey to stay the tumult, and that there he might easilie be cutt off in the middest of the throng. When this device succeeded not, he appointed some of his servants to ly in waite for him in the way at night, when he was to come late frome the queene to his loodging. The Erle of Murrey was advertised. Some of Huntlie's servants were deprehended in the porche at the entrie of the Abbey, armed. He is called before the queene. He alledged that some of his servants had put on their armour becaus they were to depart home, and had beene deteaned still upon some new occasioun. The excuse was accepted, but not approved.

MR KNOX HIS SECUND CONFERENCE WITH THE QUEENE.

The queene returned to Edinburgh. Then dancing begunne to grow hote. The queene danced excessivelie till after midnight, becaus she was advertised frome France, that persecutioun was renued, and her uncles were begunne to trouble the whole realme. Mr Knox, teaching upon these words of the secund Psalme, " And now, understand, O yee kings," etc., taxed the ignorance and vanitie of princes, and their despite against all these in whome appeared

hatred of vice and love of vertue.   Mr Alexander Cockburne, his
owne scholler, was sent by the queene to bring him doun.   The
queene had a long harang to him upon the heads of his accusatioun :
That he had spokin unreverentlie of the queene ; and had travelled
to bring her in contempt and hatred of the people.   He answered,
" Madame, this is oft the just recompense God giveth to the stubborne, that becaus they will not heare God speeking to the comfort of the penitent, and for amendement of the wicked, they are
oft compelled to heare the false report of others, to their greater
displeasure.   I doubt not but it came to the eares of Herod, that
our Master, Christ, called him a foxe; but they told him not how
odious a thing it was before God to murther an innocent.   Madame,
if the reporters had beene honest men, they would have reported
my words with all the circumstances.   But becaus they want vertue
worthie of credite in court, they must have somewhat wherewith
to pleasure your Majestie, if it were but with flatterie and lees.
Madame, if your owne eares had heard; if there be in you anie
sparke of the feare of God, of honestie, and wisdome, yee could not
justlie have beene offended.   After that I had declared the dignitie
of kings and rulers, the honour wherin God hath placed them, the
obedience which is due to them, being God's lieutenants, I demanded this questioun : ' But what accompt, alas ! sall the most part of
princes make before the supreme Head and Judge, whose throne
of authoritie so manifestlie and shameleslie they abuse, so that violence and oppressioun doe occupie the throne of God heere on this
earth ?   For whill murtherers, blood-thristie men, oppressors and
malefactors, darre be bold to present themselves before kings and
princes, and the poore sancts of God are banished, what sall we
say, but the devill hath takin possessioun of the throne of God,
which ought to be fearefull to all wicked doers, and a refuge to the
innocent oppressed ?   How can it otherwise be ? for princes will
not understand, they will not be learned as God commandeth ; but
God's law they despise, his statuts and holie ordinances they will
not understand.   They are more exercised in fiddling and flinging,
than in reading and hearing of God's most blessed Word.   Fid-

dlers and flatterers, which commounlie corrupt youth, are more pretious in their eyes than men of wisdome and gravitie, who by wholesome admonitioun can beate doun some part of that vanitie and pride wherin all are borne, but in princes taketh deepe roote and strenth, by wicked educatioun.' Of dauncing, Madame, I said, that albeit I found no commendatioun of it in the Scripture, and that in profane writters it is termed the gesture rather of these that are mad and phrenetick than of sober men, yitt doe I not utterlie damne it, providing, First, that the cheefe calling of these that use that exercise be not neglected for pleasure of dancing; nixt, that they dance not as the Philistins their fathers did, for the pleasure they take in the displeasure of God's people. If anie of these two be done, they sall receave the rewarde of dancers, that is, hell, unlesse they repent. So sall their mirth be turned in suddane sorrow, for God will not alwayes afflict his people, neither yitt will he alwayes winke at the tyrannie of tyranns. If anie, Madame, will say that I spake anie more, lett him presentlie accuse me." Manie that stood by bare witnesse that he recited the verie words. The queene, after she had looked about to some of the reporters, said to him, "Your words are sharpe eneugh, as yee have spokin them; but they were told me after another maner. I know that my uncles and you are not of one religioun, and therefore I cannot blame you to have no good opinioun of them. But if yee heare anie thing of myself that mislyketh you, come and tell myself, and I sall heare you." "Madame," said he, "I am assured your uncles are enemeis to God, and his Sonne, Christ, and that for maintenance of their owne pompe and glorie they spaire not to spill the blood of manie innocents. As to your owne person, Madame, I sould be glade to doe all that I could to your Grace's contentment. I am called, Madame, to a publick functioun in the Kirk of God, and am appointed by God to rebooke the sinnes and vices of all persons. I am not appointed to come to everie one in particular, for the labour were infinite. If it please your Grace to frequent the sermouns, then sould yee fullie understand what I like or mislyke, als weill in your Majestie as in all others. Or if your Grace will assigne to me a certane day and houre, to heare the forme and substance of doctrine which is preached in publict, I will most gladelie awaite upon your Grace's pleasure, time, and place. But to come to waite upon your chamber doore, or elles where, and then to have no further libertie but to whisper in your Grace's eare, or to tell you what others thinke or speeke of you, neither will my conscience, nor the vocatioun wherunto God hath called me suffer it. For albeit I be heere now at your Grace's commandement, yitt can I not tell what other men will judge of me, that at this time of day am frome my booke, and waiting upon court." "Yee will alwayes," said she, "be at your booke ;" and so turned her backe. Mr Knox departed with a reasonnable merrie countenance. Some Papists being offended, said, "He is not affrayed." He hearing, answered, "Why sould the pleasant face of a gentlewoman make me affrayed ? I have looked in the faces of manie angrie men, and yitt have not been affrayed out of measure."

THE INTERVIEW OF THE TWO QUEENS DISAPPOINTED.

This sommer, posts went frequent betwixt our and the English queene. Great bruite there was of an interview betwixt the two queens at Yorke, and some preparatioun made in both realmes for that purpose ; but the Queene of England and her counsell behoved to attend upon the south parts, by reasoun of some appearance of warres betwixt England and France. Duke D'Awmall caused open the English ambassader's letters, who was then lying at court ; and by his procurement, an English ship, wherin another ambassader faired, was spoiled. There being appearance of warres betwixt England and France, the queene came frome Sanct Andrewes to Edinburgh, at what time the Erle of Arran was committed to waird in the castell of Edinburgh.

THE ERLE OF MURREY APPREHENDETH FIFTIE THEEVES.

The Erle of Murrey, in the meane time, made a privie road to Hawick, upon the faire day, and apprehended fiftie theeves, of which number seventeene were drowned. Others were executed in Jedburgh. The cheefe were brought to Edinburgh, and suffered upon the Borrow Mure. The queene was nothing content with his prosperous interprises, but she could not be weill served without him at that time.

AN AMBASSADGE FROM SWEDEN.

This sommer there came an ambassader frome the King of Sweden, to propone mariage to our queene. He was honourablie enterteaned, but the propositioun pleased her not. Had she not beene great Queene of France?—Fy on Sweden! what is it? And yitt she refused not one farre inferiour.

THE ERLE OF LENNOX AND HIS LADIE COMMITTED TO THE TOWRE.

The Erle of Lennox and his ladie were committed to the Towre of London, for trafficking with Papists. The young Laird of Burr, a traveller in their bussinesse, was apprehended with some letters, wherupon arose their trouble.

THE FOURTH GENERALL ASSEMBLIE.

The Generall Assemblie was holdin at Edinburgh, in Mr Henrie Lane's hous, the penult day of June, where were present Mr Johne Spotswod, Superintendent of Lothiane, Mr Johne Wynerame, Superintendent of Fife, Mr Johne Willocke, Superintendent of Glasgow, Johne Areskine of Dun, Superintendent of Angus, Mr Johne Kerswell, Superintendent of Argile, together with other ministers, elders, and barons, commissioners of touns or shires.

In the first sessioun for the triell of ministers, elders, and superintendents, it was ordeaned that ministers sould be first tryed in their life, conversatioun, and doctrine, and, therefore, after the tryell of the superintendents, the elders of everie kirk to be charged, in God's name, to declare their conscience, what they knew tuiching their ministers' doctrine, life, 'maners, diligence in executioun of their office. If anie be accused or convicted of anie notable crime, he must be subject to the censure of the Kirk, and suffer punishment and admonitioun, as the Assemblie sall think good. Secundlie, After the ministers, the elders of everie kirk must be tryed, if anie man have ought to lay to the charge of anie of them. Thridlie, The accused, whether he be minister or elder, is to be removed out of the Assemblie till his caus be tried. If he be convicted, he sall have no vote till the Assemblie receave satisfactioun.

After triell takin of the whole number, then must everie superintendent, with the ministers and elders within his diocie, expone to the Assemblie the estat of the kirks in their bounds, the offences and crimes they know, to the end some remedie may be devised, at least supplication made to the superiour powers for redresse of the same. And for avoiding confusioun, lotts are to be cast, what diocie sould first be heard, what nixt, and so furth of the rest. It was ordeaned, that if ministers be disobedient to superintendents, in anie thing belonging to edificatioun, that they must be subject to correctioun.

It was ordeaned, that a charge sould passe frome everie superintendent to all ministers within their bounds, to warn their kirks of the order takin, to witt, that the superintendents, ministers, elders, and deacons, doe willinglie subject themselves to discipline; and if anie man have anie thing to lay justlie to their charge, that they doe the same in the nixt Assemblie, which is to be holdin in December; and that no minister leave his flocke for comming to the said Assemblie, except he have complaints to make, or elles be compleaned upon, or, at least, be warned thereto by the superintendent.

In the secund sessioun, holdin the last of June, it was answered by the Assemblie to Mr Alexander Gordoun, tuiching the superintendentship of Galloway, First, That they understood not how he hath anie nominatioun or presentatioun, either by the Lords

of Secreit Counsell or province of Galloway. Secundarilie, Albeit
he had presentatioun of the Lords, yitt he had not observed the
order keeped in the electioun of superintendents, and, therefore,
cannot acknowledge him for anie superintendent lawfullie called,
for the present. Yitt they offered their furtherance, if the kirks of
Galloway sould sute, and the lords present. It was ordeaned,
that letters be sent to the kirks of Galloway, to learne whether
they craved anie superintendent or not, and whom they sought.
He was required, before he went frome the Assemblie, to subscribe
the Booke of Discipline.

It was acted, that ministers sould be subject to superintendents,
as is prescribed in the Booke of Discipline, and forme of admissioun of superintendents. Secundarilie, That so manie ministers
as have beene accepted of their kirks, after triell offered, and libertie granted to them to receave or refuse, sall remaine as lawfull
ministers, unlesse after that time they have beene found criminall
in life or doctrine; and that suche as serve in the kirks without
publick and free admissioun, it sall be free for the kirks to reteane
or refuse them, as they be able to rander a reason wherfore they
refuse. Thridlie, That all those who have not beene alreadie examined, sall be examined in the presence of the superintendent, and
of the best reformed kirk within his bounds, neerest the place
where the minister is to be established; providing alwise, that the
judgement of the best learned who are present be sought at the
examinatioun or admissioun, and that he who is so admitted sall
not be removed, according to the order of the Booke of Discipline.
Fourthlie, That superintendents take compt in time of their visitatioun, what bookes everie minister hath, and how he profiteth frome
time to time.

In the thrid sessioun, holdin the first day of Julie, concerning
the disobedience and negligence of elders in assisting ministers to
correct offenses, and sometimes of the whole people in refusing to
be subject to discipline, it was concluded, that the minister sall
diligentlie require his elders, and everie one of them, to assist him
in all their lawfull meetings; wherin, if they be found negligent,

then sall he proceed to admonitiouns, according to Christ's rule; which if they, or anie of them, obey not, then sall the minister, with so manie of the kirk as will subscrive with him, notifie the same to the superintendent. And if he by his admonitiouns can profite nothing, that then, by his advice, the disobedients be excommunicated; and that magistrats subject to Christ's rule be not exeemed frome the same punishment. Secundarilie, Tuiching persons to be nominated to kirks, that none be admitted without the nominatioun of the people, and due examinatioun and admissioun of the superintendent; and who have beene otherwise intrused since the fiftie-eight yeere, to make supplicatioun for their provisioun, according to the forsaid act.

In the fourth sessioun, holdin the secund day of Julie, Mr Johne Scharp was asked, Whether he would serve in the Kirk of God, where the Assemblie would place him? He answered, He was content to imploy his gifts to the comfort of the Kirk; but seing the charge of the ministrie required the preaching of the Word, and ministratioun of the Sacraments, till he atteaned to farther knowledge he could not accept the same. The Assemblie finding him able to preache, and minister the sacraments, as he had done before, charged him to re-enter to the ministrie.

In this sessioun it was ordeaned, that Mr Craig sould be joyned with Mr Knox in the ministrie of Edinburgh; that Mr James Greg sould assist the superintendent of Glasgow till Michaelmasse, and thereafter teache in the parishes belonging to the Lord Areskine, till the nixt Assemblie; that Mr George Hay, the superintendent of Glasgow, Mr Robert Hammilton, minister of Mauchline and Uchiltrie, preache in the unplanted kirks of Carrick monethlie by course, till the nixt Assemblie; that Mr James Pont minister the Word and Sacraments till the nixt Assemblie; that Mr Robert Pont doe the like in Dumblane, till the nixt Assemblie. The harvest was great, and the labourers few, therefore were they driven to devise this kind of supplee and helpe.

In the sixt sessioun it is ordeaned, that Mr Johne Scharpe serve in the ministrie, where the Superintendent of Lothiane sould appoint ; and if he refused, that the censures of the Kirk be executed against him.

Mr Patrik Cockburne, Mr Thomas Hepburne, Mr David Lindsay, or elles Mr Johne Gaig, were appointed to preache in the unplanted kirks of the Merce, their moneth by course.

Johne Dowglas of Pumferston, compleaning in name of the kirk of Calder, that they are defrauded diverse times of the preaching of the Word, since their minister was elected Superintendent of Lothiane, desired the said superintendent to be restored to them againe, or some qualified minister to be provided to them. It was answered, the profite of manie kirks is to be preferred to the profite of one particular ; and that the kirk of Calder sould either be occupied by himself, or by some other qualified person in his absence, which could not be otherwise helped in this raritie of the ministrie, and that they sould have compleaned, when the publick edict was sett furth twentie dayes before his admissioun.

The Assemblie being informed, that Mr David Spence gave institution, by vertue of the Pop's Bulls, to Mr Robert Auchimmowtie, of the prebendrie of Ruffill, the 25th of June last bypast, ordeaned, that the Superintendents of Fife and Lothiane tak order with the forsaid persons respective, and informe the Justice-Clerk, if they find the mater cleerelie tryed, that he may call them to particular dyets for breaking the queen's acts ; and that the Superintendent of Lothian informe the duke therof.

The tenor of the supplication which was to be presented to the queen's Majestie and her counsell was read in open audience of the Assemblie, and approved, as followeth :—

"To the Queen's Majestie, and her most Honorable Counsell, the Superintendents and Ministers of the Evangell of Jesus Christ within this realme, together with the Commissioners of the whole Kirks, desire grace and mercie from God, the Father of our Lord Jesus Christ, with the spirit of upright judgement.

"Having in minde that fearefull sentence pronounced by the

Eternall God against the watchemen that see the sword of God's
punishment approache, and doe not in plaine words forewarne the
people, yea, the princes and rulers, that they may repent, we cannot but signifie unto your Highnesse and counsell, that the estate
of this realme is suche for the present, that unlesse redresse and remedie be shortlie provided, that God's hand can not long spaire in
his anger to strike the head and the taile; the inobedient prince
and sinfull people. For as God is unchangable and true, so must
he punishe, in these our dayes, the greevous sinnes which before,
we read, he hath punished in all ages, after he hath long called for
repentance, and none is showin. And that your Grace and counsell may understand what be the things we desire to be reformed,
we will beginne at that which we assuredlie know to be the fountaine and spring of all other evills that now abound in this realme;
to witt, that idol and bastard service of God, the masse. The
fountaine we call it of all impietie, not onlie becaus manie tak boldnesse to sinne by reason of that opinioun which they have conceaved of that idol, to witt, that by the vertue of it they gett remissioun of their sinnes, but also, becaus that under this colour of
masse, are whoores, adulterers, drunkards, blasphemers of God,
contemners of his holie sacraments, and suche others manifest malefactors mainteaned and defended. For lett anie masse-sayer, or
earnest mainteaner therof, be deprehended in anie of the foresaid
crimes, no executioun can be had: for all is done in hatred of his
religioun. And so are the wicked permitted to live wickedlie,
cloked and defended by that odious idol. But suppose that the
masse were occasioun of no suche evills, yitt, in itself it is so odious
in God's presence that we cannot cease with all instance to desire
the removing of the same, as weill frome yourself, as from all others
within this realme; taking heaven and earth, yea, and our owne
consciences to record, that the obstinat maintenance of that idol
sall be in the end to you destructioun of soule and bodie. If your
Majestic demand, why now we are more earnest than we have
beene heeretofore, we answere, (our former silence no wise excused,)
becaus we find us frustrated of our hope and expectatioun, which

was, that in processe of time, your Grace's heart sould have beene
mollifeid so farre, as that yee sould have heard the publick doctrine
taught within this realme; by the which our further hope and expectation was, that God's holie Spirit sould have moved your heart,
that you would have suffered your religioun (which before God
is nothing but abomination and vanitie) to have been tried by the
true tuichestone, the writtin Word of God; and that your Grace
finding it to have no ground nor foundatioun in the same, sould
give that glorie unto God, that yee would have preferred his truthe
unto your owne pre-conceaved vaine opinion, of what antiquitie
that ever it hath beene; wherof we, in a part now disappointed,
can no longer keepe silence, unlesse we mak ourselves criminall before God of your blood, perishing in your owne iniquitie; for we
plainlie admonishe you of the dangers to come.

"The secund that we require is punishment of horrible vices,
suche as are adulterie, fornicatioun, open whordome, blasphemie,
contempt of God, of his Word and sacraments, which, in this
realme, for laike of punishment, doe even now so abound, that sinne
is reputed to be no sinne. And, therefore, as that we see the signes
of God's wrath now manifestlie appearing, so doe we forewarne,
that he will strike ere it be long, if his law, without punishment, be
permitted thus manifestlie to be contemned. If anie object that
punishment can not be commanded to be executed without a parliament, we answere, that the Eternall God, in his parliament, hath
pronounced death to be the punishment of adulterie and of blasphemie; whose acts, if yee putt not in execution, (seing that kings
are but his lieutenants, having no power to give life where he commandeth death,) as that he will repute you and all others that foster vice patrons of impietie, so will he not faile to punishe you for
neglecting of his judgements.

"Our thrid requeist concerneth the poore, who be of three sorts:
the poore labourers of the ground; the poore desolate beggers, orphans, wedowes, and strangers; and the poore ministers of Christ
Jesus his holie Evangell, which are all so cruellie intreated by this

last pretended order takin for sustentatioun of ministers, that their latter miserie farre surmounteth the former. For now, the poore labourers of the ground are so oppressed by the crueltie of these that pay their thrid, that they, for the most part, advance upon the poore whatsoever they pay to the queene, or to anie other. As for the verie indigent and poore, to whome God commandeth a sustentatioun to be provided of the tithes, they are so despised, that it is a wounder that the sunne giveth heate and light to the earth, where God's name is so frequentlie called upon, and no mercie (according to his commandments) shewen to his creatures. And as for the ministers, their livings are so appointed, that the most part sall live a beggar's life. And all cometh of that impietie, that the idle belleis of Christ's enemeis must be fed in their former delicaceis. We darre not conceale from your Grace and honours our conscience, which is this, that neither by the law of God, neither by anie just law of men, is anie thing due unto them who doe now exact of the poore and riche the two parts of their benefices, as they call them. And, therefore, we most humblie require that some order be takin with them, not that they be sett up again to impire above the people of God; for we feare that suche usurpatioun to their former estate be neither in the end pleasing to themselves, nor profitable to them that would place them in that tyrannie. If anie thinke that a competent living is to be assigned unto them, we repugne not, provided that the labourers of the ground be not oppressed, the poore be not utterlie neglected, and the ministers of the Word so sharplie intreated as they are now; and, finallie, that these idle belleis who by law can crave nothing, sall confesse that they receave their sustentatioun, not of debt but of benevolence. Our humble requeast is, therefore, that some suddane order may be takin, that the poore labourers may find releefe, and that in everie parochin some portioun of the tithes may be assigned to the sustentation of the poore within the same; and likewise, that some publick releefe may be provided for the poore within the burghes; that collectors may be appointed to gather, and right sharpe compt

may be takin, als weill of their recepts as of their deliverance. The
farther consideration to be had to our ministers, we in some part
remitt to your wisdoms, and to their particular complaints.

" Our fourth petition is for the manses, yards, and gleebes justlie
apperteaning to ministers, without which it is impossible to them
quietlie to serve their charges : and, therefore, we desire that order
be takin therinto, without delay.

" Our fyft concerneth the inobedience of certan wicked persons,
who not onlie trouble, and have troubled, ministers within their
functiouns, but also disobey the superintendents in their visitatioun,
wherof we humblie crave remedie ; which we doe, not so muche for
anie feare that we or our ministers have of Papists, but for the love
we beare to the commoun tranquillitie. For this we cannot hide
from your Majestie and counsell, that if the Papists thinke to
triumphe where they may, and doe what they list, where there is
not a partie able to resist them, that some will thinke that the
godlie must beginne where they left, who heertofore have borne all
things patientlie, in hope that law sould have bridled the wicked ;
wherof if they be frustrated, (albeit that nothing is more odious to
them than tumults and domesticall discords,) yitt will men attempt
the uttermost, before that in their owne eyes they behold the hous
of God demolished, which, with danger and travell, God within this
realme hath erected by them.

" Last, we desire that suche as receave remissioun of their thrids
be compelled to susteane the ministrie within their bounds, or elles
we forwarne your Grace and counsell, that we feare that the people
sall reteane the whole in their hands, untill suche time as their ministers sall be sufficientlie provided. We farther desire the kirks
to be repaired, according to an act sett furth by the Lords of Secreit Counsell, before your Majestie's arrivall in this countrie ; that
judges be appointed to heare the causes of divorcement, for the
Kirk can no longer susteane that burthein, especiallie becaus there is
no punishment for the offenders ; that sayers and hearers of masse,
profaners of the sacraments, suche as have entered into bencfices
by the Pope's Bulls, and suche other transgressers of the law made

at your Grace's arrivall within this realme, may be severallie punished; for elles men will thinke that there is no truthe in making
of suche laws. Farther, we most humblie desire of your Grace and
honorable counsell a reasonable answere to everie one of the heads
before writtin, that the same being knowne, we may somewhat satisfie suche as be greevouslie offended at manifest iniquitie now
mainteaned, at oppressioun, under colour of law, done against the
poore, and at the rebellioun and disobedience of manie wicked persons against God's Word and holie ordinance. God, the Father of
our Lord Jesus Christ, so rule your hearts, and direct your Grace
and counsell's judgement, by the dytement and illumination of his
Holie Spirit, that yee may answere so, that your conscience may
be absolved in the presence of that righteous Judge, the Lord
Jesus. And then, we doubt not but yourselves sall find felicitie;
and this poore realme, that long hath beene oppressed by wicked
men, sall injoy tranquillitie and rest, with the true knowledge of
God."

This letter is extant in the Fourth Booke of Mr Knox his Historie. In the Register of the Acts of the Assemblie, we find complaints made by ministers, exhorters, and readers, of the smalnesse
of their stipend, or of not-payment of the same, becaus the thrids
were givin away by the queene; and agreement to mak supplicatioun for manses and gleebes to ministers, reparatioun of kirks,
maintenance of schooles out of the two parts of benefices; and in
burrowes, by annuel rents, and other suche things as served before
to idolatrie : for removing of idolatrie; for punishing all vices commanded by the law of God to be punished, not punishable by the
lawes of the realme; to witt, blasphemie of God's name, contempt
of the Word and Sacraments, profanatioun of the same by suche as
were not lawfullie called to the ministratioun of the same; perjurie,
taking the name of God commounlie in vaine, breache of the Sabboth by keeping commoun mercats, adulterie, fornicatioun, filthie
speeches. *Item,* To requeist the Justice-Clerk to tak order with
Mr William Scot of Balwerie, for disobedience to the Superintendent of Fife; and Mr James Mackverit in Boote, for disobedience

to the Superintendent of Argile.   Tuiching the actioun of divorcements, it was thought good, that supplication sould be made to the
Secreit Counsell, that either they would transferre the judgement
of divorcement to the Kirk and their sessiouns, or elles establishe
men of good lives, knowledge, and judgement, to order the same,
providing the saids lords provide how the guiltie persons divorced
sall be punished.

THE SUPPLICATION CENSURED BY SOME COURTEOURS.

The supplicatioun above writtin being read in publick assemblie,
was approved of all.   Some wished more sharpnesse, becaus the
time so craved.   But the courteours, speciallie Lethington, could
not abide suche hard speeking.   " Who ever saw it writtin," said
he, " to a prince, that ' God would strike the head and the taile ?'
—that ' if the Papists did what they list, men would beginne where
they left ?'   But that the queene would raise up Papists and Papistrie againe, and to putt that in the heads of the people, was no
lesse crime than treasoun ; yea, oathes were givin, that she never
meant suche a thing."   It was answered, that the prophet Isay useth
suche maner of speeking ; a man acquainted with the court, and
said to be of the king's stocke.   Howsoever it was, he spake to the
court, to judges, ladeis, princes, and preests.   If these words offend
you, ' men must beginne where they have left, in cace Papists doe
as they doe,' we would desire you to teache us, not so muche how
we sall speeke, as what we sall doe, when our ministers are beaten,
our superintendents disobeyed, and a plaine rebellion decreed
against all good order.   " Compleane," said Lethington.   " Whom
to ?" said the other.   " To the queen's Majestie," said Lethington.
" How long ?" said the whole number.   " Till yee get remedie,"
said the Justice-Clerk : " give me their names, and I sall give you
letters."   " If the sheep," said one, " sall compleane to the wolfe,
that the wolve's whelpes have devoured her lambes, the compleaner
sall stand under danger, but the offender sall have libertie to hunt
after his prey."   " Suche comparisons," said Lethington, " are un-

savourie; for I am assured the queene will never erect nor mainteane Poperie." " Lett your assurance," said the other, " serve
yourself; it cannot serve us, for her proceedings argue the contrarie." It was concluded that the supplicatioun sould be presented as it was conceaved, unlesse the secretare would frame another agreeable to the purpose. He promised to keepe the substance, but said, he would use other termes. The first conceaver
said, he served the Assemblie, and was contented his dytement
sould be changed as best pleased them, providing he were not compelled to subscrive to the flatterie of suche as regarded moe the
persons of men and weomen than the simple truthe. The supplication was givin to Lethington to be reformed. He so framed it,
that when it was delivered to the queene by the Superintendents of
Lothiane and Fife, and she had read somewhat of it, she said,
" Heere are manie faire words: I cannot tell what the hearts
meane." So faired it with his oratorie, that they were termed by
the nixt name to flatterers and dissemblers; but for that seasoun,
the Assemblie receave no other answere.

CORRICHIE FEILD.

Soone after the Assemblie, Johne Gordoun of Finlatoure, sonne
to the Erle of Huntlie, sett upon the Lord Ogilvie betwixt nyne
and ten at night, in the streets of Edinburgh, and hurt him, becaus
old Finlatour had resigned to Ogilvie, as appeared, the right of certan lands which he was persuing by the law, and like to evict.
Johne Gordoun was takin, and putt in the tolbuith; but within
few dayes brake his warde, not without the instigation of his father, as was alledged, for he was making preparatioun for the
queen's comming to the north. The queene went from Stirline in
the moneth of August toward the north. No good was meant to
the Erle of Murrey, nor to suche as depended upon him at that time.
The Hammiltons, the Gordons, the Hepburns, thristed for his overthrow. The Gwises plotted his destructioun, becaus they could not
effectuat restauratioun of Poperie, so long as he lived. They wrote

to the queene, to feed Huntlie with hopes of a matche with his sonne
Johne, that so he might be wonne to be an instrument to execute
her intentions; and sent her, beside, the names of suche as they
would have cutt off. The Pope egged her fordward. She sought
money frome the Pope, as it were, to wage warre against those
that had made defectioun from the Roman kirk, but, indeid, to susteane her pompe and prodigalitie. The Pope his grant was obscure;
but the cardinall answered plainlie, she sould laike no money to
suche warres, as soone as those whose names she had receaved in
row were killed. The queene shewed these letters to the Erle of
Murrey, and others destinated for the slaughter, either becaus she
suspected the plott to have beene bewrayed, or to give a shew of
a sincere minde. She fained a longing desire to visite the north.
She came to Aberdeen about the middest of August. She hated
the Erle of Murrey for his innocencie and uprightnesse of life; the
Erle of Huntlie, for his perfidie to her father and mother, and feared
his great power in the north. But her uncles, above all things,
sought the murther of the Erle of Murrey. The Ladie Huntlie,
in her husband's name, renued the promises made for restauratioun
of the Roman religioun. The queene accepted weill her commissioun; but, said she, it cannot stand with her dignitie to be reconciled with her sonne Johne, except he re-enter in waird in Stirline.
She thought, if the Erle of Murrey were cutt off, and Johne Gordoun
of Finlatour were keeped in wairde, she needed not to be constrained to the mariage, wherof she had onlie made some shew, for another end. Huntlie was willing to satisfie the queene, but loath to
deliver his sonne, as it were, a pledge to the Erle of Marr, uncle to
the Erle of Murrey, speciallie being yitt uncertane how the queene
would take with the slaughter of the Erle of Murrey. His sonne
refused to enter. He gathered together a thowsand men, and drew
them neare to Aberdeene. The Lord Gordoun came frome the
Erle of Huntlie to the duke, to require him to putt to his hand
in the south, as he sould doe in the north, and so Knox his
crying and preaching sould not stay them. The Bishop of Sanct
Andrewes and the Abbot of Cosraguell held secreit conventions in

Pasley. The Bishop said at open table, " The queene is gone to the north, belike, to seeke disobedience : she may, perhaps, find the thing she seeketh." Whill the queene and the Erle of Huntlie were crafting with other, the Erle of Murrey caused keepe watche about his chamber in the night.   The queene is invited by Johne Leslie, a follower of the Gordons, to come to his hous, distant twelve myle from Aberdeene.   But he, not being ignorant of their secreit purpose against the Erle of Murrey, besought them not to bring suche a blott upon his hous, as to make him to be suspected guiltie of betraying the queen's brother, no evill man, nor enemie to him.   The purpose was delayed till they come to Strabogie. Whill the queen is passing fordward, Huntlie interceedeth for his sonne ; the queen alledged her authoritie was impaired, unlesse he re-entered in some waird, and remained certan dayes, for her credite.   Huntlie refused obstinatelie, either becaus he would lay the blame of the fact upon his sonne, if the queene did not approve the murther ; or, becaus, howbeit she sould approve it, if his sonne were absent and in warde, he might be keeped as a pledge, and the other purpose would tak no effect.   The queene was so offended with his obstinacie, that when she was come within sight of Stra-bogie, she turned another way ; went through Strachyla to Enner-nesse.   The queene purposed to have loodged in the castell.   Hunt-lie was captan of the castell, and shireff in these parts.   The keeper of the castell, Alexander Gordoun, was charged by an he-rald to raunder it ; but it was not randered till the nixt day.   The captan, Alexander, for his refusall, was hanged upon the toun bridge. The Lord Gordoun and his brother Johne were, in the meane time, lying in the toun, with a great number of their freinds ; but manie deserted them, namelie the Clanchattans, and came to the queene, when they understood what their purpose was.   The barons of the countrie about resorted to her.   Huntlie beganne to assemble his folkes.   The whole malice was bent against the Erle of Murrey, Secretar Lethington, and the Laird of Pitarrow, yitt the queene beganne to be affrayed, and caused warne Stirlinshire, Fife, Angus, Mernes, Stratherne, to come to Aberdeene the fyft of October, there

to remaine the space of twentie dayes. In her returning frome En-
nernesse, she craved the castells of Finlatour and Auchindoun to
be delivered, which both were denyed. Huntlie is again charged,
under the paine of treasoun, to deliver the saids houses. Whill
Huntlie sent his servant, Mr Thomas Keir, to present the keys, in
signe of some obedience, the queene had sent Captan James Stewart his sonne, with six score souldiours, to ly about the place of
Finlatoure. Whill they were loodging in Cullen, not farre frome
Finlatoure, Johne Gordoun came with a companie of horsemen,
tooke the captan, and slue some of the souldiours. The queene
was so incensed at this fact, committed, as she alledged, under trust,
that all hope of reconciliation was past. Huntlie was charged to
present himself, and his sonne Johne, before her and her counsell,
within six dayes, under paine of rebellioun. The charge was disobeyed, and he denounced rebell. He was sought in the place of
Strabogie, but escaped. Huntlie assembled his forces, marched toward Aberdeene, of purpose to tak the queene ; hoping to appease
her after with flatterie, officious service, and the mariage of his
sonne, and fullie resolved to cutt off the Erle of Murrey, the cheefe
lett of all his interprises, by one meane or other. George Gordoun,
Erle of Sutherland, reveeled to Huntlie all the queen's purposes ;
the fittest opportuniteis for execution of his bussinesse. Letters
directed frome the Erle of Sutherland and Johne Leslie were intercepted, and their whole purpose bewrayed. Leslie acknowledged
his fault, and was pardonned. Huntlie was come to the Loche of
Skyne, with seven or eight hundreth men, the 22d of October.
When he understood what had happened, he purposed to flee to
the mountaines ; but being certifeid, that the most part of those
that were about the queene were his freinds, resolveth to trie the
event. The Forbesses, Hayes, Lesleis, went out of the toun before ten houres, putt themselves in array, but approached not to
the enemie, till the Erle of Murrey and his companie were come to
the feilds, about two, afternoone, howbeit they bragged they would
fight without helpe, and desired him onlie to behold. Huntlie resolved, the night before, to retire, but could not be wakened that

morning before ten houres. When he arose, his speeche failed
him, neither could he doe anie thing right, by reason of his cor-
pulencie. Some of his freinds left him. There remained onlie
three hundreth men. He said to them, "This great companie
which approacheth will doe us no harme: I onlie feare the other
small companie which standeth upon the hill-side. But we are a
sufficient number, if God be with us." Then upon his knees he
uttered these words, "O Lord, I have been a blood-thristie man,
and by my moyen muche innocent blood hath beene spilt: if thou
will give me victorie this day, I sall serve thee all the dayes of my
life." He confessed he was guiltie of the shedding of much innocent blood, and yitt begged power and strenth to shed more;
thinking, belike, he would satisfie God for all together !

Some were sent to keepe the passages of the water, least Huntlie
sould escape. The Lesleis, Hayes, Forbesses, perceaving the Erle
of Murrey, James Dowglas, Erle of Morton, and Patrik Lindsay,
Master of Lindsay, to have lighted, and to be on foote, sett fordward against the Erle of Huntlie and his companie, who stood at
Corrichie Burne ; some call it Farabanke. They fastened heather
kowes to their steele bonnets, to be a signe that they were freinds.
Before they came within the shott of an arrow, they cast frome
them their speares and long weapons, and fled directlie in the face
of the Erle of Murrey and his companie. The Laird of Pitarrow,
the Master of Lindsay, the Tutor of Pitcur, said, "No doubt, there
is treasoun : lett us cast doun[1] our speares to the foremost, and
lett them not come in among us." So they did, for they were
marching on foote, in order. The Erle of Huntlie, seing the great
companie flee, said, "Our freinds are honest men ; lett us encounter
the rest." Secretar Lethington willed everie man to call upon God,
to remember his duetie, and not to feare the multitude. In end he
concluded thus : "O Lord, thou that ruleth the heaven and the
earth, looke upon thy servants whose blood this day is sought, and
to man's judgement is sold and betrayed. Our refuge is now unto
thee, and our hope is in thee. Judge thou, O Lord, this day be-

[1] Level.

twixt us and the Erle of Huntlie. If ever we have sought unjustlie his or their destructioun and blood, lett us fall on the edge
of the sword. If we be innocent, mainteane and preserve us, for
thy great merceis sake." Soone after the speeking of these, or the
like words, the former ranks joyned, for Huntlie's companie came
with speed. They were driven backe by the Master of Lindsay,
and the companeis of Fife and Angus. Some of the great companie returned, but gave no strokes till Huntlie's companie was
driven backe; then they strike, and committ almost all the slaughter that was committed that day, to cleere themselves of suspicioun.
There were killed upon Huntlie's side an hundreth and twentie;
not one upon the other side. Huntlie, and his two sonnes, Adam
and Johne, were takin. The father being old, and of short breath,
becaus he was grosse and corpulent, expired in the hands of his
takers. There was no wound, nor appearance of anie deadlie
stroke. Becaus it was late, he was cast thwart a paire of creeles,
and so was carcid to Aberdeene, and was layed in the tolbuith.
His ladie blamed her cheefe witche, Jonet, becaus she had affirmed, he sould be that night in the tolbuith, without anie hurt in
his bodie. She defended herself stoutlie, and affirmed she gave a
true response, howbeit she uttered not all the truthe; for she
knew that he sould be there dead. The Erle of Murrey sent
word to the queene, and besought her humblie to conveene with
them, to give thanks to God for so notable deliverance. She
glowmed at the messinger, and would skarse speeke a good word,
or looke with a cheerefull countenance to anie she knew favoured
the Erle of Murrey, whose prosperitie was as venome to her ve-
nomed heart. Albeit she caused execut Johne Gordoun, and sindrie others, yitt was the destructioun of others sought. A wise
and religious ladie, the Ladie Forbesse, beholding, the day after
the discomfiture, the corps of the erle lying upon the cold stones,
having upon him onlie a doublet of cannvesse, a paire of Scotish gray
hose, and covered with arras worke, said, "What stabilitie sall we
judge to be in this world! There lyeth he that yesterday in the
morning was holdin the wisest, richest, and man of greatest power

in Scotland!" And, indeid, in men's judgements, there was not suche a subject these three hundreth yeeres within this realme.

A CONSPIRACIE REVEALED.

Johne Gordoun confessed before his death manie things devised by his father, his brother, and himself. Letters were found in the erle's pocket, which discovered the traffiquing of the Erle of Sutherland and others: Mr Thomas Keir, cheefe counseller to the umquhile erle, reveeled what he knew. So the conspiracie was plainlie discovered, to witt, that the Erle of Murrey, and some others, sould have beene slaine in Strabogie, and the queene takin. The queene returned soone after, leaving the treasurer, Mr James Makgill, Mr Johne Spence of Condie, and the Laird of Pitarrow, in Aberdeene, to compone for the escheats of these who were in the feilds with the Erle of Huntlie. The Erle of Huntlie's bodie was brought about in a boat, and layed in the Abbey of Halyrudhous without buriall, till the day of his forfaltoure.

LORD GORDON COMMITTED.

The queene commanded the duke straitlie to apprehend his sonne-in-law, George Lord Gordoun, if he repaired within his bounds. He apprehended him. But before he delivered him, the Erle of Murrey interceeded for his life, which was hardlie granted. He was committed to waird in the castell of Edinburgh, the 28th of November, where he remained till the 8th of Februar. At that time he was putt to an assise, and convicted of treasoun, but was committed again to the castell of Edinburgh, and therafter transported to Dumbar castell, where he was deteaned prisoner till the moneth of August.

THE ERLE BOTHWELL BREAKETH WARDE.

Whill the queene was in the north, the Erle Bothwell brake

waird, the 28th of August. Some said he brake the stanchells of
the window ; others whispered that he gott easier passage by the
gates. Howsoever it was, the queene was little offended, and he
remained in Lothiane as one not muche affrayed.

MR KNOX PREACHETH IN KYLE.

Whill the queene was in the north, Mr Knox preached in Kyle
and Galloway. He forewarned some of the nobilitie and barons of
apparent dangers, and exhorted them so to order their effaires, as
that they might be able to serve the authoritie, and represse the
enemeis of the truthe. A number of barons and gentlemen of
Kyle, Carick, and Cunninghame, conveened at Air, and after exhortatioun made, and conference had, the band following was subscrived :—

A BAND SUBSCRIVED AT AIR.

" We, whose names are under-writtin, doe promise, in the presence of God, and of his Sonne, our Lord Jesus Christ, that we
and everie one of us sall and will mainteane the preaching of his
holie Evangell, now of his mercie offered unto this realme ; and
also will mainteane the ministers of the same, against all persons,
power, and authoritie, that will oppone the self to the doctrine
proponned, and by us received. And, further, with the same solemnitie we promise, that everie one of us sall assist others, yea,
and the whole bodie of the professors within this realme, in all lawfull and just actions against all persons. So that whosoever sall
molest, hurt, or trouble anie of our bodie, sall be reputed enemie to
the whole, except that the offender will be content to submitt himself to the judgement of the Kirk, now established among us. And
this we desire to be accepted, and favoured of the Lord Jesus, and
recounted worthie of credite and honestie in the presence of the
godlie. At the burgh of Air, the ferd[1] day of September, the yeere

[1] Fourth.

of God 1562. Subscrived with all their hands that were there
present, as followeth :"

The Erle of Glencarne, Lord Boyd, Lord Uchiltrie, Failfurde,
Mathew Campbell of Lowdun, knight, Alane Lord Cathcart, Cap-
rinton, elder and younger, Cuninghamheid, Rowallan, Waterston,
Cragie, Lesnores, Achinharvie, Middetoun ; Mr Michael Wallace,
Proveist of Air, with fortie men of the honestest of the toun, the
Master of Boyd, Gathgirth, Barr, Carnell, Dreghorne, Cested,
Skeldum, Wolstoun, Karsland, Forgishall, Polquharne, Stair,
Barskimming, Kinzeancleuch, with a hundreth moe gentlemen ;
Johne Dumbar of Blantyre, Carleton and his brother, Halrig, Kers,
Kirkmichaell, Daliarbich, Corstlayes, Hopscleugh, Carbistoun, Kel-
wod, Taringanoch, &c.

MR KNOX AN INSTRUMENT OF GOOD ORDER IN THE SOUTH.

Mr Knox went from the west to Nithisdaill and Galloway. After conference with the Master of Maxwell, a man of deepe judgement and great experience, upon the apparent dangers, he wrote to
the Erle Bothwell at his desire, to behave himself as a peaceable
subject in the places committed to his charge, for so, his breaking
of warde would be the more easilie pardouned. Mr Knox wrote
to the duke, and exhorted him not to hearken to the pernicious
counsells of his bastard brother, the bishop, or of the Erle of Huntlie ; assuring him, if he did, he and his hous would come to suddan
ruine. By suche meanes, the south parts were keeped in reasonable
good order, howbeit the bastard bishop, and the Abbot of Cosraguell, did what in them lay to raise trouble. They spread fearefull
bruites : sometime that the queen was takin ; sometime that she had
randered herself to the Erle of Huntlie ; sometime that the Erle
of Murrey and all his companie were slaine. They stirred up the
Crawfurds against the Reids, for payment of the bishop's Pasche
fynes, to make a stirre in Kyle. But indifferent men favouring
peace, reconciled them.

DISPUTATION BETWEEN MR KNOX AND THE ABBOT OF COSRAGUELL.

The Abbot of Cosraguell craved disputatioun with Mr Knox, which was granted, and holdin at Mynnibole[1] three dayes. The abbot undertooke to prove that Melchisedeck offered bread and wine. He could produce no prooffe, as in the disputatioun yitt extant may appeare. He presented himself to the pulpit; but the voice of Mr George Hay so affrayed him, that after once he wearied of that exercise.

LETHINGTON'S COMMISSION TO ENGLAND.

Lethington was directed with ample commissioun both to the Queen of England and to the Gwisians. The mariage of the queene was in all men's mouths. Some would have Spaine, some the emperour's brother, some Robert Lord Dudley. Some unhappilie gessed at the Lord Darnlie. It was said that Lethington spake with Ladie Margaret Dowglas, and that Robert Melvill receaved a horse from the Erle of Lennox, or his ladie, to the secretar's use. Howsoever it was, Mr Foullar, servant to the said erle, came with letters to the queene, and obteaned licence to the erle to come to Scotland, to doe his lawfull bussinesse. That day the licence was granted, the secretar said, "This day have I takin upon me the deadlie feid of all the Hammiltons in Scotland, and have wrought them no lesse displeasure than if I had cutted their throats."

BOTHWELL DENOUNCED REBELL.

The Erle Bothwell was charged, the 26th of November, by an herald, to re-enter in waird. He disobeyed, and was therefore

[1] The ancient name of Maybole. The town is still so called by the old inhabitants of the district.

denounced rebell. Whill he was upon the seas, fairing toward France, the ship was drivin by storme of weather into England. He was deteaned, and offered to our queen, to be randered. But she answered, he was no rebell, and requested that he might have libertie to passe whither he pleased. Lethington procured this favour ; for he travelled to have freinds in everie factioun of the court, and, therefore, obteaned to him licence to passe to France.

THE COURTEOURS CALL THE PREACHERS RAYLERS.

The preachers declamed against avarice, oppressioun of the poore, excesse in ryotous cheere, immoderate dancing, whoordome ensuing therupon, and all other vices. The courteours stormed, and said, preaching was turned in railing. Mr Knox answered one day as followeth :—" It cometh to our eares that we are called railers ; wherat, albeit we wonder, yitt are we not ashamed, seing the most worthie servants of God before us, travelling in the same vocatioun, have beene so stained. But to you do I say, that the same God who, from the beginning, hath punished the contempt of his Word, and hath powred out his vengeance upon suche proud mockers, sall not spaire you ; yea, he sall not spaire you before the eyes of the same wicked generatioun, for pleasure wherof, yee despise all wholsome ad- monitioun. Have yee not seene one greater than anie of you, sitting presentlie where yee sitt, pyke his nailes, and pull doun his bonnet over his eyes, when idolatrie, witchcraft, murther, oppressioun, and suche vices were rebooked ? (He meant the Erle of Huntlie.) Was not this his commoun speeche : ' When these knaves have railed their fill, then they will hold their peace.' Have yee not heard it affirmed in his face, that God sould revenge that his blasphemie, even in the eyes of suche as were witnesses to his iniquitie ? Then was the Erle of Huntlie accused by you, and compleaned upon, as a mainteaner of idolatrie, and a hinderance of all good order. Him hath God punished, even according to the threatnings which his and your eares have heard, and by your hands hath God exe- cuted his judgement. But what amendement can be espied in you ?

Idolaters are in rest, vertue and vertuous men are contemned, vitious men bold, and without feare of punishment. And yitt, who guide the queen and court but Protestants? O, horrible slander to God, and his holie Evangell! Better it were unto you plainlie to renounce Christ Jesus, than thus to expone his blessed Evangell to mockrie. If God punishe not you, that the same age sall behold and see your punishment, the spirit of righteous judgement guideth not me." The courteours were greatlie offended. Their favourers said, their brethrein in the court were unreverentlie handled. " They did what they might: suche specking would cause them doe lesse: what was this, but to inflamme the hearts of the people against them ?"

THE FYFT GENERALL ASSEMBLY.

The Generall Assemblie conveened the 25th of December, 1562, in Edinburgh, in the old counsel hous.

TRIELL OF SUPERINTENDENTS.

In the triell of superintendents, the Superintendent of Fife was delated, that he was somwhat slacke in his visitations, stayed not at kirks for ordering necessarie effaires, muche givin to worldlie effaires, slacke in preaching, rash in excommunicating, sharper in making acts for payment of small tithes than became him. It was layed to the Superintendent of Angus his charge, first, That there were manie Popish preests unqualifeid, and of vitious life, admitted to be readers of kirks within his diocie. Secund, That young men were admitted rashlie to be ministers and exhorters, without that triell and examinatioun which is required in the Booke of Discipline. Thrid, That gentlemen of vitious life were chosin to be elders in diverse kirks. Fourth, That sindrie ministers, under his jurisdictioun, make no residence at their kirks; visite not the sick; come too late upon the Lord's day, the people wearied waiting on them, and depart incontinent after sermon. Fyft, That the youth are not instructed. Sixt, That ministers resort not to the exercise of propheceing, according to the order sett doun in the Booke of Discipline.

TRIELL OF THE ENTRIE OF MINISTERS.

In the thrid sessioun it was ordeaned, according to the fourth head of the Booke of Discipline, that all persons serving in the ministrie, who had not entered into their charges, according to the order appointed in the said Booke, be inhibited; that is to say, if they have beene slanderous before in doctrine, and have not satisfeid the kirk; if they have not been presented by the people, or a part thereof, to the superintendent, and he, after examinatioun and triell, hath not appointed unto them their charges: and that this act have strenth, als weill against those who are called Bishops as others; and ordeaneth the same to be promulgat by the superintendents, in their dioceis, and where there are no superintendents, by commissioners sent from the Assemblie; the copie thereof to be affixed upon the principall kirk doores. And if anie persoun, after inhibitioun made, contemptuouslie continue in his ministrie, the Assemblie ordeaned to proceed against him by censures to excommunication, unlesse by his letters to the commissioners or nixt superintendent, he give signification of his obedience, and promise to accept the same charge, according as they sall command him. And in that case, the Assemblie decerneth, that with libertie and freedome of conscience, and without danger of the former paine, he may continue in his ministrie to the nixt Assemblie, at which time it is ordeaned, that they present themselves before the Assemblie; and that this act comprehend all exhorters and readers.

LEETS FOR A SUPERINTENDENT TO THE NORTH.

Becaus it was compleaned, that the north countrie, for the most part, was destitute of ministers, and that the order of electioun and admissioun of the Superintendent of Aberdeene was not putt in execution, the Assemblie appointed Mr George Hay, Mr Johne Row, and Adam Heriot, to be proponed in leetes to the said kirk, and edicts to passe furth with all expeditioun; and committed the charge of inauguration of the person elected to the Superintendents of Fife and Angus, and suche learned men as they sall choose. The kirk of Old Aberdeene was appointed to be the place of admissioun. In cace either Mr Johne Row or Adam Heriot sall be elected, the Assemblie nominated Mr James Wilkie, Patrik Corston, and Robert Hammilton, to be proponed in leets to the kirks destituted of their ministrie.

LEETS FOR A SUPERINTENDENT TO GALLOWAY, &c.

For planting of kirks in the shirefdoms of Dumfreis, Galloway, and Nithisdaill, and the rest of the west dails, the Assemblie nominated in leets for the superintendentship, Mr Alexander Gordoun, intituled Bishop of Galloway, and Mr Robert Pont, minister of Dunkelden; ordeaned edicts to be sett furth for the admissioun, upon the last Lord's day of Aprile, and appointed the Superintendent of Glasgow, Mr Knox, minister of Edinburgh, Mr Robert Hammilton, minister of Uchiltrie and Mauchline, and other learned men, to be present at the inauguration of the person elected; the place of admissioun to be the parish kirk of Dumfreis. In the mean time, the Assemblie giveth commissioun to Mr Alexander to admitt ministers, exhorters, and readers, and to doe suche other things as were before accustomed in planting kirks. Heere we may see, that the bishops converted from Poprie were not suffered to exerce jurisdictioun ecclesiasticall, by virtue of their episcopall office.

PAUL METHVEN, SLANDERED FOR ADULTERIE, TO BE TRIED.

In the fourth sessioun, commissioun was givin to Mr Knox to go to Jedburgh, and to tak triell, upon the 3d of Januar nixt to come, of the slaunder raised against Paul Methven, late minister of the said burgh; and after triell to report to the sessioun, or consistorie of the kirk of Edinburgh, to whom, with the Superintendent of Lothiane, the Assemblie giveth power to decerne and pronounce sentence.

ACTS FOR SUPERINTENDENTS.

This Assemblie giveth power to everie superintendent within their owne bounds, in their synodall assembleis, with consent of the most part of the elders and ministers, to translate ministers frome one kirk to another, as they sall consider the necessitie. Ministers were commanded to obey the superintendent, tuiching their translating. It was ordeaned, that superintendents indict their synodall conventions twise in the yeere, to be holdin at suche dayes, in Aprile and October, as the superintendent sall think good; and that they give sufficient advertisement to the particular kirks, that the minister, with an elder or deacoun, may repaire to the place appointed by the superintendents, at the dayes appointed, to consult upon the commoun affaires of their dioceis.

COMMISSIONS.

In the fyft sessioun, commissioun was givin to the Superintendents of Angus, Lothiane, Glasgow, Fife, and David Foresse, to travell with the Lords of the Secreit Counsell, to know what causes sall come to the judgement of the kirk, and what order sall be takin therin, for executioun. *Item*, To travell for discharging of mercats holdin upon the Lord's day. *Item*, Commissioun givin to make supplication, both by word and writt, to the queen's Majestie, for support of the poore.

NOMINATION OF SUPERINTENDENTS.

Notwithstanding of the nominatioun of superintendents for Aberdeene, Bamf, Jedburgh, and Dumfreis, the Assemblie remitted farther advisement and nominatioun of the persons to the Lords of

the Secreit Counsell, providing the dayes appointed for admissioun
be not altered.

ACTS.

It was ordeaned, that an uniforme order sould be keeped in ministratioun of the sacraments, solemnizatioun of mariages, and buriall of the dead, according to the Booke of Geneva. *Item*, That
the communioun be ministred foure times in the yeere, within the
burrowes, and twise in the yeere in countrie parishes. The superintendents were appointed to confer with the Lords of the Secreit
Counsell, tuiching the charges to be bestowed upon the elements
at the Lord's Supper. *Item*, That no minister, or others bearing
office within the Kirk, tak in hand to cognosce, and decide in actions of divorcement, except superintendents, and these to whom
they sall give speciall commissioun, for speciall persons.

COMPLAINTS.

In this Assemblie complaints were made, that ministers wanted
stipends, or had verie small. The Comptroller, Justice-Clerk, and
Clerk-Register promised, where the thrids were remitted to the
possessors, and the queen's Majestie, to caus charge the principall
intrometters, and possessors of the tithes, to pay the ministers' stipends. It was compleaned, that manses were deteaned by parsons
or vicars, or sett in few to gentlemen. The Clerk of Register and
Justice-Clerk desired the superintendents to informe the clerk of
the rentals where these manses lay, that they might be assigned
to the queen's thrid part, and that so the ministers might come to
the possessioun of them. It was compleaned, that idolatrie was
erected in sindrie places. Some thought good, a supplicatioun
sould be presented to the queene; others demanded, what answere
was returned to the last: the presenter, the Superintendent of Lothiane, said, " None." The queen's supposts, as some of them were
ever there, excused the mater by the troubles of the north; but

putt them in hope, that betwixt the nixt parliament, suche order sould be takin as sould content honest men. Her and their practise was to drive time.

PAUL METHVEN EXCOMMUNICATED.

The triell of Paul Methven was verie difficill. His servant woman left his hous betwixt termes, had borne a childe, and alledged that she was suppressed by night. He would have purged himself in publick; but it was refused, becaus his accusers offered to prove by witnesses. Some of the witnesses affirmed, that they did see, others, that they heard them in the act. The sight of the place augmented the suspicioun. The most vehement presumptioun arose of this, that, in absence of his wife, who was gone to Dundie, he lay nightlie in the hous, without anie companie but a childe of seven or eight yeeres. The gentlewoman's brother came to the toun, ignorant of their proceedings. He was produced by the accusers, as one who was privie to the fact; for he convoyed the woman away, he caused the childe to be baptized, as if it had beene his owne; he caried frequent messages, money, and clothes, from him to her. When Paul perceaved this man produced as witnesse, he withdrew himself and left the toun. And, indeid, the man made the mater cleere. The commissioners returned to Edinburgh, and informed the sessioun. He is summoned publicklie, to heare the sentence pronounced; but he, not compeering, in the end, for his contumacie and crime, was excommunicated, and deprived of all functioun within the Kirk of Scotland, and so left the realme. How manie of the Popish rable have beene, and yitt remaine knowne whoormongers, adulterers, violaters of virgins, yea, and committers of suche abominatioun as we will not name, and yitt are called and acknowledged bishops, archbishops, cardinals, and pops!

CHATTELAT BEHEADED.

Danvill, sonne to Annas Montmorancie, Constable of France, could hardlie be drawin home from our queene, when his father sent for him. At lenth, being constrained to returne home, left behind him a broker betwixt him and the queene, Monsieur Chattelat, nephew to the famous knight, Pierr Tertal, by his daughter. But he laboured to· conquishe her affection to himself. He passed all others in credite. At a purpose dance, whereat men and weomen talke secreitlie, the queene choosed Chattelat. All this winter, skairse could anie of the nobilitie have accesse to her aire or late, becaus she was in the cabinet with Chattelat. She would ly upon his shoulder, and sometime privilie steele a kisse off his necke. Upon a night, he convoyed himself privilie under her bed; but being espied, was commanded to goe furth. The bruite rysing, the queene requested the Erle of Murrey, as he loved her, to slay Chattelat, and never lett him speeke a word. At the first he promised; but, after remembring what a crime it was to putt to death, without order of justice, fell upon his knees before the queene, and said, " Madame, I beseech your Grace, caus me not take the blood of this man upon me. Your Grace hath interteaned him so familiarlie before, that yee have offended all the nobilitie. If he be slaine secreitlie at your commandement, what will the world judge of it ? I sall present him to justice, and lett him suffer by law, according to his deserts." " O," said the queene, " yee will never lett him speeke." " I sall doe," said he, " Madame, what lyeth in me to save your honour." Poore Chattelat was convoyed to Sanct Andrewes, putt to an assise, and beheaded, the 22d of Februar, 1563. He craved licence to write to France the caus of his death, which, said he, was " *Poure estre trouvé en lieu trop suspect ;*" that is, for being found in a place too muche suspect. At the place of executioun he granted, that for his declynning frome the truthe, and following vanitie and impietie, he was now justlie punished.

He made a godlie confessioun. In end, he concluded with these words, " O, cruell dame !"

MASSE AT EASTER IN SINDRIE PLACES.

The Papists erected the idol of the masse at Easter in diverse places. The Bishop of Sanct Andrewes, the Pryour of Quhitterne, and some others of that factioun, would avow it. Some preests in the west countrie were apprehended. Intimatioun was made to the Abbot of Cosraguell, the Parson of Donquhare, and others, that the punishment which God appointed for idolaters sall be executed without stay upon complaint to the queene or counsell, wheresoever they sall be apprehended. The queene fretted at suche freedome of specche.

THE THRID CONFERENCE BETWEEN THE QUEENE AND MR KNOX.

Where force failed, the queene used craft. She sent for Mr Knox, to come to her to Lochlevin. She travelled with him two houres before supper, to be an instrument to perswade the people, speciallie the gentlemen of the west, not to putt hands in anie man for the exercise of their religioun. He willed her Grace to punishe malefactors according to the lawes, and promised quietnesse upon the part of the professours. " But if your Majestie would delude the lawes, I feare," said he, " the Papists sall understand, that without due punishment they will not be suffered so manifestlie to offend God's Majestie." " Will yee," said she, " avow, that they sall take my sword in their hands ?" " The sword of justice," said he, " Madame, is God's, and is givin to princes and rulers for one end ; which, if they transgresse, spairing the wicked, and oppressing the innocent, those who, in the feare of God, execute judgement, where God hath commanded, offend not God, although kings doe it not ; nor yitt sinne they, who bridle kings frome slaying innocent men in their rage. Samwell feared not to slay Agag, the fatt and delicate king of Amaleck, whome King Saul had saved.

Elias spaired not Jesabel's false prophets, nor Baal's preests, albeit King Achab was present. Phinehas was no magistrat; yitt feared he not to strike Zimri and Cosbie, in the verie act of their filthie fornicatioun. So, Madam, your Grace may see, that others than cheefe magistrats may lawfullie punishe, and have punished, the vices and crimes which God hath commanded to be punished; for power by Act of Parliament is givin to all judges, within their bounds to searche masse-mungers, and hearers of masse, and to punishe them according to the lawes. Therefore, it is expedient that your Majestie consider, what is the thing your Grace's subjects looke to receave of your Majestie, and what yee ought to doe to them, by mutuall contract. They are bound to obey you, but in God: yee are bound to keepe the laws unto them. Yee crave of them service; they crave of you protectioun, and defence against evill doers. Now, Madame, if yee sall denie your duetie to them, which speciallie craveth that yee punishe malefactors, thinke yee to receave full obedience of them? I feare, Madame, yee sall not." Heerewith she, being somwhat offended, went to her supper. He informed the Erle of Murrey of the whole conference, and so departed, of purpose to have returned to Edinburgh, without anie farther communicatioun with the queene. But before the sunne rysing, upon the morne, was he commanded by two directed to him, not to depart whill he spake with the queen's Majestie.

Mr Knox mett the queene at the Hauking-hill, by west Kinros, the day following. She dissembled her anger, and told him how that the Lord Ruthven had offered her a ring: "But," said she, "I cannot love him, for I know he useth enchantment; and yitt, he is one of my privie counsell." "Whome doth your Grace blame?" said he. "Lethington," said she. "That man is absent," said he, "for the present, Madame, and, therefore, I will speeke nothing in that behalfe." Then she fell to speeke of the admissioun of the Superintendent of Dumfreis. "I heare," said she, "the Bishop of Athens would be superintendent." "He is one," said the other, "Madame, who is putt in electioun." "If yee knew him," said she, "als weill as I doe, yee would never promove

him to anie office in your Kirk." " What he hath beene, Madame,"
said he, " I neither know, nor doe inquire ; for what could we doe
in time of darknesse but grop, and goe wrong? If he be not now
one fearing God, he deceaveth manie moe than me. And yitt, I
am assured, Madame, that God will not suffer his Kirk to be so
farre deceaved, as that an unworthie man sall be elected, where
there is free electioun, and the Spirit of God earnestlie incalled
upon." " Weill," said she, " doe as yee will : that man is a dangerous man." She was not deceaved ; for he had corrupted the
most part of the gentlemen, not onlie to nominate him, but also to
choose him. Mr Knox, therefore, being commissioner, delayed the
electioun, and left Mr Robert Pont, with the Master of Maxwell,
for better triell of his doctrine and conversatioun. The bishop was
verie familiar at that time with Mr Knox, and eate often at his
table, but was frustrated of his purpose at this time.

Mr Knox being willing to tak his leave of the queene, she said,
" I have one of the greatest maters that have tuiched me since I
came in the realme to open up unto you, and must have your
helpe." She confessed, her sister, the Ladie Argile, was not so
circumspect in everie thing as she wished ; " yitt," said she, " her
husband faileth in manie things." " I brought them to concord,"
said he, " that her freinds were fullie content ; and she promised
before them, she sould never compleane to anie creature, till I sould
first be made acquaint with the querell, either out of her owne
mouth, or by an assured messinger." " Weill," said she, " it is
worse than yee beleeve. Doe this muche for my sake, as once
againe to reconcile them, and if she behave not herself as becometh,
she shall find no favour of me : but in no case lett my lord know
that I employed you. As for our conference yesternight, I sall
doe as yee have required. I sall caus summoun all offenders, and
yee sall know that I sall minister justice." " I am assured, then,"
said he, " that yee sall please God, and injoy rest and tranquillitie
within your realme, which is of greater use to your Majestie than
all the Pop's power can be." But she meant no suche mater. Thus
they parted. Mr Knox, according to his purpose, in his journey

to Dumfreis, he directed a letter from Glasgow to the Erle of Argile, wherin he exhorted him to beare with the imperfections of his wife, seing he was not able to convince her of anie crime since the last reconciliatioun, and not to denie her due benevolence. This letter was not weill accepted.

LETTERS FROM QUEENE MARIE TO THE COUNCELL OF TRENT.

Upon the 10th of May, the Cardinall of Lorane exhibite to the Councell of Trent letters directed from our queene. She submitted herself to the councell, and promised to bring both England and Scotland under subjectioun to the Apostolick See, how soone she sould be promoved to the crowne of England. The Cardinall of Lorane excused her not sending of prelats or oratours to the councell, becaus all were hereticks in her countrie; yitt he promised, in her name, that she sould never declyne from the Roman religioun. The synod gave thanks; but some jested at that officiousnesse, as proceeding rather from a privat person nor from a prince, becaus there was not so muche as one of her Catholick subjects sent. Others deemed the letters to have beene begged, becaus none were sent.

MASSE-MUNGERS COMMITTED TO WAIRD.

Summons were directed furth against masse-mungers. They were summoned in the straitest forme to compeere the 19th of May. Of Pop's knights compeered the Bishop of Sanct Andrewes, the Parson of Sanquhare, William Hammilton of Camskeith, Johne Gordoun of Barskioch, and diverse others. The professors craved justice. Young Lethington was absent. The queene asked old Lethington's advice. He said she must see her lawes keeped, or elles she would gett no obedience. The bishop and his band made it nyce to enter before the Erle of Argile, who was sitting in judgement; but at lenth it behoved him to enter within the bar. A merrie man, Robert Norwell, in stead of the bishop's crosse, caried

before him a steele hammer, wherat the bishop and his band were
not a little offended. The bishop and his fellowes, after muche
dealing and dryving of time, came in the queen's will. Some were
committed to warde in one place, some in another. The Ladie
Areskine gott the bishop for her part. All this was done, that the
queene might not be urged with anie other thing concerning maters
of religioun at the parliament, which was to beginne the day following. Noblemen were forewarned; but becaus manie of them
had their owne particulars to be treated upon in the parliament, the
commoun caus was the lesse regarded.

HUNTLIE FORFALTED.

The Erle of Huntlie's corps was brought to the tolbuith, his
armes rent, he, the Erle of Sutherland, and elleven barons and
lairds of the surname of Gordoun, were forfaulted. The queene
road in pompe to the tolbuith, the Parliament hous, three sindrie
dayes. The first day she made a painted oratioun. Then might
have beene heard among her flatterers, " *Vox Dianæ!* the voice
of a goddesse!—God save that sweete face; was there ever one
that spake so eloquentlie?"

THE PROCEEDINGS OF THE PARLIAMENT.

The preachers spake freelie against the targetting of weomen's
tailes,[1] and the rest of their vanitie. Articles were presented for
reformatioun of suche vanitie, and other enormiteis. But the Erle
of Murrey had the confirmatioun of his erledome to passe, others
their owne ratifications likewise for themselves, their freinds, or
dependers. " If the queene," said they, " be urged with suche
things, she will hold no parliament; and then, what sall become of
those who medled with the slaughter of the Erle of Huntlie? Lett
that parliament passe over, and when the queene sall aske anie
thing of the nobilitie, as she must doe before her mariage, then sall

[1] Ornamenting the skirts of dresses with tassels

religioun be the first thing that sall be established." It was answered, that poets and painters erred not altogether that fained
and painted Occasioun with a bald hind head. If it be neglected
when it is offered, it is hard to be recovered. It fell furth so hote
betwixt the Erle of Murrey, some other courteours, and Mr Knox,
that they spake not familiarlie together for a yeere and an halfe
after. Mr Knox, by letter to the Erle of Murrey, discharged himself of all care of his affaires. He called to his remembrance, in
what estate he was when they conferred first together at Londoun;
how God had promoted him above man's judgement. In end, he
concludeth thus: " But seing I perceave myself frustrated of my
expectatioun, which was, that yee sould ever have preferred God
to your owne affectioun, and the advancement of his truthe to your
singular commoditie, I committ you to your owne witt, and to the
conducting of those who better can please you. I praise my God
I leave you this day victor of your enemeis, promoted to great
honour, and in credit and authoritie with your soverane. If so you
continue long, none sall be more glad than I sall be. But if after
this yee sall decay, as I feare yee sall, then call to minde by what
meanes God exalted you; which was neither by bearing with impietie, nor by mainteaning pestilent Papists." Some, invying the
great familiaritie that was betwixt them, were glade, and ceassed
not to cast oyle in the flamme, which burned, till God by the water
of afflictioun beganne to slocken it.

Least they sould seeme altogether to have forsakin God, (as in
verie deed, God and his Word was farre off frome the hearts of the
most part of the courteours, some few excepted,) they beganne to
treate of the punishment of adulterie and witchecraft, of restitutioun of gleebs and manses to ministers, of reparatioun of kirks.
An Act of Oblivioun was made of things past since the sixt day of
Marche, 1558, to the first of September exclusive, 1563, and it was
ordeaned, that the memorie of all actions, civill or criminall, which
resulted upon divisioun for religioun during that time, sall expire,
be bureid and extinct for ever. But the acts against adulterie and
witchecraft, for manses and gleebs, were so modifeid, that no acts,

and suche acts, were both alike; to witt, That committers of adulterie sall be punished to the death, after due premonitioun made to absteane from the said crime; and that others acts and lawes made therupon before be putt in execution. That no person use anie maner of witchecraft, sorcerie, or necromancie, or avow the art and knowledge therof; nor seeke anie helpe, response, or consultatioun of the said abusers, under the paine of death to the user and consulter, and to be putt in executioun by the justice, shireffs, stewarts, bailiffes, lords of regaliteis and royalteis, their deputs, and other judges ordinar competent. That no parson, vicar, nor other ecclesiastical person, sett in few or long tacks their manses or gleebes, without speciall licence and consent of the queen's Grace. That the ministers serving the cure sall have the principall manse of the parson or vicar, or so muche therof as may be sufficient; or, that a reasonable and sufficient hous be builded beside the kirk, by the parson or vicar, or others possessing the said manses in few or long tacks.

MR KNOX HIS ADMONITION TO THE LORDS.

Mr Knox, in his sermoun before the most part of the nobilitie, (for the parliament was not yitt dissolved,) discoursed upon the merceis of God, the deliverance frome tyrannie both of bodie and soule, which this realme had felt, and of the ingratitude of the multitude. " Now, my lords," said he, " I praise God that, in your owne presence, I may powre out the sorrowes of my heart. Yee yourselves may be witnesses if I lee. Frome the beginning of God's mightie working within this realme, I have beene with you in your most desperate tentations. If that I (not I, but God's Spirit in me) willed you not, ever in your greatest extremitie, to depend upon God, and promised, in his name, victorie and preservatioun frome your enemeis, so that yee would onlie depend upon his protectioun, and preferre his glorie to your owne lives and worldlie commoditie, aske your owne consciences. I was with you at Sanct Johnstoun ; Cowper Moore and the Craigs of Edinburgh are yitt recent in my minde; yea, that darke and dolourous night, wherin all yee, my lords, with shame and feare left this toun, is yitt in my minde, and God forbid that ever I forgett it! What was my exhortation to you, what hath fallin in vaine of all that God promised to you by my mouth, yee yourselves can testifie. There is not one of you against whom death and destructioun was threatned, perished in the danger, but manie of your enemeis hath God plagued before your eyes. Sall this be the thankfulnesse yee sall rander to our God, to betray his caus, when yee have power in your owne hands to establishe it as yee please? The queene, say yee, will not agree with us. Aske of her that which we may justlie by God's Word, and if she will not agree with you in God, yee are not bound to agree with her in the devill. Lett her plainlie understand so farre of your mindes, and steale not frome your former stoutnesse in God, and yee sall prosper in your enterprises. I see nothing but suche a recooling from Christ, as that the man who first and most speedilie fleeth from Christ's ensigne holdeth himself happie. Yea, I heare some say,[1] that we have not our religioun established by law or act of parliament. Albeit the malicious words of suche can neither hurt the truthe of God, nor us who depend therupon, yitt the speaker, for treason committed against God and this poore commoun wealth, deserveth the gallows. Our religioun being commanded, and so established by God, is accepted within this realme. If the king then living, and the queene now raigning, were lawful soverans, that parliament cannot be denied to be a lawfull parliament, whereby our religioun was approved. Now, my lords, to putt an end to all, I heare of the queen's mariage. Dukes, brethrein to emperours and kings, strive all for the best game. But this, my lords, will I say, (note the day, and beare witnesse heerafter,) whensoever the nobilitie of Scotland consenteth, that anie infidel (all Papists are infidels) sall be head to our soverane, yee doe so farre as in you lyeth to banishe Christ from this realme. Yee bring God's vengeance upon the countrie,

---

[1] " The Dean of Restalrig."—*Note in the MS.*

a plague upon yourselves, and perhaps sall bring small comfort to
your soverane."

Papists and Protestants were offended; yea, his most familiar
freinds disdained him for his speeches. Placeboes and flatterers
went to court, and told that Mr Knox had spokin against the queen's
mariage. The Provcist of Glencludden charged him to present
himself before the queene after noone. Uchiltrie and others accompaneid him to the Abbey after dinner. None went in with him
to the queen's cabinet but Johne Areskine of Dun, Superintendent
of Angus. The queene beganne to cry out in fume, that never
prince was so used as she was. "I have borne," said she, "with all
your rigorous speeches, uttered both against myself and my uncles;
I have sought your favour by all possible meanes; ·I offered unto
you presence and audience, whensoever it pleased you, and yitt I
cannot be quite of you. I vow to God I sall once be avenged."
Her chamber boy, Marvock, could skarse gett naipkins to hold her
eyes drie, for teares. The yowlling, beside womanlie weeping, stayed
her speech. Mr Knox having patientlie susteaned her first fume,
at opportunitie answered, "True it is, Madame, your Grace and I
have beene at diverse controverseis, yitt I never perceaved your
Grace to be offended at me. When it sall please God to deliver your
Grace frome that boundage of darknesse and errour wherin yee
have beene nourished, for laike of right instructioun, your Majestie
will find the libertie of my tongue to be nothing offensive. Out of
the preaching place, Madame, I thinke, you have not occasioun to
be offended at me; and there, Madam, I am not master of my self,
but must obey Him who commandeth me to speeke plainlie, and to
flatter no flesh upon earth." "What have yee to doe," said she,
"with my mariage?" "Please your Majestie," said he, "patientlie
to heare me. I grant, your Grace offered to me more than ever I
desired or required. But my answere was then, as it is now, that

God hath not sent me to await upon the courts of princes, or upon the chambers of ladeis, but to preache faith and repentance to suche as please to heare. In preaching of repentance, Madame, it is necessar that the sinnes of men be noted, that they may know wherin they offend. The most part of your nobilitie are so addicted to your affectiouns, that neither God's Word, nor the commoun wealth, are duelie regarded, therefore it becometh me to informe them of their duetie." "But what have you to doe with my mariage?" quoth she; " or what are yee within this commoun wealth?" " I am a subject, borne within the same," said he, " Madame : although I be neither erle, lord, nor baron in it, yitt God hath made me, how abject so ever I seeme in your eyes, a profitable member within the same. Yea, Madame, it apperteaneth to me no lesse to forewarne of suche things as may harme it, if I foresee them, than to anie of the nobilitie, for my office and calling so craveth. Therefore, Madame, to yourself I say, as I said in publick, ' Whensoever the nobilitie of this realme sall consent that yee be subject to an unfaithfull husband, they doe so farre as in them lyeth banishe the truthe, betray the freedom of this realme, and perhaps, in the end, sall bring small comfort to yourself.'" At these words, yowlling was heard, and teares might have been seene in greater abundance than the mater required. Johne Areskine of Dun, a man of meeke and mylde spirit, to mitigat her anger, praised her beautie and excellent parts, and said, that all the princes in Europ would be glade to seeke her favours. But suche maner of speeking was nothing but to cast oyle in the flamming fire. Mr Knox stood still without anie alteratioun of countenance a long seasoun. At lenth he said, " Madame, in God's presence I speeke, I never delyted in the weeping of anie of God's creatures; yea, I can skarse weill abide the teares of my owne boyes, when my owne hand correcteth them, muche lesse can I rejoice in your Majestie's weeping. But seing I have offered to you no just occasioun to be offended, but have spoken the truthe as my vocatioun craveth, I must beare, howbeit unwillinglie, with your Majestie's teares, rather than hurt my conscience, or betray the commoun wealth by silence." The queene was then more offended, and commanded him to passe out of the cabinet, and to abide her farther pleasure in the chamber. The Laird of Dun stayed; Johne Lord Coldingham went in. They remained with her neere the space of an houre. Mr Knox stood in the chamber, as a stranger whom men had never seene, for all were affrayed; yitt the Lord of Uchiltrie bare him companie. He beganne to seeke some purpose with the ladeis sitting there in their gorgeous apparrell. "O, faire ladeis," said he, "how pleasant were this life of yours, if it sould endure, and in the end ye might passe to heaven with all this gay geere. But, fy upon that knave Death, which will come whether we will or not! And when he hath layed on the arreist, the foule wormes will be bussie with this flesh, be it never so faire or tender : but the sillie soule, I feare, sall be so feeble, that it can neither carie with it gold, targetting, nor precious stones." So passed he the time, till the Laird of Dun willed him to depart to his hous till new advertisement. The queene would have had the Lords of the Articles to be judge, whether suche speeches deserved not punishment. But she was counselled to desist, and so that storme ceassed.

MATCHES PROPONED.

The Gwises, great enemeis to Queene Elizabeth, offered our queene in mariage to the King of Navarre, and to procure the Pop's sentence of depositioun of Queene Elizabeth, and divorcement from his owne hereticall wife. But the Cardinall of Loran was dealing for a matche betwixt her and Charles, Archduke, sonne to the Emperour Ferdinand. The bloodie tyranne, the Duke of Guise himself, was takin away in Februare before. Queen Elizabeth commended unto her Robert Dudley, whom she created Master of the Horse, and Baron of Denbigh.

LETHINGTON'S PRACTISES.

Soone after the parliament, Secretar Lethington returned out of England. He shewed himself a little offended that anie sould have affirmed there was anie motioun of the queen's matche with the King of Spaine: "For," said he, "it never entered in heart." His intentioun was to discredit Mr Knox, who had affirmed that such a mariage was both propouned, and, upon the queen's part, by the cardinall accepted. Whill he was absent, the nobilitie blamed him for serving the queen's affections too farre against the commoun wealth. Therefore he strenthened himself with freindship; for he travelled in England for the Erle Bothwel's libertie, and procured the Erle of Lennox his pasport to come home. He sett fordward the Erle of Atholl at court at home, so the Erle of Murrey his credite beganne to be obscured. Yitt Lethington caried a faire countenance to him. Soone after his returne, the queene sett at libertie the Bishop of Sanct Andrewes, and the rest of his band, who were before committed to prison for violating the lawes.

THE SIXT GENERALL ASSEMBLIE.

The Generall Assemblie was holdin at Sanct Johnstoun, the 25th day of June.

TRIELL OF SUPERINTENDENTS AND COMMISSIONERS.

In the triell of superintendents, Mr Alexander Gordoun, called commounlie Bishop of Galloway, to whom commissioun had beene givin before to plant kirks with ministers, exhorters, or readers, and other office-bearers, likewise for a reformed kirk within the bounds of Galloway, was compleaned upon by the Laird of Garleis, younger, that he had not ministred justice to an honest woman compleaning upon her husband for non-adherence.

COMMISSIONERS OF PROVINCES APPOINTED.

Commissioun was given to Mr Johne Hepburne, Minister of
Brechin, to plant ministers, exhorters, readers, elders, deacons, and
other members requisite and needfull for a reformed kirk, in Murrey, Bamf, and the countreis adjacent ; and to place schoolemasters,
to abolishe idolatrie in these parts.   The like commissioun was
givin to Mr Robert Pont to plant kirks in the shirefdome of Innernesse, and the countreis adjacent ; and to Mr Donald Monro, to
doe the like within the bounds of Rosse, and to assist the Bishop
of Cathnesse in preaching of the Gospell, and planting of kirks.
Commissions were givin to the Bishops of Galloway, Orkney, and
Cathnesse, for the space of a yeere, to plant kirks, etc., within their
owne bounds.   All these commissions were to endure onlie for a
yeere.   The Generall Assembleis aimed at the planting of moe
superintendents, and even in this same Assemblie, they aimed at a
superintendentship in Tiviotdaill, Nithisdaill, Annandaill, and Sel-
kirk.   Yitt could they never atteane to moe than five.   Therefore
they gave commissiouns to ministers to plant kirks, preache, visite
kirks, schooles, and colledges ; to suspend, deprive, transplant
ministers ; to confer vacant benefices ; to procure the eradicatioun
of all monuments of idolatrie in the provinces, or bounds assigned
to them.   These were called the commissioners for planting kirks,
commissioners of countreis or provinces, commissioners for visitation.   Their power was equall to the power of superintendents,
and had the like assistance of reformed kirks, of learned men nixt
adjacent, of meetings of ministers for the exercise of prophecie, of
synods, of other associats whom the Generall Assemblie now and
then appointed to joyne with them.   This was the difference :
commissioners injoyed their office onlie for a yeere commonlie.
When the commission expired, the Assemblie either renued it, or
placed another : so that I may justlie call the commissioners of
provinces, temporarie superintendents ; and were in verie deed but
servants to the General Assemblie, having a delegate power from

2

them, accessorie to the particular charge which they had over their
owne particular flockes.

These acts following were made in this Assemblie :—

1. That no contract of mariage alledged to be made secreitlie,
carnall copulatioun following, sall have faith in judgement in time
comming, till the contracters suffer as breakers of good order, and
offensive to the Kirk by their slaunder; and, therafter, that faith
sall not be givin to that promise, till famous and unsuspect witnesses affirme the same, or elles both the parteis confesse. And
incace probatioun or confessioun follow not, that the said offenders be punished as fornicators.

2. That if anie person findeth himself wronged by anie sentence
givin by the ministers, elders, and deacons of their kirk, it sall be
free to the partie so wronged to appeale to the superintendent of
the diocie, and the synodall conventioun, within ten dayes after;
and the said superintendent sall take cognitioun whether it was
weill appealed or not, and give sentence therupon. If the partie
yitt alledge himself wronged by the superintendent, and his synodall conventioun, it sall be free to him to appeale, within ten dayes
as before, to the Generall Assemblie immediatlie following; and
that the said Assemblie tak cognitioun of the said appellatioun,
whether the partie appealed weill or not; and therafter pronounce
sentence, from which it sall not be free to the partie to appeale.
If the appellant justifie not his appellatioun before the superintendent, and his conventioun foresaid, he sall inflict a paine upon him,
as he sall thinke good, beside the expenses of the partie: which
penaltie sall be delivered to the deacons of the kirk where the first
sentence was givin, to be distributed to the poore. In like maner,
the Generall Assemblie finding it evill appealed, from the superintendent and synodall conventioun, sall impose a penaltie arbitrarie
upon the appellant, to be distributed, as said is, together with the
expenses to the partie.

3. That the instruction of the youth be committed to none within the realme, neither in nor out of universiteis, but to suche as professe the true religioun now publicklie taught; and if there be anie other now presentlie occupying these places, that they be removed.

4. That no worke sall be sett furth in print, or published in writt, tuiching religioun, before it be presented to the superintendent of the diocie, advised and approved by him, and by suche as he sall call of the most learned within his bounds. And if they, or anie of them, doubt of anie point, so that they cannot be resolved cleerelie, they sall produce the said worke to the General Assemblie, where order sall be takin for resolutioun of the said doubt.— The like power was givin in Assembleis following to others than superintendents.

5. That everie superintendent warne shires, touns, parish kirks within the bounds of their jurisdictioun, to send their commissioners to the Generall Assemblie in times coming, and mak intimatioun to them of the time and place; and that the superintendents themselves repaire to the Assemblie, the first day, under the paine of a certan penaltie, to be distributed to the poore.

6. That everie superintendent consider within his bounds the kirks needing reparatioun, or re-edifeing; and therafter, that the letters givin to him gratis, made conforme to the Act of Parliament, be delivered to the collectors of the thrids within his bounds, to be executed by an officer of armes, at suche kirks as sall be needfull, and the superintendent sall thinke good: and therafter, that the said collectors deliver the letters duelie executed to the superintendents, that where it sall happin there be disobedience they may crave remeid from the Lords of Secreit Counsell.

ARTICLES FOR PETITIONS.

Articles and petitions. It is ordeaned, that supplicatioun be made to the superiour powers, for constituting judges in everie province, to heare the complaints of parteis, alledging adulterie to be committed by the husband or the wife; and that the said judges may take cognitioun in the mater, and punishe, according to the Act of Parliament. *Item,* That when anie benefice sall vaike, qualifeid persons may be presented to the superintendent of the province where the benefice lyeth, that places destitute of the ministrie may be provided. *Item,* That where two or three kirks are distant two or three myles, they may be united, and the inhabitants commanded to resort to one of them; becaus the smalnesse of manie parishes requireth not, and the raritie of ministers suffereth not, everie kirk to have a severall minister. *Item,* For remitting the thrids, or a part therof, to suche bishops as are appointed by the Assemblie commissioners, to plant kirks within their owne bounds. The comptroller was requested to assume, and assigne to himself so muche of the thrids of the benefices remitted by the queene to the professors, colleges and kirks of universiteis being excepted, as may sufficientlie susteane the ministrie; and to caus his collector to intromett therewith, and distribute the same among the ministers, as weill for times bypast as to come; which he promised to doe. The Comptroller, Justice-Clerk, and Clerk-Register being present, promised to give letters gratis to ministers requiring the same; and to cause them be executed upon the comptroller's expenses, to charge all possessors of manses to restore the same to ministers, or to build a sufficient hous to them before a sett day, as the partie sall desire, under the paine of horning.

COMMISSIONERS FOR TRYELL OF COMPLAINTS.

The Superintendent of Lothiane, the ministers, elders, and deacons of the kirk of Edinburgh, *conjunctim et divisim,* Mr James Makgill, Clerk of Register, Sir Johne Spence of Condie, the queen's Advocat, Messrs Thomas Makalzeane, David Borthwicke, Clement Littill, Richard Strang, or anie two of them, were appointed to tak cognitioun of Mr Magnus Halcro and Margaret Sinclar's appellation frome the Bishop of Orkneye's sentence, in a caus of divorce. Commission was givin to Mr Gudman, minister at Sanct Andrewes, William Christesone, minister at Dundie, Mr William

Coke, Mr William Scot, Mr Johne Dowglas, Rector of the Universitie of Sanct Andrewes, to tak cognitioun of the complaint givin in by the Superintendent of Fife, against Mr George Leslie, minister of Stramiglo, to decerne, and to notifie their decreit to the Superintendent of Angus : where we may see, that ministers were appointed by the Assemblie judges betwixt superintendents and ministers; and that not onlie the Generall Assemblie, but also others whom it pleased them to appoint, had power to judge of bishops and superintendents. The Superintendent of Fife had compleaned, that Mr George had not executed his summons against some persons in Auchtermowtie, where he was also minister ; and that he had not ministred the sacraments since December last bypast.

THE SENTENCE PRONOUNCED AGAINST JAMES HAMMILTON OF KINCAVELL PRONOUNCED NULL.

In the thrid sessioun of this Assemblie, after discussing of the articles for which processe was led, and sentence givin by umquhile James Bishop of Rosse, appointed commissioner by James Archbishop of Sanct Andrewes, at Halyrudhous, the 26th of August, 1534, against James Hammilton of Kincavell, Shireff of Linlithquho; the Assemblie pronounced the saids articles to be good and sound, no wise hereticall, and the sentence pronounced by the said Bishop of Rosse against the said James, *in pœna contumaciæ*, to be casse[1] and null, with all that followed therupon, and he to be restored *in integrum* to his honour, fame, and dignitie.   The articles for which he was condemned were these :—That Mr Patrik Hammiltoun died a good Christian, and he was content to dee the same death : That there is no purgatorie : That we ought not to pray for the dead : That man hath not free will, as the Papists meane : That he said the Lord's Prayer in the vulgar tongue : That he had bookes condemned, and suspected of heresie : That he contemned, and caused others contemne, the preaching of preaching friers—and so furth. James Gib of Carruder, one of those· who were summouned for

---

[1] Rendered void.

their interesse, to heare the saids articles approved, compeered after noone, and protested, that whatsoever was done in this Assemblie in favours of James Hammiltoun of Kincavell, sould not be prejudiciall to him and his rights whatsoever.

THE QUEENE'S PROGRESSE AND HER MASSES.

The queene, in her progresse through the west countrie, had her masse in touns and gentlemen's houses; herupon Mr Knox beganne that forme of prayer, which he ordinarilie used after thanksgiving at table :—" Deliver us, O Lord, frome the boundage of idolatrie; preserve and keepe us from the tyrannie of strangers; continue quietnesse and concord among us, if it be thy good pleasure, for a season." Some of his familiars asked him, why he prayed for quietnesse onlie for a seasoun? He answered, he durst not pray but in faith; he was assured by God's Word, that constant quietnesse could not continue in that realme, where idolatrie, after it was suppressed, was suffered to be erected again. The queene went to Argile from the west countrie to the hunting, and after returned to Stirline.

THE DEATH OF JOHNE LORD COLDINGHAME.

The Erle of Murrey, Robert Lord Halyrudhous, and Johne Lord Coldingham, went to the north, to hold Justice-Courts. Some theeves and murtherers suffered, and two witches were burnt. Johne Lord Coldinghame ended his life at Innernesse. For the queene's pleasure, he was an enemie to vertue, and a patron to impietie, to the uttermost of his power. His venome so raged, that at a certane time he burst furth in these words, " Or I see the queen's Majestie so troubled with the railing of these knaves, I sall leave the best of them sticked in the pulpit !" But at his death he asked God mercie, for that he had mainteaned her impietie, and flattered her in wickednesse against God and his servants. He charged those that were beside him to warne the queene, unlesse she left

her idolatrie, God would not faile to plague her. But she regarded
his words as wind ; yea, affirmed that they were invented by the
Laird of Pittarrow and Mr Johne Wood, whom she hated, becaus
they flattered her not in her dancing and other things. Yitt, she
said, God tooke away from her the person in whom she had greatest pleasure.

A MASSE IN HALYRUDHOUS IN THE QUEEN'S ABSENCE, OCCASION OF TROUBLE.

Whill the queene lay at Stirline, her Frenche meinzie, whom she
had left in the palace of Halyrudhous, had their masse more publick than at anie time before. When the kirk of Edinburgh had
the ministratioun of the Lord's Table, the Papists resorted in great
number to their abominatioun. Some zealous men were appointed
to wait upon the palace, and marke suche as resorted to the masse.
When they perceaved a great number to goe into the chappell, some
of them rushed in also. The preest and the Frenche dames being
affrayed, raised the shout. Madame Raillie, mistresse of the queene's
maides,—if that court could beare anie maides,—sent post to the
comptroller, the Laird of Pittarrow, who was then in the Great
Kirk of Edinburgh at sermoun, and called for his assistance, to
save her life, and the queene's palace. He, with greater haste than
need required, went doun, and tooke with him the proveist and
bailiffs, and a great number of others. When they came they
found all quiet, except that a peaceable man was talking with them,
and forbidding them to transgresse the lawes. True it is, that Patrik Cranstoun, a zealous professor, went in to the chappell, and
finding the altar covered, and the preest readie to goe to his abominatioun, said, " The queene's Majestie is not heere : how darre
thou then be so malapert as openlie to transgresse the law ?" The
queene was informed. Patrik Cranstoun and Andrew Armestrang
were summouned to find sovertie to underly the law for foresought
fellonie, hamesucken, violent invasioun of the queene's palace, and
spoliation of the same. It was concluded by the brethrein that

were in the toun, that Mr Knox, to whom charge was givin, to
give advertisements whensoever danger sould appeare, sould write
to the professors in all quarters, to informe them in what case
maters stood, and to crave their assistance; which he did as followeth :—

MR KNOX'S LETTER TO THE PROFESSORS.

*" Wheresoever two or three are gathered together in my name,
there am I in the middest of them.*

" It is not unknowne to you, deere brethrein, what comfort and
tranquillitie God gave unto us in times most dangerous, by our
Christian assembleis, and godlie conferences, als oft as anie danger
appeared to anie member of the members of our owne bodie; and
that how, since we have neglected, or at the least not frequented
our conventions and assembleis, the adversareis of Christ Jesus
his holie Evangell have enterprised and boldened themselves publicklie, and secreitlie, to doe manie things odious in God's presence,
and most hurtfull to the true religioun now of God's great favour
granted unto us. The holie sacraments are abused by profane
Papists; masses have beene, and yitt are, openlie said and mainteaned; the blood of some of our deerest ministers hath beene shed,
without feare of punishement or correctioun craved by us; and
now, last, are two of our brethrein, Patrik Cranstoun and Andrew
Armestrang, summouned to underly the law, in the tolbuith of
Edinburgh, the 24th of this instant, for forethought fellonie, pretended murther, and for invading the queene's Majestie's palace
of Halyrudhous with unlawfull convocatioun, etc.

" This terrible summons is directed against our brethrein, becaus
they, with two or three moe, past to the Abbey upon Sunday the
15th of August, to behold and note what persons repaired to the
masse; and that, becaus the Sunday before, the queene's Grace being
absent, there resorted to that idol a rascall multitude, having

openlie the least devillish ceremonie, (yea, even the conjuring of
their accursed water,) that ever they had in time of greatest blindnesse. Becaus, I say, our brethrein past, and that in most quiett
maner, to note suche abusers, thir fearefull summons are directed
against them, to make no doubt a preparatioun upon a few, that a
doore may be open to execute crueltie upon a greater multitude.
And if so it come to passe, God, no doubt, hath recompensed our
former negligence and ingratitude towards him, and his benefites
receaved, in our owne bosomes. God gave us a most notable victorie of his and our enemeis. He brake their strenth, confounded
their counsells; he left us at freedome, and purged this realme (for
the most part) of open idolatrie, to the end that we, ever mindefull
of so wondrous a deliverance, sould have keeped this realme cleane
frome suche filthinesse and damnable idolatrie. But we, alas! preferring the pleasure of fleshe and blood to the pleasure and commandement of God, have suffered that idol, the masse, publicklie to
be erected againe; and therefore justlie suffereth he us now to fall
in that danger, that to looke to an idolater going to his idolatrie
sall be reputed a crime little inferiour to treasoun. God grant
that we fall not farther: And now I, whom God of his mercie
made one among manie to travell in setting fordward his true
religioun within this realme, seing the same in danger of ruine,
cannot but of conscience crave of you, my brethrein of all estats,
(that have professed the truthe,) your presence, comfort, and assistance, at the said day, in the toun of Edinburgh, as ye tender
the advancement of God's glorie, the safetie of your brethrein,
and your owne assurance, together with the preservation of the
Kirk in her appearing dangers. It may be, perchance, that perswasiouns be made in the contrare; and that yee may be informed, that either your assemblie is not necessar, or elles that it
would offend the upper powers. But my good hope is, that neither flatterie nor feare sall make you so farre to declyne against
Christ Jesus, as that against your publick promise and solemn
band yee will leave your brethren in so just a caus. And albeit
there were no great danger, yitt cannot your assemblie be unpro-

fitable; for manie things require consultatioun, which cannot be had unlesse the wisest and godliest conveene. And this, doubting nothing of the assistance of our God, if that we uniformelie seeke his glorie, I ceasse farther to trouble you, committing you heartilie to the protectioun of the Eternall. From Edinburgh, the 8th day of October, 1563.

" Johne Knox."

VARIANCE BETWIXT THE MASTER OF MAXWELL AND MR KNOX.

When this letter was read in the toun of Air, Robert Cunninghame, minister of Failefurde, then reputed a professour of the Gospell, being present, gott the letter, by what meanes we know not, and sent it to Mr Henrie Sinclar, then President of the Sessioun of the Colledge of Justice, stiled Bishop of Rosse, a perfyte hypocrite, and conjured enemie to Christ. He was cutt of the stone in Parise, and ended his life the secund day of Januar following. He was a speciall enemie to Mr Knox, becaus he still affirmed, that a bishop receaving profite, and not feeding the flocke by his owne labours, is a theefe and a murtherer. He posted the letter to the queene, then resident at Stirline, together with his advice. The cabinet counsell concluded that it imported treasoun. The queene thought once to be revenged upon her great enemie. It was concluded, the nobilitie sould be writtin for, to countenance the condemnatioun with their authoritie. The day was appointed about the middest of December, and was keeped by manie. The Master of Maxwell, after Lord Hereis, discharged Master Knox of further familiaritie, unlesse he satisfeid the queene's Majestie at her owne sight. " I know no offence done," said the other. " No offence !" said he: " have yee not desired by your letters, the brethrein from all parts to come to Patrik Cranston and Andrew Armestrang's day ?" " I grant," said the other, " but acknowlege no offence." "No offence," said he, " to convocat the queene's lieges ?" " Not for so just a caus," said the other. " Greater maters were reputed no offence within these two yeeres." " The

case," said he, "is altered, for then our soverane was absent."
"God's Word," said the other, "not her presence nor absence,
ruleth my conscience. What was lawfull to me the last yeere is
yitt lawfull." "Weill," said the Master, "I have givin you my
counsell; doe as yee like; but I thinke yee sall repent, if yee bow
not to the queene." "I understand not, Master," said he, "what
yee meane. I never made myself adverse partie to the queene
but in religioun, wherin, I thinke, yee will not will me to bow."
"Weill," said he, "yee are wise eneugh; but yee will not find that
men will beare with you in time to come as they have done in
times bypast." "So long as I depend upon God's providence,
and prefere his glorie unto my life and worldlie profite, I little regarde how men behave themselves toward me," said the other;
"neither know I wherin anie man hath borne with me in times bypast, unlesse it be, that out of my mouth they have heard the
Word, which if in time comming they refuse, I will lament, but
the incommoditie will be their owne." They sindered, and were
not so familiar after.

THE ADVOCAT INFORMED.

Mr Johne Spence of Condie, Advocat, came as it were in secreit
to Mr Knox, to inquire how maters went. After he had heard his
declaratioun, and considered the letter, he said, "I thanke God,
I came to you with a fearefull and sorrowfull heart, fearing yee
had committed some offence punishable by the lawes, which would
have brought no small greefe to the hearts of all those who have
receaved the Word of Life out of your mouth. But I depart
greatlie rejoicing, als weill becaus I perceave yee have comfort in
the middest of your troubles, as that I cleerelie understand yee have
not committed suche a crime as is bruited, yee will be accused;
but God will assist you."

CONFERENCE BETWIXT THE ERLE OF MURREY, THE SECRETAR, AND
MR KNOX.

The Erle of Murrey and the Secretar sent for Mr Knox to the
Clerk-Register's hous. They beganne to lament that he had so
highlie offended the queene, which they feared sould end in great
inconvenience to him, if he did not wiselie prevent it. They told
him what paine and travell they had takin to mitigate her anger,
but could find nothing but extremitie, unlesse he would confesse
his offence, and putt himself in her Grace's will. " I praise my
God through Christ," said he, " I have learned not to crie, ' Con-
juratioun and treason !' at everie thing that the godlesse multitude
doth condemne, nor to feare the things that they feare. I have
the testimonie of a good conscience, that I have givin no occasioun
to the queene's Majestie to be offended at me, for I have done nothing but my duetie. So, whatsoever sall ensue, my good hope is,
that God will give me patience to beare it." " But how can you
defend yourself?" said Lethington : " Have yee not convocated
the queen's lieges ?" " If I have not a just defence," said he, " lett
me smart for it." " Lett us heare," said they, " your defences, for
we would be glade yee might be found innocent." " No," said the
other : " I am informed by diverse, that I am already condemned,
and my cause prejudged ; therefore, I might be reputed a foole, if
I sould make you privie to my defences." They seemed both offended. The secretar departed. The erle would have entered in
farther discourse of the estate of the court. ' Mr Knox answered,
" I understand more than I would of maters of the court. If yee
stand in good case, I am content : if not, as I feare yee doe not
alreadie, or elles sall not ere it be long, blame not me. Yee have
counsellers whom yee have chosin. My weake judgement both
they and yee despise. I can doe nothing but behold the end,
which I pray God be other than my troubled heart feareth."

MR KNOX ACCUSED BEFORE THE COUNSELL.

Within foure dayes, Mr Knox was called before the queene and counsell, about the middest of December. The professors of Edinburgh followed in suche numbers, that the inner close was full, and all the staires, even to the chamber doores, where the queen and counsell sate. The lords had beene reasouning among themselves before, but had not fullie satisfeid the secretar's minde. The queene had retired to her cabinet, and the lords were talking one with another; but when Mr Knox came, they were commanded to tak their places. The queene came furth: with no small pompe was placed in the chaire, having two faithfull suppostes, the Master of Maxwell at the one tore,[1] and the secretare at the other; the one sometimes occupying her eare, sometimes the other. When she saw Mr Knox standing at the end of the table, bare-headed, first she smiled, and after burst furth in loud laughter. Her placeboes gave their *plaudite*, with the like countenance. "This is a good beginning," said she: "but wote yee wherat I laugh? Yon man gart me greete, and never shed a teare himself: I will see if I can caus him weepe." The secretar whispered in her eare, and she again in his, and gave him a letter. After inspectioun, he directed his speech to Mr Knox, saying, "The queen's Majestie thinketh yee have travelled to raise a tumult among her subjects; and for prooffe, there is your owne letter. Becaus her Grace will doe nothing without advisement, she hath called you before some of the nobilitie heere present, that they may beare witnesse betwixt you and her." "Let him acknowledge his owne hand-writt," said she, "and then we sall judge of the contents of the letter." So the letter was reached from hand to hand, till it was delivered to Mr Knox. When he had taken inspectioun, he said, "I remember I dyted a letter in October to brethrein in diverse quarters, of suche things as displeased me; and good conceate have I, that the scribes willinglie would not adulterat my ori-

[1] Arm of the chair.

ginall, albeit I left diverse blanks with them: so I acknowledge
both the hand-writt and the dytement." " Yee have done more,"
said Lethington, " than I would have done." " Charitie," said Mr
Knox, " is not suspicious." " Weill," said the queene, " read your
owne letter, and then answere as yee sall be demanded." " I sall
doe the best I can," said he. He read it with a loud voice, and delivered it again to Mr John Spence, advocat; for the queene commanded him to accuse, which he after did, but verie gentlie.

After the letter was read, the queene said to the lords, " Heard
yee ever, my lords, a more despitefull or treasonable letter?" No
man answering, Lethington said, " Mr Knox, are yee not sorie at the
heart that suche a letter hath escaped your penne, and from you hath
come to the knowledge of others?" He answered, " My lord secretar, before I repent, I must be taught of my offence." " Offence!"
said Lethington: " If there were no more but the convocation of the
queen's lieges, the offence can not be denied." " Remember yourself, my lord," said the other; " there is a difference betwixt a lawfull convocatioun and an unlawfull. If I be guiltie in this, I have
offended often since I came last in Scotland; for what convocatioun
of the brethrein hath beene to this houre to which my penne hath
not served? But before this time, no man layed it to my charge as
a crime." " Then was then," said Lethington, " and now is now;
we have no need of suche convocatioun as sometimes we have had."
Mr Knox answered, " The time which hath beene is ever before my
eyes: for I see the poore flocke in no lesse danger than at anie
time before, but that the devill hath gottin a vizerne on his face.
Before, he came with face discovered, seeking by open tyrannie the
destructioun of all that resisted idolatrie: then, I thinke yee will
confese, the brethrein assembled themselves lawfullie for defence
of their owne lives. Now, the devill cometh under the cloke of
justice, to doe that which God would not suffer him to doe by
strenth."

" What is this?" said the queene. " Methinke yee triffle with
him. Who gave him authoritie to convocat my lieges? Is not that
treasoun?" " No, Madame," said the Lord Ruthven: " he convocateth

the people to heare prayers and sermons, almost daylie; and whatever your Grace or others will thinke therof, we think it no treasoun." "Hold your peace!" said the queene: "lett him answere for
himself." "I beganne," said Mr Knox, "to reasoun with the secretar, whom I tak to be a farre better dialectician than your Grace,
and said, that all convocatiouns are not unlawfull. Now, my Lord
Ruthven hath givin an instance, which, if your Grace will denie, I
will addresse me to prove." "I will say nothing," said the queene,
against your religioun, for conveening to your sermons. But what
authoritie have yee to convocat my subjects when it pleaseth yow,
without my warrant?" "I have no pleasure," said Mr Knox, "to
declyne frome the former purpose. Yitt, Madame, to satisfie your
Grace, I answer, that at my pleasure I never convocated foure persons, but according to the order appointed by the brethrein. I have
givin diverse advertisements, and great multitudes have assembled
therupon. If your Grace compleane that this hath beene done
without your commandement or warrant, I answere, so hath all that
God hath blessed within this realme, frome the beginning of this
actioun. Therefore, Madam, I must be convicted by a just law,
that I have done against the duetie of God's messinger, in writting
of this letter, before I can either be sorie or yitt repent, as my lord
secretar would perswade me. What I have done, I have done at
the commandement of the Kirk within this realme; therefore, I
think I have done no wrong."

"Yee sall not escape so," said the queene. "Is it not treasoun,
my lords, to accuse a prince of crueltie? I thinke there be Acts
of Parliament against suche whisperers." That was granted by
manie. "Wherein can I be accused?" said Mr Knox. "Read this
part of your owne letter," said the queene:—'Thir fearefull summons are directed against them, (to witt, the brethrein forsaid,) to
mak, no doubt, a preparation upon some few, that a doore may be
opened to execute crueltie upon a great multitude.' "Loe," said
the queene, "what say yee to that?"

Whill manie doubted what Mr Knox would answere, he said, "Is
it lawfull for me, Madam, to answere for myself; or sall I be damned

before I be heard?" " Say what yee can," said she, " for I thinke
yee have eneugh to doe." " I will first, then, aske of your Grace,
Madam, and of this honorable audience, whether if obstinat Papists
are not deadlie enemeis to all suche as professe the Evangell, and
earnestlie thrist the exterminioun of them, and the true doctrine
which is taught in this realme?" The queene held her peace. The
lords, with one voice, said, " God forbid that ever the lives of the
faithfull, or stopping of the preaching of the Word, stood in the
power of Papists; for just experience hath taught us what crueltie
lyeth in their hearts." " I proceed, then," said Mr Knox, " seing I
perceave all will grant it were a barbarous crueltie to destroy suche
a multitude as professe the Evangell within this realme, which ofter
than once or twice they have attempted to do by force, as things
done of late doe testifie; whereof they, being disappointed by God's
providence, have invented a more craftie and more dangerous practise; to witt, to make the prince partie, under colour of law. So,
what they could not doe by open force, they sall performe by craft
and deceate. Thinke you, my lords, that the insatiable crueltie of
the Papists within this realme sall end in the murthering of these
two brethrein, now unjustlie summouned, and more unjustlie to be
accused? I thinke no man of judgement can so esteeme, but rather judge, that by these two they intend to prepare a way to their
bloodie interprise against the whole number. Therefore, Madame,
cast up when you please the Acts of Parliament. I have offended
nothing against them, for I accuse not, in my letter, your Grace of
a cruell nature. But I affirme yitt againe, that the pestilent Papists, who have enflammed your Grace without just caus against
these poore men at this present, are the sonnes of the devill, and
therefore must obey the desires of their father, who hath beene a
manslayer and a leer from the beginning." " Yee forgett yourself,"
said one; " yee are not in the pulpit." " I am in the place," said
the other, " where I am demanded of conscience to speeke the
truthe. I speeke: impugne whoso list! I adde, Madame, that
natures otherwise gentle and meeke in appearance may, by wicked
and corrupt counsellers, be subverted and altered to a contrarie

course. Exemples we have in Nero. Now, Madame, I say plainlie,
Papists and conjured enemeis of Christ have your eares patent at
all times: assure your Grace, they are dangerous counsellers, and
this your mother found."

Lethington smirtelled, and rounded in her eare. Then she said,
"Weill, yee speeke heere faire eneugh before the lords; but the
last tyme I spake with you secreitlie, yee caused me weepe manie
teares, and said stubbornlie, Yee compted not for my weeping."
He repeated summarilie the conference they had before the Laird
of Dun concerning her matche, the occasioun of her weeping, and
what he said to her when she weeped. After that the secretar had
conferred secreetlie with the queene, he said, " Mr Knox, yee may
returne to your hous for this night." " I thanke God and the
queen's Majestie," said the other: " I pray God, Madame, to purge
your heart from Poprie, and preserve you frome the counsell of
flatterers. How pleasant soever they seeme to your eares, and
corrupt affections for the time, experience may teache to what per-
plexitie they have brought renowned princes."

Mr Knox removed, the queene went to her cabinet. Everie
man's vote was asked, if he had not offended the queene's Majestie? The lords voted all as one man, they could find no offence.
The flatterers of the court, Lethington especiallie, raged. The
queene was brought againe, and placed in her chaire, and they
were commanded to vote againe. The nobilitie being offended,
said, " What, sall the Laird of Lethington have power to command
us? Sall the presence of a woman caus us offend God? Sall we
condemne an innocent man against our conscience, for the pleasure
of anie creature?" So he was absolved againe, and they praised
God for his modestie, his plaine and sensible answeres. Among
manie placeboes and flatterers of the court, not one durst plainlie
condemne him, the same God ruling their tongues, that some time
ruled the tongue of Balaam; which, when the queene perceaved, she
upbraided Mr Henrie Sinclare, Bishop of Rosse, saying, " Trouble
not the barne, I pray you; trouble him not, for he is newlie
wakened out of his sleepe. Why sould not the old foole follow

the footsteps of others that have passed before him ?" The bishop answered coldlie, "Your Grace may understand, that it is nather affectioun to the man nor love to his professioun, that moveth me to absolve him ; but the simple truthe, which plainlie appeareth in his defence." This being said, the lords and their assessors arose and departed. The duke, the Erle of Argile, the Erle of Murrey, the Erle of Glencarne, the Erle Marshall, the Lord Ruthven, satt in counsell that day. Old Lethington, the Bishop of Rosse, the Clerk-Register, satt removed from the table. The Comptroller, the Justice-Clerk, the Advocat, and sindrie others, were standing by. That night there was neither dancing nor fiddling ; for the queene was disappointed of her purpose, which was to have had Mr Knox come in her will, by vote of the nobilitie. She raged, and the placeboes of the court stormed. They beganne againe to move him to confesse an offence, and to putt himself in the queene's will, promising the greatest punishment sould be to enter within the castell of Edinburgh, and immediatlie to returne to his owne hous. He answered, "God forbid that my confessioun sould condemne the noblemen who, upon their consciences, and with the queene's displeasure, have absolved me. Farther, I am assured, yee will not in earnest desire me to confesse an offence, unlesse yee will also have me to ceasse from preaching ; for how can I exhort others to peace and Christian quietnesse, if I confesse myself to be an author and mover of seditioun ?"

THE SEVENTH GENERALL ASSEMBLIE.

The Generall Assemblie conveened at Edinburgh, the 25th of December, in the new Tolbuith, where were present the duke, the Erles of Argile, Murrey, Morton, Glencarne, Marshall ; the Secretar, Comptroller, Justice-Clerk ; the Superintendents of Angus, Lothiane, Fife, and the West ; Alexander, styled Bishop of Galloway, Adame, Bishop of Orkney, ministers, commissioners, barons, burgesses, and gentlemen. The exhortatioun was made by Mr Willocke, Superintendent of the West. For avoiding confusion,

it was agreed that a Moderator sould be chosin, to moderat during
the time of everie Assemblie. Mr Johne Willocke, Superintendent
of the West, was chosin Moderator for this time.

QUICKE SPEECHES BETUIXT SOME COURTEOURS, BARONS, AND MINISTERS.

The just petitions of ministers were dispised at the first, with
these words :—" As ministers will not follow our counsell, so will
we suffer ministers to labour for themselves, and see what speed
they come." It was answered by the commissioners, " If the
queene will not provide for ministers, we must; for both the two
parts, and the thrid, are rigorouslie exacted of us and our tenants."
" If others," said one, " will follow my counsell, the guarde and
the Papists sall compleane als long." Then the speeker alledged,
he meant not of all ministers, but of some, to whom the queene was
no debtor; for what receaved she of burrowes ? Christopher Gudman answered, " If yee can show me what just title either the
queene hath to the thrid, or the Papists to the two parts, then I
think I sould resolve you whether she were debtor to ministers
within burghs or not." The secretare answered, "*Ne sit peregrinus
curiosus in aliena republica;*" Lett not a stranger be curious in a
strange commonwealth. Mr Gudman answered, " Albeit in your
policie I be a stranger, yitt so I am not in the Kirk of God. The
care thereof apperteaneth no lesse to me in Scotland than if I
were in the middest of England."

MR KNOX JUSTIFEID BY THE ASSEMBLIE.

Manie woundered that Mr Knox was silent when these sharpe
speeches past. He himself declared the caus. " I have travelled,"
said he, " right honorable and beloved brethrein, since my last arrivall within this realme, in an upright conscience before my God,
seeking nothing more (as he is witnesse) than the advancement of
his glorie, and stabilitie of his Kirk within this realme. Yitt of

late I have beene accused as seditious, and as one that usurped to myself power which becometh me not.   True it is, I gave advertisement to brethrein, in diverse quarters, of the rigour intended against some honest men for looking to the preest going to the masse, and observing these that transgressed this law.   That therein I have usurped farther power than was givin me, till by you I be damned, I utterlie denie; for by the charge of the Generall Assemblie, I have als lawfull power to advertise the brethrein, frome time to time, of dangers appearing, as I have to preache the Word of God in the pulpit of Edinburgh; for by you I was appointed to the one and the other.   Therefore, in the name of God I crave your judgements.   The danger which appeared in my accusatioun was not so fearfull as the words which came to my eares were greevous to my heart; for it was said, (and that by some professours,) ' What can the Pope doe more than send furth his letters, and command them to be obeyed?'"   Sir John Bellendine, Justice-Clerk, (then not the least flatterer of the court,) beganne to storme, and said, " Sall we be moved to justifie the wrong doings of men?"   " My lord," said Mr Knox, " you sall speeke your pleasure for the present : of you I crave nothing.   But if the Assemblie will not either absolve me or condemn me, never sall I, in publick or in privat, as a publick minister, open my mouth in doctrine nor in reasouning."   After long altercatioun, Mr Knox was removed.   It was found that charge was givin to him to advertise brethrein in all quarters, and therefore the fact to be not onlie his but the whole Assemblie's.   The queen's placeboes were more angrie than before; for some of them had promised to the queene to gett him convicted both by the counsell and by the Assemblie.   But being frustrated of both, she and they thought themselves not a little disappointed.

The approbatioun followeth in these words : " Anent the questioun moved by Johne Knox, minister of Edinburgh, to the whole Assemblie, whether he receaved charge of the whole kirk conveened in Edinburgh, after the beginning of reformatioun, to advertise the brethrein to conveene at what time it sould chance that anie

member of the kirk sould be troubled, and that for their counsell to
be had," &c.   To the which the Lord Lindsay, the Lairds of Kelwod, and Abbotshall, Cunninghamheid; the Superintendents of Angus, Fife, Lothiane, the West, and Galloway; Mr Johne Row, William Christesone, Mr Robert Hammiltoun, Mr Christopher Gudman, ministers, with the most part of the Assemblie, made their
declaratioun, that they remembered verie weill that the said Johne
Knox would have had himself exonered of the foresaid charge, and
that the Assemblie would no wise suffer him to refuse the same, but
that he sould continue as before, to advertise frome time to time, as
occasioun sall be givin.

TRIELL OF SUPERINTENDENTS AND COMMISSIONERS.

In the triell of superintendents, the commissioners of Fife craved
a dyett to be appointed, to give in complaints against their superintendent.   For the present, it was compleaned, that he preached not
at his visitatioun, but caused the minister of the kirk occupie the
place.   The Superintendent of the West was charged with negligence in extirpatioun of idolatrie.   He layed the blame upon the
duke and the Erle of Cassils.   The Superintendent of Angus and
Mernes was compleaned upon, that no discipline was exercised in
manie of the kirks of Angus and Mernes; that there was no conventioun of elders and deacons at kirks, for censuring of faults; that
he preached not in his visitatiouns; that being burthenned with the
visitatioun of the north, he might not attend upon the charge alloted
to him.   The questioun, whether superintendents ought to preache
in all the kirks where they did visite, was referred and discussed at
the end of the Assemblie.   The Superintendents of Lothiane and
the West desired to be disburthenned of their superintendentships.
Mr Robert Pont, Commissioner of Murrey, Innernesse, and Bamf,
declared how he had travelled in these parts, but confessed his inabilitie, in respect of the laike of the Irish tongue; and therefore desired the Assemblie to appoint another, expert in the Irish tongue,
to be commissioner.   It was compleaned, that Mr Donald Monro,

Commissioner of Rosse, was not so apt to teache as his charge required. Six of the number were appointed to trie his gifts, and to report to the Assemblie. The commissioners and brethrein of Fife presented in the fyft sessioun a roll, wherein there were diverse complaints givin in against their superintendent. His answere was, that some of these things layed to his charge lay not in his power to amend. The compleaners were commended for their zeale, and the supcrintendent admonished to be diligent in preaching and execution of his office. The Superintendent of Lothiane craved libertie to returne to his first cure. The parochiners of Calder desired likewise that he might be suffered to returne, or elles demitt the personage to another, to serve the cure at their kirk. The Assemblie answered as before, in Julie 1562.

COMMISSIONERS OF PROVINCES.

Commissions were renued for a yeere to Mr Robert Pont, to plant kirks frome Nesse to Spey; to Mr Johne Hepburne, minister at Brechin, to plant kirks in Bamf, from Spey to Etham, comprehending Strabogie land; to Mr Patrik Consteane, minister at Seres, to plant kirks frome Dee to Etham. Mr Robert Pont accepted the commissioun, with provisioun that he be not burthenned with kirks speaking the Irish tongue.

ACTS.

It was ordeaned, that ministers, exhorters, readers, having manses, make residence at the same, and visite the sicke as they may; and where the parish is great, that the minister crave the assistance of elders and deacons in the said visitatiouns.

II. Tuiching the buriall of the poore, it was ordeaned, that a beare sould be made in everie countrie parish, to carie the dead corps to the buriall place; and that these of the village or houses

nixt adjacent to the hous where the dead lyeth, or a certane number
of everie hous, sall convoy the dead corps to the buriall place, and
burie it six foot under the earth; and that everie superintendent
requeist the lords and barons within his bounds to make an act in
their courts tuiching this order, and caus their officers warne the
neerest nighbours where the deed ly, to convoy it to the grave.

III. Becaus superintendents ordeane diverse times notorious offenders to mak publick repentance in the kirk where the offence
was committed, and yitt give not significatioun of the same to the
ministers and elders of the congregatioun, wherethrough offenders
may easilie escape the making of their repentance in due time;
therefore it was ordeaned, that when anie superintendent injoyneth
anie persoun to mak publick repentance for anie offence, that he
sall signifie to the parish what he ordeaneth to be done by the offender, to the end the ministers, elders, and deacons of the congregatioun may notifie againe to the superintendent whether the
offender obeyeth his ordinance or not.

SUPPLICATIONS.

It was ordeaned, that superintendents sould present to the Lords
of the Secreit Counsell the supplications of ministers, that order
might be takin for payment of their stipends, speciallie where the
thrids were remitted to the possessours by the queen's Majestie.
Item, That supplicatioun be presented to the Lords of Secreit
Counsell, that everie minister may have his stipend assigned in the
bounds where he serveth. *Item,* That the act of parliament tuiching glebes and manses be more speciallie condescended upon. The
noblemen and others present, for interesse, were required to condescend that the poore labourers might have the tithes of the ground
for a reasonable compositioun, either in money or victuall, to be
payed to the erles, lords, barons, and other tacksmen. The duke,
Argile, Murrey, Marshall, Glencarne, Rothesse, Lord Areskine,
Ruthven, Lindsay, and the comptroller, being present, consented

for their owne parts. A full answere was deferred till a fuller conventioun. The superintendents were appointed to travell with the absents.

THE BOOKE OF DISCIPLINE TO BE REVISED.

In the fourth sessioun, the Erle Marshall, Lord Ruthven, Lord Secretare, the Commendatare of Kilwinning, the Bishop of Orkney, the Clerk of Register, the Justice-Clerk, Mr Henrie Balnaves, David Foresse, and Mr George Buchanan, or anie three or foure of them, were appointed to revise the Booke of Discipline, to consider the contents, to report their judgements in writt to the nixt Assemblie; or, if a parliament be holdin in the meane time, to the Lords of the Articles, and to beginne at the farthest before the sixt of Januar.

MINISTERS CENSURED.

Robert Ramsay was accused for entrie to the ministrie without the Superintendant of Angus his admissioun; for affirming there was a mid way betwixt Poprie and our religioun; for borrowing money from the toun of Innernesse, upon cautioun, pretending he was to buy bookes, and not returning, nor paying the same. He was suspended from his ministrie till further triell were takin by the Superintendent of Fife. Alexander Jerdane, minister at Kilspindie, notwithstanding he had maried a woman with whom he had committed fornicatioun, and made his publick repentance, was suspended frome the ministrie, till the nixt Assemblie advised farther. Other ministers, exhorters, or readers, of the north, not compeering, were suspended, till farther triell were takin by some superintendent or commissioner to be sent to these parts. David Ray, minister of Forrest, compeering, was admonished to observe a decent order and forme in teaching, with suche gravitie as become preachers of God's Word ; and to follow the text, without invectives, otherwise than the text sould require rebooke of sinne.

A VEHEMENT FROST.

In Januarie, upon the 20th day therof, the rain falling freezed so vehementlie, that the ground was like a shott of yce. The fowles of the aire deed, and might not flee. In the same moneth the sea stood still, neither flowing nor ebbing the space of twentie-foure houres.

MATHEW ERLE OF LENNOX RESTORED.

This moneth Mathew Erle of Lennox was restored, in a publick conventioun, to his patrimonie. The queene intended not onlie to putt others out of hope of successioun, by his sonne Henrie, but also to oppose him against the Erle of Murrey.

MUTUALL BANKETTING BETWEEN THE QUEENE AND THE LORDS.

In the moneth of Februare, the 15th and 18th day therof, were seene in the firmament as it were armeis joyned together, with speeres and other weapons. But the queene banketted the lords, to remove all suspicioun of displeasure for the patrocinie of Mr Knox. The lords banketted likewise the queene, and so banketting continued till Fasting-Eve. The guard and the queen's kitchen were so gripping, that ministers could not gett their stipends, notwithstanding of the promises made by the Erle of Murrey, and the secretar in the queen's name, at the Assemblie before.

MR CRAIG'S PUBLICK REBOOK.

Mr Craig, inveying against the corruptions of the time, said in publick sermoun, " Sometimes hypocrits were knowne by their disguised habits: we had men to be monkes, and weomen to be

nunnes. But now we cannot discerne the erle from the abbot, nor
the nunne from the noble woman. But seeing yee are not ashamed
of that professioun, would to God yee had therewith the cowle, the
vaile, and the rest belonging thereto, that yee might appeare in
your owne colours !" Lethington, in the audience of manie, gave
himself to the devill, if after that day he sould regarde what sould
become of ministers; but sould doe what he might that his companions have a skaire with him, lett them barke and blaw als muche
as they list. The flatterers of the court compleaned that men's
persons were so particularlie described, that all the world might
tak notice of whom the preacher meant. It was answered, " Lett
men be ashamed to offend publicklie, and then preachers sall absteane from particular descriptioun." Yitt would some of these
courteours have beene reputed the cheefe pillers of the kirk within
this realme.

MR KNOX DECLAMETH AGAINST LETHINGTON.

The flatterers of the court daylie reproached the ministers : happie was he who could invent the bitterest taunt, and disdainfullest
reproache. At lenth they beganne to jest at the terme idolatrie,
affirming men knew not what they spake when they called the
masse idolatrie. Some feared not to affirme, they would susteane
the masse was not idolatrie. Mr Knox directing his complaint in
publick to God, uttered these words :—" O Lord, how long sall
the wicked prevaile against the just? How long sall thou suffer
thyself, and thy blessed Evangell, to be despised by men—by men,
I say, who will boast themselves defenders of the truthe ? We
compleane not of thy manifest and open enemeis, but of suche as
to whome thou hath reveeled thy light ; for now it is come to our
eares, that cheefe professors will defend the masse to be no idolatrie. If so were, O Lord, miserablie have I beene deceaved, and
miserablie have I deceaved thy people, which thou, O Lord, knoweth, I have ever abhorred more than a thowsand deaths.—But,"
said he, turning his face to the speekers, " if I be not able to prove

the masse to be the most abominable idolatrie that ever was since the beginning of the world, I offer to suffer the punishment appointed by God for a false teacher.　And it appeareth to me," said he, " that the affirmer sould be subject to the same law, for it is the truthe of God which yee persecute and blaspheme; the inventioun of the devill, which, obstinatlie, against his Word yee mainteane: wherat, albeit yee now flirt and flyre, as thogh all that were spokin were but wind, yitt I am assured, as I am assured God liveth, that some that heare of this defectioun, and rayling against the truthe and servants of God, sall see God's judgements powred furth upon this realme; speciallie upon you, who cleave fastest to the favour of the court, for the abominatiouns mainteaned by you."　Albeit this vehemencie moved some to teares, yitt Secretare Lethington, in a mocking maner, said, " We must recant, and burne our bill, for the preachers are angrie."

THE EIGHT GENERALL ASSEMBLIE.

The Generall Assemblie was holdin the 25th of Junie, 1564. The invocation of the name of God, and exhortatioun, was made by Mr Knox.

A CONFERENCE WITH SOME FEW MINISTERS GRANTED TO THE COURT LORDS.

The first day of the Assemblie, the courteours and lords depending upon the court, conveened not with their brethrein.　Manie woundering at this, an ancient and honorable baron, the Laird of Lundie, said, " Nay, I wounder not of their absence; but I wounder that at the last Assemblie they not onlie withdrew themselves apart from us, but drew also from us some of our ministers, and would have them to conclude suche things as were never propouned in publick assemblie, which appeareth to me to be a thing verie prejudiciall to the libertie of the Assemblie.　Therefore, in my judge-

ment, they sould be informed of the offence, and humblie required,
if they be brethrein indeid, to assist their brethrein with their presence and counsell, for there was never greater need. If they purpose to fall backe from us, it were better we knew it now than
afterward." Thereunto the whole Assemblie agreed, and gave
commissioun to certan brethrein to declare their mindes to the
lords, which was done after noone. The courteours at the first
seemed not a little offended that they sould seeme to be, as it were,
suspected of defectioun ;. yitt the day following, they came to the
Assemblie. But they drew themselves a little before apart, viz.,
the Duke, the Erles of Argile, Murrey, Morton, Glencarne, Marshall, Rothesse, the Master of Maxwell, the Secretare, the Justice-
Clerk, the Clerk of Register, the Comptroller, and went in to the
inner counsel-house. After short consultatioun, they directed Mr
George Hay, then called the minister of the court, to desire the
superintendents and some of the learned ministers to conferre with
them. It was answered, they were conveened to deliberat upon
the commoun effaires of the kirk, and therefore could not spaire
suche men whose judgements were so necessarie, that without them
the rest sould sitt as it were idle. Therefore, willed them as of before, that if they professed themselves as members of this kirk, they
would joyne with their brethrein, and would propoune in publick
what they pleased : so they sould have the assistance of the whole
Assemblie, in all things which might stand with God's Word. But
to send a certan number might breed rather hurt and slaunder than
comfort ; for it was to be feared that all men would not stand content with the conclusions, where the conference and reasons were
heard but of a few. This answere was givin upon just reasoun ;
for no small travell was takin to draw some ministers to the factioun
of the courteours, and to susteane their arguments and opiniouns.
When it was perceaved by the most politick among them that they
could not prevaile this way, they purged themselves that they had
never meant to separate themselves frome the societie of the brethrein. But becaus they had certan heeds to propone, they thought
it more expedient, for avoiding of confusioun, to have conference

with a few, than to propone in publick. The Assemblie still replyed, they would admitt no secreet conference in these heeds which
sould be concluded by generall vote.   The lords promised that nothing sould be concluded, no vote asked, till both the propositiouns
and reasons were heard and considered of the whole bodie.   Upon
that conditioun were directed to them, with expresse charge to conclude nothing without knowledge and advice of the Assemblie, the
Superintendents of Angus, Fife, Lothiane, Mr Johne Row, Mr
Johne Craig, William Christisone, and Mr David Lindsay, ministers, and Mr George Hay.   Johne Willocke was Moderator of the
Assemblie, and Mr Knox attended upon the scribe, and therefore
were appointed to stay still with the brethrein; yitt, becaus the
principall complaint concerned Mr Knox, he was also called.

THE CONFERENCE BETWEEN THE LORDS AND SOME MINISTERS.

The ministers forenamed being conveened with the lords above-
named, Secretar Lethington began with an harang, conteaning
these heeds: First, How muche we were addebted unto God, by
whose goodnesse we have libertie of religioun under the queen's
Majestie, albeit she was not perswaded in the same.   Secundarilie,
How necessar a thing it was the queen's Majestie, by all good
offices (so spake he) of the part of the Church, and ministers principallie, sould be interteaned in that constant opinioun, that they
unfainedlie favoured her advancement, and procured her subjects
to have a good opinioun of her.   And last, How dangerous a thing
it was, that ministers sould be noted, one to disagree from another,
in forme of prayer for her Majestie, or in doctrine, concerning obedience to her authoritie.   "And in these two last heeds," said he,
" we desire you all to be circumspect; but speciallie, we must crave
of you, our brother Johne Knox, to moderat your self als weill in
forme of prayer for the queen's Majestie, as in doctrine that yee
propone concerning her estate and obedience.   Neither sall yee tak
this as spokin to your reproache, (*quia nevus interdum in corpore*

pulchro ;) but becaus that others by your exemple may imitate the like libertie, albeit not with the same modestie and foresight."

What opinioun that might engender in the hearts of the people, wise men doe foresee. The said Johne prepared for answere as followeth :

MR KNOX HIS ANSWERE TO LETHINGTON.

"If suche as feare God have occasioun to praise her, becaus idolatrie is mainteaned, the servants of God despised, wicked men placed again in authoritie and honour, (Mr Henrie Sinclar was a short time before made president, who before durst not sitt in judgement ;) and, finallie," said he, "if we ought to praise God, becaus vice and impietie overfloweth this whole realme without punishment, then have we occasioun to rejoyce, and praise God. But if these and the like use to provoke God's vengeance against realmes and natiouns, then, in my judgement, the godlie within Scotland ought to lament and mourne, and so to prevent God's judgements, least that he, finding all in like securitie, strike in his hote indignatioun, beginning, perchance, at suche as thinke they offend not."

"That is an heed," said Lethington, "wherinto yee and I never agreed : for, how are yee able to prove that ever God stroke or plagued a natioun or people for the iniquitie of their prince, if they themselves lived godlie ?" "I looked," said he, "to have had audience till I had ended the other two parts ; but, seing it pleaseth your lordship to cut me off before the middest, I will answere to your questioun. The Scripture of God sheweth me, that Jerusalem and Judah were punished for the sinne of Manasseh. And, if yee will alledge that they were punished becaus they were wicked, and offended with the king, not becaus the king was wicked, I answere, that albeit the Spirit of God maketh for me, saying in expresse words, 'For the sinnes of Manasseh ;' yitt I will not be so obstinat as to lay the whole sinne, and plagues that therof followed, upon the king, and utterlie absolve the people ; but I will grant with you, that the whole people offended with the king. But how, and in what fashioun, I feare that yee and I sall not agree. I doubt not but the whole multitude accompaneid him in all the abominations which he did; for idolatrie and a false religioun hath ever beene, is, and will be, pleasing to the most part of men. But, to affirme that all Judah committed reallie the acts of his impietie, is but to affirme that which neither hath certaintie, nor yitt appearance of anie truthe. For, who can thinke it to be possible, that all those of Jerusalem sould so shortlie turne to externall idolatrie, considering the notable reformatioun latelie before had in the dayes of Ezekias? But yitt, sayeth the text, 'Manasseh made Israel and the inhabitants of Jerusalem to erre,' Para. xxxiii. True it is; for the one part, as I have said, willinglie followed him in his idolatrie, and the other, by reasoun of his authoritie, suffered him to defile Jerusalem and the temple of God with all abominatiouns. And so were they all criminall of his sinne, the one by the act and deid, the other by suffering and permissioun; even as whole Scotland is this day guiltie of the queen's idolatrie, and yee lords, especiallie, above others."

" Weill," said Lethington, " that is the cheefe heed wherin we never agreed; but of that we sall speeke heerafter. What will yee say, as tuiching the moving of the people to have a good opinioun of the queen's Majestie, and as concerning obedience to be givin to her authoritie; as also, of the forme of prayer which commounlie yee use?" " My lord," said he, " more earnestlie to move the people, or yitt otherwise to pray than heertofore I have done, a good conscience will not suffer me. For He who seeth the secreets of hearts knoweth that, privatlie and publicklie, I have called to God for her conversioun, and have willed the people to doe the same, showing unto them the dangerous estate wherin not onlie she herself standeth, but also the whole realme, by reasoun of her indured blindnesse." " That is it," said Lethington, " wherin we find greatest fault: your extremitie against her masse, in particular, passeth measure. Yee call her a slave to Sathan; yee affirme, that God's vengeance hangeth over the realme becaus of her iniquitie: and what is this elles, but to raise the hearts of the people against her Majestie, and against them that heard?" Then there was heard an exclamatioun of the rest of the flatterers, that suche extremitie could not profite. The Master of Maxwell said, in plaine words, "If I were in the queen's Majestie's place, I would not suffer suche things as I heare." "If the words of the preachers (said Mr Knox) sall alwise be rest in worst part, then it will be hard to speeke anie things so circumspectlie (provided that the truthe be spokin) which sall escape the censure of calumniators. The most vehement, and (as yee speeke) excessive maner of prayer that I use in publick, is this, ' O Lord, if it be thy good pleasure, purge the heart of the queen's Majestie frome the venome of idolatrie, and deliver her frome the boundage and thraldome of Satan, into which she hath beene brought up, and yitt remaineth, for laike of true doctrine. And lett her see, by the illuminatioun of thy Holie Spirit, that there is no meanes to please thee but by Jesus Christ thy onlie Sonne; and that Jesus Christ cannot be found but in thy Holie Word, nor yitt receaved but as it prescribeth; which is, to renounce our owne witt, and pre-conceaved opinions, and worship thee as thou commandeth : that in so doing, she may avoide the eternall damnatioun which abideth all obstinat and disobedient to the end, and that this poore realme may also escape that plague and vengeance which inevitablie followeth idolatrie mainteaned against the manifest Word, and the open light therof.' This," said he, "is the forme of my commoun prayer, as yee yourselves can witnesse : now, what is worthie reprehensioun in it, I would heare."

"There are three things," said Lethington, "that never liked me. And the first is, Yee pray for the queen's Majestie with a conditioun, saying, ' Illuminat her heart, if it be thy good pleasure;' whereby it may appeare, that yee doubt of her conversioun. Where have yee the exemple of suche prayer?" "Wheresoever the exemples are," said the other, "I am sure of the rule, which is this, ' If yee sall aske anie thing according to His will, he sall heare you.' And our Master, Christ Jesus, commandeth us to pray to our Father, ' Thy will be done.' " "But," said Lethington, "where ever

found yee anie of the prophets so to have prayed?" " It sufficeth
me," said the other, " my lord, that the Master and Teacher both
of prophets and apostles, hath taught me so to pray." " But in so
doing," said he, " yee putt a doubt in people's hearts of her conversioun." " Not I, my lord," said the other; " but her owne obstinat rebellioun causeth moe nor me to doubt of her conversioun."
" Wherin rebelleth she," said he, " against God?" " In all the actiouns of her life," said the other, " but in these two heeds especiallie: First, That she will not heare the preaching of the blessed
Evangell of Jesus Christ: Secundarlie, That she mainteaneth that
idol, the masse." " She thinketh not that rebellioun, but good religioun," said Lethington. " So thought they," said he, " that offered their childrein unto Molech; and yitt, the Spirit of God affirmeth, that they offered them to devills, and not to God. And
this day, the Turkes thinke they have a better religioun than the
Papists have; and yitt, I thinke, yee will excuse neither of both
against God. Neither yitt justlie can yee doe the queene, unlesse
yee will make God to be partiall." " But yitt," said Lethington,
" why pray yee not for her Majestie without a doubt?" " Becaus,"
said the other, " I have learned to pray in faith. Now, faith, yee
know, dependeth upon the Word of God; and so it is that the
Word of God teacheth me, that prayers profite the sonnes and
daughters of God's electioun, of which number, whether she be or
not, I have just occasioun to doubt. And, therefore, I pray that
God would illuminate her heart, if it be his good will and pleasure."
" But yitt," said Lethington, " yee can produce the exemple of
none that so hath prayed before you." " Thereto have I alreadie
answered," said Mr Knox. " But yitt for farther declaratioun I
will demand one questioun, which is this, Whether yee thinke
that the apostles prayed themselves as they command others to
pray?" " Who doubteth of that?" said the whole companie who
were present. " Weill then," said Mr Knox, " I am assured that
Peter said thir words to Simon Magus, ' Repent therefore of this
thy wickednesse, and pray to God, that if it be possible, the thought
of thy heart may be forgiven thee.' Heere we may cleerelie see,

that Peter joyneth a conditioun with his commandement, that Simon sould repent and pray, to witt, if it were *possible* that his sinnes
might be forgivin him ; for he was not ignorant, that some sinnes
are unto death, and so without all hope of repentance or remissioun.
And thinke yee not, my lord secretar," said he, " but the same
doubt may tuiche my heart, as tuiching the queen's conversioun,
that then tuiched the heart of the apostle ?" "I would never,"
said Lethington, " heare you, or anie other, call that in doubt."
" But your will," said the other, " is no assurance to my conscience.
And to speeke freelie, my lord, I wounder if that yee yourself
doubt not of the queen's conversioun ; for more evident signes of
induratioun have appeared, and still doe appeare in her, than Peter
outwardlie could have espied in Simon Magus.   For, albeit sometimes he was a sorcerer, yitt joyned he with the apostles, beleeved,
and was baptized.   And, albeit the venome of avarice remained in
his heart, and that he would have bought the Holie Ghost, yitt,
when he heard the fearefull threatning of God pronounced against
him, he trembled, desired the assistance of the prayers of the apostles, and humbled himself (so farre as the judgement of man might
pierce) like a true penitent.   And yitt we see that Peter doubteth
of his conversioun.   Why, then, may not all the godlie justlie doubt
of the conversioun of the queene, who hath used idolatrie, which is
no lesse odious in the sight of God than is the other, and still continueth in the same ; yea, she despiseth all threatnings, and refuseth all godlie admonitiouns ?"   " Why say yee, that she refuseth admonitioun ?" sayeth Lethington : " She will gladlie heare
anie man."   " But what obedience to God," said the other, "or
to his Word, ensueth to all that is spokin unto her, or when
sall she be seene to give presence to the publick preaching ?"
" I thinke never," said Lethington, "so long as she is thus intreated."   " And so long," said the other, " yee and all others
must be content, that I pray so as that I may be assured to be
heard of my God ; that is, that his good will may be done, either
in making her comfortable to his Church, or, if that he hath ap-

pointed her to be a scourge to the same, that we may have patience, and she may be bridled."

"Weill," said Lethington, "lett us come to the secund heid. Where find yee, that the Scriptures call anie the blind slaves of Sathan; or that the prophets of God speeke of kings and princes so unreverently?" "The Scripture," said Mr Knox, "sayeth that by nature we are all the sonnes of wrathe. Our Master, Christ Jesus, affirmeth, that suche as doe sinne are servants to sinne, and that it is the onlie Sonne of God who setteth men at freedome. Now, what difference is there betwixt the sonnes of wrathe, the servants of sinne, and slaves to Satan, I understand not, unlesse that I be taught. And if the sharpenesse of the terme offend you, I have not invented that phrase of speeking, but have learned it furth of God's Scriptures. For these words I find spokin unto Paul —' Behold, I send thee unto the Gentiles, to open their eyes, that they may turne from darknesse unto light, and frome the power of Satan unto God,' Acts xxvi. Mark the words, my lord, and sturre not at the speeking of the Holie Ghost. And the same apostle writting to his owne scholler, Timotheus, sayeth, ' Instruct with meekenesse these that are contrarie minded, if that God at anie time will give them repentance; that they may know the truthe, and that they may come to amendiment, out of the snare of the devill, which are takin of him at his will,' 2 Tim. ii. If your lordship doe rightlie consider these sentences, yee sall not onlie find my words to be the words of the Holie Ghost, but also the conditioun which I use to adde, to have the assurance of God's Scripture." "But they speeke nothing against kings in speciall," said Lethington; "and yitt your continuall crying is, 'The queen's idolatrie! the queen's masse will provoke God's wrathe!'" "In the former sentences," said the other, "I heare not kings nor queens excepted; but all unfaithfull are pronounced to stand in one ranke, and to be in boundage to one tyranne, the devill. But belike, my lord," said he, "ye little regarde the estate wherin they stand, when yee would have them so flattered that the danger

therof sould neither be knowne, neither yitt declared to the people."
" Where will yee find," said Lethington, " that anie of the prophets did so intreate kings, queens, rulers, or magistrats ?"   " In
moe places than one," said the other.   " Achab was a king, Jesabell was a queene, and yitt what the prophet Elias said to the one
and the other I suppose yee be not ignorant."   " That was not
cried out before the people," said Lethington, " to make them
odious unto their subjects."   " That Elias said, ' Dogges sall licke
the blood of Achab and eate the flesh of Jesabell,' Scriptures assure
me; but that it was whispered in their owne eare, or in a corner,
I read not.   But the plaine contrare appeareth to me, which is,
that both the people and the court understood weill eneugh what
the prophet had pronounced; for so witnessed Jehu, after that
God's vengeance had stricken Jesabell."   " These were singular
motiouns of the Spirit of God," said Lethington, " and apperteane
nothing to this age."   " Then hath the Scripture farre deceaved
me," said the other, " for Sanct Paul teacheth me that whatsoever
is writtin within the Holie Scriptures, the same is writtin for our
instruction.   And my Master sayeth, that everie learned and wise
scribe bringeth furth of his treasurie both things old and things
new.   And the Prophet Jeremiah affirmeth that everie realme or
citie that likewise offendeth, as then did Jerusalem, sould likewise
be punished.   Why that the facts of the ancient prophets, and the
fearefull judgements of God executed before us upon the disobedient, apperteane not to this our age, I neither see nor yitt can understand.   But now, to putt an end to this heed, my lord," said he,
" the prophets of God have not spaired to rebooke wicked kings,
als weill in their face as before the people and subjects.   Elisæus
feared not to say to King Jehoram, ' What have I to doe with
thee ? Gett thee to the prophets of thy father, and to the prophets
of thy mother; for as the Lord of Hoasts liveth, in whose sight I
stand, if it were not that I regarded the presence of Jehosaphat,
King of Judah, I would not have looked towards thee nor seene
thee.'   Plain it is, that the prophet was a subject in the kingdom
of Israel ; and yitt, how little reverence giveth he to the king ? In

the secund of Jeremie, the prophet was commanded to crie to the king and the queene, and to say, ' Behave yourselves lowlie in justice and judgement, or elles your carcases sall be cast to the heate of the day, and to the frost of the night.' Of Sallum and Zedekias he speeketh in speciall, and sheweth unto them, in his publick sermons, their miserable ends.   And, therefore, yee ought not to thinke it strange, my lord," said he, " albeit the servants of God taxe the vices of kings and queens als weil as other offenders, and that becaus their sinnes are more noysome to the commounwealth than are all the sinnes of inferiour persons."

The most part of this reasoning Secretar Lethington leaned upon the breast of the Master of Maxwell, and said, " I am almost wearie : I would that some would reasoun in the cheefe heed, which is not yitt tuiched."   Then the Erle of Morton, Chanceller, commanded Mr George Hay to reasoun against Mr Knox, in the heed of obedience due unto magistrats ; who beganne so to doe.   Unto whom Mr Knox said, " That yee sall reasoun in my contrare, I am weill content, becaus I know you are both a man of learning and of modestie.   But that yee sall oppone yourself unto the truthe, wherof I suppose your owne conscience is no lesse perswaded than is myne, I cannot weill approve ; for I would be sorie that I and yee sould be appointed to reasoun, as two schollers of Pythagoras, to shew the quicknesse of our ingyne, as it were, to reasoun on both parts. I doe protest heere before God, that whatsoever I susteane, I doe the same of conscience ; yea, I darre no more susteane anie propositioun knowne to myself untrue, than that I darre teache false doctrine in the publick place.   And, therefore, brother, if conscience move you to oppone yourself to that doctrine which yee have heard of my mouth in that mater, doe it boldlie ; it sall never offend me.   But that yee sall be found to oppone yourself unto me, yee being perswaded in the same truthe, I say yitt againe, it pleaseth me not ; for thereof may arise greater inconveniences than either yee or I consider for the present."   The said Mr George answered, " That I would oppone myself unto you, as willing to impugne or confute that heed of doctrine, which not onlie yee, but manie others, yea,

and I myself have affirmed, farre be it frome me, for so I sould be
found contrarious to myself; for my lord secretare knoweth my
judgement in that heed."

" Marie," said the secretar, " yee are the weill worst of the two,
for I remember yitt our reasoning when the queene was in the cabinet. Weill," said Lethington, " I am somwhat better provided
in this last heed than I was in the other two. Mr Knox," said he,
" we heard your judgement upon the 13th to the Romans ; we
heard the minde of the apostle weill opened ; we heard the caus
why God established powers upon the earth; we heard the necessitie that mankinde hath of the same, and we heard the duetie of
magistrats sufficientlie declared. But in two things I was offended,
and I thinke some of the lords that were present. The one was,
yee made difference betwixt the ordinance of God and the persons
that were placed in authoritie; and yee affirmed that men might
resist the persons, and yitt not offend God's ordinance. This is
the first. The other yee had no time to explaine. But this me-
thought yee meant, That subjects were not bound to obey their
princes if they commanded unlawful things; but that they might
resist their princes, and were not ever bound to suffer."

" In verie deed," said the other, " yee have both rightlie marked
my words, and understood my minde ; for of the same judgement
have I long beene, and so yitt I remaine." " How will ye prove
your divisioun and difference ?" said Lethington ; " and that the
persoun placed in authoritie may be resisted, and God's ordinance
not transgressed, seing that the apostle sayeth, ' He that resisteth
the powers resisteth the ordinance of God ?' My lord," said he,
" the plaine words of the apostle affirme that the powers are ordeaned of God, for the preservatioun of quiet and peaceable men,
and for the punishement of malefactors. Wherof it is plaine, that
the ordinance of God and power givin to man is one thing, and
the person clothed with the power or authoritie is another : for
God's ordinance is the preservatioun of mankinde, the punishement
of sinne, and the mainteaning of vertue, which is in itself holie, just,
constant, stable, and perpetuall. But men clothed with the autho-

ritie are commounlie profane and unjust; yea, they are mutable,
transitorie, and subject to corruption, as God threatneth them by
his prophet David, saying, 'I have said yee are gods, and everie one
of you the sonnes of the Most High; but yee sall dee as men, and
yee princes sall fall as others,' Ps. lxxxii. Heere, I am assured, the
persons, both soule and bodie, are threatned with death: I thinke
that so yee will not affirme is the authoritie, the ordinance, and the
power wherewith God hath endued suche persons as I have said.
As it is holie, so it is the permanent will of God. Now, my lord,
that the prince may be resisted, and yitt the ordinance of God not
violated, it is evident. For the people resisted Saul, when he had
sworne by the living God that Jonathan sould dee: the people, I
say, swore in the contrarie, and delivered Jonathan, so that an hair
of his head fell not to the ground. Now, Saul was their owne
anointed king, and they were his subjects; and yitt, they resisted
him, in that they made him no better than mansworne."

"I doubt," said Lethington, "if, in so doing, the people did
weill." "The Spirit of God accuseth them not of anie crime," said
the other, "but rather praiseth them, and damneth the king, als
weill for his foolish vow and law made without God, as for his
cruell minde, that so severelie would have punished an innocent
man. But in this I will not insist. The same Saul commanded
Ahimelech and the preests of the Lord to be slaine, becaus they
had committed treasoun, as he alledged, by intercommuning with
David. His guarde and principall servants would not obey his unjust commandements; but Doeg, the king's flatterer, putt the king's
crueltie in executioun. I will not aske your judgement whether
the servants of the king, in not obeying his commandement, resisted
God or not, or whether Doeg, in murthering the preests, gave obedience to a just authoritie; for I have the Spirit of God speeking
by the mouth of David, to assure me, als weill of the one as of the
other. For he, in the fiftie-two Psalme, damneth the fact as a
cruell murther, and affirmeth, that God would punishe not onlie
the commander, but also the mercilesse executer. Therefore, I
conclude, that they who withstood his commandement resisted not

the ordinance of God. Now, my lord, to answere to the place of
the apostle, affirming that suche as resist the powers resist the ordinance of God, I say, that by POWER in that place is to be understood, not the unjust commandement of men, but the lawfull power
wherwith God hath armed his magistrats, as lieutenants, to punishe
sinne, and to mainteane vertue. And if anie man sould enterprise
to take frome the hands of the lawfull judge a murtherer, adulterer,
or anie other malefactor deserving death by God's law, he resisteth
God's ordinance, and procureth to himself vengeance and damnatioun, becaus he stayeth God's sword to strike. But so is it not
if men, in the feare of God, oppone themselves to the furie and
blind rage of princes; for so, they resist not God but the devill,
who abuseth the sword and authoritie of God."

"I understand sufficientlie," said Lethington, "what yee meane,
and to the one part I will not oppone; but I doubt of the other.
For if the queene would command me to kill Johne Knox, becaus
she is offended at him, I would not obey her. But if she would
command others to doe it, or by colour of justice take his life frome
him, I cannot tell if I be bound to defend against the queene
and her officers." "Under protestatioun," said the other, "that
the auditors thinke not that I speeke in favours of my self, I say,
my lord, that if yee be perswaded of my innocencie, and if God
hath givin you suche power or credite, as thereby yee might deliver me, and yitt suffer me to perish, that so doing yee sould be
criminall and guiltie of my blood." "Prove that, and wonne the
plea!" said Lethington. "The prophet Jeremie was apprehended
by the preests and prophets, who were a part of the authoritie
within Jerusalem, and by the multitude of the people. This sentence was pronounced against him: 'Thou sall dee the death, for
thou hath said, This hous sall be like Siloah, and this citie sall be
desolat without an inhabitant,' Jerem. xxvi. The princes hearing
the uproare, came frome the king's hous, and satt doun in judgement, in the entrie of the new gate of the Lord's hous. There the
preests and prophets accused him before the princes and before all
the people, in these words, 'This man is worthie to dee, for he

hath propheceid against this citie, as your eares have heard.' Jeremie answered, whatsoever he had spokin proceeded from God;
therefore, said he, 'As for me, behold I am in your hands; doe
with me as yee thinke good and right. But know yee for certane,
that if yee putt me to death, yee sall bring innocent blood upon
yourselves, and upon this citie, and upon the inhabitants therof;
for of truthe the Lord hath sent me unto you, to speeke all these
words.' Now, my lords, if the princes and the whole people sould
have beene guiltie of the prophet's blood, how sall yee or others
be judged innocent before God, if yee sall suffer the blood of suche
as have not deserved death to be shed, when yee may save it?"
"The case is not alike," said Lethington. "And I would learn
wherin the dissimilitude standeth," said the other. "First," said
Lethington, "The king had not condemned him to death : Nixt,
The false prophets, the preests, and people, accused him without a
caus, and therefore could not but be guiltie of his blood." "Neither
of these fighteth against my argument," said the other. "For albeit
that neither the king was present, nor yitt had condemned him,
yitt were his princes and cheefe rulers there sitting in judgement,
who represented the king's person and authoritie, hearing the accusatioun layed to the charge of the prophet. Therefore he fore-
warneth them of the danger, as was said before, to witt, that in
case he sould be condemned, and so putt to death, that the king,
the counsell, and the whole citie of Jerusalem, sould be guiltie of
his blood, because he had committed no crime worthie of death.
If yee thinke that they sould all have beene criminall, onlie becaus
that all accused him, the text witnesseth plainlie the contrare ; for
the princes defended him, and so, no doubt, did a great part of
the people : yitt he boldlie affirmeth, that they sould all be guiltie
of his blood if he were putt to death. The prophet Ezechiel giveth
a reasoun why all are guiltie in a commoun corruptioun. 'Becaus,'
sayeth he, 'I sought a man amongst them, that sould make up the
hedge, and stand in the gape before me, for the land, that I sould
not destroy it, but I found none ; therefore have I poured out myne
indignatioun upon them.' Heere, my lord, it is plaine, that God

craveth not onlie that a man committ not iniquitie in his owne persoun, but also that he oppone himself, so farre as in him lyeth, to
the iniquitie of others."

"Then will yee," said Lethington, "have subjects to controll
their princes and rulers." "What harme sould the commoun
wealth receave," said the other, "if the corrupt affectiouns of ignorant and godlesse rulers were moderated, and so bridled by the
wisdome and discretioun of godlie subjects, that they doe no wrong
nor violence to anie man?" "All this reasoning," said Lethington,
"is out of purpose; for we reasoun as if the queene sould become
suche an enemie to our religioun that she sould persecute and putt
innocent men to death for it, which, I am assured, she never thought,
nor never will doe. For if I sould see her beginne at that end, or
if I sould suspect anie such thing in her, I sould be als fordward in
that argument as yee are, or anie within this realme: but there is
no suche thing. Our questioun is, whether we may and ought to
suppresse the queen's masse, or whether her idolatrie sall be layed
to our charge?" "What yee may," said Mr Knox, "by force, I
dispute not; but what yee may and ought to doe by God's commandement, that I can tell. Idolatrie ought not onlie to be suppressed, but the idolater ought to dee the death, unlesse we will
accuse God." "I know," said Lethington, "the idolater ought to
dee the death; but by whom?" "By the people of God," said
the other; "for the commandement was made to Israel, as yee
may read, 'Heare, O Israel, sayeth the Lord, the statuts and commandements of the Lord thy God.' Yea, commandements are
givin, that if it be heard that idolatrie is committed in anie citie,
that inquisitioun sall be takin; and if it be found true, that then
the whole bodie of the people sall arise, and destroy that citie,
spairing neither man, woman, nor childe." "But there is no commandement givin to the people," said the secretare, "to punishe
their king, if he be an idolater." "I find no priviledges granted to
kings," said the other, "by God, more than to the people, to offend
God's Majestie." "I graunt," said Lethington; "yitt the people
may not be judge to their king, to punishe him, howbeit he be an

idolater." "God," said Mr Knox, "is a commoun judge, als weill
to the king as to the people; so that what his Word commandeth
to be punished in the one, is not to be forborne in the other." "We
agree in that," said Lethington : "but the people must not execute
God's judgements, but leave it to himself; who will either punishe
by death, by warre, by imprisonnment, or other kinde of plagues."
"I know," said Mr Knox, "the last part of your reasoun to be
true ; but for the first, to witt, that the people, or a part of the
people, may not execute God's judgements against their king, being
an offender, I am sure yee have no other warrant but your owne
imaginatioun, and the opinioun of suche as feare more to offend
princes than God."

"Why say yee so ?" said Lethington : "I have the judgement of
the most famous men in Europe, and of suche as yee yourself will
confesse both godlie and learned." And with that he called for his
papers, which being exhibited by Mr Robert Matlane, he beganne to
read with great gravitie the judgement of Luther, Melancthon, the
mindes of Bucer, Musculus, and Calvine, how Christians sould behave themselves in time of persecutioun ; yea, the Booke of Baruch
was not omitted. Then he concluded, that the gathering of these
things had cost him more travell than he had takin these seven
yeeres in reading of anie commentars. "The more pitie," said the
other : "yitt what have yee profitted your owne caus lett others
judge. As for my assertioun, I am assured yee have infirmed it
nothing; for your first two witnesses spake against Anabaptists,
who denie that Christians sould be subject to magistrats ; which
opinioun I no lesse abhorre than yee doe, or anie other living. The
others speeke of Christians subject to tyranns and infidels ; so dispersed, that they have no power but onlie to sobbe to God for deliverance. That suche indeid sould hazard anie farther than these
godlie men will them, I would not wittinglie be upon counsell.
But my assertioun hath another ground. For I speeke of a people
assembled together in one bodie of a commoun wealth ; unto whom
God hath givin sufficient power, not onlie to resist, but also to suppresse all kinde of open idolatrie. Suche a people, yitt againe I

affirme, is bound to keepe their land cleane and unpolluted. That this my divisioun may not appeare strange unto you, yee sall understand that God required one thing of Abraham and his seed, when he and they were pilgrims and strangers in Egypt and Canaan; another thing frome them after their deliverance from the boundage of Egypt, and possessioun of the land of Canaan granted unto them. At the first, and during the time of their boundage, God craved no more but that Abraham sould not defile himself with idolatrie. Neither he nor his posteritie were commanded to destroy the idols that were in Canaan or Egypt. But when God gave unto them possession of the land, he gave unto them this strait commandement, 'Beware that thou make confederacie or league with the people of this land. Give not thy sonnes to their daughters, nor thy daughters to their sonnes. But this yee sall doe unto them: cutt doun their groaves, destroy their images, breake doun their altars, and leave you no kinde of remembrance of these abominations which the inhabitants of the land used before: for thou art an holie people to the Lord thy God. Defile not thyself, therefore, with their gods.' To the same commandement, I say, are yee, my lords, and suche as professe the Lord Jesus within this realme, bound; for God hath wrought no lesse miracle upon you, both corporallie and spirituallie, than he did upon the carnall seede of Abraham. For, in what estate your bodeis and this realme were within these seven yeeres yee cannot be ignorant. Yee, and it both, were under the boundage of a strange natioun. And what tyranns raigned over your consciences, it may be God yitt once againe lett you feele, becaus yee doe not rightlie acknowledge the benefite received. When our poore brethrein before us yeelded their bodeis to the flammes of fire for the testimonie of the truthe, and when skarse ten could be found in a countrie that rightlie knew God, it had beene foolishnesse either to have craved of the nobilitie or of the subjects the suppressing of idolatrie; for that had beene nothing but to have exponed the simple sheepe as a prey to the woolfe. But, since God hath multipleid knowledge, yea, and hath givin the victorie to his truthe even in the hands of his servants, if

yee suffer the land againe to be defiled, yee and your princesse sall
drinke the same cuppe of God's indignatioun; she for her obstinat
abiding in manifest idolatrie in this great light of the Evangell of
Jesus Christ, and yee for your permissioun and mainteaning of her
in the same."

Lethington said, "In that point we will never agree. Where
find yee, I pray you, that anie of the prophets or apostles taught
suche doctrine, that the people sould be plagued for the iniquitie of
their prince; or that subjects might suppresse the idolatrie of their
rulers, and punishe them for the same?" "What was the commissioun givin to the apostles, my lord?" said he. "It was to
preache and plant the Evangell of Jesus Christ, where darknesse before had dominioun. Therefore, it behooved them first to lett them
see the light, before they sould will them to putt to their hands to
suppresse idolatrie. What precepts the apostles gave to the faithfull in particular, other than that they commanded all to flee frome
idolatrie, I will not affirme. But I finde two things that the faithfull did. The one was, that they assisted their preachers even
against their rulers and magistrats; the other, that they suppressed
idolatrie whensoever God gave them force, asking no licence at the
emperour, nor at his deputs. Read the ecclesiasticall historie, and
yee sall find a sufficient number of exemples. As to the doctrine of
the prophets, we know they spake as weill to kings as to the people.
I read that neither would hear them; therefore came the plague
upon both. But that they flattered kings more than they did the
people I cannot be perswaded. Now, God's law pronounceth
death, as before I have said, upon idolaters without exceptioun.
Now, how the prophets could rightlie interprete the law, and show
the causes of God's judgements, which ever they threatned sould
follow idolatrie, and the rest of the abominatiouns which accompanie it, (for it goeth never alone; but ever a corrupt religioun
bringeth with it a filthie and a corrupt life:) how, I say, the prophets could reprove these vices, and not show the people their
duetie, I understand not. Therefore I constantlie beleeve that the
doctrine of the prophets was so sensible, that the kings understood

what were their owne abominatiouns, and the people understood
what they ought to have done, in punishing and repressing the same.
But becaus the most part of the people were no lesse rebellious
against God than were their princes, therefore the one and the other
were conjured enemeis against God and his servants. And yitt,
my lord, the facts of some prophets are so evident, that easilie
therof we may collect what doctrine they taught; for it were no
small mater to affirme that their facts sould repugne to their doctrine."

"I thinke," said Lethington, "yee meane of the historie of
Jehu: what will yee prove thereby?" "The cheefe heed," said
Mr Knox, "which yee denie, to witt, that the prophets never
taught that it apperteaned to the people to punishe the idolatrie of
their kings, the contrarie wherof I affirme; and for probatioun, I
am readie to produce the fact of a prophet. For yee know, my
lord," said he, "that Elisæus sent one of the childrein of the prophets to anoint Jehu, who gave him a commandement to destroy
the hous of his maister Achab, for the idolatrie committed by him,
and for the innocent blood which Jesabell, his wicked wife, shed;
which he obeyed, and putt into executioun. For this, God promised unto him the stabilitie of his kingdome to the fourth generatioun. Now," said he, "heere is the fact of a prophet proving that
subjects were commanded to execute God's judgements upon their
king and prince." "There is eneugh to answere," said Lethington; "for Jehu was a king before he putt anie thing in executioun.
Farther, the fact is extraordinar, and ought not to be imitated."
"My lord," said the other, "he was a mere subject, and no king,
when the prophet's servant came unto him; yea, albeit his fellow
captans, hearing of the message, blew the trumpet, and said, ' Jehu
is king,' yitt I doubt not but Jesabell both thought and said that
he was a traitour, and so did manie moe in Israel and Samaria.
As tuiching that which yee alledge, that the fact was extraordinar,
and not to be imitated, I say it had the ground of God's ordinarie
judgement and command, which commandeth idolaters to be putt
to death. Therefore, I yitt affirme that it is imitable, and to be

followed by those who prefere the true honour, worship, and glorie of God, to the affectiouns of the flesh and of wicked princes."

"We are not bound to follow extraordinarie exemples," said Lethington, "unlesse we have like commandement and assurance." "I grant," said the other, "if the exemple repugne to the law; as if an avaritious and deceatfull man would borrow gold, silver, rayment, or other necessareis from his nighbour, and withhold the same, alledging, that so he might doe without offence, becaus the Israelits, at their departure out of Egypt, did so to the Egyptians: the exemple serveth him to no purpose, unlesse he could alledge the like caus, and the like commandement, becaus their fact repugneth to this commandement of God, 'Thou sall not steale.' But where the exemple agreeth with the law, and is, as it were, the executioun of God's judgement expressed in the same, I say, that the exemple approved by God standeth unto us in place of a commandement; for as God in his nature is constant and immutable, so can he not damne the ages subsequent for that which he approved before in his servants. But in his servants before us He, by his owne commandement, hath approved that subjects have not onlie destroyed their kings for idolatrie, but also have rooted out all their posteritie, so that none of their race was left after, to impyre above the people of God." "Whatsoever they did," said Lethington, "was done at God's commandement." "That fortifeith my assertioun," said the other; "for God by his commandement hath approved that subjects punishe their kings for idolatrie and wickednesse committed by them." "We have not the like commandement," said Lethington. "That I denie," said the other; "for the commandement that the idolater sall dee the death is perpetuall, as yee your self have granted. Yee doubt onlie who sould be the executers against the king. I say the people of God: and I have sufficientlie proven, as I thinke, that God hath raised up the people, and by his prophet anointed a king, to take vengeance upon the king and his posteritie; which fact, since that time, was never retracted. Therefore, to me it remaineth for a constant and cleere commandement to all people professing the truthe, and having power to punishe vice, what they ought to doe in the like case. If the people had interprised anie thing against God's commandement, we might have doubted whether they had done weill or evill. But seing God bringeth the executioun of his law in practise, after it was come in oblivioun and contempt, what reasonable man can doubt now of God's will, unlesse he will doubt of all things which God reneweth not unto us by miracles, as it were, from age to age? But I am assured that the answere of Abraham to the riche man, who, being in hell, desired that Lazarus, or some other from the dead, sould be sent unto his brethrein and freinds, to forewarne them of his incredible paines and torments, so to behave themselves that they come not to that place of torment—the answere, I say, givin to him, sall confound all suche as crave farther approbatioun of God's will than is alreadie expressed within his holie Scriptures. For Abraham said, ' They have Moses and the prophets ; whom, if they will not beleeve, neither will they beleeve albeit one frome the dead sould rise againe.' Even so, my lord, I say, that suche as will not be taught what they ought to doe by the commandement of God once givin, and once putt in practise, will not beleeve nor obey albeit God would send angels from heaven to instruct them."

" Yee have produced but one exemple," said Lethington. " One sufficeth," said the other. " Yitt praised be God, we laike not other ; for the whole people conspired against Amaziah, king of Judah, after that he had turned away from the Lord ; pursued him to Lachish, and slue him, and tooke Uzziah, and annointed him king instead of his father. The people had not altogether forgot the league and covenant which was made betwixt their kings and them, at the inauguration of Joash his father ; to witt, that the king and the people sould be the people of the Lord, and then sould they be his faithfull subjects. From which covenant, when first the father, and after the sonne declynned, they were both punished to death, Joash by his owne servants, and Amaziah by the whole people." " I doubt, said Lethington, " whether they did weill or not." " It sall be free to you," said the other, " to doubt as yee please. But when I find executioun according to God's law, and God himself not to accuse the doers, I darre not doubt of the equitie of their caus. Farther, it appeareth to me that God gave sufficient approbatioun and allowance of their fact; for he blessed them with victorie, peace, and prosperitie, the space of fiftie-two yeeres." "Prosperitie," said Lethington, "doth not alwayes prove that God approveth the facts of men." " Yes," said the other: " when the facts of men agree with the law of God, and are rewarded by God's owne promise expressed in his law, I say, that prosperitie succeeding the fact is a most infallible assurance that God hath approved the fact. Now, so it is, that God hath promised in his law, when people sall exterminat and destroy suche as declyne from him, that he will blesse and multiplie them, as he promiseth unto their fathers. But so it is, that Amaziah turned from God; the people slue him, and God blessed them. Therefore, yitt againe, I conclude, that God approved their fact, in so farre as it was done according to his commandement, and blessed them according to his promise."

" Weill," said Lethington, " I thinke not the ground so sicker, as that I durst build my conscience therupon." " I pray God," said the other, " that your conscience have no worse ground than this, whensoever yee sall beginne a worke like that which God, in your owne eyes, hath alreadie blessed. Now, my lord," said he, I have but one exemple to produce, and then I will putt an end to my reasoning, becaus I wearie to stand longer." He was biddin sitt doun, but he refused, and said, " Melancholious reasouning would have some mirth intermixed. My last exemple, my lord, is this :—Uzziah the king, not content with his royall estate, malapertlie tooke upon him to enter within the temple of the Lord, to burne incense upon the altar of incense; and Azariah the preest went in after him, and with him eightie preests of the Lord, valient men. They withstood Uzziah the king, and said unto him, ' It apperteaneth not unto Uzziah to burne incense unto the Lord; but to the preests, the sonnes of Aaron, who are consecrated to offer incense. Goe furth of the sanctuarie, for thou hath trans-

gressed, and thou sall have no honour of the Lord.' Heerof, my
lords, I conclude, that subjects not onlie may, but also ought to
withstand and resist their princes, whensoever they doe anie thing
expresslie repugnant to God's law or ordinances."

"These who withstood the king were not simple subjects, but
preests of the Lord, and types of Christ : suche persons have we
none this day, to withstand kings when they doe wrong," said Lethington. "That the High Preest was a type of Christ," said the
other, "I grant. But that he was not a subject, I denie ; for I am
assured, that he, in his preesthood, had no prerogative above these
that passed before him. Now, so it is, that Aaron was subject
to Moses, and called him his lord. Samuel being both preest and
prophet, subjected himself to Saul, after that he was inaugurated
by the people. Zadock bowed before David, and Abiather was
deposed from the preesthood by Salomon. All these confessed
themselves subject to their kings, albeit they ceased not to be
figures of Christ. Where as yee say that we have no suche preests
this day, I may answere, that as then kings were anointed at God's
commandement, and satt upon the seate of David, were no lesse
figures of Christ Jesus in their just ministratioun, than were the
preests in their office. Suche kings, I am assured, we have not
now, more than we have suche preests ; for Christ Jesus being
anointed in our nature by God his Father, king, preest, and prophet, hath putt an end to all suche externall things. Yitt I thinke
yee will not say, that God hath more diminished the graces of these
whome he appointeth ambassaders betwixt him and his people,
than he doth of kings and princes. Therefore, why the servants of
Jesus Christ may not als justlie withstand this day kings and princes
offending God's Majestie no lesse than Uzziah did, I see not, unlesse yee will say, that we in the brightnesse of the Evangell are
not so straitlie bound to regarde God's glorie, nor yitt his commandement, as were the fathers, who lived under the darke shadows
of the law."

" Weill," said Lethington, " I will dippe no farther in that heed.
But how resisted the preests the king ? They onlie spake to him,

without farther violence intended." "That they withstood him,"
said the other, "the text assureth me; but that they did nothing
but speeke, I cannot understand; for the text affirmeth plainlie the
contrare, to witt, that they caused him hastilie to depart out of the
sanctuarie; yea, that he was compelled to depart. Which maner of
speeche, I am assured, in the Hebrew tongue importeth more than
exhortatioun, or commanding by word." "They did that," said
Lethington, "after he was espied to be leprous." "They withstood him before," said the other. "But yitt their last fact confirmeth my propositioun; for my assertioun is this, that kings have
no more priviledge than the people to offend God's Majestie: and
if they so doe, that they are no more exempted from the punishement of the law than anie other subject; yea, and that subjects
may not onlie lawfullie oppone themselves to their kings, whensoever they doe anie thing expresslie repugning to God's commandement, but also that they may execute judgement upon them, according to God's law. So that, if the king be a murtherer, adulterer, or idolater, he sould suffer according to God's law, not as a
king, but as an offender. That the people may putt God's law in
executioun, this historie proveth; for how soone the leprosie was
espied in his forehead, he was not onlie compelled to depart out of
the sanctuarie, but was also removed frome all publict societie, and
administratioun of the kingdome; and compelled to dwell in a hous
apart, even as the law commanded, and gott no farther prerogative
in that case than anie other of the people sould have done. This
was executed in part by the people; for, no doubt, there were
more witnesses of his leprosie than the preests. We find none oppone themselves to the sentence of God, pronounced in his law
against the leprous. Therefore, yitt againe say I, that the people
ought to execute God's law, even upon their princes, when their
knowne crimes by God's law deserve death, speciallie suche as
may infect the rest of the multitude. Now, my lord, I will reasoun no longer, for I have spokin more than I intended."

"Yitt," said Lethington, "I cannot tell what may be concluded."
"Albeit yee cannot," said the other, "yitt I am assured of that

which I have provin, to witt, that subjects have delivered an innocent out of the hands of the king, and therin have not offended
God: that subjects have refused to strike innocents when a king
commanded, and, so doing, denyed no just obedience: that suche
as stroke at the commandement of the king were reputed as murtherers: that God not onlie hath of a subject made a king, but also
hath armed the subjects against their naturall kings, and commanded them to execute vengeance upon them, according to the
law.   And last, that God's people have executed God's law against
their king, having no farther regarde to him in that behalfe than if
he had beene the most simple subject within the realme.   Therefore, albeit that yee will not understand what sould be concluded,
yitt I am assured that God's people not onlie may, but also are
bound to doe the same, where the like crimes are committed, and
where he giveth them the like power."   "Weill," said Lethington,
"I thinke yee sall not find manie learned men of your opinioun."
"My lord," said the other, "the truthe ceasseth not to be the
truthe, howsoever it be that men either misknow or withstand it:
yitt," said he, "I laike not the counsell of God's servants in that
heed."   And with that he presented to the secretar the Apologie
of Magdeburg, and willed him to read the names of the ministers
who had subscrived, wherin the defence of the toun was justifeid as
most lawfull: and therwith added, that to resist a tyranne is not to
resist God his ordinance.   When Lethington had viewed the Apologie, he scripped and said, "*Homines obscuri:*" the other answered,
"*Dei tamen servi.*"

So Lethington arose and said, "My lords, yee have heard the
reasouns upon both the parts: it becometh you now to decide, and
to put an order to preachers, that they may be uniforme in doctrine.   May we, thinke yee, take the queen's masse from her?"
Whill as some beganne to give their votes, (for some were appointed to be leaders to the rest,) Mr Knox said, "My lords, I
suppose that your lordships will not doe contrare to your promise
made to the whole Assemblie, which was, that nothing sould be
voted in secreit till first that all maters be debated in publick; and

that then the votes of the Assemblie sould put an end to the controversie. I have rather showin my conscience in simple maner, than insisted upon the force of anie argument. Therefore I, for my part, utterlie disassent from all voting, till that the whole Assemblie have heard the questioun and reasouns on both parteis; for I unfainedlie acknowledge, that manie in that companie are more able to susteane that assertioun than I am." " Thinke yee it reasounable," said Lethington, " that suche a multitude as is now conveened sould reasoun and vote upon these heeds and maters, which concerne the queen's Majestie's owne persoun and effaires ?" " I think," said the other, " that whatsoever sould bind the multitude the multitude sould heare, unlesse they have resigned their power to their commissioners, which they have not done, so farre as I understand; for my Lord Justice-Clerk heard them with one voice say, that in no wise would they consent that anie thing sould be voted or concluded heere." " I cannot tell," said Lethington, " if the lords heere present, and that beare the burthein of these maters, sould be bound to their will. What say yee, my lords? Will yee vote in this mater or not ?" After long reasouning, some made for the purpose, said, " Why may not the lords vote, and then show to the Assemblie whatsoever is done ?" " That appeareth to me," said Mr Knox, " not onlie a backward order, but also a tyrannicall usurpation over the Assemblie. But as for me, doe as yee please," said he, " for as I reasoun, so I vote; yitt protesting as before, that I disassent from all voting, till the whole Assemblie understand what the questioun and reasouns are." " Weill," said Lethington, " that cannot be done now, for the time is spent. Therefore, my Lord Chanceller," said he, " aske the votes at one of the ministers, and at one of us by course." So the Rector of Sanct Andrewes was first demanded. He said, " I refere it to the Superintendent of Fife; for I thinke we are both of one judgement. Yitt," said he, " if yee will that I first declare what in conscience I judge, I thinke, that if the queene oppone herself to our religioun, which is the onlie true religioun, that in that case the nobilitie and states of the realme professing the same may justlie oppone themselves to her.

As concerning her masse, I know it is idolatrie; yitt I am not re-solved, whether that by violence we may take it from her or not." The Superintendent of Fife, and others of the nobilitie, affirmed the same. Others voted franklie, that as the masse is abominable idol-atrie, so ought it to be repressed; and that, in so doing, men did no more wrong to the queen's Majestie than these who sould by force tak from her a poysoned cuppe, when she was going to drinke it.

At last, Mr Johne Craig, fellow minister with Mr Knox, was re-quired to give his vote, who said, "I will gladelie show unto your honours what I thinke. But I greatlie doubt whether that my knowledge and conscience sall satisfie you, seing yee have heard al-readie so manie reasouns, and are so little moved with them. Yitt I sall not conceale my judgment, adhering to my brother his pro-testatioun, to witt, that our voting prejudge not the libertie of the Generall Assemblie. I was," said he, "in the Universitie of Bo-nonia, in the yeere of our Lord 1553, where, in the place of the Blacke Friers of the same toun, I saw this conclusioun following sett furth in time of their Generall Assemblie, reasouned and de-termined: ' *Principes omnes tam supremi, quam inferiores, possunt, et debent reformari vel deponi, per eos per quos eliguntur, confirman-tur, vel admittuntur ad officium, quoties a fide præstita subditis per juramentum deficiunt. Quoniam relatio juramenti subditorum et prin-cipum mutua est, ut utrinque æquo jure servanda et reformanda, juxta legem et conditionem juramenti ab utraque parte facti.*' That is, ' All rulers, be they supreme or be they inferiour, may and ought to be reformed or deposed by these by whom they are chosin, confirmed, or admitted to their office, als oft as they breake their promise made by oath to their subjects; becaus the prince is no lesse bound to subjects, than subjects are to princes. And therefore ought it to be keeped and reformed, equallie according to the law and con-dition of the oath, which is made of either partie.' This proposi-tioun, my lords, I heard sustcaned and concluded, as I have said, in a most notable auditorie. The susteaner was a learned man, Thomas de Smola, Rector of the Universitie, a famous man in that countrie. Vincentius de Placentia affirmed the assertioun to be most true and certane, agreeable both with the law of God and man. The occasioun of the disputatioun was a certane disorder and tyrannie attempted by the Pop's governours, who beganne to make innovatiouns in the countrie against the lawes formerlie established, alledging themselves not to be subject to suche lawes, by reasoun they were not constituted by the people, but by the Pope, who was king of that countrie; and, therefore, that having full commissioun and authoritie frome the Pope, they might alter and change statuts and ordinances of the countrie, without all consent of the people. Against this their usurped tyrannie, the learned among the people opponned themselves openlie. When all the reasouns which the Pop's governours did alledge were heard and confuted, the Pope himself was faine to take up the controversie, and to promise that he not onlie sould keepe the libertie of the people, but also that he sould neither abrogat anie law or statute, nor mak anie new law without their owne consent. Therefore," said Mr Craig, " my vote and judgement is, that princes are not onlie bound to keepe lawes and promises to their subjects, but also, that if they faile they may be justlie deposed; for the band betwixt the prince and the people is reciprock."

Then start up a claw-backe of the corrupt court and said, " Yee know not what yee say, for yee tell us what was done in Bononia. Wee are in a kingdome, they are in a commoun wealth." " My lord," said he, " everie kingdome is a commoun wealth, or at least sould be, albeit everie commoun wealth is not a kingdome. Therefore, I thinke, that in a kingdome, no lesse diligence ought to be used, that lawes be not violated, than in a commoun wealth; becaus the tyrannie of princes who rule in a kingdome is more hurtfull to the subjects than the misgovernement of these who, from yeere to yeere, are changed, in free commoun wealths. To assure your lordships yitt farther, that heed was disputed to the uttermost. In end, it was concluded and interpreted, that they spake not of suche things as were done in diverse kingdoms and natiouns, by tyrannie and negligence of the people, ' but we conclude,' say they,

' what ought to be done in all kingdoms and commoun wealths, according to the law of God, and just lawes of men. And if, through the negligence of the people, or by tyrannie of princes, contrarie lawes have beene made, yitt may that same people, or their posteritie, justlie crave all things to be reformed, according to the originall institutioun of kingdoms and commoun wealths : and suche as will not doe so deserve to eate the fruict of their owne foolishnesse.'"

Mr James Makgill, then Clerk-Register, perceaving the votes to be different, and the plainnesse and libertie of Mr Craig, said, " I remember this questioun was long debated before this time in my hous; and there, by reasoun we were not all of one minde, it was concluded, that Mr Knox sould write in all our names to Mr Calvine, to require his judgement in this controversie." " Nay," said Mr Knox, " my lord secretare he would not consent, alledging that the answere would depend muche upon the narrative; and therefore promised that he would write, and that I sould see it. But when diverse times I required him to remember his promises, I found nothing but delay." " True it is," said Lethington, " I promised to write, and that Mr Knox required me diverse times so to doe. But when I had deepelie advised and considered the weight of that mater, I beganne to find moe doubts than I did before, and among the rest this :—How durst I, being a subject, and the queen's Majestie's secretare, take upon me to seeke resolution of controverseis, depending betwixt her Highnesse and her subjects, without her owne knowledge and consent?" Then was there an acclamatioun of the claw-backes of the court, as if Apollo had givin his responce. " Weill," said Mr Knox, " let worldlie men praise worldlie wisdome als muche as they please : I am assured that by suche shifts idolatrie is mainteaned, Christ his truthe is betrayed, for the which, God one day will be avenged." At this and the like sharpnesse, manie offended, the voting ceassed, and everie factioun spake as affectioun moved them. In end, Mr Knox was againe desired to write to Mr Calvine, and to the learned in other kirks, to know their judgement in that questioun. He refused with this reasoun : —" I am not onlie fullie resolved in conscience myself, but also I

have had the judgements in this and all other things which I have
mainteaned within this realme, of the most godlie and learned that
be knowne to be in Europe. I came not to this realme without
their resolution; and for my better assurance I have the hand-
writt of manie. If I sould move the same questioun againe, what
sould I doe, but either shew my owne ignorance or forgetfulnesse?
And, therefore, it may please you to pardoun me, albeit I doe write
not. But I will shew you a surer way: write, and compleane upon
me, that I have taught and mainteaned constantlie suche doctrine
as offendeth you; so sall yee know their mindes plainlie, whether
they and I agree in judgement or not." Divers said the offer was
good; but no man was found to take it in hand. So that meeting
brake up. After this time, the ministers who were called precise
were holdin by the courteours as monsters. All this time, the Erle
of Murrey was so frem[1] to Mr Knox, that nather by word nor by
writt was there anie communicatioun betwixt them. Mr Knox
endeth this Fourth Booke of his Historie with this conference.

ARTICLES AND PETITIONS.

It was thought good in this Assemblie, and conforme to the acts
made before the queen's Majestie her arrivall, and approved since
her arrivall, that Christ's true religioun be *de novo* established, ratifeid, and approved throughout the whole realme; and that all idolatrie, speciallie masse, be abolished everie where, so that no other
face of religioun be suffered to be erected within this realme. And
for this effect, that the ministrie be sufficientlie provided with maintenance, and sure appointment, where they sall take up their stipends. In like maner, to desire that the transgressors of the saids
lawes be punished, speciallie in Aberdeen, the Karse of Gowrie,
Seyfeild, and other places which sall be specifeid. The Lairds of
Lundie, Abbotshall, Spott, Elphinston, Wedderburne, Fadownside,
Carnall, Kerse, Kelwod, Craig, Gairleis, Mr George Gordoun, and

---

[1] Foreign, strange.

the Proveist of Dundie, were appointed to present these articles to
the Lords of Secreit Counsell. The Erles of Murrey, Argile, Glencarne, and the Secretare, being present, and sent by the queene, to
observe what things were propouned in the Assemblie, thought
not good the articles sould be propouned after that maner, but drew
out two heeds. First, They would declare the good minde and
obedience of the Assemblie. Nixt, They would labour at her Grace's
hands for establishing religioun, according to the order established
before her arrivall. They promised also to deal with her for sett
stipends. Lethington returned a gracious answere to these heeds.
It was appointed that a requeist sould be presented to the queene,
for obteaning the gift of the friers' kirk of Kirkudbright, to be
holdin heerafter the parish kirk of Kirkudbright.

ACTS.

It was concluded, that no minister placed in anie congregatioun
sall leave the same, and passe to another, without knowledge of the
flocke, the superintendent, or whole Assemblie; and that the caus
be considered by the superintendent or the Assemblie, whether it be
lawfull or not. Mr Patrik Constane craving licence to passe to
other countreis for a time, to acquire increasse of knowledge, was
inhibited to leave his congregatioun without licence of the Assemblie.

A COMMISSION TO CONFER UPON CAUSES ECCLESIASTICALL.

In the fyft sessioun it was concluded, that the Superintendents
of Angus, Lothiane, Fife, and the West; Mrs Johne Row, George
Hay, Robert Pont, Christopher Gudman, Johne Knox, Johne
Craig, George Buchanan, Johne Rutherforde, Thomas Drummond,
Robert Hammiltoun, Clement Littell, the Lairds of Lundie, Elphinston, Carnall, Kerse, Abbotshall, conveene the day following,
after sermoun, to conferre anent the causes apperteaning to the

jurisdictioun of the kirk, and to report their judgements to the nixt conventioun.

THE COMPLAINT OF THE LABOURERS OF THE GROUND.

The labourers of the ground compleaned of the rigourous exactioun of the tithes.   The Erle of Murrey, Johne Maxwell of Tarrgles, Knight, the Erle of Menteith, the Lords Lindsay and Uchiltree, the Secretare, the Lairds of Kerse and Letham, Alexander Bishop of Galloway, and the gentlemen of the west, promised to be content of money or victuall, as indifferent men sould modifie.

Commissioun givin in the preceding Assemblie to visite the hospitall of Glasgow, was takin a compt of.   Commission is givin to trie the expediencie of the removall of a minister from one place to another.   A soliciter is chosin for the actions of the kirk, to be pleaded before the Lords of Counsell and Sessioun.   Ministers are censured, or commissioun givin to censure them.   Commissioners of provinces continued for a yeere, or appointed of new.   Mr Knox is appointed to visite the kirks of the north, and to remaine there six or seven weekes, becaus the north parts were destitute of superintendents and commissioners.

THE NYNTH GENERALL ASSEMBLIE.

The Generall Assemblie conveened at Edinburgh, the 25th of December, in the upper tolbuith.   Mr Knox made the exhortatioun.   Johne Areskine of Dun, Superintendent of Angus, was chosin Moderator.

TRIELL OF SUPERINTENDENTS AND COMMISSIONERS.

In the triell of superintendents and commissioners, it was demanded by some brethrein, whether the Commissioners of Galloway and Orkney might both duelie exerce the office of a Superintendent and office of a Lord of the Colledge of Justice.   It was ordeaned, that no questioun sould be propouned till the effaires of the Assemblie were ended; and that then it be presented in writt. And if, for shortnesse of time, it could not be decided before the end of the Assemblie, that the decisioun be referred to the superintendent of the bounds where the questioun ariseth, and a certane number of ministers within his bounds, as he sall choose to assist him; and that their reasons be reported in writt to the nixt Assemblie.

ARTICLES AND PETITIOUN.

The articles following were ordeaned to be presented to the Lords of Secreit Counsell, that they may crave answere from the queen's Majestie.   First, The Assemblie humblie required their honours to signifie to the queen's Majestie, that the transgressers of the edicts published against hearers and sayers of masse, and abusers of the sacraments, are become so manie, that it may be greatlie feared that judgements sall suddanlie follow, except remeed be provided in due time.   Secundlie, To require payment to ministers of their stipends for the times bypast, according to the promise made; and to lett the Assemblie know how the ministers sall be susteaned in times to come.   Thridlie, To require superintendents to be placed where none are as yitt placed, to witt, in the Merce, Tiviotdaill, Forrest, Tweddaill, and the rest of the dailes in the south; Aberdeen, and other parts in the north.   Fourthlie, To require suche to be punished as have shoot the doores of parish kirks, and would not open the same to preachers presenting themselves to preache the Word; as at Paisley, Aberdeene, Tirray, Dupline, and Aberdegie, &c.   Fyftlie, To require of the queen's Majestie what the Assemblie sould looke for, tuiching provisioun of benefices vacant and to vaike, &c.   Sixtlie, By what meanes the ministers sall come to the possessioun of their manses and gleebes, whether they be sett in few or not.   Lastlie, That the Act tuiching reparatioun of kirks might be putt in executioun.

ACTS.

It was ordeaned, that everie minister, exhorter, and reader, sall have one of the Psalmes bookes latelie printed in Edinburgh, and use the order conteaned therin, in prayers, mariage, and ministration of the sacraments.

2d, *Item,* That no minister sall admitt to publict repentance persons relapsed the thrid time in fornicatioun, drunkennesse, or the like crime; but that he send them to the superintendent of the diocie where the crime is committed, and that they cause the offender satisfie the Kirk for the offence committed, als manie dayes, and in that forme that the superintendent sall thinke good.

COMMISSION FOR VISITATION OF KIRKS.

Persons nominated for electioun to the Superintendentship of Aberdeen, in December 1562, were again putt in leits, that edicts might be served, and the person chosin might be inaugurated. Superintendents were appointed to try ministers, exhorters, readers; suspend for a time, or depose for anie crime, ignorance, or other insufficiencie, in the bounds of other superintendents, as was alloted to them by the Assemblie. Mr Knox was appointed to visite the kirks of Fife, Stratherne, Gowrie, and Menteith. It was ordeaned that these visiters report their diligence to the nixt Assemblie in writt.

ANSWERE TO PAUL METHVEN'S SUPPLICATION.

The Assemblie was content to receave Paul Methven to publict repentance, providing he presented himself personallie, and obeyed the forme which sould be injoyned to him; but would not delete the processe led against him out of their bookes, nor admitt him to the ministrie within this realme, till his former offence were buried in oblivioun, and some particular congregatioun requested for him.

The Assemblie willed the presenters of the supplicatioun to signifie unto him, that they were greevouslie offended that he, being excommunicated and unreconciled, had entered in the ministrie within England.

M.D.LXV.

LORD DARLY COME HOME.

Henrie Lord Darly, sonne to the Erle of Lennox, came to Scotland about the middest of Februarie, having obteaned licence for three moneth from Queen Elizabeth. Muche talke there was of the apparaunt matche betwixt the queene and him. The nobilitie repyned not, providing Queene Elizabeth consented. Queene Elizabeth did not so muche repyne at the matche, as provide that the cariage of the bussinesse might seeme cheefelie to depend upon her.

DAVID RIZIO HIS CREDIT IN COURT.

David Rizio, commounlie called among us Seigneur Davie, not being interteaned in the Duke of Savoye's court as he wished, came with the Duke of Savoye's ambassader, Moret, to Scotland, who left him heere at court, having no need of his service. He had some skill in musick. His father was an instructer of schollers in that art. He purchased favour among the musicians and fidlers, the most part wherof were Frenchemen. He insinuated himself so in the queen's favour, that he not onlie overtopped all the rest of his fellowes in credite, but also was preferred to be her secretar in forraine effaires; and upon that occasioun was oft tymes in secreit with the queene. Sindrie of the nobles attended upon him, and convoyed him to and fro. The Erle of Murrey signifeid by his verie countenance, that he disdained him, wherat not onlie the seigneur, but also the queene herself, was offended.[1]   To strenthen

[1] The behaviour of other Scotish noblemen towards the Italian upstart was still

himself against these who hated him, he insinuated himself in the favours of Lord Darly so farre, that they would ly some times in one bed together. He assureth him, that by his procurement the queene had fastenned her eyes upon him. He did what he could to sow dissensioun betwixt Lord Darly and the Erle of Murrey. The erle perceaving how matters went, and that his admonitions were not regarded, left the court. The queene was weill content; for she intended now to strenthen herself by a factioun of the nobilitie, that she might accomplishe her designes. For this caus, the Erle Bothwell was called home out of France, Sutherland out of Flanders, George Erle of Huntlie restored.

THE ERLE OF MURREYES DEATH CONTRIVED.

The Erle Bothwell had conspired against the Erle of Murrey. He is accused by the erle. When the queene could not disswade him from pursuing, she terrifeid sindrie noblemen, by her letters, from keeping the day of law; yitt Bothwell, conscious of his owne guiltinesse, durst not abide the triell. The favour caried by the people to the Erle of Murrey was a mater of great displeasure to the queene. His death was contrived after this maner. He was to be called for to Sanct Johnstoun, where the queene was resident for the time. Lord Darly sould enter in conference with him, and a little after, as offended with his free speeches, sould fall in chyding with him. Then sould Seigneur Davie give him the first stob, and others follow, till he were dispatched. The erle, advertised by some freinds at court, holdeth on notwithstanding in his journey, till Patrik Lord Lindsay disswaded him. Then he turned off the way to Lochlevin, and fained as if he had beene sicke. Becaus some freinds came to visite him, the bruite was spread incontinent, that he stayed there to intercept the queene and Lord Darly, when

---

more unequivocal.—" Some of the nobilitie (says Melvil) would frown upon him; others would shoulder and shoot him by, when they entered the queen's chamber, and found him alwayes speaking with her."—*Sir James Melvil's Memoirs*, p. 107. Edin. 1735.

they were to returne to Edinburgh. The feilds are searched. Howbeit there was no appearance of anie suche thing, the queene came
to Edinburgh in all haste, as if there had beene some imminent
and certane danger.

THE TENTH GENERALL ASSEMBLIE.

The Generall Assemblie conveened at Edinburgh in the neather
tolbuith, the 25th day of June, where exhortation being made by
the Superintendent of the West, he was chosin Moderator.

PETITIONS.

The nobilitie who were present were requeisted to be humble
suters to her Highness, for execution of the Acts latelie made
against the violaters of the Sabbath, committers of adulterie and
fornicatioun. Everie superintendent was desired to sute for commissiouns to judges within their jurisdictions, to punishe the committers of the saids crimes according to the tenor of the saids lawes
and acts. *Item,* To compleane, that the tithes assigned before in
some parts for payment to ministers, were givin by her Grace to
some gentlemen, and to understand her Grace's will theranent.
The Superintendents of Angus and the West, Christopher Gudman, and Mr Johne Row, minister at Perth, were appointed to
forme some articles to be presented to the queene's Majestie, which
they did, in tenor as followeth :—

Imprimis, That the papisticall and blasphemous masse, with all
Papistrie and idolatrie, and Pope's jurisdictioun, be universallie
suppressed and abolished throughout the realme, not onlie in the
subjects, but also in the queene's Majestie's owne person ; and all
persons which sall be deprehended to transgresse or offend in the
same be punished : and that the sincere Word of God and true religioun now received may be established, ratifeid, and approved
throughout the whole realme, as weill in the queene's Majestie's
owne person as in the subjects, without anie impediment ; and

that the people be astricted to resort, upon the Lord's day at least, to the prayers and preaching of God's Word, as they were astricted before to the idolatrous masse: and these heeds to be established by Act of Parliament, with consent of the Estats, and the queene's Majestie's ratificatioun.

Secundlie, That sure provisioun be appointed for sustentatioun of the ministrie, als weill for the time present as for the time to come; and that suche persons as are presentlie admitted have their stipends assigned unto them in the places where they travell, or, at the least, in the nixt adjacent, that they have no occasioun to crave the same at the hands of others: and that the benefices now vacant, or that have vaiked since the moneth of Marche 1558, or that heerafter sall happin to vaike, be dispouned to qualifeid persons, able to preache God's Word, and discharge the office of the ministrie, according to the triell and admissioun of their superintendents; and that no bishoprick, abbacie, pryorie, nor deanerie, provestrie, or anie other benefices, having manie kirks annexed to them, be dispouned whollie in time to come to anie one man; but that, at least, the kirks therof be severallie disponed to severall persons, that everie one having charge may serve at his owne kirk, according to his vocatioun; and to this effect, that the gleebes and manses be givin to ministers, that they may make residence at their kirks, and discharge their conscience in the exercise of their calling: and also, that the kirks may be repaired accordinglie; and that a law be made and established for this effect.

Thridlie, That none be permitted to have charge of schooles, colledges, or universiteis, or yitt privatlie or publiclie instruct the youth, but suche as shall be tried by the superintendents or visiters of the kirk, found sound and able in doctrine, and admitted by them to their charges.

Fourthlie, For sustentatioun of the poore, that all lands founded for hospitalitie be restored againe to the same use; and that all lands, annuel rents, or anie other emoluments perteaning anie wise some time to the friers, of whatsoever order they have beene of, or annuel rents, alterages, obits perteaning to preests, be applyed to the sustentatioun of the poore, and upholding of schooles, in the touns and other places where they ly.

Fyftlie, That suche horrible crimes as now abound in this realme without correctioun, to the great contempt of God and his holie Word, as idolatrie, blaspheming of God's name, manifest breache of the Sabboth-day, witchecraft, sorcerie, and inchantment, adulterie, incest, whoordome, maintenance of brothells, murther, slaughter, reafe, spoilzie, with manie other detestable crimes, may be severelie punished; and judges appointed in everie province or diocie, with power to execute, and that by Act of Parliament.

Lastlie, That some order be devised and established for the ease of the poore labourers of the ground, concerning the reasonable payment of their tithes, now rigourouslie exacted without their advice and consent.

Walter Lundie of that Ilk, William Cuninghame of Cuninghameheid, William Durhame of Grange, George Hume of Spot, James Baron, burgesse of Edinburgh, were appointed to present these articles to her Highnesse, and to report an answere before the dissolving of the Assemblie, if they may convenientlie : if not, to report to the eldership of Edinburgh, that they may signifie the samine to the superintendents.

AN ACT DEPENDING UPON THE PETITIONS.

Becaus sindrie ministers desired libertie to remove to places destitute of the Word, where they might be susteaned by the godlie, it was ordeaned, that no minister, exhorter, or reader, placed presentlie at anie kirk, sall attempt to remove till answere be receaved againe from the queene's Majestie to the articles directed to her ; and that after, none remove without the advice of the superintendent of his diocie, and his license in writt, under the paine of deprivatioun.

QUESTIONS DECIDED.

Adam Bishop of Orkney, Maisters Johne Craig, Christopher Gudman, Johne Row, George Buchanan, and Robert Pont, were ordeaned to conveene apart everie morning, to decide questions propouned, or to be propouned; and to report their decisions to the Assemblie, that the samine may be insert in the register. They reported their decisions in the thrid sessioun. They determined, that parteis proceed not orderlie in mariage, who nather obteane the consent of their parents, nor make sute to the sessioun of the kirk, to concurre with them in their lawfull proceedings. *Item*, That no minister·ought to injoy anie benefice or stipend belonging to anie kirk, except he remaine at the said kirk, to discharge his office. And if he be transplanted by the Assemblie or superintend-ent to another congregation, whereby he may not discharge his charge in both, that he be deprived of the one benefice or stipend, providing he be sufficientlie answered of one stipend. *Item*, Though it was not found contrarie to the Word of God, that a man abusing his father's brother's daughter seven yeeres, and begetting childrein upon her, may marie her, yitt becaus it hath not beene accustomed in this realme, and diverse inconveniences may ensue upon this libertie, it was referred to the civill magistrat, or to a parliament; granting libertie, notwithstanding, to the persons in whose name the questioun was propouned, to joyne in mariage, after their pub-lict repentance, provyding it be not a preparative to others, till farther order be takin by the civill magistrat. Tuiching the re-queist of the commissars of Edinburgh, that everie minister or reader sould have a register of the names of the deceassed in the parish where they dwell, the day of the moneth, and the yeere, and deliver the copie therof to the Procurator Fiscall, that pupills and creditors be not defrauded; it was answered, they could not lay suche a charge upon their brethrein, in respect none or few of the ministrie had manses or gleebes to make residence. But how soone they obteaned their manses, they sall desire them, as they sall be required, to doe conforme to the said requeist.

MINISTERS CENSURED.

Ministers compleaned upon in this Assemblie were to be tried and censured for these offences following: viz., for not repairing to the exercise of prophecie, or not repairing to Synodall and Generall Assembleis; or for not ministring the communioun for six yeeres bypast; or for deserting their flocke, and not discharging their office.

THE QUEENE MARIED TO LORD DARLY.

When the time of the queen's mariage drew neere, that there might be some show of publick consent, a great number of the nobilitie were conveened at Stirline; but suche as either would willingly consent, or durst not contradict. Manie assented, upon conditioun that no alteratioun be made in religioun: manie assented without anie suche exceptioun. Andrew Lord Uchiltrie professed plainlie he would never assent that anie of the Popish faction sould be their king. The Erle of Murrey perceaving that libertie of voting would be restrained, and fearing troubles might ensue if the Queene of England did not consent, absented himself from the conventioun. Yitt had he promised to procure her consent, providing sufficient suretie were made for religioun. Muche disputation there was among men about her mariage. Some thought after the death of her first husband, she ought to have the like libertie that weomen of low degree have. Others said, the case was not like, becaus in choosing herself a husband she choosed also a king to the realme; and that it was more equitable that the people sould choose a husband to one woman, than one woman a king to all the subjects. There came an ambassader out of England, in Julie, to expostulat, that they being so neere of kin to his mistresse, and in equall degree of consanguinitie, sould precipitat the mariage

without her consent; and to admonishe them to weygh more
deepelie so weightie a mater. When this ambassader had effectuat nothing, Sir Nicolas Throgmorton was sent to recall the Erle
of Lennox and his sonne, under the paine of forfaultrie of all they
had in England, in respect the time of their licence was expired.
But they insisted in their purpose. In the meane time, to diminishe the disparagement of the matche, she caused Lord Darly be
proclamed Duke of Rothesay and Erle of Rosse; or, as others
write, first made him knight, afterward Lord Ardmannoch, Erle of
Rosse, Duke of Rothesay. Witches in both the realmes had fore-
told, that if the mariage were celebrated before the end of Julie,
both the realmes sould reape great benefite thereby; if otherwise,
great inconveniences would follow. A day was sett, before which
it was bruited the Queene of England sould dee; which savoured
rather of conspiracie than soothsaying. Our queene herself feared
her uncles would cast in some impediment if it were delayed. But
Seigneur David assured them, that both the father and the sonne
were zealous Catholicks, of a noble familie, great freindship and
superioritie, weill beloved in both the realmes; so there was no
impediment more feared that way. The Bishop of Dumblane was
sent to Rome for a dispensatioun, becaus the queene and Darly
were in the secund degree of consanguinitie; which was obteaned.
The mariage was solemnized upon the 27th of Julie. They were
proclamed the day following in Edinburgh, Henrie and Marie,
King and Queene.

THE CHASE-ABOUT ROAD.

Not onlie manie of the nobilitie, but also of the commouns, were
offended, that by the voice of an herald, at the queen's commandement, Lord Darly sould have been proclamed king without consent of the estats in Parliament. The number of malcontents was
the greater, becaus manie of the nobilitie were absent, or did not
countenance either the mariage or the proclamatioun: viz. the Duke
of Chatelerault, the Erles of Argyle, Murrey, Alexander Erle of Glen-

carne, Andrew Erle of Rothesse, the Lord Uchiltree, and sindrie others. Heralds were sent to call them in. They refuse, and are condemned to banishment. The king and queene goe to Glasgow with foure thowsand men, to persue so manie rebells as remained at Paisley. An herald was sent, to command the castell of Hammiltoun to be delivered. The Hammiltons breathed nothing but crueltie. No assured peace could be had in their judgement but by cutting off both king and queene; "For the inimitie of kings," said they, "could not be extinguished but by death." The Erles of Murrey and Glencarne knowing verie weill the Hammiltons aimed at their owne particular profite, and abhorring their governement and all crueltie, perswaded to a mylder course, for the king and queene had not yitt committed anie suche crimes as tended to the overthrow of the commoun weale, but suche as might be cured by gentler remedeis. Farther, they were perswaded there were manie in the other campe would endevoure to procure peace and reconciliatioun. The Hammiltons departed malcontent; the duke himself, with other sixteene of his freinds, remained with the noblemen. They goe to Hammiltoun, frome thence to Edinburgh, to consult farther. The captan of the castell shooteth daylie at them. Their freinds were not able to conveene with suche speed as was requisite. At the instant requeist of Johne Lord Hereis, they went out of Edinburgh to Dumfreis.[1] The king and queene returne to Glasgow, where the Erle of Lennox was made Wardane of the West Marches. They returne to Stirline, and therafter make their progresse through Fife, where noblemen and barons were compelled to sweare and promise assistance, if there came anie armie frome England. Some were fynned, some confynned, as they favoured the lords. The goods and movables of suche as had fled to England were made a prey. About the 9th of October the king and queene went with an armie to Dumfreis. The Lord Hereis cometh furth to meete the queene, as it were to interceed for the lords; but he treated for a part of the patrimonie which belonged to his father-in-law, which he obteaned. He returneth to the lords, showeth to them he cannot helpe them,

---

[1] For the declaration of the lords at Dumfries see Appendix, letter A.

adviseth them to flee to England, and promiseth to follow and joyne his fortouns with theirs, so soone as he could sett his effaires in order. So the duke, the Erles of Murrey, Glencarne, Rothesse, the Lord Uchiltrie, the Abbot of Kilwinning, the Laird of Grange, Cunninghamheid, Pittarrow, Mr James Halyburton, Tutor of Pitcur, and others, went to Carlill, where they were receaved courteouslie by the Erle of Bedford, then Lieutenant of the North. The king and queene returne about the end of October. This road was called the Chase-about Road. The lords went from Carlill to Newcastell: frome thence the Erle of Murrey and the Abbot of Kilwinning were sent to the Queene of England, to intreate her intercessioun, which she promised, but could not obteane favour. The duke sent after the Abbot of Kilwinning, with letters to the queene, wherin he submitted himself, and so obteaned pardoun to him and his freinds, and licence to passe to France, there to remaine the space of five yeeres.

THE ELEVENTH GENERALL ASSEMBLIE.

The Generall Assemblie was holdin at Edinburgh, in the upper tolbuith, the 25th of December. Johne Areskine of Dun, Superintendent of Angus, was chosin Moderator.

THE TRIELL OF SUPERINTENDANTS AND COMMISSIONERS.

In the triell of superintendents and commissioners, the Superintendent of Angus confessed he had not visited anie kirk these two moneths bypast; but withall alledged, that his visitatioun could not be verie profitable, in respect it behoved him to loodge, in time of visitatioun, with his freinds for the most part, who had most need of correctioun and discipline. Therefore he besought the Assemblie to provide some other to that office. But Alexander, Commissioner of Galloway, excused his not visiting with the building of his nephewe's hous.

THE QUEEN'S ANSWERES TO THE PETITIONS OF THE FORMER ASSEMBLIE.

Follow the answeres givin by the queen's Majestie to the articles presented to her Grace, by the Commissioners of the Assemblie, holdin in June last bypast.

To the first, desiring the masse to be suppressed and abolished, als weill in the head as in the members, with punishement of the controveeners, &c., as alsua that religioun now professed be established by Act of Parliament, it is answered :—

First, For her Majestie's owne part, that her Hignesse is no wise yitt perswaded of the truthe of our religioun, nor that anie impietie is in the masse; and therefore beleeveth that her loving subjects will in no wise preasse her to embrace anie religioun against her owne conscience, and so draw her upon perpetuall unquietnesse and remorse of conscience. And to deale plainlie with her subjects, her Majestie neither will, nor may forsake the religioun wherin she hath beene nourished and brought up, and beleeveth to be weill-grounded; knowing, that besides grudge of conscience which may be wrought by change in religioun, that she sall lose the freindship of the King of France, the ancient allya of this realme, and of other great princes, her freinds and confederats, who would take it in evill part, of whome she may looke for support in all her necessiteis. And having no assurance of anie thing that may countervaile the same, she will be loath to hazard the freindship of her freinds in one instant; beseeching all her loving subjects, seing they have had experience of her goodnesse, that she neither hath in times bypast, nor yitt meaneth heerafter, to preasse the conscience of anie man, but to suffer them to worship God in suche sort as they are per-swaded to be best, that they will also not prease her to offend her owne conscience.[1]

---

[1] Yet Mary, as appears by a letter from the Earl of Bedford, ambassador at the Scottish court, addressed to Sir William Cecil, was earnestly employed in alluring the courtiers back to the Romish faith. " The queene (he writes) there useth

As for establishing of religioun in the whole bodie of the realme, that they themselves know, as appeareth weill by their articles, that it cannot be done by her assent onlie, but requireth necessarilie the consent of the three estats in parliament. Therefore, so soone as the parliament sall hold that wherupon the three estats sall agree among themselves, her Majestie sall graunt, and alwayes assure, that no man sall be troubled for behaving himself in religioun according to his conscience, or that anie man's life or heritage sall be in hazard for religion.

As to the secund article, it is answered, that her Majestie thinketh it no wise reasonable, that she sould defraud herself of so great a part of the patrimonie of the crowne, as to denude her owne hands of the patronages of benefices ; for her owne necessitie, in bearing her port and commoun charges will require, that she reteane them in her owne hands. Nothelesse her Majestie is weill pleased, that consideratioun being had of her owne necessitie, a speciall assignation be had to ministers, for their reasonable sustentatioun, in places most commodious for them, where with her Majestie sall not intromett.

To the thrid article, her Majestie sall doe therin as sall be agreed upon by the estats of parliament.

To the fourth article, her Majestie's liberalitie towards the poore sall be alwayes als farre extended as can be reasonablie required at her hands.

To the fyft and sixt article, her Majestie referreth the ordering to the parliament.

THE REPLIES TO HER ANSWERS.

Mr Johne Row, minister at Sanct Johnstoun, was appointed to

some speeche to some, and other she useth to take them by the hands, to leade them with her to masse." The blundering zeal of her husband must have counteracted, rather than seconded, her efforts ; for Bedford adds, " The Lord Darneley sometyme would shutt up the noblemen in chambres, thereby to bringe them to heare masse ; but suche kinde of persuasions take no place with them."

penne a reply to these answeres, becaus they satisfeid not the Assemblie; and to present the same in writt to the Assemblie, to be considered, before it be presented to the queen's Grace. The reply penned and approved followeth :—

"First, Where her Majestie answereth, that she is not perswaded in our religion, nor understandeth anie impietie to be in the masse, but that the same is weill grounded, etc., this is no small greefe to the hearts of her godlie subjects, considering that the trumpet of Christ's Evangell hath beene so long blowne in this countrie, and His mercie so plainlie offered in the same, that her Majestie remaineth yitt unperswaded of the truth of this our religioun. For our religioun is nothing elles but the same which Christ Jesus in the last dayes reveeled frome the bosome of his Father, wherof he made his apostles messingers, and which they preached and established among the faithfull, to continue till the secund comming of our Lord Jesus Christ. Which differeth from the impietie of the Turkes, the blasphemie of the Jewes, the vaine superstitioun of the Papists, in this, that our religion onlie hath God the Father, his onlie Sonne Jesus Christ our Lord, his onlie Spirit speaking in his prophets and apostles, for authors therof, and their doctrine and practise for the ground of the same ; which no other religion upon the face of the earth can justlie challenge, or plainlie prove. Yea, whatsomever assurance the Papists have for their religion, the same have the Turkes for the maintenance of their Alcaron, and the Jewes farre greater warrant for the defence of their ceremoneis, whether antiquitie of time, consent of people, authoritie of councels, great numbers or multitude consenting together, or anie other like clokes they can pretend. Therefore, as we are dolorous that her Majestie is not perswaded of this our religioun, so most reverentlie we require, in the name of the Eternall God, that her Highnesse would embrace the meanes whereby she may be perswaded of the truthe, which we presentlie offer to her, als weill by preaching of the Word, which is the cheefe meane appointed by God to perswade all his chosin childrein of his infallible veritie, as by publict disputation against the adversareis of this our religion, deceavers of her

Majestie, whensoever her Grace sall think it expedient. As for
the impietie of the masse, we darre be bold to affirme, that in that
idol there is great impietie ; yea, it is nothing elles but a masse of
impietie, from the beginning to the end. The author, the sayer,
the action itself, the opinion conceaved therof, the hearers and
gazers upon it, avow sacrilege, pronounce blasphemie, and committ
most abominable idolatrie, as we have ever offered and yitt offer
to prove evidentlie. And where her Majestie feareth that the
change of religion sall dissolve the confederacie and alliance she
hath with the King of France and other princes, etc.—assuredlie,
Christ's true religioun is the undoubted meane to knitt up surelie
perfyte confederacie and freindship with Him who is King of all
kings, and who hath the hearts of all princes in his owne hands ;
which ought to be more pretious to her Majestie than the confederacie of all the princes of the earth, without which, neither confederacie, love, nor kindnesse can endure.

" Concerning her Majestie's answere to the secund article, where
as she thinketh it no wise reasonable to defraud herself of the patronages of the benefices, which her Majestie esteemeth to be a
portioun of her patrimonie ; and that her Majestie is minded to reteane a good part of the benefices in her owne hands, to susteane
commoun charges, etc. To the first point, it is not our meaning
that her Majestie or anie other patron within the realme sall be defrauded of their just patronages. But we meane, that whensoever
her Majestie or anie other patron doth present anie persoun to anie
benefice, that the person presented sall be tried by learned men in
the kirk, suche as presentlie are the Superintendents appointed for
that use. And as the presentatioun of the benefices perteaneth to
the patron, so the collatioun, by law and reasoun, perteaneth to the
kirk, wherof the kirk sould no more be defrauded than the patrons
of their presentatioun. For otherwise, if it sall be leasome to present absolutelie whome they please, without triell or examinatioun,
what then may we looke for but meere ignorance, without all order
in the kirk? As to the secund point, the reteaning of a good part
of the benefices in her owne hands, it abereth so farre from good

conscience, the law of God, and the commoun law and publict order, that we are loath to open up the ground of the mater by manie circumstances. Therefore we most reverentlie wishe that her Majestie would consider the mater with herself and her wise counsell, that howsoever the patronages of benefices may apperteane to herself, yitt the reteaning of them in her owne hands, undispouned to qualifeid persouns, is ungodlie, and contrare to all publict order; and, finallie, confusioun to the poore soules of the commoun people, who, by this meanes, are provided with teachers to instruct them in the way of salvatioun. And, where her Majestie concludeth in her secund answere, that she is content that a sufficient and reasounable sustentatioun be appointed for ministers, by assignations in places most commodious, consideration being had of her owne necessitie; as we are verie desirous that her Grace's necessitie be releeved, so our duetie urgeth that we notifie to her Grace the right order which sould be observed by her in this behalfe, which is this: The tithes are to be reputed properlie the patrimonie of the kirk, wherewith, before all other, these that travell in the ministrie, and the poore indigent members of Christ's bodie, ought to be susteaned, kirks repaired, and the youth brought up into letters. Which things being done, other necessiteis may be reasounablie suppleed, according as her Grace and godlie counsell sall thinke expedient. Alwise, we cannot but thank her Majestie most reverentlie for her liberall offer of assignatioun to be made to ministers for their sustentatioun. Which not the lesse is conceaved in so generall termes, that without condescending more speciallie upon the particulars, no executioun can follow therupon. And so, to conclude at this present, we desire earnestlie her Majestie's answere to the saids articles to be reformed; beseeching God, that as they are reasonable and godlie in themselves, so her Majestie and the estats presentlie conveened may be inclynned and perswaded to approve and accomplishe the same."

PETITIONS.

· The Lord Lindsay, and David Murrey, brother to the Laird of Balvaird, were appointed to present a supplicatioun in name of the Assemblie to the queene and counsell, for payment of ministers' stipends, and for order to be takin, that suche as putt violent hand in ministers for reproving of vice; that suche as have receaved assignations of their bygane stipends from the former collectors may have execution of their assignations; and that assignatioun be appointed, as was promised in her Highness' last answers to the petitions of the Assemblie.

ACTS.

It was ordeaned, that the superintendent call the disobedient minister, exhorter, or reader before him, and some of the neerest discreet ministers; and if, being convicted of disobedience, he refuse to satisfie according to their injunctions, that he be suspended from his ministrie and stipend till the nixt Assemblie; at the which the superintendent sall notifie the whole proceeding, that by their censure he may be farther corrected, or elles restored to his former estate, according to the evidence of his repentance; providing the kirk be provided in the meane time by the superintendent.

2. That everie superintendent within his owne bounds inquire diligentlie if ministers and exhorters having stipends, manses, and gleebes, teache the youth in countrie parishes; and if they doe not, that he compell them to doe the same, under the paine of removall, and others to be placed in their rowme.

3. That all persons which have heeretofore joyned themselves to the kirk, and after revolt, offering their childrein to be baptised by Popish preests, or receaving the abominable sacrament of the altar, or approving in anie sort Popish wickednesse, after due admonition givin by the superintendent of the diocie, or principall reformed kirk, sall be excommunicated, if no repentance be offered.

4. That no minister celebrat the mariage of two parteis dwelling

without his parish, without sufficient testimoniall of the minister or ministers from whom they are come, that their bannes were orderlie proclamed, and no impediment found, under the paine of depositioun from his office, losse of his stipend, and other punishments, as the Generall Assemblie sall thinke good.

5. It was found that, according to God's Word, none might marie his wife's brother daughter, or wife's sister daughter; and that, if anie such mariage was contracted, the samine ought to be null.

QUESTIONS DECIDED.

Sir Johne Bellendine of Auchinoull, knight, Justice-Clerk, Mr James Makgill of Rankeillour Neather, Clerk of Register, Mr Johne Spence, Advocat, Mr Thomas Makcalzeane, Maisters Johne Row, Johne Craig, William Christesone, David Lindsay, ministers, and David Forrest, were appointed to convene upon Wednesday, to decide questions, and to report answers. They reported their decisions as followeth:

" 1. That no minister, receaving sufficient sustentatioun for preaching of the Evangell, may with safe conscience leave his flocke, or the place appointed for his ordinar residence, whatsoever patrocinie or oversight he have, through corruptioun often times, or negligence of rulers, so to doe.

" 2. Seing our Master pronounceth that he is but a mercenarie, who seing the woolfe comming, fleeth for his owne safeguarde, and that the verie danger of life cannot be a sufficient excuse for suche as fall backe, we no wise thinke it lawfull that suche as have putt their hand to the pleugh sall leave that heavenlie vocatioun for indigence and povertie. They may lawfullie leave an unthankfull people, and seeke where Christ Jesus his holie Evangell may bring furth good fruict; but lawfullie they may not change their vocatioun.

" 3. Whensoever fearefull crimes are committed, as murther, adulterie, or the like, if it be in the countrie, the minister, reader, or

exhorter of that place, or, if there be none there, the minister of the
place nixt adjacent, ought to give significatioun of the fact to the
superintendent of that diocie; who, without delay, ought to direct
his summouns, to charge the persons slaundered to compeere before him at a certane day and place.   Or, if they be committed in
touns or burghes, where order is established, the sessioun therof to
call the offenders accused or suspected; who, if they compeere, or
either alledge just defence, or show themselves unfainedlie penitent, then may the superintendent, or kirk reformed, without the
superintendent, dispense somewhat with the rigour of the punishment, secluding the offender onlie from participatioun of the sacraments, till farther triell of his repentance; and that their sentence
be pronounced in the kirk where the offence is knowne.   But if the
offender be stubborne, if he compeere not, or shew himself little
tuiched with his offence, then ought the superintendent, with advice of the nixt reformed kirk, decerne him or them to be secluded
from all participatioun or communicatioun with the faithfull members of Christ.   If the person or persons secluded from the sacrament be negligent in seeking reconciliatioun with the kirk, behave
themselves insolentlie, or otherwise than becometh penitent persons, the kirk, after admonitioun, may proceed to the uttermost.

" 4. When childrein, baptized by a Papisticall preest, or in Papisticall maner, come to the yeeres of understanding, they sould be
instructed in the doctrine of salvatioun, and what is the corruptioun
of Poperie, which they must publicklie damne, before they be admitted to the Lord's Table.   Which if they doe, they need not the
externall forme to be reiterated; for no preest ministreth baptisme
without water, and the forme of words, which are the principall externall parts of baptisme.   We ourselves were baptized by Popish
preests, whose corruptions and abuses now we damne, cleaving onlie
to the simple ordinance of Jesus Christ, and to the veritie of the
Holie Spirit, which maketh baptisme to worke in us the proper
effects therof, without anie iteration of the externall signe.   If
suche childrein come never to knowledge of true doctrine, they are
to be left to the judgement of God.

"5. As for oppressours of childrein, their civill punishement ought to be ordeaned and appointed by the civill magistrat. As for the slaunder, the offenders ought to be secluded from participatioun of the sacraments, till they have satisfied the kirk, as sall be injoyned.

"6. Persons lying in fornication, under promise of mariage, which they differe to solemnize, sould satisfie publicklie in the place of repentance, upon the Lord's Day, before they be maried."

MINISTERS CENSURED.

Mr Patrik Creigh, minister of Rathow, was ordeaned to make satisfaction in the kirk of Edinburgh two severall Sabboth dayes, and upon the thrid, in the kirk of Dummenie, for celebrating mariage betwixt Robert Patersone and Jonet Littill, in Dummenie kirk, without proclamatioun of bannes, or satisfactioun made to the kirk of Edinburgh, according to the decreit of the last Assemblie.

MINISTERS APPOINTED TO TRIE THE COMPLAINT OF A SUPERINTENDENT.

It was ordeaned, that according to the complaint of the Superintendent of Fife, Johne Melvill, minister at Craill, sould be inhibited to proceed to the solemnizatioun of mariage betwixt Robert Arnot and Ewphame Corstorphine, till Mr Johne Dowglas, Rector of the Universitie, and Mr James Wilkie, regent, trie the superintendent's complaint, and the other woman's claime, alledging the said Robert's promise; giving them power to pronounce sentence, and to proceed to censure against the disobedient. Heere yee may see, the superintendent's complaints were tried by others than superintendents.

A PUBLICK FAST INDICTED.

Mr Johne Craig, one of the ministers of Edinburgh, Mr Johne

Dowglas, Rector of the Universitie of Sanct Andrewes, Mr Robert Melvill, Deane of Aberdeene, William Christesone, minister at Dundie, Mr David Lindsay, minister at Leith, Mr Gilbert Gardin, minister of Monyfuth, Mr Thomas Makcalzeane and Johne Marjoribanks, commissioners of Edinburgh, were appointed to collect the causes of a publict fast. They declared the necessitie of a publict fast in the fourth or last sessioun. Therefore the Assemblie ordeaned Mr Knox and Mr Johne Craig, ministers of Edinburgh, to sett doun the forme of the exercise which was to be used at the fast, and to caus Robert Lickprivick print it. This treatise of fasting is extant in our Psalme bookes. The causes mentiouned at that time were these following:

First, Becaus that, in the beginning, they had not refused God's graces, but contrariwise, with such fervencie receaved them, that they could beare with no kinde of impietie; and, for suppressing of the same, had neither respect to freind, possessioun, land, nor life, but putt all in hazard, that God's truthe might be advanced, and idolatrie suppressed. But now, since carnall wisdome had perswaded them to beare with manifest idolatrie, and to suffer the realme, which God had once purged, to be polluted again with that abominatioun; (yea, some whom God had sometimes made instruments to suppresse that impietie, had beene cheefe men to conduct and convoy that idol throughout all the quarters of the realme, yea, to the houses of them who sometimes detested the masse as the devill and his service,) they had found God's face angrie against them. That, when they followed God, and not carnall wisdome, God made a few in number fearefull to manie; fooles before the world to confound the wise; and suche as before never had experience in armes, to be so bold and prosperous in all their enterprises that the expertest soldiour feared the poore plew man. Yea, God faught for them both by sea and by land, and moved the hearts of strangers to support them, and spend their lyves for their releefe. But now, wisdome, manheid, strenth, freinds, honour, and blood, joyned with godlinesse, were fallin before their eyes, that they might turne to God. Before, they had some hope that God

2

would move the queen's Majestie's heart to heare the Gospell of
Jesus Christ, and so to abandoun idolatrie. But now, she hath
answered in plaine words, she will mainteane and defend that religioun wherin she was nourished; and, in tokin therof, there is
erected, of late dayes, a displayed banner against Jesus Christ.
For knowne deceavers of the people are authorized to spew out
poysoun against Christ, his eternall truthe, and true messingers;
the idol of tho masse now again, in diverse places, is erected; the
best part of our nobilitie exiled, and the queene favoureth flattering
friers and corrupt Papists more than pure preachers.

Further, There is an intentioun to suppresse, through all Europ,
all that abhorre Papisticall impietie, and to raze them from the face
of the earth, according to the decree of the Councell of Trent,
which sall be put in executioun first in France, by the Catholick
king, Philip of Spaine, and some of the Frenche nobilitie. The
Pop's armie, and the Dukes of Savoy and Ferrara their forces, sall
assault Geneva, and sall not leave it till it be sacked, and no living
creature in it be saved. Frome France they sall mak expeditioun
against the Germans, to reduce them to the obedience of the Apostolick See; and so sall they proceed through other natiouns, never
ceasing, till all be rooted out who will not make homage to that
Roman idol. Their practises alreadie in France make manifest
their crueltie. The Pop's cardinals and horned bishops offer the
greatest portion of their rents for susteaning of the warre, as may
appeare by these words neere the end of that decree : " And to the
end that the holie fathers for their part appeare not to be negligent, or unwilling to give their aide and supporte to so holie a warre,
or to spaire their owne rents and money, have added, that the cardinalls sall content themselves with tho yeerlie rent of five or six
thowsand ducats, and the richest bishop of two or three thowsand
at most ; and to give franklie the rest of their revenues to the maintenance of the warre, for extirpation of the Lutheran and Calvin-
ian sect, and for the establishing of the Roman church, till suche
time as the mater be conducted to a good and happie end."

Farther, Greater inobedience and ingratitude was never shewed

to God's messingers than hath beene of late, and yitt is, within this
realme.   Whoordome and adulterie are but pastymes of the flesh;
slaughter and murther is esteemed a small sinne to anie man hath
a freind in court; feasting and ryottous banketting in court, countrie, and touns; increasse of the poore to suche a number as the
like hath not beene seene in this land.

Mr Knox was ordeaned to penne a comfortable letter, in name
of the Assemblie, to incurage ministers, exhorters, and readers, to
continue in their vocatioun, which in all liklihood they were to
leave off for laike of payment of their stipends; and to exhort the
professors within this realme to supplee their necessiteis.   He was
appointed likewise to visite, preache, and plant kirks in the south,
where there was not a superintendent, and to remaine so long as
occasioun might suffer.   The tenor of the letter followeth :

" The Superintendents, Ministers, and Commissioners of Kirks
      Reformed within the realme of Scotland, assembled in
      Edinburgh, the 25th day of December 1565, to the Mini-
      sters of Jesus Christ within the same realme, desire grace
      and peace from God, the Father of our Lord Jesus Christ,
      with the perpetuall comfort of the Holie Spirit.

" The present miserie, and greater troubles appearing shortlie to
follow, crave (deare brethrein) that everie one of us exhort and
admonish another, that we recoole not backe in the beginning of
this battell which is come upon us, unlooked for of manie.   And
therefore it is that we, your brethrein, partakers with you of the
afflictions of Jesus Christ, understanding the extremitie wherin the
whole ministers within this realme now stand, for want of reasonable provision for themselves and their poore famileis, have thought
expedient to communicat our mindes with you by this our letter:
which is, that first yee sall diligentlie marke these words of the
apostle, saying, ' No man sall be crowned, unlesse he strive lawfullie;' and also that fearefull sentence of our Maister, Jesus Christ,

saying, 'No man putting his hand to the pleugh, and looking
backe, is apte for the kingdome of God.' We have once professed
ourselves warrioures against Satan, and labourers in the husbandrie
of the Lord our God, who of his mercie hath opened our mouths
to exhort others, to contemne this wicked world, and to contend to
enter in at that heavenlie Jerusalem. God hath honoured us so
that men have judged us the messingers of the everlasting Lord.
By us hath he disclosed idolatrie, by us are the wicked of the world
rebooked, and by us hath our God comforted the consciences of
manie that were oppressed with ignorance and impietie. Consider
then, deere brethrein, what slaunder and offence sall we give to the
weaker, what occasioun of rejoycing sall the enemeis have, and to
what ignominie sall we expone the glorious Evangell of Jesus
Christ, if that we for anie occasioun sall desist, and ceasse from
publick preaching of the same. We that admonishe you are not
ignorant, neither altogether without experience, how vehement a
dart povertie is, and what troublesome cogitatiouns it is able to
raise, yea, even in men of greatest constancie. But yitt, deere
brethrein, we ought earnestlie to consider with what conditiouns we
are entered into this most honorable vocatioun, and what we cheefelie seeke in preaching of the blessed Evangell. For, if we lay before
us other conditions than Jesus Christ laid before his apostles, when
he sent them furth first to preache the glade tydings of his kingdome, and if we seeke and imagine to ourselves better entreatment
of this wicked generatioun than we find the deerest servants of God
have gottin in the world, we ather deceave ourselves, or elles declare ourselves not to be true successours of these whose doctrine
we propone to the people. They were sent furth as sheepe amongst
the middest of woolves. To them it was pronounced that they
sould be hated, they sould be mocked; men sould curse and persecute them for the testimonie of the truthe; which threatnings we
find not to have beene vaine, but to have fallin upon the cheefe
members of Jesus Christ, as the Acts of the Apostles beare testimonie. And thinke we that the same Evangell which they
preached can have anie other successe in our ministrie than it had

in theirs? In gifts we must confesse ourselves farre inferiour to
these lights of the world, in diligence and painfull travell we cannot be compared; and yitt we looke to be partakers of the kingdome
which God hath prepared for suche as patientlie abide the againe
comming of our Lord Jesus.   And sall we in nothing communicat
with them? They were sometimes whipped, sometimes stoned, oft
cast in prisoun, and the blood of manie sealed up their doctrine.
And sall we, for povertie, leave the flocke of Jesus Christ, before
that it utterlie refuse us? God forbid, deere brethrein: for what
sall discerne us frome the mercenereis and hyrelings, if our constancie in adversitie sall not doe it? The hyrelings, in time of
quietnesse, teache the truthe as we doe.   In gifts and utterance
they commounlie exceed.   In life and conversatioun they may for
a seasoun be irreprehensible.   What is it, then, that maketh them
hyrelings? Our Maister and Saviour Christ Jesus answereth, saying, ' The mercenarie seeth the woolve comming, and fleeth, becaus he is a mercenarie.'   Then, the leaving of the flocke when the
woolfe cometh to invade, proveth suche as were holdin pastors to
be nothing but hyrelings.   We denie not but if in one citie wee be
persecuted, we may flee unto another; yea, if one realme cast us
furth, we may receave the benefite of another; but ever still with
this conditioun, that we cast not frome us the professioun that publictlie we have made, neither yitt that we ceasse to feede the flocke
of Jesus Christ, and to gainstand the teachers of false doctrine, so
farre furth as in us lyeth.   But heerinto standeth the questioun:
Whether may we, whom God hath called unto this honour, that
he hath made us ambassaders of his good will unto this unthankfull
generation, desist from our vocations, becaus we cannot be provided of reasonable livings, as God hath commanded, and our travells deserve? The Spirit of God uniformlie through the Scriptures
will answere us, that Elias was sent to be fed by the ravens; Elisæus
and his fellow schollars were compelled to gather herbes to make
pottage; Paul did oft live by the worke of his owne hands.   But
we never found that they receaved dimissioun frome their vocatioun.   Seing, then, deere brethrein, that God hath not yitt

tempted none of us with the extremiteis that we find others before us to have suffered and overcome, lett us be ashamed so suddanlie to faint, even in the brunt of the battell. The price of Jesus Christ his death and passioun is committed to our charge. The eyes of men are bent upon us, and we must answere before that Judge who will not admitt everie excuse that pleaseth us, but will judge uprightlie, as in his Word before he hath pronounced. Lett us therefore stand fast, not onlie in the truthe, but also in defence and advancing of the same, which we cannot doe if we cease frome our publict vocatioun. Lett us, deere brethrein, stand fast in the same, and committ our bodeis to the care of Him who feedeth the foules of the aire, and hath pronunced that he knoweth wherof we have need, and will provide for us. He preserved us in the darkenesse of our mother's bellie; he provided our foode in their breasts, and instructed us to use the same, when we knew him not. He hath nourished us in the time of blindnesse and impietie; and will he now despise us, when we call upon him, and preache the glorious Gospell of his deere Sonne, our Lord Jesus? Nay, deere brethrein; he neither will nor can, unlesse that infidelitie cutt us off from his mercifull providence. Lett us consider that the whole earth is the Lord's, and all the fulnesse of the same: that he is able to move the hearts of men as best pleaseth him. He is able to blesse and multiplie things that are nothing in the eyes of carnall men. It is but povertie that is yitt threatned us, which, if we be not able to contemn, how sall we abide the furie and terrour of death, which manie thowsands before us have suffered, for the testimonie of the same truthe which we professe and teache, and despised all worldlie redemption, as the Apostle speaketh? This is but a gentle triell, which our Father taketh of our obedience; which if we willinglie offer to him, the bowells of his Fatherlie compassioun will rather caus the heavens, yea, the rocks and rivers to minister unto us things necessarie to the bodie, than that he will suffer us to perishe, if we dedicate our whole lives unto him. Lett us be frequent in reading, which, alas! over manie despise; earnest in prayer, diligent in watching over the flocke committed to our charge; and lett our sobrietie and temperat life ashame the wicked, and be exemple to the godlie; and then there is no doubt but the Eternall our God sall remedie this extremitie. He sall confound our enemeis, and sall shortlie convert our teares and mourning in joy, to the glorie of his owne name, and to the comfort of our posteritie to come, through the onlie merits and intercessioun of Jesus Christ our Lord, whose Holie Spirit comfort you and us to the end.

"At Edinburgh, in our Generall Assemblie, the 25th day of December, 1565.

"JOHNE KNOX.

"At the command of the publict Assemblie."

M.D.LXVI.

DAVID RIZIO'S PRACTISES AND HIS END.

David Rizio, commounlie called Seigneur Davie, having gottin the court in a maner solitarie, at least free of malcontented nobles, adviseth the queene to cutt off some of the nobilitie, for a terrour to others. Becaus the Scotish guarde would not be readie to putt in executioun suche a designe, he counselled her to send for strangers, namelie Italians, becaus they were commounlie voide of all sense of religioun, brought up under tyranns, accustomed to mischeefe; who being farre frome home might be soone stirred up to attempt anie thing. Becaus they were his owne countrie men he thought he might move them to doe what he pleased. They come out of Flanders, one by one, least the purpose sould have beene discovered. There was greater danger to offend one of them than to offend the queene herself. As the Seigneur his credite increassed daylie with the queene, so the king's decreassed, for soone after the mariage she repented of the matche. Howbeit at the first the king's name was sett before the queene's, in all their writtings and patents, yitt soone after, the queene's name was sett before the king's. At lenth, the queene pretended, that manic things

were pretermitted, or not done in due time, through his absence at
hawking and hunting, and therefore moved him to be content that
she subscrive for both; so he might follow his pleasures without
hindrance of the commoun effaires. He was loath to offend her,
and upon light occasiouns was sent farre frome court, wherby his
favour became unprofitable, and his wrathe not to be feared.
David Rizio, her secretarie in Frenche and other forraine effaires,
was appointed to have a stamp with the king's name, to use when
need required. The king is sent to Peebles, to hawke in sharpe
winter, with a small traine, where there was skarstie of good inter-
teanment. The queene for some moneths admitted a number to
her table, and among the rest, this Seigneur; at lenth, him onlie,
and some one other, sometimes in her cabinet, sometimes in Davie's
chamber. He excelled the king in houshold stuffe, apparell, and
number of good horse. Secretar Matlane, partlie finding himself
prejudged by this Savoyard in the effaires of his office, partlie for
the favour he then careid to the Erle of Murrey, now banished,
laboured to perswade the Erle of Morton and Lord Hereis to cutt
off this base stranger. The Erle of Morton, being als wise as he
was wylie, answered, he would doe what he could for restoring the
Erle of Murrey with the queene's good will; but he knew it would
offend her to putt hands in Seigneur Davie. The secretar addresseth himself to David Rizio; sheweth to him his office was
strange in this countrie, and yeelded little profite. He counselled
him to move the queene to alienate her countenance frome the
Erle of Morton, presentlie Chanceller, and a favourer of the Erle
of Murrey, and with the king to pursue his right to the Erledome
of Angus, by his mother, sole heretrix to her father, the Erle of
Angus : so Morton would be glade to seeke his freindship, and to
quite the office to him. But that he might be capable of it, the
queene must endemize him, and give him some stile of an erle in
Scotland. David beganne to work. The queene charged for the
Castell of Tamtallan, under pretence that Morton receaved not the
rebells in it, nor that they tak it. It was randered to the Erle of
Atholl. Some report that the king was moved to proclame his

breeves, as heyre to Archibald Erle of Angus, his grandfather;
others report they were proclamed before his mariage.   It behoved
the Seigneur to rise by degrees.   The queene would have bought
to him Melvill, lying within foure myle of Edinburgh, but the
owner would not consent, wherat the queene and this Seigneur
were not a little offended.   The people beganne to speeke broadlie,
and to call to remembrance the preferment of Cochrane, a cour-
teour, who was hanged over Lawder Bridge, in the dayes of King
James the Thrid.   Upon a certane night, the king hearing that
Davie was gone in to the queen's chamber, went to it, having the
key to open it: findeth it shutt, and barred within, as it wont not
to be.   Wherupon he conceaved high indignatioun, and at last
concluded with the Lord Ruthven, Patrik Lord Lindsay, brother-
in-law to the Erle of Murrey, his owne father, and George Dowglas,
called the Postulat, to slay him.   Their purpose was to have takin
him comming out of a tenise court, where he haunted; but it was
reveeled, and fiftie men with halberts appointed to attend upon him;
for the most part of the king's servants were corrupted by the
queene, so that nothing was so secreitlie contrived, but als soone it
was discovered.   The nixt remedie was, to labour for restoring of
the noblemen then banished, who were to be forfaulted at the parliament which was to be holdin in Marche.   The Frenche and
English ambassaders interceeded for them.   The Queene of England sent letters in their favours, which our queene, knowing the
nobilitie were not ignorant of the mater, read in audience of manie.
Davie interrupted her; for he was verie bold with her, and would
rebooke her often more sharplie than her owne husband.   The king
and his complices laboured to draw in the Erle of Mortoun with
them.   The erle had beene alienated somwhat by the king's insist-
ing in his title to the Erledome of Angus.   They sent to him Andrew Ker of Fadownside, and Sir Johne Bellendine, Justice-Clerk.
Through their earnest dealing, he is moved to come to the Erle of
Lennox his chamber, where the king was.   The king and his father
for themselves, and for his mother, quitt all the title they had to
the Erledome of Angus, in favour of Archibald, then erle.   He

consenteth to assist the king with all his power, upon the conditions following: First, That religioun be established and preserved in the same estat it was in before the queen's arrivall ; Secundlie, That the banished noblemen be restored ; Thridlie, That the king tak the fact upon him, and warrand them from all perells. The king subscrived these conditions most willinglie.

The nobilitie conveening to the parliament, Davie gropped their mindes, how they were affected to the banished lords. He assured them the queene would needs have them to be condemned ; and, therefore, whosoever opponed would but purchase to themselves her indignation. By suche dealing, he tried who were best affected, that either they might be sett aside if they were courageous or terrified. Others were baited with hope of favour. Whill he was busie with the Lords of the Articles, it was thought expedient to apprehend him with diligence : the fittest time, when the guarde sould be removed from him, and he at the queen's table. Their purpose was to bring him to judgement, and execute him at the Croce of Edinburgh. Whill Davie was with the queene in her cabinet, and with them the Countesse of Argile, her base sister, at supper in the Abbey of Halyrudhous, the eight of Marche, the Erle of Morton came to the Abbey with his freinds and dependents. First, he tooke the keyes from the porter, and appointed a sufficient number of men to attend the inner court, to resist, if anie tumult were raised by the contrare partie ; for the Erles of Huntlie, Atholl, and Bothwell, were in sindrie parts of the palace, in the meane time. Morton went with a number of his freinds to the chamber of presence, where he walked. The king went up to the queen's chamber from his owne, by a privie staire or trap, which was patent onlie to himself. Patrik Lord Ruthven accompaneid with the Master of Ruthven, Andrew Ker of Fadownside, George Dowglas, called the Postulat, followed. The queene was somewhat affrayed at the first sight, when she saw the Lord Ruthven, leane, and ill-coloured by reasoun of his longsome sickenesse, and yitt in armour. She asked what the mater meant. Some standing by said, he was raving through the vehemencie of a fever.

He commandeth Davie to arise, telling him, that place was not for him. The queene ariseth incontinent, and steppeth in betwixt him and them. The king biddeth her be of good courage, for nothing was intended against her. Davie grippeth the queene about the waist : Fadownside bendeth backe his middle finger, so that for paine he was forced to forgoe his grippe. Then is he drawin out to the nixt chamber, and frome thence to the utter chamber. In the meane time, the noise of a fray rising, Huntlie and Bothwell would have beene furth, to whom assembled the cookes with speates, and some other rascalls ; but were soone drivin backe by the Erle of Morton's freinds and dependers, who were appointed to attend upon the inner court, and for feare fled out at the backe windows. Lethington supped with Atholl, partlie that he might beare witnesse to his behaviour, if the queene suspected him, partlie to reteane the erle in his loodging, from offering or suffering violence. He injoyned his attenders to be quiet till it came to actioun, and then to arme themselves, and to come as it were suddanlie to the fray, but, indeid, to joyne with the Erle of Morton. These who were bringing furth Davie, hearing the noise of a tumult, but ignorant of the meaning, and fearing he might be rescued out of their hands, wounded him to death with dagers, in the chamber of presence. This was done speciallie by the Lord of Morton's freinds, but farre by his intentioun ; for it was their purpose to make him a publick spectacle to the people. After the Lord Ruthven came out of the cabinet, being wearie of standing and stirring, he satt doun. The queene called him a perfidious tratour, and upbraided him with his contemptuous behaviour. He excused himself with the weaknesse of his owne bodie. He exhorted her, to advise with the nobilitie in the publick effaires of the realme, and not to be drawin away with vagabound knaves, who had nothing to lose neither in credit nor in patrimonie, and so could not give a sufficient pledge of their fidelitie ; and to take heed to the calamiteis which had befallin kings of this realme before, for their governement without advice of the nobilitie. The queene being farther inflamed with these speeches, they departed. At the rumour of this tumult, the citicens of Edinburgh ranne to their armes, and came doun straight to the palace. The king spoke to them out at a window; told them that the queen and he were in safetie; what was done was done by his directioun; what it was, they sould know in the owne time. So they departed.

Some report that Johne Damiot, a Frenche preest and a sorcerer, had forewarned Seigneur Davie to bewar of the bastard. He thought so to provide that the Erle of Murrey, whom he interpreted to be the bastard, sould never be restored to doe him anie harme. But the bastard that gave him the first wound was George Douglas, base sonne to the Erle of Angus, as is reported. The same preest, or (as others report) one called Seigneur Francis, advised him to order his bussinesse, and to gett him hence. He answered, he was not affrayed of the noblemen; they were but dukes: strike one of them, all the rest would ly in. He replyed, " Yee will find them geese: if yee handle one of them, the rest will flee upon you, and plucke you so, that they will not leave a feather nor down upon you."

SOME NOBLEMEN BANISHED FOR THE SLAUGHTER OF SEIGNEUR DAVIE.

The Erle of Murrey and others banished, returned home the day after the slaughter, and the day following compeered in the Tolbuith, readie to answere if anie processe of forfaulture were led against them. But none were there to persue, so they went to their loodgings. The queene sent for the Erle of Murrey, and putt him in hope she would be directed heerafter by the nobilitie, whereby she obteaned greater libertie. But als soone as she had caused assemble her guarde, she escaped by a posterne doore in the night. The Lord Seton, accompaneid with two hundreth horse, was attending upon her. Frome thence she was convoyed, first to Seton, and then to Dumbar, and the king compelled with threats to goe with her. When she is at Dumbar she gathereth her forces, and pretendeth that she is reconciled with the banished lords, that she may find the lesse resistance in persuing the committers of the last fact. They give place to the time and fled, some to England; the Erle of Morton, the Lord Ruthven, the Master of Ruthven, the Lairds of Fadownside, Elphingston, Whittinghame; some to the Highlands, to lurke there for a seasoun. Their goods were confiscated, their offices dispouned, their friends wairded or confyned. Howbeit some of them were no complices at the fact, as Sir David Hume of Wedderburne. He was committed, first to Dumbar, and then to Kenmure, in Galloway. Thomas Scot, Shireff-Depute of Perth, and Sir Henrie Yair, a preest, servant to the Lord Ruthven, were hanged and quartered, and their heads sett upon a pricke, the one upon the towre in the Abbey, the other upon the Nether Bow, becaus they were suspected guiltie of the murther. All men were discharged by proclamatioun to affirme that the king was partaker or privie to the last fact; wherat manie smiled.

DAVIE HIS CORPS LAYED BESIDE QUEENE MAGDALENE.

After the flight of the noblemen, the queene caused to tak up in the night Seigneur Davie his corps, which had beene buried before the Abbey kirk doore, and lay it neere to Queene Magdalene; which ministered no small occasioun to the people of bad constructions.

LORDS RECONCILED.

In Aprile, the queene sent for the Erles of Argile and Murrey, and reconciled them with the Erles of Huntley, Bothwell, and Atholl.

THE BANISHED LORDS WARNED TO DEPART OUT OF ENGLAND.

About the beginning of May, the queene sent Mr Johne Thorntoun to England and France, to crave that her rebells be not interteaned in their realmes. The Queene of England sent Henric

Killegrew to our queene, and promised to caus them depart. She sent likewise to themselves, to warne them to depart before mid-sommer. But the reporter said to them, England was long and braid. They went out of Newcastell, but lurked not farre from Anwicke. Before their departure frome Newcastell, the Lord Ruthven departed this life. He made a Christian end, thanking God for the leasure granted to him to call for mercie.

THE FIRST PUBLICK FAST.

The first and secund Lord's day of May was celebrated univer-sallie the first publick fast which we had after the Reformation, which exercise became frequent afterwards. The causes are tuiched before. Earnest prayer was made at this fast for a safe deliverie of the queen's birth.

MR KNOX HIS PREFACE TO THE FOURTH BOOK OF HIS HISTORIE.

This moneth Mr Knox formed the preface to the Fourth Booke of his Historie, by which we may understand the state of the present time; the tenor wherof followeth :

" In the former Bookes, gentle reader, thow may cleerelie see how potentlie God hath performed in these our last and wicked dayes, als weill as in the ages that have past before us, the promise that is made to the servants of God, by the Prophet Isay, in these words :—' They that waite upon the Lord sall renue their strenth : they sall lift up their wings as the eagles ; they sall runne and not wearie, they sall walke and not faint.' This promise, we say, suche as Satan hath not utterlie blinded may see performed in us, the professours of Christ Jesus within the realme of Scotland, with no lesse evidence than it was in anie age that ever past before us. For what was our force, what was our number, yea, what wisdome or worldlie policie was into us, to have brought to an end so great an interprise, our verie enemeis can beare witnesse. And yitt, in how great puritie did God establishe amongst us his true religioun,

als weill in doctrine as in ceremoneis, to what confusioun were idolaters, adulterers, and all publick transgressers of God's commandements within short time brought, the publick order of the kirk, yitt
by the mercie of God preserved, and the punishments executed
against malefactors, can testifie to the world.   For as tuiching the
doctrine taught by our ministers, and tuiching the administratioun
of the sacraments used in our kirks, we are bold to affirme, that
there is no realme this day upon the face of the earth that hath
them in greater puritie.   Yea, we must speeke the truthe, (whom-
soever we offend,) there is none (no realme we meane) that hath
them in the like puritie.   For all others (how sincere soever the
doctrine be that by some is taught) reteane in their churches, and
the ministers therof, some footsteps of the Antichrist and dregges
of Papistrie.   But we (all praise to God alone) have nothing within our churches that ever flowed from that Man of Sinne.   And
this we acknowledge to be the strenth givin unto us of God, becaus
we esteemed not ourselves wise in our owne eyes; but understanding
our owne wisdome to be but meere foolishnesse before our God,
layed it aside, and followed onlie that which we found approved by
himself."

THE FIRST PETITION OF THE PROTESTANTS OF SCOTLAND.

" In this point could never our enemeis caus us to faint.   For
our first petition was, that the reverend face of the primitive and
apostolick kirk sould be reduced againe to the eyes and knowledge
of men.   And in that point we say, our God hath strenthened us,
till that the worke was finished, as the world may see.   And as
concerning suppressing of vice, yea, and abolishing of all suche
things as might nourishe impietie within this realme, the acts and
statuts of the principall towns reformed will yitt testifie.   For what
adulterer, what fornicator, what knowne massemonger, or pestilent
Papist, durst have beene seene in publick, within anie reformed
town within this realme, before that the queene arrived?   And this
victorie to his Word, and terrour to all filthie livers, did God worke

by suche as yitt live and remaine witnesses, whether they will or
not, of the foresaids works of God. We say, our God suffered none
of these whom he first called to the battell to perishe or to fall, till
that he made them victors of their enemeis. For even as God
suffered none of these whome he called frome Egypt to perishe in
the Reid Sea, how fearfull that ever the danger appeared, so suffered he none of us to be oppressed, nor yitt to be takin from this
life, till that moe Pharaoes than one were drowned, and we sett at
freedome, without all danger of our enemeis; to lett both us and
our posteritie understand that suche as follow the conducting of
God can not perishe, albeit they walked in the verie shadow of
death. But from whence, alas! cometh this miserable dispersioun
of God's people within this realme this day, in May 1566? Good
men are banished; murtherers and suche as are knowne unworthie
of commoun societie, (if just lawes were putt in due executioun,)
beare the whole regiment and swing within this realme."

THE COURTEOURS THAT SEEMED TO PROFESSE THE EVANGELL,
AND DID IT NOT, WERE THE CAUSE WHEREFRA TROUBLES WITH-
IN SCOTLAND DID FLOW.

"We answere, becaus that suddanlie the most part of us declyned
from the puritie of God's Word, and beganne to follow the world,
and so again shooke hands with the devill and with idolatrie, as in this
Fourth Booke we will heare. For whill that Papists were so confounded, that none within the realme durst more avow the hearing
or saying of masse, nor the theeves of Liddisdaill durst avow their
stouth, in the presence of an upright judge, there were Protestants
found, that ashamed not at tables and other open places to aske,
' Why may not the queene have her masse, and the forme of her
religioun? What can that hurt us and our religioun?' And from
these two, *Why* and *What*, at lenth sprang out this affirmative,
' The queen's masse and her preests we will mainteane : this hand
and this rapper sall fight in their defence.' The inconveniences
were showin both by tongue and by penne. But the adversareis

were judged men of unquiet spirits; their credite was defaced at
the hands of suche as before were not ashamed to use their counsell in maters of greater importance than to have refused the
masse. But then—' my lord, my maister, may not be thus used
—he hath that honour to be the queen's brother. And, therefore,
we will, that all men sall understand that he must tender her as his
sister; and whosoever will counsell him to displease her, and the
least that apperteaneth to her, sall not find him their freind; yea,
they are worthie to be hanged that would counsell him,' &c.
These, and the like reasons, tooke suche deepe root in flesh and
blood, that the truthe of God was almost forgott. And from this
fountaine (to witt, that flesh and blood was, and yitt, alas! is preferred to God and to his messingers, rebooking vice and vanitie)
have all our misereis proceeded."

THE CORRUPTIONS THAT ENTERED IN THE QUEEN'S COURT.— THEOLOGY OF THE COURT.

" For as before, so even yitt, although the ministers be sett to
beg, the guard and the men of warre must be served. Though the
blood of the ministers be spilt, it is the queen's servant that did it.
Although masse be multiplied in all quarters of the realme, who
can stoppe the queen's subjects to live in the queen's religioun?
Although innocent men be imprisouned, it is the queen's pleasure:
she is offended at suche men. Although under pretence of justice
innocents sall be murthered, the lords sall weepe, but the queen's
minde must be satisfeid. Nobles of the realme, barons, and counsellers, are banished, their escheats dispouned, and their lives most
unjustlie persued.[1] The queene hath lost her trustie servant Davie:
he was deere unto her, and, therefore, for her honour's sake, she
must show rigour to revenge his death. And yitt, farther, albeit
that some know that she is plainlie purposed to wracke religioun
within this realme, (for to that Roman Antichrist she hath made

[1] When two ranks of the lords were banished, anno 1566, was this writtin.—
Note in the Original.

l

her promise, and from him she hath takin money to uphold his pompe within this realme,) yitt will they lett the people understand, that the queene will establishe religioun, and provide all things orderlie, if she were once delivered. If suche dealing (which is commoun among Protestants) be not to prefere flesh and blood to God, to his truthe, to justice, to religioun, and to the libertie of this oppressed realme, lett the world judge. The plagues have beene, and some part are present, that were before threatned; the rest approache. And yitt, who frome the heart cried, 'I have offended!' the Lord knoweth. In Thee onlie is the trust of the oppressed, for vaine is the helpe of man."

THE BIRTH OF KING JAMES THE SIXT.

In the moneth of June, the time of the queen's child-birth approaching, she wrote to the cheefe of the nobilitie to come to Edinburgh; and upon the 19th day, betwixt elleven and ten of the clock, was delivered of a male childe, who after raigned in her place. The lords and people came to the Great Kirk of Edinburgh, to give thanks to God, and to pray for gifts and graces to him. The artillerie was shott off, and fires of joy sett furth.

THE TWELFT GENERALL ASSEMBLIE.

The Generall Assemblie was holdin at Edinburgh, in the counsell hous, the 25th day of June, where were present the Erle of Huntlie, Chancellor, Archibald Erle of Argile, Alexander Bishop of Galloway, Adam Bishop of Orkney, Johne Commendatare of Lindores, James Balfour of Pittendreigh, knight, all of the Privie Counsell, beside superintendents, commissioners of touns and kirks, and ministers. Johne Areskine of Dun, knight, Superintendent of Angus and Mernes, was continued Moderator.

THE TRIELL OF SUPERINTENDENTS.

In the triell of superintendents, the Superintendent of Fife confessed his owne inabilitie to discharge his office, and desired the Assemblie to denude him of it.

PETITIONS.

The lords present were requeisted to sute for a gracious answere to the replyes made to her Majestie's answeres at the last Assemblie. Some brethrein were appointed to requeist the Lords of the Secreit Counsell, Sessioun, Justice, that no excommunicat person have libertie of anie processe before their honours, till they be reconciled to the kirk; cheefelie where excommunication is notore, and objected against them. It was ordeaned that a letter sould be writtin and sent to the noblemen, in whose bounds some Popish preests haunted or remained, and abused the sacraments, and celebrated mariage for lucre, sould be takin order with.

THE ORDER OF PAUL METHVEN'S REPENTANCE.

Paul Methven requested to be receaved, as a poore sheepe, in the bosome of the Kirk. He compeereth personallie at the ordinance of the Assemblie, and prostrat himself before the whole brethrein, with weeping and yowling. Being commanded to rise, he could not expresse his minde for greefe and sorrow. He is biddin goe to his loodging, till his supplicatioun were considered. Some brethrein were appointed to sett doun the order of his repentance and publick satisfactioun, and to report to the Assemblie, which they did, and the tenor followeth :—

"The commissioners appointed by the Generall Assemblie for ordering of Paul Methven his repentance, &c., in consideratioun of the said Paul his lamentable supplicatioun to the Assemblie,

humble submissioun of himself to the same, and absence out of the
realme the space of two yeeres or more, ordeane and appoint the
minister of Edinburgh to notifie to the people upon the Lord's
day, after sermoun, the said Paul his supplicatioun; and how the
Generall Assemblie hath ordeaned to receave him to repentance,
upon the conditions underwrittin. And, therefore, to admonish all
faithfull brethrein, that within the nixt eight dayes they notifie to
him, if they know, or be surelie informed of the said Paul his conversatioun and behaviour since his departure out of this realme,
which might impede receaving of him to repentance, which sall be
in this maner: to witt, the said Paul, upon the said two preaching
dayes, betwixt the Sondayes, sall come to the kirk doore of Edinburgh, when the secund bell ringeth, clothed in sackloth, bare-
headed and bare-footed, and there remaine till he be brought in to
the sermoun, and placed in the place of publick spectacle, above the
people, in time of everie sermoun during the said two dayes; and
the nixt Lord's Day therafter, sall compeere in like maner; and,
after sermon, sall show signes of his inward repentance to the
people, humblie requiring the congregatioun forgivenesse. Which
being done, he sall be clothed in his owne apparell, and receaved
into the societie of the kirk, as a livelie member therof. And that
the same order be observed in Dundie and Jedburgh, alwise secluding him from all functioun in the ministrie in the kirk, and also
from participation of the Lord's Table, till the 25th of December
nixt to come, when the Generall Assemblie sall conveene; to which
they ordeane the said Paul to come, and bring with him sufficient
testimoniall from authentick persons in these places where he, in
the meane time, sall chance to remaine, anent his conversation and
behaviour, at which time the Assemblie sall tak farther order."

QUESTIONS DECIDED.

Mr Johne Dowglas, rector of the Universitie of St Andrewes,
Mr George Hay, minister of Ruthven, Mr George Buchanan, Mr

Robert Pont, and Mr Robert Hamilton, were appointed to sitt apart at sett times, to receave and decide questiouns, and to report their decisions to the Assemblie. They decided as followeth :—

First, That a woman may not joyne herself to another husband, without a sufficient testimoniall of the death of her former husband, howbeit he hath beene absent out of the countrie nyne or ten yeeres.

Secundarilie, That a minister ought to travell in the Word where he injoyeth a benefice, or receaveth sustentation, unlesse the Kirk appoint otherwise.

Thridlie, That none seeking donatioun or confirmation of benefices frome the Popish church be admitted to the ministrie.

A FAST.

It was appointed a publick fast sould be holdin the two last Sabboth dayes of Julie, in respect of the dangers imminent wherewith the Kirk is like to be assaulted ; and that the Lord's Supper be ministred upon the same day, if it can be done convenientlie.

THE KING DISCOUNTENANCED, AND BOTHWELL IN CREDIT WITH THE QUEENE.

The queene, after the deliverie of her birth, receaved humanelie all visiters. Onlie the poore king, her husband, could find no gratious countenance in her, or her traine. Bothwell was the cheefe guider of the court. About the beginning of August, she went out to Newhaven, beside Leith, and entered in a boat prepaired for her by foure notable pyrants, the Erle of Bothwel's dependers. She arrived at Alloway, where she remained certane dayes. Her husband followed with speed by land, but had no sooner refreshed himself, when he was commanded to returne. She returneth to

Edinburgh within few dayes, but loodged not in the palace, but in a privat man's hous, named Johne Balfoure. Frome thence sho removed to another loodging, where the exchecker held, beside David Chalmers' loodging, a depender of the Erle of Bothwel's, which had a backe passage to the orchards and gardens belonging to the queen's loodging. Bothwel had accesse when he pleased to the queene. The king her husband, by reasoun of her chyding and frowning, was constrained to lurke solitarie in Stirline.[1]

BOTHWEL HURT AND THE QUEENE SICKE.

About the beginning of October, the queene intended to hold a justice court at Jedburgh. Bothwell was sent to Liddisdail, to apprehend some theeves, to be presented to court. But he was wounded by a base theefe whom he hurt after he was takin, not expecting anie injurie. He was caried to Hermitage. The queene being then in the castell of Borthwicke, hasted with all speed to Jedburgh, and frome thence to Hermitage, notwithstanding the seasoun of the yeere, the difficulteis and dangers of the way, with a small traine. She returneth to Jedburgh, and prepareth all things needful for transporting him thither. At this time she fell greevouslie sicke. Of this her sickenesse mention is made in the treatise of Fasting in our Psalme bookes, and of Whoordome and Murther raigning in the Court. It was said at court, notwithstanding Bothwell was beaten by a base theefe yeelding up the ghost, yitt was he abler to ly oftener in carnall dealing with a woman than anie other in the court. He is brought to Jedburgh. The king hearing of the queen's sickenesse, posted with speed to Jedburgh, hoping that, in this time of her humiliatioun, her heart might be bowed.

---

[1] "The queene and her husband (says the Earl of Bedford, then at the Scottish court, in a letter to Cecil) agree after thold maner, or rather worse: she eateth but verie seldome with him, but lyeth not, nor kepeth no companie with him, nor loveth anie suche as love him. He is so farre out of her bookes, as, at her going from the castell of Edenboroughe to remove abrode, he knew nothing thereof. It cannot for modestie, nor with the honour of a queene, be reported what she said of him."

But the queene provided that no man sould rise to salute him, nor
give him loodging. Suspecting the Erle of Murray his courteous
nature, she moved his ladie to faine herself sicke, that he might be
disappointed of anie loodging there.[1] He had beene destitute that
night, if one of the Humes had not fained some pretence of hastie
departure out of the toun, to the end he might leave him his loodging. The king returneth the day following towards Stirline. The
same day, Bothwell was caried out of his owne loodging to the
queen's, when neither the queen was weill recovered of her sickenesse, nor he of his wounds and strokes.

THE QUEENE PROFESSETH SHE WOULD BE RID OF THE KING.

About the beginning of November, they came from Jedburgh
to Kelso, where the queen receaved letters from her husband.
When she had read them before the Erle of Murray, the Erle of
Huntlie, and the secretar, she professed plainlie, that unlesse she
was freed of him some way, she could have no pleasure to live;
and, if she could find no other remedie, she sould putt hand
into herself. About the end of November, they came to the
place of Craigmillar. There she renued her former speeches before Huntlie, Argile, Murrey, and the secretar, and showed what
way she might be freed of her husband; to witt, by divorcement,
in respect they were so neere of kin, that they could not marie together according to the canon law, which might be easilie brought
to passe, as she supposed, the Popish dispensatioun being destroyed.
But one moved a scruple, that so her sonne sould be reputed a bas-

---

[1] Mary's hatred of her husband sorely lacked in many instances that dignity which
we generally attach to her character. The following instance, related by Bedford in
a letter to Cecil, is a curious illustration of her temper on this point :

"One Hickeman, an English merchaunt there, having a water spangell that was
verie good, gave him to James Melvyn, who afterward, for the pleasure that he sawe
that the king had in suche kind of dogges, gave him to the king. The queene therupon fell mervelouslie out with Melvyn, and called him dissembler and flatterer, and
sayed, she could not trust him who would give any thing to such one as she loved
not."

tard, as one not borne in lawfull matrimonie. So this project succeeded not. The king cometh from Stirline to Craigmillar, hoping
to find her somwhat changed; but is threatned with want of all
kinde of maintenance, unlesse he returne and stay at Stirline.

THE BAPTISME OF THE PRINCE.

About the beginning of December the prince was baptized.
The English ambassader, the Erle of Bedford, brought with him a
font of gold curiouslie wrought, and enambled, weyghing three hundreth, threttie-three unces. The poore king was forbiddin to come
furth in publick, under pretence that his apparrell was not answer-
able, neither to his estate, nor to the celebritie of the time. The
blame was layed upon merchants and craftsmen. The nobilitie
were forbiddin to convoy him out or in. The ambassaders were
forbiddin to hold conference with him, howbeit they were all together in one castell. Bothwel, in the meane time, wanted nothing
to beare out a great port. It is reported by persons worthie of credite, that that day the prince was baptized, there was sitting in the
entrie of the castell a poore man asking almous, having a young
childe upon his knee, whose head was so great, that the bodie of
the childe could skarse beare it up. A certane gentleman perceaving, could not refraine himself from teares, for feare of the evills he
judged to be portended.[1]

---

[1] Amidst the daily banquets, dances, and triumphs, on this joyful occasion, Melvil
describes a pageant that gives us a poor idea of the taste of Mary's Frenchified court.
" At the principal banquet there fell out a great grudge among the Englishmen : for,
a Frenchman called Bastian, (perhaps Sebastian, on the night of whose marriage,
soon after, Darnley was murdered,) devised a number of men formed like Satyrs,
with long tails, and whips in their hands, running before the meat, which was brought
through the great hall upon a machine or engine, marching, as appeared, alone, with
musicians clothed like maids, singing and playing upon all sorts of instruments. But
the Satyrs were not content only to make way or room, but put their hands behind
them to their tails, which they wagged with their hands, in such sort, as the Englishmen supposed it had been devised and done in derision of them ; weakly apprehending that which they should not have appeared to understand."—*Melvil's Memoirs*, p.
152. Another exhibition given by the queen to the French ambassador, on Darnley's being invested with the order of St Michael, was still more indecorous. " Upon

THE KING POYSONED.

The king, despairing of favour, and finding himself so farre contemned, resolved to goe to Glasgow, to his father, the Erle of Lennox.   At his departure frome Stirline, the queene caused tak all
the silver plait frome him, and give him tinne insteid therof.   He
had not riddin a myle frome Stirline, when he was tormented with
great paine through all his bodie.   It is easilie appeared to proceed not frome anie ordinarie or naturall disease.   When he come
to Glasgow, his bodie brake out in foule spots, and his torments
waxed so greevous, that small hope there was of his recoverie.
James Abernethie, physician, being sent for, and demanded what
was his judgement, said plainlie, he had gottin poysoun.   The
queen's owne physician was sent for, but was forbiddin to goe.

BOTHWEL ACCOMPANEITH THE QUEENE TO TULLIBARDIN.

The ceremoneis of the baptisme being finished, the Erle of Murrey accompaneid the Erle of Bedford to Sanct Andrewes; Bothwell accompaneid the queene to Drummenie and Tullibardin.   She
returned to Stirline within eight dayes, about the beginning of
Januar.

THE THIRTENTH GENERALL ASSEMBLIE.

The Generall Assemblie was holdin at Edinburgh, in the counsell house, and beganne the 25th day of December.   The Superintendent of Angus and Mernes was continued Moderator.

the ellevint day of the said moneth, (says the Diurnal,) the king and queene in lyik
manner bankettit the samin ambassatour; and at euin our soveranis maid the maskrie
and mumschance, in the quhilk the quenis Grace and all her Maries and ladies *were
all cled in men's apperell;* and everie ane of thame presentit ane quhinger, bravelie
and maist artificiallie made and embroiderit with gold, to the said ambassatour and
his gentilmen, everie ane of thame according to his estate." Was it strange that the
Reformers scowled at these doings, and condemned them as foolish and flagitious? Or
was Knox devoid of taste, who wished to supersede them by schools and colleges?

ASSIGNATION OF MONEY AND VICTUALS OFFERED TO MINISTERS BUT IN SHEW.

Assignation of money and victualls being offered by the queene and her counsell, the Assemblie thanked the lords who had takin paines to purchase the said assignatioun, requeisting them to continue, till they brought that worke to some perfectioun. They protested, notwithstanding, that this acceptatioun of the forsaid assignatioun prejudge not the libertie of the kirk to sute for that which justlie perteaneth to the patrimonie of the same, in time and place convenient, at anie time heerafter. The Assemblie appointed the Bishop of Galloway, the Superintendent of Lothiane, the Lairds of Carden and Keir, to goe to Stirline and seeke the extract of the said assignation from the Comptroller and Clerk of Register, that letters may be raised therupon; and to report their answere to the church-sessioun of Edinburgh, that the commissioners which are to be appointed for divisioun of the said assignatioun may be advertised. The commissioners were chosin and appointed to conveene at Edinburgh, within tenne dayes after advertisement, to divide the said assignatioun of money and victuals among ministers, exhorters, and readers, according to their discretioun. This offer was made onlie to gull the ministers, for there were other purposes in brewing.

THE JUDGEMENTS OF THE ASSEMBLIE CONCERNING THE TITHES.

It was asked, whether if the tithes perteane properlie to the kirk; and sould be applyed onlie to the sustentatioun of the ministrie, the poore, and the schooles, and reparation of kirks, and other godlie uses, at the discretioun of the kirk? It was answered affirmativelie, without contradiction. Nixt, it was asked, if so be, whether the ministers, which are the mouth of the kirk, may, with safe conscience, keepe silence, seing the patrimonie of the kirk unjustlie

takin up, and waisted in vaine uses, by suche persons as beare no
office in the kirk; the ministrie in the meane time ceasing frome
exercise of their office through necessitie, the poore perishing
through hunger, the soules of people perishing, and kirks falling
down to the ground? It was answered, that they ought not to
keepe silence, but to admonishe everie man of his duetie, and desire everie man to seeke that which justlie perteaneth to the sustentatioun of the forsaids. It was asked, whether the kirk might require of all possessors the tithes to be payed onlie to the kirk, and
inhibite all others to intromett therewith; and in case of disobedience, what order sall be takin? It was answered, that after due
admonitioun, and denyall of obedience, the censures of the kirk
sould be used.

QUESTIONS DECIDED.

The Bishops of Galloway and Orkney, the Justice-Clerk, Maisters Robert Pont, David Lindsay, William Christesone, George
Leslie, William Ramsey, and David Forest, were appointed to receave and decide questions. They reported their decisiouns as followeth :—

That the woman lying now two yeeres in whoordome with another man, her husband having past to Denmarke foure yeeres
since, but now deceased, may not marie the other man, till it be
tryed by the sessioun of the kirk, if, in her husband's time, or before the knowledge of his deceasse, she had anie carnall copulation
with the man.

2. That the man forwarned not to marie his father's brother's
wife, and yitt mareing, he and she sould be delated, both to the
Justice-Clerk and the kirk.

3. That suche as have communicat at the Lord's Table, and
after become witnesses at the baptisme baptised by a Papisticall
preest, in a privat place, sall, after admonitioun, underly the censures of the kirk.

4. That superintendents admonishe that none within their jurisdictions joyne in mariage anie partie offending, severed for adulterie, under the paine of depositioun.

A READER CENSURED.

The reader of Bathket (was) censured for baptising of childrein,
and solemnizing of mariage, he being but a simple reader, and taking silver for the same, frome persons that were without the pa-
rishe.

COMMISSION TO REVISE MR WILLIAM RAMSAYE'S BOOKE.

The Assemblie appointed the Bishops of Galloway and Orkney,
the Justice-Clerk, David Forrest, Mr John Row, David Lindsay,
Robert Pont, William Christesone, to revise the answere made by
Mr William Ramsay, one of the Masters of Sanct Salvator's Col-
ledge, to Henrie Bullinger, tuiching the apparell of preachers in
England.

THE CONFESSION OF HELVETIA APPROVED.

The Assemblie being advised with the interpretatioun of the
Confessioun of the Tigurine kirk made by Mr Robert Pont, ordeaneth the same to be printed, together with the epistle sent by
the Assemblie, allowing the same, providing a note be putt in the
margin of the said Confessioun, where mentioun is made of the
remembrance of some holie dayes, etc. In this Confessioun, superioritie of ministers above ministers is called an humane appointment; confirmatioun, a device of man; baptisme by weomen is
condemned; prolixe prayers, hindering the preaching of the Word;
canonicall houres, that is, prayers to be chanted, and often repeated
at sett times, as the Popish maner is, heaping up of ceremoneis to
the prejudice of Christian libertie, observation of sancts' dayes.
But this Assemblie would not allow the dayes dedicated to Christ,

but tooke exception against that part of the Confessioun ; yea, our
Assembleis meete often upon the 25th of December, so that manie
of the ministrie could not be at home in their owne parishes, to
teache upon Christ's nativitie. This Confessioun, called commounlie the Latter Confessioun of Helvetia, was allowed not onlie by
the Kirk of Scotland, but also Geneve, Savoy, Pole, Hungarie ;
but not the Kirk of England, becaus of the manie corruptions
mainteaned by them, which are condemned in it.

The Assemblie ordeaned a letter to be directed to the bishops of
England, to entreate them to deale gentlie with the preachers,
their brethrein, about the surplice and other apparell. Mr Knox
penned the letter at the desire of the Assemblie, the tenor wherof
followeth :—

"The Superintendents, Ministers, and Commissioners of Kirks
within the realme of Scotland, to their Brethrein, the
Bishops and Pastors in England, who have renounced the
Roman Antichrist, and doe professe with them the Lord
Jesus in sinceritie, desire the perpetuall increasse of the
Holie Spirit.

"By word and writt it is come to our knowledge, reverend pastors,
that diverse of our deerest brethrein, amongst whom are some of the
best learned within that realme, are deprived from ecclesiasticall
functioun, and forbiddin to preache ; and so by you are stayed to
promote the kingdome of Jesus Christ, becaus their conscience will
not suffer them to putt on, at the commandement of authoritie, suche
garments as idolaters in time of blindnesse have used in their idolatrie. Which bruite cannot be but most dolorous to our heart,
mindfull of that sentence of the apostle, ' If yee byte and devoure
one another, tak heed least yee be consumed one of another.'
We purpose not at this present to enter into the ground which we
heare, by either partie, to be agitated with greater vehemencie
than weill liketh us : to witt, whether suche apparell is to be

counted among things which are simplie indifferent or not. But in the bowells of Jesus Christ we crave, that Christian charitie may so prevaile in you, (in you, we say, the pastors and leaders of the flocke in that realme,) that yee doe not to others that which yee would not others to doe to you. Yee cannot be ignorant how tender a thing the conscience of man is. All that have knowledge are not alike perswaded. Your conscience reclameth not at the wearing of suche garments. But manie thowsands, both godlie and learned, are otherwise perswaded, whose consciences are continuallie stricken with these sentences, ' What hath Christ Jesus to doe with Beliall ?' ' What fellowship is there betwixt darknesse and light ?' If suirclothes, corner-cap, and tippet, have beene the badges of idolaters in the verie act of their idolatrie, what hath the preacher of Christian libertie, and open rebooker of all superstitioun, to doe with the dregges of that Romish beast ; yea, what is he that ought not to feare either to tak in his hand, or his forehead, the print and marke of that odious beast ? Our brethrein who refuse of conscience that unprofitable apparell, doe neither damne nor molest you that use suche vaine trifles. If yee sall doe the like to them, we doubt not but therin yee sall please God, and comfort the hearts of manie who are wounded with the extremitie which is used against these godlie, and our beloved brethrein. Colour of rhetorick or manlie perswasioun we will use none ; but charitablie we desire you to call that sentence of Peter to minde : ' Feede the flocke of God which is committed to your charge, cairing for it, not by constraint, but willinglie ; not as though yee were lords over God's heritage, but that yee may be exemples to the flocke.' Further, we desire you to meditat upon that sentence of the apostle, ' Give no offence neither to Jew, nor to Grecian, nor to the Kirk of God.'

" In what conditioun of time yee and we both travell in promoting of Christ's kingdome, we suppose yee be not ignorant. Therefore, we are the more bold to exhort you to walke more circumspectlie, than to trouble the godlie for suche vaniteis : for all things which may seeme lawfull edifie not. If the commandement of the authoritie urge the consciences of you and your brethrein,

with further than they can beare, we unfainedlie crave of you that
yee remember, that yee are called the 'light of the world,' and the
'salt of the earth.'   All that are in civill authoritie have not the
light of God shining before their eyes, in their statuts and commandements, but their affectiouns savour over muche of the earth,
and of worldlie wisdome; and therefore we thinke yee sould boldlie oppone your self not onlie to all that power that will or darre
extoll the self against God, but also against all suche as darre burthein the consciences of the faithfull, farther than God hath burthenned them by his owne Word.   But heerin we may confesse
our offence, that we have entered in reasouning farther than we
purposed and promised at the beginning.   And, therefore, we
shortlie returne to our former humble supplicatioun, which is, that
our brethrein who among you refuse the Romish rags may find of
you, the prelats, suche favour, as our Head and Maister commandeth everie one of his members to show one to another; which
we looke to receave of your gentlenesse, not onlie for that yee feare
to offend God's Majestie in troubling of your brethrein for suche
vaine triffles, but also, becaus yee will not refuse the humble requeist of us, your brethrein and fellow-preachers of Christ Jesus,
in whom, albeit there appeareth no great worldlie pompe, yitt, we
suppose, yee will not so farre despise us, but that yee will esteeme
us to be of the number of these that fight against that Roman Antichrist, and travell that the kingdome of Christ Jesus may be
universallie advanced.   The dayes are evill, iniquitie aboundeth,
Christian charitie groweth cold.   Therefore, we ought the more
diligentlie to watche, for the houre is uncertan when the Lord
Jesus sall appeare, before whom yee, your brethrein, and we, must
give acompt of our administration.   And thus, in conclusioun, we
once again crave favour to our brethrein; which granted, yee, in
the Lord, sall command us in things of double more importance.
The Lord Jesus rule your hearts in his true feare to the end, and
give to you and to us victorie over that conjured enemie to all true
religioun, to witt, over that Roman Antichrist, whose wounded
head Satan by all meanes laboureth to cure again.   But to de-

struction sall he and his mainteaners goe, by the power of the Lord Jesus, to whose mightie protectioun we heartilie committ you. From Edinburgh, out of our Generall Assemblie, and thrid sessioun therof, the 27th of December, 1566.

"Your loving brethrein and fellow-preachers in Christ Jesus :—

" Johne Craig.	James Melvill.
" Robert Pont.	William Christesone.
" Nicol Spittell.	Johne Row.
" David Lindsay.	Johne Areskine.
" Johne Wynrame.	Johne Spotswod."

A SUPPLICATION TO RECALL THE COMMISSION GRANTED TO THE BISHOP OF SANCT ANDREWES.

It was ordeaned, that humble supplicatioun sould be made to the Lords of Secreit Counsell, tuiching the commissioun of juris-dictioun supponned, granted to the Bishop of Sanct Andrewes, to the effect their honours may stay the same, in respect that the causes for the most part judged by his usurped authoritie perteane to the true kirk. And howbeit for hope of good things, the As-semblie did oversee the queen's commissioun givin to suche as were for the most part brethrein, yitt can they no wise be content that the Bishop of Sanct Andrewes, a conjured enemie to Christ, use that jurisdictioun, and als, because in respect of that coloured com-missioun, he might usurpe again his old usurped authoritie; and the same might be the meane to oppresse the whole kirk, by his corrupt judgement. The tenor of the supplicatioun followeth :—

" The Generall Assemblie of the Kirk of Scotland, conveened at Edinburgh, the 25th of December, 1566, to the Nobilitie of this realme that professe the Lord Jesus with them, and hath renounced that Roman Antichrist, desire constancie in faith, and the spirit of righteous judgement.

" Seing that Satan by all our negligences (right honorable) hath

so farre prevailed within this realme of late dayes, that we doe
stand in extreme danger not onlie to lose our temporall possessiouns,
but also to be deprived of the glorious Evangell of Jesus Christ,
and so we, and our posteritie, to be left in damnable darknesse ;
we could no longer conteane ourselves, nor keepe silence, least, in
so doing, we might be accused as guiltie of the blood of suche as
sall perishe for laike of admonitioun, as the prophet threatneth.
We, therefore, in the feare of our God, and with greef and anguish
of our heart, compleane unto your honours ; yea, we must compleane unto God, and to all his obedient creatures, that that conjured enemie of Jesus Christ, and cruell murtherer of our deare
brethrein, most falslie stiled Archbishop of Sanct Andrewes, is reponed and restored by signature past to his former tyrannie : for
not onlie are his ancient jurisdictions, as they are termed, of the
whole Bishoprick of Sanct Andrewes granted unto him, but also
the executioun of judgement, confirmatioun of testaments, and
donatioun of benefices, as more amplie in his signature is expressed.
If this be not to cure the head of the venemous beast, which once
within this realme, by the potent hand of God, was so brokin doun
and banished, that by tyrannie it could not have hurt the faithfull,
judge yee. His ancient jurisdiction was, that he, with certan collegues, collaterals, might have damned of heresie upon probation,
as pleased him and them ; to tak all that were suspected of heresie.
What they have judged to be heresie heertofore, yee cannot be
ignorant, and whether they remaine in their former malice or
not, their fruicts and travells openlie declare. 'The danger may
be feared,' say yee ; 'but what remedie ?' It is easie and at hand,
right honorable, if yee will not betray the caus of God, and leave
your brethrein, which will never be more subject to that usurped
tyrannie, than they will to the devill himself. Our queene, belike,
is not weill informed. She ought not, nor justlie may not, break
the lawes of this realme ; and so, consequentlie, she may not sett
up against us, without our consents, that Roman Antichrist againe.
For in a lawfull and most free parliament that ever was in this
realme before, was that odious beast deprived of all jurisdiction,

2

office, and authoritie within the realme. Her Majestie, at her first arrivall, and by diverse proclamations sensyne, hath expresslie forbiddin anie other forme and face of religion than that which she found publictlie established at her arrivall. Therefore she may not bring us (the greatest part of the subjects of this realme) backe againe to boundage, till that als lawfull and als free a parliament as justlie damned that Antichrist and his usurped tyrannie, have givin decisioun betwixt us and him. If heerof, and of other things which no lesse concerne yourselves than us, yee plainlie and boldlie admonishe our soveran, and without tumult onlie crave justice, the tyrans darre no more be seene in lawfull judgement, than darre the owles in the day light. Weygh this mater as it is, and yee will find it more weyghtie than to manie it appeareth. Farther, at this present, we compleane not, but humblie crave of your Honours a reasonable answere, what yee will doe in cace suche tyranns and devouring woolves beginne to invade the flocke of Jesus Christ within this realme, under what title soever it be; for this we boldlie professe, that we will never acknowledge suche, either pastors to our soules, or yitt judges to our causes. And if for denyall therof we suffer either in bodie or in goods, we doubt not but we have not onlie a Judge to punishe them that unjustlie trouble us, but also an Advocat and strong Champion in heaven, to recompense them who for his name's sake suffer persecution; whose Holie Spirit rule your hearts in his true feare to the end. Your Lordships' answere yitt againe we crave. Givin in the Generall Assemblie, and thrid sessioun therof, at Edinburgh, the 27th of December."

Mr Knox wrote another letter, wherin he advertised what was the danger which might ensue of the gift and power granted to the bastard Bishop of Sanct Andrewes, as followeth :—

" The Lord cometh, and sall not tarie. Blessed sall he be whom he sall find fighting against impietie.

" To deplore the misereis of these our most wicked dayes, (beloved brethrein,) can neither greatlie profite us, nather yitt releeve us of our present calamiteis; and yitt utterlie to keepe silence

cannot laike the suspicioun of apostasie, and plaine defectioun frome
God, and frome his truthe once by us publicklie professed. For
now are maters that in yeeres bypast have beene denyed so farre
discovered, that he who seeth not the plaine subversioun of all true
religioun within this realme to be concluded, and decreed in the
hearts of some, must either confesse himself blind, or elles an enemie to the religioun which we professe. For besides the open
erecting of idolatrie in diverse parts of this realme, and besides the
extreme povertie wherin our ministers are brought, by reasoun that
idle belleis are fed upon that which justlie apperteaneth to suche
as truelie preache Christ Jesus, and rightlie and by order minister
his blessed sacraments, that cruell murtherer of our brethrein,
falselie called Bishop of Sanct Andrewes, most unjustlie, and against
all law, hath presumed to his former tyrannie, as a signature past
for his restitutioun to his ancient jurisdiction (as it is termed) more
fullie doth proport. What end may be looked for of suche beginnings, the halfe blind may see, as we suppose. And yitt, we have
heard, that a certan summe of money and victuals sould be assigned by the queene's Majestie, for sustentatioun of our ministrie.
But how that anie suche assignatioun, or anie promise made therof,
can stand in anie stable assurance, when that Roman Antichrist, by
just lawes once banished frome this realme, sall be intrused above
us, we can no wise understand. Yea, farther, we cannot see what
assurance can anie within this realme that hath professed the Lord
Jesus have, of life or inheritance, if the head of that odious beast
be cured among us. And, therefore, we yitt again, in the bowells
of Christ Jesus, crave of you to looke unto this mater, and to advertise us againe with reasonable expeditioun of your judgements,
that in the feare of God, and with unitie of mindes, we may proceed to crave justice, and oppone ourselves to suche tyrannie as
most unjustlie is intended against us : for, if we thinke not that
this last erecting of that wicked man is the verie setting up againe
of that Roman Antichrist within this realme, we are deprived of
all right judgement. And what is that elles but to separat us and
our posteritie frome God ; yea, and to cutt ourselves frome the
freedome of this realme? We desire, therefore, that the wisest

among you consider the weight of this caus, which long hath beene neglected, partlie by our sleuth, and partlie by beleeving faire promises, by which, to this houre, we have beene deceaved. And, therefore, we ought to be the more vigilent and circumspect, especiallie seing that a parliament is proclamed.

"We have sent to you the forme of a Supplicatioun and Articles, which we would have presented to the queene's Majestie. If it please you, we would yee sould approve it by your subscriptions; or if yee would alter it, we desire you so to doe, and we sall allow whatsoever yee sall propone, not repugnant to God. If it sall be thought expedient that commissioners of countreis sall conveene, to reasoun upon the most weightie maters that now occurre, the time and place appointed by you, and due advertisement givin unto us, by God's grace there sall no fault be found in us; but as frome the beginning we have nather spaired substance nor life, so minde we not to faint unto the end, to mainteane the same, so long as we can find the concurrence of brethrein; of whome (as God forbid) if we be destitute, yitt are we determined never to be subject to that Roman Antichrist, nather yitt to his usurped tyrannie. But when that we can doe no farther to suppresse that odious beast, we minde to seale with our blood to our posteritie, that the bright knowledge of Jesus Christ hath banished that man of sinne, and his venemous doctrine, frome our hearts and consciences. Lett this our letter and requeist beare witnesse before God, before his angells, before the world, and before your owne conscience, that we require you that have professed the Lord Jesus within this realme, als weill nobilitie as gentlemen, burgesses, and commouns, to deliberat upon the estat of things present; and speciallie, whether that this usurped tyrannie of that Roman Antichrist sall be anie longer suffered within this realme, seing, that by just law it is alreadie abolished.

"2. Whether that we sall be bound to feed idle belleis upon the patrimonie of the kirk, which justlie apperteaneth to ministers.

"3. Whether that idolatrie, and other abominations which now are more than evident, sall by us anie longer be mainteaned and defended.

" Answere us as yee will answere unto God, in whose feare we
send these our letters unto you, least that our silence sould be
compted for consent unto suche impietie.   God take frome our
hearts the blind love of ourselves, and all ungodlie feare.   Amen.
Lett us know your mindes with expeditioun."

MR KNOX HIS LICENCE TO GOE TO ENGLAND.

Mr Knox obteaned licence frome the Assemblie to passe to England, upon conditioun he returne before the 25th of Junie nixt following.   It appeareth by the former Assemblie, that by some occasioun, the exercise of his ministrie in Edinburgh was suspended
for a while.   For there we find, that Mr Johne Craig, minister of
Edinburgh, desired that Johne Cairns, exhorter, might be joyned
with him as collegue, in respect he was alone.   This hath come,
belike, through the malice of the court, displeased with his free rebooke of sinne.[1]

Superintendents were injoyned to warne, or cause to be warned,
all bishops, abbots, priours, and other beneficed persons lifting up
tithes within their jurisdiction, to compeere at the nixt Generall
Assemblie.

M.D.LXVII.

THE PRINCE TRANSPORTED.

Whill everie man looked that the king sould have ended his
dayes, the queene pretended everie day she was to ryde to Glasgow.   But being uncertan of the event of things, her first care
was, to have her young sonne transported out of Stirline to Edin-

---

[1] The following brief entry in the Diurnal of Occurrents, for the year 1565, ex-
plains the cause of this suspension :—" Upoun the xix. day of August the king came
to Sanctgellis' kirk, and Johne Knox preachit; quhairat he was crabbit, and causit
discharge the said Johne of his preitching."   This perhaps was Darnley's greatest
exertion of influence during the heyday of his very short-lived favour with the queen,
and a part of the nobility.

burgh Castell. She pretended the wackenesse[1] and coldnesse of
the aire ; but the like was no lesse incommodious in Edinburgh Castell. He is transported frome Stirline in Januar.

THE QUEENE VISITETH HER HUSBAND AT GLASGOW.

The king is like to overcome the force of the poysoun, by the
vigour of his youth, and to recover his health. The queene heareth, that he had intentioun to passe to France or Spaine, and had
some dealing with the English men for that effect, who had a shippe
lying into Clyde Firth. This bruit was spread by his enemeis ;
yea, some offered to kill him, if, when the queene sent for him, he
refused to come. The queene, after she had sent sundrie letters,
to purge herself of her unkindenesse, went to Glasgow, and tooke
with her the Hammiltons, the cheefe enemeis of his father's hous,
and among the rest, the bastard bishop, who had beene latelie reconciled to her. What was the maner of her visitation she herself
sheweth, in a letter writtin to Bothwell, whom she left behind, to
prepare a loodging for him in Edinburgh. In this letter, she telleth
him that the king had sent for one of her servants, Joachin, and
inquired if she were come for reconciliation or not ; and whether
Bothwell was come, and whether she had takin Paris and Gilbert
in service : how that when she come to him, he said, that the sight
of her was so joyfull to him, that he thought he sould dee for verie
joy, and was sorie that she was so sad ; how that he requeisted her
to come to him after supper againe, which she did : that he imputed
the caus of his sicknesse to her strangeness : that he would make
no other testament, but leave all to her : that he confessed that he
had offended her, but not in that which he had constantlie denyed :
that he had offended some of her subjects, but the fault was forgivin by her, and promised never to committ the like offences
againe : that he sought no other thing of her but fellowship at bed
and boord, otherwise he sould never rise out of that bed : that he
suffered meekle paine becaus he had made her a God : that the

[1] Dampness.

caus wherefore he offended her is, becaus when he is offended, he
can find no comfort nor assistance at her hands, which greeved
him : that he denyed constantlie he had anie intentioun to flee
away in an English ship, but denyed not he had conference with
some English men : that Minto told him, that one of the counsell
had brought to her a warrant to subscrive, to command him either
to enter in waird, or, if he obeyed not, to slay him : that he was desirous to have her loodge beside him, but that she refused, and advised him to take purgatioun : that she said to him, that she would
tak him for that effect to Craigmillar, where he might have physi-
cians neere at hand, and she herself might visite him : that she never
saw him in better health, nor ever heard him speeke with greater
submissioun : that his father bled at the nose and mouth that day,
which she willed him to conjecture what that did presage : that
she did what she could to exeme all feare and doubts out of his
minde : that he was not greatlie deformed, yitt had gottin muche :
that he had almost killed her with his breathe, but that she satt
not before him, but in a chaire, at his bed end : that he feared his
owne life, and that which was in working, but with two or three
faire words was made againe free of suspicioun : that he goeth
wood when Lethington is named : that she was working late at
night upon a bracelett, which she was to send to him, and willeth
Bothwell to remember of the loodging at Edinburgh.   Manie love
words she useth to Bothwell in this letter, and willeth him not to be
miscarreid with his owne wive's fained teares, or her brother the Erle
of Huntlie his speeches, and refereth sundrie things to the bearer.
She wrote other two letters also to Bothwell at the same time.

THE MURTHER OF THE KING.

When the queene with great difficultie had, partlie by upbraid-
ing and compleaning, partlie by flatterie, perswaded the king her
husband of her renewed affectioun, he was content to be transported
to Edinburgh, howbeit he had not yitt fullie recovered his health.
He was careid in a litter, and brought to a loodging appointed for

him in Edinburgh, in the Kirk of Feild, neere the town wall, the most desert place of the toun. Manie of his servants forsmelling danger, left him. The few that remained could by no meanes gett the keyes of the loodging. The pretence of choosing this loodging was, the wholesomnesse of the aire. A posterne gate was made in the toun wall, that he might goe furth to the feilds, when he pleased, to refreshe himselfe, as was pretended. The time was no lesse fitting than the place, for Argile, Atholl, Huntlie, Bothwell, Flee-ming, Glames, Livingston, Arbrothe, the Bishop of Sanct Andrewes, and sindrie others of the nobilitie, were in the toun, in the meane time, so that others might have beene brought under suspicioun as weill as the guiltie. Whill as he was writting to his father, and assuring him, by manie evidences, of the queene's sincere love, the queene cometh in, and after she had read his letters, kisseth him, embraceth him often, and sheweth, that she now perceaved there rested no scruple or suspicioun in his heart. The Erle of Murrey addresseth himself to his journey toward Sanct Andrewes, to visite his ladie lying neere the point of death. The queene deteaneth him to dismisse honorablie, as she pretended, the Duke of Savoye's ambassador, who was sent to the baptisme of her sonne, but came too late. He stayed, howbeit the caus was not so weightie, as to stay him frome visiting his wife lying in childbed. The queene visiteth the king daylie, and reconcileth him and Bothwell. The queene's base brother, Lord Robert, reveeled to him secreitlie what was intended against him, and willed him to provide for the safetie of his life, als weill as he might. But he could conceale nothing frome the queene. Lord Robert is called for, and denyeth that he had spokin anie suche thing. After they had givin other the lee, they putt their hands to their weapons. The queene calleth for the Erle of Murrey to ridde them. None other was present but Bothwell, who was readie to have dispatched either the one or the other, as he sould be found inferiour. The queene caused carie her bed out of the palace to the king's loodging, to the chamber be-neath the chamber where the king lay. She made more travell nor she needed; for the king might have lyin in the palace neere herself, where the aire was more wholesome. Upon the Lord's day, the ninth of Februar, the Erle of Murrey being advertised that his ladie had parted with her birth, would not be stayed at the queene's requeist one day longer, but tooke journey presentlie before sermoun.

That day was Sebastian, one of the queene's minstrellers, mareid. The queene passed over the day at the briddell, in the palace. After supper, she went up frome the palace to the Kirk of Feild, to the king's loodging. She shewed not suche kindnesse to him seven moneths before as then. She kissed him, and gave him a ring. Among other speeches, she said, that about the same time bygane a yeere, David Rizio was slaine. As soone as Paris, a Frenche man, one of the partakers of the murther, came in her sight, when she was in the king's chamber, she would needs be gone, for she had forgottin a peece of duetie, and had not daunced after supper, and convoyed Sebastian's bride to her bed, according to the fashioun. The queene's bed had beene brought out of the loodging, and a courser placed in the roome of it. The king, after her departure, beganne to recount to his servants manie speeches which passed that day, which might cherishe his hope of restitutioun to his former place in the queene's affectioun; yitt the mentioun of Seigneur Davie's slaughter seemed unseasonable, and marred all the pleasure he could otherwise reape of anie thing she had done or spokin. After the queene returned to the palace, accompaneid with the Erles of Argile, Huntlie, and Cassils, she had conference a long time with Bothwell. When he came to his owne chamber, he changed his apparell, and came to the toun, accompaneid with some of his complices. Two other companeis came sindrie wayes to the place appointed. Some went into his chamber, and strangled him, and another servant, lying in another bed beside, when they were sound sleeping. After that, they careid them by a posterne gate to the yards nixt adjacent: then was the hous blowin up in the aire. The loodgings neere hand did shake, and these who were sleeping in the toun were wakened with astonishment. Bothwell returneth another way than he went. The queene calleth for the

noblemen that were in the palace, and sent some to learne what
the noise and tumult meant. Bothwell was sent for among the
rest. These who were sent found the king lying naked in a yaird,
with the shirt upon him, and his clothes and shoes lying apart beside him, neither burnt nor singed. Everie man concluded in his
owne minde that he was not blowne up, as Bothwell imagined they
would conceave. His bodie was nather bruised nor brokin. Bothwell relateth to the queene what he had heard and seene, as one
ignorant, and woundering at the mater. The queene went to bed,
and sleeped, till a great part of the day was spent.

In the meane time the bruite was spread, and the report careid to
England before the nixt day, that the king was murthered by the
Erles of Murrey and Morton's device. But if they had beene the
authors of this vile murther, why were they not apprehended, or
charged to underly triell? It is true that Morton, in Junie before,
obteaned libertie to returne home by Bothwell his procurement,
upon conditioun he came not within a mile to court. Bothwell was
carefull to gaine freinds, at least to avert enemeis, by some benefite. Howbeit Morton understood what was in working, yitt durst
he not reveele it to the king, for he saw by experience his futilitie,
in reveeling to the queene what Lord Robert had discovered to
him. His persuing of Bothwell after may cleare him sufficientlie
of the vile imputation of art, part, or counsell of Bothwell. Farre
lesse could this imputation be fastened upon the Erle of Murrey.
The commouns of the countrie spaired not to affirme that Bothwell, with knowledge and consent of the queene, together with his
complices, were the authors and actors of this vile murther. The
bastard Bishop of Sanct Andrewes loodged that night in the Erle
of Arran's loodging, the neerest loodging to the hous which was
blowin up in the aire; where as before, he wount to loodge in some
conspicuous part of the toun, where there was greatest repaire to
hunt for salutatiouns. Light was seene in his loodging till the
hous was blowin up; and then the lights were putt out, and his servants and dependers, who had beene watching till that time in their
armour, forbiddin to goe furth. Is it likelie the Erles of Murrey

and Morton would have made this bastard bishop privie to the conspiracie, if they had contrived anie? Thus have yee heard the maner of murthering King Henrie, upon the tenth of Februar, as Buchanan hath sett it doun in his Detectioun and his Historie. Manie particulars were discovered after, which we reserve to their owne places. The circumstances alreadie mentioned may serve for an apologie for the Erles of Murrey and Morton. They brought him not to Edinburgh, they appointed him not his loodging. If the Erle of Murrey had aspired to the crowne, he would have caused blow up the hous some night when the queene lay there.

THE KING BUREID.

When manie of the commoun people had gazed long upon the king's corps, the queene caused it to be brought doun to the palace by some pyoners. She beheld the corps without anie outward signe of joy or sorrow. When the lords had concluded among themselves that he sould be honorablie bureid, the queene caused his corps to be careid by some pyoners in the night, without solemnitie, and to be layed beside the sepulchre of David Rizio. If there had beene anie solemne buriall, Buchanan had wanted witt to relate otherwise, seing there would have beene so manie witnesses to testifie the contrare; therefore the contriver of the late Historie of Queene Marie wanted policie heere to convoy a lee.

THE ERLE OF ATHOLL DEPARTETH MALCONTENTED.

The nixt night after the murther, the palace being watched, as the maner is in time of tumult, with armed men, the Erle of Atholl's servants heare, as it were, some undermyning the wall of his chamber without; wherupon his servants watched all that night. The day following, he went to the toun, and soon after conveyed himself away secreitlie out of the toun. He was most greeved, becaus he was neere of kin to the king, and the cheefe procurer of the matche.

CONSPIRACIE AGAINST MURREY.

When the Erle of Murrey returneth from Sanct Andrewes to court, armed men were seene about his loodging. But, becaus his domesticks watched all the night, by reasoun he was sore vexed with the gutt, his enemeis were disappointed. Upon another night, Bothwell pretending he would goe visite him, becaus he was diseased with the gutt, intended to cutt him off with his owne hand. But, by the way, he was advertised that he was removed to Lord Robert's loodging, to be free of the noise and dinne of the palace.

THE QUEENE CANNOT ENDURE LONG A COUNTERFOOTE MOURNING.

The queene, according to an ancient custome, sould have keeped herself fourtie dayes within, and the doores and windowes sould have beene closed, in tokin of mourning; but the windowes were opened, to lett in light, within the fourth day. Before the twelfth day, she went furth to Seton, not regarding what the people either thought or said; Bothwell never parting from her side. There she went out to the feilds, to behold games and pastymes. In the meane time cometh Monsieur le Crocke, who had beene sent diverse times before out of France. He showed how odious the fact was in forraine countreis. The queene returneth to Edinburgh, but, within few dayes, went furth again to Seton. The king's armour, horse, and houshold stuffe, were bestowed upon the murtherers. A certane tailyeour, when he was to reforme the king's apparrell to Bothwell, said, jesting, he acknowledged heere the custome of the countrie, by which the clothes of the dead fall to the hangman.

SLIGHT INQUISITION TO FIND OUT THE MURTHERERS.

Soone after the murther, Bothwell and some of his complices

went to the Erle of Argile, Lord Cheefe Justice, and craved inquisitioun to be made, as if they had beene ignorant and innocent themselves. Some sillie poore weomen were examined. They tempered their language as they could; yitt some words escaped which the inquisitors expected not. They were dismissed as rash and foolish. The king's servants, so manie as escaped the danger, were demanded how the murtherers could gett entrance? It was answered, They had not the keyes. It was asked, "Who had them?" They answered, "The queene." Farther inquisitioun was in shew delayed, but in effect suppressed. Least the triell sould seeme altogether to be deserted, a summe of money was offered, by publick proclamatioun, to anie would detect the murtherers. No man durst accuse Bothwell, yitt the people spaired not to speeke freelie. Libells and pictures were affixed on conspicuous places: sundrie, walking through the streets in the darke night, proclamed the names of the guiltie. Sharper inquirie was made to find out the authors of these libells, pictures, and night proclamatiouns, than to find out the murtherers: no paines, no expenses were spaired. All who could write faire, or draw pictures within the toun, were tried. An edict was published by open proclamatioun, that no man sett furth, or read anie of these libells, under the paine of death.

THE CASTELL OF EDINBURGH DELIVERED TO THE QUEENE.

The queene dealeth with the Erle of Marr's freinds for the castell of Edinburgh, for the erle himself was lying sicke at Stirline. It was agreed, at lenth, that her sonne sould be delivered to him at Stirline, providing some of his speciall freinds were delivered as pledges in the meane time. So the castell was delivered to the queene, which ought not to have beene done without [consent] of the estats; for upon that condition it was committed to his custodie.

BOTHWELL CLEANGED BY AN ASSISE.

The Erle of Lennox not darring come neere the court, urgeth, notwithstanding, by missives, that the queene would caus Bothwell be committed to waird, and deteaned therin till he suffered triell. Seing it could not be longer shifted, it was hastened before the parliament, which was to be holdin the 13th of Aprile. The Erle of Lennox, his mother, and neerest kinsmen, ought to have beene summouned to compeere within fourtie dayes, to accuse either by themselves, or by some procurators. But the erle himself onlie is summouned to compeere the 13th day of Aprile, and discharged to come accompaneid otherwise than with his domestick servants. Bothwell, in the meane time, jetteth up and doun the street with great companeis of men. The Erle of Lennox, fearing to come among his foes without his freinds, and looking for no sincere dealing, compeered not; so Bothwell was both defender and accuser. Robert Cunninghame, a gentleman of the hous of Lennox, took instruments and documents, that they proceeded not according to order of law and justice : that the defender had strenthened himself against all feare of punishment; and the accuser durst not compeere to accuse, for feare of his life. He protested, whatsoever sentence sould be pronounced in favour of the defender, it sould be null, and of no force. They proceed notwithstanding; and, least it sould be thought that they had committed wilfull errour, they protested that they absolved him for laike of an accuser. Some alledged, that they were appointed judges of a murther committed the 9th of Februar, when as the murther wherof he was accused was committed the 10th of Februar. By suche trickes he was not clenged, but the slaunder augmented. Betwixt the summoning of the assise and the day appointed for triell, there was a libell affixed in publick, wherin the cheefe that were upon the assise were published as guiltie of the same murther. Notwithstanding of the murmuring of the people, of libells, of protestations, and instruments takin, he was absolved by five erles, five lords, five barons, a great number of them being his freinds and favourers. Then another libell was affixed publicklie, accusing the lords of wilfull manswearing, to colour knaverie; and want of all regarde of the credite of the coun-

trie.[1] Some of the lords flattered Bothwell, without anie regard to
conscience or credit of the countrie; others were in feare, becaus
Bothwell was great in court.

BOTHWELL'S CHALLENGE TO A SINGLE COMBAT.

Howbeit Bothwell was absolved by the assise, when he came
furth out of the tolbuith, he caused sett up a cartell subscrived with
his owne hand, wherin he offered to fight in singular combat with
anie gentle man undefamed, that durst say he was author of
the king's murther. No man durst answere him apertlie at this
time; yitt an honorable gentleman, whose name was then unknowne, affixed upon the Croce an answere, and offered to prove,

---

[1] Both of these libels are contained in Calderwood's larger History. We copy the
first as a specimen of the pasquinades of this period.

> I hold it best ye give him assise
> Of them that wrought the interprise ;
> And consented to that foule band,
> And did subscrive it with their hand ;
> And other sillie, simple lords,
> Who feare their hanging into cords.
> God is not glee'd thogh ye him clenge ;
> Beleeve me, weill He will revenge
> The slaughter of that innocent lambe :
> *Mihi vindictam, et ego retribuam.*
> Ye wold faine clenge ; I love it the war ;
> It makes it the more suspect by farre.
> The farther in filth ye stampe, but doubt,
> The fouller sall your shoes come out.
> Ye, being chiftan of that tryst,
> Ye braid* of him that speired at Christ.
> " *An sum ego, Jesu Christe ?*"
> Who answered, " *Juda, tu dixisti.*"
> Here I advertise yow in time,
> If that ye clenge him of that crime,
> Ather for love, or yitt for terrour,
> I sall protest for wilfull errour.

> * Have resemblance.

4

by the law of armes, that he was the cheefe author of that foule and horrible murther, howbeit an inqueist, for feare of their lives, had slightlie quitt him. Becaus the King of France and the Queene of England had, by their ambassaders, craved a triell and condigne punishment, he humblie craved of their Majesteis, that they would desire of our queene a day might be appointed with her consent, and some place in their dominiouns, where the same may be tried by the law of armes, in their Highnesse presence, or their deputeis. He promised, upon the faith of a gentleman, to keepe the day and the place, providing safe conduct be granted by their Majesteis. He promised likewise, that the rest of the murtherers sould have the like offer made to them.

HUNTLIE RESTORED.

At this time a parliament was holdin at Edinburgh, wherin nothing was done, but the Erle of Huntlie restored to his father's lands. Howbeit the queene had promised to abrogat Popish lawes, and to establishe the authoritie of the reformed kirk, she denyeth now that she promised anie suche thing. When two proclamations, made since her arrivall, were alledged, she biddeth the commissioners of the kirk come again another day ; but it was not her purpose to grant them audience.

THE LORDS CONSENT TO THE MATCHE BETWIXT THE QUEENE AND BOTHWELL.

About the same time, Bothwell invited the nobilitie to supper. When they were weill cheered, he presented to them a writt, to be subscrived. That they might be the more willing, he thanked them for their bygane favours, and letteth them know, that by giving their consents, they might winne to themselves the queen's favour. They were astonished with such an unexpected petition ; yitt some made for the purpose, putt to their hand. The rest not knowing what number there were of flatterers, and everie one suspecting another, all followed and subscrived. The day following, calling to remembrance what they had done, they protested inge- nuouslie, they would not have subscrived, if they had not thought it would have beene acceptable to the queene : for it might be not onlie prejudiciall to the commoun weale, but also might be layed to their owne charge, that they had betrayed the queene, and, in a maner, driven her to a base mariage, in cace discord sould arise betwixt her and Bothwell; and that she reject him as she did her first husband. Therefore, it was thought expedient now in time to seeke a ratificatioun of that which they had done, sub- scrived with her owne hand. It was easilie obteaned, and with commoun consent committed to the custodie of the Erle of Ar- gile. The tenor of the band followeth :—

THE WRITT SUBSCRIVED BY THE LORDS.

" Wee, under-subscriving, understanding that the noble and mightie Lord James Erle of Bothwell, Lord Hales, Crichton, and Liddisdaill, Great Admirall of Scotland, and Lieutenant to our Soverane Ladie over all the marches therof, being not onlie bruited and calumniated by placats presentlie affixed on publick places of the burgh of Edinburgh, and otherwise slaundered by his evill willers and privie enemeis, as art and part of the haynous murther of the king, the queen's Majestie's late husband, but als being delated of the same, by speciall letters sent to her Highnesse by the Erle of Lennox, who thereby earnestlie craved and desired the said Erle Bothwell to be tried of the said murther, is by condigne inqueist, and assise of diverse noblemen, his peeres and others, barons of good reputatioun, found innocent and guiltlesse - of the odious crime objected to him, and acquitt therof, conforme to the lawes of this realme : who, also, for farther triell of his part, hath offered him readie to defend and mainteane his innocencie against all that will impugne the same, by the law of armes ; and so, hath omitted nothing for the perfyte triell of his accusatioun, that anie noble man of honour, by the lawes, ought to underly and accomplishe.

And we, considering the ancietie and noblenesse of his hous, the honorable and good service done by his predecessors, and himself in speciall, to our soverane ladie, and for defence of this her Highnesse' realme against the enemeis therof, and the amitie and freindship which so long hath persevered betwixt his hous and forbeares, and everie one of us, and our predecessors in particular; and on the other part, seing how all noblemen standing in the reputatioun, honour, and credit, of their soverane, are commounlie subject to susteane, als weill the vaine bruites of the unconstant people, as the accusatiouns and calumneis of their latent adversareis, invyfull of their place and vocatioun; which both being practised against the said Erle Bothwell, we acknowledge ourselves of freindship oblished and astricted to withstand and represse; and therefore to be bound and oblished, and by the tenor heerof, upon our honours, faith, and truthe, in our bodeis, and as we are noblemen, and will answere to God, oblishe us and promitt, that in cace heerafter anie maner of person or persons in whatsomever maner sall happin to slaunder, backbyte, or calumniat the said erle, as participant art or part of the said haynous murther, wherof ordinarie justice hath acquitt him, and for which he hath offered to doe his devoire, by the law of armes, in maner before expreemed: Wee, and everie one of us, by ourselves, kin, freinds, and assisters, partakers, and all that will doe for us, sall tak effald,[1] plaine, and upright part with him, to his defence and maintenance of his querrell, with our bodeis and goods, against all his privie or patent calumniators, bypast or to come, or anie others whatsomever, presuming anie thing in word or deid to his reproche, dishonour, or infamie. Moreover, weighing and considering the time present, and how the queen's Majestie, our soverane, is now at God's pleasure destitut of an husband, in which solitarie estate the commoun weale of this our native countrie may not permitt her Highnesse alwayes to continue, but at some time her Majestie, in apparence, for the commoditie of her realme, must yeeld unto a mariage: And, therefore, in cace the former affectionat and heartlie service of the said erle done to her Majestie frome time to time, and his other good qualiteis and beha-

[1] Sincere.

viour, may move her Majestie so farre to humble her self, as preferring one of her owne subjects unto all forraine princes, to tak to husband the said erle, we, and everie one of us, under-subscriving, upon
our honours, truthe, and fidelitie, as said is, oblishe us, and promitt,
not onlie to fortifie, advance, and sett fordward the mariage, to be
compleit and solemnized betwixt her Highnesse and the said noble
erle, with our votes, counsell, fortification, and assistance, in word
and deid, at suche time as it sall please her Majestie to think it convenient, and how soone the lawes sall leave it to be done ; but in cace
anie would presume directlie or indirectlie, openlie, or under whatsomever colour or pretence, to hinder, hold back, disturbe, or impede
the same mariage, we sall in that behalf esteeme, hold, and reput
the hinderers, disturbers, and adversaries therof, our commoun
enemeis, and evill willers ; and, notwithstanding, sall advance, fortifie, and sett fordward the said erle thereto, so farre as it may
please our soverane ladie to allow : and in that querrell, sall spend
and bestow our lives and goods, against all that live or dee may,
as we sall answere to God, and upon our honours and fidelitie :
And in case we doe in the contrare, never to have reputatioun,
honestie, nor credit, in time heerafter ; but to be accompted
unworthie and faithlesse creatures. In witnesse of which things,
we have subscrived thir presents with our hands, as followeth :—
At Edinburgh, the 20th day of Aprile, the yeere of God 1567
yeeres.   Before thir witnesses,

George Erle of Huntlie.
Archibald Erle of Argile.
Arroll.
Crawfurd.
Cassils.
Morton.
Sutherland.
Cathnesse.
Johne Lord Glames.
Robert Lord Boyd.
James Lord Ogilvie.

Sanct Andrewes. (This subscrip-
   tion is counterfoote in the
   principall.)
Joannes Episcopus Rosensis.
William Bishop of Aberdeen.
Alexander Candidæ Casæ.
William Bishop of Dumblane.
Alexander Episcopus Brechinen-
   sis.
Johne Bishop of the Isles.

13 Mensis Maij, Anno Domini 1567.

" Having seene and considered the band above writtin, promitteth in the word of a prince, that she nor her successours, sall never impute crime nor offence to * * in caus therof their subscriptioun or consent givin to the mater conteaned, * * or their heyres sall never be called nor accused therefore; nor yitt * * subscriving be anie deragation or spott to their honours, or they esteemed * * of * * notwithstanding whatsomever things may tend or * * In witnesse wherof, her Majestie hath subscrived the samine * * ."

BOTHWELL DIVORCED FROM HIS LADIE.

Katharine Gordoun is compelled by the Erle of Bothwell, her husband, to intend an actioun of divorcement before the commissars. She accuseth him of adulterie, and obteaneth divorcement. She persueth him likewise before the judges delegat by the bastard bishop of Sanct Andrewes, alledging that he had carnall copulatioun with a neere kinswoman of his before their mariage, and, therefore, she could not be his lawfull wife. Lett the reader judge upon what intentioun this commissioun of jurisdictioun was givin to the bastard bishop before the murther of the king, and before the last Generall Assemblie. By the lawes of the realme he had no power to constitut judges, for anie suche causes. This actioun was intended and ended within tenne dayes. She was moved to persue for divorcement, partlie for feare of her life, partlie, that the restitutioun of her brother to his father's lands might not be hindered. So it appeareth this processe was led before the Parliament.

THE QUEENE INTENDING TO BRING HER SONE FROM STIRLINE IS DISAPPOINTED.

After that the Lords had consented to the matche, the queene went to Stirline, of purpose to bring her sonne with her to Edinburgh. Johne Erle of Marr admitted her to the sight of her sonne; but suspecting her intentioun, had so provided that he was master and commander. The queene dissembleth her purpose, and returneth. A greevous paine seazed upon her within foure myle to Stirline. Whether it proceeded of her travell, or greefe becaus she was disappointed, it is uncertane. After she recovered of her paine, she cometh fordward to Linlithquo.

BOTHWELL LEADETH THE QUEENE, AS IT WERE, CAPTIVE TO DUMBAR.

When the queene came to Linlithquo, she sent Paris, her servant, with a letter to Bothwell. Bothwell cometh soone after, to witt, upon the 24th of Aprile, accompanied with six hundreth horse; and stayeth at Almond bridge till the queene came fordward out of Linlithquo: taketh her, and leadeth her, as it were, captive to Dumbar. This fact was thought a device of Johne Leslie, Bishop of Rosse; for it being the order of our countrie, when a man getteth his remissioun, the most haynous crimes are expressed by name, and the other crimes included in generall termes, the conspirators ashamed to expresse the king's murther, committed this fained rapt, a crime of lese-majestie, in shew wherof, they doubted not to gett a remissioun suppose it were expressed; and so, the murther might be included in this, or the like generall claus, " *And for all other unlawfull deeds.*" The sounder part of the nobilitie conveened at Stirline, sent to the queene, to understand whether she was takin and holdin captive against her will. If against her will, they offer to sett her at libertie. She answered, she was takin against her will; but hath beene sensyne so courteouslie used, that she had no great caus to compleane. The lords tooke this confessioun as a ground of their interprise, which they keeped closse till a fitt opportunitie.

THE QUEENE DECLARETH HERSELF TO BE SETT AT LIBERTIE.

The shew of the queen's captivitie was a stay to the finishing of the mariage; therefore Bothwell convoyeth the queene to Edinburgh, that the queen being sett at libertie nothing sould be alledged to be extorted. But few or none suspected anie constraint. By the way his freinds and dependers cast from them their speares and lances, least that maner of convoy might argue against them that she was captive. They convoy her up to the castell, which then was in the Erle of Bothwell his custodie. The day following, she cometh doun frome the castell, presenteth herself before the lords, and declareth herself to be free, and at libertie.

THE MARIAGE BETWEEN THE QUEENE AND BOTHWELL SOLEMNIZED.

The reader of the kirk, Johne Cairns, obstinatlie refusing to proclame the bannes of mariage, the elders and deacons layed the burthein upon Mr Johne Craig, minister. He yeelded, but withal professed he would declare some impediment to stay the mariage. The queene and Bothwell could by no meanes drive him from his alledgance; yitt make they preparatioun for the solemnitie. Upon the 12th day of May, Bothwell was created Duke of Orkney. Upon the 16th day, James Hepburne, Lord Hales, Erle of Bothwell, Duke of Orkney, and Marie Stewart, Queene of Scotland, were joyned in the band of matrimonie, by the Bishop of Orkney, who accepted this peece of service when all others had refused. Others alledged just impediments; speciallie that he had yitt two wives alive, and the thrid he had separat from him, alledging or confessing adulterie to his owne turpitude. Manie of the nobilitie were gone out of the toun. Some few of Bothwell his freinds and favourers staying behind, were invited to the bridell. The Frenche ambassader, La Crocke, denyed his presence, howbeit he was one of the Gwise's factioun, becaus her owne freinds and the King of

France mislyked, and the people abhorred her mariage. The Bishop of Orkney, at the mariage, made a declaratioun of the Erle of Bothwell his repentance for his former offensive life; how he had joyned himself to the Kirk, and embraced the reformed religioun: but they were maried the same day, in the morning, with a masse, as was reported by men of credite. What doctrine sounded in the pulpits in these times, may be easilie considered, by the chapters chosin for the fast, which was celebrated the secund and thrid Lord's day of May. The note of the chapters is extant in our Psalme-bookes, at the end of the treatise of Fasting.[1]

THE QUEENE EXCUSETH THE DISPARAGEMENT OF THE MARIAGE TO THE KING OF FRANCE AND THE GWISES.

The queene, knowing verie weill what evill opinioun the King of France and the Gwises would conceave of this mariage, sent William Bishop of Dumblane to them, with instructions how to excuse her, and to grace the mater it self. The instructions are prolixe, sett doun at large by Buchanan, and translated by Holinshed. The instructions are forged, and full of lees, as the reader may perceave, if he will read and examine them.

A BAND SUBSCRIVED BY THE QUEENE, BOTHWELL, AND OTHER LORDS.

The queene and Bothwell convocated a number of the nobilitie, and presented unto them a band, to be subscrived and sworne unto ; viz., to defend the queene and Bothwell, and all their deeds ; wherin they, on the other part, were bound to favour and protect the confederats. The most part being induced before, subscrived ; the rest followed for feare. The Erle of Murrey was sent for to Seton. Courteours directed by the queene to him, asked, if he

---

[1] These chapters were, Ezek. iii. ; Zeph. i. ; Numbers xvi. and xxv. ; Josh. vii. ; 1 Sam. iv–vii. and xv. ; 1 Kings xv. ; 2 Chron. xxvi ; Isa. iii. ; Jerem. xxxiv. ; Hos. iv. ; Amos vi. ; Obad. ; Mich. ii. ; Zachar. v. ; Ezra iv. ; Nehem. ix.

would subscrive the band. He answered, he could not, with honestie subscrive a band with the queene, whom he ought otherwise
to obey in all things lawfull. At her requeist he was content to
be reconciled with Bothwell, and to stand to anie thing he had
promised; but to make a band with him, or anie other subject, he
thought it prejudiciall to the commoun weale. The queene spake
to him faire manie dayes: Bothwell himself assayed what he could
procure at his hands. After manie ¦purposes, he said, "I committed not that fact of my owne motive, or for my self alone."
The other frowned with his countenance. Bothwell seeketh occasioun of a plea, and skarse absteaneth from opprobrious speeches: the
other answered coldlie and calmlie, but upon no conditioun would
subscrive the band. When he perceaved that troubles were like to
arise, he craved licence frome the queene to goe to Sanct Andrewes,
or if it pleased her, to Murrey. At lenth he purchased licence to
goe to France, upon conditioun he stayed not long in England.

THE QUEENE AND BOTHWELL SET THEMSELVES AGAINST THE
NON-SUBSCRIVERS.

When the queene and Bothwell were rid of the Erle of Murrey,
whom they muche feared, becaus he was popular, they sett themselves against others who had not subscrived, namelie, these who
had banded together for the prince; to witt, the Erles of Argile,
Atholl, Glencarne, Marr, Lord Lindsay, and Lord Boyd. But
Argile, the day after he joyned with them, reveeled all their designes to the queene. Boyd was allured with manie faire promises
to her factioun. There were also others no lesse suspected by the
queene and Bothwell; Alexander Lord Hume, Walter Ker, Laird
of Cesfurd, Walter Scot of Balcleughe, becaus they lay neere to
Liddisdaill or Lothiane, where Bothwell had heritage or freindship. Bothwell being minded to make a road into Liddisdaill to
repaire his discredit he had receaved the yeere before,[1] the cheefe

---

[1] Bothwell's misadventure among the thieves of Liddisdale, excited so much mer-
riment and scorn, and is so frequently alluded to by cotemporary writers, that the

of the clans were commanded to enter in the castell of Edinburgh, to remain for a seasoun, least, as was pretended, they sould hinder the successe of his expeditioun; and that, in their absence, their dependers might be acquainted with the commandement of others. But they, suspecting some other thing, went home in the night, all except Sir Andrew Ker of Phairnihirst, who was judged not ignorant of the murther of the king, and Walter Ker, Laird of Cesfurde, a weill meaning man, suspecting nothing. The Lord Hume refused to come in. All men were charged by proclamation to prepare themselves against the 12th of June, to ryde with Bothwell to Liddisdaill. The queen and Bothwell went to Borthwicke castell, which is distant from Edinburgh seven myle, upon the 6th of June, with artillerie and men of warre.

following particular accoount of it from the Diurnal may perhaps not improperly be introduced here :

" Upoun the samyn day, James Erle Bothwell, Lord Hailis of Cryghtoun, being send be our soveranis to bring in certane thevis and malefactouris of Liddisdaill, to the Justice Air, to be puneist for their demeritis, and he being serchand the feildis about the Hermitage, efter that he had takin certane of the saidis thevis, and had put thame in the place of the said Hermitage in presoun, chancit upon ane theif callit Johne Elvat of the Park. And efter he had takin him, the said Johne speirit gif he wald saif his lyff; the said Erle Bothwill said gif ane assyiss wald mak him clene, he was hertlie contentit; bot he behuvit to pas to the queenis Grace. The said Johne heirand thaj wordis, slipis fra his horse to have rune away; bot in the lychting, the said erle schot him with ane dag in the body, and lichtit doun to have taken him agane ; and followand feirselie upoun the said theif, the said erle slipit ower ane souch, and tomblit doun the same, quhair throw he was sa hurt that he swounit. The said Johne persaveand himself schot, and the erle fallin, he geid to him quhair he lay, and gaif him thrie woundis, ane in the bodie, ane in the heid, and ane in the hand ; and my lord gaif him twa straikis with ane quhingar at the paip, and the said theif depairtit; and my lord lay in swoun quhill his servantis come and carijt him to the Hermitage. At his coming thairto, the saidis thevis quhilk was in presoune in the Hermitage had gottin furth thairof, and wes maisteris of the said place, and wald not let my Lord Bothwell in the said place, quhill ane callit Robert Ellot of the Schaw come and said, that gif thaj wald let in my Lord Bothwell, he wald saif all thair lyvis, and let thame gang hame ; and sua thaj let my lord in ; and gif he had not gottin in at that time, he and all his companie had been slane. And the said theif that hurt my Lord Bothwell, deceissit within ane myle, upone ane hill, of the woundis gottin fra my Lord Bothwell of befoir.''

THE QUEENE AND BOTHWELL FLEE TO DUMBAR.

When the queene was staying at Borthwicke castell the lords
of the other factioun gather together two thowsand men, before
the queene understood of their gathering. The lords sould have
mett at Libberton. Morton came to the appointed place. The
Lord Hume came to the castell of Borthwicke, accompaneid with
eight hundreth men armed with jacke and speere, of which number
an hundreth gentlemen came with young Cesfurde, to assist him.
The Lord Hume not having a sufficient number to keepe all passages about the castell, and being withall somewhat negligent, becaus he feared the Lord had deserted the cause, Bothwell first escaped, and then the queene, disguised in man's apparrell, followed
to Dumbar. The lords sould have met together at Libberton;
but the Erle of Atholl, either his fearefulnesse or sleuth, stayed
them at Stirline longer than the appointed time. Howbeit the
diett was not keeped, yitt they came fordward with the greatest
part of their armie to Edinburgh. When the Lord Hume heard
that Bothwell had escaped, he returneth from Borthwick castell,
and mett the lords upon the elleventh of June.

BOTHWELL PROCLAIMED AUTHOR OF THE KING'S MURTHER.

When the lords were conveened at Edinburgh, they proclaimed
the Erle of Bothwell to be the cheefe author of the murther of the
king, and that their intentioun was to be avenged upon him for
that murther.[1]

TRANSACTION BETWEEN THE LORDS AND SIR JAMES BALFOUR FOR THE CASTELL OF EDINBURGH.

Sir James Balfour had the custodie of the castell of Edinburgh
committed to him by the Erle Bothwell. He was a cheefe actor
in the murther; yitt not being recompensed as he wished, and

[1] For this Act of the Lords, see Appendix, letter B.

Bothwell having attempted to remove him, he removed so manie
as favoured the queen's factioun, and beganne to transact with the
lords about the randering of the castell.   In time of this transactioun, he lett out at a posterne gate the Erle of Huntlie, the Bishop of Sanct Andrewes, the Bishop of Rosse, whom he had receaved in when the lords came to Edinburgh.

THE QUEENE TAKIN AT CARBARIE HILL.

   The lords found not suche concurrence out of all quarters as they
expected, and suche worthie enterprise required; for manie favoured the other partie, or suspended their aide, till they saw farther.   They wanted likewise artillerie and munitioun necessarie for
the siege.   When they beganne to deliberat upon dissolving their
armie, the queen cometh fordward with her forces.   She had two
hundreth harquebusiers, under the conduct of Captan Anstruther.
Her forces consisted of two thowsand five hundreth men, but the
most part were commouns.   The Lords Seton, Yester, Borthwicke; the Lairds of Basse, Waughton, Ormeston in Tiviotdaill,
Wedderburne, Langton, Blanerne, and Sir Andrew Ker of Hirsill,
were the cheefe.   If she had stayed her forces had encreassed;
but she being confident in this number, determined to marche to
Leith.   Mr Edmund Hay, the Erle Bothwel's procurator, made
her beleeve that at the verie bruite of her comming the confederat lords would take the flight.   When they came through
Glaidsmure, an hundreth pund land of old extent was promised,
by open proclamatioun, to him that sould slay an erle or lord;
fourtie pund land to him that sould slay a baron, ten pund land to
him that sould slay a gentleman, the escheat of a yeaman to him
that slayeth a yeaman.

   The lords being advertised, a little before midnight, of their
comming, the trumpets were blowin, the commoun bell knelled.
They went out on foote, till they came to the Stoods, to the number of two thowsand men.   There were no harquebusiers among
them, except some voluntars of Edinburgh.   The Erles of Morton,

Atholl, Marr, Glencarne, the Maister of Montrose, Lords Hume, Ruthven, Lindsay, Sempill, Sanquhair, Lairds Tullibardin, Cesfurde, Dumlanrig, Grange, were the cheefe leaders. They went furth at two houres of the morning, stayed till five, and sent furth in the mean time to trie where the other partie was. When they heard they were at Seton, they sent for their horse, and marched till they came to Mussilburgh bridge, where they refreshed themselves a little, till seven houres. About this time, the queene came furth of Seton to Fawside, or Carbarrie Hill, above Mussilburgh. The lords marching toward Preston, perceaving the queen's armie standing upon the top of Carbarrie Hill, arrayed, returne, and cast about to ascend where the hill was not steepe, but not till after noone, that the sunne might shine upon their backes. Foure hundreth men were allowed to young Dumlanrig, Manderston, and Huttonhall, to disturbe and breake the array of their gunners. The Erle of Morton and Lord Hume were conductors of the avant-guarde; the Erles of Marr, Atholl, Glencarne, Lindsay, Sempill, Sanquhare, Ruthven, &c., conducted the rere-guarde. Monsieur le Crocke desired the mater to be takin up without blood, and promised to procure pardoun for all offences bypast, and that they sould incurre no danger for taking armes against her for that day. Morton answered, They tooke not armes against the queene, but against the murtherer of the king. If the queene would deliver him to be punished, or seperat herself frome him, they would continue in due obedience; otherwise, there could be no reconciliatioun. Glencarne said, They came not in armes to crave pardoun for anie offence, but rather to give pardoun to suche as had offended. The ambassader, knowing the equitie of their caus, left them, and went unto Edinburgh.

The queen's armie stood upon Carbarrie-hill, where the English armie camped some yeeres before : the lords' armie stood over against them, on the north side of Cowsland. Bothwell came furth weill mounted before the armie, and by a cryer, offered the singular combat, for triell of his innocencie. James Murrey of Tullibardin, the man who before had affixed upon the Croce of Edinburgh an

answere to his challenge, accepted the offer: the other refused,
pretending he was not his equall in degree of honour. Then his
brother, William Murrey, Laird of Tullibardin, offered to fight,
and alledged his hous to be more ancient than his. He still refused,
and craved an erle; speciallie, he provoked the Erle of Morton.
He accepteth the offer, and craveth to fight on foote, with two-
handed swords. But Patrik Lord Lindsay besought the lords of
courtesie, and in recompence of all the service he had done, or
could doe, to honour him with that combat, claiming it also as due
to him, in respect of his kindred with the defunct king. It was
granted. The Erle of Morton gave him Archibald Erle of Angus,
called Bell-the-Cat his sword, which frome that time furth, the
Lord Lindsay caried about with him continuallie. When he was
in readinesse, the queene called for Bothwell, and said he was her
husband; he sall not fight with anie of them. She perswaded him
to withdraw himself secreitlie out of the feild; for she had tried,
that few except his owne freinds and dependers were willing to
fight; at least, were desirous the battell might be delayed till the
nixt day, that Huntlie and the Bishop of Sanct Andrewes come
with new forces, if Bothwell, in the meane time, would not decide
the questioun by single combat. She weeped, fretted, upbraided
the barons and lairds : then she sent to the lords, desiring them to
send to her William Kirkaldie of Grange, pretending she would
conferre with him upon conditiouns. He is sent, and they stay in
a lower place, to avoide the shott of her artillerie and feild peeces.
Whill the queen was conferring with Grange, Bothwell conveyed
himself secreetlie from the armie, and hasted with speed to Dumbar, himself alone, becaus he would trust none; yitt others report
with seven or eight. After he had takin the flight, sindrie shrinked
away by hundreths, fourteis, and thretteis. One was sent frome
the queen's armie with a long picke, and cast it doun before the
horsemen of the other armie, in tokin the victorie was theirs. The
queen cometh with Grange to the lords, in a short pitticoate, little
syder than her knees. She was receaved with respect by Morton
and Hume, leaders of the avant-guarde. She desired libertie to

goe to the Hammiltons, who were said to be neere hand at Corstorphine, to give them thanks for their willingnesse to serve her,
promising faithfullie to returne, and desired the Erle of Morton to
be cautioner. He refuseth, seing Bothwell was fled, and their enemeis wanted her to be a head, which was a great advantage. Then
she upbraided them with benefites which she had bestowed upon
them. When she came to the rere-guarde, all cried out, to burne the
whoore and murtherer of her husband. An ensigne was caried
before her wheresoever she went, by two men, stented betwixt two
speeres, wherin was painted her husband lying dead under a tree,
and beside him her young sonne at his head, heaving up his hands,
and above his head these words, " Judge and revenge my cause, O
Lord!" She could skarse be holdin upon horsebacke, for greefe
and faintnesse. So soone as she recovered, she burst furth in
teares, threats, reproaches, as her discontentment moved. All the
way she lingered, looking for some helpe. She came to Edinburgh
about ten houres at night, her face all disfigured with dust and
teares. The throng of the people was so thicke, that it behoved
the armie to marche single, man by man.

A BLIND TUMULT IN EDINBURGH AFTER HER ENTRIE.

The day following, that is the 16th of June, a discord arising
betwixt two men, the one cried, " A Hume!" wherupon the Lord
Hume went to the street with his freinds, and would suffer none
to come to the street for the space of three houres. A great tumult there was at the knelling of the bell; everie man mervelled
what the mater meant. It was supposed afterward that this tumult was devised purposlie, that the queene might escape.

THE ENSIGNE STENTED AGAIN BEFORE HER.

The ensigne was again displeyed over against her window, which,
when she perceaved, she closed herself againe. Her spirit was not
yitt throughlie dauntoned; for when she entered in her loodging

a certan woman spaired not imprecatiouns against her: she turned, and threatned to caus burne the toun, and then slocken the fire with the blood of (its) perfidious inhabitants.

THE QUEENE IMPRISONNED IN LOCHLEVIN.

Great diversitie of opinions there was among the lords what sould nixt be done. Mortoun would have her life spaired, with provisioun of securitie to religioun. It was answered, so long as she was alive some would attempt her libertie; and then, if she escaped, all promises would be eluded, and imputed to feare or compulsioun : yea, some said, that as he was a stayer of justice he sould feele the justice of God striking him with the sword. If it be unlawfull to execute her, then her deteaning sall be unlawfull, and all that they had done might be called in questioun. It was, notwithstanding concluded, that she sould be sent to Lochlevin, and committed to the custodie of William Dowglas, Laird of Lochlevin. The Lords Ruthven and Lindsay convoyed her.

AN INVENTAR OF THE QUEEN'S JEWELLS TAKIN.

The lords went doun to the Palace of Halyrudhous, and tooke up an inventar of the plait, jewells, and other movables. Upon the 24th day of June they threw doun sindrie things in the queen's chappell, where the queene had her masse.

CAPTAN BLACADER TAKIN.

About this time Captan Clerk went to the seas, and brought in Captan Blacader, and some others, guiltie of the murther of the king. They were convicted, but denied obstinatlie.

DUMBLANE DELIVERING HIS MESSAGE, IS INTERRUPTED.

The Bishop of Dumblane, sent, as yee have heard before, to

3

France, craved a day to be sett, for hearing his instructions and message. When he beganne to mak his harang before the king and his mother the queene; to extoll Bothwell, to excuse the contracting and finishing of the mariage without their knowledge, the queene interrupted him, and produced the letters which she had receaved out of Scotland, wherin was declared, that Bothwell had takin the flight, and the queen was takin captive. He, astonished with suche unexpected newes, held his peace. Some girned, some laughed: no man thought anie thing had befallin which she had not deserved. The king and queene had receaved letters from Le Crocke and Captan Cockburne.

BOTHWEL'S SILVER CASKET INTERCEPTED.

About the same time Bothwell sent to the Castell of Edinburgh for a silver casket, which belonged sometime to the King of France, as the letters upon it testified. In it were conteaned the queen's letters to Bothwell, contracts, songs, &c., which Bothwell keeped, fearing her inconstancie, to be a testimonie against her, howbeit she had desired him to burne the letters after he had read them. Sir James Balfour delivered the casket to the messinger, but withall advertised some of the lords what he was careing to Bothwell. The casket is intercepted, wherin were found the letters and songs, whereby manie secreits of the conspiracie against the king were farther detected, and the whole proceeding represented almost in a livelie maner to men's eyes. I find in a certane manuscript, that the messinger was Mr Thomas Hepburne, Parson of Aldham-stocke.

BOTHWEL PROCLAMED THE MURTHERER OF THE KING.

Upon the 26th day of June the Erle Bothwell was declared by open proclamation, not onlie the cheefe author of the murther, but also the committer of it with his owne hands, and a thowsand crownes were offered to anie that would bring him in.

THE FOURTEEN GENERALL ASSEMBLIE.

The Generall Assemblie was holdin at Edinburgh in the neather Tolbuith, the 25th day of June.

A MISSIVE SENT TO THE LORDS AND BARONS.

Another Assemblie was indicted to be holdin the 20th day of the nixt moneth. It was ordeaned, that missives sould be sent to erles, lords, barouns, and commendatars of abbeyes, to require their presence at the nixt Assemblie, and assistance to suche maters as are conteaned in the missive. Commissioners were appointed to direct or deliver the missives to the persons nominated to them. The tenor of the missive followeth :—

" My Lord, (or Worshipfull Sir,)—After our most heartlie commendatiouns of service in the Lord Jesus ; having now of long time travelled both in publick and privat with all estats, continuallie craving of them, and of your Honour in speciall, that the course of the Evangell, now once by the liberall mercie of God restored to this realme, might continue to your and your posteriteis comfort ; and that, for the furtherance and maintenance therof, a perfyte policie and full libertie might be granted to this reformed kirk within Scotland, the ministrie and poore provided for sufficientlie, as God and all other policie and civill lawes ordeane and require, and that all superstitioun, idolatrie, and monuments therof might be utterlie removed and banished out of this realme, which God of his infinite mercie hath so lovinglie and willinglie called from darknesse to light ; this mater, indeid, was liked by all men. But suche impediments made the enemie of the kirk in his members, to stay the good work of God, that moyen could there none be had ; but by the contrare, at everie light occasioun, the ministrie frustrated of all livelihood and sustentatioun, the lame and impotent members of Christ lying in the street as doung, perishing for hunger and cold,

yea, and the whole flocke of Christ Jesus within this realme continuallie threatned with the executioun of that most cruell decreet
of the last Councell of Trent, wherin was determined and decreed
to make a sacrifice of all the professors in Europ, by the tyrannie
of that Roman Antichrist. We are not ignorant how farre the
samine was attempted by way of deid within the realme of France;
how farre now in Flanders, and in parts neere adjacent thereto;
and also what practising to that effect hath beene continuallie these
three yeeres bypast, and even now of late dayes within our bowells,
by our commoun conjured enemeis, als weill within as without the
realme; how they were bent to their interprise, if God of his mercie
had not prevented, beyond all our knowledge and expectatioun,
their cruell and craftie practises. Upon which consideratiouns, the
Assemblie at this present conventioun of the Kirk accustomed at
the course of time occurring, hath found needfull and expedient to
repaire the decay and ruine of that warke so vertuouslie begunne
among us, by an universall.concurrence and consent of the whole
professors of Christ Jesus within this realme, and by the same
meanes to meete the foresaid dangers hanging over our heads, proceeding from the craft of our implacable enemeis, as weill within as
without the same; and to that effect hath ordeaned a Generall Assemblie of the whole professors of all estats and degrees within the
kirks of Scotland to be holdin heere, in this toun of Edinburgh,
upon the 20th day of the nixt moneth of Julie, whereby a perpetuall order may be takin for the libertie of the Kirk of God, sustentatioun of the ministers, and decaying members therof; and that
a sure unioun and conjunctioun may be had amongst the whole
members, whereby they may be able to withstand the rage, the
craft, and violence of our forsaid enemeis. And becaus it hath
pleased the goodnesse of God so to move your lordship's heart, that
yee are become a notable instrument and member of this kirk; as
our hope is, and our prayer sall be, that yee may continue increass-
ing from vertue to vertue, to life everlasting, we thought it our
duetie, in name of our whole brethrein heere conveened, to notifie
to your lordship the appointment of the said Assemblie, and in the

name of the Eternall, our God, to recommend to your care and so-
licitude the building of this ruinous hous of God within this realme ;
requiring also, in his name, that yee will give your personall presence, your labours, and concurrence to that effect in the forsaid Assemblie, to be holdin the said day, that the whole bodie may be comforted by the presence and good advice of so notoure a member therof. And, becaus we doubt nothing but your lordship sall be present,
showing experience of your good part in all times past, we ceasse
to trouble you with a long letter, referring the rest to be declared
by our brethrein, the commissioners of the kirk, who to this effect
are directed to your lordship, and others our brethrein in these
parts. And we, for our part, sall earnestlie pray to God to augment in you his love, and blesse your lordship to the comfort of his
kirk. Amen. From Edinburgh, the 26th of June 1567.

"By your lordship's to command in Christ Jesus : in name and at
command of the rest of the brethrein heere assembled. *Sic subscribitur,*

"John Areskine of Dun.	Johne Knox.
Mr Johne Spotswod, Superintendent	Johne Row.
of Lothian.	Mr Johne Craig."
Mr Johne Dowglas, Rector of St Andrews.	

QUESTIONS DECIDED.

Mr Johne Row, Mr Johne Dowglas, Rector of the Universitie
of Sanct Andrewes, Mr Johne Craig, William Christesone, minister of Dundie, Mr Robert Hammiltoun, minister at Irwing, Mr
Robert Hammilton, minister at Sanct Andrewes, Mr James Melvill, minister at Tannados, were appointed to decide questiouns.
They reported their decisions as followeth :

I. That fornicators promising to the minister to absteane in time
comming from all societie with the woman, and to marie her in
cace of carnall deale with her therafter, may not be compelled to
marie upon suche promises suppose of carnall deale, after the pro-

mise made, but the offender is to be censured according to the qualitie of the offence.

II. It being asked, whether it be lawfull to a man to marie
her whom before, in his wive's time, he had polluted by adulterie,
his wife now being deid? it was answered, The Assemblie will not
grant that thing to be lawfull which God's law damneth; neither
yitt admitt anie suche mariages, for causes conteaned in the law.

III. It being asked, whether a man divorced for adulterie may
marie again? it was answered, The Assemblie will not resolve heerin
suddanlie; yitt, for the present, inhibiteth all ministers to meddle
with suche mariages till farther resolutioun.

A fast was indicted to be observed at Edinburgh upon the Lord's
Day following, the 20th day of Julie.

THE LORDS DIVIDED IN TWO FACTIONS.

The queene was earnestlie requested, but obstinatlie refused to
separat her caus from Bothwell's, professing she had rather beg
with him nor raigne without him. The hatred of the people was
now by processe of time turned into pitie. Some of the nobilitie
deplored her calamitie, who before deteasted her crueltie. This
proceeded rather of inconstancie, than affectioun or passioun truelie
moved one way or other, whereby it appeared they had respect
onlie to their owne particular profite before. Manie inclynned to
the strongest partie. The consenters to the murther, and sub-
scrivers of the band after the murther, seemed to be the strongest.
Sundrie fearing her deliverie would bee wrought some time by one
meane or other, were carefull to preoccupie her favour. Sir William Matlane, secretar, had joyned himself before to the lords, for
hatred of Bothwell. Bothwell, despairing to recover his former
place and dignitie, fled to Orkney, and from thence to Zetland.
Being redacted to great straits, the best shift he could make was
to be a pyrat. The secretar now being rid of him, writteth to the
queene, offereth his service; sheweth how stedable it might be, by
the apologue of the mowse delyvering the lyon takin in the netts.

The Erle of Morton taketh great paines to reteane in Edinburgh suche as were embarked in the caus. The heads of the other factioun conveened at Hammiltoun. The lords that remained in Edinburgh craved their advice, presence, and assistance, to the effaires of the countrie. They would neither read letter nor heare messinger, but reproached the lords despitefullie. They charged them with arrogancie, that they sould come first to the cheefe citie of the realme, and send for them, who were moe in number, and greater in power. They were the more insolent, becaus manie of the nobilitie lay quiett, and did not concurre with them. The lords requested the ministers to write to them conjunctlie and severallie, and to requeist them to lay aside privat grudges in so perellous a time; but the ministers could obteane nothing at their hands. Yitt they dissolved, becaus not yitt resolved of the queen's owne mind. Their meeting was, notwithstanding, a warning to the lords to provide for some imminent danger.

The sounder part of the nobilitie perceaving they could not move the queene to separat her caus from Bothwel's, they deale with her to resigne the crowne and authoritie to her sonne, under colour of infirmitie of bodie, love to her sonne, care to prevent dangers and troubles which were like to arise; and to committ the governement of the countrie, in the meane time, in his minoritie, to whom she thought good. Loath she was to dimitt, but at last consented, as these letters following, of commissioun and procuratioun, beare witnesse:

THE CONSTITUTION OF PROCURATORS AUTHORIZED, IN THE QUEEN'S NAME, TO RENOUNCE THE CROWNE TO HER SONNE.

"Marie, by the grace of God, Queene of Scots, to all and sindrie our judges and ministers of law, lieges, and subjects whom it effeires, to whose knowledge thir our letters sall come, greeting. Forsameekle as, since our arrivall and returning within our realme, we, willing the commoun commoditie, wealth, profite, and quietnesse therof, lieges and subjects of the samine, have imployed our

bodie, spirit, whole senses, and forces, to governe the same, in suche
sort, that our royall and honorable estate may stand and continue
with us and our posteritie, and our loving and kinde lieges might injoy the quietnesse of true subjects : In travelling wherin, not onlie is
our bodie, spirit, and senses so vexed, brokin, and unquietted, that
longer we are not of habilitie by anie meane to endure so great and
intolerable pains and travells wherwith we are altogether wearied ;
but als great commotiouns and troubles by sindrie occasiouns in the
meane time have ensued therin, to our great grief : And, seing it hath
beene the pleasure of the Eternall God of his kindlie love, mercie,
and goodnesse, to grant unto us of our owne persoun a sonne, who,
in cace by the hand of God we be visited, will, and of right and
equitie must and ought to succeed to us, and to the governement
of our realme : And knowing, that all creatures are subject to that
immutable decreet of the Eternall, once to rander and give up this
life temporall, (the houre and time wherof is uncertane ;) and, in
cace by deceasse we be takin from this life, during the time of his
minoritie, it may be doubted greatlie that resistance and trouble
may be made to our said sonne, now native prince of this realme,
in his tender yeers, (being so destitute of us,) to succeed to that
rowme and kingdome which most justlie of all lawes apperteaneth
to him : Which inconvenient, by God's helpe and good providence,
we minde to prevent in suche maner, that it sall not ly in the power
of anie unnaturall subjects to resist God's ordinance in that behalfe.
And, understanding that nothing earthlie is more joyous and happie
to us, nor to see our said deerest sonne in his owne life-time peaceablie placed in that rowme and honourable estate whereto he justlie
ought and must succeed : We, of the motherlie affectioun we beare
toward our said onlie sonne, have renounced and dimitted, and by
thir our letters freelie of our owne motive will, renounceth and di-
mitteth the governement, guiding, and ruling of this our realme of
Scotland, lieges, and subjects therof, and all intromissioun and dispositioun of anie casualteis, properteis, benefices, offices, and all
things apperteaning, or heeretofore is knowne, or heerafter sall happin to apperteane thereto, in favour of our said deerest sonne, to

that effect, that he may be planted, placed, and possessed therin; use and exerce all things belonging thereto, as native king and prince of the samine, and siklyke as we, or anie of our predecessours, Kings of Scots, have done in anie time bypast. Attoure, that this our dimissioun may take the more solemne effect, and that none pretend ignorance therof, we have givin, granted, and committed, and by thir our letters give, grant, and committ our commissioun, full, free, and plaine power, generall and speciall command, to our trust cousins, Patrik Lord Lindsay of the Byres, and . William Lord Ruthven, and to ilk one of them, conjunctlie and severallie, to compeere before so manie of the nobilitie, clergie, burgesses, and other people of our realme, as sall happin to be assembled to that effect, in our burgh of Stirline, or anie other place or places where it sall be thought most convenient, at anie day or dayes; and there, publicklie in their presence, for us in our name, and upon our behalfe, dimitt and renounce the governement, guiding, and ruling of this our realme, lieges, and subjects therof, all intromissioun with the propertie, casualtie, or other things apperteaning to us thereby; and all right and title that we had, have, or may have, by anie maner of way thereto, in favours of our said sonne, to that effect, that he may be inaugurated, placed, and rowmed therin, and the crowne royall delivered to him, and be obeyed in all things concerning the samine, as we or our predecessors have beene in times bypast. And likewise, by thir presents, give, grant, and committ our full, free, and plaine power, to our right trust cousins, James Erle of Morton, and Lord of Dalkeith, Johne Erle of Atholl, &c., Johne Erle of Marr, &c., Alexander Erle of Glencarne, William Erle of Menteith, Johne Maister of Grahame, Alexander Lord Hume, Adam Bishop of Orkney, the Proveists of Dundie, Montrose, or anie of them, to receave the said renounciatioun and dimissioun in favours of our said sonne; and after the receaving therof, to plant, place, and inaugurat him in the kingdome, and with all ceremoneis requisite to putt the crowne royall upon his head, in signe and tokin of the establishing of him therin; and, in his name, to make and give to the said nobilitie, clergie, burgesses, and others our lieges, his princelie and kinglie oathe debtfullie and lawfullie, as effeeres; and to receave their oathes, for due and lawfull homage to be made by them to him in all times comming, as becometh subjects to their native king and prince: And generallie, all and sindrie other things to doe, exerce, and use, that for sure performance and accomplishment heerof may or can be done, firme and stable, holding, and for to hold, all and whatsomever things they, in our name, in the premisses leid[1] to be done, in the word and faithfull promise of a prince: And ordeane thir our letters (if need sall be) to be published at all places needfull. Subscrived with our hand, and givin under our privie seale, at Lochlevin, the 24 day of Julie, and of our raigne the 25th yeere, 1567."

THE TENOR OF THE COMMISSION WHEREBY QUEENE MARIE CONSTITUTE REGENTS.

"Marie, by the grace of God, Queene of Scots, to all and sindrie our judges and ministers of law, leiges, and subjects whom it effeeres, to whose knowledge thir our letters sall come, greeting. Forsameekle as by long, irkesome, and tedious travell takin by us in the governement of this our realme and lieges therof, we are so vexed and wearied, that our bodie, spirit, and senses are altogether become unable longer to travell in that rowme: And, therefore, we have dimitted and renounced the office of governement of this our realme, and lieges therof, in favours of our onlie most deere sonne, native prince of this our realme. And becaus of his tender youth and inabilitie to use the said governement in his owne person during his minoritie, we have constitut our deerest brother, James Erle of Murrey, Lord Abernethy, &c., regent to our said sonne, realme, and lieges forsaids. And in respect that our said deerest brother is actuallie furth of our realme, and cannot instantlie be present to accept the said office of regentrie upon him, and use

---

[1] Left.

and exerce the same during our said deerest sonne's minoritie, we, whill his returning within our realme, or in cace of his deceasse, have made, constituted, named, appointed, and ordeaned, and by thir our letters make, constitut, name, appoint, and ordeane our trust cousins and counsellers, James Duke of Chattelherault, Erle of Arran, Lord Hammiltoun, Mathew Erle of Lennox, Lord Darly, &c., Archibald Erle of Argile, Lord Campbell and Lorne, &c., Johne Erle of Atholl, James Erle of Morton, Alexander Erle of Glencarne, and Johne Erle of Marr, regents to our said deerest sonne, realme, and lieges.   And, in cace our said brother, James Erle of Murrey, come within our realme, and refuse to accept the said office of regentrie upon his singular person, we mak, constitute, name, appoint, and ordeane our trust cousins and counsellers forsaid, and our said brother, regents of our said deere sonne, realme, and lieges; giving, granting, and committing unto them, or anie five of them conjunctlie, full power for our said sonne; and in his name to receave resignatiouns of lands, and make dispositions of wairds, non-entreisses, releeves, mariages, benefices, escheats, offices, and other casualteis and priviledges whatsomever, concerning the said offices, signatures therupon to make, subscrive, and caus be past through the seales: And to use and exerce the said office of regentrie in all things, priviledges, and commoditeis siclyke, als freelie, and with als great libertie as anie regent or governour to us and our predecessours used the samine, in anie time bygane; promitting to hold firme and stable, in the faith and word of a prince, whatsomever we or our said trust cousins doe in the premisses: Charging therefore you, all and sindrie our judges and ministers of law, leiges, and subjects forsaid, to answere and obey our said trust cousins, regents forsaid, in all and sindrie things concerning the said office of regentrie, during our said deerest sonne's minoritie, and ay and whill he be of the age of seventeene yeeres compleet, as yee, and ilk one of you, will declare you loving subjects to our said most deere sonne, your native prince, and under all paine, charge, and offence that yee, and ilk one of you, may committ and inzin against his Majestic in that part.

" Subscrived with our hand, and givin under our privie seale, at Lochlevin, the 24th day of Julie, and of our raigne the 25th yeere."

The commissioun in which the Erle of Murrey was appointed to be regent, in the minoritie of the king, is extant in our printed Acts of Parliament, wherunto I referre the reader. The letters of dimissioun, and constitution of procurators, are extant in the Acts printed at Edinburgh, *anno* 1568 and 1575.

THE FYFTEENTH GENERALL ASSEMBLIE.

The Generall Assemblie conveened the 21st day of Julie at Edinburgh, in the upper tolbuith. Mr Johne Row, minister at Sanct Johnstoun, was chosin moderator.

A CONFERENCE APPOINTED.

In the first sessioun it was ordeaned, that the brethrein of everie shire should choose some out of their number, and the ministers likewise choose so manie from among themselves, to reason and conferre upon the effaires of the kirk ; and to forme articles in writt, and present the same to the Assemblie, to be considered.

ARGILE AND ARBROATHE SENT TO EXCUSE THEIR ABSENCE.

In the secund sessioun, the commissioners appointed to deliver their missives to the erles, lords, barons, and other brethrein nominated, exhibited their rolls. The Erle of Argile his letter excusing his absence was read, wherin he alledged, that the brethrein alreadie assembled in Edinburgh were in armes, and, so farre as he understood, the rest were to come likewise in the same maner. Seing he had not beene privie to their proceedings, nor had yit joyned himself to them, therefore, he could not at this time be present ; in the meane time, desireth that no innovations be attempted, till the meeting of the other brethrein ; so muche the rather, becaus their adversareis would not allow of their proceedings: promisseth, in the meane time, to continue in the maintenance of true religioun. The Commendatar of Arbroathe alledged the like reasons for his absence.

In the fyft sessioun, the articles advised upon by suche as were chosin in the first sessioun were read publictlie, in presence of the whole nobilitie and brethrein assembled; were allowed and subscrived. It was ordeaned, that the commissioners appointed in the last Assemblie sould everie one of them have an authentick copie of the Articles subscrived by the clerk of the Assemblie, or Alexander Hay, scribe to the Secreit Counsell; and that the saids commissioners require all and sindrie erles, lords, barons, and other faithfull brethrein, who excused themselves for not giving their personall presence to this Assemblie, to subscrive the saids Articles with the rest of their brethrein, according to their promises made by word or by writt; with certificatioun to them that refuse, that the kirk heerafter will not repute them as members of their bodie; and to returne the rolls of the saids Articles, subscrived by the scribe of the Assemblie, to the effect their subscriptions may be sett doun in register with the rest.

THE TENOR OF THE ARTICLES, AND NAMES OF THEM THAT SUBSCRIVED PRESENTLIE.

The noblemen, barons, and others undersubscriving in this present Assemblie, have agreed and condescended to the Articles after following. At Edinburgh, the 25th of Julie, 1567.

"In the first: Forsameekle as there was a parliament holdin in this realme before the queene's Majestie's arrivall in the same, by the estats conveened for the time, authorized with her Highness' owne power and commissioun, in which parliament it was concluded, that the religioun of Jesus Christ, then universallie receaved within this realme, sould be universallie established and approved within the same; and all Poprie, with the Pope's usurped jurisdictioun, all idolatrie, and in speciall, the blasphemous masse to be abolished and putt away, as the acts made therupon proport; which acts, together with the queene's Majestie's power to hold the same parliament, the noblemen, barons, and others undersubscriving, will to be extracted, and putt in full executioun, as a publict law; and that the transgressers therof be punished according to the same, throughout the whole realme, without exceptioun. Which parliament, in all things concerning Christ's true religioun, they sall defend and mainteane to their uttermost, in the first parliament which sall be holdin, and at all other times and occasiouns convenient.

"*Item,* That the Act alreadie made anent the thrids of the benefices within this realme, speciallie for sustentatioun of the ministrie, may be duelie putt in executioun, according to the order of the Booke of the Appointment of Ministers' Stipends, als weill of them that are to be appointed, as for these that are alreadie placed; and that the ministers be first duelie answered, and sufficientlie susteaned with the same, to the releefe of their present necessitie, ay and whill a perfyte order may be takin and established, anent the full distributioun of the patrimonie of the kirk, according to God's Word: and that also the ordinance made by the queen's Majestie and her counsell, concerning small benefices not exceeding the value of three hundreth merks, be duelie putt in execution, als weill concerning the benefices which have vaiked since the date of the said ordinance, as these that sall happin heerafter to vaike; and siclyke the Act made concerning the annuells, obits, and altarages of burrows.

"*Item,* How soone a lawfull parliament may be had, or that the occasioun may otherwise justlie serve, the noblemen, barons, and other brethrein undersubscriving, sall labour and preasse to the uttermost, that the faithfull kirk professing Christ Jesus within this realme sall be putt in full libertie of the patrimonie of the kirk, according to the Booke of God, and the order and practise of the primitive kirk; and that nothing sall passe in parliament, untill the effaires of the kirk be first considered, approved, and established; and in the meane time, the professors undersubscriving consent and offer to reforme themselves according to the Booke of God, which they sall putt in practise, and that the refusers and contraveeners be secluded frome the bosome of the kirk. And, moreover, in the said nixt parliament, or otherwise, at the first occasioun, order sall be takin for the ease of the poore labourers of the ground, for the payment of their tithes in a reasonable maner; and how the same sall not be sett over their heads, without their advice and consent.

" *Item,* That none be admitted, nor permitted heerafter to have charge over schooles, colledges, universiteis, or yitt openlie and publictlie to instruct the youth, but suche as have beene tried by the superintendents and visiters of the kirk; suche as sall be found sound, and able to teache, and as sall be admitted by them to their charges.

" *Item,* That all crimes, vices, and offences committed against God's law, may be severelie punished according to the Word of God; and where lawes are presentlie concluded for the said punishment, and judges also constituted for that effect, that executioun follow therupon as effeeres: and where neither law is made, nor judges appointed for suche crimes as are punishable by the law of God, that in the first parliament judges sall be appointed, and lawes made for the same, as God commandeth in his Word.

" *Item,* That seing the horrible murther of the king, the queen's Majestie's husband, is so odious not onlie before God, but also before the whole world, and will bring perpetuall infamie and shame to this whole realme, if the same murther sall not be punished accordinglie; therefore, the noblemen, barons, and others undersubscriving, sall with all their forces, strenth, and power, concurre and assist others to further and mainteane the punishment of the said murther, upon all and whatsomever persons which sall be found guiltie of the same; seing the plague of God cannot depart frome the countrie or toun where innocent blood is shed, before it be clenged by shedding the blood of the offenders.

" *Item,* Seing it hath pleased Almightie God, of his mercie, to give a native prince to this countrie, apparent to be our soverane;

to the end he be not cruellie and shamfullie murthered, as the king his father was, the nobilitie, barons, and others under-subscriving, sall assist, mainteane, and defend the prince, against all that would violentlie oppresse him, or doe him injurie.

" *Item*, That all kings, princes, and magistrats, which heerafter in anie time to come sall happin to raigne and beare rule over this realme; at their first entrie, before they be crowned and inaugurated, sall make their faithfull league and promise to the true kirk, that they sall mainteane and defend, and by all lawfull meanes sett fordward, the true religion of Jesus Christ, presentlie professed and established within this realme, even as they are oblished and astricted by the law of God, in Deuteronomie, and in the secund chapter of the First Booke of the Kings ; as they crave obedience of their subjects. So the band and contract to be mutuall and reciprock, in all times comming, betwixt the prince and God, and also betwixt the prince and the faithfull people, according to the Word of God.

" *Item*, That the prince whom God hath givin us, als weill for his securitie as good educatioun, sall be committed to wise, ancient, godlie, and learned men, to be brought up in the feare of God and vertue, whereby he may so profite in his youth, that when he sall come to his yeeres of majoritie, he may be able to discharge himself sufficientlie of that honorable place wherunto he sall be called, and prove that good king, which with all their hearts they wishe him to be.

" *Item*, The nobilitie, barons, and other brethrein under-subscriving, in the presence of God, have faithfullie promised to conveene themselves together, with their power and force, to beginne to root out, destroy, alluterlie subvert all monuments of idolatrie, and namelie, the odious and blasphemous masse ; and, therafter, to goe through the whole realme, to all and sundrie places wheresoever idolatrie hath beene fostered and mainteaned, and cheefelie where masse is said, to execute the reformatioun forsaid, without exceptioun of place or persoun; and sall to the uttermost of their power remove all idolaters, and others not admitted to the ministrie, from all functioun, as weill privat as publick, that they hinder

not the ministers anie maner of way in their vocatioun; and in
place of the premisses, sett up and establishe the true religioun of
Jesus Christ throughout the whole realme, by placing of superintendents, ministers, and other needfull members of the kirk, seing
the hoast of the Lord sall passe throughout the whole countrie to
this effect; and also, sall proceed to the punishement of idolaters,
according to the lawes pronounced against them.   And siclyke sall
punishe, and caus to be punished, all other vices which presentlie
abound within this realme, which God's law, and the civill lawes
of this realme, commandeth to be punished; and, cheefelie, the
murther of the king latelie committed: and, in like maner, promise
faithfullie to reforme schooles, colledges, and universiteis throughout this whole realme, to expell and remove idolaters that have
charges, and others, who as yitt have not joyned themselves to the
true kirk of Christ; and plant faithfull instructers in their rowmes,
to the effect the youth be not infected with poysonable doctrine at
the beginning, which afterward cannot be purged.

   " Morton, Glencarne, Marr; Alexander Lord Hume, William
   Lord Ruthven, Sanquhair, Patrik Lord Lindsay, Grahame,
   Lord Innernieth, Uchiltrie; Sir James Balfour, James Makgill, Tullibardin, Comptroller, William Matlane, Johne Areskine, Johne Wishart, Glenbervie, Johne Cunningham of
   Drumquhassil, William Kirkaldie, Johne Cathcart of Carleton, William Moncreif, Dumlanrig, Barganie, Andrew Wood
   of Largo, Andrew Stewart, Robert Fairlie of Braid, Archi-
   bald Wood, George Barclay of Mathirs, George Torrie of
   Kelwod, George Hume of Spot, Mr William Lundie, Gil-
   bert Kennedie of Dalquharne, Johne Melvill of Raithe,
   Quhittinghame, Ressyth, Barrow, Pittincreif, Andrew Ker
   of Fadounside, Thomas Scot of Harin, Robert Campbell,
   Henrie Grahame, Johne Foulerton of Dreghorne, Alexander
   Guthrie of that Ilk, William * * of Craigings, William
   Durhame of Grange, Thomas Distinton, Thomas Scot of
   Thirlestane, George Straton of that Ilk, Alexander Crich-

ton of Carko, Mr Johne Wood, Alexander Ugston of Fetter-
carne, Patrik Kinninmonth, Robert Lindsay, Treasurer,
Johne Collesse, William Meinzeis, Johne Melvill, William
Edmiston of Duntreth, Robert Murrey of * * Thomas
Kennedie of * .* Johne Schaw of * * Johne Stew-
art of Minto, Gilbert Ogilvie of that Ilk, James Chalmer
of Gaithgirth, Commissioners of touns. For Edinburgh:
Alexander Clerk, Bailiffe, Mr Clement Littill, Mr Johne
Preston, Mr Richard Strang.

"For Aire: Paul Reid, Richard Bannatyne, Gilbert Makmillan.

"For Irwing: Alexander Cunninghame, Alexander Commendatar of Culrosse.

"For Glasgow: Mr David Wemes, James Boyd.

"For Jedburgh: Williame Howburne, Alexander Forrester."

"Names of these that subscrived afterward, at the desire of the
commissioners:—

"William Churneside of East Nisbet, Kenneth Makceinzie,
Robert Monro of Foullis."

THE STIPENDS OF THE SIXTIE-SIXT YEERE MODIFEID.

In the fourth sessioun, commissioun was givin to revise the rolls
of ministers' stipends for the three-score six yeere, the tenor wherof followeth:—

"At Edinburgh, the 24th day of Julie, the whole Assemblie in
one voice thought meet, tuiching the assignatioun of money and
victualls made by the queen's Majestie for the sustentatioun of the
ministrie the three-score six yeere, that the distributioun therof
sall be made by the collectors alreadie appointed, according to the
tenour of the rolls of appointment of stipends, which the superintendents and commissioners, that sall be appointed, sall receave
from the keeper of the booke of the ministers' stipends; and after
the saids superintendents and commissioners have diligentlie marked these that are dead, or have not diligentlie waited on their

charges, as they will answere to God, and the Assemblie therupon, to deliver the rolls to the said collectors, everie one within his owne bounds, commanding the collectors to pay everie minister, exhorter, and reader, the thrid part of that which is appointed in the rolls forsaids, the superplus to be made compt of to the Assemblie."

THE CORONATION OF THE PRINCE.

Upon the 26th of Julie, the lords went to Stirline, to the coronatioun of the prince. He was crowned upon the 29th day. Mr Knox made an excellent sermoun before the coronatioun. After sermoun, the Superintendent of Lothiane, the Superintendent of Angus, and the Bishop of Orkney, sett the crowne on his head. The lords tuiched the crowne in signe of their consent; after them the burgesses. The Erle of Morton and the Lord Hume tooke the oath for him, that he sould mainteane and defend the religioun then preached and professed in Scotland, and persue all suche as sould oppugne the same. Mr Knox and other preachers repyned at the ceremonie of anointing, yitt was he anointed. Before he was crowned, certane letters of commissioun and procuratioun were read, which had the queen's seale hanging at them. One concerned the resignatioun of the crowne in favour of the prince.

THE ERLE OF MURREY RETURNETH HOME.

The Erle of Murrey being advertised of the estat of the countrie, addresseth himself to his journie. He was courteouslie receaved in the court of France, yitt not with that respect that was caried to Duke Hammiltoun; for they thought the duke's factioun was the stronger, and would be to them more trustie. After he had takin his fairweill, the Archbishop of Glasgow, who caried himself as ambassader for the Queen of Scots, informed the king and the Gwises, that the Erle of Murrey, howbeit absent, was the head of the other factioun; that he was sent for by them to be their chiftane: that whatsoever was done in former times was done by his credite and authoritie. Some were sent after to recall him ; but he embarked at Deepe, before the king's letters were brought thither. He was honorablie interteaned in England by the way. He came to Scotland upon the 10th of August.

THE ERLE OF MURREY PROCLAMED REGENT.

When the Erle of Murrey came home, the Papists thought he would be an instrument to sett the queene at libertie. But the lords were glade they had gottin him, a man so weill beloved of the people, and indued with manie good vertues, to be their chiftane. He was desired to accept the governement of the realme, becaus he would be least subject to the invy of men, partlie in respect of his neerenesse in blood, partlie in respect of the good estimatioun he had acquired in former times. He craved time to advise. In the meane time, he writteth to the heads of the other factioun, but speciallie to Argile, whom, in respect of old freindship, he was loath to offend. He craveth their presence and advice in some commodious place, to consult upon publick effaires ; but they refusing, and the pupill's factioun urging him to accept upon him the governement, he at last consented. He was proclamed Regent at Edinburgh Croce, the 22d day of August, with great pompe ; and therafter at other croces in the countrie. The Hammiltons and the Maister of Maxwell would not suffer the heralds and officers of armes to proclame, where they had commandement, either the prince, king, or the Erle of Murrey, regent. About this time, there was a conventioun holdin so frequent, that the like had not been seene in our countrie in the memorie of man.

SINDRIE SUMMONED FOR THE KING'S MURTHER.

The same day, the 22d of August, Skirline Rickerton, and some other gentlemen, sould have beene tried by an assise, for the murther of the king, but were continued till October. But the Laird of Ormeston in Teviotdaill, Sir Patrik Hepburne of Quhytcastell, the Laird of Tallow, younger, with diverse others, were denounced rebells, and putt to the horne, for non-compeerance.

A CONVENTION HOLDIN.

The heads of the other factioun conveened at Hammilton. They fretted, that some few, and not of the mightiest, sould without their consent rule as they pleased. They travelled to draw others to their factioun; but manie resolved rather to be spectators than actors for a time. At lenth they write to the lords that Argile was readie to conferre with the Erle of Murrey. Their letters were rejected, becaus they styled him not Regent. Argile, not being ignorant what had offended them, came to Edinburgh, with some others of his factioun. When he had receaved satisfactioun of the lords, and considered better that they had done nothing in contempt of the absents, but that necessitie moved them to make haste, he came to the conventioun, which beganne the 25th of August. At this convention, the regent's authoritie was confirmed. It was agitated, what order sould be takin with the queene. Manie inclynned to have her executed: some, to cover their owne guiltinesse, to be ridde of suche a witnesse; some, for justice' sake; some, for suretie of religioun; suche as favoured the Hammiltons, that they might be so muche the neerer to the crowne. Others thought it sufficient to deteane her in waird, speciallie the Erle of Morton.

BOTHWELL FLEETH TO DENMARK.

Upon the fyft of September, the Laird of Grange, accompaneid with diverse gentlemen, went to Zetland, to apprehend Bothwell. He escaped, and went to Denmark, where he was committed to waird, becaus he declared not plainlie whence he came, and whether he was going. But afterward, being knowne by some merchants, he was committed to closse prison, where he died tenne yeere after, mad, and miserable for filth, wanting necessareis, and other commoditeis.[1]   They tooke notwithstanding three ships; apprehended the young Laird of Tallow, and diverse others.

THE CASTELL OF EDINBURGH RANDERED.

The same fyft day of September, Sir James Balfour, commounlie called Parson of Fliske, having receaved a great summe of money frome the regent, randered the castell of Edinburgh.   The regent soone after constituted the Laird of Grange captan.

THE CHEEFE SUBJECTS ACKNOWLEDGE THE KING'S AUTHORITIE.

The cheefe men of Lothiane, Merce, and Tiviotdaill, were writtin for to come in to Edinburgh, to acknowledge the king's authoritie, which they did.   Waughton was committed to waird, becaus his freinds came not in.   But he escaped, and was receaved into Dumbar castell, by the captan therof, the Laird of Quhytlaw. The castell of Dumbar was delivered the first of October.   The Hammiltons had sent to the Queene of England, to crave her aide, becaus it was supposed she would favour the queene's caus, as a commoun caus to kings and queenes.   They gott not suche answere as they expected; therefore, upon the 10th of September, Mr Gawin Hammilton came in for the Hammiltons, the Erle of Argile, Lords Livingston and Boyd.   They protested, first, for the queen's libertie; nixt, that the crowning of the king be not prejudiciall to the Hammiltons' title and right.   The lords answered they were not minded to deprive anie man of his right.   Upon the 14th of October, the Lord Hereis, notwithstanding of his former oppositioun, came to Edinburgh, and acknowledged the king and regent's authoritie.

[1] For the Earl of Bothwell's testament and latter will, see Appendix, letter C.

THE REGENT APPREHENDETH FOURTIE-THREE LIDDISDAILL THEEVES.

The regent, accompaneid with Morton, Hume, and Lindsay, surprised fourtie-three theeves in Hawick, upon the mercat-day, the 30th day of October; twentie-two of the surname of Elliots, six of the surname of Crosers, the rest of other surnames. Ellevin were hanged, seven drowned, one slaine in the taking, three or oure led to Edinburgh, the rest clenged by an assize.

A PARLIAMENT.

A parliament was holdin the 15th day of December, at Edinburgh. All the nobilitie came in, except the Erles of Cassils, Eglintoun, Rothesse, Lords Seton, Fleming, and two or three other. This parliament beganne with invocatioun of God's name. Mr Knox made the exhortatioun. He exhorted the lords to beginne at the effaires of religioun. The burgesses of Dundie and Perth striving for the neerest place to the Tolbuith, whill they were to stand in armour, were charged to depart off the toun.

THE WORTHIE ACTS AND PROCEEDINGS OF THIS PARLIAMENT.

In this parliament, the dimissioun of the crowne, made by vertue of the queene her commissioun and procuratioun, was ratifeid as lawfull and perfyte; the coronatioun of the king, the nominatioun, constitutioun, and ordinatioun of James Erle of Murrey in the regentrie, during the king's minoritie, were likewise ratifeid and confirmed. The acts made in the yeere 1560, tuiching the abolishing of the Pope his jurisdictioun and authoritie, the abolishing of the masse, punishement of heerers and sayers of masse, were renewed. The Confessioun of Faith was againe ratifeid. Suche as opposed to the Confessioun of Faith, or refused to participat in the holie sacraments, as they were then ministred, were declared to be no members of the kirk within this realme, so long as they keeped themselves so divided frome the societie of Christ's bodie. It was ordeaned, that appellatiouns of laicks patrons, in cace the persons presented by them, to the superintendents or others having commissioun frome the kirk to that effect, sall end at the Generall Assemblie, by whom the caus sall be fullie decided.

Item, That all kings, princes, or magistrats, occupying their place, sall, at the time of their coronatioun, and recept of their princelie authoritie, take their great oath in the presence of God, that they sall mainteane the true religioun, the preaching of the holie Word, the due and right administratioun of the sacraments now receaved; sall abolishe and withstand all false religioun contrarie to the same; sall rule the people according to God's Word, lovable lawes, and constitutiouns of the realme, not repugnant to the said Word; sall procure to their power the peace of the kirk and commoun weale; sall preserve and keepe unviolated the rights, rents, and priviledges of the crowne; sall represse reefe, oppressioun, and all kinde of wrong; sall procure justice and equitie to be keeped; sall root out hereticks and enemeis to the true worship of God, that sall be convicted by the true kirk of the forsaid crimes.

Item, That none beare publict office removeable of judgement, but suche as professe the religioun and doctrine now presentlie established. That none be admitted to procure, nor admitted notar, or created a member of court, at anie time comming, unlesse he professe the religioun forsaid; providing this act be not extended to persons that have their offices heritablie or in liferent.

Item, That the thrids of the whole benefices in time comming sall be payed first to the ministers, notwithstanding anie discharge givin by the queene to whatsoever person or persons of the thrids, or anie part therof, ay and whill the kirk come to the full possessioun of their owne proper patrimonie, which is the tithes; providing the ministers their collectors make yeerelie compt in the exchecker of their intromissioun, that the superplus may be applyed to the king's use.

Item, That none be permitted nor admitted to have charge in uni-

versiteis, colledges, or schooles, in burgh or countrie, or to instruct
the youth privatlie or publicklie, but suche as sall be tried by the
superintendents, or visiters of the kirk.

Item, That no other jurisdictioun ecclesiasticall within this realme
be acknowledged other than that which is, and sall be within the
samine kirk established presentlie, or which floweth therefrome, concerning the preaching of the Word, the correctioun of maners, administratioun of the sacraments; wherin the said jurisdictioun consisteth. Commissioun was givin to Sir James Balfour of Pittin-
dreigh, knight, Pryor of Pittenweeme, Marke, Commendatar of
Newbottle, Johne, Pryor of Coldinghame, Lord Privie Seale, Mr
James Makgill of Rankeillour Neather, Clerk-Register, William
Matlane, younger of Lethington, Secretar, Sir Johne Bellendine,
Justice-Clerk, Johne Areskine of Dun, Mr Johne Spotswood, Superintendent of Lothiane, Johne Knox, Mr Johne Craig, to searche
more speciallie, and consider what other speciall points or causes
sould apperteane to the jurisdictioun, priviledge, and authoritie of
the said kirk, and to report their judgement to the nixt parliament.

Item, It was ordeaned, that patrons having provestreis or prebendreis of colledges, altarages, or chaplanreis, at their gift and dispositioun, present bursers to them, to studie in anie colledge or universitie
of the realme, so long as the patron, principall, and masters of the colledges sall agree, notwithstanding anie foundatioun or confirmatioun
past in anie time bygane. The lawes, acts, and constitutions,
canons civill and municipall, with other constitutions contrare to
the religioun presentlie prófessed, were cassed and annulled. It
was declared that secunds in degrees of consanguinitie and affinitie,
and all degrees without the same, might lawfullie marie. It was
declared that the prince entereth in his perfyte age at the 21st
yeere compleet. It was provided for the indemnitie of those who
had leveid warre, apprehended the queene at Carbarrie Hill, and
deteaned her in Lochlevin. All things invented, spokin, writtin,
or done, since the 10th of Februare last bypast, by the erles, lords,
barons, noblemen, and others, faithfull and true subjects, " or anie

of them to that effect, and all things depending therupon, was justifeid, in so farre, as by diverse her privie letters writtin with her owne hands, and sent by her to James, sometime Erle Bothwell, cheefe executor of the horrible murther of her husband, als weill before the committing therof as after, and by her ungodlie and dishonourable proceiding to a pretended mariage suddanlie and unprovisedlie therafter, it is most certane, she was privie art and part of the actuall device and deid of the forenamed murther of the king, her lawfull husband, and father to our soverane lord, committed by the said James, sometime Erle of Bothwell, his complices and partakers; and therefore justlie deserveth whatsoever hath beene done to her in anie time bygane, or sall be used towards her for the said caus in time comming, which sall be used by the advice of the nobilitie, in respect that our soverane lord's mother, with the said James, sometimes Erle of Bothwell, went about, by indirect and coloured meanes, to colour and hold backe the knowledge of the truthe of the committers of the said crime. Yitt all men in their hearts were fullie perswaded of the authors and devisers of that mischeevous and unworthie fact, awaiting whill God sould move the hearts of some to enter in the querrell, for revenging of the same. And in the meane time, a great part of the nobilitie, upon just feare to be handled and demaimed, in semblable maner as the king had beene of before, perceaving also the queene so thralled, and so blindlie affectionat to the privat appetite of a tyranne, and that both he and she had conspired together to suche horrible crueltie, being there with all garnished with a companie of ungodlie and vitious persons readie to accomplishe all their godlesse commandements, of whom he had a sufficient number continuallie waiting upon him for the same effect; all noble and vertuous men, abhorring their tyrannie and companie, but cheefelie suspecting that they who had so treasonablie putt doun and destroyed the father, would make the innocent prince, his onlie sonne, the principall and almost onlie comfort sent by God to this afflicted natioun, to taste of the same cuppe, as the manie invented purposes to passe where he was, and also where the noblemen were, in that open confusioun, gave sufficient warning and declaratioun."[1]

In the twentie act, the charge givin by the Erles of Morton, Atholl, Marr, Glencarne, Lords Ruthven, Hume, Lindsay, Sempill, and diverse other honorable barons and gentlemen, upon the 16th day of June last bypast, by their letters subscrived to William Dowglas of Lochlevin, to receave our soveran lord's mother in his keeping, within his fortalice and place of Lochlevin, and to keepe it, till he be sufficientlie exonered and discharged of her said keeping, is declared to be duelie and reasonablie directed, and to have proceeded from just, true, and sincere ground ; and that he had done his duetie in obeying the said charge. The queen's declaratioun made upon the 28th day of Julie, that she was on no wise treated nor compelled by the said William Dowglas of Lochlevin, nor anie other at his procurement, to doe anie thing contrare to her pleasure, since her comming to the place of Lochlevin, is remembred in this act.

These acts were printed the sixt of Aprile following, by Robert Lickprevick, printer to the king's Majestie, and were printed again in the yeere 1575. About the time of these changes was printed also that Dialogue, " *De Jure Regni apud Scotos*," writtin by Buchanan, which he dedicated after to the young king, in the yeere 1579, he was so farre from repenting that he wrote it.

THE SIXTEENTH GENERALL ASSEMBLIE.

The Generall Assemblie conveened the 25th of December, at Edinburgh, in the Neather Tolbuith. Mr Johne Row, minister at Perth, was chosin Moderator.

TRIELL OF SUPERINTENDENTS.

In the triell of superintendents and commissioners, Adam, called

---

[1] These are the verie words of the 19th Act.—*Note in the MS.*

Bishop of Orkney, was delated for not visiting the kirks of his countrie, from Lambmesse to Allhallowmesse. *Item,* That he occupyed the rowme of a Judge in the Sessioun. *Item,* Becaus he reteaned in his companie Francis Bothwell, a Papist, upon whom he had bestowed benefices, and whom he had placed in the ministrie. *Item,* Becaus he solemnized the mariage betwixt the queene and the Erle of Bothwell. He was absent for the present, at this time.

Alexander of Galloway, commissioner, delated, that he had not visited these three yeeres bygane the kirks within his charge, that he had left off the visiting and planting of kirks, and had haunted court too muche; and had now purchased to be one of the Sessioun and Privie Counsell, which cannot agree with the office of a pastor or bishop: that he had resigned Inchaffray in favours of a young childe; and sett diverse lands in few, in prejudice of the kirk.

When the Bishop of Orkney came to the Assemblie, he pretended he might not remaine in Orkney all the yeere, by reasoun of evill air, and weakenesse of his bodie. He denyed that he understood that Francis Bothwell was a Papist, or that he placed him in the ministrie, yitt he was deprived of all functioun in the ministrie, for solemnizing the mariage betwixt the queene and the Erle Bothwell, contrarie an act made against the mariage of the divorced adulterer, ay and whill he satisfie the Assemblie for the slaunders committed by him. The Bishop of Galloway granted he offended, in all that was layed to his charge. Yitt upon some considerations not expressed in the register, his commission was continued at this time till the nixt Assemblie, and he admonished to be diligent in visitatioun.

Mr Johne Craig, Mr David Lindsay, Mr George Buchanan, Principall of Sanct Leonard's Colledge, and Mr George Hay, or anie two of them, were appointed to direct their edicts to all ministers, elders, and deacons of kirks, which are under the Superintendent of Fife his charge, to compeere at Cowper, the 22d day of Januar, with their complaints against the said superintendent, to

trie and report to the nixt Assemblie.—Heere we may see commissioun givin to ministers to trie superintendents.

The Superintendent of Angus presented a supplicatioun in writt,
or rather a dimissioun of his office of superintendentrie, by reasoun
he was not able to discharge that office, in respect of his age and
infirmitie.   The Assemblie, notwithstanding, would not accept his
dimissioun, for diverse reasons, which sould be made knowne to
him, but continued him till farther advisement.

Mr Knox was appointed to assist the Superintendent of Lothiane,
in his visitatioun from Stirline to Berwicke.

Mr Johne Craig, at the ordinance of the Assemblie, presented
in writt his proceedings, tuiching the proclaiming of the bannes
betwixt the queen and the Erle Bothwell, in tenor as followeth :—

"To the end that all that feare God may understand my proceedings in this mater, I sall shortlie declare what I did, and what
moved me to defend the same, leaving the finall judgement of all
things to the kirk. First, Being required of Mr Thomas Hepburne,
in the queen's name, to proclame her with the Lord Bothwell,
I plainlie refused, becaus he had not her hand-writt ; and also,
becaus of the constant bruite, that the lord had both ravished
her, and keeped her in captivitie. Upon Wednesday nixt, the
Justice-Clerk brought me a writting subscrived with her hand,
bearing in effect, that she was neither ravished nor yitt deteaned in
captivitie, and therefore charged me to proclame. My answere
was, I durst proclame no bannes (and cheefelie suche) without
consent and command of the kirk. Upon Thursday nixt, the kirk,
after long reasoning with the Justice-Clerk, and amongst the brethrein, at lenth concluded, that the queen's minde sould be published to her subjects, the three nixt preaching dayes. But becaus
the Generall Assemblie had inhibited all suche mariages, we protested, that we would neither solemnize nor yitt approve that mariage, but would onlie declare the princesse' minde, leaving all
doubts and dangers to the counsellers, approvers, and prescrivers

of the mariage. And so, upon Friday nixt, I declared the whole minde and progresse of the kirk, desiring everie man, in God's name, to discharge his conscience before the Secreet Counsell. And to give boldnesse to others, I desired of the lords there present, time and place to speeke my judgement before the parteis; protesting, if I were not heard and satisfeid, I either would desist frome proclaming, or elles declare my minde publicklie before the kirk. Therefore, being admitted after noone before my lord and the counsell, I layed to his charge the law of adulterie, the ordinance of the kirk, the law of ravishing, the suspicioun of collusioun betwixt him and his wife, the suddane divorcement and proclaming within the space of foure dayes, and last, the suspicioun of the king's death, which his marriage would confirme. But he answered nothing to my satisfaction. Wherupon, after manie exhortatiouns, I protested, that I could not but declare my minde publictlie to the kirk. Therefore, upon Sunday, after I had declared what they had done, and how they would proceed whether we would or not, I tooke heaven and earth to witnesse, that I abhorred and deteasted that mariage, becaus it was odious and slaunderous to the world. And seing the best part of the realme did approve it, either by flatterie or by their silence, I desired the faithfull to pray earnestlie, that God would turne to the comfort of this realme, that thing then intended against reasoun and good conscience. And becaus I heard some persons grudge against me, I used thir reasouns for my defence:—First, I had brokin no law, by proclaming of thir persons at their requeist. Secundlie, If their mariage was slanderous, I did weill, forewarning all men of it in time. Thridlie, As I had of duetie declared to them the prince's will, so did I faithfullie teache them, by word and exemple, what God craved of them. But upon Tuisday nixt, I was called before the counsell, and accused, that I had passed the bounds of my commissioun, calling the princesse her mariage odious and slanderous before the world. I answered, The bounds of my commissioun, which were, the Word of God, good lawes, and naturall reasoun, were able to prove whatsoever I spake; yea, that their owne conscience could

not but beare witnesse, that suche mariage would be odious and
slaunderous to all that sould heare of it, if all the circumstances of
it were rightlie considered.   But whill I was comming to my probatioun, my lord putt me to silence, and sent me away.   And so,
upon Wednesday, I first repeated and ratifeid all things spokin,
and after exhorted the brethrein not to accuse me, if that mariage
proceeded, but rather themselves, who would not, for feare, oppone
themselves, but rather sharped their tongues against me, becaus I
admonished them of their duetie, and suffered not the cankered
conscience of hypocrits to sleepe at rest ; protesting at all times to
them, that it was not my proclaming, but rather their silence, that
gave anie lawfulnesse to that mariage : for as the proclaming did
take all excuse frome them, so my privie and publict impugnation
did save my conscience sufficientlie.   And this farre I proceeded in
this mariage, as the kirk of Edinburgh, lords, erles, and barons, will
beare me witnesse.

" Now, seing I have been shamefullie slaundered both in England
and Scotland, by wrong informatioun, and false report of them
that hated my ministrie, I desire, first, the judgement of the kirk ;
and nixt, the same to be published, that all men may understand
whether I be worthie of suche a bruite or not."

COMMISSION TO TREAT UPON THE JURISDICTION OF THE KIRK.

It was thought expedient, that certane brethrein be appointed to
concurre at all times with suche persons in parliament, and secreit
counsell, as my lord regent's Grace hath nominated, for suche
effaires as perteane to the kirk, and jurisdictioun therof, and for decisioun of questiouns which may occurre in the meane time ; to
witt, Maisters Johne Knox, Johne Craig, the Superintendents of
Angus and Lothiane, Maisters David Borthwick, Thomas Mackal-
zeane, David Lindsay, George Hay, Johne Row.   In the thrid
sessioun, the Lairds of Braid, Quhittinghame, and Elphingston,
Mr Alexander Arbuthnet, and Johne Brand, ministers, were joyned
to them.   Commissioun was givin in the twelve act of the last par-

liament, to consider what causes apperteaned to the jurisdictioun and authoritie of the kirk.

MINISTERS CENSURED.

Mr Patrik Creigh, minister at Rathow, was suspended from his ministrie and lifting his stipend, for solemnizing the mariage of Mr James Lindsay, and a woman whom he had abused in fornicatioun, without proclamatioun of bannes, or testimoniall therof; and upon a feriall day, contrare to the order established in the kirk, namelie, an act made in December, 1565.

ARGILE AND HIS LADIE CENSURED.

The Erle of Argile being accused for separatioun frome his wife, answered that the blame was not in him. As for other scandalous offences, was content to submit himself to the discipline of the kirk. The Assemblie ordeaneth the Superintendent of Argile to trie and take satisfactioun. The Countesse of Argile compeering, acknowledged that she had offended God, and slaundered the kirk, by assisting the baptisme of the king in Papisticall maner, with her presence. The Assemblie ordeaned her to mak her publict repentance in the Chappell Royall of Stirline, in time of sermoun, before the time of the nixt Assemblie, upon the Lord's day, as the Assemblie sall appoint the Superintendent of Lothiane.

COLLECTORS OF THE THRIDS APPOINTED BY THE ASSEMBLIE.

Twelve or thretteen brethrein were appointed to conveene, and choose collectors, for uplifting and inbringing the thrids of benefices in everie province. Commissioun and power was granted to everie collector within the bounds assigned to him, to intromett and uptake all and sindrie the thrids of whatsomever benefices lying within the bounds assigned to them; together with the whole fruicts of commoun kirks, and all other commoun rents, whole

fruicts and rents of friers' lands, places, and livings, whole superplus omitted, and benefices or chappelreis not givin up in rentall,
lying within the bounds above specifeid, which are now by parliament givin and assigned to the ministrie of the kirk, of the crop
and yeere of God 1567 yeeres instant, and siclyke yeerelie in time
comming, whill it be lawfullie discharged ; to make, give, and subscrive acquittances and discharges therupon : and, generallie, to
doe all things which to the office of collectorie, in suche cases, by
law or consuetude, is knowne to perteane, providing he observe the
injunctiouns prescrived to him. In the injunctions it was required,
that everie collector be knowne to be of sound religioun ; that they
sall doe their office without suspicioun of fraud or avarice ; mak
payment to everie superintendent, commissioner of the kirk, minister, or reader, serving within their bounds, of the stipends appointed to them, quarterlie, at foure times in the yeere, at their
owne houses, least they be forced to seeke abroad : that where
their rentall beareth victuall, they sall not have power to sell the
victuall, or anie part therof, or set price therupon, but by advice of
the Assemblie, and suche as they sall depute commissioners therto,
in everie province ; and sall sell no victuall, till the minister be first
furnished, or ellis refuse to receave the same, upon the prices which
sall be appointed.   That if the poore labourers be not able for
povertie to deliver the bolls, he sall take no higher price than is
appointed, nor lay up in girnell where he may have the sett price :
that they sall not deale fraudulentlie, to force ministers, through
necessitie, to give acquittances of greater summes than they sall
happin to receave ; or to take the victualls upon deerer prices than
sall be prescrived, under the paine of two hundreth punds, to be applyed to godlie uses.   That they sall give accompt to the Assemblie,
or others appointed by the Assemblie, of their particular intromis-
sions with the forsaid thrids, and make thankfull payment of the
superplus resting in their hands above the payment of the ministrie, or ellis give in letters of horning, sufficientlie executed
and indorsed, for their diligence.   That they resigne their office in
the hands of the Assemblie whensoever they sall be charged, or

2

found negligent or fraudulent. That they find some sufficient landed man or burgesse, cautionĕr, one or moe, if one be not sufficient, for the faithfull administratioun of their office, under paine of refounding all domages, scathes, and interesses which the kirk, or anie member therof, sall susteane through their default; the samine being summarilie liquidat and knowne, and losse of their office *ipso facto*, and under paine before expressed.

Mr Clement Littill, Alexander Sim, and Richard Strang, were appointed procurators to defend and pursue all actiouns perteaning to the kirk. Mr George Mackesone was chosin solister. James Nicolsone, comptroller, keeped the rentalls of the thrid of benefices and assumptiouns therof.

The ministrie having suffered povertie a long time, are now refreshed with the allowance granted by the last parliament. The manie benefites they found by the changes in the commoun wealth, moved the Assemblie to send a letter to England to Mr Willocks, to requeist him to returne; the tenor wherof followeth :—

" *Videbam Satanam sicut fulgur de cœlo cadentem.*"

" As the Lord our God hath at all times beene, frome the beginning of this his worke of reformatioun, and restitutioun of the puritie of his true worship and religioun within Scotland, loving brother in the Lord, most beneficiall and bountifull toward this realme, so hath he now, by this last most miraculous victorie and overthrow, powred furth in greatest abundance the riches of his mercie, in that not onlie he hath driven away the tempest and storme, but also hath quietted and calmed all surges of persecutioun, as now, we may thinke weill our shippe is receaved, and placed in a most happie and blessed port. Our enemeis, praised be God, are dashed; religioun established; sufficient provisioun made for ministers; order takin, and penaltie appointed for all sort of transgressioun and transgressers; and above all, a godlie magistrat, whom God, of his eternall and heavenlie providence, hath reserved to this age, to putt in executioun whatsoever He by his law commandeth. Now,

then, loving brother, as your presence was to us all in time of
truble most comfortable, so it is now of us all universallie wished;
but most earnestlie craved by your owne flocke, who continuallie,
at all Assembleis, have declared the force of that conjunctioun, the
earnestnesse of that love, the pith of that zeale and mutuall care,
that bindeth the pastor with his flocke, which nather by processe
of time is diminished, nor by separatioun and distance of places re-
stringed, nor yitt by anie tyrannie and feare dissolved.   True it is,
that at this their most earnest and just petitioun, we have ever still
winked this while past; not but that to us all your absence was
most dolorous.   But, in respect of troubles, we judged more meete
to await for suche opportunitie as now God, in this most wonderfull victorie of his Evangell, hath offered.   Therefore, seing all impediments are removed, and your flocke still continueth in earnest
sute for you, and now everie where throughout the realme commissioners and superintendents placed, and one offered to them, and
by them refused altogether, awaiting for you, we could no longer
stay, but agree to this their desire.   In sute wherof, nather through
feare have they fainted, nor by charges retarded, nor yitt by anie
kinde of offer desisted.   And, as we have beene moved to grant to
them that which they have thus humblie and continuallie suted, we
cannot but perswade our selves but yee will satisfie the same.   Nather can we thinke that the sheepheard will refuse his flocke, that
the father will reject the just petitioun of his sonne, least of all, that
the faithfull servant of God will shutt up his eares at the voice and
commandement of the Kirk, or yitt denie his labours to his owne
countrie.   The time is proper now, to reape with blythenesse that
which by you before was sowin in teares, and injoy the fruict of
your most wearisome and painfull labours.   It sall be no lesse pleasant to you, to see your owne native countrie at libertie and freedome, which yee left in mourning and sobbing, under the heavie
burthein of most cruell servitude, than comfortable to behold the
religioun of Jesus Christ throughout all the realme floorishing, vertue encreassing, vertuous men in reputatioun; and, finallie, to embrace these dayes which, howsoever by your self have beene most

piouslie desired, yitt could yee never looke to obteane the same.
Now, at last, to conclude; unlesse yee will be an enemie to your
countrie, yee will not refuse these requeists.   Unlesse you will be
stubburne and disobedient, yee will not contemne the commandement of the kirk.   Unlesse yee will be carelesse and unthankfull,
yee will not despise the humble, continuall, and earnest sute of
your flocke.   And, last of all, we assure our selves, that yee are not
so astricted and addicted to your owne particular, as that this generall and commoun caus sould be in anie wise by you neglected.
Now sall yee see the kaip-stone of that worke wherof yee layed the
foundatioun.   Thus we cannot looke for anie other answere than
yee sall give by your self, and that with all expeditioun possible.
Our state, yee know, is not so sure, but we ever stand upon our
watches.   But that, we know, will not stay you, seing your compt
is so layed.   Thus we committ you to the protectioun of our Lord
Jesus.   At Edinburgh, in our Generall Assemblie, and seventh
sessioun thereof."

M.D.LXVIII.

SOME OF THE MURTHERERS OF THE KING EXECUTED.

The thrid day of Januar, 1568, Johne Hepburne of Bolton,
Johne Hay of Tallow, James Dalgleish, and Thomas Powrie, were
beheaded and quartered for the king's slaughter.   They said there
were none at the murther but nyne—Bothwell, Johne Hay of
Tallow, Johne Hepburne of Bolton, James Dalgleish, Thome
Powrie, the Laird of Ormeston and Teviotdaill, and Hobe Ormeston, his father brother, a Frenche man called Paris, and one Patrik
Wilson of Hadinton.   The maner of the king's slaughter, they said,
they knew no other but by blowing up the hous with powder.
How he was brought furth to the garden they could not tell.   They
said also, that he sould have been slaine before in the feelds : that
sindrie lords consented therunto, and sould have sent, everie one

of them, two men, to putt their designe in executioun, but it tooke
not effect; and that this traine was devised after.

THE LORD FLEEMING REFUSETH TO RANDER THE CASTELL OF DUMBARTANE.

The Commendatare of Arbrothe, one of Duke Hammilton's
sonnes, went through England to France, to seeke support against
the regent.[1] In hope of good successe to his negotiatioun, the Lord
Fleeming, captan of the castell of Dumbartan, refused to rander it.

Mr Knox, in a letter writtin to a certane freind in England, the
14th of Januare, hath these words following: "I have the testimonie of a good conscience, that in writting that treatise, against
which so manie worldlie men have stormed, and yitt storme, I nather sought myself, nor worldlie promotioun; and becaus, as yitt,
I have nather heard nor seene law nor Scripture to overthrow my
grounds, I may appeale to a more indifferent judge than to Doctor
Jewell. I would most gladelie passe through the course that God
hath appointed unto my labours, in meditatioun with my God, and
giving thankes to his holie name, for that it hath pleased his mercie
to make me not a lord-like bishop, but a painfull preacher of his
blessed Evangell; in the functioun wherōf, it hath pleased his Majestie, for Christ his Sonne's sake, to deliver me frome the contradictioun of moe enemeis than one or two; which maketh the more
slow, and lesse carefull to revenge by word or writt, whatsoever injurie hath beene done against me in my owne particular. But if
that men will not ceasse to impugne the truthe, the faithfull will pardoun me if I offend suche as for pleasure of fleshe feare not to of-

---

[1] Sir Nicolas Throgmorton, writing from Edinburgh, thus forewarns Cecil of the
character of the Hamiltons, and the mission here mentioned :—" As for the Hamyl-
tons and theyre faction, theyre condycions be suche, theyre behavyor so inordynate,
the moost of them so unhable, theyre lyvynge so vycyous, theyre fydelytye so tyckle,
theyre partye so weake, as I count yt loste whatsoever is bestowed upon them.
Shortlye yow are lyke to have with yow an handsome yonge man of that surname
named John Hamylton, to procure to set yow on fyer, to get some money amongest
them to countenance theyre doinges, which serve lytle for our purpose."

fend God. The defence and maintenance of superstitious triffles produced never better fruict in the end than I perceave is budding amongst you: schisme, which, no doubt, is a fore-runner of greater desolatioun, unlesse there be speedie repentance. God comfort that dispersed little flocke, amongst whom I once lived with quietnesse of conscience and contentment of heart; and amongst whom I would be content to end my dayes, if so it might stand with God's good pleasure: for, seing it hath pleased his Majestie, above all men's expectatioun, to prosper that worke, for performing wherof I left that companie, I would even als gladelie returne to them, if they stand in need of my labours, as ever I was glade to be delivered from the rage of myne enemeis. I can give you no reasoun that I sould so desire, other than that my heart so thristeth."

THE QUEENE ESCAPETH OUT OF LOCHLEVIN.

The regent determined to hold justice-airs throughout the countrie. Whill he was at Glasgow, readie to minister justice, and the countrie about warned Lennox, Renfrew, Cliddisdaill, the queene escaped out of Lochlevin. George Dowglas, youngest brother to the Laird of Lochlevin, brother uterine to the regent, allured with her faire speeches and fashiouns, tooke in hand to worke her libertie, not without knowledge of his mother. He provided first for remissioun to his speciall freinds, and promise of advancement to himself; and that the forfaltoure of the Erle of Mortoun sould not prejudge the hous of Lochlevin, which was neerest in taillie to the erledome. William Dowglas, called the laird's bastard brother, but in truthe a foundling, and no Dowglas, had the credite of the keyes manie times. George Dowglas seduced him. This William gott the keyes, to lett out a gentle woman of the queen's, but he lett out her self disguised in a gentle woman's apparell; shutteth the gates, casteth the keyes in the loche, roweth her to land, where George Dowglas receaved her. He had before beene removed by the regent's advice, and at his brother's command, out of the castell; but stayed in Kinrosse, at the loche side, and had no lesse in-

telligence than before. The Laird of Tullibardin was with him.
They were accompaneid with nyne horsemen onlie. The Lord
Seton, and James Hammilton of Orbiston, laying secreetlie among
the hills, mett her, when a signe was made unto them; and convoyed her to Nidrie, the Lord Seton's hous, and frome thence, the
nixt day, that is, the thrid of May, to Hammiltoun, which is distant
from Glasgow eight myles. The regent was in the meane time in
Glasgow, holding a justice court. The cheefe plotters and devisers of her libertie were Secretar Matlane and Sir James Balfour.
Tullibardin, for his difference in religioun, and other privat querell,
estranged from the governour, joyned himself to the queen's factioun. The Hammiltons assisted her for their owne particular
aimes. Huntlie and Argile were privie to the murther of the king.
The first maried a Hammiltoun, the other was borne of a Hammiltoun.

THE REGENT GATHERETH FORCES.

When the regent heard of these newes, it was deliberated what
sould nixt be done; for manie had slipped from the regent to the
queene, at the first report of the newes, and the most part of the
countrie people were gone out of the toun to their owne bussi-
nesses. Robert Lord Boyd his departure frome the regent to the
queene discouraged manie, becaus he had beene inteere with the
regent, and privie to all his purposes, notwithstanding he had givin
a proofe of inconstancie in former times. To colour his defectioun,
he wrote to the Erle of Morton, that he could doe better service
than if he had remained still. When the queene came to Hammiltoun, she was accompaneid with five hundreth horse. Manie
resorted to her daylie. It was bruited that manie were comming
from remote parts to her. It was thought dangerous, that the regent being thus deserted by some, and the countrie not yitt warned
to concurre, sould stay in Glasgow, their enemeis daylie repairing to
Hammilton. They advised him therefore to retire to Stirline.
Others alledged, their departure would have a shew of flight, and

that there was great moment in the beginnings of things. They had the Cunninghams and Semples, the barons and gentlemen of Lennox, the king's owne peculiar patrimonie; and some others in the countrie neere hand, in readinesse when they sould be called, till farther supplee come. William Dowglas, Laird of Dumlanrig, before he was demanded, said, "If yee depart, I will goe to the queen, as my Lord Boyd hath done." The Erle of Morton alledged, that the queen's forces lay farre off; the toun of Glasgow was weill affected toward them, and haters of the Hammiltons; the Cunninghams, Semples, Lennox men, Dowglasdaill, Stirlinshire, were neere hand, and might keepe the toun, till their freinds in remoter parts might be sent for. This advice was followed, and their freinds, speciallie in Merce and Lothiane, advertised. The queen sent furth her proclamatiouns, and also privat missives to sindrie, promising remissioun for bypast offenses, and to some rewards. The regent sent out proclamatiouns likewise, which were printed. All and sindrie the king's leiges were discharged to assist, fortifie, mainteane, or obey anie pretended authoritie of the king's mother, under whatsomever colour or pretence, under paine of treasoun and lese-majestic. All that were suborned, perswaded, or allured to the treasonable conspiraceis and interprises of her assisters, and conspirators against the king his person or authoritie royall, were warned to come within fourtie-eight houres nixt after the proclamatioun, or so soone as by good appearance it could come to their knowledge, and confesse their error to the regent, and pardoun upon that conditioun was promised. Another proclamatioun was sett furth, at the same time, declaring the purpose and intentioun of these who assisted the king's mother, the tenor wherof followeth :—

A PROCLAMATION.

"James, by the grace of God, King of Scots, to all and sindrie faithfull and true leiges, to whose knowledge thir our letters sall come, greeting. Forsameckle as the occasioun of the present troubles oc-

curred within our realme is not unknowne to you, and what work God
hath wrought in time bygane, since the horrible and cruell murther
treasonablie perpetrated on the persoun of the king, our most deere
father, of worthie memorie: That execrable fact, as it is deteastable
in God's sight, so ought all men that either feare God, or have respect to civill societie among men, to abhorre the persons that still
would mainteane the authors and devisers of that beastlie crueltie;
and by the contrare, advance and promote the righteous querrell of
us, their native prince and lawfull king, descended of the right lyne
of the most noble and valient princes of this regioun, as a speciall
confort and mercie sent by the favour of Almightie God to this afflicted natioun.

" And howbeit the cruell murtherers of our most deere father, their
favourers and assisters, had conspired the same cuppe to us to taste
of, to transferre the crowne frome the righteous lyne to suche as
long had beene ambitious therof, yitt that same God that preserved
our innocent persoun from their mercilesse hands, hath respected
the equitie of our caus, and mainteaned the same, to his glorie and
our safe-guarde, when in man's sight both we, and they that professed our obedience, and avowed our querell, were most likelie to
have beene overthrowne. But becaus the malicious hearts of our conspired enemeis not onlie proceed in their wickednesse and rebellioun
against us and our authoritie, but also seduce the true and simple
people, our lieges, to follow them, slaunderouslie speeking of us, as
that our title were in doubt, we have thought good to notifie and
make knowne the certantie of the whole mater, for satisfactioun of
them whose judgement yitt remaineth in suspense; that being resolved of the naked and simple truthe, they may give place to the
right, and absteane from errour, and putt a difference betwixt our
true subjects seeking God's glorie and our due obedience, and the
rebellious factioun treasonablie seeking to bereave us of our lawfull
crowne and proper inheritance, under a craftie pretence of the
queene our mother's title; unto whom (God wott) they beare no
better good-will nor unto us, saving in so farre as her presence
may move a controversie, wherin by processe of time, having both

us and her cutted off, they may winne the game, and possesse the garland long hoped for. But what end sall God putt to suche usurpers, all ancient historeis, both godlie and profane, declare, in similitude. Was ever innocent murther left unrevenged? Or was it ever in the power of man so farre to blind the eyes of the Almightie, but when the iniquitie of man was come to fulnesse, His potent hand quicklie confounded both the policie and force of his wicked creatures?

"That coloured cleanging of James sometime Erle Bothwell, cheefe murtherer of our deere father, upon the 12th day of Aprile, the yeere of God 1567 yeeres, could not assure that godlesse and wicked man, nor mak his cankered conscience rest without terrour; the whole world perceaving his pretence no other thing but as a mask to blind the eyes of God and man; the murtherer seeking his owne purgatioun, the accustomed order of the law perverted, in that sufficient warning was not givin to our deerest goodsir, and others the kin and freinds of our said deere father, to follow and persue the murtherers, and the verie time of the committing of that crueltie not expressed. Nather yitt could that unhonest and pretended mariage, suddanlie and unprovisedlie therafter accomplished, either blind God, or yitt satisfie the people that continuallie craved vengeance of God for that sakelesse blood and concealed murther; not yitt the ravishing, or rather mocking of God and the world, could colour shame and dishonour, when it was so farre proceeded. That honour, conscience, and greatnesse, were all tint for the inordinat affectioun borne to that tyranne. Loath we are to condescend more speciallie; but, alas! what profitteth silence when there is no repentance? Not words and reports of men, but writt remaineth, conteaning the discourse of that lamentable trajedie, and unnaturall crueltie, the truthe wherof no processe of time will consume, nor age weare away. And when that unlawfull divorce was made, and more than unlawfull mariage compleet, what estat our innocent person stood into, the eternall God best knoweth, and all godlie men may judge. Our father latelie murthered, and the queene, our mother, coupled with him that was the cheefe author

of that mischeevous deid; she thralled and subject to him, circuited
with a companie of ungodlie and wicked persons, notorious pyrats,
murtherers, and others readie to execute all their dulefull commandements; diverse of our nobilitie aberring with the wicked time,
others departing furth of the realme, or privilie reposing themselves
to see the end of that confusioun; at last, by necessitie constrained,
it behoved them, rather late nor never, to provide for our suretie,
whom God had granted to them as native prince, that we sould
not fall in the mercilesse hands of these who slue our father; to separate that tyranne and godlesse man from the queene our mother,
and to putt our persoun in suretie. For which purpose, a great
number of our true and faithfull subjects being conveened on the
feilds against the said erle, after he had refused combat of a lord
and baroun of parliament, and gentleman undefamed, howbeit, before he had offered himself therunto by his cartell and proclamatioun, he escaped, and our said mother came to the noblemen, and
others our lawfull subjects conveened for that effect; who refusing
to leave the ungodlie and unhonest companie of the murtherer of
our father, and minassing suche as had beene carefull of our preservatioun, by commoun consent she was putt in suretie whill farther deliberatioun might be had of the mater. Shortlie therafter,
God manifested the murther more cleerelie; and not onlie the report of diverse actuallie present therat, and manie other things gave
presumptioun, but writt declared the truthe, resolving manie of the
doubts they stood into.

"Alwise, the queene our mother seing the trubles occurred in her
governement; how contrariouslie things succeeded, and how evill
her subjects lyked of her governement, dimitted the crowne of this
kingdome, with all honours, priviledges, and commoditeis therof, in
our favours; according to the which, by a great number of the three
estats of our realme purposelie conveened to execute her commissioun, we were lawfullie inaugurated with the crowne royall of this
our kingdome, and our deerest cousin, James Erle of Murrey, Lord
Abernethie, nominated, elected, sworne, and admitted in regent to
us, our realme and lieges, until our age of seventeene yeeres; and,

according to his commissioun, did all that was in him to mainteane
the good and godlie peace standing betwixt us and all Christian
princes, our nighbours, freinds, and confederats, to interteane justice and quietnesse in the state of our commoun weale, for the commoditie and safeguarde of true men and vertuous persons, and punishment of brokin men, troublers of the countrie, and others, transgressers of the lawes.   Which our coronation, inauguratioun, and
possessioun of the crown of this our realme, is, by Acts of a lawfull,
free, and plaine parliament, found and declared to be duelie, rightlie, and orderlie done and executed, and als lawfull and valuable in
the self in all respects, and we als righteouslie invested and possessed in this kingdom as our said mother, goodsir, grandsir, or
anie other our most noble progenitors, native princes of this our
realme, were, and have beene before ; or, as if she, the tyme of the
said coronatioun, had beene departed furth of this mortall life, or
had compeered personallie in presence of the three whole estats of
this realme assembled in parliament, and made the said dimissioun,
notwithstanding anie maner of title, actioun, or interesse to anie
other thing that presentlie, or can heerafter be objected in the contrare.   And als, that the nominatioun, constitutioun, and ordinatioun of our said deerest cousin in regent to us, our realme and
lieges, during the time of our minoritie, and the acceptatioun of the
said office by him, was, is, and in all time comming sall be reputed,
holdin, and esteemed lawfull, sufficient, and perfyte ; and als sufficientlie and righteouslie done, and to have als great availl, force,
strenth, and effect in all respects and conditiouns, as anie things
done by whatsomever regents, governours, and protectors of this
our realme, in the minoritie and lesse ages of anie others, native
princes of the same : ratifeing, approving, and confirming the said
nominatioun and acceptatioun in all points.   And als, in the same
free and lawfull parliament it was found, declared, and concluded,
that the causes and occasiouns of the conventiouns and messages of
the erles, lords, noble men, barons, and others faithfull and true
subjects, and consequentlie their taking of armes, and comming to
the feilds with open and displayed banners, and the caus and occa-

sioun of the taking of the persoun of the queen, our mother, upon
the 15th day of June last bypast, and holding and deteaning of her
within the hous and fortalice of Lochlevin continuallie sensyne, and
in time comming, and generallie, all other things invented, spokin,
writtin, or done by them, or anie of them, to that effect, since the
10th day of Februarie, the yeere of God 1566 yeeres, upon the
which, umquhyle the king, our most deere father, was treasouna-
blie, shamfullie, and horriblie murthered, unto this day and date
of the said Act, tuiching her, and deteaning of her persoun, that
the caus, and all things depending theron, or that anie wise might
perteane thereto, was, to our greefe, in her owne default. The
causes wherof, as they are patent to God, so, alas! they are over-
manifest to the world.

"What the parliament hath concluded presentlie needeth not to
be expressed at greater lenth. It is conteaned in writt and print,
and manie others nor the inhabitants of this countrie have knowledge of the same. But what suretie is able to gainstand treasoun;
or what bands and subscriptiouns can perswade them to be true,
that are facile with their hands to subscrive, and with their tongues
to speeke, the thing they think not? The shame is their owne, and
the spott and ignominie will last unto their posteriteis. If anie of
the degree of nobilitie, or anie other our meanest subjects, had beene
oppressed, disdained, or handled otherwise nor the ancient lawes of
the countrie prescrived, then men might have had occasioun to
wearie of our governement, and to have sought alteratioun. But
what is he that, in his conscience, is able to compleane, or accuse
that estat of unjust dealing or uncourtesie? Yitt seditious men of
unquiet spirit, invyfull to see the poore people of this our realme
injoy that quietnesse and good dayes wherin they had an interesse,
but moved partlie of ambitioun, partlie in hope of gaine, and sakelesse revenge of them that never offended them, and cheefelie to
stay the said ordinar course of justice, treasonablie against the
tenour of the said Acts of parliament, practised and conspired the
libertie of the queene, our mother; and in conclusioun, by fraudulent and craftie meanes brought the same to passe in suche sort, as

she was not onlie convoyed to Hammiltoun, but there, through the
perverse counsell of suche as had beene participant of our said father's murther, so farre induced, that she intended by force to bereave us of our crowne wherewith we are rightfullie possessed, and
for the more speedie executioun of the purpose, conveened their
force, not onlie of suche as long have thristed for our place, but of
others dissembled freinds and unnaturall subjects.   To what end
their treasounable insurrectioun and rebellioun hath succeeded, all
our good subjects understand[1] * * * * * * * * * * * * * * *
* * * * * * * * * * * * * nather we, nor none professing
our obedience, nor ¦avowing our querrell, ever sought; but, being
sharpelie assaulted and persued, for preservatioun of our innocent
persoun, and that rowme and authoritie wherin God hath placed
us, it behoved our regent, the noble men, and faithfull subjects assisting him, to resist their crueltie and invasioun.   What womanlie
mercie was in the person of her that, alas! thought the shedding of
Scotish blood a pleasaunt spectacle? What favour and clemencie
can men looke at her hands, that stirreth this seditioun against her
onlie lawfull sonne; or what securitie can noblemen or godlie men
thinke themselves in, she bearing the regiment by whose occasion
our most deere father, being a portioun of her owne fleshe, was so
used? God hath his counsells to putt in executioun, and alreadie
hath begunne to execute his judgements.   Suche as feare God, and
would the lawfull and righteous blood royall continued in the successioun of our crowne, will willinglie obey us, and furth-sett our
authoritie.   The same God that hath overcome the rebellious factioun once, will yitt represse their insolencie, if they tend to farther
untruthe and conspiraceis ; and we doubt not but yee will assist us
in their contrare, to their opprobrie and confusioun.

" Our will is heerefore, and we straitlie command and charge
you all and sundrie our lieges and subjects forsaid, as yee will answere to God, and upon your allegiance and bound duetie to us,
that none of you tak upon hand to arise, assist, fortifie, mainteane,
or obey our said mother, or anie conspirators, movers of seditioun

---

[1] Here a blank occurs in the original.

and insurrectioun, under colour of whatsomever other pretended
authoritie nor ours, under the paine of treasoun; and that Lyoun
King of Armes, his brethrein, heralds, macers, pursevants, and messingers whatsomever, make publicatioun heerof at the mercat croces
of the head burrowes of our realme, and others places needfull, that
none pretend ignorance of the samine.   Givin under our signet,
and subscrived by our said deerest cousin and regent, at Glasgow,
the   day of May, and of our raigne the first yeere, 1568."

A TRUE COPIE OF THE MUTUALL BAND BETWIXT THE CAPTAN OF
THE CASTELL AND TOUN OF EDINBURGH.

" At Edinburgh, the 8th of May, the yeere of God 1568 yeeres:
It is appointed, agreed, and finallie contracted and bound up, betwixt the Right Honorable Sir William Kirkaldie of Grange, Knight,
Captan of the Castell of Edinburgh, for himself, kin, freinds, servants, assisters, and partakers, on the one part; and the Right Honourable Simon Preston of Craigmillar, of that Ilk, Knight, Proveist of the Burgh of Edinburgh, for himself, the bailiffes, counsell,
and communitie, and whole inhabitants of the said burgh, on the
other part, in maner, forme, and effect, as after followeth :—
" That is to say, Forsameekle as it is not unknowne to them;
how that the queen, our soveran's deerest mother, with certan of
the nobilitie, her assisters and partakers, seeke by all meanes, force,
and power they may, to depose our said soverane of his authoritie
royall, and for more haistie performing therof, are alreadie conveened in armes, for the invasioun of our said most undoubted soveran's regent and governour, James Erle of Murrey, &c., and all
others his partakers and assisters, touns, castells, citeis, and whole
lieges of this realme, who will not obey and assist them in their unnaturall and ungodlie proceedings : For eshewing wherof, fortificatioun, mainteaning, and defending of our said undoubted soverane,
now in his tender age, and his regent foresaid, the saids captan
and proveist for themselves, and taking the burthein upon them for
the others above-writtin, according to their bound duetie and oath

of fidelitie givin to their most undoubted and native soverane, for
maintenance of him and his authoritie royall, are bound, oblished,
and sworne by the faithe and truthe of their bodeis, lyke as by
thir presents they bind, oblishe, and sweare by their great oathes,
in all time comming, to tak effald, true, and plaine part together,
for defence of our said soverane his authoritie and persoun royall ;
and either of them, with their whole force, substance, and power,
to fortifie, assist, and mainteane others with their bodeis and goods ;
and to concurre, and passe together at all times, and to all places
needfull, not onlie for defence of the said castell, toun, lieges, habi-
tatioun, and substance therof, but also for the maintenance, defence,
and aide of our said soveran his authoritie royall, and regent foresaid, against all and sindrie that sall pretend to invade, molest, or
persue them, or anie of them ; and to aid and support others, with
whatsomever things necessar in their possessiouns, or sall be possible for them to doe, for defence of others, as need sall require.
And, further, that neither of them sall heare, see, nor acknowledge
the domage or hurt of others, in their persons, lands, or goods, but
sall incontinent warne others with all haist possible, lett, stop, and
mak impediment to the samine, at their utter power : And, finallie,
sall nather contract, compone, take appointment, or make agreement
by others ; but sall with their whole powers fortifie, defend, and
mainteane others in the causes above-writtin, but fainzie or dissimulatioun, contrare and against all that live or dee may, that sall
happin, or pretend to trouble or molest our said soverane in his authoritie royall, his said regent, assisters, and partakers, this toun,
castell, lieges, and whole inhabitants therof, for the causes foresaid.
In witnesse of which, to thir present letters, indentours, and contract subscrived with our hand, our signet is affixed, at the said
burgh, day, yeere, and place foresaid, before thir witnesses, Sir
William Matlane of Lethington, younger, Knight, Mr James Makgill of Rankeillour Neather, Clerk of Register, Mr Archibald Dowglas, Parson of that Ilk, and David Forrest, Generall, with others
diverse.

    " WILLIAM KIRKALDIE.   CRAIGMILLAR, KNIGHT."

Forces were gathered on both sides. Als soone as the Lord Hume came to Glasgow, accompaneid with six hundreth men of Merce and Lothiane, the regent purposed to marche toward Hammiltoun, and force the queen's factioun to fight. The forces of the other factioun consisted of six thowsand men; the regent's skarse of foure thowsand. The other factioun, confident in their owne forces, intended to convoy the queene to Dumbartane, that ther-after they might ather fight, or draw at lenth the warre, as they thought fittest; resolving to encounter the regent, if he would needs fight by the way. The regent attended upon them in Glasgow Mure, deeming that they would come that way. But when he perceaved them to marche on the south side of Clyde, he sent some footemen and horsemen before, to trouble them in the way, and to take the hill above Langside. The great armie followed, marching among little knows and hollow valeyes, and were not seene, till they were neere to the hill, howbeit the queen's forces were marching toward the same place. The Erle of Argile, lieutenant for the queen, being overtakin of a suddaine with an apoplexie, stayed the armie a certane time, and so the regent's armie prevented them, and tooke the vantage of the ground. There were in the battell with the Erle of Argile, Lieutenant, the Erles of Cassils, Eglinton, and Rothesse; Lords Seton, Somervell, Yester, Borthwick, Livingston, Sanquhere, Boyd; the Shireff of Air, the Lairds of Basse, Waughton, Dalhowssie, Lochinvar, Rosling. The avant-guarde was led by Claud Hammilton of Paisley, secund sonne to the Duke of Chattelerault, and Sir James Hammiltoun of Evindaill; with them, the Hammiltons, their freinds and followers, to the number of two thowsand men. They bragged, that they alone would defeate the adverse partie. The Lord Hereis had the conduct of the horsemen, all almost borderers, dependers and tennents to my Lord Maxwell, his brother. James Stewart of Cassilton, and Arthure Hammiltoun of Myrrinton, had the conduct of the shott, to the number of three hundreth. The regent's avant-guarde was con-

ducted by the Erle of Morton, Alexander Lord Hume, Patrik Lord
Lindsey, Robert Lord Sempill. In the rere-ward, with the regent,
were Johne Erle of Marr, Alexander Erle of Glencarne, William
Graham Erle of Menteith; the Master of Grahame, Lords Uchiltrie, Cathcart; Lairds Barganie, Blaquhan, Cesfurd, Luse, Bu-
quhanan, Pitcur, Lochlevin, Lethington; Sir James Balfour, the
barons and gentlemen of Lennox, and the citicens of Glasgow.
The shott was placed in the yairds of Langside. The horsemen,
about two hundreth, were conducted by William Dowglas of Dumlanrig, Alexander Hume of Manderston, Johne Carmichaell of that
Ilk. The regent had six peeces careid in carts; the queen had
seven. The queen's armie being disappointed of the hill, stood
upon a know. When the great ordinance were shott, the regent's
harquebusiers went, and skirmished before the queen's avant-
guarde. Her harquebusiers were drivin backe. So, upon the
other side, the regent's horsemen at the first encounter gave.
ground; but perceaving the other casting about to invade the
foote, with helpe of the bow-men drave them backe. In the meane
time, the queen's avant-guarde marching through a strait lane,
were much annoyed by the regent's harquebusiers. The regent's
avant-guarde made haste, and receaved them, after they had come
out of the strait lane, upon the north-east side of Langside village,
with long speares. There was no yeelding on either side for the
space of halfe an houre, so that when speares were brokin, they
cast whingers, brokin peeces of speeres, stones, or whatsoever came
to their hand, at the faces of their enemeis. The Lord Hume was
hurt on the·face, and almost felled with a stone. The regent's
harquebusiers shott continuallie from the dykes and hous toppes.
Makfarlane with his Hieland men fled from the wing, where they
were sett. The Lord Lindsay, who stood neerest to them in the
regent's battell, said, "Lett them goe: I sall fill up their place better;" so he stepped fordward with a companie of freshe men, and
charged the enemie with long weapons, so that they, having spent
their speeres before, and almost overthrowne by the avant-guarde
and harquebusiers, were drivin backe, and turned to flight. The

regent's battell perceaving the enemie to flee without order, brake array and followed.   Moe were slaine in the flight than in the battell, and the most part by the Hieland men, who perceaving the victorie to fall on the regent's side, returned and persued.   If the regent had not sent speedilie to all parts a command to spaire, moe had beene slaine; yitt the number of the slaine was about three hundreth, but moe takin prisoners.   The Lords Seton, Rosse, Sir James Hammiltoun, the Shireff of Air, the Shireff of Linlithquho, the Master of Cassils, the Laird of Innerweeke, the Laird of Trabrown, James Hammiltoun of Bothwelhauch, were takin.   On the regent's side were slaine onlie one man, a tenent to the Erle of Morton, in Preston in the Merce, named Johne Ballon.   Among the few that were hurt were Alexander Lord Hume, and Andrew Stewart, Lord Uchiltree, who was hurt by the Lord Hereis.   The queene standing about a myle from the battell to behold, fled, and was convoyed by the Lord Hereis to Dundrennan.   The regent returned to Glasgow, and after publict thanksgiving for so notable a victorie, spent the rest of the day in taking order with prisoners.   The cheefe men, speciallie of the surname of Hammiltoun, were detened, and after committed to sindrie wairds.   The Frenche ambassader came about the end of Aprile to meete with the queene, but could not gett accesse, till the estats, which were to conveene the 20th of May, consented.   He traffiqued betwixt the two factiouns, pretending he was a peace-maker; but perceaving the regent's forces to be weaker, he encouraged the queene to fight.   But now, being disappointed of his hope, he made haste the nearest way to England, without bidding the regent fare weill.   He was robbed by the way; but Dumlanrig caused restore to him all that was takin frome him.   This battell was fought the thriteenth of May.

THE CASTELLS OF HAMMILTON AND DREFFANE RANDERED.

The day following, the regent sent to summoun the castell of Hammiltoun, the keyes wherof were offered the nixt day.   In the castell of Hammiltoun were found some of King James the Fyft

his household stuffe. About the same time, the castell of Dreffane
was randered.

BOTHWELHAUCH AND OTHERS PARDONED.

Upon the 22d day of May, the Shireff of Linlithquho, Innerwicke,
Bothwelhauche, and six others, were putt to an assise, convicted,
their hands bound, and pardouned at the requeist of Mr Knox,
wherof he repented after; for Bothwelhauche slew the good regent, as sall be declared in the owne place.

HODDOM ROAD.

The regent having charged by proclamatioun the lieges to meete
him at Biggar, the 10th of June, he went out of Edinburgh the
11th of June. At this time the castell of Boghall, Crawfurd, Sanquhare, Lochwod, Hoddom, Lochmabane, Annand, were randered
and spared, upon hope of obedience promised. Skirline castell was
razed, and Kenmure, for exemple to others. His forces consisted
of five thowsand horsemen, and a thowsand shott. This expeditioun, becaus of the skairstie of victuall, when they came to Hoddom, a hous belonging to the Lord Hereis, was called Hoddom
Road.[1]

---

[1] In this military progress, a house devoted to destruction was spared, under a curious pretext, related by Lord Herries himself, in the following words, in his History
of the Reigns of Mary and James VI. :—

" The Lord Herreis' hous of Terreglis, the Regent give full orders to throw it
doune. But the Laird of Drumlanrig, who was the Lord Herreis' uncle, and much
in favour with the Regent, told that the Lord Herreis wold take it for a favour, if
he wold ease him of [his] pains, for he was resolved to throw it downe himselfe, and
build it in another place. The Regent sware he scorned to be a barrowman to his
old walls ! And so it was safe."—*Herries's Memoirs, Abbotsford Club Publication,*
p. 106.

A PARLIAMENT HOLDIN.

The parliament was continued till the 16th day of August. Manie meanes were used by the other factioun to mak impediment. Argile cometh to Glasgow with six hundreth horse, and had conference with the Hammiltons; but they could resolve upon nothing. The Erle of Huntlie came accompanied with a thowsand horse; but his passage by the bridge and foords of Tay was stopped by the Lord Ruthven, and others of the nobilitie and gentrie lying neere hand. The Queen of England, at the requeist of the rebells, craved a delay, and that sentence sould not rashlie be pronounced against them, till she were perfytlie informed of the whole proceedings; for the queene, her cousin, had compleaned to her of wrongs done to her by her subjects: for our queene at this time was in England. She feared to stay in Scotland, and doubted of the Lord Hereis' fidelitie.[1] Least the rebells sould be encouraged, the parliament was holdin at the day appointed. There was sharpe reasouning, whether all that had takin armes against the king, and had not sought pardoun, or acknowledged the king's authoritie, sould be forfaulted. Secretar Matlane, favouring secretlie the rebells, wrought so, that his advice prevailed; to witt,

---

[1] The subtlety, selfishness, and double-dealing of this nobleman are sufficiently evident in the course of this History, in which he makes a prominent figure. His character is thus graphically sketched in one of the letters of Throgmorton :—" The Lord Heryes ys the connynge horseleache and the wysest of the wholle faction; but as the Quene of Scotland sayethe of hym, there ys no bodye can be sure of hym; he taketh pleasure to beare all the worlde in hande; we have good occasyon to be well ware of hym. Sir, yow remember how he handled us when he delyvered Dunfryse, Carlaverocke, and the Harmytage, into our handes; he made us beleave all should be ours to the Fyrthe, and when wee trusted hym best, how he helped to chase us awaye, I am sure you have not forgotten. Heere, amongest his owne countreymen he ys noted to be the most cautelous man of hys natyon. It may lyke yow to remember, he suffred hys owne hostages, the hostages of the Lard of Loughanver and Garles, hys nexte neyghboures and frendes, to be hanged for promesse broken by hym. Thys muche I speake of hym, because he ys the lykelyest and most dangerous man to enchaunte yow."—Here Throgmorton seems to fear that Herries might be too cunning even for Sir William Cecil!

that a few sould be condemned for the present, to strike a terour
in others, and the rest be putt in hope of pardoun.   The rebells
were muche encouraged by this delay, for they looked for assistance out of England and France; yea, they thought their owne
power sufficient to overthrow the other factioun.   The regent punished some by a light fyne, others he laboured to bring to the acknowledgement of the king's authoritie.

ARGILE'S LETTER TO CRAWFURD.

What were the practises of the rebells to stay this parliament
may be seene in the letter following, writtin by Argile to Crawfurd :—

" My Lord, after our heartilie commendatiouns : We have thought
it expedient to mak your lordship participant with our proceedings
of the nobilitie in thir west parts, in the queen's Majestie our soveran's service, and for the securitie of us that are her favourers and
faithfull subjects.   For this 28th of Julie instant, we have conveened, with all the great men of the nobilitie and great barons of
the west parts, suche as my lord Duke's freinds of Chattelerault,
Erles Eglinton, Cassils, Lords Fleeming, Boyd, Sanquhare, Master of Hereis, Lairds Lochinvar, Johnstoun, with manie other
great barons, who all are bent to sett fordward our soveran's service, and be constant therin ; and it was thought expedient among
them all, to renew the samine band among themselves, for our soveran's service, which was made before herself in Hammiltoun.

" *Item*, They thought good to write to the King of Spaine, and
the Duke of Alva, in favours of our soverane ladie, and for help
and support of men and munitioun.   And becaus they were hastilie to be sent away, we gott not leasure to send them to you, to be
subscrived, but caused them to be subscrived, which we doubt not
but yee will confirme and ratifie.   And siclyke we have writtin to
the Queene of England right sharpelie.

" *Item*, There is a great part of the nobilitie that are faithfull
subjects to our soverane, summoned to this pretended parliament,

the 16th of August nixt, (which we are all deliberated to stay,) that we and our freinds of the nobilitie sould be forfaulted, with suche our faithfull subjects that are true and faithfull to our native borne prince and heretrix. And to that effect, we will have all the folkes we can make to be readie against the 10th of August, to come to suche places as sall be appointed, with twentie dayes victuall. And this is the commoun caus to all our freinds conveening, or that favour us; and the noble men, our freinds, will resist the said forfaultour to the utter power of their lyves. Heerefore we pray your lordship, and all the nobilitie about you, and under your charges, with all your freinds and others the queen's Grace's favourers, who love us and our freinds, our lyves and our heretages, to mak all our force readie against the said 10th day of August, that therefore my Lord Huntlie and all these parts may meete and come together; and to come to Sanct Johnstoun, or therabout; and that your lordship have some harquebusiers, under charge of some captane, to be in your companie; and at the least, to stay all erles, lords, prelats, that have vote in parliament, that no man come to their pretended parliament.

"Farther, we have caused make proclamatioun at all burrowes, that no man of anie burgh come to their parliament, or to send them men or money in anie sort, or yitt to tholl anie officers of armes to proclame anie of their letters within their touns, but allanerlie in our soveran ladie's name. And if they doe the contrare, they to be used with fire and sword, to the rigour. And we desire your lordship to doe the samine in the touns beside your lordship in the north, as Dundie, Montrose, Forfar, Brechin; and the copie therof sall be sent to your lordship. Farther, please your lordship to make the lords and barons about your lordship partakers and assisters to our soveran ladie the queen of thir our proceedings; and your lordship doe siclyke in the bounds yee have commissioun of, and haste us answere again. Off Dunnoun, the last of Julie, 1568.

"Your lordship's assured at power,

"ARGILE."

THE SEVENTEEN GENERALL ASSEMBLIE.

The Generall Assemblie conveened at Edinburgh, in the neather tolbuith, the 1st of Julie, 1568. Mr Johne Willock, Superintendent of the West, was chosin Moderator.

TRIELL OF THE SUPERINTENDENT OF FIFE.

In the first sessioun, the commissioners appointed by the last Assemblie to trie the complaints givin in, or to be givin in, against the Superintendent of Fife, produced the executioun of their commissioun. Others were appointed to revise their proceedings. He was accused of negligence in visitatioun, and carelesseness in censuring adulterers.

ACTS.

It was thought meet, that this order sould be followed in choosing commissioners with power to vote in the Generall Assemblie, for eshewing of confusioun :—

I. That none have place or power to vote except superintendents, commissioners appointed for visiting of kirks, ministers brought with them, and by them presented as persons able to reasoun and to judge. With the forenamed sall be joyned commissioners of burghes and shires, together with commissioners of universiteis. Ministers and commissioners of shires sall be chosin at the synodall conventioun of the diocie, with consent of the rest of the ministers and gentle men that sall conveene at the said synodall conventioun. Commissioners of burghes sall be appointed by the counsell, and kirk of their owne touns. None sall be admitted without sufficient commissioun in writt. And least this sould turne to a perpetuall commissioun of a few and certane persons, it is concluded, that ministers and other commissioners be changed from Assemblie to Assemblie.

II. It was ordeaned that superintendents command readers to absteane from all ministratioun of the sacraments, under paine to be accused as abusers, and criminall, according to the act of parliament.

III. Tuiching the questioun of murther committed upon suddantie, and satisfactioun to be made for the same, it was answered, that the crime being confessed, and the persoun orderlie convicted, he sall be admonished by the superintendent, or the nixt reformed kirk, where the slaughter was committed, to absteane from all participatioun of the sacraments till he satisfie the kirk, as sall be injoyned to him; that the admonitioun be published where the crime was committed, and where the recent bruite therof was spread, that men may understand the kirk winketh not at the shedding of innocent blood. If the crime be denied, and yitt the bruite therof be constant, and as it were publict, the suspected sall be commanded to absteane frome the use of the sacraments till farther triell may be had, or elles till he be solemnelie purged of the bruite. As for suddane murther, and that which is committed purposelie, the answere was remitted to an act made before.

IV. Tuiching the forme of receaving the murtherer, the manslayer, or adulterer, it is ordeaned, that none that hath committed slaughter, adulterie, or incest, or heerafter sall committ the same, sall be receaved to repentance by anie particular kirk, till first they present themselves before the Generall Assemblie, there to receave their injunctions, and, therafter, sall keepe the same order that was prescrived to Paul Methven for his repentance; this being added, that he or they sall beare in their hands, at all time of their publict repentance, the same or like weapoun wherewith they committed the murther.

V. As for oppressours of childrein, they are to be admonished to make publict repentance in sackcloath, bare-footed and bare-headed, so oft as the particular kirk sall appoint.

VI. It was ordeaned, that no office-bearer in the kirk subscrive anie assignatioun, or give charge to anie collectour, to answere anie man of anie portioun of the patrimonie of the kirk, but suche as beare office in the kirk, and that according to the rolls givin to them, subscrived by the keeper of the register of ministers' stipends.

VII. It was thought necessar, that order sould be takin, that commoun kirks and tithes vacant since the last parliament, through neglect of presentatioun, sall be disponed to qualified men, able to discharge their calling to the comfort of the people.

VIII. It was ordeaned, that superintendents and commissioners caus suche as injoy benefices, and have gifts enabling them to the ministrie, to be present at the nixt Assemblie, to accept the office according to their abilitie.

IX. It was ordeaned, that no ministers, exhorters, readers, or other persons, trouble or molest the Generall Assemblie heerafter with suche things as superintendents may and ought to decide in their synodall conventions. And if anie doe otherwise heerafter, that their bills be rejected. Some brether were appointed to read the bills givin in to this Assemblie, to writt their answere according to their judgement on the backe, and to report to this present Assemblie.

THE BOOK INTITULED " THE FALL OF THE ROMAN KIRK" TO BE REVISED.

Thomas Bassandine, printer, was commanded to call in the bookes printed by him, entituled " The Fall of the Roman Kirk," wherin the king is called " Supreme Head of the Primitive Kirk," &c., and to keepe the rest unsold, till he alter the foresaid title. *Item,* To delate the bawdie song, " Welcome, Fortune," &c., printed in the end of the Psalme Booke, without license ; and that he absteane in times comming from printing anie thing without licence of the supreme magistrat, or, if it concerne religioun, of suche as sall be appointed by the Assemblie to revise. Mr Alexander Arbuthnet was appointed to revise the forenamed tractat, and to report to the Assemblie.

THE BISHOPS OF GALLOWAY AND ORKNEY TRIED AND CENSURED.

The Commissioner of Galloway was ordeaned to come to Edinburgh all the time of the nixt parliament, and show his diligence in the charge committed to him in that province; and to answere, whether he will await on court and counsell, or upon preaching the Word and planting kirks. The Superintendents of Angus, Fife, and Lothiane, were appointed to report his diligence and answeres to the nixt Assemblie, and, in the meane time, commissioun was givin to Mr Johne Row to visite Galloway. The Bishop of Orkney is restored again to the ministrie, but ordeaned at some convenient time, upon the Lord's day, when he may convenientlie, for weaknesse of bodie, preache in the kirk of Halyrudhous, and after sermon confesse his offence for solemnizing the mariage betwixt the queen and the Erle Bothwell, which he promised to doe.

THE TREATISE OF EXCOMMUNICATION TO BE REVISED.

Maisters Johne Willocke, Johne Craig, Johne Row, Robert Pont, James Greg, William Christesone, and David Lindsay, were appointed to revise the forme and order of excommunicatioun, which is penned by Mr Knox, at the desire of the Assemblie, and to report their judgements. The treatise is extant in our Psalme Bookes. In it is mentioun often made of the ministrie, sessioun, and kirk; but of superintendents, onlie where there is no reformed kirk. Where there is mentioun made of superintendents, there is mentioun also made of assessors joyned with them. Our first reformers dreamed not of the sole power of a bishop to excommunicat, nor of privie excommunicatioun by officialls.

The Superintendents of Angus, Fife, and Lothian, Mrs Johne Craig, Johne Row, ministers, were appointed, together with the Laird of Barganie, to present the heeds following to the lord regent's Grace, and to report his answeres to the Assemblie :—

1. Lett his Grace know the heavie and greevous complaint of the ministers concerning the assignatioun, whereby they are altogether disappointed of their stipends; for the assignatioun standing, the thrids are not able, as they are ordered, to pay the ministers halfe their stipends, and in some parts not the quarter therof.

2. It is thought verie unreasonable that the Papists, enemeis to God's kirk and this commoun wealth, and others that labour not in the ministrie, sall possesse freelie, without impositioun of anie burthein, the two part of the benefices, and the labourers in the kirk sall not possesse the thrid. Heerefore the Assemblie desireth my lord regent's Grace will take suche order, that the commoun charges may be susteaned upon the two parts of the benefices possessed by the Papists, so that the thrid may remaine free, to be dispouned by the kirk: not that the ministers desire more than their reasonable stipends, but that the superplus may support the schooles and the poore, according to the will of God; and that the collectors of the kirk sall mak compt yeerelie therof, so that my lord regent's Grace, and the counsell, sall know the disposition of the same.

3. *Item,* To show my lord regent's Grace, that there are sindrie benefices vacand, and speciallie the benefices of the commouns pertaining to cathedrall and metropolitan kirks; that his Grace would present qualifeid men to them, with advice of this Assemblie; otherwise, that the kirk may dispone them, as falling to them, by reasoun that none have beene presented these six moneths bypast; and also, to present qualified persons to the kirks of the nunreis presentlie vacand, as presentlie to Northberwick.

4. *Item,* That my lord regent's Grace will give commissioun or authoritie to certane persons for reformatioun of the Colledge of Aberdeene; that the corrupt office-bearers, regents, and others, be removed, and other qualified persons placed in their rowmes, that the youth may be instructed in godlinesse and good letters.

5. *Item,* To desire my lord regent's Grace, for suppressing of vice, whereby the plague of God may be withdrawin from the realme, to be carefull to see diligent executioun of justice upon

committers of suche odious crimes, as sall be exhibited to his
Grace, in bill, by the superintendents and commissioners of touns.

6. *Item*, That his Grace would caus suche of the counsell as
were appointed, conveene with these that were appointed by the
Assemblie, to treate of the jurisdictioun of the kirk; to decide
therin, that time and place be condescended upon to that effect;
and that this be done before the parliament hold.

7. *Item*, To advise with my lord regent's Grace and counsell, that superintendents may be placed where none are as yitt
placed.

8. *Item*, To understand what is to be done anent augmenting or
appointing of ministers' stipends, as need requireth.

The answeres made by the regent's Grace and the counsell to
the forsaid articles follow :—

" At Edinburgh, the eight day of Julie, the lord regent's Grace,
my Lord Sempill, my Lord Glames, the Secretar, Lord Uchiltrie,
and my Lord Balmerinoth, being on the Secreit Counsell.

" Anent the complaint made by the kirk, for laike of payment
of the thrids of benefices to the sustentatioun of the ministrie, the
persons addebted for payment of the same being at the horne, and
no further diligence used for obteaning of payment, my lord regent's Grace, with advice of the Lords of Secreit Counsell, ordeaneth the treasurer to receave all letters of horning which are to
be presented by whatsomever collectors, ather of the three-score
six yeere crop, or three-score seven, or in time comming; and upon
the said letters of horning, to direct letters to officers of armes, or
to the shireffs, or other ordinar judges, to uptake the escheats of
the persouns denounced and putt to the horne; and of the first and
readiest of the escheats, to pay to the collectors the summes aught-
and, for which the saids persons were putt to the horne; freelie
taking up the remanent to our soverane lord's use, at the least,
taking so meekle above the valour of the debt, as will make the
expenses upon the executioun of the letters in uptaking the escheat,
so that no expenses in executioun of the said letters be made otherwise but of the escheat goods of the persons denounced.

" All commoun kirks sall be givin to qualified ministers; and
als, when anie prebendreis are founded on the fruicts or tithes of
kirks, as Dumbervie and Ormeston in Lothiane, as the prebendrie
vaiketh to be uptakin by the collectors.

" Ordeans a commissioun to be formed for reformatioun of the
Colledge of Aberdeene, and for placing of godlie and qualified masters therin.

" The roll of the committers of the vices to be presented to my
lord regent's Grace, who sall caus the Justice-Clerk proceed in
forme of justice against them.

" My lord regent's Grace sall give warning to the persons named
in the parliament, to conveene the 8th day of August.

" Forsameekle as superintendents cannot presentlie be appointed, the Assemblie must appoint commissioners for the self same
purpose, as the Assemblie sall thinke good to give commissioun,
till the nixt Assemblie.

" Anent the appointing or augmenting of ministers' stipends; by
advice of my lord regent's Grace and counsell, the Clerk of Register, the Laird of Pittarow, and Mr Henrie Balnaves, were appointed, together with suche as the Assemblie sould thinke meet,
or anie two of them."

The regent's letter anent chaplanreis.

" We, understanding that there are some chaplanreis properlie
perteaning to the king's Majestie's presentatioun, and some at this
present to be dispouned, have thought good to require your opinioun, how we sall proceed in that behalfe, presentlie, and in time
comming, that ignorantlie we doe nothing which the kirk may
justlie find fault with heerafter.

                                    " JAMES, REGENT."

Mr Knox, in a letter writtin to Mr Johne Wood, staying in
England, for the time imployed by the regent, hath these words
following :—

" My words (viz. upon the Evangell of Johne, concerning the
treasonable departing of Judas from Christ) were these : ' I feare

that suche as have entered with us in professing the Evangell, as
Judas did with Christ, sall depart and follow Judas, how soone the
expectatioun of gaine and worldlie promotioun faileth them. Time
will trie farther, and we sall see over muche. We looke daylie for
the arrivall of the duke and his Frenchemen, sent to restore Satan
to his kingdome, in the persone of his deerest lieutenant—sent, I
say, to represse religioun, not from the King of France, but frome
the Cardinall of Lorane, in favour of his deerest nice. Lett England take heed, for assuredlie their nighbours' houses are on fire. I
would, deere brother, that yee sould travell with zealous men, that
they may consider our estate. What I would say, yee may easilie
conjecture. Without support, we are not able to resist the force
of the domesticall enemeis, (unlesse God worke miraculouslie;)
muche lesse are we able to stand against the puissance of France,
the substance of the Pope, and the malice of the hous of Gwise,
unlesse we be conforted by others than by ourselves. Yee know
our estate, and, therefore, I will not insist to deplore our povertie.
The whole comfort of the enemeis is this, that by treasoun or other
meanes they may cutt off the regent, and then cutt the throat of
the innocent king. How narrowlie hath the regent escaped once,
I suppose yee have heard. As their malice is not quenched, so
ceasseth not the practise of the wicked, to putt in executioun the
crueltie devised. I live as a man alreadie deid from all effaires
civill; and, therefore, I praise my God; for so I have some quietnesse in spirit, and time to meditat upon death, and upon the
troubles I have long feared and foresee. The Lord assist you with
his Holie Spirit, and putt an end to my travells, to his owne
glorie, and to the comfort of his kirk; for assuredlie, brother, this
miserable life is bitter unto me."

After the queene arived at Warkington in Cumberland, accompanied with sixteene persons, Captan Read was appointed to attend upon her, with fiftie souldiours, and to convoy her to Carlill,
and from thence to Bolton Castell, which belonged to the Lord
Scroope, where she remained till she was committed to the Erle of

Shrewsburie. She sent up her heavie complaints to court. Suche as fled out of the countrie reported likewise that there was great injurie done to her through the malice of her subjects, and that she was charged unjustlie with haynous crimes. Queen Elizabeth, partlie moved with her complaints, partlie beleeving misreports, and feering the evill which might follow upon suche an exemple, required the regent to send some men sufficientlie instructed, to declare to her the order of their proceedings, and to answere to suche reproaches as were layed to his owne charge. Albeit it was thought hard to call in questioun things alreadie justified in parliament, and that before forraine kings and judges, often enemeis to our natioun, yitt becaus the Cardinall of Lorane ruled the court of France at his pleasure, and the queene had a great factioun at home, it was not expedient to offend the Queene of England. When the cheefe of the nobilitie refused this ambassadge, the regent professed he would goe himself. He choosed nyne persons to accompanie him: James Dowglas Erle of Morton, Patrik Lord Lindsay, William Matlane of Lethington, secretare, Adam Bishop of Orkney, Robert, Commendatare of Dumfermline, Mr James Makgill of Rankeillour, Mr Henrie Balnaves, and Mr George Buchanan. Secretare Lethington was verie unwilling, but he was perswaded by faire promises of lands and money; for it was not expedient to leave behind them a factious man, that inclynned secreitlie to the queen's factioun. They went in England the 27th of September, accompanied with an hundreth horse. The regent was advertised, that the Erle of Westmerland had directioun from Thomas Hawart, Duke of Norfolk, to ly in wait for him; yitt he came to Yorke the secund of October, the place appointed for hearing the controversie. At the same verie houre came thither also Thomas Ratcliffe, Erle of Sussex, and Sir Rawfe Sadler, Chanceller of the Dutchie of Lancaster. The duke comming the same verie houre to the towne when the regent came, thought he could not be free of slaunder if anie thing were then attempted. Their purpose was, that the regent being slaine, and our queen's letters to Bothwell intercepted, she might the

more easilie be cleered of anie crime might be layed to her
charge; but their machinatioun succeeded not.   Our queene and
the duke, at this time, were treating of a matche by secreit messingers.· Upon the thrid of October compeered Johne Bishop of
Rosse, William Lord Livingston, Robert Lord Boyd, Johne Lord
Hereis, Gawin, Commendatare of Kilwinning, Sir Johne Gordoun
of Lochinvar, and James Cockburne of Skirline, knights, commissioners for our queene. The English commissioners caused read
their commissioun, and deliver the authentick copie therof. The
commissioun was, to treate and conclude with the commissioners
of both sides upon all maner of hostiliteis, differences, controverseis,
maters debatefull and contentious, of what nature so ever the same
be, or have beene, betwixt her sister the Queene of Scotland, and
anie of her subjects, on the one part, and the Erle of Murrey, and
anie other subject of Scotland refusing to obey her, on the other
part: and also, upon anie caus or mater depending undecided or
ended betwixt her and her sister, or betweene anie of their subjects
on either part; or for the further confirmatioun or reformatioun,
augmentatioun of anie treatie of peace heeretofore made and concluded; or for the contracting and establishing of anie other new
treatie or confederatioun, for increasse of amitie, peace, and concord
betwixt them, their realmes and subjects.

After reading and delivering of the copie of the said commissioun,
they required the saids commissioners for the Queene of Scots to
produce their commissioun; and they tooke to produce the same on
Wednesday nixt, the 6th of October.   James Erle of Murrey,
James Erle of Morton, Adam Bishop of Orkney, Patrik Lord Lindsay, Mr Robert Pitcarne, Commendatare of Dumfermline, compeered as commissioners for the young king before the English
commissioners, in the Deane of York's hous, and produced their
commissioun. The effect of their commissioun was, to declare before the Queen of England's commissioners the true causes moving
diverse of the nobilitie to put on armes, wherupon followed the deteaning and sequestratioun of the queene his mother's person for
a time; with all causes, actiouns, circumstances, and others their

proceedings whatsomever towards her, or anie subject of the realme, sithence that time, and to commune, treate, and conclude therupon with the Queen of England her commissioners; as also to treate and conclude upon all differences, causes, or maters whatsomever, depending betwixt the subjects of either their realmes, or for further confirmatioun or augmentatioun of anie treatie of peace heeretofore made and concluded; or for contracting or perfyting anie other new treatie or confederatioun, als weill for the maintenance of true religioun publictlie professed by the inhabitants of both the realmes, and resisting of anie forraine power, or other power that may be stirred up within the samine, to disturbe the present quietnesse granted to both realmes in the unitie of the said religioun, as also, for increasse of amitie, peace, and concord.

Upon Tuesday the 6th of October, at nine houres before noone, in the said Deane of York's hous, in presence of the commissioners of England, the commissioners for our queen produced their commissioun, wherin power was givin to the forenamed, or anie foure of them, to conveene with the English commissioners; to treate, indent, conclude upon all suche heeds and articles as sall be found best for the furth-setting of the glorie of God, the reductioun of her disobedient subjects to their debtfull obedience; for good amitie als weill for byganes as to come, betwixt them and all their obedient subjects; and to treate upon the peace to be made betwixt her and her deerest sister, their realmes and subjects, and all other things perteaning to the weale of the same.

After noone, the Deane of York receaved, in presence of the commissioners of both the parteis, the oath of the commissioners of England, that they sould proceed uprightlie in all this conference. Therafter, they required the Queen of Scotland's commissioners to give their oathe. But, becaus they were to make some protestatioun, in name of their soverane, before they entered to anie act in this conference, they tooke the day following, to witt, the 7th of October, to give in the said protestatioun, with the oath, as was required. The Erle of Murrey, and his colleagues in commissioun, were required presentlie to give their oath, which was receaved by

the Deane of York; viz., that they sould make a plaine and ample
declaration of the true causes moving them and others of the nobilitie of Scotland to putt on armes, and to sequestrat the Queen of
Scotland her person for a time; that they sall proceed sinceerlie
and uprightlie, and that they sall not hide or conceale anie thing
which is meet and requisite to be opened and declared, for the
better knowledge of the truthe of the saids causes and controversie.
Upon the 7th of October, the commissioners for our queen compeered before the English commissioners, at nine houres before noone,
in the Deane of York's hous, and protested, that howbeit their mastresse was content that the controversie betwixt her and her disobedient subjects be considered and dressed by her sister and consignesse the queen's Majestie of England, or her Grace's commissioners authorized thereto, before all others, yitt they protested solemnelie, that thereby they intended on no wise that the queen's
Majestie, their soveran, sould recognosce herself to be subject to
anie prince on earth, in respect she was a free princesse, having the
imperiall-crowne givin her of God, and acknowledgeth no other superiour, and, therefore, that her posteritie be not prejudged in their
soveranitie on no wise heereby. Then they gave their oath to
make a plain and ample declaratioun of the true causes whereby
they, and others of the nobilitie of Scotland, tooke occasioun to
putt on armes for mainteaning of the queen's Majestie their soverane in her authoritie; and all others their proceedings in this caus,
and difference standing betwixt their said soveran and a part of her
subjects; to deale sinceerelie and uprightlie; to hide or conceale
nothing meete and requisite to be opened and declared, for the
better knowledge of the truthe of the saids causes in controversie.
The same day, after noone, the commissioners for the Queen of
England made a protestatioun, as an answere to the protestatioun
made by our queen's commissioners. They protested they nather
did nor would admitt or allow the samine in anie wise hurtfull or
prejudiciall to the right, title, and interest incident to the crown of
England, which the queen's Majestie, and all her noble progenitors,
had clamed, had, and injoyed, as superiours over the realme of Scot-

2

land : and the same superioritie they protest to belong and apperteane to the queen's Majestie, in the right of the crowne of England.[1]   Then the English commissioners required our queen's commissioners to give in their complaint upon the subjects of Scotland
who had offended her, which they did the day following, Fryday the
8th of October; protesting, it sould be leasome to them to augment
the same at their pleasure; which protestatioun was admitted.
And, therefore, they produced the complaint in forme as after followeth :—

THE COMPLAINT GIVIN IN BY THE QUEEN OF SCOTS' COMMISSIONERS.

" We, the commissioners appointed for the queen's Majestie of
Scotland, our soverane ladie, in her Highnesse' behalfe, show to
your Grace, and my lords commissioners for the queen's Majestie
of England, that James Erle of Murrey, Johne Erle of Marr, Alexander Erle of Glencarne, the Lords Hume, Ruthven, Lindsay,
Sempill, Cathcart, Uchiltrie, with others their assisters, assembled
in armes a great part of the queen's Grace her subjects; declared
by their proclamatiouns, it was for her Grace's releefe; unbesett the
gate in her passage betwixt her Grace's castells of Dumbar and
Edinburgh ; there tooke her most noble persoun; committed her in

---

[1] This bone of national contention was produced at the commencement of the trial.
" The first day of the meeting," says Melvill in his Memoirs, " the Duke of Norfolk
required, that the regent should make homage in the king's name to the crown of
England, thinking he had some ground to demand the same, seeing the said regent
there to plead his cause before the council of England. Whereat the regent grew
red, and knew not what to answer; but Secretary Lidington took up the speech, and
said, That in restoring again to Scotland the lands of Huntington, Cumberland, and
Northumberland, with such other lands as Scotland did of old possess in England, that
homage should gladly be made for the said lands : but, as to the crown and kingdom
of Scotland, it was freer than England had been lately, when it paid St Peter's penny
to the Pope."—Independently of English patriotism, which may have inspired such a
demand, the duke's subsequent conduct makes it certain that he had other and more
selfish motives. If Murray had assented, his own credit, and that of his party, would
have been utterly ruined : if he had peremptorily refused, the duke might have hoped
that a trial, which was to place Mary's character in jeopardy, would be averted.

waird, in her owne place of Lochlevin; after, intrometted with her
coine-hous, pressing yrons, gold, silver, coined and uncoined; past
to the castell of Stirline, and made their fashioun of crowning of
her young sonne, the prince, being then but of thretteene moneths of
age.   James Erle of Murrey tooke upon him the name of regent,
usurping thereby the supreme authoritie of that realme, in the
name of that infant; intrometted with the whole strenths, munitions, jewells, and patrimonie of the crowne, als weill propertie as
casualitie.   And, when it pleased Almightie God to releeve her
Grace out of the strait thraldome where her Highnesse was deteaned elleven moneths so hardlie, that none of her true subjects
might have accesse to speeke her Highnesse, therefore in Hammiltoun made open declaratioun, that her former constrained writtings
in prisoun were altogether against her will, and done for feare of
her life; affirmed the same by solemne oath; yitt, for the godlie
zeale and naturall affectioun her Grace bore to her native realme
and subjects, gave power to the Erles of Argile, Eglintoun, Cassils,
and Rothesse, to agree and conforme a pacificatioun with the other
erles and their partakers : passing to Dumbartane, left the hie way,
for avoiding trouble; the saids Erles of Murrey, Morton, Glencarne,
Marr, with their adherents and partakers, unbesett her passage,
and by their men of warre which they had waged with her Grace's
owne silver, overthrew her power, slue sindrie right honest and
true men, tooke others prisoners, and ransoumed them ; condemned
to death, under colour of their pretended law, great landed barons
and gentlemen, for no other caus, but onlie for serving of their native
prince.   Thir, their unreasonable and unduetifull proceedings,
caused the queen, our mastresse, to come in this realme, to require
of the queen's Majestie, her most deerest sister, and in blood neerest consignesse in the world, (their promises of love, freindship,
and assistance so effectuouslie effirmed,) favours and support, that
she may injoy peaceablie her realme, according to God's calling;
and that her subjects may be caused recognosce their debtfull obedience, reforme to her Majestie and her true subjects the wrongs
they have done, as sall be givin in speciall, that we and they may

live under her Highnesse in one calling, as good subjects, under that head that God hath appointed us, is her Majestie's, and our desire." *Sic subscribitur,*

> " Johne, Rossen   Hereis.
>   Levingston.   Kilwinning:
>   R. Boyd.   Skirline."

Upon Moonday, the elleventh of October,.the commissioners for the king gave in their answere to the complaint forsaid, as followeth :—

THE ANSWERE GIVIN IN BY THE ERLE OF MURREY AND HIS COMPLICES, TO THE COMPLAINT MADE BY THE COMMISSIONERS FOR THE QUEEN'S MAJESTIE OF SCOTLAND.

" It is notified to all men, how som whiles King Henrie, father to our said soverane lord, was horriblie murthered in his bed. James, some time Erle Bothwell, being weill knowne for cheefe author therof, entered in suche great credit and authoritie with the queene, then our soverane, that within three moneths after the murther of her husband, the said erle presentlie interprised to ravishe her persoun, and led her to Dumbar castell, holding her there as captive a certan space ; during which, he caused divorce be led betwixt him and his lawfull wife, and suddanlie with the end therof, accomplished a pretended mariage betwixt him and the queen. Which strange and haistie proceeding of that godlesse and ambitious man, after murthering of the queen's husband in suche sort, to atteane to her owne mariage, the governement of the realme, and power over their sonne, our soverane lord's persoun ; the which ignominie spokin among all nations of that murther is, although all the nobilitie had beene alike culpable therof, so moved the hearts of a good number of them, that they thought nothing more godlie, nor more honorable in the sight of the world, than by punishing the said erle, cheef author of the murther, to releeve others sake-

lesselie calumniated therof; to putt the queene to freedome, out of
the boundage of that tyranne, that presumptuouslie had interprised
to ravishe and marie her, whose lawfull husband he could not be,
nather she his lawfull wife; and to preserve the innocent persoun of
our native prince, furth of the hands of him that murthered his
father. For which purpose, taking armes, the said erle came against
us, leading the queene, then our soverane, in his companie, as a defence and cloke to all his wickednesse, accompanied with a great
force that he had brought to the feilds, with great ordinance, and
waged men of warre: where, to decide the querell which was onlie
intended against him, and the remanent knowne murtherers, without bloodshed of anie innocent man, it was offered, at two severall
times, by the noble men seeking the punishment of the murther,
to trie the mater with him in singular battell, according to the law
of armes, as he by his cartall before had proclamed: which being
shifted, delayed, and in the end utterlie refused by him, he escaped
by flight; and the queene, preferring his impunitie to her owne
honour, would see him convoyed. And to the end he sould not
be followed nor persued, she came herself to the noble men assembled against him, who convoyed her to Edinburgh; and being
there, informed her of the verie causes that had drivin them to
that forme of dealing; humblie requiring that she would be content
to see the said erle, and others her husband's murtherers, punished,
and that pretended and unlawfull mariage wherin she was impro-
visedlie entered to be dissolved, for her owne honour, the safeguarde of her sonne, the quietnesse of her realme and subjects: To
which no other answere could be obteaned, but rigorous menacing
on the one part, avowing to be avenged on all them that had
shewed themselves in that caus; and, on the other part, offering to
leave and give over the realme and all, so that she might be suffered
to possesse the murtherer of her husband. Which her inflexible
minde, and extremitie of necessitie, compelled them to sequestrat
her for a seasoun from the companie, and having intelligence with
the said Erle Bothwell, and others his fautors, whill farther triell
might be takin, and executioun made for the murther. During

which time, finding herself by long, irkesome, and tedious travell,
takin by her in the governement of the realme and lieges therof, so
vexed and wearied, that her bodie, spirit, and senses were altogether unable longer to occupie the governement of the realme; and
perceaving, by things that had past before that time, betwixt her
and her people, that nather she could weill allow of their doings,
nor they like of her fashiouns; and for other consideratiouns moving her for the time, therefore demitted and remitted the office of
governement of the realme and lieges therof, in favours of her owne
and most deere sonne, the prince of the same. And becaus of his
tender youth, and inabilitie to use the said governement in his owne
person, during his minoritie, constitute me, the said Erle of Murrey, (being then absent furth of the realme, and without my knowledge,) Regent to his Grace, realme, and lieges: and whill my returning, or in cace of my deceasse, or not-acceptatioun, made and
constitute diverse others noblemen Regents; as her severall commissions to that effect, subscrived with her hand, and under the
privie seale, beare; and that voluntarilie, no compulsioun, violence,
or force used or practised to move her therto. According to which
dimissioun and resignatioun, the king, now our soverane lord, was
duelie, rightlie, and orderlie crowned, invested, and possessed in
the kingdome; and I, the said Erle of Murrey, lawfullie placed, entered, and admitted, to the said office of Regencie, was not onlie
receaved and universallie obeyed over the whole realme, as lawfull
and sufficient, even by the most part of these, that in these six
moneths last bypast have withdrawin their debtfull obedience
from his Grace's authoritie, and interprised to establishe and sett up
another; but also, in a lawfull, free, and plaine parliament, wherat
they were present, the same coronatioun and acceptatioun of the
Regencie were, by perpetuall lawes made, and publict acts sett
furth, decerned to be lawfullie, sufficientlie, and righteouslie done;
as also other things intended, spokin, writtin, or done by anie of
them to that effect, since the 10th day of Februar, 1566, upon
which day the said umquhile King Henrie, then the queen's lawfull husband, was murthered, unto the date of the said act, and in

all time to come, tuiching the said queene, and deteaning of her
person, that caus, and all things depending thereon, the intromissioun or dispouning upon her propertie, casualteis, or whatsomever
things perteaning, or that in anie wise might apperteane to her;
like as at more lenth is conteaned in the acts, lawes, and constitutions concluded, made, and sett furth in the said parliament.

" Which acts and lawes, with our soveran lord's authoritie, and
the regiment of me, the said Erle of Murrey, were universallie
obeyed over all the realme without contradictioun, whill some of
the nobilitie and others that, in the said parliament, by free votes,
and otherwise by their hand-writtings, had acknowledged and advanced the king's authoritie, and regiment established in his name,
impatient to see the poore people of the realme injoy quietnesse
and good ease, and disdaining to see justice proceed as it was begunne, and likelie to have continued, to the punishment of manie
offenders over the whole countrie, according to the lawes ; first
practised to bring the said queene out of Lochlevin, contrarie to
the acts made in the parliament; and then by open force to destroy and subvert the publict governement and authoritie of our soverane, established by the estats, against their promised obedience
and hand-writtings; and for that purpose, proceeded in all kinde
of hostilitie, whill upon the 13th day of May last bypast, that God,
respecting the equitie of the caus, confounded their interprise, and
granted the victorie to the king, and suche as constantlie continued
in his obedience. That, since that time, they have persevered in
their rebellioun, abstracting their debtfull obedience from our soveran lord, and his authoritie, practising all kinde of things that may
subvert and overthrow the same, in holding of houses, proclaming
of other authoritie, running to the feilds in warlike maner with displeyed baners, taking and imprisoning of officers of armes, and
other free persons, raising of impositions of burrowes, and, under
pretence of law, summouning of houses, banishing and rigorouslie
persuing of diverse the king's good subjects, for no other caus but
onlie the serving of the king, their native soveran lord. It is therefore required, in his Highnesse' behalfe, that he, and his regent in

his Highnesse' behalfe, may peaceablie injoy and governe his realme, according to God his calling ; and his Majestie's disobedient subjects may be caused recognosce their debtfull obedience, and what the order of justice condemneth may receave full executioun. Protesting alwise, that notwithstanding this our answere, we may adde to the same, as occasioun sall serve, and as need may require."— *Et sic subscribitur,*

" James, Regent.   Dumfermline.
    Ad. Orcaden.   Patrik Lindsay."

Upon Saturday the 16th day of October, our queen's commissioners exhibited before the English commissioners a reply and true declaratioun, answering the alledgances made by the Erle of Murrey and his adherents, the tenor wherof followeth :—

" Wheras, in the answere presented to your Grace, and others the commissioners of the queen's Majestie of England, to the complaint givin in by us in our soveran's name, declaring thereby, that our soveran's umquhile late husband was murthered, &c. Her Highnesse, we, and others her true subjects, doe most sorrowfullie lament that tragedie, minding, with the advice and counsell of the queen's Majestie of this realme, most rigorouslie to punishe the same : and, if her Grace had not beene troubled in her authoritie, the same would have tane effect ere now. And, becaus in the said answere they alledge our said soverane voluntarilie, uncompelled, to have resigned and committed the governement of her realme and lieges to her sonne the prince, and constituted James Erle of Murrey regent during his minoritie ; with other invented clauses, to her Highnesse' dishonour and disadvantage : First, adhering to our former protestatioun, that our said soverane being a free princesse, with an imperiall crowne granted her by God, acknowledgeth no superiour on earth, and therefore may not be content that her Majestie's estate and crowne come in questioun before anie judge, yitt, neverthelesse, for declaring of the truthe and veritie to the queen's Majestie of this realme, your Grace, and my lords commissioners,

of suche things alledged by them against our soverane, we doe reply as followeth:

"That where it is alleged, that the complices of the Erle of Murrey took occasioun to putt themselves in armes against the queen's
Highnesse, their soverane, because James Erle Bothwell being in
such credite and authoritie with his soverane; being knowne (as
they affirme) the cheefe author of the horrible murther committed
on her said husband, &c. Which can on no wise excuse their unnaturall and disobedient fact, for their part. For, if he was principall author of the murther, the same was never knowne, nor manifested to her Highnesse: But the contrare did weill appeare to
her Majestie, by reasoun the said Erle Bothwell being suspected,
indyted, and orderlie summouned by the lawes of that realme, was
acquitt by an assise of his peeres, and the same notified and confirmed by act of parliament, by the greatest part of the nobilitie,
als weill of the principalls which now withdraw themselves sensyne
frome the queen's Majestie their soveran's obedience, as others her
faithfull subjects, who also consented and solicited our said soverane to accomplishe the said mariage with him, as a man most fitt
in the realme of Scotland; in so doing, promising him service, and
her Highnesse loyall obedience. And manie of themselves gave
their bands unto him, to defend him against all these whatsomever
might challenge or persue him therafter for the said crime, as their
hand writts can testifie. And further, they, nor none of them be-
for the mariage, or after, came to her Highnesse, (as the part of
true subjects sould have done;) knowing at that time, (as they
affirme the contrare,) ather privatlie or openlie, to find fault with the
said erle concerning the murther forsaid; or yitt, in anie wise seemed
to greeve or disallow the said mariage, unto suche time they had
practised the keeper of the castell of Edinburgh, and proveist of
the toun, to be their assisters; and they secreetlie tooke armes, and,
upon suddane in the night, with their forces invironed the castell of
Borthwicke, where her Majestie was in quiett and peaceable maner:
so that their first warning was by sound of trumpet, and their sight
in armes. And her Grace escaping to Dumbar, wherethrough they

could not atteane to their conspired purpose, returned suddanelie
to Edinburgh, raised their bands of men of warre, sett out their
proclamatiouns, affirming the same to be for her releefe, unbesett
her way betwixt her Grace's castells of Dumbar and Edinburgh.

" And her Majestie willing, for the tender love her Highnesse bare
her subjects, to stanche all effusioun of blood among them, did not
preferre the impunitie of the Erle Bothwell to her owne honour, in
seing him convoyed away, as in their answere is conteaned. For
they, being in the feilds in arrayed battell against her Majestie,
sent the Laird of Grange to her Highnesse, and desired her Grace
to caus the Erle Bothwell passe off the feilds, alledging him suspected of the said crime, untill the time the caus might be tried;
and that her Grace would passe with them, and use the counsell of
her nobilitie, and they sould honour, serve, and obey her Majestie
as their princesse and soverane. And upon their promises, for
eshewing of bloodshed, as said is, her Majestie consented thereto,
and passed with the said Laird of Grange to them; who at the
samine time tooke the Erle Bothwell by the hand, and bade him
depart, promising, that no man sould follow nor persue him: and
so, by their owne consent, he past away. And, if they had beene
minded to persue him onlie, they would not have left the doing of
all diligence was possible, wherethrough he might have beene tane.
But fra they had gottin her Majestie's persoun in their hands, they
made no more travell nor persute against him, so long as he was in
the countrie neere them, where he remained a great space, and might
[have] apprehended him more easilie; nor when long time, he being
furth of the realme, and unrecoverable, made a coloured maner of
seeking him upon the sea, as now appeares manifest it was not him
they sought, but their owne particular profite. Wherethrough, to
all men of whole judgement, it may appeare her Grace prefered
not his escaping and impunitie to her owne honour: for whatsoever
was last done in that behalfe, it may be justlie layed to their owne
charge. And therafter, at her first comming to them on the feilds,
the Erle of Morton said to her Majestie, with great reverence, ' Madame, heere is the place your Grace sould be in; and we will honour,

serve, and obey you, as ever the nobilitie of this realme did anie of
your progenitors before, in their names.' Her Majestie passing
with them to Edinburgh, being loodged in a simple burgesse's hous,
setting aside her owne palaces and castells, rudelie and rigorouslie
intreated by them, it was no wounder, incace her Majestie had
givin them quicke and sharpe answeres, (as we beleeve not unreasonable,) but was alwise content, tuiching the thing alledged by
them, to offer the same to be reformed by the triell of the whole
nobilitie, her Grace being present, and heard: And to that effect
directed her secretare, Lethington, to their counsell, that held her
captive at that time, and was alluterlie refused therof; and made
no offer to leave the realme that her Grace might possesse the Erle
Bothwell, as they alledge. And, therefore, her Grace was secreitlie convoyed per force, and against her will, in the night, and
imprissouned within the fortalice of Lochlevin.

" Where they alledge, her Grace, finding herself irkesome, and
wearie of the governement of her realme, and lieges thereof, for
which, and other consideratiouns moving, her Majestie dimitted
the same in favours of the prince, her sonne, constituting the said
Erle of Murrey his regent during his minoritie, willinglie, and uncompelled therto; it is manifest the truthe to be otherwise, as evidentlie may appeare by many sundrie and infallible reasouns. For,
first, her Majestie is not of suche age, nor subject to maladeis and
sicknesse, (thankes to God,) nor so unable of her persoun for to
refuse that which God had givin to her Highnesse to rule. And
it is certane, that before the subscriving of the alledged dimissioun,
that the Erle of Atholl, the Lairds of Tullibardin and Lethington,
the principalls of her counsell, sent Robert Melvill to her Highnesse with a ring, and tokins, counselling her Highnesse to subscrive suche writtings as would be presented to her Grace for dimissioun of her crowne, for to putt off that present death which
was prepared for her Highnesse if she refused the same; assuring
her, whatsomever her Majestie did in captivitie, might not prejudge her Highnesse in no sort. And, also, the said Robert Melvill brought at that same time a writting from Sir Nicolas Throg-

morton, writtin with his owne hand, desiring her Highnesse to subscrive whatsoever they would require her unto; for the estate wherin her Grace was then could not prejudge her Grace, whatever her Majestie subscrived. To whom her Grace sent answere in writt, that her Highnesse would use his counsell; and prayed him to declare to her deerest sister, the queen's Majestie of England, his mastresse, how her Highnesse was handled by her subjects, and what estate her Grace was in for the time. Sir Nicolas shew the same to the queen's Majestie of this realme, her Highnesse being at that time minded to send an armie in Scotland, for delivering our soverane furth of prisoun, were not her Majestie was surelie advertised, incace her Highnesse had so done, the blood of our mastresse had payed the wages of her Grace's souldiours. Anent the presenting of the saids writtings of dimissioun of her crowne to her Majestie by the Lord Lindsay, he minassed her Grace, that if she would not subscrive, he had command presentlie to putt her in the towre, and would doe the same; and counselled her Grace to fulfill their desires, or elles worse would follow shortlie : which her Highnesse subscrived with manie teares, never looking what was conteaned in the writtings; declaring plainlie therafter, if her Grace ever came to libertie, she would never abide thereat, becaus it was against her will. And als, the Laird of Lochlevin, being then her keeper, would not come present, and desired a writting of her Highnesse, to testifie he was not present the time of her subscriptioun, becaus he knew the same to be done against her will, and that the samine sould not be imputed to him in times coming : which writting he obteaned. And if probable appearance sould have place, her Grace's conditioun had beene verie strait and miserable in the said dimissioun, wherin nather her Highnesse had reserved anie portioun of her revenue wheron to have lived, nor obteaned thereby her libertie, nor yitt sure promise nor assurance of the safetie of her life. Which premises being considered, our said soveran hath no wise prejudged her title and estate in the said forced dimissioun, which nather law of God nor man doeth approve. For at her furth-comming of the said prisoun, in presence of a great part of her Highnesse' nobilitie in Hammiltoun, she revoked the said pretended dimissioun of the crowne, and all that followed therupon, affirming that same, by a solemne oath, to have beene done for feare of her life.

"The pretended coronatioun of her Highnesse' sonne, in respect of the premises als weill unduelie as unorderlie led, can prejudge her Majestie no wise. For where, in that realme there are moe erles, bishops, and lords, having vote in parliament nor an hundreth, of the which the whole, or at least the greatest part, sould have consented thereto, and to all other publict actiouns of consequence, were onlie foure erles, of whom the most honorable hath not the seventh or eight place in parliament among the erles, or the first of twentie votes among the whole estats; six lords onlie, who were all at her Grace's taking, together with one bishop, and two or three abbots and pryors; which could be no sufficient number to determine and conclude so weightie a caus : protestatiouns being openlie made, whatsomever was done at the said coronatioun contrarie her Majestie's estat royall, her persoun, or yitt in effirming a regent, sould not in anie wise prejudge her Majestie's self, nor her estat royall, nor yitt the neerest lawfullie descended of her Majestie's progenitors' blood, Kings and Queens of Scotland; becaus her Grace had beene long time bygane, and at that time, straitlie and rigorouslie keeped within the fortalice of Lochlevin, where none of her faithfull subjects, nor the King of France his ambassador, being present for the time, nor the Queene of England's, that came therafter to that effect, might have free accesse to her Highnesse, to know whether the said dimissioun was willinglie done or not by her Majestie; as authentick instruments, in presence of the forsaids number of the nobilitie there present takin, will report. For if her Grace had willinglie dimitted the samine, (as her Highnesse did not,) her Grace could not have nominated the said Erle of Murrey regent; for there were others to have beene preferred to him, who were more lawfull, and had more right thereto, and worthilie used the governement of that realme in our soveran's minoritie. Wherethrough the said pretended corona-

tioun, the alledged investing, and wrongous electioun of the said
regent, nor the effirming therof by pretended parliament, was nather duelie, rightlie, nor orderlie done, (as in their answere they
affirme,) nor yitt obeyed universallie within the whole realme; becaus a great part of the nobilitie, and speciallie of the most principalls, never obeyed, voted, nor subscrived with them, but ever en-
rolled, and held their compts in the queen's Majestie their soveran's name. And others who did compeere in the said pretended
parliament tooke instruments and protestatiouns, both in articles,
and at the voting time of the parliament, that they consented not
to anie hurt of the queen's Majestie's persoun, estat royall, nor
crowne, farther than her Highnesse would approve herself, being at
libertie; nor yitt would vote in anie thing concerning her Grace's
honour or life; but plainlie oppouned themselves in the contrare,
howbeit they have caused insert otherwise in their pretended Acts,
and will suffer their clerks in no wise to give the saids protestatiouns.

"And where it is alledged, that certan of the nobilitie, favourers
of the queen's Majestie, their soverane, were impatient to see the
poore people injoy quietnesse, and disdaining to see justice to proceed to the punishment of offenders over the whole realme; by
the contrare, the eternall God knoweth, and men on earth doe testifie, what murther and bloodshed, what thift and reafe, what destructioun of policeis, in casting doun of cathedrall kirks and true
barons' houses, and taking up true men's goods to satisfie their
souldiers, have beene committed since the publict coronatioun, and
usurped authoritie or regiment; as by the particulars will appeare,
when they sall be givin in, the like wherof in chronickle hath never
beene heard, seene, nor writtin, thir manie hundreth yeeres. And,
as to the last alledged offences committed by our said soveran's
lieges, true subjects, in withdrawing them from the said pretended
authoritie, in holding of houses, comming to the feilds in warlike
maner, taking and imprisoning of officers, making proclamations
against their authoritie; we affirme the same, so farre as it was by
the commandement of our soveran Ladie in executioun of justice, to

be most justlie, duelie, and orderlie done, as they that had lawfull power and authoritie of her Highnesse granted thereto. And whosoever have done anie suche acts, not authorized by her Majestie, we affirme the same most wrongouslie and unjustlie done.

" It is therefore required, in her Highnesse' behalfe, that her Grace may be fortified and supported by the queen's Highnesse of England, to peaceablie injoy and governe her realme and lieges therof, according to it that God hath called her Grace unto ; and their usurped and pretended authoritie to be null from the beginning, and all that followed therupon ; and that the wrongs committed by them, as weill· toward her Highnesse' self, as other her faithfull and obedient subjects, may be repaired, according to all equitie and reasoun, that no farder trouble ensue therupon : Alwise protesting to adde to thir premises, as time and need sall require."

The complaint, answere, and reply, I have extracted out of the Bishop of Rosse his memorialls, left in writt. The complaint and reply are in some parts probable ; for it may be, the queene dimitted not willinglie her authoritie. Yitt seing she deserved a greater punishment in the judgement of manie, the pretences of dimissioun were devised where no need was. As for the rest, the preceeding narratioun, drawin out of Buchanan, and other manuscripts, may furnishe a sufficient rejoynder to the reply. Loath was the regent and the other commissioners to discover the whole truthe, they were so carefull to absteane from discrediting her too farre.

Upon Tuisday, the 19th of October, the English commissioners declared, that it was the Queene of England's will that the commissioners for both parteis sould send two of their collegues to Londoun, to her Majestie, within eight dayes ; and that the conference begunne at Yorke sould ceasse till the returning of the commissioners. The commissioners for the queen of Scots went from Yorke to Bolton, and upon Thursday the 21st of October communicated the mater with their mastresse. With her advice, Johne Lord Hereis and Johne Bishop of Rosse were sent. The

Erle of Murrey sent William Matlane of Lethington, younger, and Mr James Makgill of Rankeillour. The regent sent Mr James Makgill with him, not so muche to assist him, as to watche over him, and to espie what would be his cariage; for the secretar was greatlie suspected before he came to England; and since he came the suspicioun was augmented. For never a night passed almost so long as they remained at Yorke, wherin he had not secreetlie communicatioun with our queen's cheefe commissioners, and forewarned them what the regent intended to doe. Yitt would not the regent seeme to take notice of his privie traffiquing, becaus there was no hope of anie ingenuitie in him, but rather feare, that he would deale more closelie after. He went out to the feilds, under pretence of hunting with the Duke of Norfolke, but in effect, it was to consult how to dresse that present bussinesse. It was concluded, as most expedient, to draw in lenth, so that nather the caus sould seeme to be deserted, nor yitt an end putt to the controversie. The secretar informeth the Bishop of Rosse, that he may advertise the queen what course was most expedient, and not to cast off all hope for protracting of time. The end of this device was, that the regent being wearied, might returne, without perfyting his bussinesse; or troubles arising at home might recall him. The Bishop of Rosse his missive to the queene tossed from hand to hand, came at last to the regent's hands, whereby, yitt farther, Lethington his perfidie was discovered.

The Lord Hereis and the Bishop of Rosse compeered before the Queene of England, accompaneid with her nobilitie, in her great chamber of presence, at Hampton Court, the last of October. They presented their mastresse her letter, wherin she declared, that she had sent them to await upon her pleasure and commandement. They desired to know her will and pleasure. Her Majestie answered, after long communing, that she would declare the caus moving her to send for them by some of her counsell, who sould come and conferre with them. Lethington and Mr James Makgill went to the queen upon Moonday, the first of November.

Her Highnesse did signifie likewise to them, that she sould caus them be certified, by her counsell, of her minde and will. Upon Tuisday, the 2d of November, Sir William Cecil, Principall Secretar, and Sir Rawfe Sadler, two of her Highnesse' Privie Counsell, sent from the queene, came to Kingstone, and declared to the Bishop of Rosse and Lord Hereis, there remaining, that her Highnesse thought meete, that the causes of her sister, the Queen of Scotland, sould be treated neere by to her self, where the commissioners might have conference with her Highnesse, and her advice in all their proceedings. They desired, to that effect, they would obteane a new commissioun, in the same forme as they had at the conference at Yorke, changing onlie the place and the number of commissioners, and to send for a greater number of their collegues. A new commissioun was formed, conforme to the other. The Lord Boyd and the Commendatar of Kilwinning were sent from our queene, to be joyned with the Bishop of Rosse and Lord Hereis. Sir Rawfe Sadler was sent to Kingstoun, upon the 22d of November, to declare to them, that it was her Highnesse' pleasure to have her Highnesse' commissioners sitt at Westminster, beside the citie of Londoun, and that the conference beginne on Thursday nixt. The commissioners for our queene went to Hampton Court; and upon Tuisday, the 23d of November, declared unto the queene, that they understood Westminster to be a judiciall place, where causes criminall and civill are to be treated; and therefore might be prejudiciall to their soverane to enter in anie judiciall place. And siclyke desired, that since the Erle of Murrey, the principall of her disobedient subjects, and other his adherents, had gottin alreadie presence of her Majestie, and admitted to speeke of their soverane as they pleased, that, therefore, her Majestie would grant to their soverane, to come in proper persoun to the presence of her Highnesse and nobilitie, to declare her owne innocencie. The regent was come before this time to Londoun, with a small traine, for he had sent backe a great number of his companie from Yorke. The Queene of England answered, the place sould be a chamber, where

5

never yitt judgement was holdin. But as to their soveran's presence, she could not goodlie admitt the same, untill her causes were
tried and ended.

Johne Lord Hereis, Robert Lord Boyd, Johne Bishop of Rosse,
and Gawin, Commendatare of Kilwinning, compeered upon Tuisday, the 25th of November, at Westminster, in the utter chamber,
beside the Parliament Hous, before the Duke of Norfolke, the Erle
of Sussex, the Erle of Leicester, Sir Nicolas Bacon, Keeper of the
Great Seale, Edward Lord Clinton, Admirall, Sir William Cicill,
Principall Secretar, and Sir Rawfe Sadler, her Highnesse' counsellers
and commissioners. The English commissioners produced and read
their commissioun. After the reading of the said commissioun, the
Lord Keeper desired the commissioners for the Queen of Scotland
to exhibite and produce their commissioun, to the effect they might
enter in conference. It was answered, they would gladlie produce
the same; but ere they would enter in anie conference, they
would declare and propone some things necessarilie required to give
light, together with some protestations. The summe of the commission was, that she had constituted Robert Lord Boyd, John Bishop
of Rosse, &c., her commissioners, to treate and conclude upon suche
heeds as sall be found best for the furth-setting of God's glorie, the
reductioun of her disobedient subjects to their debtfull obedience;
for good amitie, by tie, betwixt them and her obedient subjects, and
to treat upon all maters and causes in controversie betwixt her and
her subjects; alwise so, that it doe not tuiche her title to the
crowne. Farther, to treate betwixt the peace to be made betwixt
her and her deerest sister, and the two realmes. The Bishop of
Rosse, in presence of the English commissioners at Westminster,
the 25th of November, proposed, in name of the rest of his collegues, that they were come to declare and lament the unjust dealing of certane disobedient subjects against their mastresse, whom
she had of her liberalitie promoved to high honours and profites.
But they, upon their former evill deservings, fearing her Grace
would revocke and withdraw her liberalitie and patrimonie which
they possesse, have takin upon them to putt hands in her most no-

ble person, imprison her, and corrupted the keepers of her castell, who treasonablie delivered to them her jewells, pose, and munitions, and have usurped her supreme authoritie; and to colour their wicked proceedings, have slaundered her honour: That their undutifull proceedings caused her to come to this realme, to desire of the queen's Majestie, her deerest sister, her support, that she may peaceablie injoy her owne realme, and that her rebellious subjects may recognosce their debtfull obedience: That their mastresse had desisted frome seeking support from anie other princes, upon the confidence she had in her, and the promises of freindship past betwixt them in former times: That the queen's Majestie of England thought best their soveran's caus sould be sett fordward, by conference and appointment to be givin to her disobedient subjects, rather nor by force of armes: That therupon, they were appointed commissioners by their mastresse, and were readie to enter in conference conforme to their commission, providing, and solemnelie protesting, they nather enter in judiciall place, nor are to proceed in anie maner of way in forme of judgement, or before anie judge or judges, but as commissioners of a free princesse, with their Honours as commissioners to the queen's Majestie of England, in forme of treatie allanerlie. They presented the protestatioun subscrived with her hands, and desired the samine to be receaved and admitted, before they enter in anie further conference. The protestatioun was read and admitted, with this protestatioun for answere :—

" We, the commissioners of the Queen's Majestie of England, doe not meane to proceed judiciallie as judges, or in judiciall place, but as commissioners, according to our commissioun, alwise adhering to the protestatioun made by certane of us, her Majestie's commissioners at Yorke. *Sic subscribitur,*

" S. N. Bacon.	E. Clinton.
Norfolk.	M. Cicill.
Sussex.	R. Sadler."
R. Leicester.	

Therafter, the English commissioners gave their oath to proceed uprightlie in this conference, after the same tenor as was givin by the commissioners at Yorke. The commissioners for our queene siclyke gave their oath, under protestatioun, as at Yorke, and therafter presented the complaint and reply, givin in and exhibited at Yorke. It rested therefore to the Erle of Murrey and his collegues to mak answere or farther eeke or augmentatioun to their former alledgances, if they thought good.

The regent, after he came from Yorke, refused to answere, or detect anie farther than he had done at Yorke, unlesse the Queen of England would grant to protect the young king, incace he proved cleerelie that she was worthilie displaced. In the meane time, our queene, by Sir James Balfour, preassed to trouble the countrie at home. She writteth to Bothwel's freinds, and other rebells, to vexe the other partie as they might; createth lieutenants in sindrie parts of the kingdome; causeth rumors to be spread, that the regent and the cheefe of his companie were committed to the Towre of Londoun. Becaus this report would soone vanishe, another was devised, to witt, that the regent promised to make Scotland tributarie to England, and to deliver some castells, and the young king himself, in pledge. The regent, perceaving himself thus besett with difficulteis, resolved to dispatche his bussinesse the best maner he could. He craveth to be dismissed. The commissioners still urge him to declare the causes wherupon the proceedings of the nobilitie and parliament were grounded, otherwise they could not determine. Wherupon the Erle of Murrey and his collegues exhibited and presented an eeke to their answere givin at Yorke, together with a protestatioun made at the exhibiting of the said eeke.

THE EEKE GIVIN IN BY THE REGENT AND HIS COLLEGUES TO THE
ANSWERE PRESENTED BY THEM AT YORKE.

" Whereas in our former answere, upon good respects mentiouned in our protestatioun, we keeped backe the cheefest causes and grounds wherupon our actions and whole proceedings were founded; wherewithall, seing our adversareis will not content themselves, but by their obstinat and earnest preassing we are compelled, for justifeing of our caus, to manifest the naked truthe, it is certane, and we boldlie and constantlie affirme, that as James, sometime Erle Bothwell, was the cheefe executer of the horrible and unworthie murther perpetrated upon the person of umquhile King Henrie, of good memorie, father to our soverane lord, and the queen's lawful husband, so was she of the foreknowledge, counsell, device, perswader, and commander of the said murther to be done, maintenar and fortifier of the executers therof, by impeding and stopping of the inquisitioun and punishement due for the same, according to the lawes of the realme; and, consequentlie, by mariage with the said James Erle Bothwell, delated and universallie esteemed cheefe author of the above-named murther, wherethrough they beganne to use and exerce an uncouth and cruell tyrannie in the whole state of the commounwealth; and with the first (as weill appeared by their proceedings) intended to caus the innocent prince, now our soverane lord, shortlie to follow his father, and so to transferre the crowne frome the right lyne to a bloodie murtherer and godlesse tyranne. In which respects, the estats of the realme of Scotland, finding her unworthie to raigne, decerned the dimissioun of the crowne, with the coronatioun of our soverane lord, and establishing of the regiment of that realme in the person of me, the said Erle of Murrey, during his Highnesse' minoritie, to be lawfullie, sufficientlie, and righteouslie done; as in the acts and lawes, made therupon, more largelie is conteaned."

Subscribed thus,

"James Regent.
Mortoun.
Ad. Orcad.

Dumfermline.
Patrik Lindsay."

THE PROTESTATION MADE BY THE REGENT AND HIS COLLEGUES, AT THE PRESENTING OF THE EEKE FORESAID.

" Albeit our whole proceedings, frome the beginning of our interprise, directed onlie for punishment of the king's murther, and
by just executioun therof, to drive the slander of that abominable
fact frome the whole natioun upon the heads of a few, according
to their deserts, may serve for a sufficient testimonie to the world
how unwilling we have alwise beene to staine the king our soveran
lord's mother's honour, or to publishe to strangers maters tending
to her perpetuall infamie, yitt sall it not be amisse, upon this present occasioun, to tuiche breeflie what hath beene and yitt is our
meaning therin.   Suche was our devotioun toward her, als weill
for privat affectioun, whereby everie one of us was led to wishe her
weale, as also for publict respects, that rather ere we would spott
her honestie with the societie of that detestable murther, we were
content to winke at the shrewd reports of the world, who not being
privie to the ground wherupon our actions were founded, and so
for laike of informatioun misconstruing our doings, blazened us as
tratours and rebels to our native prince, in whose persoun we had
putt hand without anie deserving.   It had beene easie for us to
have wiped away these and the like objections with a few words, if
we would have uttered mater which we keeped in store for the
latter cast.   But so desirous were we to cover that shame, that we
were content to beare a part of her burthein, suffering the world
still to live in doubt of the justice of our querell, and consequentlie
to speeke everie one as their affectiouns were inclynned ; so farre
furth, that when we were preassed by the queen's Majestie of England and King of France their ambassaders, why we deteaned the
queene in Lochlevin, we never came furth for answere to them, but
onlie, that her affectioun was so excessive toward Bothwell, cheefe
author and executer of the murther, that she being at libertie, it
would not be possible to punishe him ; and, therefore, it behoved us
for a seasoun to sequestrat her persoun, till he might be appre-

hended. In what danger this dealing was like to cast us is more
than evident; whereas, we could looke for nothing but plaine hostilitie frome France, and the Queen's Majestie of England's minde
was cleere alienated frome us, for laike of due informatioun; and
by reasoun of our silence keeping backe the cheefe caus of our
rhotioun, which being hid frome her eares, and not uttered to the
world, it was feared she would call the justice of our caus in doubt.
And so, if she should disallow of our doings, we were left destituted
of her Majestie's aide, at whose hand we principallie looked to receave confort in all times of danger, being the prince of Christendome who hath greatest interest to persecute the punishement of
that murther, in so farre as the king in whose persoun it was perpetrated had that honour to be so neere of her Majestie's blood;
beside that, that he was borne her subject, whereby, by God's ordinance, she is bound to crave his blood out of the hands of the
murtherers. In the same moderatioun we could still be content to
conteane our selves, if the continuance of Scotland in the state of a
kingdome, and the professioun of the true religioun, would permitt
it. For we remember what persoun she is whom this mater cheefelie
tuiched; the mother of the king, our soverane; and to whom, in particular, the most part of us are bound, for benefites receaved at her
hand; and therefore cannot but privatlie beare her good will; yea, so
farre, that if the perpetuall exile of anie one of us, or yitt of a number, furth of our native countrie, might redeeme her honour, without danger of the king our soveran's persoun and whole estate, we
would willinglie banishe ourselves to that end. And, therefore, before we enter furth into the ground of this mater, which to this
houre we have fled, we protest solemnlie that we have no delite to
see her dishonoured, and that we come not willinglie to her accusatioun of so odious a crime; but that we are thereto inforced
by her owne pressing, and our adversareis, who will not content
themselves with our former answere, which they know to be true;
but, for defence of our owne just caus, compelleth us to utter that
most odious mater; protesting also, that whatsoever shall follow
therupon be not imputed to us heerafter, but rather to our said ad-

versareis, in whose default her shame sall be disclosed. Whereby they sufficientlie declare how little they care what become of her, howsoever they give themselves out to the world to be of her partie, for pressing us to come to that answere, which they know we have just caus to make, and will make, in the end. And so, to produce suche evidents as they know we have, it is indirectlie to preasse earnestlie her perpetuall infamie, wherof, as of before, we protest that they, and not us, be esteemed the cheefe procurers, etc. At Westminster, the 26th of November 1568." Subscrived thus,

> " James Regent.	Dumfermline.
> Mortoun.	Patrik Lindsay."
> Ad. Orcad.

The Lord Hereis, after the presentatioun of this eeke, at the desire of the Bishop of Rosse was heard before the English commissiouners at Westminster, the 1st of December. He with great vehemencie inveyghed against the Regent and his collegues, and their partakers at home. He alledged that they had slaundered his mastresse to excuse their owne treasons : that they were the first inventors, writters with their owne hand of that devilish band, the conspiracie of the slaughter of that innocent gentleman, Henrie Stewart, (so he called him,) late spous to our soverane, and presented it to their wicked confederat, James Erle of Bothwell : that after the slaughter of her secretare, in her owne Grace's presence, becaus she would have made a revocatioun of the patrimonie of the crowne bestowed upon some of them, they laboured to cutt her off : that it was not the punishement of the slaughter of her husband which moved them to this proud rebellioun, but the usurping of their soveran's supreme authoritie, and to possesse themselves with her great riches.

The Bishop of Rosse desired that the queene, his soverane, might be admitted to the queen's presence, her nobilitie, and ambassaders of forraine countreis, for their satisfactioun, and declaratioun of her innocencie. The commissioners for the queene went

to Hampton Court, and presented a supplicatioun, tending to the
same effect : that their soverane Ladie may be permitted to come
in proper persoun before her Highnesse, her nobilitie, the ambassaders of other countreis now resident within her realme ; and seing
her rebells had takin upon them unjustlie and boldlie to accuse
their native soverane, that they may be stayed and arrested, to
answere upon suche haynous attemptats as sall be layed to their
charge.   The queene gave answere to their supplicatioun upon the
fourth day of December, in presence of a number of the Lords of
her Privie Counsell.   The summe of her answere was, that seing
the commissiouners for the other partie had givin in an eeke or additioun to their former answere, it cannot weill stand with her honour, or their mastresse's, that the mater should be now takin up or
appointed, and that she sould travell to come to her presence, till
it be knowne how they will prove, and what they have for them
to verifie their answere and additioun ; that she sould send for them
and enquire, and therafter she would give them an answere.   They
urged that their soverane might be present before her Majestie, before they were farther heard, affirming, that they would neither
accept nor give answere to whatsoever they would alledge, for im-
probatioun in that behalfe, whill her Highnesse' self were admitted
first to her Majestie's presence, becaus they had speciall commandement to that effect.   The Queene of England replyed, she would
not urge them to answere by their commissioun ; yitt she would
heare the other partie, how they could prove what they had alledged, both for her owne satisfactioun and for their mastresse's
weill.   The commissioners for our queene still urged that their
mastresse might be heard, protesting, whatsoever was done therafter before her Highness' commissioners, sould not prejudge their
soveran in anie sort.

  Upon the 6th of December, they went to the commissioners at
Westminster, signefeing to them, that according to the articles, instructiouns, and commandement givin by their soverane Ladie, they
had presented a petitioun to the queen's Highnesse.   But seing
they could not obteane a direct answere, but her Majestie declared

she would receave probatioun upon the eeke givin in by the other partie, and consider the same, before their soverane sould be heard, they still required all conference sould be stayed till she were heard; and that her rebellious subjects sould not be heard to give in anie pretended probatioun, for proving of their additioun, till their soverane were present and heard : protesting, that incace their lordships proceed, whatsoever hath, or sall be done heerafter, sall not prejudge their mastresse' honour, persoun, crowne, nor estate; and that for their owne part, they dissolve and discharge this present conference, having speciall command thereto, by their soverane, in case forsaid.   The English commissioners answered, they could not receave suche a declaratioun, becaus it conteaned some words different from the queen's Majestie's answere to their supplicatioun.   Upon Tuesday, the 9th of December, the Bishop of Rosse and Lord Boyd past to Westminster, and presented before the commissioners another writting, bearing the supplicatioun, petitioun, protestatioun, dissolutioun, and discharge of the conference, in the same forme, word by word, except there is left out in this last writting the words following :—" And that her Majestie declareth she would receave their probatioun upon their said eeke, and consider the same, before our soverane sould be sent for to be heard."   Upon Thursday, the 16th of December, the commissioners for the Queene of Scots, being desired by the Queene of England to come frome London to Hampton Court, to receave a direct and resolute answere to their supplicatioun, because the former was dilatorie, went to Hampton Court.   The Queene, in presence of her counsell, pronounced this answere as followeth :—

THE TENOR OF THE QUEEN'S MAJESTIE'S SUPPLICATION.

Apud Hampton Court, 16 *Decembris,* 1568.

The summe of her Majestie's answere to the Bishop of Rosse, the Lord Boyd, Lord Hereis, and the Abbot of Kilwinning, in the presence of the Lord Keeper of the Great Seale, the Duke of Norfolke, the Marquesse of Northampton, the Erles of Sussex, Bed-

ford, and Leicester, the Lord Clyntoun, Lord Admirall, and Lord
Hawart, Lord Chamberlane, Sir William Cicill, Knight, Principall
Secretare, Sir Rawfe Sadler, Knight, Chanceller of the Dutchie of
Lancaster, and Sir Walter Myldmey, Knight, Chanceller of the
Exchecker, was, that where the requeist latelie exhibited to her
Majestie consisted upon two points, the one, that the queene, their
mastresse, might come to the presence of her Majestie, and there
make answere to the maters wherewith she was charged ; the
other, if that were not admitted, that they might be permitted
to forbeare from anie farther conference heerin, her Majestie had at
the same time answered, (as they weill know,) that she thought it
more meete to have the said queen's subjects reproved for their
audacious maner of accusatioun of the queene, their soverane, the
samine being but generallie in words, than (as though the same were
to have beene credited) to have had her come up to answere in persoun. According to which answere, then so givin, her Majestie
told them that she had caused the lords, her commissioners, furth-
with to call the Erle of Murrey and his companie before them, and
verie sharpelie to charge them for their so audacious proceedings,
as being disloyall and contrare to the duetie of true and good subjects, and not to be suffered to passe unpunished. Wherupon, the
said erle and his collegues being accordingly reproved, answered,
that none of them meant at anie time to have uttered anie thing in
reproofe of the queene ; but being directlie charged by their adversareis with suche great crimes, as they could not passe over without condemning themselves unjustlie : And, therefore, according
to a protestatioun which they had before that time to that effect
exhibited, and to avoide and quitt themselves of the same crime,
they were unwillinglie forced, for their owne just defence, to proceed as they have done ; and for maintenance therof, they had produced and shewed to the saids lords, her Majestie's commissioners,
suche maters as are verie great, and appearand presumptions and
arguments, to confirme the former commoun reports of the crimes
imputed to the said queene. Of which maters, her Majestie, by
the declaratioun of her commissioners, had also understanding, to

her great admiratioun, and no small greefe, never looking to have heard of suche kinde of maters, and so manie against her. And now, considering they were come againe to require a farther answere, her Majestie said they sould have a resolute answere, in this sort. Her Majestie would caus the same maters to be opened and discovered to her, if so that she would be content to agree to make direct answere thereto; for so her Majestie thought it necessarie, and also wished it to be sufficient, as might acquitt and discharge her. For the maner wherof, she said, she would propone to them three maner of wayes : The one was, for her to send some trustie and sufficient persoun, or moe, thereto authorized with her answeres. The other was, for herself to give her answere to suche noble men as her Majestie would (if she so liked) send to her. And the last was, To appoint and authorize, ather these her late commissioners, or anie other, to mak answere before her Majestie's commissioners. But as for her comming to her presence ; considering, at the first when she came into this realme, her Majestie could not find it then agreeable to her honour, she being then defamed onlie by commoun report both heere and abroad, in most parts of Christendome, much lesse could she now thinke it ather meete or honorable to her to come to her presence, considering the multitude of maters and presumptiouns now latelie produced against her, suche as gave her Majestie to thinke of. And, therefore, her Majestie required them to receave this her answere, and to make report, by sending the samine to her, or otherwise, as they would, all or some of them to carie the same to her; thinking it alwayes verie necessar for her to answere; for otherwise, whosoever sould advise her to forbeare making of answere, having so manie wayes to doe the same, onlie because she might not come to her Majestie's presence, howsoever they sould seeme and appeare to be good servants for her safetie, they sould rather be thought and judged (for some other respects) to betray her. And therewith her Majestie required them to consider weill, as her servants, of this that she said : for it cannot be weill takin in the world for a reasonable excuse, if she be innocent, (as her Majestie wisheth her to be found,) to suffer herself to be made culpable of suche crimes, onlie for laike of comming to her Majestie's presence, and in no wise to cleere her self to the world by anie maner of answere. Nather could she find, how the queene more readilie sould procure her owne condemnatioun, than to refuse to mak answere. And so, with manie moe suche like words and speeches, uttered at great lenth, not heere remembred, her Majestie's earnest meaning did appeare, that she would gladelie the said queene might acquitt her self by some reasonable answere: And so ended.

After this answere givin to their supplicatioun, the Bishop of Rosse, in name of the rest of the commissioners, his collegues, propouned certan artickles to the queen's Majestie. First, he urged, as before, that unlesse their soveran were permitted to have her Highnesse' presence, their commissioun and instructiouns would permitt them to deale no farther in this conference, but to dissolve the samine, in cace forsaid, lyke as they had done amplie before. Nixt, seing the proceedings are not conforme to their mastresse' meaning and expectatioun, so that, as it appeareth, their soverane sall not be restored hastilie to her owne estate, but also her true and faithfull subjects sall be oppressed by usurpers, with her owne pose, jewells, and strenths, it will please her Majestie not to be offended, if their soverane seeke the aide of other Christian princes. Thridlie, that these who so oft have beene remitted by their soveran for their so haynous crimes, can not be found able to be competent accusers; and that they doubt not, when her Majestie hath weill considered the whole mater, her Highnesse will not admitt suche an exemple prejudiciall to all princes. Fourthlie, if her Majestie thinketh she can not goodlie restore their mastresse, by her Highnesse' aide and support, to her owne estat and realme, that at least her Majestie will permitt her to passe in her owne countrie, for maintenance of her faithfull subjects, daylie oppressed in her absence by usurpers. Fyftlie, if her Majestie findeth not that good, to lett her passe to France where her dowrie lyeth, that she may live a honorable life, according to her estate. They craved an answere in writt, for discharge of their duetie, conforme to their commissioun; and that they may have her Highnesse' pasport to retire to their owne countrie, seing their mastresse' bussinesse taketh no effect. The queen

answered, that she could not thinke them trustie servants nor counsellers to her good sister, or carefull of her honour, that would labour with her to appoint with her subjects, seing they have accused
her of suche crimes.   As for the other heeds, she could not give answere till she were certified by their mastresse, whether she would
answere to suche things as were layed to her charge, by one of the
three wayes conteaned in her Majestie's answere : And, to that effect,
granted to them a passport to passe to Boltoun, to report her answere ; but would not be content that anie of them sould depart
unto Scotland.   The Lord Boyd and the Bishop of Rosse prepared
themselves to depart from Londoun ; but the Queen of England
sent to them, and desired Lord Hereis and the Bishop of Rosse to
returne to Hamptoun Court the 23d day of December.   They returned, and the Lord Boyd departed from London the 22d day,
with the queen's answere to his mastresse.   Upon the 23d day,
when they came to Hamptoun Court, the Duke of Norfolke, the
Marquesse of Northampton, the Erle of Leicester, Lord Hawart,
the Lord Chamberlane, and Mr Cicill, Secretarie, were appointed
by the queen's Majestie to conferre with them.   The duke's Grace
declared unto them, that the Erle of Murrey had meaned to the
queen's Majestie and counsell that it was come to his knowledge,
that it sould be murmured and bruited that he and his companie
sould be guiltie of the murther which they had layed to the queen's
charge, and understood the same to proceed of them and their collegues, and therefore enquired if anie of them would lay anie thing
to the charge of the other partie.   It was answered, that they had
receaved writtings and instructions this day from their mastresse,
dated at Boltoun, the 19th of December, wherin they had speciall
command to lay the same to their charge ; and, conforme thereto,
would accuse them in presence of the queen's Majestie and her
counsell, and would answere to their alledged calumneis.   Upon
the 25th of December, the Lord Hereis, the Bishop of Rosse, and
Abbot of Kilwinning, being admitted to the presence of the queen's
Majestie and her counsell, produced their mastresse her speciall
writtings and instructiouns sent unto them.

THE TENOUR OF THE WRITTING PRESENTED, BEARING THE AN-
SWERE TO THE EEKE OF THE QUEENE OF SCOTLAND'S REBELS
FOR THE MURTHER.

" Traist cousins and counsellers, we greete you weill.   Since the
copie yee sent unto us of the unlawfull and false accusatioun presented against us by some of our rebels, together with the declara-
tiouns and protestatiouns made by you theron, before the Queen of
England our good sister's commissioners, wherin yee have followed
our intentioun and charge which we sent you by our former de-
pesche.   And, therefore, incace that the presence of our good sister
were refused us, we wrote to you, to shew her first the wrongs done
to us ; and nixt, in publict, before the nobilitie, and ambassadors of
uncouth princes : praying you thereanent, to continue in accom-
plishing our said intentioun, which yee know; and referres to your
wisdoms and judgements to amplifie the instructions which yee
have of us.   But, to the effect our rebels may see that they have
not closed our mouths, yee may offer to eeke to your reply that
which the additioun deserveth made by the Erle of Murrey and his
complices, to the pretended excuse and cloke of their wicked actiouns, falset, and disloyaltie.   Providing that, if it by question
come to the prooffes, indices, appearances, or suspiciouns, although there be no competence betwixt tratours and their naturall
prince, the presence of our good sister be permitted to us, to declare the justice of our caus to her self and no other, not having
consented the assemblie and conventioun of commissioners to other
effect than to inform them of the veritie ; before our which good
sister, the saids rebells have gottin the credite to come, accuse, and
calumniat us.   Moreover, that there be sufficient leasure givin us
to answere and verifie their impostures and crimes which we have
to lay to their charge, with respects which sould be keeped anent
suche a queene as we are.   In this meane time, that our rebells be
not fortifeid, assisted, nor favoured against us, by anie of our good
sister's ministers.   Which are asked by us, becaus we will not that

1

our said good sister, nor no prince in the world, sall esteeme that
we thinke our reputatioun of so little value, to putt the same in the
hands of anie living creature, so farre as we may perceave.   And
albeit that we lippin our person, life, and hazard of our estate to
our good sister, we would be loath that she sould thinke that we
deserve not it that we hold deerest, which is our honour, and is deliberat to defend the samine our self, or, at the least, assist you
therin, not doubting of your integreteis toward us; and that yee
have mater eneugh to confound the imprudencie of our tratours, as
weill in this additioun as yee did in that which was past at Yorke.
And if our good sister grant you this reasonable requeist in writt,
wee thinke good, that having caused the commissioners know that
yee have understood our intentioun, on that which hath beene added
by the Erle of Murrey and his complices, wherof ye had no instructioun before, as of a thing so horrible, that nather yee nor we
thought it sould have fallin in the thoght of the saids rebells, and
that yee would not the samine sould ceasse, but answere; which
yee may dresse conforme to the points as after followeth :—

ANSWERE TO THE EEKE PRESENTED BY THE ERLE OF MURREY
AND HIS ADHERENTS.

" Forsameekle as the Erle of Murrey and his adherents, our rebellious subjects, have eeked unto their pretended excuses produced
by them, for colouring of their horrible crimes and offences committed against us, their soveran ladie and mastresse, in suche words :
—' That as the Erle of Bothwell hath beene principall executer of
the murther committed in the person of umquhile Henrie Stuart,
our husband, so we knew, concealed, devised, perswaded, and commanded the said murther.'   The answere which we thinke good
be givin them in our name theron is, that in all times, when the
Erle of Murrey and his complices have said, spokin, or writtin,
that we knew, concealed, devised, perswaded, or commanded the
said murther, they have falselie, tratorouslie, and mischantlie[1]

[1] Wickedly.

leed, imputing unto us maliciouslie the crime wherof they themselves are authors, inventers, doers, and some of them proper
executers. And where they alleged that we impeshed[1] and stopped
inquisitioun and due punishement to be made of the said murther,
it is another calumnie, to the which having sufficientlie answered
by the reply produced at Yorke, wherin they were stricken dumbe ;
and likewise in that which they rehearse of our mariage with the
Erle Bothwell, thinke not necessar theranent to make them farther answere, but to referre the said, (if they thinke good to consider,) that it was answered to them on both thir two points in the
said reply. And as to that where they alledge we sould have
beene occasioun to caus our sonne follow his father hastilie, they
cover themselves theranent with a wett seck. And that calumnie
sould suffice for proofe and inquisitioun of all the rest. For the
naturall love of the mother toward her barne confoundeth them ;
and the great thought that we ever had of our sonne sheweth how
shamefullie they are bold to sett furth, not onlie that which, conforme to the malice and impietie of their hearts, they judge in
others by their owne proper affectioun, but of that wherof in their
conscience they know the contrarie ; lyke as the words of Johne
Matlane, Pryor of Coldinghame, who being in France a littill before our imprisoning, boore witnesse in sindric things, how they
were deliberat to mak insurrectioun, and that he had letters of
their sure purpose ; eeking therto, that howbeit they had no just
occasioun to make the samine, yitt, at the least, there were three
appearand pretexts to draw the people to their side. The first,
that, making to understand, to deliver us frome the hands of the
Erle Bothwell, who ravished us : The secund, to revenge our
said husband's death : And the thrid, to preserve our sonne, whome
they knew we had putt surelie in the Erle of Marr's hands. All
the saids things, they said, were against the Erle Bothwell, and
for the weale, rest, and suretie of me and my sonne, as they made
the commoun people beleeve, by their publict proclamations. But
their actiouns sensyne have declared the contrarie, and Johne

---

[1] Impeded.

Matlane spake as weill-informed : for to the veritie, this was but fained and false semblance that they did, to gett the Erle Bothwell, so that they desired onlie to obteane our persoun and usurpe our authoritie, as was suffieientlie declared by the said reply. And howbeit they beleeve yitt to dissemble the pernicious and cruell will they have, als weill toward the barne as toward the mother, there is no man of judgement discovering the things bypast, but he may easilie perceave their hypocrisie; how they would fortifie themselves in our sonne's name till that their tyrannie were better established, even as they have done after our good bountie and traist we had in them. They would have slaine the mother, and the barne both, when he was in her wombe, and did him wrong ere he was borne. Which act sheweth manifestlie itself, by the crimes wherof they are culpable before God and man, and that they are falselie sett against our innocencie. Finallie, where they say, that the estats of our realme finding us unworthie to raigne, decerned our dimissioun of our crowne to our sonne, and establishing of the regiment of the realme in the persoun of the Erle of Murrey, it sall be answered therto, that the dimissioun which they caused mak was subscribed per force, wheron the said Erle of Murrey hath founded his regencie; and declareth sufficientlie they proceeded not therein by way of parliament, but by violence; and sall content themselves, that by the said reply it was shewin them their pretended Assemblie of the Estats is illegitime, against the lawes and statuts of the realme, and ancient observatioun therof, to which the greatest part of the nobilitie was against and opposite to the same. And heeron conclude, as yee did on your reply, requiring support frome the Queene of England, our good sister, conforme to the promise of freindship betwixt her and us; protesting to adde to this answere, as time, place, and need sall require.

" And so committeth you to the protectioun of God Almightie. Off Boltoun, the 19th of December, 1568.

" Your good maistresse,

(Subscribed) " MARIE, R."

(And writtin thus on the backe :)

" To our right trust Cousins, Counsellers, and Commissioners, the Bishop of Rosse, Lord Hereis, and Abbot of Kilwinning."

The eeke, together with the protestatioun made by the regent and his collegues, after they came frome Yorke, the answere to their eeke, and their recriminatioun, I have extracted out of the Bishop of Rosse his memorialls, that the reader thinke not that I have defrauded him of the informatioun of the other partie. Anie judicious reader may perceave a bold and bare recriminatioun without proofe or evidences. Now, I will sett doun summarilie what Buchanan reporteth :—

The regent being urged to declare the causes moving the nobilitie to take armes, to committ to prisoun and depose the queene, and to purge himself of calumneis, declared the whole maner; produced the depositiouns of suche as were executed for the murther of the king; the decreet and Act of Parliament, wherunto manie of his accusers and calumniators did subscrive; and the silver caskett which the queene gave to Bothwell, wherin were conteaned her missives to Bothwell, writtin in Frenche, with her owne hand, and some love sonnets in Frenche, some secreets concerning the king's slaughter, the rapt after the murther, and three contracts of mariage : one before the murther, writtin with her owne hand; the secund before the divorcement of Bothwell, writtin with Huntlie's hand; the thrid, a little before the mariage, which was not concealed in the meane time. Buchanan could not be ignorant of these proceedings ather at home or in feild, when he was with the regent. As he was ingenuous and upright, not givin to avarice or bribes, so did he never repent afterward of anie thing he had writtin, in his booke intituled The Detectioun, but insert afterward the substance of it in his Historic, which was printed when he was neere his death.

When these things were produced, and read before the English counsellers and commissioners, the whole mater was made so evident, that there remained no doubt. And, indeid, we can find nothing in the Bishop of Rosse his owne memorialls after this, but fretting and fooming, and suche frivolous defences and impertinent harangs, as can give no satisfactioun to anie reader of anie meane judgement. The Bishop of Rosse tooke upon him to answere, not as a commissioner, as he reporteth himself, but for his mastresse' honour, and informatioun of the Queene of England, in a letter presented to her Majestie. He alledged the presumptions alledged were not so vehement as the law doth require to convict anie privat persoun : that it could not be verifeid that the letters were writtin with her owne hand : that it was not likelie that her Majestie would hazard her estate or credite upon suche writts, or suche an abominable fact : that his mastresse affirmed that the letters were forged, and that sindrie could counterfoote her handwritt : that it is not unlikelie that these who had putt hand in their prince, imprisouned her persoun, would not spaire to counterfoot her hand-writt : that they could not be lawfull accusers nor witnesses, being first accused of great crimes, as imprissoning of their prince, and suche other deeds as they are culpable of. And if they would preasse to verifie their caus by comparisoun of letters, that the same is no wise sufficient, *cum de jure fallacissimum sit genus probandi, per conjurationem literarum :* that writtings which are writtin in forme of missive letters or epistles make no faith, speciallie where in the same no words depositive, or giving expresse commande, are conteaned, as in these may be seene ; and als that they are not subscrived by her, sealed, or signetted, no certane date of yeere, moneth, or day, sett doun.

Thir were the frivolous defences made for the letters which were produced, which anie man reading the preceeding historie may easilie confute. The depositiouns of suche as were executed for the murther, the complices in the conspiracie, the rapt after the murther, the three contracts of mariage, and other circumstances, were past over with silence. Our queene in the meane time stirred up her factioun at home by her letters, putting them in hope of her returne within short time ; for the matche betwixt her and the Duke of Norfolke made her confident. She desired them not to make anie scruple for the truce takin betwixt them and the other

partie, but to tak so manie castells and holds as they might, that
incace of warre they might be the more able to resist or overcome
their adversareis.   Argile came to Glasgow with fyfteene hundreth
men ; others beside repaired to him.   The Hammiltons desired
him to invade and spoile the barons and gentlemen of Lennox;
but his freinds disswaded him, in respect they had beene freindlie
to his hous for manie ages bygane. After few dayes, not resolving,
they dissolved without anie further effect.   Suche practises at
home bewray that they diffided the susteaning of their cause
a-field.   I will heere subjoyne a part of a letter writtin by a Lon-
donner to his freind, after the apprehensioun of the Duke of Norfolk, which followed not long after ; the which letter was printed.

A PART OF A LETTER WRITTIN BY ONE IN LONDOUN, TO HIS FREIND,
CONCERNING THE CREDIT OF THE LATE PUBLISHED DETECTIOUN
OF THE DOINGS OF THE LADIE MARIE OF SCOTLAND.

" The booke itself (meaning the discoverie of the murther of the
king, with the oratioun of evidence) is writtin in Latine, by a
learned man in Scotland, Mr George Buchanan; one privie to the
proceedings of the Lords of the King's Secreit Counsell there, weill
able to understand and disclose the truthe ; having easie accesse
also to all the records of that countrie that might helpe him.   Besides that the booke was writtin by him, not as of himself, or in his
owne name, but according to the instructiouns to him givin by
commoun conference of the Lords of the Privie Counsell of Scotland ; by him onlie for his learning penned, but by them the mater
ministered, the booke overseene and allowed, and exhibited by them
as mater that they have offered, and doe continue in offering, to
stand to, and justifie before our soverane Ladie, or her Highnesse'
commissioners in that behalfe appointed.   And what prooffe they
have made of it alreadie, when they were heere for that purpose,
and the said author of the said booke one among them, when both
parteis or their sufficient procurators were heere present, indifferentlie to be heard, and so were heard indeid, all good subjects may

easilie gather, by our said soverane Ladie's proceedings, since the said hearing of the caus; who, no doubt, would never have so stayed her requeist, but rather would have added enforcement, by ministring aide to the Ladie Marie of Scotland, for her restitutioun, (the president and honour of princes, and her Majestie's owne former exemple of sinceritie, used in defence of the Scotish queene herself in Scotland, against France, and her maintenance of the Frenche king's honour and libertie, against the hie attempts of some his Popish subjects considered:) nor would have lived in suche good amitie with the young King of Scotland, the regents, and the true lords, mainteaners of that side, if these haynous offences alledged in that part had not beene proveable; or, if the young kind had beene an usurper, or his regents and other lords of that factioun tratours, as they must have beene, if all be false that is objected against the said Ladie Marie. I recite not what subscriptiouns and assents have bene to confirme the booke, and the maters in it conteaned. Beside that, I doe you to witt, that one writtin copie therof in Latine was now upon his late apprehensioun found in one of the Duke of Norfolk's men's houses, and thither sent by his commandement, a little before his apprehensioun, to be secreetlie keeped there, with diverse others pamphlets and writtings. Which thing not onlie addeth credite to this booke, that it was not counterfoote, but also giveth shrewd suspicions that the duke could not so weill lyke the woman, being suche a woman, as for her person's sake to venture the overthrow of suche a floorishing state wherin he stood before; but that some other greater thing it might be, that he liked, the greedinesse wherof might temper his abhorring of so foule conditiouns, and of so great a danger to himself, to be sent after his predecessors. The Bishop of Rosse likewise doth both know that the duke had this booke, and can tell how the duke came by it. The other mater of the contracts, letters, songs, &c., have, among other, these proves. Livelie witnesses of great honour and credite can tell, that the verie casket there described was heere in England shewed, the letters and other monuments openned and exhibited, and so muche as is there said to have beene writtin or subscrived by the said Ladie Marie, the Erle Bothwell, or others, hath beene, by testimoneis and oaths of men of honour and credite in that countrie, testified and avowed in presence of persons of most honorable estat and authoritie, to have beene writtin and sub- scrived as is there alledged, and so delivered without rasure, diminu- tioun, addition, falsifeing, or alteration in anie point. And a num- ber there be in England of verie good and worshipfull calling, be- side the commissioners thereto appointed, that have seene the ori- ginalls themselves, of the same hands whose this booke doth say them to be. Which things have beene heard and understood by these who can tell, and these whose truthe in reporting is above all exceptioun."

THE CONTROVERSIE BETWIXT THE REGENT AND THE DUKE.

The Duke of Chattelerault living privatlie in France, attended upon with a man or two, was drawin to the Frenche court, and stirred up to mainteane a factioun against the regent, speciallie now when the regent was in England. Whill he is returning home through England, he is importuned by his freinds to solicite the queene to move the regent to resigne the regencie to him, seing that place was due to him, as neerest in blood and nixt in succes- sioun. The mater was debated before the counsell of England. But the queene, by her counsell, declared that he craved an unjust thing, and that he sould not looke for anie aide of her.

THE GENERALL ASSEMBLIE CONTINUED.

The Generall Assemblie sould have conveened at Edinburgh, the 25th of December; but, in respect of the stormie weather, and the bruite of the plague, verie few conveened. Therefore, they con- tinued the Assemblie till the 25th of Februar. Onlie a letter sent from William Erle of Glencarne was read, his zeale commended for putting the kirk in possessioun of the thrids of the Bishoprick of Glasgow, and a commissioun givin to the said erle and some others, to modifie, appoint, and sett prices upon the victuals of the thrids assigned to the sustentatioun of the ministrie in Cliddisdaill, Renfrow, Kyle, Carict, and Cuninghame, in suche sort that the labourers of the ground may find ease, and ministers be not defrauded of payment.

M.D.LXIX.

Howbeit the Queene of England thought our queene unworthie of anie aide, yitt, remembring her former prosperitie, and fearing that the exemple of depriving princes sould creepe farther, and being solisted by the Frenche ambassader, tempered her sentence with a neutrall answere, saying, she saw nothing for the present to be reprehended in the proceedings of the nobilitie of Scotland; but desired, that the regent might leave behind him some, to answere to suche crimes as he sall be charged with, seing that he may not stay himself, becaus the troubles at home doe require his presence. The Bishop of Rosse, in his memorialls, reporteth that the regent and the rest of his collegues, commissioners, came before the queen's Majestie's counsell of England, where Sir William Cicill, secretar, at the queen's Majestie's command, and her Highnesse' counsell, gave them suche answere in effect as followeth, upon the 10th of Januare :—

" Whereas, the Erle of Murrey and his adherents come in this realme at the desire of the queen's Majestie of England, to answere to suche things as the queene, their soveran, objected against them and their alledgances : for so muche as nothing hath beene deduced against them as yitt, that may impaire their honour or alledgances, and on the other part, there had nothing beene sufficientlie produced nor showne by them against the queen, their soverane, whereby the Queene of England sould conceave or tak anie evill opinioun against the queene, her good sister, for anie thing yitt seene and alledged by the Erle of Murrey, yitt, in respect of the unquiett estat and disorder of the realme of Scotland now in his ab-

sence, her Majestie thinketh meete not to restraine anie farther the
said erle and his adherents' libertie; but suffer him and them at
their pleasure to depart; relinquishing them in the same estate in
the which they were of before their comming within this realme,
till she heare farther of the Queen of Scotland's answeres to suche
things as have been alledged against her."

THE REGENT CLEERED OF CALUMNEIS.

But we proceed with Buchanan's relatioun, as more worthie of
credit. The regent perceaving that the queene did protract time,
onlie to the end that she might give her judgement according to the
event of things as she sall find her own advantage, was instant
that his adversareis, who had traduced him in secreit, both to some
counsellers and to the Frenche ambassader, might alledge in publict what they had to lay to his charge: for he was not so desirous
to returne home, as to be cleered of suche aspersiouns as his enemeis did cast upon him, howbeit otherwise he might hardlie stay,
both in respect of his owne privat and publict effaires. At lenth,
the queen's procurators were called, and desired to show if they
had anie reasoun to burthein the regent with the murther of the
king. They answered they had nothing to say, but would then
accuse when it pleased the queene their mastresse to command
them. He answered, he was ever readie to defend; but in the
meane time, if they knew anie thing, he desired it might be now
alledged, when he was present before suche an honorable companie,
than to mutter it in privat and secreet conventicles, when he sould
be absent. When they had refused a long time, and the counsellers beganne to be offended, they answered, they knew nothing of
themselves whereby it might be presumed that the regent nor anie
of his companie was guiltie of that murther. So the counsell brake
up, and no farther accusatioun of the regent was heard from that
time furth. The describer of the Chameleon sayeth, that by the
force of the reasouns, and cleerenesse of the deductioun of the whole
actioun of the caus, the regent was so persuasive, that by Lething-

ton's advertisement, our queene discharged her commissioners to
proceed anie farther, and differe it to a more commodious time.
For it was weill knowne that the Queene of England and her
counsell had allowed of the regent's proceedings; and that the ambassader of Spaine, astonished at the haynousnesse of the crime, refused to interceed for her, and the Frenche ambassader excused
himself, for that he was commanded by his maister.

THE REGENT'S PASPORT.

After that the regent had cleered his owne caus, he obteaned
libertie to returne. The Queene of England had promised to the
regent and the rest of the commissioners, his collegues, that the
duke sould not gett his pasport to returne before they had gottin
theirs. He was charged to stay still till they had takin leave, becaus he minded no other thing by preventing them, but to trouble
the countrie in their absence; for she was offended, that the truce
was not keeped during the conference.

THE QUEENE OF ENGLAND AND THE REGENT TRADUCED.

After that the regent had obteaned licence to returne, Queene
Marie's missives sent to Scotland were intercepted, and sent to the
regent. She compleaned to the heads of her factioun at home that
the Queene of England had dealt otherwise with her than she promised; that some of her courteours had diswaded her to send an
armie with her to Scotland. She willed them, notwithstanding,
not to shrinke, for she hoped to be assisted another way. She
willed them to make als great a stirre as they might, and hinder
the regent his returne by all meanes they could devise. In one
letter, she preassed to perswade them that the regent had entered
in factioun with the Queen of England; had offered to putt the
young king in her hands; to deliver to her the castells of Edinburgh and Stirline, and to receave English garrisons in them; and
to do their endeavoure to putt in her hands all the rest of the strenths

of the realme : that the regent sould be legitimated, and proclaimed successour, if the young king died without issue ; and that he sould hold the kingdom in fealtie and homage of the Queene of England. These calumneis were published by Archibald Erle of Argile, Justice-General and Lieutenant to Queene Marie, and aggredged,[1] to stirre up the subjects against the regent.

THE QUEENE OF ENGLAND CAIRFULL OF HER OWNE AND THE REGENT'S CREDIT.

The Queene of England, perceaving by the letters intercepted, that she was charged with breache of promise, and that Queene Marie bragged of assistance from others, was offended that her owne credite was impeached ; and woundered whence the aide sould come, wherin the Scotish queene was so confident; for the secreets of the conspiracie which soon after brake furth were not yitt seene. Whill the regent was upon his journey, returning home, Queene Elizabeth caused print the purgatioun following, both for her owne and the regent's credite.

THEIR PURGATION.

" The Queen's Majestie of this realme of England, understanding that there are published sindrie maters in the realme of Scotland, contrare to all truthe and meaning of the said queene, as it appeareth, maliciouslie devised to blemishe the honour and sinceritie 'of her Majestie, and to bring the Erle of Murrey in hatred with his owne freinds, being native good Scotish men, hath thought it good to let it be openlie notified to all persons, English and Scotish, that are disposed to heare the truthe, that howsoever it be said or writtin by anie persoun, of whatsoever estate the same be, that anie secreit practice had beene made betwixt her Majestie and the Erle of Murrey, whereby it sould be convented and accorded that the Queen of Scots' sonne sould be delivered into her Majestie's

---

[1] Aggravated.

hands, to be nourished in England, as she sould thinke good; and
that the castells of Edinburgh and Stirline sould be in English
men's keeping; and that the castell of Dumbartan sould be as-
seidged, takin, and randered to her Majestie's behoove; and that
the Erle of Murrey sould be declared ligitime, to succede to the
crowne of Scotland after the deceasse of the young prince or king
without barnes; and in that case, the Erle of Murrey sould declare
to hold the realme of Scotland in fea of her Majestie, as Queen of
England; her Majestie, as she is, and intendeth to be, during her
life, a prince of honour and maintainer of truthe, doth, in word of
a Queene, lett all persons know, that all thir aforesaids things
above specified are altogether false and untrue; and are devised
by persons of meere malice and rancour, being disposed to nourish
factiouns and discord, and hating the good quietnesse and concord
betwixt the two realmes. And this her Majestie likewise assureth
all persons, that, as of these untruthes and falsets there was never
conventioun nor accord betwixt her Majestie and the said erle, nor
betwixt him and anie her ministers, to her Majestie's knowledge,
so was there not at all anie conventioun or compact, by word or
writting, made betwixt her Majestie and the said erle, for anie
thing since his last comming into this realme; althogh it is truthe,
that some motiouns have beene made, as weill by the Erle of Lennox and the ladie his wife, being, as it is knowne, parents to the
late murthered father of the prince, as by others, that if heerafter
it sould be seene that the said prince could not safelie continue in
Scotland, from the attempts of the murtherers of his father, and
others his mortall enemeis, that there he might be nourished in
England, under the custodie of suche as now have the charge of
him, and are knowne to have most tender care of him. But heerof was there never more of conventioun nor accord; nather yitt
was there heard of her Majestie anie word of the Erle of Murrey,
or of anie of his companie, to allow of anie removing of the samine
prince out of Scotland, or out of the charge of them that now have his
custodie. And likewise, her Majestie assureth all maner of persons,
that she esteemeth all other reports false, that are said also to be

made, of anie league and intelligence betwixt the Erle of Murrey
and the Erle of Herfurde;[1] with other suche like improveable devices and slanders : all which her Majestie would have to be of all
honest persons, both English and Scotish, (that love truthe and hate
falset,) esteemed for false, and to be seditiouslie and malitiouslie
devised, invented, and published.   Finallie, this her Majestie willeth all persons to understand, that in this case, betwixt the Queene
of Scots and her sonne, there hath laiked no good meaning, nor yitt
doeth, to have had the same weill ended, for quietnesse to the whole
natioun of Scotland, or to the dignitie therof; the lett and impediment of which good end, her Majestie would all good persons to
understand not to have come of her or her counsell, as heerafter
sall more manifestlie appeare. . Givin at Hampton Court, the 22d
day of Januar, the elleventh yeere of her Majestie's raigne."

THE REGENT RETURNETH SAFE.

The Queen of England understanding, by letters intercepted,
and other reports, that the regent was in danger, for her owne credite sent to the Wardans, that when he came neere to the borders
and suspect places, they sould have a care to see him safelie convoyed.   The courteours offered him companie to convoy him ; but
courteouslie he refused, and entered in his journey about the middest
of Januar.   The Lord Hume being advertised that the rebellious
lords had waged two hundreth Liddisdail men, to ly in wait for the
regent betwixt Morpeth and Berwick, advertised the Lord Hounsdane, governour of Berwick, and sent post to the regent himself.
Wherupon he was convoyed to Berwick with a great companie, according to the queen's directioun.   But he was in greater danger of
Norfolk and the Popish factioun.   The describer of the Chameleon

---

[1] Among the reports sent down to be propagated in Scotland was the following :
That the Earl of Hertford and Murray had entered into a mutual agreement to
maintain each other's claims, the former to the crown of England, and the latter to
that of Scotland; and that Cecil, whose daughter Hertford had agreed to marry,
was the contriver of the plot.

reporteth, that the Erle of Westmerland, ryding through the regent's companie, not farre frome Durhame, thoght it not safe to matche with them. The regent came to Scotland the secund day of Februare. The fourth day after, the pest stayed, which in his absence had takin away, in Edinburgh and the Cannogate, two thowsand five hundreth and fiftie persons.[1]

A CONVENTION.

Upon the 10th of Februare there was a conventioun holdin at Stirline. The regent made a relatioun of all their proceedings in England, which were allowed.

PREPARATION FOR CIVILL WARRES.

James Hammiltoun, Duke of Chattelerault, came to Scotland the 17th day of Februarie. His freinds assembled unto him incontinent. Our queene constituted him her deputie. He charged, by publict proclamatioun, that none sould be obeyed but he, and suche as sould be substituted by him. Upon the 21st of Februar the regent commanded, by proclamatioun at the Croce of Edinburgh, the king's lieges to repaire to Glasgow, the 10th of Marche. The lords collected a summe of money, for waging of souldiours, and prepared themselves for the hardest conflict.

THE EIGHTEENTH GENERALL ASSEMBLIE.

The Generall Assemblie was holdin at Edinburgh, the 25th of Februar. Mr David Lindsay was chosin Moderator.

---

[1] The scarcity and dearness of provisions, with which this visitation was accompanied, must have fearfully aggravated the miseries of disease, as the following extract from the Diurnal will show :—" In all this yeer preceiding, the pest being in Edinburgh and Leith, and Cannongate, thair was ane verie greit darth in this realme, sua that the boll of eit meill wes sauld for iij. pundis xij. shillings, the boll of quheit for iiij. pundis x. shillings, and the boll of beir for iij. pundis."

SUPERINTENDENTS TRIED.

Mr Johne Spotswod, Superintendent of Lothiane, was delated for slacknesse in visitatiouns, &c. He alledged none-payment of his stipend for three yeeres bypast; and that diverse times he had exhibited to the Justice-Clerk the names of haynous offenders, but could find no executioun.

A MINISTER CENSURED.

Mr Andrew Blakhall, Minister at Ormeston, was ordeaned to compeere before the church sessioun of Edinburgh, to confesse his offence, for solemnizing mariage betwixt two parteis of their congregatioun without testimoniall of proclaiming their bannes; and to promise not to committ the like offence again.

AN ACT.

Concerning proceeding by degrees in schooles to the degree of a Doctor of Divinitie, it was ordeaned, that the brethrein of the colledges of Sanct Andrewes conveene, and forme suche order as they sall thinke meit; and that they present the same to the nixt Assemblie, to be revised and considered, that the Assemblie may eeke or diminish as they thinke good; and that the order allowed may therafter be established.

A COMMISSION TO PROCEED AGAINST HUNTLIE.

Commissioun and power was givin to the Superintendent of Angus, Mr George Hay, Minister at Ruthven, Mr Robert Pont, Commissioner of the kirks in Murrey, and Adam Heriot, Minister at Aberdeene, to require the Erle of Huntlie to restore the collectors of the kirk to their places; and if he refuse, to summoun him to compeere before them, or anie two of them, where and when they sall thinke meit, to answere tuiching the premisses; with certificatioun if he compeere not, nor yitt restore the said collectors to their owne places, due admonitiouns preceiding, that they sall proceed to the sentence of excommunicatioun.

THE DUKE'S LETTER.

In the fourth sessioun a letter was read, which was sent frome the Duke of Chattelerault, the tenor wherof followeth :—

"Brether, we thought it expedient to certifie you, that being in France, and hearing of the great troubles in this our native countrie, of conscience and duetie were compelled to come home, desirous to pacifie the same at our power, first, to the glorie of Almightie God, and nixt, to the releefe of the right sore and lamentablie oppressed true subjects, whose innocent blood, and innumerable heirshippes, oppressiouns, wrongs, stouthe, which have beene and are daylie committed upon them, are to us so greevous and intolerable a burthein, both in conscience and honour, that we rather refuse not onlie this our native realme, but also the whole world, ere it were not reformed. And albeit, in my absence, I have susteaned wrong, I assure you myne owne particular, nather in blood, lands, or geere, is so heavie to me, as the great danger this whole kingdome standeth in, if by the grace of Almightie God, and helpe of the old and native Scotish blood, it be not foreseen and releeved in time. Hearing of your conventioun, brethrein, at this time, I have sent this bearer to you, to declare this to be our full and determined minde, to follow by the grace of God, First, That the Word of God may have free passage through this whole realme ; and that the sacraments may be ministred according to the institutioun of Christ Jesus his Sonne, our Saviour: Nixt, That everie true subject of this realme may live without feare upon that which justlie is his owne, according to God's calling and commandement. In this caus of this present diversitie betwixt our native soverane and a part of her subjects, for which we are heartilie sorie; as Almightie God knoweth, we are innocent of foreknowledge of anie doing, so we wishe all others to be suche like. Our desire is, that

all hostilitie and troubles might be pacifeid, according to the
command of Almightie God; and that the whole estats in quiett
and peaceable manner may conveene; and, first calling for his
grace, and Holie Spirit of righteous judgment, might consider the
ground and beginning of this altogether evil deid,—I meane the
slaughter of the queene's late husband; what hath proceeded therupon sensyne, and what God would of reasoun sould be done therefore.   And this to be devised, ather by the whole estats, or twentie-
five of the wisest of the nobilitie, chosin by the whole people of the
realme, wherunto we of the nobilitie, and all that continue under
our obedience to the queene, our soverane, sall, for God's caus and
the commoun weale, be found agreeable.   To avoide wrangous
judgement, that we write this to you because of proclamations
that the Erle of Murrey hath caused to make in diverse shires of
this realme, to have the people at Glasgow the 10th day of Marche,
we would yee sould consider we doe it not for that caus.   For
first, as yee know, that before and since thir troubles beganne, we
have never beene in this countrie before the 25th day of this instant
of Februar, wherethrough we might have shewed our minde heerin, and all the people of Scotland were gathered together, both for
nativenesse of blood, for good deservings of my forbeares and my
self, there is the strenth of the world, where I could wishe myself,
and finde me most sure.   And if the said Erle of Murrey would tak
upon him to invade me, or anie of my freinds or dependers, or
anie true men in this realme, as I cannot thinke he will, then
trust I that the nobilitie or people will not assist him therto whill
first they find a caus worthie, and it be declared by the ancient
lawes of the realme.   And though we desire thir conventiouns and
forces of menne of warre to be turned against theeves and oppressours of the realme, wherunto we sall be most readie with our
bodeis and geir, to the devoire of noble and true men, yitt, if he
will persevere to persue us, we doubt not in God and the justnesse
of our caus, to find all noble and true men so favourable to us that
it sall not be in his power to doe us wrong, upon particular malice,
altogether without deserving.   Therefore, we require you in God's

behalfe to make some of our effaires and minde patent to the people; and if yee find out on our part, sought heere and offered, that which to our Christian professioun perteaneth, duetie requireth that yee come and reasoun upon the same with us, where yee sall find us reasonable in all causes, according to God's Word and equitie; to whose divine protectioun we committ you.

" Your Christian brother,

" JAMES HAMMILTOUN.

" From Hammiltoun, the 27th of Februar, 1569."

A COMMISSION TO DEALE WITH THE DUKE, ETC.

In this letter we may see a faire professioun and goodlie pretences; but in the meane time, the secreit drift was, to move the ministers to dehort the people frome repairing to Glasgow, as they were commanded by proclamatioun. The Assemblie giveth commissioun to the Superintendents of Lothiane and Fife, and Mr Johne Row, to goe to the regent, and to learne what is his Grace's pleasure tuiching this letter. And, according as his Grace sall direct, to goe to the duke, and conferre with him, and suche of the nobilitie as they sall find present; and by all meane possible to reconcile them to the regent, and to bring them to the acknowledgement of the king, and his regent's authoritie; and to doe farther as the said commissioun sall proport.

In the sixt sessioun it was ordeaned, that the letter directed to the lords who had made defectioun frome the king's Majestie, after it be returned frome the regent's Grace, sall be registered among the Acts of the Assemblie, and that it be printed. I find not this letter in the copie of the register: but I take it to be the letter following, which the Superintendent of Lothiane sent to the noblemen and barons within his bounds; and that the letter was penned by Mr Knox, as appeareth by the stile, howbeit it was directed by particular Superintendents, commissioners, and ministers.

" Mr Johne Spotswod, Superintendent of Lothiane, To
all that professe, or have professed the Lord Jesus, and have
refused the Roman Antichrist, called the Pope, within the
diocese committed to his charge, desireth grace, mercie, and
peace, frome God, the Father of our Lord Jesus Christ ; together with the Spirit of righteous judgement.

"That fearefull sentence pronounced by God himself unto his
prophet Ezechiel, against the watchman that seeth the sword
coming, and doth not blow the trumpet, and plainlie warne the
people, (Ez. xxxiii.) compelleth me to write unto you, beloved in
the Lord, this my rude letter, becaus that my corporall presence
and weake voice cannot be extended to you all, in these dangerous and most wicked dayes. To you, I say, I am compelled to
crie by my penne, that the sword of God's just judgement is come,
and hath devoured some, according to the forewarning of his messingers ; and, alas ! I feare is yitt drawin, and readie to devoure
moe. The first part of this cannot be denied, and the secund also
hath great probabilitie ; and yitt, I feare that everie man seeth not,
or at least will not confesse the verie caus, nather of the one, nor
yitt of the other. We see a wicked woman, whose iniquitie knowne,
and lawfullie convicted, deserved moe than ten deaths, escaped
frome prison. This is the First. Negligence of the keepers, as it
is not to be excused, so may it weill occupie the Secund place
before man. Practises of deceatefull men, together with her owne
villanie, justlie may occupie the Thrid rank in that wicked fact.
But none of all thir sould have had place to worke, if the mouth of
the Lord had beene obeyed. For if she had suffered, according as
God's law commandeth murderers and adulterers to dee the death,
the wickednesse takin furth frome Israel, the plague sould have
ceassed ; which cannot but remaine, so long as that innocent blood
tratorouslie shed is not punished, according as God hath commanded. And so I feare not to affirme, that the reservatioun of that
wicked woman, against God, and against the voices of his servants,

2

is the first and principall caus externall, which man can see, of the
plague and murther latelie begunne.

And yitt, when I confesse it to be the *first* externall caus, I meane
not that it is the onlie and sole caus of this present and appearing
calamitie. For, albeit that the devill himself had beene loosed (as
no doubt he was) in the person of that most wicked woman, yitt
could not he nor she greatlie have troubled this commoun-wealth,
unlesse that she had beene assisted with the presence, counsell, and
force of suche as have professed the Lord Jesus, and, by all appearance, had renounced that Roman Antichrist and his damnable
superstitioun. For, albeit that all the Papists within the realme of
Scotland had joyned with her, the danger had not beene great.
For, although in number the wicked might have exceeded the faithfull, yitt, when the servants of God sould have had battell onlie
against the Canaanites, Jebusites, Amorites, and against the rest
of that profane and adulterous generatioun, they could no more
have feared now, than that the little flocke hath feared from the
beginning of this controversie, which now, by God's power, thir
nine yeeres they have susteaned against all the pestilent Papists
within the same. But, alas! the sword of dolour hath pearced, and
yitt pearceth manie hearts, to see brethrein seeke with all crueltie
the blood of their brethrein; yea, to see the hands of suche as were
esteemed the principall within the flocke to arme themselves
against God, against his Sonne Christ Jesus, against a just and
most lawfull authoritie, and against the men who looked of them
not onlie quietnesse and peace, but also maintenance and defence
against all invasioun domesticall and forraine. The consideratioun
of this their most treasonable defectioun from God, from his truthe
professed, and frome the authoritie most lawfullie established, causeth the hearts of manie godlie to sob and mourne, not onlie secreitlie, but also openlie to crave of God the conversioun and repentance of suche as have assisted that most wicked woman, who
ambitiouslie, cruellie, and most unjustlie hath aspired, and yitt as-
pireth to that regiment, wherefra, for impieteis committed, most
justlie, and by suche order as no law can reprove, she was deposed.

And, therefore, in the bowells of Christ Jesus, I exhort all in generall, and suche as are under my charge in speciall, who have communicated with her odious impieteis, that they deepelie consider their fearefull defectioun from God, and from his lawfull magistrats, by his Word and good order erected within this realme; and that they, by condemnatioun and publict confessioun of their follie, travell speedilie to returne again to the bosome of the kirk, and to the obedience due unto the magistrats, from which they have most tratorouslie declyned; assuring suche as sall be deprehended to remaine obstinat into their former wicked interprise, that in our nixt letters their names sall be expressed and proclamed before all congregations. Wherewith, if they be not moved to repentance, then will we (albeit with greefe of heart) be compelled to draw the sword committed to us by God, and to cut them off from all societie of the bodie of Jesus Christ; and, for their stubburne rebellioun, give them to the power of Satan, to the destructioun of the flesh, that they, (confounded in themselves,) by unfained repentance, may returne again from their wicked wayes, and so escape condemnatioun in the day of the Lord Jesus: whose Omnipotent Spirit move the hearts of all that looke for the life everlasting to consider that his comming approacheth. Amen. Givin at Calder."

PETITIONS.

In the fyft sessioun certane heeds were formed, which were to be presented to the regent's Grace and counsell, and commissioners appointed to present the same, and crave answere: the tenour of which heeds followeth:

First, That suche as have benefices, and doe nothing but pay their thrid, may be compelled to beare farther burthein with the kirk, and for support of the poore. For it seemeth altogether unreasonable that idle belleis sall devoure and consume the patrimonie of the kirk, whill the faithfull travellers in the Lord's vineyarde suffer extreme povertie, and the needie members of Christ's bodie are altogether neglected.

That suche as have manie benefices may be compelled to dimitt all except one.

That order may be takin that the collectors be obeyed, who now are universallie disobeyed, as weill by Protestants as Papists.

That remedie may be provided against the oppression of the Erle of Huntlie and others, who have removed the collectors of the kirk, and tyrannouslie placed their owne.

That it may please his Grace and the Secreit Counsell, that the kirk, from admonitiouns may proceed to farther censures against the said erle, and all others guiltie of the like oppressioun may be publictlie denounced excommunicat, in cace of his or their contempt.

That the Assemblie, without offence of his Grace, may appoint their brother, Mr Robert Pont, minister, where his labours may be more fruictfull than they can be for this present, in Murrey.

That remedie may be provided against the chopping and changing of benefices, selling of the same, diminishing of the rentals, setting of long tacks in defraud of ministers, both for the time present and for the time to come; against the which, except substantiall remedie be provided, not onlie sall the kirk suffer domage, but also that portioun which might support the commoun effaires of the realme sall be craftilie sold.

That order may be takin with suche as are alreadie excommunicated, and doe contemne the censures, may be punished.

That order may be takin that suche odious crimes as this day provoke God's displeasure against the whole land may be punished, as God hath commanded. If his Grace send us to the justice-clerk, experience hath taught us sufficientlie what he hath done heeretofore in suche maters.

That the jurisdictioun of the kirk may once be separated frome that which is civill.

That the questioun of adulterie may be once decided, at least in that heed, whether the adulterer sall be admitted to the benefite of mariage, or not.

THE ORDER OF THE PUBLICT FAST.

In this sessioun also it was concluded that a generall fast sould be proclamed through all the countrie, and beginne in Lothiane, Fife, and suche other places as may receave advertisement, the 13th of Marche. That the exercise accustomed at the first fast be used; and that superintendents and commissioners of provinces appoint the same order to be used als oft as occasioun requireth, without anie farther appointment of the Generall Assemblie.

THE DUKE TRANSACTETH WITH THE REGENT.

Upon Moonday the 9th of Marche, the regent, accompanied with Morton, Hume, and other noblemen, went out of Edinburgh to Stirline. Frome thence they went to Glasgow. They tooke with them five peece of ordinance. The Hammiltons, for all their brags, could not make their partie good. By the travells of Lethington, and some others that favoured them, it was granted that the duke sould come in safetie to Glasgow, providing he would acknowledge the king's authoritie. He, the Erle of Cassils, and Lord Hereis, came to Glasgow; promised to ratifie and acknowledge the king's authoritie; that they and their freinds sould come to the convention which was to be holdin at Edinburgh in Aprile, and to reasoun upon all controverseis, the king and regent's authoritie ever excepted. The like offer was made to others of their factioun. Argile and Huntlie were offended with the duke for transacting with the regent without their consent; for letters were sent frequentlie from the queen, to encurage them with hope of farther aide. The rumor of the matche betwixt her and Norfolk was now farther spread.   ·

THE DUKE WAIRDED.

At the conventioun appointed the 14th day of Aprile, were present the regent, the Erles of Morton, Marr, Cassils; the Duke,

Lords Hereis, Hume, Lindsey, Ruthven, Methven, Graham, Oliphant, with manie other lords, beside barons and gentlemen. The duke differred the performance of his promises; desired a delay till the 10th of May, that the rest of the nobilitie who were of his minde might be present, that the agreement may be made with all their consents, and untill he had tried the queen's minde. It was answered, that Huntlie and Argile were expected in vaine, for they would see to their owne estat a part by themselves. It was demanded, what he would doe incace the queene would not approve their transactioun. He confessed that he had not made suche promises but for feare of the armie lying at Glasgow, neere to his hous. Seing that nather he had givin pledges to performe the appointment, as was compromitted, nor would presentlie performe anie part, he was committed to waird in the castell of Edinburgh, upon Moonday the 18th of Aprile, and the Lord Hereis likewise, for the like reasons. The Bishop of Sanct Andrewes was commanded to keep his loodging; but upon his owne promise was sett at libertie. The Erle of Cassils by oath and subscriptioun approved the king's authoritie.

ARGILE AND HUNTLIE SUMMONED.—HUNTLIE COMPEERETH NOT.

Huntlie and Argile had troubled the countrie in the regent's absence; for Huntlie spoiled Mernes and Angus, and bare himself like a king in the north. He appointed Crawfurd and Ogilvie lieutenants on this side of Dee. What Argile did we have mentiouned before. They are charged to come to Sanct Andrewes the tenth of May. Argile came, and becaus he had done no great harme, onlie his oath was takin to be obedient to the king without anie fraud or deceate, otherwise to be compted infamous. Huntlie compeered not. Lethington and others, favouring the other factioun, alledged, impunitie was the surest way for concord and peace; that it was hard to overthrow him; yea, he might flee to the Hïelands, and lurke for a time, or to some forraine king, and purchase his aide, if he were overthrowne. It was answered, his father was overthrowne with little adoe. The Hieland people might easilie be induced to betray him for a peece of money. Forraine kings had work aneugh at home. It was no clemencie nor great policie to suffer good subjects, obedient to the king's authoritie, to be oppressed, the oppresser spaired, and others emboldenned to doe the like. That howbeit the regent would pardoun the contempt of the king's authoritie and his persoun, yitt the domage which good subjects had receaved cannot be remitted. When a generall remissioun to Huntlie, and all his freinds and followers, could not be obteaned, it was agreed in end that Huntlie sall tak order for himself, his domesticks, and feals, for satisfactioun of suche as had received wrong, and that the rest of his followers deale for themselves. This was thought by the regent and his partie the fittest way to dissolve factiouns.

THE REGENT'S ROAD IN THE NORTH.

The regent went to the north the secund or thrid of June, accompanied with the Erle of Morton and other freinds, and two companeis of harquebusiers. All that were guiltie of oppressioun in his absence were summouned to Aberdeen, Elgin, and Innernesse; fynned, and forced to satisfie compleaners. Huntlie and the cheefe of the clans delivered pledges.

LETHINGTON'S SECREIT PRACTISES FOR THE QUEEN.

Whill the regent was in the north, Lethington was bussie among the noble men, to procure their defence against the Erle of Morton, with whom, as he alledged, he was at variance. But it was bruited, not without caus, that he was dealing for the queen's restitutioun, and for subscriptions to a band tending to that effect. At this time he drew the Laird of Grange, Captan of the Castell of Edinburgh, to the queen's factioun. The queen herself had writtin to sindrie of her favourers to meete her at an appointed time and place, to bring her home. It was reported that the Duke

of Norfolk was to marie the queen, and to bring with him five thowsand men.

THE ANSWERE TO QUEEN ELIZABETH AND QUEEN MAREIS LETTERS.

When the regent was at Elgine, Robert Lord Boyd brought to
him letters from the queene and court of England. He was advertised by freinds from court that the Duke of Norfolk's conspiracie was so cunninglie convoyed, that by all appearance it could :
not be disappointed. Heerupon a conventioun was appointed to
to be holdin at Perth. The regent returneth to Perth the 25th
day of Julie. At this conventioun were read the letters of both
the queens. The Queen of England craved three things in behalfe of the Queen of Scots : That ather she might be whollie restored to her owne place ; or suffered to rule joyntlie with her
sonne, and to injoy the title of queene, in publict acts and patents,
and in the meane time that the regent reteane the governement till
the young king were full seventeene yeeres of age ; or elles, that
she might be permitted to live privatlie at home, and maintenance
may be assigned unto her. The last heed was granted, providing
she would be content to accept of it. The rest were obstinatlie
denyed by the sounder part of the nobilitie, becaus not onlie the
young king's authoritie, but also his life, sould so be endangered.
Queene Marie, in her letters, craved judges to be appointed, to
cognosce upon her mariage with Bothwell, and to decerne her
free, if it cannot be justified by law. Some were offended that she
stiled herself Queen, and in a manner commanded them as subjects ;
some would not have her deigned with an answere. So manie as
favoured her seemed to wonder that they would refuse that which
they sought of her before. As for anie stile in her letter, they offered to procure a new procuration from her, conceaved in suche
termes as sould content them. It was answered, there was no
haste : it behoved Bothwell to have sixtie dayes after citatioun for
compeering, becaus he was out of the countrie. Within that space
she had leasure to send a new commissioun ; seing she had past

over two yeeres alreadie with silence, she might suffer delay that long.   If she minded in earnest to be ridde of Bothwell, she might write to the King of Denmark, and requeist to putt him to death for the murther of her first husband, and then she might marie whom she pleased : otherwise it was her purpose to live in a doubt-full mariage with some other, fast or loose, as pleased her.   It was the more suspicious, that she would have the sentence pro-nounced by suche judges, to whose sentence she needed not to stand, being banished, but if she pleased.   The English queen was to be forewarned, who might ather further or hinder the mater. Some secreit fraud seemed to lurke in this her sute ; therefore it was not expedient to be hastie or rash, for manie secreit purposes might come to light in processe of time.   Lethington and the rest of her favourers opposed mightilie, and raged, but prevailed not. Alexander Hume of Northberuick was sent to England with the answere.

WILLIAM STEWART BURNT.

William Stewart, Lyon Herald, was apprehended in Dumbar-tane, for conspiring the regent's death.   He was convicted by an assise of witchecraft, and burnt.

THE NINETEEN GENERALL ASSEMBLY.

The Generall Assembly was holdin at Edinburgh, in the neather counsell-hous, the fyft of Julie.   Mr William Christesone, mini-ster at Dundie, was chosin Moderator.

TRIELL OF SUPERINTENDENTS AND COMMISSIONERS.

In the triell of superintendents, the Superintendents of Lothian and Fife were delated for slacknesse in visitatioun, and reparatioun of the fabrick of kirks.   Mr Johne Kerswell, Superintendent of Argile, was rebooked for accepting the Bishoprick of the Iles, not making the Assemblie forseene; and for ryding at, and assisting of parliament holdin by the queen, after the murther of the king. Mr Alexander Gordoun, some time commissioner of Galloway, was ordeaned to come to the nixt Assemblie; and in the meane time, exhibited to exerce anie functioun in the kirk, conforme to the Act made against him, in the Generall Assemblie holdin in Julie, 1568, in which he was discharged to exerce the office of a commissioner in that countrie, or to tak up the thrids which he had for that office, incace he compeered not before the last sessioun of the said Assemblie.

ACTS.

It was ordeaned, that suche as come to the Assemblie repaire in due time; otherwise, to proceed against them. 2. That persons guiltie of capitall crimes, summouned by superintendents and elders of reformed kirks, to compeere before this or anie other Assemblie heerafter; if they compeere not, that the superintendents or ministers proceed to excommunication against them, and to notifie to the supreme magistrat, who are alreadie excommunicated for their offences, that farther punishment may be inflicted.

THE PRINCIPALL AND REGENTS OF ABERDEEN DEPOSED FOR POPRIE.

The decreet and sentence pronounced by the lord regent's Grace and his counsell, the last of June, and by the Superintendents of Angus and Mernes, the 3d of Julie, against Mr Alexander Andersone, Principall of Aberdeene, and some of the regents, was allowed. The regent, when he was in the north, caused call them before the counsell, and required of them subscriptioun to the articles following :—

"We, whose names are underwrittin, doe ratifie and approve from our verie hearts the Confessioun of Faith, together with all other acts concerning our religioun, givin furth in the parliaments holdin

at Edinburgh, the 24th day of August, 1560, and the 15th day of
December, 1567 ; and joyne our selves as members to the true kirk
of Christ, whose visible face is descrived in the said acts ; and sall,
in time comming, be participant of the sacraments now most faithfullie and publictlie ministred in the said kirk, and submitt us to the
jurisdictioun and discipline therof."

They compeered, but refused. Therefore, the lord regent's Grace,
with advice of the lords, decerne and declare, that the said persons
are and sall be deprived, and presentlie are deprived, *ipso facto*,
of all instructioun of the youth within the realme, and of all honours, digniteis, functions, pre-eminenceis, faculteis, and priviledges
within the said colledge ; and ordeane letters to be directed, charging them to remove, desist, and ceasse therefra. Conforme to the
decreit of the counsell, was the other sentence pronounced in presence of Mr Alexander Andersone, principall, and Mr Andrew Andersone, regent, the rest not compeering, as followeth :—

" I, Johne Areskine, Superintendent of Angus and Mernes,
having commissioun of the kirk to visite the shirefdom of Aberdeen and Bamff, by the advice, counsell, and consent of the ministers, elders, and commissioners of kirks present, decerne, conclude,
and for finall sentence pronounce Mr Alexander Andersone, some
time principall, Mr Andrew Galloway, sometime sub-principall,
Maisters Andrew Andersone, Thomas Owsten, and Duncan Norie,
sometime regents in the colledge of Old Aberdeen, are not to be
reputed as members of this kirk : And therefore seclude them,
and everie one of them, from using anie office or jurisdictioun in
the colledge of Old Aberdeen ; and inhibite them, and everie one
of them, to teache publictlie or privatlie in time comming in that
colledge, or anie other part within this realme ; and ordeane them
to remove furth of the said colledge with all diligence, that other
godlie and weill qualified persons may be placed therin, for up-bring-
ing of the youth in the feare of God, and good letters. This our
sentence pronounced, we ordeane to be published and intimated to
the saids persons, and to the congregations of New and Old Aberdeen, publictlie, the nixt Soonday, the 3d of Julie nixt, 1569."

Commissioun was givin to the Superintendent of Lothian, Mr Knox, Mr Johne Craig, and Mr David Lindsey, to revise the acts of the Generall Assembleis; and note the acts which concerne the commoun effaires of superintendents and ministers, and caus the samine to be printed ; and also the forme of excommunicatioun, with the inauguration of superintendents and ministers.   Commissioun was givin to the Superintendents of Angus, Fife, Lothian, Argile, Mr Knox, Mr David Lindsay, Robert Fairlie of Braid, William Dowglas of Whittinghame, the Lairds of Keir and Lundie, Mr Robert Hammiltoun, minister at Sanct Andrewes, Thomas Wallace, commissioner of Sanct Andrewes, Mr Johne Row, minister of Sanct Johnstoun, Patrik Murrey, Commissioner of Sanct Johnstoun, Mr Andrew Hay, Minister of Renfrow, Mr David Wemes, Minister of Glasgow, Mr William Christesone, Mr Gilbert Gardin, James Baron, burgesse of Edinburgh, David Ramsay, burgesse of Dundie, and the Laird of Barganie, to present to the regent and the nobilitie, which are to be assembled at Perth, the 25th of this instant moneth of Julie, the articles following :—

Imprimis, Tuiching the heeds which my lord regent's Grace sent to the Kirk Assemblie, with Mr Johne Wood, the Assemblie hath givin their full power to their commissioners sent presentlie to his Grace, to resolve fullie therupon, conforme to the answeres givin to the said Mr Johne Wood.

Item, The Assemblie desireth the contract made in this Generall Assemblie, concerning the assignation of ministers' stipends, to be ratified and approved, with letters therupon, as is conteaned in the same.

Item, That the manses and gleebs may be givin to the ministers, for their residence at their kirks ; and that the law heerupon may be made cleere, that it may have executioun : and in like maner concerning the reparatioun of kirks.

Item, That all that have benefices be compelled to pay their thrids, so that payment be made of the yeeres bygane, as weill as to come.

Item, That order may be taken for sustentatioun of the poore, and that a portioun of the tithes be appointed to that effect.

And, in like maner, that the poore labourers of the ground may have intromissioun, to leade their owne tithes, upon reasonable compositioun.

Item, That some auditors of the Exchecker be appointed to convene with the auditors of the kirk, to heare the collectors of the kirk their compt.

Item, That immunitie may be granted to the commissioners of the kirk sent to Generall Assembleis, that during the time of the Generall Assembleis they be not molested in civill actions.

Item, That superintendents may be planted through the whole realme, as are alreadie in some parts.

Item, That commissioners may be appointed throughout the whole realme, to cognosce in causes of divorcements.

Item, That suche as have benefices, and doe nothing but pay their thrid, may be compelled to beare some further burthein with the kirk, and cheefelie for the support of the poore.

Item, That suche as have pluralitie of benefices may be compelled to demitt all save one.

Item, That remedie may be provided for chopping and changing of benefices and selling of the same ; diminishing the rentall, setting long tacks in defraud of the kirk ; and that all tacks sett since the assumptioun of the thrids may be disannulled, with expresse inhibitioun against the same in time comming.

Item, That order may be takin, that suche odious crimes as this day procure God's heavie displeasure against the whole land, may be punished as God commandeth.

Item, That the jurisdictioun of the kirk may be separated from that which is civill.

Item, That the questioun concerning adulterers may be once decided, as weill concerning the punishement of the adulterers, as whether the adulterer sall be admitted to the benefite of mariage again, or not.

The tenor of the act made for assignatioun of stipend followeth :—

" Forsameikle as this long time bygane the ministers have beene

universallie defrauded of their stipends; and now, at last, it hath
pleased God to move the hearts of the superiour powers and estats
of this realme, to grant the thrids of the whole beneficies within
this realme to the ministers and ministrie, by plaine and publict parliament, as at more lenth is conteaned in the said parliament holdin
at Edinburgh in the moneth of December, 1567: In respect wherof, this present Assemblie findeth it most needfull and expedient
that all superintendents, ministers, exhorters, and readers, sall have
their owne particular assignatiouns appointed to them, to receave
the same frome the hands of the labourers, tacksmen, or others addebted in payment of the saids thrids; and, therefore, in one voice,
by this act giveth their full power and commissioun to everie superintendent and commissioner of kirks within their own bounds,
that they and everie one of them, by advice and consent of their
commissioners of provinces appointed in the synodall conventiouns,
give and make particular assignations to everie minister, exhorter,
and reader within their owne bounds, as they sall find expedient,
under the superintendent's subscriptioun and ministers' forsaid,
with all clauses needfull and expedient thereto, which sall be als
sufficient as if the samine were expede[1] by the Generall Assemblie
of the kirk. And as concerning the superintendents and commissioners of kirks, their provisioun and assignatioun to be made
by the Generall Assemblie of the kirk.

"And to the effect this act may take full perfectioun, the Assemblie requireth most humblie my lord regent's Grace and Secreit Counsell to interpone their authoritie heereto, that the assignatiouns forsaid, generall and particular, may be exped in forme
of provisioun *ad vitam* under the privie seale; with ordinance therupon, that letters may be directed at everie man's instance under
all the foure formes, as is granted to the possessours of the two
part. And als, to the same end, that his Grace and his counsell
forsaid would decerne the thrids of benefices forsaid within this
realme, to be separated and divided reallie, and with effect, frome
the two part, so that the kirk may intromett with the thrid part,

---

[1] Expedited.

as the old possessours doe with the two part; the superplus alwise
to be comptable for the commoun effaires, conforme to the act of
parliament. And, for accomplishement therof, the Assemblie giveth
commissioun to the forsaid brethrein appointed to goe to the conventioun at Sanct Johnstoun, with the articles before registred,
that among the rest they may obteane the confirmatioun of
this act."

Answere givin by the lord regent's Grace, with advice of the
Lords of Secreit Counsell, and others of the nobilitie assembled in
the convention at Perth, the penult day of Julie.

" Tuiching the Act made in the Generall Assemblie, concerning
the assignatioun of ministers' stipends, my lord regent's Grace,
with advice of the Lords of Secreit Counsell, and others of the
nobilitie and states assembled at this present conventioun, ordeane
the assignatioun to be putt in forme, and therafter to be presented
to the Exchecker, to be seene and considered by the lords audi-
ters therof, to the effect that the order being found good and
reasonable by them, and suche of the kirk as sall happin to be
present with them, provisions may therafter be made and exped
therupon, according to the meaning of the said act; providing that
commissioners or procurators of the kirk, at the said Exchecker,
present the names of the whole kirks in Scotland, and how manie
ministers are presentlie therat, to the end it may be knowne what
kirks are presentlie provided, and what desolat and destitut of the
ministrie; and also, show a perfyt order, how they would the ministers sould be payed by the thrids or otherwise; or have all the
writts in readinesse, which may cleere doubts for farther resolution.

" Tuiching the articles, desiring that the manses and gleebs
may be givin to ministers for their residence at kirks, and that the
law therupon may be made cleere, that it may tak executioun,
and likewise concerning the reparatioun of kirks, my lord regent's
Grace, with advice forsaid, promiseth that he sall caus foure, three,
or two godlie, discreit, and wise men within the bounds of everie
superintendent's charge, passe with the superintendent or commis-

sioner within the countrie or province, and visit the manses and
gleebs of all the kirks within the same, to the effect they may report to my lord regent's Grace and lords forsaid what is the particular quantitie of everie manse and gleeb; by whom the same is
presentlie occupied and inhabited, and by what right and title; as
also, how muche they thinke sufficient for the loodging and commoditie of everie minister and reader; and if they may, to appoint
the minister or reader with the possessor of the manse and gleeb;
and as they doe, to report, upon whose report his Grace sall hold
hand, to see the kirk and ministers presentlie putt in possessioun of
so muche of the said manses and gleebs as sall be thought necessar
by the said superintendents and visiters, for the loodging and com-
modie of the minister or reader, as said is, where there is no title
to impede the same. And incace the same title by law be reduce-
able, or may be declared null, his Grace sall hold hand to see justice ministred therupon with expedition. And where the mater
standeth in terms, that the present possessors cannot be removed
by order of law, without an explanatioun of the act of parliament,
his Grace sall travell to have the same act explained and made
cleere at the nixt parliament, to the effect it may tak executioun
in all times heerafter. And toward the reparatioun of kirks, his
Grace understandeth that there are acts of Secreit Counsell sufficient in that behalfe alreadie, if the samine sall be putt in execution.

"Tuiching the article desiring that superintendents may be planted
throughout the whole realme, my lord regent's Grace is content
that so be done, the persons being godlie and learned.

" Tuiching the article desiring that commissioners may be planted
throughout the whole realme, to cognosce in causes of divorcements, my lord regent's Grace promiseth to tak sufficient order
in that behalfe, by one of the Lords of the Sessioun, at the nixt
sitting doun therof.

" Tuiching the article desiring that remedie may be provided
against chopping and changing of benefices, and fewing of the same,
diminishing of the rentalls, setting of long tacks in defraud of the

kirk, and that all tacks sett since the assumption of the thrids may be disannulled, with expresse inhibitioun against the same in time comming; my lord regent's Grace ordeaneth the said article to be weill dilated and extended, and presented to the nixt parliament, where the same sall have a good answere and resolutioun, which presentlie cannot be done, through default of a speciall and expresse law against suche abuses.

"Tuiching the article desiring that the jurisdictioun of the kirk may be separated from that which is civill, my lord regent's Grace ordeaneth the persons nominated in the act of parliament to conveene the time of the nixt Exchecker, and define and limitat the said jurisdictioun according to the Word of God and the said act of parliament.

"ALEXANDER HAY.

"*Extractum ex Libro Actorum Secreti Consilij.*"

In the fyft sessioun, Mr Johne Wood presented the regent's letter; and according to the credit givin, proponed certane heeds to the Assemblie, wherunto answeres were givin. The tenor of the letter followeth :—

"After our most heartilie commendations : Seing we are not able to present the Assemblie approaching, as our intentioun was, we thought convenient breeflie to give you signification of our meaning in writt, of the which we pray you tak good consideratioun, and accordinglie to give your advertisement. Yee are not ignorant, as we suppose, what hath beene the estat of the Kirk of God within this realme, both before we accepted the burthein of regiment and sensyne : how, first, the thrids of benefices were granted, and the ministers thereby partlie releeved, and susteaned in suche sort, that nothing enlaiked that our travells could procure. The first order, indeid, was diverse wayes interrupted and brokin; but cheeflie in that yeere when we were exiled in England, wherethrough the whole ministers that yeere were frustrated of their livings. Shortlie, the estat of governement altering at God's pleasure, and the king our soveran lord being inaugurated with the

crowne of this kingdome, the first thing that we were carefull of
was, that the true religioun might be established, and the ministers
of the Evangell made certan of their livings and sustentatioun in
times comming. ' Yee know at the parliament we were most willing that the kirk sould be putt in full possessioun of the proper
patrimonie; and towards the thrids we exped in our travell, and
enlaiked onlie a consent to the dissolution of the prelaceis; wherinto, although we were earnestlie bent, yitt the estats delayed, and
would not agree therunto.   And since that time to this houre, we
trust yee will affirme that we have pretermitted nothing that will
advance the religioun, and putt the professours therof in suretie,
whereanant the whole, one onlie inlaike hath beene in the civill
troubles that God that suffered the countrie to be plagued with.
Now, the mater being after so great rage brought to some stay
and quietnesse, it is convenient that we returne where maters left,
and preasse to reduce them to the estat they stood in.

    " One thing we must call to remembrance, that at suche time
as we travelled in the parliament, to caus the estats to agree that
the thrids sould be decerned to perteane to the ministrie, they
plainlie oppouned them to us in respect of the first act, alledging
that with the sustentatioun of the ministrie there was also regarde
to be had to the support of the prince, in susteaning of the publict
charges; which, if they had not some releefe by that meane, the
revenue of the crown being so diminished, and the ordinar charges
come to suche greatnesse of force, they would be burthenned with
exactions.   And so, this dangerous argument compelled us to promitt to the estats, that we would tak upon us, the act being granted to the kirk, they sould satisfie and agree to anie thing sould be
thought reasonable, for supporting the publict charges of the
prince.   And according to this, the commissioner depute for the
maters of the church agreed to certan assignations of the thrids,
for support of the king, and us bearing the authoritie.   Which order
had beene sufficient for the whole, if the civill trouble had not occurred.   Yitt the disobedience growing so universallie, we are
content to susteane our part of the inlaike and losse for the time

bypast. But becaus there hath beene murmure and grudge, for that thing assigned to the king's hous and ours, and some other needfull things of the state, as that thereby the ministrie was frustrated of their appointed stipends, some communicatioun was had at Sanct Andrewes, and nothing yitt concluded whill the Generall Assemblie of the kirk; which now moveth us to write to you in this forme, praying you rightlie to consider the necessitie of the caus, and how the same hath proceeded from the beginning; having respect, that the kirk will be verie evill obeyed without the king's authoritie and power; and that now the propertie of the crown is not able to susteane the ordinarie charges: how in the beginning, the thrids had not been granted, if the necessitie of the prince had not beene one of the cheefe causes; and at the parliament, the estats, as before we have writtin, stake to consent that the whole thrids sould be declared to perteane to the ministrie, whill first we tooke in hand, that they being made without condition in favours of the kirk, the same would again condescend to so muche as might be sufficient to the support of the publict effaires, in furth-setting of the king's authoritie: and that, therefore, yee will now agree and condescend to a certan and speciall assignation of it, that sall be imployed to this use, the quantitie wherof, diverse of your selves, and this bearer, Mr Johne Wood, our servant, can informe you; that therafter yee may distribute to everie man having charge in the Kirk of God his stipend, according to the conditioun of the placc he serveth in, at your wisdom's discretion. Heerby all confusioun, that long hath troubled the state of the kirk, toward the stipends, sall be avoided; and some speciall provisioun being made for susteaning of the publict charges, we may the better hold hand to see the kirk obeyed of that wheron the ministers sould live, as we have beene willing heertofore, and as we beleeve your collectors sall report, that during our travells in the north countrie, they have found our affections, good-will, and travell, in their furtherance.

" Farther, we must putt you in minde breefelie of a mater occurred at our late being in Elgine. One Nicol Sutherland, in Forresse, was putt to the knowledge of an assise, for incest, and with him the woman. The assise hath convicted him of the fault. But the questioun is, whether the same be incest or not; so that we behoved to delay the executioun whill we might have your resolution at this Assemblie. The case is, that the woman was harlott of before to the said Nicol's mother brother. Heerin Mr Robert Pont can informe you more amplie, to whose sufficiencie we remitt the rest.

" Moreover, at our comming to Aberdeen, there came one, named Porterfield, a minister provided of before to the vicarage of Ardrassane; and required of us, that he might also have the vicarage of Stevinson, seing both was a mater meane aneugh to susteane him, and becaus the kirks were neere, that he might discharge the cure of both; we having him commended by diverse great men to the same, but thought good to advertise you, that this preparative induce not evill exemple and corruption. Alwise, incace suche things occurre heerafter, lett us understand what yee would have us to do ; as in like maner toward the chaplanreis that sall happin to vaike, wheranent, becaus there is no certan order prescrived, some confusioun standeth, some desiring them for lyftime, some for infants that are not of the schooles, and some for seven yeeres. We are sometimes preassed to receave or confirme assignations or dimissioun of benefices, the preparative wherof appeareth to bring with it corruption ; and so we would be resolved how to proceed.

" Before our comming from Fife, and sensyne, we have beene verie willing to doe justice on all persons suspected of witchecraft; as also upon adulterers, incestuous persons, and abusers of the sacraments : wherin we could not have suche expedition as we would have wished, because we had no other probabilitie to trie and convict them, but a generall delation of names, the persons suspected not being for the most part tried and convicted by order of the kirk of before. This hindered manie things that otherwise might have beene done. And, therefore, we pray you appoint and prescrive how the judgement of the kirk may proceed and be executed

against all suche trespassers, before complaint be made to us, that
when we come to the countrie we may caus execute the law, and
be releeved of the triell and inquisitioun heeranent.   We thought
expedient to give you this for advertisement, and so remitt the
whole to your care; committing you to the protectioun of Eternall
God.   From Aberdeen, the last day of June 1569.

" Your assured freind,

" JAMES, REGENT.

" Farther, yee sall credit the bearer toward the bussinesse of my
Lord of Huntlie and the Abbot of Deir."

These are the heeds proponned by Mr Johne Wood, in my lord
regent's Grace his name to the kirk, conveened the 5th day of
Julie, at Edinburgh, 1569, with the resolutions and answeres
thereto.

Imprimis, That a sufficient summe be takin off the whole thrids
of benefices and rents now in your hand by the last act of parliament, and particular presentations since that time, and granted for
certan yeeres to my lord regent, now present, for support of the
publict charges; and that the summe may be assigned in place and
rowme commodious.

It is answered by the kirk, that in just consideratioun of my lord
regent's Grace his necessitie in the publict charges he presentlie
beareth, they have consented, and consent, that the whole summes
of silver and money craved and desired by his Grace in the last
conventioun of some of the lords for that effect, in Sanct Andrewes,
in the moneth of May last was, be granted and allowed, and readilie
answered by the collectors, when the same sall be appointed and assigned.   And for the more commodious assignatioun therof, ordeans
an ample and sufficient commissioun to be made to the commissioners, that sall passe from this present Assemblie to the conventioun to be holdin at Perth the 25th day of this instant: givand
and grantand full power to the saids commissioners, or most part of
them, to assigne the forsaid summes of victuall and money upon

suche benefices and thrids as sall be most commodious for the kirk
and the regent's behove, with consent of his Grace ; and the same
assignatioun to stand, ay and whill the kirk sall tak farther order
heerwith : providing alwise, my lord regent sall not passe, nor solist
the kirk to dispone anie farther of their rents, nor confirme anie
other pension grauntcd furth of the saids beneficcs or thrids whatsomever, further than law will compell the kirk to doe.

Item, A speciall and resolute answere to the question of incest intended against Nicolas Sutherland.—Answered, The kirk findeth
it incest, and so hath resolved.

Item, A speciall answere tuiching the interpretation of double
benefices, by Mr Johne Porterfeild, minister at Dumbartane.—Answered and concluded, That no suche gifts sall be in time comming ;
and that which is givin is dissolved alreadie.

Item, Tuiching the chaplanreis which sall happin to vaike.—Answered, The kirk agreeth that the chaplanreis be disponned to the
colledges or to the poore, conforme to the act of parliament, and
no otherwise.

Item, An order to be takin tuiching the dimissioun or resignatioun of benefices.—Answered, The kirk understandeth that all
dimissioun and resignatioun of benefices must be made in the hands
of the kirk, the patronages alwise reserved to the lawfull patrons.

Item, To know what actions yee receave to be enquired of by
the ministrie ; and that the delations be so amplie tane, as a dittay
may be sufficientlie formed therof, that the civill sword may follow.
—Answered, It is referred to the conventioun at Sanct Johnstoun.

Item, Tuiching the desires of my Lord Huntlie and Deir.—Answere, Becaus of my lord regent's Grace his requeist, the kirk
would gladelie doe that thing which lay in their power. But by
reasoun of the rigorous handling of my Lord of Huntlie, in the great
necessitie of the kirk in these parts, and of the great povertie which
the poore brethrein susteane presentlie in these bounds, the kirk
can no wise remitt the thing that perteaneth to the poore ministers.
And likewise of my Lord of Deir, who debursed his money to the

enemeis of God, to persecute his servants and banishe them out of the realme.

Item, What they will doe tuiching my lord regent's supplicatioun in favours of George Robesone of Dundie.—Answered, The kirk agreeth heerunto in respect of manie circumstances, providing alwise this be not a preparative to anie others.

Item, A declaration how my lord regent's answers please them tuiching the precept granted to Mr James Harvie.—Answered, The discharge of the writting givin to the said Mr James and his complices pleaseth the kirk verie weill, and thanketh his Grace thereof.

THE ANSWERE RENEWED TO QUEENE ELIZABETH'S DEMANDS.

When it was made knowne to the regent and the counsell that the Queen of England was not satisfied with the answere givin to her three demands, nor weill pleased with the messinger, the counsell conveened at Stirline. It was concluded, as before, that the last heed might easilie be transacted. The secund needed no advisement. For in what securitie could the young king be, having joyned with him in authoritie a craftie woman, in the flowre of her age, assisted with a strong factioun threatning to restore her by force, when she is now denuded of her authoritie? In what securitie sall he be when she sall be maried to another husband; speciallie such a husband as may double her forces, and will not be content that his owne issue be excluded from right of successioun? Seing the secund heid is so full of inconveniences, there is no question to be made of the first. Robert Pitcairne, Commendatar of Dumfermline, a wise and trustie man, was sent with this answere.

LETHINGTON COMMITTED AND DELIVERED BY GRANGE.

The regent, understanding that the queen's factioun did grow stronger daylie, sent to Perth, to Secretar Lethington, to come to

Stirline; for he was suspected to be the contriver of all the plotts and conspiraceis in England and Scotland. Howbeit the regent's clemencie was too weill knowne to him, he doubted what to doe. Yitt he went, and brought with him the Erle of Atholl, a Papist and consulter with witches, to interceed for him, incase he were putt to anie strait. When he was sitting in counsell, upon the thrid of September, he was accused guiltie of the king's murther by Thomas Crawfurd, a depender of the Erle of Lennox, wherupon he was committed prisoner to a chamber in the castell of Stirline. Sir James Balfour, parson of Fliske, was committed to the castell of Blacknesse. These two, beside that they were guiltie of the king's murther, were the cheefe devisers of the late conspiraceis and insurrections. Lethington was brought to Edinburgh, and was committed to the custodie of Alexander Hume of Northberwick. But William Kirkaldie, Laird of Grange, captan of the castell of Edinburgh, came to Alexander's loodging about ten of the clock at night, and brought with him counterfoote letters, signed with the Erle of Murrey's hand. The other, not being ignorant how intcere he was with the regent in former times, but ignorant of his late defection, delivered Lethington to him. He tooke him with him to the castell, to the great greefe of all good men, uncertan whether to be more offended with Grange his boldnesse, or the regent his lenitie. Sir James Balfour, at the earnest intercessioun of his freinds, and for the freindship he shewed when he was captan of the castell, was sett at libertie.

THE REGENT'S ROAD IN THE BORDERS.

Upon the 14th of September, the regent went to the Merce, where he found the Lord Hume, a godlesse man, estranged from him; for he had beene of late drawin by Lethington to the queen's factioun. From Merce he went to Teviotdaill, to take order with theeves mainteaned by Sir Thomas Ker of Phairnihirst, and Sir Walter Scot of Balcleuch. They were both upon the queen's factioun. He went from Hawick the 20th day of September, and marched

through the dales, the English ryding through the English marches
in the meane time, least fugitives and outlawes sould escape. He
brought with him to Edinburgh threescore and twelve pledges,
whom he sent over the water, to be keeped for keeping of good
order in the borders.

GRANGE BEARETH HIMSELF STILL AS A FREIND.

The regent being loath to abandoun his old and inteir freinds,
sent often to Grange the informations he had receaved of his subscriving to a band contrived by the other factioun. He still and
stifflie denyed, bearing himself as a freind to the king, and mainteaner of his authoritie.

FLEEMING AND BOGHALL FORFAULTED.

I find in a certan manuscript, that the Lord Fleeming and
Johne Fleeming of Boghall were denounced tratours, and fore-
faulted the 17th of September, in a parliament holdin at Edinburgh; and that their armes were rivin at the Croce, in presence of
the regent and the lords.

THE SECRETAR'S DAY OF LAW PROROGATED.

Upon the 21st of November, the day appointed for Lethington
to underly triell and the verdict of an assise, manie noblemen and
gentlemen repaired to Edinburgh, whom he had writtin for to
mainteane him, as he alledged, in his innocencie. His freinds
were all that were unfreinds to the king, or privie to the murther.
Hume came with the Hepburns and other freinds to Edinburgh.
Atholl, Huntlie, and the Hammiltons, came to Linlithquo; but,
being charged by the regent to come no neerer, stayed.   The Erle
of Morton, with three thowsand, lay at Dalkeith, waiting till the
regent sent for him. The regent, finding the convocatioun of his
freinds and favourers so great by expectation, sent for the cheefe

noblemen in the toun, and spake to them, in effect, these words :
" When yee interprised the revenge of the king's slaughter, I was
in France. Yee desired me to come home, and take upon me the
regiment. Yee caused me tak an oath, that I sould to the uttermost revenge the murther of the king ; and yee, on the other part,
swore to fortifie me. Now, there is a gentleman accused of this
murther, but yee have convecned to hinder justice. Therefore yee
sall understand I will continue this day of law to another time. If
he be cleane he sall suffer no harme ; but if he be found guiltie it
sall not ly in your hands to save him."

THE ERLE OF NORTHUMBERLAND TAKIN.

The Duke of Norfolk was apprehended in England, the 11th of
October ; the Erle of Northumberland in Scotland, about the end
of December, for a conspiracie contrived against Queene Elizabeth,
wherin Queene Marie had a hand. The progresse was this : When
Queene Marie was at Bolton, the Lord Scroop's castell, the matche
betwixt her and the Duke of Norfolke was propouned to her by the
Ladie Scroop, sister to the Duke of Norfolk. The Bishop of Rosse,
and one Robert Ridolph, a Florentine, who lay at Londoun under
the name of a merchant factor, laboured to perswade the duke to
like of this matche. When Secretar Lethington went with the
regent to England last, he laboured privilie as muche as he could
with the duke, by conference with the queene, by letters sent by
Robert Melvill. Ridolph was sent by the Pope, Pius Quintus, to
promove the Roman religion in England, becaus he could not have
his Nuncio there, nor anie other publict person, to traffique in suche
a bussinesse. Ridolph stirred up some noblemen to a conspiracie,
and brought to passe that the conspirators sould draw on the Duke
of Norfolke to their societie, and make him the head therof, to
whom they promised mariage with the Scottish queene. The Pope
stirred up the King of Spaine to promise aide to the conspirators,
that his effaires might succeed the better in the Neatherlands. He
shewed to the Frenche king what duetie he owed to the Queene of

Scots, and what benefite he may reape by her restitutioun. Then the
Pope sent furth his bulls of excommunicatioun, wherin he absolved
the subjects from their oath of allegiance to Queen Elizabeth. The
bulls were sent to Ridolph, to disperse them through England.
When the regent was in England, the secreets of this conspiracie
were not knowne; yitt, upon a bruite of mariage betwixt our queen
and the Duke of Norfolke, the queen not long after caused convoy
her from Boltoun to Tudburie, where she was keeped in the custodie of George Erle of Shrewsburie. Howsoever the Duke of
Norfolk made a shew of profession of the true religioun, yitt was he
in heart a Papist. His sonnes were brought up in Papistrie; the
cheefe men of trust in his hous were Papists; the last wife he maried
was a Papist, and now, he is als bent to marie a Papist; his cheefe
complices in the conspiracie were Papists. Queene Elizabeth rebooked him for attempting the matche without her knowledge.
He promised to desist, but keeped, notwithstanding, a secreit
course of writting, and receaving letters from the Queen of Scots
by secreit characters, all which, together with a commentarie sent
to him by the Scottish Queen, the duke commanded his secretarie,
Higford, to burne. But he layed them under the matt, in the
duke's chamber; and being apprehended, reveeled where they
were, as George Carleton, Bishop of Chechester reporteth, in his
booke intituled, " A thankfull Remembrance of God's Mercie," &c.
The duke was apprehended the elleventh of October. Queen Elizabeth sent for Thomas Percie, Erle of Northumberland, and
Charles Neveill, Erle of Westmerland, about the 14th of November, supposing, that if they were innocent, they would come to
court; if guiltie, their purpose would sooner breake out. They,
suspecting the plott to be reveeled, brake furth in open rebellioun,
before anie helpe, which they looked from forane parts, could come
to them. They came with displayed banner to Durhame, burnt
the Bible and Service Booke, had masse in Darnton, tooke Barnard
castell by compositioun. The Erle of Sussex, the queen's Lieuten-
ant-Generall in the north, discovered the craft and pretences of the
rebels, the 17th day of November. They were putt to flight, and

were conducted by blacke Ormeston, an outlaw, and one of the murtherers of the king, to Liddisdaill. Martine Elliott and others, who had givin pledges to the regent, warned Ormeston, that if he conveyed them not out of the countrie, he sould doe the worst he might to him and them; wherupon the Erle of Northumberland was forced to flee to Hector Armstrang of Hairlaw. The Erle of Westmerland changed his coat of plait and sword with Johne Aside, and shifted from place to place, like a Scotish borderer. The Queen of England sent a post to the regent, and desired him either to take or expell her rebells. All the lieges on this side of Forth were charged, by proclamation, to meet the regent at Peebles, the 20th day of December. Johne Carmichael of that Ilk, at the instigatioun of the Erle of Morton, perswaded Hector Armestrang to deliver the Erle of Northumberland.[1] So the regent returned to Edinburgh the penult of December, and brought Northumberland with him. Whill the regent was in the borders, Westmerland shifted from place to place, and lurked speciallie with Phairnihirst and Balcleuche. He escaped after to the Low Countreis, where he was susteaned by a poore pensioun givin him by the King of Spaine. At the Duke of Norfolk's arraignement, a letter was produced, writtin to him from Queen Marie, wherin she signified her greefe, that the Erles of Westmerland and Northumberland were up in armes before the duke had raised his forces. The Queen of England was so weill pleased with the ap-

---

[1] Among the border thieves, the duty of protecting a guest composed the greater part of their moral code, so that Armstrong's dereliction was regarded by his lawless brethren with astonishment and horror. " This act of treacherie in Hector," says Lord Herries, in his History, " was so foullie constructed by all the rest of the border men, that from this tyme all men disdained his companie, even his own nearest kinsmen; and to this day he is spoken of as an example of treasone! For amongst these border men, their word of protection to any man in distress that comes amongst them is held sacred; and before they breake their faith, in this kynd, they will rather undergoe any hazard whatsomever."—A stronger motive than even fear of the regent's displeasure had probably animated Armstrong and his companions to this obnoxious deed; for Bannatyne informs us, in his Memoriales, " These countriemen lost nothing of this truble; for thai got his (the earl's) gold, his jewelis, and his wyve's jewelis, estemed to a grit sowme."

prehending of Northumberland, that she sent to the regent, to assure him of her assistance, and that all the forces of England sould be at his command.

M.D.LXX.

THE MURTHER OF THE GOOD REGENT.

Upon Moonday, the secund day of Januar, the regent went over the Queen's Ferrie, where William Dowglas of Lochlevin mett him, and receaved the Erle of Northumberland, to be keeped in the fortalice of Lochlevin. From thence he road to Dumbartane, becaus he was putt in hope that the castell would be randered to him upon conditions, by the Lord Fleeming. He returned disappointed, and remained at Stirline till the 22d day of Januar. In the meane time, the Hammiltons, and suche as were in the castell, or had their sonnes there, conspired to cutt him off. James Hammilton of Bothwellhauche, sister sonne to the bastard Bishop of Sanct Andrewes, undertaketh the execution. He lay in wait for the regent returning from Dumbartan, first in Glasgow, then in Stirline. But his interprise not succeeding he cometh to Linlithquo, which depended muche upon the Hammiltons, where his uncle, the Bishop of Sanct Andrewes, had a loodging not farre from the hous where the regent wont to loodge. The regent is advertised before he arose out of his bed, that if he road through the toun he would be shott at. The advertiser offered, if he would appoint some to goe with him, he sould bring the tratour to him out of the loodging where he was loodged. The regent would needs hold fordward in his progresse to Edinburgh, saving onlie that he purposed to ride out at that same port whereby he entered, and cast about the toun. Yitt did he not hold on in this purpose, ather becaus he confided in the protection of the Almightie, or becaus the multitude of horsemen attending upon him was so throng in the streets. He intended to ryde by the place suspected with speed, but was hindered by the throng. So Bothwellhauche shott at him with a hacquebutt,

through a tirleis¹ window, from a stair wherupon were hung sheetes
to drie; but in truthe to hide the smooke, and mak the place the
lesse suspected.   The regent is shott a little under the navell, and
neere the reines, and with the same bullet, the horse upon which
George Dowglas of Parkheed, base brother to the Erle of Morton,
was ryding.   The murtherer fled out at a posterne gate, where he
mounted upon a horse which he had gottin from Johne Hammilton,
Abbot of Arbrothe, to carie him away with speed.   He was receaved by the Hammiltons at Hammilton, with great applause and
commendatioun.   The regent lighted and returned to his loodging
on foote, as if he had no feeling of paine.   When he was often remembred of lenitie and great indulgence toward his greatest enemeis, namelie, the same murtherer, he answered, that he no wise
repented of his clemencie.   After that this good Josias had set his
hous in order, and recommended the young king to the nobles who
were present, he randered his spirit in the hands of the Lord, about
ellevin houres at night, the 23d day of Januar.

This worthie governour was commounlie called the " Good Regent."   His courage in the civill warres, tempered with a care of
peace, was commended by all good men.   He compelled all the rebells to acknowledge the king's authoritie the first yeere of his governement, and brought under obedience the cheefe ringleaders of
the queen's factioun, howbeit they changed not their owne fals-
hood.   When he had rest from civill insurrections and commo-
tions, he attended continuallie upon counsell and sessioun.   His
hous was like a little sanctuarie, where were not heard so muche
as lascivious speeches.   When the chapter was read after dinner
or supper, it was his custome to propone questions, and to seeke resolution of anie difficultie at the learned, of whom he had some
usuallie at his table.   His liberalitie was rather excessive nor within measure.   He was affable to his owne domesticks, and yitt rebooked them more sharplie than anie other, when they gave offence.
He was weill-beloved of the English, for interteaning peace betweene the two realmes, and for his other vertues.

¹ Trellissed.

5

THE HAMMILTONS' PRETENCES BEFORE AND AFTER THE MURTHER.

The Hammiltons had conveened in great number to Edinburgh before the slaughter, under pretence to see their cheefe sett at libertie. But als soone as the murther was committed, they sent to the rest of the Hammiltons, pretending to disswade them from all fellowship with the murtherer, but in truthe to advertise them to be readie to tak up armes at all occasions, as they sould be warned. Whill the regent was at Dumbartan, Glasgow, Stirline, Linlithquo, the Abbot of Kilwinning travelled with Mr Knox, that he might interceed for his freinds. Mr Knox said, " Abuse not my travells, my lord : although I be a poore man, yitt am I the servant of God, and would be loath to be spotted with anie dishonestie. If your freinds intend anie mischeefe, what greefe sall it be to me, to be noted a traveller for men in whom there is no truthe ! But be it as it will, I sall not ceasse to meane weill to all honest men of that surname. I have nothing to do with your bishop, so long as he remaineth enemie to Christ Jesus. I will doe what lyeth in me for all others that will acknowledge the king's authoritie, and serve the regent. But I protest before God, who is the onlie witnesse now betwixt us, that if there be anie thing attempted by anie of that surname against the persoun of that man, that in that cace, I discharge my self to you and them for ever ; for I am als assured as that God liveth, if yee be not quiett, the destruction of that hous approacheth." These words were spokin eight or ten dayes before the murther. The abbot made faire promises, but returned not againe to Mr Knox till the murther was committed. Then he desired conference ; but Mr Knox refused, and returned answere by the messinger as followeth :—" I have not now the regent to make sute unto for the Hammiltons." The bastard bishop and the duke's sonnes sent missives to their freinds and favourers, craving their assistance and concurrence for defence of the commoun weale, as they pretended. In some letters they called the

murther a " sudden alteratioun," and " the taking away of their
enemie." The duke sold or wedsett land to Johne Somervell,
Laird of Camnethen, and with the money, together with other
summes collected among his freinds, ordeaned the bastard bishop
his brother, and his sonnes, to wage souldiours, and to have them
in readinesse upon all occasioune.

BALCLEUCHE AND PHAIRNIHIRST PRIVIE TO THE CONSPIRACIE.

In the night after the slaughter, Sir Walter Scot of Balcleuche,
and Sir Thomas Ker of Phairnihirst, made an incursion in the borders of England, not so muche for greedinesse of a bootie, as to
provoke the English, and to kindle warres betwixt the two countreis, as had beene before appointed by the Bishop of Sanct Andrewes, and others of that factioun. When some said, the regent
would tak order with this breache; " Tush !" said one of their followers, " the regent is als cold as the bitt in my horse mouth."
They had beene not long before in the castell of Edinburgh, where
all the mischeefe was brewed, whereby it is apparent they were not
ignorant of the conspiracie.

MR KNOX HIS PRAYER.

How heavie and dolorous was the heart of Mr Knox, after the
murther of the regent, may be perceaved by this forme of prayer,
which he used after dinner and supper, when the thanksgiving for
bodilie sustenance was ended :—

" O Lord, what sall we adde to the former petitions we know
not; yea, alas ! O Lord, our owne consciences beare us record,
that we are unworthie that thou sould ather increasse or yitt continue thy graces with us, by reasoun of our horrible ingratitude.
In our extreme misereis we called, and thou in the multitude of
thy merceis heard us. And first thou delivered us from the tyrannie of mercilesse strangers, nixt, from the boundage of idolatrie,
and, last, from the yoke of that wicked woman, the mother of all

mischeefe; and in her place, thou did erect her sonne, and to supplee his infancie, thou did appoint a regent indued with suche
graces as the devill himself can not accuse, or justlie convict him,
this onlie excepted, that foolish pitie did so farre prevaile in him
concerning executioun and punishment, which thou commanded to
have beene executed upon her, and upon her complices, the murtherers of her husband. O Lord, in what miserie and confusioun
found he this realme, and to what rest and quietnesse now, by his
labours, suddanlie brought the same, all estats, but the poore
commouns, speciallie can witnesse! Thy image, Lord, did so
cleerelie shyne in that personage, that the devill, and the wicked to
whom he is prince, could not abide it. And so,. to punishe our
sinnes and our ingratitude, who did not rightlie esteeme so pretious a gift, thou hath permitted him to fall, to our great greefe, in
the hands of cruell and tratorous murtherers. He is at rest, O
Lord, and we are left in extreme miserie: be mercifull to us, and
suffer not Satan utterlie to prevaile against thy little flocke within
this realme; nather yitt, O Lord, lett blood-thristie men come to
the end of their wicked interprises. Preserve, O Lord, our young
king. Although he be an infant, give unto him the Spirit of sanctificatioun, with increasse of the same as he groweth in yeeres.
Lett his raigne, O Lord, be suche, as thou may be glorified, and
thy little flocke comforted by it. Seing that we are now left as a
flocke without a pastor, in civill policie, and as a shippe without the
rudder in the middest of the storme, lett thy providence watche,
Lord, and defend us in thir dangerous dayes, that the wicked of
the world may see, that als weill without the helpe of man as with
it, thou art able to rule, mainteane, and defend the little flocke that
dependeth upon thee. And becaus, O Lord, the shedding of innocent blood hath ever beene, and yitt is, odious in thy presence,
yea, that it defileth the whole land where it is shed and not punished, we crave of thee, for Christ thy Sonne's sake, that thou will so
trie and punishe the two treasonable and cruell murthers latelie committed, that the inventers, devisers, consenters, authors, and mainteaners of treasonable crueltie, may be ather throughlie converted

or confounded. O Lord, if thy mercie prevent us not, we cannot escape just condemnation, for that Scotland spaired, and England hath mainteaned, the life of that most wicked woman. Oppone thy power, O Lord, to the pride of that cruell murtherer of her owne husband: confound her factioun and their subtile enterprises, of what estat and conditioun so ever they be; and lett them and the world know, that thou art a God that can deprehend the wise in their owne wisdome, and the proud in the imaginatioun of their wicked hearts, to their everlasting confusioun. Lord, reteane us that call upon thee in thy true feare: lett us grow in the same. Give thou strenth to us to fight our battell; yea, Lord, to fight it law-fullie, and to end our lives in the sanctificatioun of thy holie name."

A CONFERENCE FORGED BY MR THOMAS MATLANE.

Immediatlie after the murther of the regent was caried from hand to hand a letter, conteaning a counsell givin by the Lord Lindsey, the Laird of Pittarrow, Mr Knox, Mr Johne Wood, the Tutor of Pitcur, Mr James Makgill. The contriver counterfooteth the tongues, countenance, and affections of suche as gave counsell to the regent, as followeth :—[1]

"After most heartilie commendations: I promised to advertise you of the proceedings heere in court principallie. As concerning my lord, your cousin, they will you to understand, that at this time there is no hope of anie good wayes for him. And this I know, not onlie by diverse reports of courteours, and so muche as

---

[1] This clever production, which looks like a harmless *jeu d'esprit*, was, in fact, an atrocious attempt to blacken the memory of the murdered regent, while the style and manner of each speaker was so strikingly sketched, that many appear to have been mystified by its plausibility, and to have regarded it as the description of a real event.   Three copies of this pretended conference have been published of late years, two of which are in the first volume of the Bannatyne Collection, and the third in Bannatyne's Memoriales, edited by Robert Pitcairn, Esq., and published by the same society.   As might be expected from a pasquinade hastily copied by different in-dividuals, and circulated in private as a contraband article, the readings of the dif-ferent versions in some points disagree.   Calderwood has probably copied that of the Memorials, and adapted the spelling to his own time.

I can perceave my self by my lord regent's owne speeking, but also by a discourse of counsell holdin verie secreetlie, wherunto, I trust, no man in this realme is privie but they which namelie were called thereto, and I, who was covered.

"About foure dayes since, in this toun, my lord regent went in a privie chamber, and with him thir six persons; my Lord Lindsay, the Laird of Pittarrow, Mr Johne Wood, Mr Knox, Mr James Makgill, and the Tutor of Pitcur, which are the men in the world he beleeveth most into. When they were entered, he desired them to place themselves, for he would reteane them the space of three or foure houres. It chanced that I was sleeping into a bed within the cabinet, so weill hid, that no man might perceave me; and after I was wakenned with the bruite of their entrie, I might easilie heare everie word that they spake. Then first my lord regent sayeth to them, 'I have conveened you at this time, as the men of the world in whom I putt most confidence, and whom I beleeve would fainest have my estat standing, to give me your faithfull advice familiarlie, for my advancement and standing. Yee see how manie ly out from me, and manie that were with me in the beginning of this actioun are miscontent with my procceedings; wherefore, I would desire you to declare to me your opinions how I may best stand, and sett fordward the purpose yee wote of.'

"And after he had thus spokin, he commanded my Lord Lindsay to speeke first, who said, 'My lord, yee know of old, that I was more rash nor wise. I cannot give you a verie wise counsell, but I love you weill eneugh. To be short, what sould yee doe but use counsell, which yee will never? Therefore, I thinke manie times, the devill gart me make you regent. My lord, mak us quite of thir Matchiavelian and bangester[1] lords, that will circumveene you with their policie, and wracke you with force; and when yee fall to them, bourd not with them. For, by God's bread, if yee take them in mowes, I will goe to the Byres, and hauke, as I did this last time at Stirline. But gar them daunce headlesse, and then ilk good fellow may gett a lumpe of their lands, which will

[1] Turbulent.

gar them fight like swine, and other men will be sure of the spang
of their taile.[1] And if there be anie stout carle that will fight, sett
me till him, and yee sall see that I sall give him a targatt and
scrotchard :[2] and if he be a hote man, I will lett him play him a
while, syne take him a cowpe-darier. And when the principals
are past, yee may doe with the gogeis[3] what yee list. If we had
this old Craig[4] in our hands, I would like maters the better. Yee
know I will not speeke Grange. But lett him ly there whill the
principals be dispatched, then give him an heele wedge. But yitt,
I thinke to be even with him, for taking the Erle of Rothesse' part
against me.'[5]

"Yee will not beleeve, when he putt on his bonnet, how great
a laughter was in the hous. And syne, my lord regent sayeth,
'Yea, weill, sirs ; for all his rashnesse in speeking, he kenneth weill
aneugh wherat he would be :' and then they swore all, with one
voice, The devill speed them, but my lord hath spokin weill !'[6]

"Nixt my lord regent caused Johne Knox to speeke ; who,
looking up to the heaven as he had beene beginning a prayer be-

---

[1] Grasp of their tail, i. e. a sure hold of them. This expression alludes to the sport
of swine-chasing at fairs and wakes, in which the animal was only to be caught by
the tail, which was greased, to make the feat more difficult.

[2] A scrotchard was some weapon of offence. By this swash-buckler phrase of
target and scrotchard, Lindsay perhaps means that he will give them both parry and
thrust.

[3] Silly fellows. The bangster lords he has already disposed of, and the Machiave-
lians he leaves to wiser heads.

[4] By the Craig he probably means the Castle of Edinburgh, as by a natural
transition he immediately passes to its governor, Kirkcaldy.

[5] The blunt-witted but stout-hearted Lord of the Byres, who was so effective a
champion of the Reformation, has been distorted into every form that wit or malig-
nity could devise, chiefly, it is to be suspected, from the alleged harshness of his
dealings with Queen Mary. The following sketch of him, from among many others,
will illustrate this bitterness of party feeling :—" He had," says the historian Black-
wood, " the figure and shape of a man, and could speak ; but as for any thing else,
he was so stupidly brutal, that he differed in nothing from that animal of whom Mar-
cus Varo speaks, which had a soul given him in place of salt, to keep his carcase
from stinking."

[6] Putting such an oath into the mouths of such grave personages was a slip of the
pen that could only be justified by the fact, that hard swearing was a very pre-
valent fashion, from which only the more strict of the reformers were free.

fore sermoun, (for by a hole I might behold their countenance, and
so see what they did;) and after he had keeped silence a good
space, he beginneth with a sture and brokin voice, and said, 'I
praise my God greatumlie that hath heard my prayer, which often
times I powred furth before the throne of His Majestie, in anguish
of my heart ; and that hath made his Evangell to be preached with
so notable a successe, under so weake instruments ; which, in deed,
could never have beene done, except your Grace had beene constituted ruler over his church, especiallie indued with suche a singular and ardent affectioun to obey the will of God, and voice of
his ministers. In respect wherof, I embrace, as the servant of
God, your Grace's good-will and zeale to the promotioun of God's
glorie, and as Johne Knox favoureth your Grace better than anie
man upon the face of the earth. Now, to explaine to your Grace
my judgement concerning your owne standing, which being so
joyned with the establishing and standing of the kirk ; yea, seing
the weelfare of God's kirk so dependeth upon your Grace, that,
yee circumveened, it is not able to endure anie long time ; therefore, it seemeth to me necessar, both for the honour of God, the
comfort of the poore brethrein, and the utilitie of this commoun
weale, that first your Grace, nixt your estat, be preserved in equali-
tie of time, and not to prescrive anie diett of fyfteene or seventeene
yeeres, leaning more to the observatioun of politick lawes, than the
approbation of the Eternall God. As I could never away with
thir jollie witts, and politick braines, which my Lord Lindsay
calleth Matchiavel's[1] disciples, so would I wishe they were out of
the way, if it were possible. And I trust surelie, if first your
Grace, and syne the nobilitie of that confederation, had past to
work with als great magnanimitie as I uttered my judgement simplie
and assuredlie in my sermouns made expresslic for that purpose,
the mater had beene farther advanced nor it is, or sall be this long
time, if God send not better successe than my sorrowfull heart
perceaveth. Siclyke, these of the nobilitie who would hinder your

---

[1] Maitland of Lethington, the dreaded and distrusted of all parties, had already
acquired the name of Machiavel.

Grace's pretence, though they seem not so in the eyes of the blind world, I have preached openlie, and yitt daylie crave of God, that they may be confounded with that wicked woman unto whom they cleave so obstinatlie, and that their posteritie may drinke of the cuppe prepared for the judgement and punishement of their child-rein. Heerin I agree with my Lord Lindsay, who spake imme-diatlie before. But me thinke, to establishe true religioun, to ob-teane this, I say, we must have a farther respect and consideration than this; that is, that the governement be established in your person, so long as yee live. For when this bairne, whom we call now king, sall come to age, doth anie man thinke that he will leave off royall insolencie, and suffer himself to be ruled by the simplicitie of the Evangell? What good hope can we have of the childe borne of suche parents? I will not speeke of the suspicioun that may be concerning the man that was killed. But though he be his whose he is called, what can we looke for, but, as it were, the heretage of the slaine's lightnesse, and the mother's iniquitie? If Johne Knox his counsell be followed, the estat of the Evangell, and professors therof, sall never be givin over to suche a hazard. Better it is to content ourselves with him of whose modestie we have had good experience, both in wealth and trouble, than to change from the gravitie of an aged ruler, to the intemperancie of an unbridled childe. Your Grace hath perceaved, how the Blast of my Trum-pet against the Regiment of Weomen is approved of all the godlie. I have writtin, in like maner, and have it readie for the printing, a booke, wherin I prove, by sufficient reasons, that all kings, princes, and rulers, goe not by successioun; and that birth hath no power to promote, nor bastardie to seclude, men from the government. This will waken others to panse[1] more deepelie upon the mater. Besides this, we sall sett furth an Act in the Generall Assemblie; and both I, and the rest of the brethrein, sall ratifie the same in our daylie sermons, till that it be more nor sufficientlie perswaded to the people. This being solemnlie done, the Booke of God open-ed and layed before the nobilitie, who will say the contrare, except

[1] Think.

he that will not feare the weightie hand of the magistrat striking
with the sword, and the censure of the kirk rejecting him, as the
scabbed sheepe from the rest of the flocke, by excommunicatioun?
This sall also serve, in eventure the king depart off this life, (as
we are all mortall,) to keepe us furth of the hands of Lennox and
Hammilton, whose imperfectiouns are both notorious.   Then your
Grace being thus advanced by God, we doubt nothing but yee sall
be thankfull, in punishing but pitie all that displease the church,
and provide that the servants of God be honorablie entreated with
a portioun of this commoun wealth, according to their calling.'
And so he held his peace.

"Then my lord regent said, ' Yee know I was never ambitious.
I will not oppone my self to the will of God, reveeled by you, who
are his true ministers.   But, Johne, heare yee; tell your opinioun
in the pulpit.'   Which, when he had promised to doe, the Laird of
Pittarrow was desired to speeke, who said,—

"' Sir, and it please your Grace, that which our brother Mr
Knox hath spokin hath ever beene my opinioun: for, to be plaine,
except that yee be so weill hefted in the authoritie, that yee cannot be takin furth of it, I cannot see how this commoun wealth can
stand.   But for bringing this mater to passe, beside the furtherance
that standeth in the minister's hands, yee must have some other
respect; that is, that yee have the strenths in your hands.   Stirline is weill, so long as yee and my Lord of Marr agree so weill together as yee doe; but I would wishe that the king were in your
owne hands.   For your Grace knoweth what guiding my ladie hath
of your uncle, and yee know whose sister she is.   Edinburgh,' sayeth he, ' hyme! hyme!' shaiking his head; ' it were better that
both the hous and the plenishing therof were in your brother's hand,
or some other that loveth you weill, as your brother doth.   To gett
Dumbartane, I would not sticke for geere, yea, albeit I sould give
als muche as Sir James Balfour gott.¹   A king seeking treasoun
may find land.   And yee like, yee may ay gett your hand beyond

¹ Balfour, for surrendering the castle of Edinburgh, was rewarded with the lands
of Strathkinnes and Ballone.

my Lord Fleeming. I heare say, the Lord of Morton is traffiquing to gett the hous of the Basse; which, if he doe, he will stoppe some devices your Grace knoweth. And, therefore, were I in your Grace's stead, I sould be betwixt the kow and the corne. I tell you that that old craig is a good starting hole: at the least, it would serve to keepe them that yee would be sure of. And if there be anie other great strenth within this realme, I would have that by some moyen in my hands. But, besides the strenths, yee must have respect to some great houses, that will never lett you come to honour, so farre as they may, suche as Hammilton, Lennox, Argile, Huntlie, that pretend to the crowne; and other men that have over great power in this countrie, as Morton, Atholl, Hereis, Hume, Phairnihirst, Lethington, Sir James Balfour, Tullibardine, and diverse others, whom your Grace hath in tickett. This I would yee handled as it hath beene oft times devised.'

" Nixt him spake the Tutor of Pitcur on this maner : ' My lord, when Hannibal went to conqueisse Italie, he made himself strong with men of warre, wherunto he gave wages. Scipio, when he past to Africa, and to destroy Carthage, did the like. Even so, my lord, if your lordship will do weill, make yourself strong with waged men, both on horse and foote. And so, I thinke, with some strangers, yee may easilie conquer this countrie.'

" When he had shortlie spokin to this effect, Mr Johne Wood beganne, and said, ' My lord, I trust my uprightnesse in your service hath sufficientlie perswaded your Grace that I am no flatterer, and upon the other part, addicted to no factioun; wherethrough both I will, and may give your Grace a faithfull counsell for your behove, whom I love enteerelie in my heart, both for your owne Grace's good nature, and profite of the commoun wealthe. For in good faith, as I have said often times, if I knew there were anie vice in you, I sould never serve you. I wrote long since a long discourse how yee sould behave yourself, of the which I will remember you at this present of a few heeds, in stead of my counsell. Zenophon, in a little prettie booke, intituled Cyripaideia, writteth, that a captan that desireth to vanquishe his enemeis sould use strenth, moyen, subtilitie, craft, deceate, leesings, soothsayings, oathes, liberalitie, and crueltie. This precept I would your Grace sould note. Secundlie, I have ever said, that this natioun cannot be dauntoned with babishnesse. Propone to yourself the Duke d'Alva's exemple. Yee must come in there, and be bold among them, and that will gar all their hearts tremble, and their haire start widdershin. Thridlie, The prince can never doe anie notable enterprise, except he be right politick. Yee must have a factioun both within the countrie and without, to repose upon. And now, to speeke how to putt thir things in executioun. To speeke of the last heed, the men yee are to repose upon, in Scotland, are the precise Protestants; for the nobilitie and their bands of men are a packe of false, greedie tratours: without the countrie, the Queen of England and Ladie Katherine's [1] factioun; for what recks you who brooke the crowne of England, so they be your freinds? I would not yee sould cast away yourself, for conquissing of kingdoms to the queene's sonne. It is meete also to be confederated with the princes of Almanie that are of the religioun, and the King of Denmarke; and ere yee faile, lett some of Scotland or Orkney slippe with him, for yee gett not meekle profite of it. The best way to gett silver is, to caus the king's rents to be lifted by a faithfull man, to your behove. I cannot tell where yee sall gett one better than my father, the Laird of Pittarrow.[2] Nixt, gar tak all the benefices to the crowne; for why sould thir idle belleis brooke these rowmes in the kirk's name? And give the ministers the thrid, and hold the two part to yourself. The kirk lands that are fewed, make you to reduce them all; for that way, yee sall have the whole fewes in your owne hands, or get great summes of money

---

[1] Katherine Gray, sister of Lady Jane Gray, and heiress of the house of Suffolk, was one of the claimants to the crown of England, the superior right of Mary Stuart being set aside. Her history is one of the most tragical that occurs during this fearful period of oppression and bloodshed. She died in the Tower in 1567; but her claims, which descended to her children, were strongly advocated by the Protestant party in England, in preference to those of the Scottish queen, on account of the Protestantism of the Suffolk family.

[2] For Pittarrow's talents as a financier in this way, see *ante*, p. 172.

in compositioun. And syne, of thir noble men who have offended, and riche burgesse carles, lett none passe without debursing of silver. And I trust, if yee behave yourself wiselie, yee may gett everie yeere some little pott of wine [1] out of England to pay your men of warre. Feede France with faire words, and looke als muche to the admiral's factioun [2] as yee may. As for the nobilitie, yee see they are divided in two parts. Some are great men and puissant, some are feeble and gogeis. Of the one sort are they that my father, the Laird of Pittarrow, hath reckoned, and the rest, that your Grace hath in bill. Let these childer want the heads, which sall both make you quite of their cummer, (*quia mortui non mordent,*) and sall caus others stand in awe. Make the simple band a coine hous, and gar them pay everie yeere a good tribute. Moreover, yee must change all the offices both of court and sessioun, and others in the countrie. Putt in men of your owne creatioun ; feede the simple with faire words ; boast the faint-hearted, dispatche the men of spirit, and make a new forme in this countrie. As for the strenths, my father hath spokin weill ellis. But I must eeke this one word concerning the Laird of Grange, to trappe him. Cause Alexander Clerk, Mr Knox, David Murrey, and others of his acquaintance, both write and say he is evill spokin of through the countrie for lying out frome your Grace, and that cannot stand with his honour ; and able[3] he will give credite. Which if he doe, and yee gett him once in your hands, yee know what is devised. I need to speeke no farther. If yee will know other things in speciall, take the paines to read my discourse once againe, and I sall come to-morrow to your Grace's rysing, and explaine it point by point, that yee may be the more resolute.'

" And after he had done, my lord regent sayeth, ' Now, Clerk of

---

[1] *Pot de vin* is an expression still used in France to designate the present given to the broker on the conclusion of a bargain. Perhaps this is a sly allusion to the gratuities which Murray was alleged to have received for his compliances with the wishes of Elizabeth.

[2] Admiral Coligny.

[3] Perhaps. The word is now usually *aiblins*,

Register, lett us heare you : becaus ye are a wylie cheild, we keeped
you to speeke hindmost, to speeke plainlie; for sorrow a bodie
heareth us but our selves, nor yitt sall heere.' But I thought,
' Sorrow fall you, and God save me, that lyeth heere, and heareth
weill eneugh all that is spokin!' Then the Clerk-Register said,
' My lord, I am an evill discourser, but I will speare a question :
If you would save your owne life and state ?' ' Yea,' quoth my
lord regent. ' Then, my lord, yee must putt them out of the way
that may or hath desire to hinder you. The time hath beene
when I would my Lord of Morton had beene weill. But now,
since he trusteth other men, or his owne phantasie, better than me,
and runneth not your course, lett him passe among the rest, sync
wyte the nifferers. As to the strenths, in good faith yee must
have men of your owne impositioun. I grant all these that are of
Matchiavell's doctrine will say that they have done your Grace
good service. But the clerk, Blair, said, ' Matchiavel is an evill
booke, and I would he had beene burnt seven yeeres since.' That
be there and heere, good yeere. Remember yee what the old Bishop of Dumblane said, in the yeere of God 1556, when I was
commissioner at the border : ' Princes sould not be windie,' quoth
Mr Henrie : alas ! in good faith, he was a good companion ; he
could have told you his minde. They say they have manie against
you : weill, I am als old as thir folkes, and have seene the fashioun
of Scotland als weill as another. Though they have the tongue, I
can tell the taile. Yee will gett als manie to tak your part as the
contrare will be against you, and one moe. Tak there an answere.'

"In a word, when they had all done, my lord regent said, it was
an heavie burthein that lay upon him, and yitt he would underly the
same, als long as he might, and depend upon their counsels allan-
erallie ; praying them to advertise him when he keeped not all his
kowes ; for the thing they spake he judged all to be true.

"By this day's talking yee may judge what was meant. I cannot write all that was spokin, but this was the effect, so farre as I
remember. Surelie maters are evill guided heere, and I can perceave nothing but great crueltie, deceate, and dissolutioun. Sup-

pose I beare a faire countenance, and have a reasonable dresse in court, yitt I mislyke verie farre the things I saw, and would wishe all the nobilitie knew what I know, concerning their owne wracke. I trust they sould not be so airch to putt remedie to thir inconveniences. Advertise, my lord, your cousin of this, and desire him to provide for himself; for heere there is nothing but ' Geld him !' Thus, fareweill."

MR KNOX HIS PURGATION.

The Abbot of Kilwinning sent this letter, or fained advertisement, to the Erle of Argile. He sent it to the Erle of Marr. His brother, Alexander Areskine, howbeit a Papist, after he had read it, said, "Heere are the most malicious lees that ever man invented !" David Forrest, called the Generall, gave the copie of it to Alice Sandelands, Ladie Ormeston, and affirmed it to be true. She brought it to Mr Knox, and asked if it was true. He answered, "Yee sall know my answere afterward." So, the nixt preaching day, he rehearsed the contents of it, and declared that the devill, the father of lees, was the cheefe inventer of that letter, whosoever was the penman, and threatned that the contriver sould dee in a strange land, where he sould not have a freind neere him to hold up his head. The author, Mr Thomas Matlane, brother to Lethington, was present and heard. When he was going out at the kirk doore, he confessed to his sister, the Ladie Trabrowne, that he had forged that letter. But, as the servant of God denounced, it came to passe; for he departed out of this life in Italie, whill he was going to Rome.

THE BURIALL OF THE GOOD REGENT.

Upon Tuisday the 14th of Februar, the regent's corps was careid from the Abbey of Halyrudhous to the Great Kirk of Edinburgh, and was bureid in the south ile. Mr Knox made a sermon before the buriall upon these words, " Blessed are these that dee in the Lord."

Manie of the nobilitie were present. He moved three thowsand persons to shed teares for the losse of suche a good and godlie governour. This epitaph following, made by Mr George Buchanan, was engraven in brasse, and sett above his tombe:

JACOBO STEWARTO, MORAVIÆ COMITI, SCOTLÆ PROREGI, VIRO ÆTATIS
SUÆ LONGE OPTIMO AB INIMICIS, OMNIS MEMORIÆ DETERRIMIS, EX
INSIDIIS EXTINCTO, CEU PATRI COMMUNI, PATRIA MŒRENS POSUIT.

LETHINGTON PURGETH HIMSELF BEFORE THE COUNSELL.

After the buriall of the good regent the lords assembled to consult upon the effaires of the countrie. Lethington was brought doun from the castell to the counsell. He purged himself of privitie to the murther of the king or the regent, or stirring up of rebellioun in England. The Lord Uchiltrie desired him to give his oath, for their greater satisfactioun, which he did; and offered to underly triell, whensoever the freinds of the deceassed king sould crave it. So he was sett at libertie.

A REASONING UPON THE REVENGE OF THE MURTHER OF THE REGENT.

William Dowglas of Lochlevin, and his brother Robert, craved summar execution of justice against the murtherers of the regent, seing the most part of that surname had beene denounced tratours, before the murther. All agreed that the offender sould be punished; yitt were they otherwise of diverse opinions. Some would have had a day appointed to suche as were suspected of the murther. The names of sindrie were delated. Others were of opinioun that they sould not await upon anie day of law, to be granted to them who had alreadie takin armes to defend that deed which they had alreadie done; and that they sould rise in armes, not onlie against them, but also against all suche as had beene before de-

nounced rebells. The barons and gentlemen were earnest this
way. Atholl, inspired by the secretar, would have them to delay
till there were a fuller assemblie of the nobilitie. The Erle of Morton was of opinioun that the confounding of manie faults would
tak away the principall; and to joyne others guiltie with the murtherers might bring on civill warre; and therefore advised all things
to be done by order of law, and the 1st of May to be appointed
for a full conventioun. The barons were offended at delay of time;
preferred a bill to the lords, and craved, First, That the murtherers,
and all that were privie to it, mainteaned or assisted the same, sould
be openlie condemned by their letters, in the king's name. Nixt,
That none, under paine of treason, tak upon them to mak anie innovatioun in religioun, or derogat from the authoritie already established. Thridlie, That all men sould abhorre the societie of the
Hammiltons, till their cheef, and suche as were suspected guiltie,
had purged themselves sufficientlie. Fourthlie, That the mainteaners and resetters of the murther sould be persued with all hostilitie. Last, That they would not consent that anie infidele or
wicked man, favourer of the queen's factioun, sould be advanced to
governe in the king's name. But the secretar, soule to the Erle of
Atholl, wrought so in that obstinat and witlesse man, that nothing
could be done till a fuller conventioun. Manie were offended at
this delay, becaus it would be said that all things were done at
the pleasure of the king's enemeis: that they had thus protracted
time, to the end that the greefe for the murther of the regent
might vanishe away by little and little.

THE ELECTION OF THE REGENT DELAYED.

At this conventioun they had almost condescended, that one of
these whom the queen had chosin tutors, before her resignatioun,
sould be chosin regent, provyding he had not declynned to the
queen's factioun. But Lethington, mynding nothing but commo-
tioun, alledged that the rest of the nobilitie were to be warned,
least they sould querrell the electioun. Atholl and some few as-

sented.   The rest made no great opposition, judging it expedient
to tak away all occasioun of calumniating, howbeit they saw no
benefite to be reaped by this delay.   .

THE ENGLISH AMBASSADER'S DEMANDS. ·

Queene Elizabeth had sent ambassaders, before the death of the
good regent, to demand the deliverie of her rebels.   He gave them
audience at Stirline, but willed them to attend for an answere at
Edinburgh ; but he is cutt off by the way, and they departed.   Sir
Thomas Randolph, a man weill acquainted with the fashiouns of
our countrie, and weill beloved of our nobilitie, was sent in ambassadge, and came to this conventioun.   He offered, in his mastresse'
name, becaus her Majestie was not ignorant of the tumults latelie
raised, that if, by reasoun of the troublesome time, they could not
compell the disturbers of the peace to make satisfactioun for the
wrongs done at the late invasions of the borders, to joyne her forces
with theirs.   If they could not doe this muche she would persue
them with her owne armie, without anie harme to others.   Therafter he advised them to be carefull to defend and preserve true religioun, peace, and obedience to their prince.   He shewed how
odious a crime treason was.   No resolute answere could be givin
before the 1st of May, becaus no regent was as yitt chosin.

A FAINED OFFER OF THE OTHER PARTIE TO REVENGE THE
MURTHER.

At the dissolving of the conventioun the Erles of Morton, Atholl,
and Cassils, Lords Ruthven, Methven, and Uchiltrie, and the commoun officers, were left counsellers, to keepe the countrie in some
order.   But Cassils and Atholl left them.   The Hammiltons with
their band, Argile, Boyd, Phairnihirst, Balcleuche, Lochinvar, assembled in Glasgow, the 17th of Februar.   Frome thence was a
letter directed to Morton and the secretar, subscrived by Argile
and Boyd, bearing that they were ignorant who were guiltie of the
l

murther of the regent, and would gladelie concurre with the rest of
the nobilitie, to consult and advise with them, upon the searching
and punishing of the same, if they would come to Linlithquo,
Fawkirk, or Stirline, for they would not come to Edinburgh. Morton went to the castell, to consult with the secretar, but they could
not agree upon an answere.

PHAIRNIHIRST'S DEMAND.

At this same time Sir Thomas Ker of Phairnihirst wrote from
Linlithquo to his father-in-law, the Laird of Grange, desiring him,
if he could, to procure that the Queen of England would stay her
armie, and upon that conditioun offered to quiett the borders :
otherwise he would continue in his attempts, not doubting but good
subjects, obedient to the queene their soverane, would aide him ;
and hoping that there would aide come shortlie out of France to
them.

THE TWENTIETH GENERALL ASSEMBLIE.

The Generall Assemblie, which sould have holdin in Stirline the
25th of Februar, was continued till the first of Marche, to be holdin
in Edinburgh, becaus none were conveened but three or foure, by
reasoun of the troublesome time. So the Assemblie held at Edinburgh the first of Marche. Mr Johne Craig, minister of Edinburgh, was chosin Moderator.

THE ORDER OF THE ASSEMBLEIS PROCEEDINGS.

Mr Knox, Maisters Johne Craig, Johne Row, William Christesone, were appointed to consult upon the order of proceeding in
actiouns to be treated in the Assemblie; which they did, as fol
loweth :—

First, That the moderator of the last Assemblie sall make tn
exhortatioun in the nixt Assemblie; which being ended, the As-

semblie sall proceed to the choosing of a new moderator, and so furth, from Assemblie to Assemblie.

Nixt, Sall follow the triell of superintendents and commissioners for planting of kirks; with the complaints, if there be anie, of superintendents, commissioners, or anie others, upon ministers.

Thridlie, The penitents remitted to their superintendents or ministers at anie preceeding Assemblie, sall be receaved according to the order appointed by the last Assemblie; and injunctions sall be givin to other notorious criminall persons, that ather are summouned by the superintendents, commissioners of kirks, or of their owne free will moved with hatred of their vice, present themselves to the Generall Assemblie.

Fourthlie, Suche things as were not decided at the preceeding Assemblie, and remitted to the nixt, or referred thereto by the Lords of Sessioun, auditors of the Excheeker, or otherwise, sall be decided and decerned upon.

In the Fyft place, Collectors sall be called to give in their accompts for their diligence; namelie, the names of suche as they have putt to the horne, that a remedie may be provided; and als, that they may be discharged or continued, as occasioun sall serve.

In the Sixt place, The complaints of countreis for want of superintendents sall be heard and provided for, according to the necessitie of the countrie which requireth; and appellations, made frome the Synodall Assemblies to the Generall, sall be receaved.

In the Seventh place, Questions proponed the first and secund day of the Assemblie sall be decided by suche as sall be appointed to that effect.

In the Eight place, All bills and complaints sall be read and answered.

THE BISHOP OF ORKNEY'S ANSWERES TO THE OFFENCES LAYED TO HIS CHARGE.

The Bishop of Orkney presented his answeres to the offences layed to his charge. To the First he answered, That it is true, that, in the 58th yeere of God, before the reformatioun of religioun, he was, according to the order then observed, provided to the bishoprick of Orkney; and, when idolatrie and superstitioun were suppressed, he suppressed the same also in his bounds, preached the Word and ministred the sacraments; planted ministers in Orkney and Zetland, dispouned benefices, and gave stipends out of his rents to ministers, exhorters, and readers; and when he was commissioner, visited all the kirks of Orkney and Zetland twise, to the hazard of his life, in dangerous stormes on the seas, whereby he contracted sicknesse, to the great danger of his life, till he was suspended from the exercise of the said commission in the yeere 1567, by reasoun of his infirmitie and sickenesse, contracted through the aire of the countrie, and travells in time of tempest; at what time he desired some other place to travell in, which was then thought reasonable. As for dimitting of his office, he denyed that ever he dimitted to my Lord Robert the same, or anie part therof; but that the said Lord Robert violentlie intruded himself on his whole living, with bloodshed, and hurt of his servants; and after he had craved justice, his and his servants' lives were sought in the verie eyes of justice, in Edinburgh; and then was constrained, of meere necessitie, to tak the abbacie of Halyrudhous, by advice of sundrie godlie men, becaus then we could not have the occasioun of a Generall Assemblie.

As to the Secund, he denyed that he had abandonned absolutlie the preaching of the Word, or that he intended so to doe; but was to bestow his travells in preaching, as the abilitie of his bodie, and sickenesse wherunto he was subject, would suffer or permitt. He confessed, that, in the 1563 yeere of God, he was required by the king's mother to be a Lord of the Sessioun, which he accepted, with advice of godlie and learned men, compting it not repugnant or contrarious to anie good order as yitt established in the kirk; and alledged, that diverse others having benefices have done the like, and are not condemned for so doing. Yea, he doubted not to affirme, as the office itself was allowable, so it sould be profitable for the kirk, that manie preachers of the Evangell were placed in the Sessioun. *Item*, Seing superintendents and ministers are, and may be, temporall judges in other inferiour offices, and no fault layed to their charge, he woundered why it sould be compted a fault in him onlie. As for the latter part of the secund article, he answered thus: " With pardoun and reverence of the Assemblie, I may declare that I never delyted in suche a stile, nor desired anie such arrogant title: for I acknowledge my self to be a worme of the earth, not worthie anie reverence: giving and attributing to my God onlie all honour, glorie, and reverence, with all humble submissioun."

To the Thrid article he answered, That it is true he had sett an assedatioun of the fruicts of the bishoprick of Orkney to the said Lord Robert, for the yeerlie payment of certan dueteis conteaned in his tacke. And albeit the said Lord Robert, for payment of a part of the yeerlie duetie foresaid, assigned unto him a certane pensioun, which his bairns had assigned unto them, of the fruicts of the abbacie of Halyrudhous, of which pensioun they had confirmatioun by act of parliament, and were in reall possessioun, without impediment, diverse yeeres; with provisioun also, that incace it sall happin the pensioun be evicted frome them, the said Lord Robert sall pay to him so muche silver, victuall, and goods of the fruicts of the bishoprick of Orkney, as extend to the just valuatioun of the said pensioun; which thing is done, and permitted universallie throughout the whole realme, that anie ecclesiastical person may sett a part of his benefice in tacke, for the yeerelie payment of a just duetie. And so, there is nothing bought or sold in defraud of ministers. But by the contrare, he being troubled by vertue of letters of horning, at the instance of the collectors of the kirk, and also at the instance of Lord Robert's bairns, charging him to make double payment, he meaned himself to the Lords of Sessioun, desiring both the parteis to be called before them, and to decide who had just title. Which actioun was yitt depending before the Lords, to his great hurt. For, in the meane time, his whole living is sequestrated; and, incace the collectors of the kirk evict, he will gett recourse and payment of the fruicts of the bishoprick; and that he

had made no other plea or impediment, by himself or by his procurators.

To the first part of the Fourth article he answered, That he had
no commissioun to plant or visite, since his entrie to the said abbacie ; but if they would give him a conjunct charge with the Superintendent of Lothiane, he sould so travell, that they sould be
satisfied. As to the secund part, he answered, That the whole
thrids of the benefice of Halyrudhous are to be payed furth, ather
to the collectors of the kirk, or to the Lord Robert's bairns. And
attoure, the most part of the fruicts of the two part of the said abbacie is assigned and givin furth in pensiouns to diverse persouns
before his provisioun ; and yitt hath payed to the ministers their
stipends, as they were wont to receave furth of the said abbacie,
and hath augmented some ministers' stipends : and also, if the
plea depending before the Lords were decided, would be als liberall
in the sustentatioun of ministers as become him, having respect to
the rent of the benefice ; and withall desiring, that so manie ministers, some times channons of the place, having a great part of the
living therof assigned out of certane kirks now altogether destituted, might be charged to serve rather in the said kirks than in
others, as other channons doe in other kirks wherof they receave
their living ; and promised, if so were done, to augment their stipends largelie.

As to the Fyft, he answered, That he was but of late come to
the benefice, and the most part of these kirks were pulled doun by
some greedie persons, at the first beginning of the reformatioun,
which have never beene helped or repaired sensyne ; and few of
them may be repaired by his small portioun of the living, but speciallie the Abbey Kirk of Halyrudhous, which hath beene these
twentie yeeres bygane ruinous, through decay of two principall
pillers, so that none were assured under it ; and two thowsand
punds bestowed upon it, would not be sufficient to ease men, to the
hearing of the Word, and ministratioun of the sacraments. But
with their consent, and helpe of an established authoritie, he was
purposed to provide the meanes, that the superfluous ruinous part,

to witt, the quire, and the croce kirk, might be dispouned by faithfull men, to repaire the remanent sufficientlie; and that he had
also repaired the kirk of Sanct Cuthbert's and Libberton, that they
were not in so good cace these twentie yeeres bygane. And farther, that there was an order to be used for reparatioun of kirks,
wherunto the parochiners were oblished as weill as he; and when
they concurred, his support sould not be enlaiking.

As to the last, he denyed that he spake anie thing but that
which he spake in the last Assemblie, in their owne audience. God
forbid that he sould be a detracter of God's ministers for anie privie
injurie done to him, as he alledged none; and if there were anie,
he would rather burie them, than hinder the progresse of the Evangell. As for absenting himself from their preaching, he answered,
he onlie keeped his owne parish kirk where he had receaved the
sacraments.

These were his answeres to the heeds of the complaint made
upon him. For he was charged with the simonaicall change of
the bishoprick of Orkney with the abbacie of Halyrudhous, and
dimitting the same in the hands of an unqualifeid person; and
had, *simpliciter*, left the office of preaching, giving himself daylie to
the exercise of the office of a Lord of the Sessioun, which required
the whole man, and cannot both be discharged by one man : That
he reteaned still the stile of the bishoprick, and stiled himself with
Roman titles, as, " Reverend Father in God," which belong not to
the ministers of Christ : That he nather planted kirks destituted of
ministers in either of the two, nor susteaneth them that are alreadie
planted : That the kirks are decayed, and made, some sheepe-
folds, some so ruinous that none darre enter into them, for feare
of falling; speciallie Halyrudhous, although the Bishop of Sanct
Andrewes, in time of Papistrie, sequestrat the whole rents of the
said abbacie, becaus the glasse windowes were not holdin up and
repaired : That he traduced the ministers of Edinburgh, as ministers passing the bounds of God's Word, in their publict preaching, and absented himself from their sermons. The rest may be
understood by his answeres.

Mr Knox, Mr Johne Craig, Mr David Lindsay, were appointed to trie the sufficiencie of these answeres, and to report to the nixt Assemblie. In this accusatioun we may perceave, that the office of a Lord of the Sessioun, and of a bishop or minister, were thought incompatible in one man's persoun; and that the stile which is now givin to our prelats, "Reverend Father in God," was compted a Roman or Antichristian stile.

The commissioners appointed in the last Assemblie to give answere to my lord regent's Grace's desires, produced the said answeres, with his Grace's promises conteaned therin; together with the assignation of money and victualls to the king's Majestie's hous, the regent's Grace and others, both subscrived with his hand. First, They condescended, that the assignations before granted for the king's Majestie's hous, and other commoun effaires, stand in forme as before; and that during the kirk's will. *Item*, That the summes appointed for my lord regent's owne hous, extending to five thowsand merks or thereby, which the collector sould have payed, sall be payed. Becaus thir premisses are granted, my lord regent promiseth faithfullie, not to charge the kirk with anie farther duetie of the thrids; but if a superplus remaine, the ministers being payed, it sall be bestowed to suche godlie uses as the Assemblie thinketh best, by his Grace's advice. And to the effect that good payment may be givin of the whole, my lord regent's Grace promiseth to travell to the uttermost of his power, that obedience may be givin, and that the lawes made against disobedients sall be executed. Farther, his Grace giveth power to choose or depose, if need be, their owne collectors, and to call them to accompt when they thinke good, without prejudice of the generall compt yeerelie to be made in the Exchecker. In like maner, his Grace condescendeth to the particular assignatioun of ministers, where they may be convenientlie gottin, without prejudging the assignations before granted, and the summes granted to my lord regent's Grace his house, providing the forsaids assignatiouns, *ipso facto*, be dissolved, whensoever the assigncy obteaneth anie benefice sufficient for his stipend, or that the Assemblie sall think

otherwise. *Item*, That ministers' and superintendents' stipends
sall be modified and appointed by suche as the Generall Assemblie,
having warned his Grace and counsell therunto, sall appoint.

JAMES, REGENT.

Mr David Lindsey was appointed to present certan articles to
the Lords of Sessioun, and to require their answeres. The articles
and answeres follow :—

" First, The thrids are decerned to perteane to the ministers, by
a law past *in rem judicatam*, and have receaved executioun of a
decreit, and sentence of liquidat summes and victualls ; against the
which, your lordships, by your daylie practick, use to give no suspensioun, without consignatioun of the summes decerned : and notwithstanding there are so manie suspensions of this executioun for
the thrids givin, that both your lordships are troubled with the
processe, and the poore ministers defrauded of that wheron they
sould live : For remedie wherof, the Assemblie most humblie requireth your lordships to take suche order heerin, as that no suche
suspensions be givin for the thrids in times comming, except the
compleaner, desiring the suspensioun, make payment to the collector of so muche as is out of questioun, if it stand in difference of
the questioun of the rentals ; and consigne in the Clerk of Register's hands so muche more, as sall happin to be decerned, or find
cautioun in Edinburgh responsable therefore : And likewise, consigne or find cautioun, if he clameth the whole thrid, to be discharged for the whole : and that none of thir passe upon light
causes, but be read in presence of your whole lordships, before the
bills be past and delivered." 16 *Martii* 1569. AGREED.

" *Item*, That no letters past upon your lordships' decreits, givin
upon new provisions or summouns, warrand all parteis to heare
letters givin, except there be speciall provisioun and exceptioun
made of the thrid therin ; or ellis, that the compleaner have sufficient testimonie, that his thrid is allowed in his stipend, or remitted
by some good order, and show the kirk's admissioun and ordinance

therupon : And for observing therof, that your lordships would take suche order with your owne clerks of the sessioun, that no letters passe by the provisioun foresaid; and that the cautions be givin or sufficientlie notified in writt to the clerk of the collectorie, or to the procurators of the kirk, to the effect that the kirk may call therefore, when time is." AGREED.

" *Item*, That your lordships will give letters, at the instance of the procurators of the kirk, to charge all beneficed persons that as yitt have not givin in their rentals, to produce and give in the same, at a certaine day to be appointed by your lordships thereto ; with certificatioun if they faile, your lordships will direct letters to uptake and inbring the whole fruicts of their benefices to the use of the ministrie, conforme to the first act and ordinance made for uplifting of the thrids : And, in the meantime, that yee would give command to the commissars to sequestrat the whole fruicts of their benefices forsaids, not givin up in rentall, as said is, with letters of full inhibitioun, by your own deliverance, that none answere, obey, or make payment of anie part of the fruicts of the saids benefices, unto the time the possessors pretending right thereto give in sufficient rentals therof; and ather give particular assumptioun, or cautioun for thrids, as the kirk will stand content with." AGREED.

" *Item*, That according to your lordships' order alreadie made, tuiching the calling of the kirk's actiouns, and promise made therupon, that yee will caus the same be observed, to witt, that everie day of the sessioun yee will call one of the kirk's actions to be givin in by the solisters and procurers of the kirk, as weill of the particular as generall causes therof. And becaus it is weill knowne to your lordships, that fra yee enter in other causes, it is not possible to you to gett anie other called, therefore your lordships will condescend and ordeane the said actiouns of the kirk to be daylie called first, before anie other, so that they be not differed to the end, wherethrough, both the actiouns ly uncalled, and your lordships are troubled and slaundered, that yee doe nothing in the kirk's

causes. Answere, THE LORDS WILL DOE SUCHE DILIGENCE TO
SATISFIE THIS ARTICLE AS THEY MAY, GOODLIE.

> " *Georgius Gibsonus, Scriba Consilii, de mandato*
> *Dominorum Consilii.*"

ACTS.

Some adulterers and incestuous persons compeared in linnen
cloathes, bare-headed and bare-footed, with testimonialls of their
honest behaviour during the time of their publict repentance since
the last Assemblie, according to the injunctions givin them. They
desired to be receaved to the societie of the faithfull, willing to obey
farther injunctions, if it was the will of the Assemblie. The Assemblie ordeaned the saids persons, and all others who heerafter sall fulfill
their injunctions, and not stubbornlie contemn the admonitions of
the kirk in suffering the sentence of excommunicatioun to be pronounced against them, to make their publict repentance in sackcloath, at their owne kirks, bare-headed and bare-footed, three severall preaching dayes ; and after the thrid day, to be receaved in the
societie of the kirk, in their owne clothes : That others, who have
beene excommunicated for their offences, sall present themselves in
sackcloath, bare-headed and bare-footed. It was concluded, that
murtherers, incestuous persons, and adulterers, not fugitive from
the lawes, but continuallie suting to be receaved to publict repentance, sall be receaved to give the signes of their repentance in their
owne kirks, according to the order appointed before by the Generall Assemblie to suche persons ; at which time the minister sall
notifie, publictlie, their crimes, that the civill magistrat pretend not
ignorance. The particular injunctions to be used by everie particular kirk, tuiching the triell of the repentance of these that are
admitted, or heerafter sall be admitted, by the Generall Assemblie
to publict repentance, for slaughter, incest, adulterie, and other
haynous crimes, are these, to witt, If they be excommunicated,

they sall stand bare-headed, at the kirk-doore, everie preaching day, betwixt the Assembleis, secluded from prayers before and after sermoun; and then enter in the kirk, and sitt in the publict place of repentance, bare-headed, all the time of the sermoun, and depart before the latter prayer. Others that are not excommunicated sall be placed in the publict place of repentance, where they may be knowne from the rest of the people, bare-headed, the time of the sermouns, the minister remembring them in his prayer, after the preaching. And the saids persouns sall bring their minister's testimoniall to the nixt Assemblie, of their behaviour in the meane time, according to the act made thereupon in Julie 1569. In that Assemblie, some adulterers and incestuous persons, excommunicated for their offences, desiring to know what the Assemblie would injoyne them, the Assemblie ordeaned them to repaire to their superintendents, or to the ministers, elders, and deacons, of their owne kirks respective, and receave injunctions from them, how they sould behave themselves till the nixt Assemblie; and that they might bring a testimoniall from their ministers of their behaviour to the Assemblie; and that they present themselves to the nixt Assemblie, bare-headed and bare-footed, in linnen cloaths, humblie requeisting the Assemblie for farther injunctions, and to be receaved into the bosome of the kirk.

It was concluded and ordeaned, that all collectors be warned to compeare at all Generall Assemblies heerafter, to know the minde of the Assemblie tuiching their offices, and other effaires perteaning to them in the kirk, under paine of deprivation from their offices. The Superintendent of Fife, Mrs Johne Row, David Lindsey, and James Nicolsone, were appointed to consult with the Clerk-Register, for ordering suche things as were referred to the Assemblie by the lords' auditors of the Exchecker, and cheeflie tuiching the diminishing of the rentals of the thrids. As for the selling of victuals from yeere to yeere, the Assemblie thinketh it expedient, that everie superintendent or commissioner, where there is anie, and that failing, the next superintendent or commissioner adjacent, with the assistance of suche assessors as they sall thinke good to assume, sall appoint the prices yeerelie of victuals, and notifie the samine to the collectors, in suche secreit maner as they sall think expedient.

It was concluded, that superintendents and commissioners of kirks, in time comming, sall, with the ministers of their provinces, or most part of them in their synodall conventions, choose and depose their collectors, as occasioun sall serve. The Assemblie appointed everie superintendent and commissioner in their owne provinces, with the assistance of so manie ministers as they sall choose, to tak particular assumpts of the thrids of all benefices not yitt assumed, and to report the samine to the nixt Generall Assemblie.

It was ordeaned, that everie superintendent or commissioner for the time modifie the stipends, augment or diminishe the same, as occasioun sall serve, with the assistance of the brethrein presentlie nominated, providing they report the said stipends, the ministers' names heerafter to be planted, the augmentatioun or diminution of the stipends to the register of the ministrie and their stipends; noting the time of appointing of the stipend, the entrie of everie minister, and time of augmentation of the stipend, to the effect that they and the collectors may have the extract and rolls therof.

It was ordeaned, that no minister provided, or that sall heerafter be provided, to anie benefice, sall sett in tacks anie maner of way their gleebs or manses, or yitt anie part of the fruicts and emoluments therof, in diminution of the rentals, under the paine of deprivatioun from the benefice for ever. It is also decerned, that the tacks sett in maner forsaid be null and of no effect, as sett by him who hath no power.

QUESTIONS DECIDED.

The brethrein appointed to decide questions exhibited their resolutions as followeth :—

1. That suche as will not forbeare the companie of excommunicated persons sall, after due admonitioun, be excommunicated, unlesse they promise to forbeare.

2. That the person, committer of the murther of the good regent, is to be excommunicated in all notable touns ; and the excommunicatioun is to be notified in parish kirks, where there is order established. That the rest who had anie art, part, or counsell therin, or mainteane the same, are to be proceeded against, as they may be lawfullie convicted.

3. That ratificatioun of things granted by my lord regent's Grace to the kirk is to be craved, and farther, as the Assemblie sall thinke good.

4. That the childrein of excommunicated persons may be receaved frome a faithfull member of the kirk to be baptized.

5. If parteis be contracted, bannes proclamed, and the day appointed for solemnizatioun of the mariage in presence of the congregatioun, the woman refuse to take the man, the mater is to be refered to the commissars, and the woman to be punished, upon triell of the caus, according to the order of the kirk.

6. That it is to be meanned to the lords, by way of supplicatioun, that the tithes of the abbaceis now vacant, and not provided, sall be employed to the sustentation of the ministrie.

7. A single woman committing adulterie with a maried man, sould be punished as weill as the man, and receave injunctions of the Generall Assemblie.

8. If a man have repudiated his wife without caus, lett the minister labour for reconciliatioun, and the partie offended compleane to the judge competent.

9. A promise of mariage being made before the reader and elders, and the parteis contracting compeering before the minister and sessioun, require their bannes to be proclamed ; which being done, carnall copulatioun hath followed, by confessioun of both parteis ; but when they are required to proceed to the solemnization, the woman refuseth : the partie refusing ought to be admonished, or

ellis gett a decreit from the judge competent, that they sould not marie, under the paine of excommunicatioun.

10. If after promise of mariage made before witnesses, and proclaming of bannes, no carnall copulatioun following, the parteis desire to be free, lett them be free, *si res es integra*, and their unconstancie be punished.

11. Two men having lyin with two sisters, anie of them may marie the daughter of the other man, begottin upon another woman, and not upon anie of the two sisters.

12. A minister having a benefice in one shire, and another in another shire, may not be chosin to the thrid office, viz. of a superintendent or commissioner, except the particular kirks be provided, according to the time.

13. In respect of the great offences committed in disturbing the commoun peace, and breaking the unitie which God hath made betwixt the realmes, and that by these who have avowed themselves professors of the Word of God, who have not allanerlie often times committed the forsaid offences, but still to aggredge the same, have receaved, receave, and mainteane (despising heerin God and the present authoritie) the rebels of England; lett the minister reprove, where anie suche offenders are, without exceptioun of persons, conforme to God's Word, prudentlie.

14. If anie persoun having alreadie a sufficient stipend, and therafter called to the office of a superintendent or commissioner, sall have a new stipend appointed, or sall be content with the old, if it be sufficient for the office; or at the most receave suche augmentatioun, as the burthein of the office requireth? It is answered, Lett this be considered at their electioun or admissioun.

15. A man having two benefices in sindrie shires, under sindrie superintendents, serving for one of them, if he sall have the thrid of the other discharged? This questioun was answered before.

16. It is not lawfull for ministers to leave their vocatioun, and exerce other offices and charges within the commoun weale, with-

out consent of the Assemblie. And, in times comming, it is needfull that all who sall serve in the ministrie be publictlie admitted.

17. A certan man, whose wife was banished out of Dundie, ten yeeres since, for certane crimes committed by her, hath begottin a child upon another woman, about two yeeres since, not knowing whether his wife was living or deid ; for which offence he was punished by the magistrat, and hath made diligent inquirie, according to the injunctions givin to him, to learne whether she was living or deid, and can come to no certan knowledge therof : asked, Whether the Assemblie will injoyne him anie farther satisfactioun ; and whether he may have libertie to marie? Answere, Edicts are to be served for further searching of the woman, and further punishment for proceeding in mariage is to be suspended to the nixt Generall Assemblie.

MINISTERS AND ABUSERS CENSURED.

Mr George Leslie, minister of Kilconquhar, was admonished to mak residence at his kirk ; and incace of disobedience, it was ordeaned that he be suspended or deposed. Johne Flint, vicar, pensioner of Ayton, summoned to compeere for abusing the sacraments, compeered, and was ordeaned to absteane from all functioun within the kirk, till the Superintendent of Lothiane trie his abilitie and learning.

Johne Adam of Mauchline, excommunicated for presenting his childe to be baptized by a Popish preest, in Papisticall maner, presented himself before this Assemblie, to receave injunctions for the forme of his repentance.

COMMISSION.

Andrew Lord Uchiltrie, George Hume, Laird of Spott, Robert Fairlie, Laird of Braid, William Lawder, Laird of Hattoun, Andrew Ker, Laird of Fadownside, the Superintendent of Lothiane, Mr Knox, Mrs George Hay, David Lindsey, Johne Row, were ap-

pointed to conveene before the nobilitie presentlie assembled in
Edinburgh, and whensoever they sall assemble heerafter, till the
nixt Assemblie ; and in their name present some articles, require
and receave answeres, and report the samine to the nixt Assemblie.

A CONVENTION AT EDINBURGH.

Upon the thrid of Marche, the bastard bishop, with the Hammiltons, the Erle of Argile, and Lord Boyd, assembled at Linlithquo. A servant or freind of the Lord Boyd's had killed one Gib-
bie, a souldiour, wherupon arose no small tumult among the Hammiltons' souldiours, and others defenders of this Boyd. The nixt
day, the Hammiltons, with their bishop, returned to their dwelling-
places in Cliddisdaill. Some alledge, that a claus conteaned in the
safe-conduct granted to all men to repair to Edinburgh was the
occasioun of their returning. The claus was this, That no man
lying under the doome of forfaultrie sould injoy that benefite. So
they durst nather marche fordward nor stay still. Huntlie, Ogilvie, Crawfurd, Atholl, Hume, Seton, Lethington the soule of all
the godlesse band, repaired to Edinburgh. The Erle of Morton
was in Edinburgh before, slenderlie accompanied, till the Erle of
Marr and Glencarne with their freinds come. The heads of both
parteis mett together upon the fourth of Marche, to consult upon
the commoun effaires : but they could come to no determinatioun,
becaus the other partie pretended that Argile was absent, whose
presence was needfull. The Erle of Huntlie tooke franklie in hand
to bring Argile to the rest of the lords, and went furth, the 12th
of Marche, out of Edinburgh to Linlithquo, but returned without
him ; for so his counseller, the secretar, thought best : for it was
his intention onlie to drive time, till he might find opportunitie
to work a change in court. He keeped counsell apart with the
queen's factioun. He pretended the inabilitie of his bodie ; but
the truthe was, they could doe nothing without him, more than the
wheele can doe without the axe-tree. He was lustie eneugh at his

table, both at noone and even.   He spaired not openlie to say at his table, that suche as had fled from England, had als honest and just a caus as ever banished men had.   When it was objected, that they had burnt ministers' bookes, deflowred men's wives, erected the idol of the masse; " Tush," said he, " they did that in the beginning, to purchase to themselves the moe freinds. But consider," said he, " the tenor of their secund proclamatioun."   Now, he himself formed this secund proclamatioun, wherof he maketh mentioun. The night after the Erle of Huntlie had returned from the Erle of Argile, there arose suche a feare among the godlesse band, that the most part of the night they lay in their jackes.   Huntlie, Atholl, Ogilvie, Crawfurd, Lochinvar, and the rest of that factioun, departed out of Edinburgh upon the morne, without anie further consultatioun, and Sir James Balfour in companie with them.[1]   At this conventioun, which continued from the 4th of Marche to the 15th, it was reasouned and disputed, upon what ground, and by what authoritie, they might appoint a regent or regents?   Some alledged the commissioun granted before, by the queen, about three yeeres since, whereby eight noblemen were designed to be tutors. Others objected, that that commissioun was expired, the regent being dead, and that it could have no strenth ; and therefore desired the mater to be refered to a lawfull and full parliament. And this was the secretar's shift, stoutlie mainteaned by Robert Matlane.   Others were of a diverse judgement from both the former ; to witt, that the present electioun of a regent or regents sould not depend upon the queen's commissioun, which, in the judgement of all godlie men, was invalide from the beginning ; nor be stayed till a parliament, becaus there was imminent danger in driving of time ; but that suche as from the beginning had acknowledged the king's authoritie, and had remained constantlie under obedience to the same, sould, without farther delay, putt order to all maters.   This

---

[1] Sir James Balfour of Pittendreich was a man so notorious for changing sides, and profiting by every change, during this mutable and self-seeking period, that it was commonly said of him, " He could wag as the buss wagged."

counsell was neglected, becaus it proceeded from a poore man. In this meane time arose a bruite, that the Erle of Lennox was to returne out of England, which greatlie vexed the secretar's braine.

GOOD MEN LAMENTING THE DEATH OF THE REGENT.

In the time of this conventioun, Mr Knox receaved letters from Doctor Vinfred, Mr Willock, and Mr Gudman, all three regraiting the death of the regent. Mr Gudman wrote thus :—" The flowre of Scotland, the crowne of nobilitie, the power of peace, the paterne of a godlie governement, and signe of God's favour, hath takin his leave and gone, I doubt not to our mercifull God whom he served. But woe to these devilish heads which have devised this foule, devilish murther! Woe to that unnatural monster, enemie to God and his countrie, and fullie possessed with Satan, that hath been the instrument! Woe to the whole nobilitie, and all that professe the name of God's people, if this be not extremelie sought furth and revenged, as was the abused wife of the Levite among the Benjamites! Lett the devisers of the murther tak heed ; for God seeth them, and his servants smell them furth."

LETHINGTON AND GRANGE THEIR PRACTISES.

The secretar, and the captan of the castell, now wrapped in factioun with him, stirred up two fire-brands, Phairnihirst and Balcleuche, to mak incursions upon the borders of England. They spared not to speeke reproachefullie of the Queen of England, and to call our noblemen her vassals or feals. They threatned to seeke aide out of France and Spaine, if the other sent for forces out of England.

THE REBELLIOUS LORDS' LETTER TO THE QUEEN OF ENGLAND.

About the end of Marche, the lords of the queen's factioun sent this letter following to the Queen of England. It was dyted by the secretar. They sett to the names of some who had no medling with them in the subscriptiouns, to make the Queene of England beleeve that their number was greater nor it was, for Marshall and Forbesse had nothing to doe with them.

"It may please your Majestie: The present dangerous estate of this our native countrie, joyned with the consideration of the future, with threatnings to both realmes, fearefull accidents, (if the love of our countrie move us not on both parts to foresight it, to avoide the perell afore hand,) compelleth us to have recourse to your Majestie, as the princesse in Christendome who hath best meanes, and, as we thinke, of good reasoun sould have the best will, to quenche this heate begunne among us, before it burst furth into a flamme, which is able, ere it be long, to sett both countreis on fire. We confesse the first like to be ours, seing the fire is alreadie kindled in our hous. Yitt the consequent therof is like to draw your Majestie's estate in the fellowship of the same danger, by reasoun of the nighbourhead, and other respects, which the situatioun of the two kingdoms in one Ile hath made commoun to both. It is no time now to us to hide the burning, wherof the smooke hath alreadie begunne to discover itself. Nather can we be perswaded, that your Majestie will refuse us that comfort which, by your concurrence, will suffice to remove our inconvenient, and consequentlie your owne, whose realme is nixt nighbour to this. Christian charitie will not allow, nather policie permitt, that whereas we require water at your hands, to represse the rage of the flamme, you bring oyle, timber, and other materialls, to increasse and nourishe it; for so doing, with our losse of the lesse, yee sall procure to your self the subversioun of more.

"Your Majestie is not ignorant how this estat is divided in factions; not onlie the persons of the nobilitie, but descending from them, the gentlemen and commouns universallie, in the whole lieges; and not so inequallie divided, that the one is so farre like to overmatche the other. But the victorie must be doubtfull, if maters be brought once to that part, that force must try whose querrel is best. The factions are grounded upon the diversitie of two titles pretended to the crowne, by the mother and the sonne: a pitifull caus, God knoweth, and yitt led by the thrawardnesse of time and our unhappe; which not the lesse must end betimes, or ellis, within a short time it is like to bring manie of us to an end. We find in ourselves small conformitie to appease the difference, for that the most part are particularlie inclynned, for privat or publict respects, to the parteis; and doe see no towardnesse to anie amendiment. By the contrare, it doth appeare evidentlie, that so long as there are two clames, so long sall the two factiouns endure; and it is probable, that so long as there are two factiouns at home, neither factioun sall lacke maintenance abroad, but sall find some prince or forraine potentat, who by his countenance will feede their humor. Wherupon must follow, of necessitie, that by one meane or other, a number of strangers sall be drawin in this realme. How dangerous this sall be for us we know, and what prejudice therof may ensue to your Highnesse we remitt to your wise consideratioun, wherin we will not appeare otherwise too curious discoursers. This farre onlie we will tuiche: The foresight of this commoun danger sould induce us on all sides to a commoun consent, to provide the remedie against the same, which, in our opinioun, can be no other, but by removing the causes of divisioun, to make the effect to ceasse; to witt, by the reducing of the two clames to one, putt away the whole fundament of the factiouns.

"There is nather prince, potentat, nor people in Christendome, that hath the like interesse to desire it, nather yitt the like meanes to performe. It is profitable for your Majestie, that strangers have no pretended colour wherefore to enter in this Ile, or to sett foot on drie land, so neere your Majestie's countrie. It is honourable for your Majestie to sett at an accord the two persons who are made the parteis, being your nixt cousins, and most tender to you by blood. It is easie to your Majestie to bring it to passe, als weill

for your credite and authoritie with all the parteis, as that the principall partie is in your realme.   We thinke it not convenient to prescrive to your Majestie anie certan rule to follow in this case;
for we consider what your Majestie is to whom we write, and what
persons we are that doe write.   Yitt, for our opinioun, we see no
more convenient meanes to reduce this realme to uniformitie, and,
consequentlie, to procure the quietnesse of the whole Ile, than that
your Majestie will enter in suche conditiouns with the queen's Highnesse of Scotland, as may be honorable for all parteis, sure for your
Majestie, safe for the nobilitie of this realme, and appearand to continue the godlie amitie betwixt the two realmes, which is most commodious for both.

  " We are the more bold to enter with your Majestie in this heed,
for that a good part of us saw, the last yeere, a certan platt, under
the forme of articles, projected, tending to this end, and sent hither
from your Majestie to the late regent, by his servant, Mr Johne
Wood; wherof, albeit at that time there was not so great consideration had in an assemblie of a part of this nobilitie conveened at
Sanct Johnstoun to that effect, as the weight of the same, and
your Majestie's persoun, being the directer, did require, yitt find
we in the same mater, so great moment, worthie to be intreated of.
And most humblie praying your Majestie to take the same once
againe in your hand, and follow furth the same trade, which we
thinke the neerest, yea, the onlie meane to divert us frome the
desperat course wherin we are ather alreadie, or like shortlie to enter,
for laike of a good unioun amongst ourselves, we trust, no faithfull
counsellor you have will advise your Majestie to enter the turn-over
of a divided estat, to bestow your forces, men, or money, in an un-
necessar and unprofitable exploit.   And unprofitable it will prove
in the end, if your Majestie sall joyne your fortune with a small
portioun of this realme, where ye may have the whole at your devotioun, if yee will; to witt, if yee goe about to unite us as one
flocke, under the obedience of one head, by entering in conditions
with the Queene of Scotland, wherby the different clames betwixt
her Highnesse and her sonne may ceasse from henceforth.   In do-

ing wherof, your Majestie sall oblishe us (and so we protest) to doe unto your Highnesse what service we sall be able, standing with our obedience due to our soverane.

" And so, after our humble commendations to your Majestie, we committ you to the protection of God.   Written towards the end of Marche 1570.

" By your Majestie's humblie to command :

" Erles Huntlie.	" Erles Sutherland.	" Lords Yester.
Argile.	Eglinton.	Fleeming.
Atholl.	Lords Hume.	Hereis.
Arroll.	Seton.	Boyd.
Crawfurd.	Ogilvie.	Somervell.
Marshall.	Rosse.	Innernieth.
Cathnesse.	Borthwicke.	Forbesse.
Cassils.	Oliphant.	Gray.

" William Matlane, Comptroller.   Balfoure."

THE FAMOUS AMBASSADER MONSIEUR VIRACK SENT TO THE
REBELLS.

About the same time, there came from France a varlett of the king's chamber, named Monsieur Virack. He was receaved in Dumbartane as an honorable ambassader, and was conveyed by the Lord Fleeming to Nidrie, the Lord Seton's place. The secretar was unable of his bodie, yitt must he be careid hither in a coache. There the Lord Seton and the secretar conferred with this famous ambassader! What was the subject of their consultation was un-knowne; but within foure or five dayes after, Phairnihurst and Bal-cleuche road in England, and burnt Harram. The northland lords, mainteaners of the queen's authoritie, wrote to the Lords of the Sessioun, to superseed all ministration of justice, till they might waite upon their freinds' actiouns, and have an established autho-ritie. When the secretar came frome Nidrie, he conferred with the captan of the castell, at St Cuthbert's kirk. Upon Moonday

therafter, the captan's freinds, with others of that factioun, came to
Edinburgh, to punishe the deacons of the crafts, for a ryott committed in staying of victualls. It was reported that the captan was
the cheefe man that sent away the victualls.

THE REBELLIOUS LORDS' DECLARATION OF THEIR INTENTION.

The rebellious lords appointed a conventioun to be holdin at Linlithquo the tenth of Aprile. They declared by open proclamation the causes of their conveening, and by what order they intend
to proceed heerafter, in all their actiouns tending to God's glorie,
and defence of the realme, the observatioun of peace with all confederat friends and allyaes, and tranquillitie of the realme. They
acknowledged, that the first honorable caus interprised by some
other noblemen in the pursute of the Erle Bothwell, who had presumptuouslie putt hands in the queen's Majestie, deteaned her as
captive, envirroned her with a guarde of men of warre, constrained
her by just feare, against her will, to enter suddanlie with him
in a pretended mariage, which was not tolerable, neither could
the issue be lawful; to releeve her Highnesse from his boundage
and tyrannie, and to sequestrat her persoun from his societie, till
he were punished or expelled, was an actioun worthie of praise.
But the order of their actioun sensyne make manifest, that these
were but pretences. Yitt are they content, that the ground and
originall caus, als weill of the principall controversie, as of the particular and inferiour dissentiouns, may be coldlie reasouned, and
wiselie considered in a peaceable conference, where bragging sall
not lett noble men to speeke their mindes and judgements; and to
open the grounds of maters and circumstances in suche sort, as the
necessiteis in all respects being duelie regarded, the best, or least
of the evills, may be embraced or accepted. They purge themselves of anie intentioun to alter religioun; yea, affirme that they
may challenge to themselves that honour, that, under God, they
were the cheefest and first instruments of the promotioun, continuance, and establishing therof; that they preferred the advance-

ment of it to their lands and lives, and that it is yitt more deere to
them : yea, if the noblemen now conveened, which are of the first
places and greatest number, sould intend alteratioun of religioun, in
whose power beside sould it stand to withstand it ? They professed
they were desirous of the unioun of the realme ; that all noblemen,
and other good subjects, may injoy their owne ranks, callings, and
places, in peace and quietnesse; that to this effect they offerred to
conveene, with others of the nobilitie that differ frome them in
judgement, in convenient time and place, and would stay so long as
they may, if they can see anie hope of familiar and peaceable conference : that the grounds and occasiouns of the late controverseis
being disclosed, the necessitie of the state, and everie nobleman
particularlie interessed weyghed and regarded, an uniforme resolutioun may be takin by commoun consent, for the furthsetting of
God's glorie, for the queen's Majestie's estate, that she remaine
not as a barren stocke ; that the successioun of the crowne may be
the more strong, and he whome God, of his mercie, hath graunted
to us for our confort alreadie, may be honorablie provided, as weill
for the safetie of his person as continuance of his estate : that the
godlie peace standing betuixt this realme and all other commoun-
wealths may be interteaned, and mutuall concord among all noblemen and other lieges in the countrie ; that justice may proceed, and
be ministred, according to the lawes ; and that everie nobleman,
and others, may possesse in suretie their lands, lives, rents, and
goods : that, ere perrell sould fall to anie of the other partie presentlie separated from them, they would rather yeeld to lesse than
reasonable conditions, and will be content to be partakers of all
suche hazards and dangers that the others can thinke themselves
subject unto, so that they will receave upon them a portioun of
anie difficultie or inconvenient possiblie may fall, tending to the
suretie of the others, and repose of the whole estat.   Then they
protested if this overture sould be contemned, and so, proper meanes
of re-unioun of the nobilitie and quietting the estat refused, and
therupon they be constrained to provide for the realme and their
owne sureteis, and so strangers be brought in on all sides, that the

blame be imputed to the refusers. That none pretend ignorance, they ordeane an herald, macer, or other officer of armes, to passe to the mercat croce of the burgh of Edinburgh, and all other burrowes and places needfull, and there, by open proclamatioun, make publicatioun, requiring all the lieges judge of their intention, according to the equitie of the mater; concurre, fortifie, promove, and sett fordward the same; and no wise assist whatsoever others that sall attempt anie thing in the contrare, under anie kinde of pretence, cloke, or authoritie, or otherwise; certifeing them that doe in the contrare, they would esteeme them as seditious, and enemeis to the publict peace. They ordeaned likewise, that the said officers of armes command and charge, that none of the lieges tak in hand to alter or innovat the forme of the true Christian religioun publictlie preached and receaved within this realme, or attempt anie thing against the lawes made in that behalfe; with certificatioun to them that doe the contrare, that they sall be punished according to the same lawes.

A CONVENTION OF THE REBELLIOUS LORDS AT LINLITHQUO.

At the convention holdin at Linlithquo, conveened Huntlie, Argile, Atholl, Ogilvie, Crawfurd, Hume, Seton, and the Secretar. The Lord Fleeming brought with him from Dumbartan the Erle of Westmerland, who was not yitt gone out of the countrie. There was also Leonard Dakers, secund sonne to William Lord Dakers, who encouraged Westmerland and Northumberland in their rebellioun, undertooke to kill the Lord Scroop, and fortifeid Naworth Castell; but was forced to flee into Scotland, the 22d of Februar last bypast, encountered in the feilds by the Lord Hounsden. The Lord Hereis was sett at libertie a little before. The secretar, as he went to Linlithquo, mett with the captan of the castell at St Cuthbert's kirk, and laboured with him, as was conjectured, that the Linlithquo lords might be receaved in Edinburgh. At this conventioun, they beganne to treat of that which they did whisper in secreit, to witt, to raise warre against the English, that the mur-

ther of the king and the regent might be ather forgottin, or men's
mindes being bussied with the warres, might languish in the pursute therof. But becaus they could not throughlie resolve in the
particular circumstances, they determined to goe to Edinburgh,
that their proceedings might have the fairer countenance, it being
the cheefe burgh of the kingdom, and the captan of the castell
being their secreit freind, howbeit he bare the people in hand, that
he was for the king. They sent to the proveist and counsell of the
toun, to understand if they would suffer them to come in to their
toun in a peaceable maner, to hold counsell. It was answered,
they would exclude none carefull of the commoun peace and tranquillitie of the realme, providing there were none in their companie
justlie suspected of the regent's murther, or none of the English
rebels; that they published no proclamations anie wise derogating
from the king's authoritie; that they beate no drumme, for waging
of men; and that they attempt nothing against religioun, or the
persoun of anie inhabitant. The conditiouns, howbeit hard, were
accepted. The Hammiltons and English rebels were excluded by
this their answere.

THE REBELL LORDS CONVEENE AT EDINBURGH.

The lawlesse band, with their gracelesse garrisoun of three hundreth Irish men, came to Edinburgh upon the 13th of Aprile. The
Lords Hume and Seton convoyed the English rebells to Leith.
They supposed they might draw the citicens of Edinburgh what
way they pleased; yitt could they not perswade them to deliver
to them the keyes of the toun and ports, notwithstanding the captan of the castell, their proveist, travelled to that effect. Upon
Saturday, the secund day after their comming, notwithstanding of
their acceptatioun of the conditions, they called the bailiffes and
counsell of the toun before them, and with stormie words, demanded how they durst tak upon them to prescrive an order to the nobilitie; and if they would stand to their last answere? They answered, they would heare their proveist before they gave anie direct

answere, seing they had not writtin without his advice. The lords, speciallie the Lord Hereis, emboldenned with this cold answere, craved, First, that they might have the keyes of the ports in their custodie; Nixt, that they may have libertie to beate a drumme; Thridlie, that the English may be permitted to come in to the toun, and spend their money; Lastlie, that the toun may be patent to all Scotishmen. They answered as before, and consulted the most part of that day. The bailiffes keeped the keyes of the ports, and no drumme was beaten. But the captan of the castell promised them safeguarde, so long as they remained within the toun, and that was a sufficient recompence. It was bruited, that he sold the castell for two thowsand crownes, and for the pryorie of Sanct Andrewes, to be givin to him and his heyres in few.[1] The English rebels were receaved secreitlie in Edinburgh. All this time there was great resort to Lethington. He was lying sicke of the gutt. His hous was therefore called the schoole, and himself the schoole-master, and suche as repaired to him, his disciples.

QUEENE ELIZABETH'S DECLARATION OF HER INTENTION OF SENDING AN ARMIE TO THE BORDERS.

The Queen of England published the declaration of her minde concerning the sending of an armie towards the borders, which was givin at Hampton Court, the 10th of Aprile, and printed afterward in Edinburgh. Her Majestie declared, " That some English rebels, having had former intelligence to beginne and prosecute

---

[1] Bannatyne, who, in many parts of his Memoriales, bewails, in pathetic exclamations, the defection of this chivalrous soldier, alludes to this bargain in the following words :—" Alas! Sir Williame Kirkaldie! (some tyme stout and true Laird of Grange!) miserable is thy fall, who now drawis in yocke with knowin and manifest traytoris, that sum tyme had place amonges honest heartis, yea, amongis the sanctis of God, and now are reputed as one of (the) most treasonabill traytouris yat ever lived ; who, for the pleasure of that father of traytouris, the Secretare, left (yea, betrayed) the Regent that promoted thé ; and now is bruited to sell the castle for two thousand crownes, and for the pryorie of Sanct Androis, to be gevin to thé and thyne in few! Judas joyed nocht long the pryce of innocent blood!'

their rebellioun with some disordered rebellious persons living upon the frontiers of Scotland, are mainteaned in Scotland by the said rebellious persons. That seing a great part of the ancient nobilitie and states of Scotland nourished peace and concord betwixt both the realmes, and are desirous to conserve the commoun peace in their native countrie, yitt seing they are not able presentlie, according to justice and the good order of the treatie, speedilie to represse and stay the said outlawes and disordered persons upon the borders, from open maintenance of the said English rebels, and from the invasioun of England ; and that some men of no meane calling within the bodie of the realme, taking their commoditie by the murther of the last regent, and, as seemeth, naturally invying the continuance of the commoun peace betwixt the two natiouns, and being affected with privat ambitioun and unquiett humours, doe stirre up with all their industreis certan factions, and great troubles in the bowells of their countrie, and thereby give confort not onlie to the English rebels, but also to Scotish outlawes, theeves, and disordered persons, to continue in their wickednesse and disorders, als weill against their owne native countrie, as against the subjects of England ; and that it is likelie that they will misconstrue and slaunder her Majestie's intent at this time, in leveing and sending certan of her forces to the borders, for defending of the same from anie further invasioun, and therewith to persue according. to justice her rebellious subjects, and according to the lawes of armes the invaders of her realme ; howbeit her Majestie hath givin prooffe, in former times, that she never sought nor covetted anie particular interesse in that realme for her self, as she easilie might, but to her great charges delivered and made free that realme, yitt, becaus the simple multitude, which are commounlie seduced by the craftier sort, having pretence of some rule, may feare evill or harme to follow to good people, or to the publict state of the crowne, by her armie now to be conducted towards that realme : Therefore assureth, in the word of a prince, all maner of persons, that her intentioun and certane meaning is, to use and treat all the subjects of Scotland als lovinglie and peaceablie as her

owne, excepting onlie suche notorious outlawes, theeves, enemeis
and peace-breakers, as have latelie with her rebells invaded and
spoiled her realme; and suche others of that natioun as have, and
sall support her rebells, contrarie to the treateis betwixt both the
realms : and that her Majestie hath givin strait charge to the Erle
of Sussex, Lieutenant of the north parts of her realme, and Captan
Generall to her said armie, to use the good subjects of Scotland that have, or sall keepe peace with her Majestie and her subjects, favourablie, as need sall require, howsoever some seditious
members of that realme sall otherwise misreport, or craftilie sall
procure to be by others misreported, who indeid in their slanderous
inventions are to be justlie suspected to the whole natioun, that
for their onlie privat ambitioun of rule and gaine, they will, upon
pretences, without caus labour to bring into the same suche strangers, with forces of sindrie sorts, as may shortlie hazard the whole
estate there, and reduce that ancient crown and natioun into a subjectioun, a perpetuall, miserable, and tributarie servitude."

A CONFERENCE APPOINTED BETWIXT BOTH PARTEIS, BUT NOT HOLDIN.

This declaratioun was brought to Scotland in time of the conventioun.   The generalitie of it displeased the godlie.   But it was
nothing pleasant to the Linlithquo lords, speciallie to Lethington
and the captan; for they had hounded out Balcleuche and Phairnihirst, to invade the English borders.   Atholl all this time spaired
no travell to draw the lords standing for the king to this conventioun holdin at Edinburgh : but they refused to come before the
first of May, the day appointed by commoun consent for the parliament, unlesse there were some necessitie to prevent the time.
If there were anie mater of moment which might not suffer delay,
they desired them to communicate the same with the Erle of Morton, who was then resident at Dalkeith.   A day was appointed for
conference betwixt the lords of both sides; but the rebell lords

thought it a derogatioun from their authoritie and credit to goe to
the Erle of Morton.

GRANGE HIS TREACHERIE.

The lords of the queen's factioun, when they would faine exclude the other lords out of the toun, and yitt could not draw the
citicens to take part with them, they intend to send for a greater
number, and to be masters of the toun by violence. They were
emboldenned in this enterprise by the captan of the castell, proveist of the toun, who sett at libertie, without anie publict warrant
of authoritie, the Lord Hereis, under colour, that his sonne was to
be delivered in pledge for him, the Shireff of Air his sonnes, and
Sir James Hammilton, upon Wedinsday, the 19th of Aprile; and
the day following, the duke, who made an harang or powred out
his complaint frome three after noone till six, to his great god, the
secretar. The Lord Hume was sett at libertie about the same
time; the Lord Seton a little before. The captan of the castell
had said, he sould bide by the king als long as anie man; which
imported, that in a publict defectioun, it was no shame to him to
follow the rest: and yitt, when others stood, he proved a tratour.
Siclyke, when he was admonished to be thankfull to the former
regent, who had placed him in that office; " I must," said he, " be
a freind to my freinds; and yitt sall I be true to him als long as
he liveth." Shortlie after followed the murther of the good regent. It was conjectured he understood more in that mater than
commoun men.

THE REBELS LEFT EDINBURGH FOR FEARE.

Whill the lords of the queen's faction were thus dealing and de-
vising, the rumor of the comming of the English armie confounded
all their devices. Hume and Hereis went home to defend their
owne castells and possessiouns. A portioun of the money which

5

was collected to wage souldiours was givin to the Lord Hume, to fortifie the castell of Hume. Phairnihirst and Balcleuche craved aide, or some forces to be sent to Lawder to ostentat warre, or a portioun of the commoun collectioun. When they could obteane none of these, they departed in great anger, to defend their owne as they might. The rebell lords sent two messingers to England, one to the queen, and another to the Erle of Sussex : to the queen, to stay the armie from comming doun ; to Sussex, to crave a truce, till the queen were informed of their estat. In their letters to the queen, they craved that all acts and conclusions agreed upon these two yeeres bygane might be rescinded, howbeit some of themselves had agreed unto them, and that a new decreet might be formed. They sett to the names of sindrie who were of the contrarie factioun, or neutrall, supposing, that in respect of the distance of place, the fraud would not soone be discovered, and the letters sent there would not be made commoun in men's hands. In the meane time, came Monsieur Lansack his servant out of France, with letters from the King of France, directed not onlie to the cheefe rebells, but also to indifferent men. Suche as had not yitt joyned themselves were requested to concurre. Promises were made of greater aide than was craved. The messinger added of his owne head, that there was peace and tranquillitie through all France ; and that he doubted not but souldiours sould be levied, to be sent to Scotland, before his returne. Howbeit the wiser sort gave no credite, yitt they were content that the simpler sort sould be deluded. But the returne of their messingers out of England, without obteaning their requests, marred all their mirth ; for the Erle of Sussex thought it an idle thing to interteane an armie, no conditions being offered by the enemie. The letters directed to the queen were found to be full of vain ostentatioun ; for the English were not ignorant of proceedings heere. The copie of their letters was sent to the lords, mainteaners of the king's authoritie. When they saw them disappointed of the favour they expected, that the English armie would come, that manie of their factioun had gone home to defend their owne houses, that the citicens of Edinburgh

did not favour them, that the lords, defenders of the king's authoritie, were to come to Edinburgh the first of May, they went to
Linlithquo; judging that place to be most convenient to assemble
their confederats there, to stoppe the passage of those who were
to passe to the conventioun, which was to be holdin at Edinburgh,
and to bring their devices to some fine. The Erle of Atholl and
Tullibardin departed out of the toun the 20th of Aprile. The
Lord Seton assembled his forces at the Palace of Halyrudhous.
He bragged that he would enter in the toun, and caus beate a
drumme, in despite of all the carles. He had in companie with
him the Ladie Northumberland. By the captan's moyen they were
receaved. But the burgesses keeped a strait watche everie night,
which they did, since the duke was sett at libertie, and his freinds
repaired to the toun. The duke went to Linlithquo the 29th of
Aprile, accompanied with seven score of horsemen, and fourtie or
fiftie souldiours.

THE PROCEEDINGS OF THE TWO CONVENTIONS OF THE LORDS CONTRARE TO OTHER.

The lords, defenders of the king's authoritie, conveened at Edinburgh in the beginning of May; the rebellious lords stayed at Linlithquo. They charge the other with seditioun and troubling of
the countrie. The lords standing for the king's authoritie offered
to satisfie anie man that would compleane of anie injurie done by
them, at the sight of indifferent men; to agree to anie conditions
which may serve for publict peace, providing nothing were dero-
gated from the king's authoritie, and the rest, who had separated
themselves, would concurre to the revenge of the murther of the
king and of the regent. But the Linlithquo lords sett furth proclamatiouns, charging all the subjects to obey the queen's lieutenants, the Erles of Arran, Argile, and Huntlie, and indicted a parliament to be holdin the first day of August at Linlithquo. They
tooke this boldnesse upon them, after that the English armie had
departed out of Scottish ground. The lords conveened at Edin-

burgh answered, that they would have no farther commouning with open and perjured tratours, suche as they were everie one, the duke onlie excepted, who had not sworne obedience to the king. Upon Moonday, the 8th of May, they caused declare, by open proclamation at the Croce, that the Linlithquo lords intended no other thing but to cloke and colour their devilish devices, and the foule murthers of the king's father and regent. All heralds, macers, messingers, and other officers of armes, were discharged to make anie proclamations at anie mercat croce within the realme in the queen's name, under paine of death. Shireffs, proveists, bailliffes, and other officers, were discharged to suffer anie proclamations to be made within their jurisdictions prejudiciall to the king's authoritie, under the paine of treasoun. Upon Tuisday, the 9th of May, to trie the affections of the inhabitants of the toun, the oathes of the bailliffes, deacons of crafts, and other cheefe men, were takin, that they acknowledge the king's authoritie. The Linlithquo lords craved of the captan of the castell, that the toun of Edinburgh might be patent to them, according to the promise made unto them before their departure. Some denied there was anie suche mater motiouned; others more privie, granted it was motiouned, but that no promise was made. A thrid sort alledged, that howbeit there had beene suche a promise made, yitt they were not bound to stand to it, becaus, when it was made, they knew nothing but that they were faithfull subjects to the king; but now they had declared themselves by their publict proclamations mainteaners of the queen's authoritie, solemnelie abrogated by parliament.

The captan stormed at this answere. It is true, when they would faine have gone out of the toun with honestie, manie pretences were devised. At last, this shift was found out by the secretare, the proveist himself, and Sir James Balfour, that the bailliffes, counsell, and communitie, sould requeist the proveist, and the proveist sould requeist the lords, to depart in peace out of the toun, but no farther. The lords conveened at Edinburgh sent Robert Pitcairn, Commendatare of Dumfermline, to the Queene of

England, to intreat her aide for suppressing of the commoun enemie; and to signifie to her their good minde toward her, in so
farre that they would not choose a regent, but by her appointment
or consent.

CASTELLS TAKIN OR RAZED.

Whill the lords were dealing against other, the Erle of Sussex,
Lieutenant of the North, Lord Hounsdane, Wardane of the East
Marche, and Sir Johne Foster of the Middle Marche, wasted the
lands and razed the castells belonging to Balcleuche, Phairnihirst,
and their assisters. Gilbert Gray was willed by the Lord Hume
to doe as William Drurie, Marishall of Berwick, would prescrive
to him. Mr Drurie communicat the mater with the Erle of Sussex. So the castell of Hume was randered and spoiled, farre by
the Lord Hume's expectatioun, who looked for greater favour at
their hands, knowing them to be secreit favourers of the Duke of
Norfolke. The Lord Scroope spoiled the Laird of Johnstoun's
lands in the west.

THE HAMMILTONS ASSAILE THE CASTELL OF GLASGOW IN VAIN.

Upon Saturday, the 13th of May, William Drurie, Marishall of
Berwick, came to Edinburgh with three hundreth horse, and a
thowsand foote, and the Erle of Lennox with them. The Hammiltons and their complices, after communing with the Lord Fleeming, made a suddan and secreit assault at the castell of Glasgow,
which they purposed to demolishe, least it sould be anie wise stedable to the Erle of Lennox. The captan was absent, and manie
of the garrisoun were excluded, by reasoun of the suddantie of the
assault. Yitt was the castell valiantlie defended by twentie-foure
men, and manie of the assaillers slaine or wounded. When it was
bruted at the first, that Minto his sonnes, and the rest of his companie, were slaine in the castell, Mr David Borthwick, an Hammilton in his heart, said, "Lett them fast now; lett them fast now,

for they have gottin a bloodie sacrifice!"   There was a fast at this
time in Edinburgh.

THE ENGLISH ARMIE MARCHETH TOWARD GLASGOW.

Upon Tuisday, the 16th of May, the English armie departed
from Edinburgh towards Glasgow.   Upon advertisement of their
comming, the Hammiltons left the seige of the castell, and their
Sow prepared for undermyning, eating draffe.[1]   The secretare
practised what he could to stay the English armie.   First, he spread
a bruite, that they were come to searche the Queene of England's
rebels.   When that device could not serve, he affirmed to the marishall, that the lords of the king's factioun (so he called them) were
not able to assist him with two hundreth horse.   The captan of
the castell wrote little lesse to Berwick, to Mr Randulph.   But before they past Linlithquo, howbeit the time was verie short, the Erle
of Morton his companie exceeded the double of that number.   When
they came to Glasgow, the Erles of Lennox, Glencarne, and Sempill, mustered in presence of the English armie foure thowsand
men, foote and horse.   The duke and Argile fled to Argile.   Huntlie fled to the north, als soone as the English armie drew neere to
Edinburgh.

THE CASTELL OF HAMMILTON RANDERED.

After consultatioun how to proceed against the rebells, and suche
as were suspected of the first and last murther, it was concluded,
that no rigour sould be used till the offenders refused reasonable
conditions.   First, That they underly the law for the murther of
the king or the regent, for anie art or part of the same.   Nixt,

---

[1] This was a joke uttered by a wag upon the present occasion.   The sow was a
sort of *testudo*, under which the miners were enabled to advance close to the walls ;
and is supposed to have received its denomination from its powers of rooting up and
undermining.   The punsters of the middle ages made merry with the name of the
engine, as in the present instance.

That suche as have takin armes against the king's authoritie, underly suche correction as sall be prescribed by the Lords of Secreit Counsell, and find sufficient securitie for their obedience in times comming.   Thridlie, That they observe the peace betwixt the two realmes ; and if anie have resett, fortifeid, or mainteaned the Queen of England's rebells, contrarie to the treateis, that pledges be entered by them, till they performe what sall be appointed by the Queen of England and her officers on the one part, and Robert, Commendare of Dumfermline, now ambassader for the king, on the other part.   Last, That for observatioun of the premisses, they sall enter themselves, or others for them, as the lords sall judge sufficient, as pledges, to be placed where it sall be thought expedient ; and, in the meane time, that they subscrive a band of obedience to the king, and renounce all other bands and subscriptions made to whatsoever person or persons, prejudiciall to the king, his state and nobilitie.   Space being granted to suche as would offer obedience, it was concluded, that the obstinate Hammiltons sould be punished in their substance, and by demolishing of their castells and houses, becaus their persons could not be apprehended.   Hammilton castell was defended stronglie in the beginning, by Andrew Hammilton of Myrrinton, having under him fiftie souldiours.   The English brought with them feild peeces, but they were not sufficient to batter.   Order was takin to bring great ordinance from Stirline.   In the meane time, the English compancis made some mutinie for pay, by the secreit instigatioun, as was thought, of Sir William Drurie, who secreitlie favoured the English rebells.   But money being provided for them, they were moved to stay.   When the two peeces of great ordinance were planted for batterie, the captan offered to rander the hous, upon conditioun to have their lives spaired.   The conditioun was granted, upon conditioun that they sould not beare armes against the king therafter ; and that they sould depart out of the realme for a certane time, wherunto they were sworne, as writteth Holinshed. The castell was spoiled, and therafter blowne up with powder. The palace and toun were burnt by the furious multitude, without

consent of their captans. Whether at this time, or in May, 1568,
I am not certane becaus of diverse reports, when the castell was
spoiled, there was found in it some apparell and houshold stuff belonging to King James the Fyft, which the duke, when he
resigned the governement, swore solemnelie, he had randered
whollie. At this time, Bothwellhauche, Roploche, Stennois, and
sindrie other houses belonging to the Hammiltons in Cliddisdaill,
were cast doun and spoiled.

LORD SEMPILL TAKIN.

The same day the armie returned from Glasgow, these that defended the castell of Hammilton besett the Lord Sempill, ryding
home securelie after this expeditioun, and careid him prisoner to
Dreffane, where he remained certane dayes ; and after was led to
Argile by the Lord Boyd, and keeped twelve moneths prisoner.

THE DEPARTURE OF THE ENGLISH.

The armie returned to Edinburgh the 19th of May. The English departed the 1st of June. Before the armie returned to Edinburgh, the bird in the cage, the secretar, tooke his flight from the
castell of Edinburgh, and lighted at lenth in the Blair of Atholl.

THE ERLE OF LENNOX CREATED LIEUTENANT.

The Commendatare of Dumfermline returned out of England,
and reported that the queene woundered that they had not informed her of their estat now foure moneths after the death of the
regent : that being solicited by the Spanish and Frenche ambassaders, she had promised audience to the Scottish queene, providing
she would move the noblemen, her favourers, to absteane from all
hostilitie, and to recall whatsomever proclamatioun they had published of late, and to leave maters in the same estat they were left
in before the death of the regent : that they would deliver the

English rebels; and if they agreed, pledges sould be delivered for
securitie. Therefore, till this treatie were ended, requested the
lords to absteane from armes, and the election of a regent, promising to be carefull that this prorogation of time sould be no
wise prejudiciall to them. Loath they were to offend her; yitt
needfull it was that one sould be placed in authoritie, becaus, by
this delay, the queen's factioun was emboldenned to creat lieutenants, to publishe proclamatiouns, and to usurpe a regall authoritie under the queen's name; and in the meane time, the favourers
of the king were discouraged, and it was to be feared that they
would make defectioun. Whill they were thus distracted with
doubts, they were certified out of England, that the Pop's bull was
affixed at the Bishop of London's palace-gate, and Paul's Churche-
yarde, for which Johne Felton was shortlie after apprehended.[1]
Ladie Marie, our king's mother, was thought to be privie to this
fact. Skarse could the lords be conteaned anie longer from choosing a regent. At last they resolve upon a middle course; and
presuming of her favour and freindship, they constitute the Erle of
Lennox lieutenant for twentie dayes, in which space they looked
for better newes; for they considered, if the English rebels were
delivered, all the Papists in England would be estranged from the
Scotish queen; if not delivered, there would be no treatie. They
assured themselves likewise, that the English queene would not
sett her free without sufficient pledges, which she was not able to

---

[1] This bull of deposition and excommunication against Elizabeth had for some time
been a dead letter, until Pius V. found a man hardy enough to publish it in London.
The extreme consternation produced upon the English Council, from its having been
affixed upon these public places, was so great, that an instant search was made among
the Inns of Court for the offender; a copy of the bull was found in the possession of
one of the students, who, on being racked, confessed that he had received it from
John Felton, a gentleman of property, living in the neighbourhood of London. Felton was put to the torture, to confess his accomplices; but as nothing could be extracted from him, he was sentenced to the death of a traitor. To show that no per-
sonal malice had inspired him, Felton before his execution drew a diamond ring from
his finger, valued at L.400, and sent it as a present to Elizabeth. It is supposed
that he had received the copies of the bull from the Spanish ambassador's chaplain,
who instantly left the kingdom to escape the consequences.

give. Another conventioun was appointed to be holdin the tenth of Julie, and letters were directed to England.

QUEEN ELIZABETH'S ANSWERE TO THE LORDS' LETTERS.

The Queen of England sent a letter to the Erle of Sussex, the secund of Julie, wherin an answere was givin to the Erle of Lennox, and the rest of the noblemen conveened with him. Her Majestie allowed their desire to have a speciall governour to be chosin, becaus of the inconveniences fell furth by the delay ; that she was weill content with anie they would choose, but in her opinioun, the Erle of Lennox, grandfather to the young king, is meetest for to have the governement for his safetie, ather alone, or joyntlie with others ; not that she will prescribe to them this choice, except they sall of themselves fullie and freelie allow therof : that finding that realme ruled by a king invested by coronatioun, and other solemniteis used and generallie so receaved by the whole estats, it was not her meaning, by yeelding to heare the complaints or informations of the queen against her sonne, to doe anie act whereby to mak confusioun of governements, or to suffer it to be altered by anie meanes that she may impeshe, as belongeth to her honour, and by her late actions hath manifestlie appeared, untill, by some justice and cleere caus, she sall be directlie induced otherwise to declare her opinioun. Sho willed the Erle of Sussex to give this answere in her name to the Erle of Lennox, and the rest of the noblemen.

THE ERLE OF LENNOX PROCLAMED REGENT.

This missive being read publictlie, was interpreted diverslie. Some thought it freindlie and plaine eneughe ; others thought it seemed to tend to this end, to receave the king's mother upon conditions. In end, it was concluded, that her missive sould be interpreted to the best part, till farther danger appeared. So, with commoun consent, the Erle of Lennox was chosin regent during the king's minoritie, from the 15th day of Julie, at which time he tooke his oath for maintenance of the lawes and liberteis of the realme, but speciallie of religioun. The lords promised to assist him to the uttermost of their power. After noone, he was proclamed Regent at the Mercat Croce of Edinburgh.

APPENDIX.

A.

" THE nobilitie and congregatioun professing the right religioun
of Jesus Christ within this realme of Scotland, presentlie persued
of their lives by the queene their soverane, to all princes, realmes,
and nations, to whose knowledge these presents sall happin to
come ; as also, to the residue of the same realme, their native brethrein, as yitt not joyned with them in the cause, wishe grace from
God the Father, mercie and favour from the Lord Jesus, with the
spirit of true knowledge and righteous judgement.

" Becaus we have beene now long (and yitt still are) persued
most rigorouslie, extremelie, and against all right and equitie of
our lives, as seditious rebells and tratours to our prince, commoun
wealth, and countrie ; and understanding that it cannot be but the
bruite therof sall shortlie be sparsed throughout all countreis, and
we burthenned with their odious titles of seditioun, rebellioun,
and treasoun : And least therethrough we sould be made odious
in the eares and sight of all good and vertuous princes, and other
professors of the same veritie that we doe, we have thought good,

in these few heeds, to notifie and declare the principall and cheefe causes that have moved us hitherto; which being weill considered and weyghed by you, and everie one of you, we doubt not but it sall be certanlie perswaded to you all, that these former crimes and titles are wrongfullie and unjustlie layed to our charge, and that we have done, nor intended nothing but that of duetie becometh the faithfull of God and true subjects to doe to their prince, native countrie, and commoun weale of the same.

" The first and principall caus is, the mainteanance of the true religioun, according to the writtin will of God, expressed in his Word, which we require by publict law to be established, als weill for us as for our posteriteis, according to the queen's Majestie's promise made at Stirline to the nobilitie and ministers in May last; and that all idolatrie and superstitioun, with all kinde of false wor-shippings of God, may be cleerelie abolished through all this realme, lyke as our sute hath beene to her Majestie continuallie, since her first arrivall in this her Grace's realme. For after our sore troubles and heavie travells not long past susteaned by us, for the same caus, it pleased God to shew his mercifull countenance toward us, and to establishe his true religioun through this whole realme, by parliament of the assemblie of the estats, which we now professe, and cheefelie are persued for; and thereby to abolishe the Papisti-call, with plaine determinatioun, who ever sould presume to prac-tise the same, or anie part therof, sould dee the death. This we injoyed, by the mercie and great favour of our God, inviolablie, a long space before the queen's Majestie's comming home out of France, so that none within this whole realme durst have beene so bold to have declared himself openlie to have professed anie part therof. And our soverane mistresse likewise, at her arrivall, by her publict ordinances and proclamations, inhibited, that none sould make innovation or alteratioun of that publict forme of religioun forsaid, which she then found publictlie erected, under the like paine of death; wherewith we gladelie quietted our selves, and en-deavoured our selves by all meanes possible to serve her Majestie in feare, love, and obedience knowne, that none of her Highnesse'

progenitors was ever so weill, and with so great quietnesse, obeyed
and served, as her Grace hath beene hitherto. But that ungodlie
and wicked religioun wherin her Grace hath beene brought up, beganne hastilie, after her arrivall, to crave one quiett masse to her
owne household onlie. And we, hoping that the mercie of God by
processe of time sould have converted her therefra, alas! (to the
great dishonour of God, as his heavie displeasure powred out upon
us this day testifieth,) past over with silence, and to the great
greefe of our conscience oversaw the same. For, from thence, it
proceeded plainlie to all that resorted to her chappell royall unpunished, from saying to singing; and from her chappell to all the corners of the country that listed. And when we craved punishment
of the transgressors, according to the act of parliament, and her
Highnesse' owne proclamations, even when we would obteane them
convicted in judgement, and the partie offending confesse the crime,
and comming in will therefore, we could have no executioun of the
lawes against them; and by the contrare, our poore brethrein, accompaneing the magistrats of the toun of Edinburgh, onlie apprehending a Papisticall preest in the verie actioun of idolatrie, contrarie to the said ordinance and act, and onlie setting him at the
Mercat Croce of the said toun, to be exponed but to mocking of
weomen, childrein, and commoun people, without anie further executioun of the said lawes, were persecutted most cruellie, and their
deaths threatned without mercie, if we of the nobilitie had not earnestlie interponed our great labours and sutes for their defence. If
this, and the like other her Majestie's proceedings in maters of religioun, (which were heere over tedious singularlie to repeate,) be not
the verie plaine way to suppresse the true religioun, and us, the professors therof, and to erect again the Papisticall, all men of judgement, als weill as we, might easilie have perceaved and plainlie
seene. Which also is now plainlie uttered, by the apprehending
and taking of some of the ancient and aged barons out of their
housses and beds, and that under silence of night, without all order
of law; the wairding and deteaning of them without anie crime
knowne, or that may be alledged, saving onlie the professioun of

the right religioun. And what meaneth ellis the dispositioun of the thrids of the benefices, which were promised and appointed by her Highnesse and counsell for the sustentatioun of the ministers, but for povertie to make them leave the preaching of the Word, and so to abolishe the true religioun of God? Or to what end intendeth the plaine inhibiting and discharging of Johne Knox, minister of Edinburgh, that he sall preache no more, then but at their pleasures, and when ever they will, to inhibite the remanent preachers in like maner, and to discharge all men of heareing of them, and so to tak away the preaching of the Word, and to destroy and suppresse the whole religioun? And that all men may understand the gravitie of our caus of religioun which we susteane, we would, it sould be knowne to them, that it is not onlie weightie to us, by the reasoun of our conscience, and duetie toward our God; but also in respect of the danger of the not establishing therof by law, bringeth to us, our lives, and ancient heritages, which altogether ly under the danger of forfalture, by lawes made in the time of Papistrie and blindnesse, so long as the same remaine unabrogated, and the other established being the contrarie. What marvell then is it, that we endeavoure our selves to our whole powers, and so earnestlie doe insist to have the forsaid true religioun ratified and confirmed by publict law, and the contraric abrogated? And this muche as tuiching the actioun of religioun.

" Secundarilie, Concerning the policie and commoun wealth, we that are of the cheefe of the nobilitie and counsellers of this realme, to whom of duetie it apperteaneth to have a speciall care of the publict effaires of the same, and of the preservatioun of the estate therof, als weill by reasoun of our birth and blood, as also by defence of the countrie, (in whose hands hath stand the defence therof by our blood shedding,) having advisedlie considered the great misorder and danger ensuing to the estat forsaid by diverse enormiteis and misorders, can doe no lesse, than by all meanes possible sue the same to be repaired and redressed. As for the first, her Majestie, to the great greefe of our hearts, leaving the wholsome advice and counsell of her Majestie's ancient nobilitie and barons, of whose faithfull and good service her Grace hath had long and good experience, and her Majestie's subjects, ease, repose, and justice, with diverse other great commoditeis, hath done, and yitt doeth in most part in her weightiest effaires, follow the advice and counsell of suche men, strangers, as have nather judgement nor experience of the ancient lawes and governance of this realme, nor naturall love toward her Majestie nor subjects therof; but being men of base degrie, and seeking nothing but their owne commoditeis, expone the greatest and weightiest effaires of governement and justice to their owne privat commoditeis. Of their sinister counsell hath ensued the misorder following: First, The most weightie mater of her Majestie's mariage was so inconsideratlie handled and haisted, contrare to promises, that beside the note of inconstancie wherewith our soverane is bruited, she hath incurred the disfavour and displeasure of forane princes, which are like to bring the incommoditeis of mortall warres, as it is notoriouslie knowne, als weill unto her Majestie, as unto all others that be of anie judgement within this realme. The same hath givin great occasion of divisioun and schisme within the same realme. And what dangers to the estat royall, and inconveniences to the whole realme are like to follow therupon, are easilie to be judged.

" Of the same sinister counsell doeth proceed, that her Majestie, without the advice of her estats, yea, without the advice of the nobilitie ather demanded or givin, hath made and proclamed a king over us, giving unto him, so farre as in her Highnesse lyeth, power over our lands, lives, and heritages, and whatsoever is deerest unto us in the earth. In the which doing, the ancient lawes and liberteis of this realme are utterlie brokin, violated, and transgressed, and the libertie of the crowne and state royall of Scotland manifestlie overthrowne, while he was made king over us, that nather hath the title therof by anie lineall descent of blood and nature, nather by consent of the estats. And what extremitie and wrong proceedeth therof to all the subjects, may be easilie seene also by that which alreadie beganne to be practised upon us, in that diverse of us, the ancient nobilitie, and sindrie of the barons and gentlemen of this our native countrie, are spoiled of their housses and goods, without anie caus expressed, and against all ancient lawes.

"Of the samine fountane of sinister counsell foresaid doeth proceed the dilapidating and waisting of the patrimonie and propertie of her Majestie's crowne, which within these eight moneths bypast is diminished more than the thrid part therof, to the manifest danger of the estat, and great greefe and hurt of the lieges. Which now doeth presentlie appeare, by the taxing and tousting[1] of her Majestie's barons and other lieges, which are tousted for repairing of that which was so indiscreitlie of the patrimonie forsaid dilapidated, as Edinburgh, and other severall persons have alreadie felt.

"And as the propertie and patrimonie of the crowne is thus dilapidated, even so are the benefices and patrimonie of the kirk waisted, bought, and sold, and finallie bestowed on them that are most unworthie and most unable to discharge anie suche vocatioun, and are enemeis to the right religioun.

"Of the same fountane of sinister counsell doeth proceed the divisioun that is raised betweene nobilitie and nobilitie, barons and barons, merchants and craftsmen, with the remanent estats of this realme, which is notoriouslie knowne to have been sought, procured, sett fordward, and brought into executioun by the forsaid counsellers in diverse parts of this realme, for their privat gain, and other respects. And also, it is not unknowne to diverse and sindrie, how (of the same sinister counsell) that the lives of diverse of the nobilitie have beene with all extremitie sought, whill as men of base degree, and voide of all good qualiteis, being placed in high degree, and unmeete rowmes for them and their qualiteis, can never thinke themselves in full securitie so long as men of vertue and honour, to whom of right that rowme ought to apperteane, sall stand a fordell,[2] to controll their abusings and wicked proceidings.

"And, finallie, it is also notoriouslie knowne to the whole realme, that few or no crimes so odious to these counsellers (except onlie to the true worshipping of God) but that remissiouns are able to be

---

[1] Assessing.   [2] Stand in precedence.

obteaned, and have beene obteaned, by the meanes of the forsaid
evill counsellers; and that for their particularitie, and for gaine and
brybes : now, persons so unworthie of offices and great charge, and
wherupon the justice of this realme cheefelie dependeth, they have
found, and daylie doe find, place and rowme to their sutes, and have
obteaned, and daylie obteane, the said rowme; which must bring
subversioun to the estat royall, and to the whole realme in the end.

"These enormiteis, and infinit moe, have, and doe give us just
occasions to assemble ourselves together, and, as it were, in one
bodie and one consent, to seeke by all possible meanes the reformatioun of the same; for the craving wherof, we are thus rigorouslie
persued, our lives sought with great extremitie, our housses, lands,
and heritages tane, our freinds most wrongouslie and extremouslie
used, and for no other crime that we have committed, ather against
the queen's Majestie, or our commoun wealth, or anie member therof. And, considering that this is the truthe, and cannot be denied,
we cannot doubt but all they that serve God unfainedlie, or minde
to have anie part in this commoun wealth, of what estate, degree, or
conditioun soever they be, will, in heart and minde, and personall
presence, concurre with us, to the obteaning of reformatioun of the
enormiteis foresaid, as they would be compted right worshippers,
and faithfull members of this commoun wealth. Protesting, in th
presence of Almightie God, that we crave not this reformatioun
for anie ambitioun, nather desire we to seeke the lives, lands, honours, rowmes, nor digniteis of anie Scotishman; but the maintenance of God's truthe, the good successe, godlie libertie, and re-
nowne of this our native countrie; declaring and assuring all Scotish
men, that if they refuse to concurre with us for the forsaid causses,
we can nather judge them faithfull to God, true to their soverane,
loving to this our commoun native countrie, nor keepers of their
promises made unto us in the caus of God, as the manifest part of
their owne hand-writts doe testifie. And if, for laike of concurrence, we sall be compelled to seeke support of other realmes, for
maintenance of the foresaid just causses, then, we protest also, that

their fearefull hearts, that nather regard God nor the commoun wealth, is the caus therof.

"Off Dumfreis, the 19th of September 1565."

B.

AN ACT THAT THE LORDS OF SECREIT COUNSELL MADE IN THE TOLBUITH OF EDINBURGH THE 12TH DAY OF JUNE 1567, DECLARING JAMES ERLE BOTHWELL TO BE THE PRINCIPALL AUTHOR AND MURTHERER OF THE KING'S GRACE, OF GOOD MEMORIE, AND RAVISHING OF THE QUEEN'S MAJESTIE.

" The which day, the Lords of Secreit Counsell and nobilitie, understanding that James Erle Bothwell putt violent hands in our soveran ladie's most noble person, upon the 24th day of Aprile last bypast, and therafter wairded her Highnesse in the castell of Dumbar, which he had in keeping; and by a long space therafter convoyed her Majestie, environed with men of warre, and suche freinds and kinsmen of his as would doe for him ever in suche places where he had most dominioun and power, her Grace being destitute of all counsell and servants; into the which time, the said erle seduced by unleasome wayes our said soverane to an unhonest mariage with himself; which from the beginning is null, and of none effect, for sindrie causses knowne as weill to other natiouns and realmes, as to the inhabitants of this commoun weale, and als expresse contrare to the law of God, and true religioun professed in this realme, which they are in minde to manteane to the uttermost point of their life. Attour, the said lords and nobilitie are assuredlie informed, that the same James Erle Bothwell, for to bring the mariage betwixt our said soveran ladie and him to effect, was the principall author, deviser, and instrument of the cruell and most abominable murther, committed upon umquhile our soverane lord, King Harie Stewart, of good memorie, which appeareth to be of veritie, becaus that the said James Erle Bothwell being maried and conjoyned with a wife, the time of the murther forsaid, hath sensyne, and speciallie when he had the queen's Majestie's person into his hands, caused a pretended divorcement to be made, and wrongouslie led, all the processe and sentence therof begunne, ended, and sentence givin therinto within two dayes: Which confirmeth the informatioun to the saids lords and nobilitie of the said Erle Bothwell. Als, he not being content and satisfied with the cruell murther done upon our said soverane, King Henrie Stewart, ravishing, wairding, and seducing of the queen's Majestie to an unlawfull mariage, and holding her yitt in captivitie, is now, as the saids lords and nobilitie are informed, making some assembleis of men, trysting and perswading them to assist him; which we looke, can be for no other effect, but for to committ the like murther upon the sonne as was upon the father; to the which, the saids lords and nobilitie minde with their forces to resist, and als to deliver the queen's Grace furth of most miserable boundage forsaid. Therefore ordeane a macer and officer of armes to passe to the mercat croces of Edinburgh, Perth, Dundie, Sanct Andrewes, Stirline, Glasgow, &c., and other places needfull, and there, by opin proclamatioun, command and charge all and sindrie lieges in this realme, as weill to burgh as to land, that they be in readinesse, upon three houres warning, to passe fordward with the saids Lords of Secreit Counsell and nobilitie, to deliver the queen's Majestie's most noble persoun furth of captivitie and prissoun; and upon the said Erle Bothwell, and all his complices that sall assist him, to bring them to underly the lawes of this realme, for the cruell murther of our said umquhile soverane, King Henrie, and ravishing and deteaning of the queen's Majestie's person; and to obviat and resist this most wicked interprise, which, we are informed, he intendeth to doe against the prince. Attour, we command all and sindrie suche as will not assist to the revenge of the premisses, and to deliver the queen's Grace's person furth of thraldome, together with all suche as are assisters, complices, or partakers with the said

Erle Bothwell, that they, within foure houres after publicatioun of this present Act, voide and rid themselves furth of this burgh of Edinburgh ; with certificatioun, incace they failzie, that they sall be holdin and reputed as enemeis, and punished-in bodie and goods as effeirs."

Imprinted at Edinburgh by Robert Lickprevick. 1567.

C.

BOTHUEL HEPBURNE'S TESTAMENT AND LATTER WILL.

" The Confession of the Lord Bothuell before he died, in the presence of foure lords of Denmark, with manie others in Malmye Castell, under the King of Denmark's jurdisdiction, writtin more at length in the Latine and Danish toung ; and these be their names ; Berreis, governour of Malmye Castell, Pittabray of Alsenburgh Castell, Presizbraw of Vaseull Castell, Mons. Guilliam of Starne Soncostre Castell ; with the Bishop of Shone, and foure baliffs of the town ; desiring him, that he would declare his confession, and say nothing but the trueth concerning the King and Queene, and Child, her sone.

" He took it upon him at his death, that the queene did never know nor consent to the death of the king ; but he, and his freinds by his appointment and device, and likewise diverse lords, consented therunto, who were not there present at the doing of the deid ; and these be their names ; the Lord James, (after regent,) the Lord Morton, the Erle of Glencarne, the Erle of Argile, the Lord Robert, the Laird Lethingtoun, the Lord Boyde, the Laird of Grainge, the Erle of Huntlie, the Erle of Crawfurd, the Laird of Balcleuch, the Laird of Phairniherst, with manie others.

" He confessed, that all the freindship that he had at the queen's hands was by meanes of witchcraft, and all kind of inventions belonging therto; and that he found the meanes to putt his maried wife away.

"He confessed, that, after the mariage, he sought all the means possible to destroy the young child, and manie lords of Scotland, and that by treason.

"He confessed, that he had deceived manie gentlewomen both in France and England, and manie other vile facts, which, he said, were too long to rehearse, asking God forgivenesse; and confessed likewise, that he had takin away two ladies' daughters out of Denmark into Scotland, and made them both beleeve he would marie them, and defloured them, and manie gentlewomen in Scotland.

"He confessed, that he had deceived two of the burrow masters' daughters of Lubeck, with manie moe deeds in that place; which, he said, would be too long to declare at length. For these expressed, and all his offenses he did since his birth, he asked forgivenesse, and forgave all the world; and was sorrowfull for his offenses: received the Sacrament that this was good and true, and therafter died."

This confession I found in a peice paper writtin in evill shaippen letters, and the construction farre ruder, that skarse could I make out the sense: and, indeed, it appeareth to be forged, partlie to free the queene, partlie to lay an imputation upon the Erles of Murrey and Morton. But how free the Erle of Murray was, and how farre Morton was acquainted with the mater, yee may reade in the story.

END OF VOLUME SECOND.

EDINBURGH PRINTING COMPANY,
12, South St David Street.

Lightning Source UK Ltd.
Milton Keynes UK
UKHW020354100821
388593UK00002B/197